"The Book of Revelation's Hidden Warning for America"

THE TRUMPET II

THE **PROPHECY CONTINUES—** **AMERICA'S FINAL HOUR** UNVEILED

LORI ANN MOESZINGER

THE RIDGE
PUBLISHING GROUP

THE RIDGE PUBLISHING GROUP
COUER D'ALENE, IDAHO

THE RIDGE
PUBLISHING GROUP

The Ridge Publishing Group
Visit us at https://www.RidgePublishingGroup.com

The Ridge Publishing Group is headquartered in Coeur d'Alene, Idaho, 83814 USA.

The name, house mark, logo, and all associated trademarks—including *Guardians of Biblical Truth* and *New Narrated Study Bible (NNSB)*—are trademarks or service marks of The Ridge Publishing Group.

All Scripture quotations are taken from the Holy Bible, King James Version (KJV), translated out of the original tongues and published in 1611, with the former translations diligently compared and revised.

Cover design by Eric Moeszinger
Interior design and images by Guardians of Biblical Truth

ABOUT THE NEW NARRATED STUDY BIBLE (NNSB)

Guardians of Biblical Truth Publishing Group, an imprint of The Ridge Publishing Group, proudly presents the NEW NARRATED STUDY BIBLE (NNSB)—a bold, immersive translation of Scripture arranged in chronological order and enriched with vivid fictional narrative. Unlike any Bible you've encountered, the NNSB preserves the full integrity of God's Word while illuminating biblical events, people, and prophetic themes through engaging storytelling. This creative approach makes Scripture more accessible to every generation, helping readers experience the redemptive story from beginning to end.

Library of Congress Cataloging-in-Publication Data

Names: Moeszinger, Lori Ann, author
Title: *The Trumpet II: The Prophecy Continues—America's Final Hour Unveiled*

Description: The Book of Revelation NNSB edition. | Idaho : The Ridge Publishing Group, 2025. | Includes biblical text reference.

Identifiers: LCCN 2025909986 | ISBN 978-1-956905-61-8 (hardcover) | ISBN 978-1-956905-62-5 (softcover) | 978-1-956905-63-2 (e-book)

Subjects: Religion, Biblical Studies, Prophecy | Religion, Eschatology | Religion, Christian Theology, Apocalyptic and Eschatology | Fiction, Christian, Futuristic

Printed in the United States of America

To the faithful remnant who continued reading—who pressed deeper, searched harder, and listened longer. This book is for you—those who understand that the sound of the trumpet is not just coming . . . it has already begun to echo across the earth.

Contents

AUTHOR'S NOTE

What you are about to read is presented in the form of a story, but at its core, it is a deep and reverent exploration of the Book of Revelation.

All scripture quotations are taken from the 1611 Authorized King James Version (KJV), with slight revisions for clarity—similar to the approach used in modern translations such as the NLT, NIV, NKJV, NASB, ESV, or NEB. Indented sections contain direct Scripture, while the surrounding narrative includes interpretation, explanation, and storytelling—drawn from my vision, my research, my spiritual insight, and my voice.

One of the most profound discoveries I made while writing *The Trumpet* is the remarkable interconnectedness between the Book of Revelation and the Old Testament. Nearly every verse echoes earlier prophecies, divine patterns, and foreshadows of what is to come—together painting a unified picture of God's redemptive plan and prophetic timeline. For this reason, I have included select Old Testament references throughout, to highlight the inseparable bond between the Testaments.

As we explore America's prophetic role in the end times, it's important to understand that this book is only the beginning. *The Vanishing: The Day Will Begin Like Any Other—Until the Rapture Silences the World* will further explore biblical cycles, Shemitah years, and our current place in prophetic history.

It is my prayer that *The Trumpet I: The Ancient Prophecy That Reveals America's Final Hour* (covering Revelation 1–11) and *The Trumpet II: The Prophecy Continues—America's Final Hour Unveiled* (covering Revelation 12–22) will bring biblical prophecy to life—awakening insight, stirring conviction, and equipping readers with wisdom for what is coming and how to prepare.

Preface

In *The Trumpet I: The Ancient Prophecy That Reveals America's Final Hour*, we raised a sobering and long-avoided question: Is America in the Bible? For many, the idea still seems implausible—perhaps even unthinkable. And yet, Scripture, when studied with prophetic clarity and historical insight, begins to tell a very different story.

Volume I laid the foundation: it traced the spiritual parallels between America and ancient Israel, identified prophetic patterns of judgment, and revealed how the first eleven chapters of the Book of Revelation speak not only to global events, but also to America's spiritual condition and prophetic destiny.

Now, in Volume II, the trumpet continues to sound—but its tone is sharper, and its message more urgent. We move beyond Christ's letters to the Church, beyond the breaking of the seal judgments and the trumpet blasts, into the heart of end-time prophecy. These are not distant symbols or abstract metaphors—they are divine signals, timely and unmistakable:

the rise of the beast,
the woman clothed with the sun,
the fury of the dragon,
the desecration of the holy,
and ultimately—the final judgments and the glorious return of the King.

WHAT THIS BOOK REVEALS

The Trumpet II: The Prophecy Continues—America's Final Hour Unveiled is not fiction, but it remains deeply narrative. Through the unfolding dialogue between Irene and Ann, readers are invited into the prophetic visions and symbols of Revelation 12–22. These chapters, often considered cryptic, are in truth alive with meaning—and increasingly relevant for our time. What once felt far off is now converging in real-time.

As you journey through the final chapters of Revelation, you will discover:

- The true identity and mission of the Antichrist and the False Prophet— and how their influence is already reshaping today's world.
- The invisible spiritual war behind global unrest, deception, and persecution.
- Israel's prophetic role—and how America's alignment reflects its standing in God's timeline.
- The fall of Mystery Babylon—and the sobering implications for our nation—America.
- The climactic Battle of Armageddon, the Second Coming of Christ, the Millennial Kingdom, and the dawn of eternity.

We have not been left in the dark. Revelation was never meant to confuse— it was meant to reveal. It is a divine unveiling. And within its final chapters, we encounter both terror and triumph: a cosmic war between good and evil, a final invitation to repentance, and the unstoppable emergence of God's eternal Kingdom.

A PROPHETIC BLUEPRINT IN TWO VOLUMES

Together, *The Trumpet I* and *The Trumpet II* form a unified vision: one message, one timeline, one urgent call to prepare. These books are more than end times commentaries—they are a trumpet blast to the heart of the Church, to a nation on the brink, and to a world in need of truth.

So, the questions remain:

- Is America facing its greatest reckoning?
- Will we recognize the signs before the silence falls?
- Are we ready for the return of the King?

The final trumpet is sounding.
The Kingdom is near.
The time to awaken is now.

Chapter 11

Revelation 12
Parenthetical—The Woman,
the Man Child, and the Dragon

THE WAR AMERICA CAN'T ESCAPE—A quiet study room. *Trumpet II* lies open on the table, Revelation 12 marked with a ribbon. Irene leans forward, eyes narrowed in thought.

"So, here we are. *Trumpet II*." She flips the page slowly. "And you're starting it with this . . . strange vision of a woman, a dragon, and a child?"

"Yes, Irene. Revelation 12 is the turning point. We've moved past the trumpet judgments. Now, God opens a window to the war behind the scenes. A panoramic vision. A symbolic conflict that reveals the root of everything."

Reading the first verse aloud:

> And there appeared a great wonder in heaven; a woman clothed with the sun, and the moon under her feet, and upon her head a crown of twelve stars. (Revelation 12:1)

"This isn't just a woman, is it?"

"No. She represents Israel—God's covenant people. The imagery of the sun, moon, and stars traces back to Joseph's dream in Genesis 37. The twelve stars? They symbolize the twelve tribes of Israel. This woman is on the verge of birthing something eternal—something heaven has anticipated since the beginning."

Irene leaned in, curious. "And the child?"

"The Man Child is Christ—the Messiah, born from Israel. He's the One destined to rule all nations with a rod of iron. The great red dragon? That's Satan. He's known this from the beginning—and he's been trying to devour the Messiah ever since. Through Pharaoh. Through Herod. Through every shadow war etched into history."

"So Revelation 12 pulls back the veil . . . and reveals the spiritual warfare that's been raging behind everything this whole time?"

"Exactly. We're seeing the unseen battle. Satan wasn't just after Israel—he was after the seed of the woman. And even though he failed to stop Jesus' First Coming, he knows his time is short. That's why the tone shifts here—he intensifies his war against the woman, her offspring, and all who follow Christ."

"So this isn't just ancient history—it's a living prophecy? One that's still unfolding right now?"

"Yes. Revelation 12 bridges the past, the present, and the future. It reminds us that everything happening on earth has always had a supernatural backdrop. The dragon is still enraged. And now, the war is against the faithful—those who 'keep the commandments of God and hold to the testimony of Jesus Christ.'"

Quietly, Irene asked, "And where does America fit into this war?"

"That's what *Trumpet II* will explore. Because as the dragon tightens his grip on the nations, America's prophetic role is becoming clearer—and more urgent—than ever before."

She turned the page with purpose.

"Then let's begin. The veil has been lifted. I'm ready to see."

THE WAR IN HEAVEN: A BATTLE AGES IN THE MAKING

We now cross a prophetic threshold. With the sounding of the seventh trumpet, the first half of the Tribulation has ended. *Trumpet I* covered that initial 3½-year span—marked by the seven seal judgments, the seven trumpet judgments, the rise and ministry of the 144,000 sealed servants during the trumpet period, and the powerful 3½-year witness of the Two Witnesses in Jerusalem.

But now—both groups are gone. Their mission is complete. The stage is set for what remains: the second half of Daniel's 70th Week—the final 3½ years of the Tribulation, which Jesus called "the Great Tribulation" (Matthew 24:21).

However, before the final terrors unfold on earth, Revelation 12 lifts the veil on the spiritual realm. What follows is not a new sequence of judgments, but a panoramic vision—a revelation of the cosmic war that has fueled everything leading up to this moment.

The war described in Revelation 12 is not spontaneous—it is the culmination of an age-long spiritual struggle. Though Scripture gives us glimpses throughout redemptive history, Revelation 12 unveils the climactic turning point: the moment when Satan is cast down from heaven and permanently barred from access to the heavenly realms.

Though Jesus said, "I saw Satan fall like lightning from heaven" (Luke 10:18), and though Colossians reveals that Christ triumphed over principalities and powers at the Cross (Colossians 2:15), Satan has continued to function as the "accuser of the brethren," granted mysterious access to the heavenly courts (Job 1:6–8; Revelation 12:10). For thousands of years, he has stood before God—accusing the saints day and night.

But in Revelation 12, the tide turns.

The War in the Heavens

The heavens have long been occupied by spiritual beings of both divine and fallen order. Satan, though cast from his former glory, still occupied space in the heavenly realms and exercised influence as "the prince of the power of the air" (Ephesians 2:2). He established thrones, dominions, and spiritual principalities—seats of power from which he strategized against the work and people of God (Ephesians 6:12; Colossians 1:16).

This war is waged between two supernatural armies. On one side stands Michael the Archangel—his very name meaning "Who is like God?"—a declaration of divine allegiance and unrivaled strength. He leads the armies of heaven. On the other side stands Lucifer, the adversary, commanding the one-third of the angels who fell with him at the beginning (Revelation 12:4).

Why Satan Was Cast Out

Isaiah gives us insight into the origin of Satan's rebellion:

> How are you fallen from heaven, O Lucifer, son of the morning! How are you cut down to the ground, which did weakened the nations! For you have said in your heart: I will ascend into heaven, I will exalt my throne above the stars of God: I will sit also upon the mount of the congregation, in the sides of the north. I will ascend above the heights of the clouds; I will be like the Most High. (Isaiah 14:12–14)

Satan's fall was the result of pride and ambition. He sought to usurp God's throne—not through brute force, but through deception and manipulation, drawing with him a third of the angelic hosts. Though he was cast down, God, in divine wisdom and longsuffering, still allowed him access to the heavenly realms for a time.

But in Revelation 12, during the second half of the Tribulation—the Great Tribulation—God commands Michael and his angels to expel Satan completely. From that moment on, he is no longer permitted in heaven—not in the highest heaven, the cosmic realms, or even the atmospheric skies. His access is revoked. His influence is severed. His place is found no more in the heavens.

The Heavenly Hosts: Orders and Beings

Scripture identifies a vast array of spiritual beings:

In the Kingdom of God:

- Seraphim (Isaiah 6:1–3)
- Cherubim (Ezekiel 10)
- Living Creatures (Revelation 4:6–8)
- Angels and Archangels (Hebrews 1; Jude 9)
- Spirit Horses and Chariot Hosts (2 Kings 2:11; Revelation 19)

In the Kingdom of Darkness:

- Principalities, Powers, Rulers of Darkness (Ephesians 6:12)
- Thrones and Dominions (Colossians 1:16)
- Demons and Unclean Spirits (Matthew 12:43)
- Fallen Angels in Prison (2 Peter 2:4; Jude 6–7)

These are divided into three categories:

1. Those loyal to God.
2. Those aligned with Satan.
3. Those bound in chains in Tartarus awaiting final judgment.

The Nature of the War

This is not a symbolic struggle. It is a literal war—a clash of spiritual force, not of philosophy or theory. Revelation 12:7–9 describes a real battle in the unseen realm: Michael and his angels fighting against the dragon and his angels—and prevailing.

This is no metaphor. It is a supernatural conflict involving actual angelic beings. Satan and his armies are not defeated by human strength, but by divine decree. No longer will the accuser be permitted to stand before God. He is forcibly cast to earth—restricted, confined, and enraged.

In this final chapter of his rebellion, Satan is:

- Prohibited from leaving the earth.
- Barred from re-entering the heavenly realms.

- Preparing for his last stand at Armageddon.

This pivotal moment signals that God is cleansing the heavens—scrubbing even the spiritual realms in preparation for Christ's millennial reign.

The Power and Limits of Satan

Let us not forget: Satan is not God's equal. He is not omnipresent, omniscient, or omnipotent. He cannot create—he can only corrupt, manipulate, distort, and deceive. Though he drew one-third of the angels in his rebellion, he cannot create more. God retains two-thirds—and holds the power to create anew. Satan's army is finite and fading. He is not a rival; he is an imposter. He is limited. He is bound. He is destined for defeat.

Key Angelic Engagements in Scripture

1. Jacob wrestled with an angel—a mysterious encounter that left him changed forever (Genesis 32:24–30).
2. Angels rescued Lot from Sodom, guiding him out before judgment fell (Genesis 19).
3. An angel appeared to Joshua as the commander of the Lord's army before the battle of Jericho (Joshua 5:13–15).
4. One angel struck down 185,000 Assyrian soldiers in a single night (2 Kings 19:35).
5. Michael assisted Gabriel in spiritual warfare against the prince of Persia (Daniel 10:12–14).
6. Angels will return with Christ to wage final war at Armageddon (Revelation 19).

This war in heaven described in Revelation 12 marks a decisive turning point in the spiritual battle. Once Satan is cast out, he is never again granted access to accuse the people of God. His fury now turns to the earth—focused on Israel and the faithful remnant. But his end is certain. The victory is not only in heaven—it is coming to earth. Christ is preparing to reign. And every demonic power will soon be brought low.

Irene leaned back in her chair, brow furrowed.

"Ann, I'm trying to wrap my head around something . . . Revelation 12 says Satan is cast out of heaven. But didn't that already happen—like, before the garden of Eden? So which heaven is he cast out of *this* time?"

I smiled gently, flipping open my Bible.

"That's a great question. The key is understanding that Scripture speaks of more than one 'heaven.' In fact, it describes *three*."

Irene raised an eyebrow.

"Three? I thought heaven was just . . . heaven."

I nodded. "Most people do. But the Bible actually distinguishes three realms when it refers to 'heaven.'"

Irene leaned in, interested. "Okay, explain."

I held up three fingers.

"The *first heaven* is our atmosphere—the sky, where birds fly and clouds move. Genesis 1:20 calls it 'the open firmament of heaven.'"

"The *second heaven* is what we'd call outer space—the stars, planets, galaxies. Psalm 19:1 says, 'The heavens declare the glory of God, and the firmament shows His handiwork.'"

"Then there's the *third heaven*—what Paul referred to in 2 Corinthians 12:2:"

I knew a man in Christ above fourteen years ago, (whether in the body, I cannot tell; or whether out of the body, I cannot tell: God knows) such as one caught up to the third heaven. (2 Corinthians 12:2)

"It's the spiritual realm—the throne room of God."

Irene leaned forward, intrigued. "Wait—so you're saying Satan *still* had access to that third heaven?"

My voice turned somber. "Yes. Even though he was cast out of his position and glory in the original rebellion—Isaiah 14 and Ezekiel 28 talk about that—God, in His sovereignty, still allowed Satan limited access to the heavenly courts."

Irene flipped quickly to the Book of Job.

"Like in Job 1—where Satan presents himself before God?"

I pointed to the text.

"Exactly. Verse 6 says:"

Now there was a day when the sons of God came to present themselves before the LORD, and Satan came also among them. (Job 1:6)

"It shows us that even after his fall, he could still accuse God's people before His throne."

Irene looked uneasy. "So then, in Revelation 12 . . . what's being cast out if he already fell once?"

I closed my Bible slowly. "What Revelation 12 describes is the *final* expulsion. This isn't just a loss of rank or glory—it's total eviction. Satan is cast out from *every* realm of heaven. No more access to the third heaven, or the cosmic realms, or even the atmospheric heavens. He is confined to the earth itself."

Irene whispered. "No more accusing the brethren before God?"

I nodded. "Revelation 12:10 says, 'The accuser of our brethren is cast down, who accused them before our God day and night.' That role—gone. His access is revoked. And he's *furious*—because he knows his time is short."

Irene stared out at the garden. "And now he's stuck here. With us."

My voice was quiet. "That's why Revelation says, 'Woe to the inhabitants of the earth.' The enemy is here. And he's raging."

A silence settled between us for a moment. Then Irene looked back down at her notepad. "I came across something else. Some scholars say Satan might've already been in Eden—*before* Adam was formed. That something happened between Genesis 1:1 and 1:2. What do you think?"

My eyes lit with recognition. "That's called the *Gap Theory*. It's the idea that a massive judgment occurred between 'In the beginning God created the heavens and the earth' and 'the earth was without form and void.'"

> In the beginning God created the heavens and the earth. And the earth was without form, and void; and darkness was upon the face of the deep. And the Spirit of God moved upon the face of the waters. (Genesis 1:1–2)

Irene's brow furrowed. "So . . . they're saying something catastrophic happened *between* those verses?"

I nodded. "Right. That the original creation was perfect—and Satan's rebellion brought devastation. Genesis 1:2, then, is not the beginning, but the aftermath: the earth in chaos, awaiting restoration."

Irene flipped a few pages, thinking. "I always assumed Genesis 1:2 was just the starting point. But you're saying it might describe a ruined creation?"

I leaned forward. "Yes. The Hebrew word for 'was'—*hayah*—can also be translated 'became.' So it could read, 'The earth *became* formless and void.' That opens the door to the idea that Lucifer's fall wrecked a previous order, and the six days of creation were actually God *reordering* the earth for mankind."

Irene blinked. "And that connects to Ezekiel 28?"

I turned my Bible. "It describes a radiant being in Eden—'full of wisdom and perfect in beauty'—until iniquity was found in him. Many believe that's a reference to Satan before his fall. But it might not be the same Eden that Adam knew—it could be a *pre-Adamic* Eden."

> Son of man, take up a lamentation upon the king of Tyre, and say unto him, Thus says the Lord GOD; You seal up the sum, full of wisdom, and perfect in beauty. You have been in Eden the garden of God; every precious stone was your covering, the sardius, topaz, and the diamond, the beryl, the onyx, and the jasper, the sapphire, the emerald, and the carbuncle, and gold: the workmanship of your

tabrets and of your pipes was prepared in you in the day that you were created. You are the anointed cherub that covers; and I have set you so: you were upon the holy mountain of God; you have walked up and down in the midst of the stones of fire. You were perfect in your ways from the day that you were created, till iniquity was found in you. (Ezekiel 28:12–15)

"Though addressed to the King of Tyre, this passage is widely interpreted as a symbolic depiction of Satan before his fall. It is one reason some theologians suggest the existence of a pre-Adamic Eden—possibly distinct from the Eden described in Genesis 2–3."

Irene's voice dropped. "So the Eden in Ezekiel may have existed *before* Genesis 1:3?"

I nodded. "Possibly. Think of it as the first world—corrupted by Satan. Then God judged it, and in six days, began to restore it for humanity."

Irene's eyes widened. "And all of that could've happened . . . in the space between two verses."

I smiled gently. "A pause that changed everything. It reframes the Cross, too. Jesus didn't just redeem mankind—He came to defeat the ancient enemy who corrupted creation in the first place."

Irene exhaled, slow and reverent. "There's so much hidden in those early verses. Truths I've read a hundred times . . . but never really seen."

I closed my Bible and looked at her. "Scripture is like that. It's layered. And every time we return to it, God reveals another thread in the tapestry."

We sat in thoughtful silence, the garden around us glowing with late-afternoon light—revelation lingering like sunlight on the page.

THE REVELATION OF JESUS CHRIST REVEALS:

^{12:1} And there appeared a great wonder (sign) in heaven; a woman clothed with the sun, and the moon under her feet, and upon her head a crown of twelve stars.

Revelation 12 opens with a "great sign" (Greek: *semeion*) appearing in heaven—a radiant woman, clothed with the sun, with the moon under her feet, and a crown of twelve stars on her head. This striking image is symbolic, not literal, and has sparked much interpretation. However, the most biblically grounded identification of this woman is that she represents *Israel*.

This description closely mirrors Joseph's prophetic dream in Genesis 37:9–10, where the sun represents Jacob, the moon represents Rachel, and the eleven stars represent Joseph's brothers—making Joseph the twelfth. In that dream, the family of Israel is portrayed using the same celestial imagery later echoed in Revelation 12:1, further reinforcing the woman's identity as Israel.

And he dreamed yet another dream, and told it to his brethren, and said, Behold, I have dreamed a dream more; and, behold, the sun and the moon and the eleven stars made obeisance to me. And he told it to his father and to his brethren: and his father rebuked him, and said unto him, What is this dream that you have dreamed? Shall I and your mother and your brethren indeed come to bow down ourselves to you to the earth? (Genesis 37:9–10).

This connection firmly identifies the radiant woman as Israel—a nation frequently portrayed in Scripture as a woman: married, then widowed, divorced, and ultimately restored.

Some interpret the woman in Revelation 12 as Mary, since she gave birth to Christ, or as the Church, the Bride of Christ. However, both views encounter theological challenges:

- Mary did not flee into the wilderness or experience the prolonged persecution described in later verses.
- The Church is never depicted as a mother in Scripture. Instead, she is consistently portrayed as a virgin (2 Corinthians 11:2) and as the Bride of Christ (Ephesians 5:25–27).

The woman in Revelation 12 is not the bride but the mother of the "Man Child"—a title pointing to national Israel. It is through Israel that the Messiah came, and it is Israel that will play a pivotal role in the end-time narrative.

Throughout the Old Testament, Israel is consistently portrayed as a woman in various stages of covenant relationship with God:

- As wife, married to the LORD—her Maker and Redeemer (Isaiah 54:5).
- As unfaithful and estranged (Jeremiah 3:1–8).
- As restored and wooed back to covenant faithfulness (Hosea 2:14–23).
- As a mother in labor, bringing forth new life (Isaiah 66:7–8).

This prophetic imagery aligns closely with the woman in Revelation 12, reinforcing the interpretation that she represents Israel.

The radiant woman is a powerful symbol of God's covenant people—Israel—through whom the Messiah came and who will once again take center stage during the Tribulation Age. The heavenly sign marks a turning point in redemptive history, foreshadowing the intensifying spiritual warfare ahead and the ultimate fulfillment of God's sovereign plan.

OLD TESTAMENT FORESHADOWS REVELATION:

Before she travailed, she brought forth; before her pain came, she was delivered of a Man Child. Who has heard such a thing? Who has seen such things? Shall the earth be made to bring forth in one day? Or shall a nation be born at once? For as soon as Zion travailed, she brought forth her children. (Isaiah 66:7–8)

In this passage, "she" symbolically refers to Zion—another name for Israel. The image of a woman giving birth to a Man Child closely parallels Revelation 12:1–2, where the radiant woman (Israel) brings forth the Messiah. This prophetic language anticipates both the supernatural birth of Christ and the future restoration and prominence of Israel in the end times. While Genesis 37:9–10 provides the celestial symbolism, Isaiah 66:7–8 reveals the prophetic theme of sudden travail and divine deliverance. Together, they deeply reinforce the meaning of Revelation 12:1 and the woman's identity as national Israel.

Irene leaned over the pages of her study Bible, eyes scanning the name *Israel* again and again throughout the text.

"Ann," she said, brow furrowed, "I keep seeing *Israel* everywhere. But where did the name actually come from?"

I smiled, already turning to the book of Genesis. "That's a great question. The name *Israel* came directly from God. He gave it to Jacob—Abraham's grandson—after a life-changing encounter."

Irene tilted her head. "Wait—Jacob? As in 'Abraham, Isaac, and Jacob'? I didn't realize he was the one called Israel."

I nodded. "Yes. After wrestling all night with the Angel of the Lord, Jacob was given a new name—Israel. It's in Genesis 32. Let me read it to you."

I flipped to the passage and read aloud:

And He said, Your name shall be called no more Jacob, but *Israel*: for as a prince you struggled with God and with men, and have prevailed. (Genesis 32:28)

Irene's eyebrows lifted. "So the name *Israel* means . . .?"

I replied, "It means 'He struggles with God' or 'God prevails.' It captures Jacob's transformation—from a deceiver to someone forever changed. He walked away with a limp—but also with a calling."

Irene leaned back, thoughtful. "That makes sense. So what about *Israelites* and *Israeli*? Where do those come in?"

I continued, "After Jacob—now Israel—had twelve sons, their descendants became known as the *children of Israel*. Over time, the term *Israelites* came to refer to the Hebrew people as a whole, especially during key events like the Exodus and the conquest of the Promised Land."

Irene nodded slowly. "So all of the tribes came from one man—Jacob, who became Israel."

I smiled again. "Exactly. The term *Israeli* is more modern. It refers specifically to a citizen in the modern state of Israel—established in 1948."

Irene thought aloud, "So Israel is a man, a people, and a nation."

I pointed to my Bible. "Yes—and even more than that, Israel is a prophetic clock. God's covenant with Israel traces all the way back to Abraham, 4,000 years ago. The promises, the Messiah, the land—it all centers on that name."

Irene whispered, "It's more than a name. It's a destiny."

I nodded, gently closing my Bible. "And it's woven into every chapter of prophecy—including the one we're reading now."

THE REVELATION OF JESUS CHRIST REVEALS:

[12:2] And she being with child cried, travailing in birth, and in pain to be delivered.

This verse continues the symbolic vision from Revelation 12:1, where the radiant woman represents Israel. Now, she is pictured in the agony of labor—crying out in pain, travailing to bring forth a Child. This is more than a depiction of physical childbirth; it represents Israel's deep spiritual and prophetic struggle. The birth reflects both the coming of the Messiah through Israel and the nation's ongoing travail in redemptive history, especially leading into the Tribulation.

In context, the Child she bears is the long-awaited Messiah—Jesus Christ—who came through the lineage of Israel (Romans 9:4–5). The phrase "travailing in birth" echoes a recurring Old Testament motif, where Israel is pictured in labor during times of deep suffering and anticipation of redemption (see Isaiah 26:17–18; Micah 4:9–10). This imagery underscores not only the pain of the nation's past but also its prophetic role in bringing forth the Redeemer.

This verse paints a vivid picture of both national and spiritual agony—a people yearning for the promised Redeemer while enduring centuries of bondage, persecution, and oppression. From Egypt to Babylon, through Roman occupation and relentless spiritual warfare, Israel's path to bringing forth the Messiah was marked by deep suffering, longing, and prophetic expectation.

OLD TESTAMENT FORESHADOWS REVELATION:

Therefore will He give them up, until the time that she which travails has brought forth: then the remnant of His brethren shall return unto the children of Israel. (Micah 5:3)

Micah 5:3 refers to a period of divine delay "until she who is in labor has given birth." This parallels Revelation 12:2, where the woman—symbolizing Israel—is shown in the pain of labor, giving birth to the Man Child (Christ). Both passages highlight Israel's prophetic role in bringing forth the Messiah and foreshadow the emergence of a faithful remnant in the end times. Together, they point to the ultimate restoration of God's covenant people in the unfolding redemptive plan.

Irene leaned forward, intrigued. "Ann, I've heard people talk about Israel being delivered as a nation—and something called the 'super sign' in prophecy. What is that exactly?"

I nodded. "Yes—many Bible scholars refer to the rebirth of Israel in 1948 as the *super sign* of the end times. It's one of the most astonishing fulfillments of prophecy in modern history. On May 14, 1948, Israel became a nation again— after nearly 2,000 years of dispersion. No other nation in history has vanished from the map and then been reborn in the same land, with the same language and national identity."

"And didn't that tie into the dry bones prophecy in Ezekiel?"

"Exactly. Ezekiel 37 speaks of a valley of dry bones—symbolizing Israel's national death and God's promise to breathe life back into it. That vision began to take shape in 1948, when Israel became a nation again. And in 2009, something remarkable happened: for the first time since the Diaspora, more Jews were living in Israel than outside of it. It was like a final prophetic piece snapping into place.

> Then He said unto me, Son of man, these bones are the whole house of Israel: behold, they say, Our bones are dried, and our hope is lost: we are cut off for our parts. Therefore prophesy and say unto them, Thus says the Lord GOD; Behold, O My people, I will open your graves, and cause you to come up out of your graves, and bring you into the land of Israel. And you shall know that I am the LORD, when I have opened your graves, O My people, and brought you up out of your graves, And shall put My Spirit in you, and you shall live, and I shall place you in your own land: then shall you know that I the LORD have spoken it, and performed it, says the LORD. (Ezekiel 37:11–14)

"Ezekiel 37:1–14 is a prophetic metaphor for the national resurrection and restoration of Israel, widely interpreted by many scholars as pointing toward both the physical return of the Jewish people to their land and their spiritual revival in the end times."

Irene eyes widened. "And then, exactly 70 years later—on May 14, 2018— President Trump officially recognized Jerusalem as Israel's capital and ordered the U.S. embassy to be moved from Tel Aviv to Jerusalem?"

"Yes. No other U.S. president or major world leader had officially recognized Jerusalem as Israel's capital. But President Trump did—on the exact same date, 70 years later. That wasn't just political—it was prophetic. In Scripture, seventy is a number of completion, especially significant in relation to Israel."

"That's stunning," Irene said, shaking her head in amazement. "So Israel is the only nation in all of recorded history—spanning 6,000 years—to disappear completely and then be restored with the same name, people, language, and land?"

I said with gravity. "Yes, Irene. That has never happened to any other nation. It's living proof that God keeps His promises—and that the prophetic clock is ticking."

Irene's voice was hushed. "So . . . the *super sign* was really the beginning of the end."

I nodded. "Or more accurately—the beginning of the beginning. The unfolding of the final chapters in Bible prophecy."

Irene leaned in with curiosity. "Ann, you mentioned the word *Diaspora*. What exactly does it mean?"

I nodded thoughtfully. "The *Diaspora* refers to the scattering of the Jewish people from their homeland, Israel, to nations all over the world. The word comes from the Greek *diaspeiro*—meaning 'to scatter abroad.' And that's exactly what happened."

Irene's brow furrowed. "When did it start? After the Romans destroyed the temple?"

I smiled. "That was a major turning point. In AD 70, after the Roman siege of Jerusalem, many Jews were killed, enslaved, or fled—marking the beginning of the great Diaspora. Then, after the Bar Kokhba Revolt in AD 135—another failed rebellion against Rome—Jews were banned from Jerusalem entirely and scattered even further."

I continued. "But the scattering began even earlier—long before the Romans. The first major wave happened when the Assyrians conquered the northern kingdom of Israel in the 8th century BC (2 Kings 17). Then, in the 6th century BC, the Babylonians captured the southern kingdom of Judah and exiled its people (2 Kings 25)."

Irene blinked. "So the Jews were already being scattered long before Jesus?"

I nodded. "Exactly. The scattering had begun centuries earlier. In fact, it was prophesied. Deuteronomy 28:64 says:"

> And the LORD shall scatter you among all people, from the one end of the earth even unto the other; and there you shalt serve other gods, which neither you nor your fathers have known, even wood and stone. (Deuteronomy 28:64)

"It was a consequence of their disobedience—but even in judgment, God had a redemptive plan."

Irene's voice softened. "But He also promised to bring them back, didn't He?"

I turned the pages of my Bible and pointed.

"Yes. Jeremiah 16:15 says, 'I will bring them again into their land that I gave unto their fathers.' And we've seen that begin to unfold—especially in 1948 when Israel was reborn as a nation."

Irene sat back, awestruck. "So the Diaspora wasn't just a historical exile—it was a fulfillment of prophecy. And their return is too."

I nodded. "Exactly. The scattering proves God's Word is true—and so does the regathering."

Irene leaned forward, eyes narrowing thoughtfully.

"Ann, I've been wondering . . . Israel today is just a tiny strip of land—barely the size of New Jersey. But didn't God promise Abraham something much bigger? The Promised Land . . . wasn't it supposed to stretch far beyond what Israel occupies now?"

I nodded, already flipping to a marked page in my Bible.

"You're absolutely right. What modern Israel occupies today is only a fraction of what God originally promised to Abraham. The full boundaries of the Promised Land are clearly outlined in Scripture—and that covenant promise has yet to be fully fulfilled. It remains prophetic."

"So, where exactly are those borders described?"

I pointed to Genesis 15.

"Right here. God is speaking to Abram—before his name was changed to Abraham."

I read aloud:

In the same day the LORD made a covenant with Abram, saying, Unto your seed have I given this land, from the river of Egypt unto the great river, the river Euphrates. (Genesis 15:18).

Irene blinked.

"Wait . . . from the river of Egypt to the Euphrates? That's massive!"

I nodded.

"It really is. If you map it out, the full extent of that promise includes not just modern-day Israel, but parts of Egypt, Saudi Arabia, Jordan, Syria, Lebanon—even parts of Iraq. Israel has never fully possessed all that land—not even during the reigns of King David or Solomon."

Irene leaned back, stunned.

"So we're talking about a future fulfillment then?"

My tone grew reverent.

"Yes—it's prophetic. The full inheritance of the land covenant will be fulfilled when the Messiah returns and establishes His Kingdom on earth. It's part of the millennial reign. What God promised Abraham in Genesis has not been forgotten."

Irene whispered.

"And no one can stop it?"

I smiled gently.

"No. God's covenants are everlasting. He repeated the promise to Isaac in Genesis 26:3, and again to Jacob in Genesis 28:13. It's an unbreakable thread woven throughout Scripture."

I pulled out a map. Irene studied it in silence, her eyes tracing the borders with growing focus.

THE BOOK OF REVELATION

North America and Eurasia
(Europe, Asia, the Middle East, and northern Africa)

The large circles show the Bible Lands. The central square marks the full covenant land God promised to Abraham's descendants (Genesis 15:18–21). This promise remains unfulfilled and awaits its future fulfillment during the Messianic Kingdom (Ezekiel 47–48).

"So this is what remains after the trumpet judgments—North America and Eurasia. The very regions linked to the sons of Noah . . . the lands of the Bible."

I nodded and brought up the image of Pangaea.

THE BOOK OF REVELATION

Supercontinent—Pangaea

Supercontinent—Pangaea, the landmass that existed when all continents were joined as one.

"This is how it began at creation—one landmass. Then judgment came after the Flood, in the days of Peleg, and the earth divided into seven continents. But now, after the sixth seal judgment—those violent earthquakes and eruptions—it's as if God has reset the geography, pulling us back toward a unified landmass. Though not entirely."

I continued. "Then came the fire—the first four trumpet judgments. A third of the land burned. A third of the oceans turned to blood. A third of the rivers poisoned. A third of the sky darkened. Cold. Chaos. Death."

Irene's brow furrowed. "And you believe that one-third means the southern portion of the landmass? Australia, Antarctica, India, South America, southern Africa . . . all gone?"

"Yes, Irene. It fits. What remains corresponds to the territories of Shem, Ham, and Japheth—North America and Eurasia: Europe, Asia, the Middle East, and northern Africa. It's as if God is turning the spotlight back to the Bible Lands, narrowing His focus to the nations descended from Noah's sons. The final stage of redemptive history is being set."

Irene nodded slowly. "A progressive geographic funnel. Eden to Eden. Genesis to Revelation. Restoration through judgment."

I smiled gently. "And mercy woven into wrath . . . He promised never again to destroy the earth with water—"

Irene cut in, quoting:

> But the Day of the Lord will come as a thief in the night, which the heavens shall pass away with a great noise, and the elements shall melt with fervent heat; the earth also, and the works that are therein, shall be burned up. (2 Peter 3:10)

"Fire. This time, by fire."

"Fire is everywhere in Revelation, Ann. It erupts from the sixth seal judgments—lava, earthquakes, volcanoes. It falls during the trumpet judgments—comets, asteroids, burning stars. Even the Two Witnesses? Fire comes from their mouths."

I nodded. "It's judgment, yes—but it's also cleansing. A holy fire, refining the earth before the kingdom comes."

"And now, we're watching history repeat itself. God offers a fresh start, humanity falls short, and judgment follows—again and again. Yet through it all, one thread remains unbroken: His mercy."

I leaned in closer. "We're watching the systems of man collapse—and the Kingdom of God emerge. The Antichrist may rise from the ashes, but his power is limited. His reign is short. God's plan is unfolding."

Irene nodded slowly. "And it's so precise. From the genealogies to the geography. From judgment to restoration."

I closed my Bible. "And when the sixth trumpet sounds, the Euphrates takes center stage—Babylon's ancient playground, the cradle of rebellion. With it, another third of humanity perishes. Think about it: 8 billion people before the Rapture, reduced to 6 billion. Then the fourth seal brings it down to 4.5 billion. After the sixth trumpet? Just 3 billion remain."

I paused, letting the numbers settle. "And that doesn't even count the 1.5 billion Tribulation martyrs throughout the seven-year period. And the bowl judgments haven't even begun."

I looked up, voice steady. "But even then, God is still calling. Still reaching. In wrath, He remembers mercy. This isn't just the end—it's the final invitation before the King returns."

Irene tilted her head thoughtfully. "Wait a second—wasn't Peleg mentioned in Genesis 10? The one where it says, 'in his days the earth was divided'?"

I nodded. "Exactly. Genesis 10:25 says:"

And unto Eber were born two sons: the name of one was Peleg; for in his days was the earth divided; and his brother's name was Joktan. (Genesis 10:25)

"Most scholars believe that 'division' refers to the scattering of nations following the Tower of Babel incident."

Irene's eyes widened. "So Peleg was alive during the Tower of Babel?"

I smiled. "Yes. Most biblical chronologists place the Tower of Babel around 2242 BC—roughly a century after the Flood, which occurred around 2348 BC. Peleg lived from 2243 BC to 2004 BC, so his entire lifetime overlapped with those early post-Flood generations, including the events at Babel."

Irene's eyes widened. "That makes sense. God confuses the languages, scatters the people, and the nations are born. And Peleg's name becomes a marker in time."

I nodded. "Exactly. And depending on your interpretation, that 'division' could refer either to the cultural scattering—nations formed through language barriers—or possibly to a physical division of the earth's landmass. Some believe that the continental shifts after the Flood accelerated around Peleg's day. Others see it strictly as the dispersion at Babel. Either way, Peleg and the Tower of Babel are closely linked."

"So," Irene said slowly, "we have judgment at Babel through language confusion . . . the birth of ethnic nations . . . and that sets the stage for God to call Abraham out from among them."

I smiled. "Exactly. It's divine strategy. Every name and event in Genesis is like a breadcrumb pointing to Messiah. And Peleg? He's more than a name—he's a timestamp in redemptive history."

———◆◆◆———

THE REVELATION OF JESUS CHRIST REVEALS:

12:3 And there appeared another wonder in heaven; and behold a great red dragon, having seven heads and ten horns, and seven crowns upon his heads.

"Another wonder in heaven." The word "wonder" (Greek: *semeion*) implies a symbolic vision—not a literal event, but a deeper spiritual reality being revealed through imagery. The first "wonder" was the radiant woman (Israel); this second wonder reveals her cosmic adversary.

"Great red dragon." The term "dragon" is a well-known symbol of chaos, destruction, and ancient evil. The color red is associated with bloodshed and violence, indicating Satan's murderous nature (John 8:44). This is not merely a mythical creature—it is a representation of real spiritual warfare led by a personal being: Satan.

"Seven heads and ten horns" refer to the global political structure Satan influences. The seven heads are commonly understood to represent seven historical empires that have opposed and persecuted God's people—typically identified as: Egypt, Assyria, Babylon, Medo-Persia (Medes and Persians), Greece, Rome, and the final empire (Revelation 17–18).

"Ten horns." In biblical symbolism, horns often represent power and authority—especially that of kings or political rulers (Daniel 7:7, 24). The ten horns in both Daniel and Revelation point to a regional alliance of ten kings who rise with and support the Antichrist during the final 3½ years of the Tribulation. This is not a global empire, in the traditional sense, but a concentrated coalition rooted in the Middle East—specifically within the territories of ancient biblical empires, often referred to as the "Bible Lands."

This aligns with the view that the final world empire referenced in Revelation 17–18 is America, a nation with global influence but ultimately judged and destroyed before Christ's return (see Revelation 18). The ten horned empire of the Antichrist, then, is distinct from America—a localized, end-time confederation that dominates the Middle East and fulfills its prophetic role in opposition to Israel and the coming King.

"Seven crowns upon his heads." The crowns (Greek: *diademata*) symbolize illegitimate authority. This is Satan's false claim to dominion over the kingdoms of the world (Luke 4:5–6). The fact that these crowns are on the heads (not horns) points to past imperial powers Satan has influenced.

This symbolic portrait of the dragon shows us the visible political and historical structures through which Satan works and has worked. He operates through empires, kings, and governments—but his true aim is spiritual: to devour, accuse, and destroy the people of God. Revelation 12 sets the stage for the conflict between Satan and Israel, and ultimately, between Satan and Christ.

OLD TESTAMENT FORESHADOWS REVELATION:

Speak, and say, Thus says the Lord GOD; Behold, I am against you, Pharaoh king of Egypt, the great dragon that lies in the midst of his rivers, which has said, My river is my own, and I have made it for myself. (Ezekiel 29:3)

Ezekiel refers to Pharaoh, the king of Egypt, as a "great dragon," linking the symbolism of a powerful, oppressive ruler with that of a mystical or monstrous beast. The dragon in Revelation 12:3 represents Satan, working through world empires, just as Pharaoh was a tool of satanic oppression against God's people

(Israel). Both passages depict hostile powers opposing God's purposes and His covenant people. The imagery of a dragon as a political or spiritual adversary finds its roots in Old Testament prophetic tradition—especially in Ezekiel, where it is used as a metaphor for prideful earthly rulers who defy God.

THE REVELATION OF JESUS CHRIST REVEALS:

[12:4] And his tail drew the third part of the stars of heaven, and did cast them to the earth: and the dragon stood before the woman, which was ready to be delivered, for to devour her child as soon as it was born.

This verse unveils Satan's twofold agenda:

1. **His role in the ancient rebellion**—The phrase "his tail drew the third part of the stars of heaven" is widely understood to refer to Satan's initial rebellion—when he led one-third of the angelic host in defiance against God. These "stars" symbolize the fallen angels who became demonic forces aligned with him (Isaiah 14:12–14; Ezekiel 28:12–17).

2. **His violent opposition to the Messiah**—The dragon standing before the woman (symbolizing Israel), ready to devour her child, represents Satan's relentless effort to destroy the promised Redeemer from the moment of His birth.

Satan's opposition is not vague or abstract—it's specific. His warfare targets the *woman* (Israel) and *her child* (Christ). This scene offers a prophetic snapshot of spiritual conflict manifesting in real history. The phrase "to devour her child as soon as it was born" directly parallels Herod's massacre of the infants in Matthew 2—a demonic scheme to destroy the young Messiah. Yet God, in His sovereignty, intervened and preserved the child:

- The Magi were warned in a dream.
- Joseph was told by an angel to flee to Egypt.
- Jesus was supernaturally preserved (Matthew 2:11–16).

Other attempts on Jesus' life—like the mob in Luke 4:29–30 seeking to throw Him off a cliff—also reflect this spiritual war. Time and again, Satan tried to derail God's plan, but divine protection prevailed.

This verse affirms that Jesus' incarnation was more than a moment in history—it was a cosmic turning point in the war between good and evil. Revelation now moves toward the climax of that long-standing conflict.

OLD TESTAMENT FORESHADOWS REVELATION:

Why do the nations rage, and the people imagine a vain thing? The kings of the earth set themselves, and the rulers take counsel together, against the LORD, and against His anointed, saying, Let us break their band asunder, and cast away their cords from us. He that sits in the heavens shall laugh: the LORD shall have them in derision. (Psalm 2:1–4)

The dragon standing before the woman (Israel) to devour the Child in Revelation 12:4 mirrors the rebellion described in Psalm 2:1–4. This psalm prophetically portrays the nations and their rulers—under the influence of Satan— conspiring against the LORD and His Anointed (the Messiah). While Psalm 2 emphasizes earthly resistance, it reveals the deeper spiritual conflict that undergirds it. Together, these passages underscore Satan's relentless efforts to thwart God's redemptive plan through Christ, both spiritually and politically.

THE REVELATION OF JESUS CHRIST REVEALS:

^{12.5} And she brought forth a Man Child, who was to rule all nations with a rod of iron: and her Child was caught up to God, and to His throne.

Revelation 12:5 gives a powerful yet succinct snapshot of Jesus Christ's mission, identity, and exaltation. The "woman" (as established in verse 1) represents Israel, and the Man Child she brings forth is clearly Jesus the Messiah, based on the context and supporting scriptures.

One of the clearest identifiers of the Man Child is the phrase "who was to rule all nations with a rod of iron." This imagery is a signature attribute of Christ's future reign:

- Psalm 2:7–9 foretells the Messiah's inheritance of the nations and His authority to rule them with a rod of iron.
- Revelation 2:26–27 and Revelation 19:15 reinforce this prophetic role, highlighting Christ's unyielding righteousness and divine justice.

No one else in Scripture is described in these exact terms. This expression is uniquely reserved for Jesus, marking a prophetic flashpoint that affirms His destiny as the sovereign King over all the earth.

The second half of the verse compresses a monumental truth: "her Child was caught up unto God, and to His throne." This refers to Christ's ascension after His resurrection (Acts 1:9–11), when He returned to heaven and sat down at the right hand of the Father. It also reflects the end result of His redemptive work—He is enthroned and glorified, now awaiting the day of His return in glory to rule the nations.

Notably, Revelation 12 does not detail Christ's earthly ministry, crucifixion, or resurrection—it moves directly from His birth to His ascension. This is not a dismissal of His redemptive work but a deliberate literary and prophetic device. Just as the Apostles' Creed offers a doctrinal summary by highlighting only the most vital points of His identity and work, Revelation here gives a prophetic summary, emphasizing His origin (Israel), His destiny (to rule), and His current position (enthroned).

This abbreviated description also points to the mystery of Christ's two comings. In the Old Testament, prophets saw only the Second Coming of the Messiah—His triumphant return as King. The Rapture and the Church Age were hidden mysteries later revealed through the apostles, especially Paul (Ephesians 3:4–5). Even John the Baptist struggled to reconcile the meek and suffering Jesus with the conquering Messiah he expected (Matthew 11:2–3).

This verse marks a prophetic transition. After Christ's rejection by Israel (at His First Coming), the prophetic "clock" paused. Revelation 12 picks up where the clock resumes—during the Tribulation, also known as Daniel's 70th Week. God begins to remove the veil from Israel's eyes, preparing them to receive the One they once rejected (Romans 11:25).

The Book of Revelation ultimately unveils Jesus not as a Suffering Servant, but as the coming King, who returns to establish His Millennial Kingdom (Revelation 19–20). Revelation 12:5 is the prophetic anchor of that reality. The Child who was caught up to God is the same one who will return to rule the nations—with a rod of iron, with justice, and with glory.

OLD TESTAMENT FORESHADOWS REVELATION:

For unto us a Child is born, unto us a Son is given: and the government shall be upon His shoulder: and His name shall be called Wonderful, Counselor, the Mighty God, the Everlasting Father, the Prince of Peace. Of the increase of His government and peace there shall be no end, upon the throne of David, and upon His Kingdom, to order it, and to establish it with judgment and with justice from henceforth even forever. The zeal of the LORD of hosts will perform this. (Isaiah 9:6–7)

Isaiah 9:6–7 offers a powerful Old Testament prophecy that clearly foreshadows the identity and mission of the "Man Child" in Revelation 12:5. This passage describes the birth and divine authority of the Messiah—Jesus Christ—emphasizing both His humanity ("a Child is born") and divinity ("a Son is given").

The government "upon His shoulder" and His eternal reign on the throne of David mirror the declaration in Revelation 12:5 that the Child is destined "to rule all nations with a rod of iron." Isaiah's royal titles—"Mighty God," "Prince of Peace"—point to Christ's future rule of justice and peace, aligning with the victorious destiny seen in Revelation. Together, these verses form a prophetic arc: from the promise of Messiah's birth in Isaiah to His triumphant rule in Revelation.

THE REVELATION OF JESUS CHRIST REVEALS:

[12:6] And the woman fled into the wilderness, where she has a place prepared of God, that they should feed her there a thousand two hundred and threescore days.

This verse follows the birth and ascension of the Man Child (Jesus Christ) and now returns focus to the woman—identified earlier in the chapter as Israel (Revelation 12:1). Her flight into the wilderness represents a literal, prophetic event in the second half of the Tribulation, when Israel will face intense persecution and must flee for her survival.

Again, the woman here is not the Church, but national Israel. Just as Israel fled Egypt in the Exodus and was sustained by God in the wilderness (Exodus 16–17), she will again be driven into a place of divine protection during the Great Tribulation. This flight aligns with Jesus' warning in Matthew 24:15–21, where He instructed those in Judea to flee when they see the "abomination of desolation," a reference to the Antichrist desecrating the future rebuilt temple.

Then let them which be in Judea flee into the mountains: Let him which is on the house top not come down to take anything out of his house. (Matthew 14:16–17)

"A thousand two hundred and threescore days." This duration—1,260 days— is 3½ years, the second half of Daniel's 70th Week (Daniel 9:27). This exact time period appears repeatedly in Revelation (11:2–3, 13:5), describing the timeframe when the Antichrist reigns and persecutes the saints, especially Israel.

This time period is also seen in symbolic terms as:

- 42 months (Revelation 11:2, 13:5).
- Time, times, and half a time (Revelation 12:14; Daniel 7:25).

"Where she has a place prepared of God." God Himself prepares a specific, protected place for the Jewish remnant during this time. While the exact location is not named, many scholars suggest Petra in modern-day Jordan, due to its defensible terrain and prophetic references to Edom (southern Jordan), Moab (central Jordan), and Ammon (northern Jordan) escaping the Antichrist's reach (Daniel 11:41). Wherever it is, God supernaturally protects and sustains this remnant—just as He did during the Exodus with manna and water in the desert.

"That they should feed her." The plural "they" indicates divine or angelic provision. Just as angels ministered to Jesus (Matthew 4:11) and Elijah was fed in the wilderness (1 Kings 19:5–8), Israel will again be nourished by supernatural means. This wilderness will be both a refuge and a revelation—where physical provision and spiritual understanding converge.

This verse underscores God's faithfulness to His covenant people, even during their time of greatest distress. Though Israel is under judgment and persecution during the Tribulation, God has not forsaken her. The woman fleeing into the wilderness reflects both God's justice and His mercy: judgment is falling on the earth, but a remnant of Israel is being preserved for ultimate restoration and redemption (Romans 11:26).

THE BOOK OF REVELATION

Petra: Israel's Wilderness Rose-Red Refuge

This line drawing shows Petra, the ancient city in Edom (modern-day Jordan). Many believe it is the place in Revelation 12:14 where God protects Israel during the Great Tribulation—a divinely prepared refuge for the woman from the dragon.

OLD TESTAMENT FORESHADOWS REVELATION:

Then said the LORD unto Moses, Behold, I will rain bread from heaven for you; and the people shall go out and gather a certain quota every day, that I may test them, whether they will walk in My law, or not. (Exodus 16:4)

The woman (Israel) fleeing into the wilderness mirrors Israel's Exodus from Egypt into the desert. Just as God prepared a place for ancient Israel in the wilderness, He prepares a place again during the Tribulation. The phrase "that they should feed her" in Revelation parallels God's supernatural daily provision of manna to Israel during their wilderness journey.

THE REVELATION OF JESUS CHRIST REVEALS:

[12:7] And there was war in heaven: Michael and his angels fought against the dragon; and the dragon fought and his angels.

This verse marks a turning point in the prophetic timeline of the Book of Revelation. The spiritual conflict that has raged since the fall of Lucifer now escalates into open warfare in heaven itself. This is not symbolic or metaphorical—it is a real, literal war between angelic beings, a cosmic battle with eternal consequences.

- Michael and his angels—Michael is one of the only angels in Scripture referred to by name and is designated as an *archangel* (Jude 9). He is consistently portrayed as a warrior angel and the protector of Israel (Daniel 10:13, 21, 12:1). In this scene, he leads the heavenly host in battle against the forces of evil. His role here confirms his status as a principal angelic leader under God's authority.
- The dragon and his angels—The dragon is Satan, described in verse 9 of this chapter. He is not alone—he commands a third of the angels who fell with him (verse 4), now known as demons. This war reveals Satan's desperate final stand against the Kingdom of God, attempting to retain access to the heavenly realm even as his time draws short.

"And there was war in heaven." This war takes place in heaven, not on earth. It is a spiritual battle in the unseen realm. Up until this point in history, Satan has had access to the heavenly courts, where he functions as the "accuser of the brethren" (Revelation 12:10; Job 1:6–12; Zechariah 3:1). But here, God initiates the final eviction notice. This is not the original fall of Satan from heaven (Isaiah 14; Ezekiel 28), but his final expulsion from the heavenly realms, signaling the last phase of judgment before Christ's return.

This war doesn't begin by accident. God permits it, signaling the midpoint of the Tribulation—3½ years into Daniel's 70th Week. This time corresponds with "the time of Jacob's trouble" (Jeremiah 30:7), where God turns His attention toward the purification and restoration of Israel.

OLD TESTAMENT FORESHADOWS REVELATION:

And at that time shall Michael stand up, the great prince which stands for the children of your people: and there shall be a time of trouble, such as never was since there was a nation even to that same time: and at that time your people shall be delivered, every one that shall be found written in the book. (Daniel 12:1)

Daniel 12:1 provides a prophetic foundation for Revelation 12:7, where Michael once again rises as Israel's divine defender during the most intense period of tribulation the world has ever seen. This verse underscores Michael's appointed role as protector over Israel and links his end-time appearance to a period of unprecedented trouble—"a time of trouble such as never was." Revelation 12 captures the heavenly war that triggers Satan's final expulsion from the heavenly realms to earth, intensifying his persecution of Israel. Daniel 12:1 confirms both the severity of the Tribulation and God's sovereign plan for Israel's ultimate deliverance.

THE REVELATION OF JESUS CHRIST REVEALS:

^{12:8} And prevailed not; neither was their place found any more in heaven.

This verse marks a turning point in the heavenly conflict. Satan and his angels "prevailed not"—they were decisively defeated by Michael and his angelic host. This isn't a symbolic or metaphorical struggle. This is a real, spiritual war, and it ends with Satan's complete loss of access to the heavenly realms.

The phrase "neither was their place found any more in heaven" indicates a permanent expulsion. Up until this point, Satan still had access to the heavenly courts to accuse the saints (Job 1:6–12; Zechariah 3:1). But now, after millennia of spiritual warfare, his place—his legal standing and spiritual access—has been revoked. The war is not just lost—it results in the total eviction of Satan and his followers from heaven itself.

This corresponds with the midpoint of the Tribulation, when Satan is cast not just out of the third heaven (God's throne room), but out of all heavenly realms, including the second heaven (cosmic space) and the first heaven (earth's atmosphere). He is now incarcerated to earth, no longer free to roam.

This turning point shifts the Tribulation into its most intense phase—the Great Tribulation, the final 3½ years foretold by Jesus in Matthew 24:21:

For then shall be great tribulation, such as was not since the beginning of the world to this time, no, nor ever shall be. (Matthew 24:21)

Satan, cast down and enraged, will unleash persecution, especially upon Israel (the woman of Revelation 12) and those who hold to the testimony of Jesus Christ. His loss of position results in an increase in aggression. He knows his time is short (Revelation 12:12), and he acts like a cornered beast, seeking to devour and destroy.

This verse confirms: heaven is now scrubbed clean of Satan's presence. The war is won in heaven—but the battle shifts to earth.

OLD TESTAMENT FORESHADOWS REVELATION:

Now there was a day when the sons of God came to present themselves before the LORD, and Satan came also among them. And the LORD said unto Satan, Where comes you? Then Satan answered the LORD, and said, From going to and fro in the earth, and from walking up and down in it. (Job 1:6–7)

In Job 1:6–7, Satan still had access to the heavenly court, where he accused the righteous (like Job). In Revelation 12:8, that access is permanently revoked—"neither was their place found any more in heaven." This contrast reveals a prophetic shift: from tolerated accuser in Job to defeated enemy cast down in Revelation. This paints a full picture of the enemy's fall from tolerated presence to total exclusion—a fulfillment of God's long-declared judgment.

THE REVELATION OF JESUS CHRIST REVEALS:

[12:9] And the great dragon was cast out, that old serpent, called the Devil, and Satan, which deceived the whole world: he was cast out into the earth, and his angels were cast out with him.

This verse marks a decisive turning point in the cosmic conflict between God and Satan. The dragon—clearly identified as "that old serpent" from Eden (Genesis 3:1), also called the Devil (accuser) and Satan (adversary)—is permanently cast out of the heavenly realms. His expulsion is absolute. No longer can he stand before God to accuse the saints, as he did in Job 1:6–12 and Zechariah 3:1–2. The great deceiver of the whole world is now forcibly confined to the earth, setting the stage for intensified spiritual warfare during the final days.

This expulsion is not symbolic—it is actual and final. It begins the second half of the Tribulation—the Great Tribulation—and coincides with intensified demonic oppression and persecution of Israel (the woman of Revelation 12).

This verse also reveals the global nature of Satan's deception—"which deceives the whole world." This aligns with what Jesus said in Matthew 24:24—the false Christs and false prophets will rise and, if possible, deceive even the elect. The devil's expulsion marks the unleashing of deception, destruction, and wrath on a scale the earth has never seen.

Now bound to the earth, Satan becomes like a cornered, enraged beast—"knowing that his time is short" (Revelation 12:12). His fury will be especially directed at Israel and all who hold to the testimony of Jesus Christ (Revelation 12:17). But even in this, God is in control. Satan's exile is part of God's plan to expose and eradicate evil, purify the remnant of Israel, and prepare the world for the return of the rightful King.

OLD TESTAMENT FORESHADOWS REVELATION:

How are you fallen from heaven, O Lucifer, son of the morning! How are you cut down to the ground, which did weaken the nations! (Isaiah 14:12)

Both passages describe Satan's fall from heaven. Isaiah 14:12 uses the name Lucifer, traditionally associated with Satan before his rebellion. The phrase "cut down to the ground" parallels "cast out into the earth." The reference to weakening the nations mirrors "deceives the whole world" in Revelation 12:9.

THE REVELATION OF JESUS CHRIST REVEALS:

12:10 And I heard a loud voice saying in heaven, Now is come salvation, and strength, and the Kingdom of our God, and the power of His Christ: for the accuser of our brethren is cast down, which accused them before our God day and night.

This verse marks a profound turning point in the war between good and evil. It is a declaration of victory, not just for heaven, but for God's redemptive plan as a whole.

"And I heard a loud voice saying in heaven." This heavenly proclamation erupts in response to Satan's final expulsion from heaven (verse 9). The voice could be that of an angelic host or perhaps the collective voice of the redeemed, but it signals overwhelming joy and celebration. Why? Because something monumental has occurred—the accuser has been evicted.

"Now is come salvation, and strength, and the Kingdom of our God." This phrase doesn't mean salvation is only now becoming available—rather, it announces the full arrival and visible manifestation of God's reign.

This is an eschatological shift—a declaration that:

- The plan of redemption is reaching its fulfillment.
- Satan's access to the heavenly courtroom has been revoked.
- The reign of Christ is about to be physically and publicly established.

This moment reflects Revelation 11:15, where the seventh trumpet sounds and the announcement is made: "The kingdoms of this world are become the kingdoms of our LORD and of His Christ."

"And the power of His Christ." This highlights that Christ's authority is now being fully exercised. The Greek word for "power" here is *exousia*—delegated authority. The final phase of Jesus' reign—the one where He physically rules on earth—is being activated. His enemies are being subdued, starting with Satan's removal from heaven.

"For the accuser of our brethren is cast down." This is the critical reason for heaven's rejoicing: Satan—the relentless prosecutor of the saints—has been cast down. He no longer has access to accuse believers before God. But now—his courtroom privileges are revoked. Heaven's throne room is now free of his poisonous accusations.

"Which accused them before our God day and night." This phrase speaks to the unceasing nature of Satan's attacks against God's people. His strategy has always been to slander, condemn, and shame the saints in an attempt to undermine God's mercy and righteousness.

But with Satan cast down, the spiritual atmosphere in heaven changes. No more accusations. No more opposition. No more slander. Only worship, justice, and preparation for the return of the King.

Revelation 12:10 is a heavenly proclamation of victory—a cosmic shift in spiritual authority and warfare. It confirms the defeat of the accuser and celebrates the coming visible reign of Christ. With Satan cast down, heaven rejoices because the final stages of redemption are in motion, and the glorious Kingdom of God is preparing to manifest on earth.

OLD TESTAMENT FORESHADOWS REVELATION:

And he showed me Joshua the high priest standing before the Angel of the Lord, and Satan standing at his right hand to resist him. And the LORD said unto Satan, The LORD rebuke you, O Satan; even the LORD that has chosen Jerusalem rebuke you: is not this a brand plucked out of the fire? (Zechariah 3:1–2)

This passage directly foreshadows the heavenly courtroom scene described in Revelation 12:10, where Satan—the accuser—is finally cast down, silenced, and defeated. The "accuser of our brethren" role is shown active in Zechariah 3:1–2, and Revelation records its permeant end.

THE REVELATION OF JESUS CHRIST REVEALS:

12:11 And they overcame him by the blood of the Lamb, and by the word of their testimony; and they loved not their lives unto the death.

This verse stands as a powerful, threefold declaration of how believers triumph over Satan—through Christ's sacrifice, faithful testimony, and complete surrender, even unto death.

1. **By the blood of the Lamb**—"Neither by the blood of goats and calves, but by His own blood He entered in once into the holy place, having obtained eternal redemption for us" (Hebrews 9:12).

Victory begins at the Cross. The "blood of the Lamb" refers to the finished work of Jesus Christ—His sacrificial death that satisfies divine justice, secures our redemption, and silences Satan's accusations. The enemy's greatest weapon was sin, but the blood of Jesus disarms him completely, cleansing believers from all guilt and restoring them to right standing before God.

2. **By the word of their testimony**—"It is written . . ." (Matthew 4:4, 7, 10). "And take the helmet of salvation, and the sword of the Spirit, which is the Word of God" (Ephesians 6:17). "He put on righteousness as a breastplate, and a helmet of salvation upon his head . . ." (Isaiah 59:17).

The believers wield the Word of God both as sword and shield—declaring truth in the face of deception, standing on Scripture even under persecution. Their testimonies are not merely personal stories, but Spirit-filled affirmations of Christ's power, truth, and redemptive plan. Just as Jesus overcame Satan in the wilderness by quoting the Word, so do these saints prevail through faithful proclamation.

Their testimonies may also include faithfulness unto martyrdom, echoing the boldness of the Two Witnesses in Revelation 11, whose prophetic witness shook the world despite opposition and death.

3. **They loved not their lives unto the death**—"Likewise reckon you also yourselves to be dead indeed unto sin, but alive unto God . . ." (Romans 6:11). "For I know whom I have believed, and am persuaded . . ." (2 Timothy 1:12). "But none of these things move me, neither count I my life dear unto myself . . ." (Acts 20:24).

Their willingness to die reveals the ultimate devotion and unshakeable trust in God's eternal promises. They were not clinging to their earthly lives, but looking forward to the crown of life. Their faith in Christ surpassed the fear of death—a mark of true discipleship. This is the faith of martyrs, prophets, apostles, and Tribulation saints alike.

This also ties to the promise that those written in the Book of Life will be delivered (Exodus 32:32; Daniel 12:1), having overcome by faith, not by force.

Revelation 12:11 shows us the heavenly record of earthly faithfulness. In a world dominated by evil and deception, God's people overcome:

- By Christ's redeeming blood (past victory),
- By declaring His truth boldly (present witness), and
- By laying down their lives if necessary (eternal hope).

This is not just a strategy for the end times saints, but a timeless pattern of overcoming for every believer.

OLD TESTAMENT FORESHADOWS REVELATION:

Yea, for your sake are we killed all the day long; we are counted as sheep for the slaughter. (Psalm 44:22)

This verse beautifully mirrors the spirit of Revelation 12:11. It highlights the steadfast loyalty of God's people, even unto death. Just as the faithful in Revelation overcome Satan by the blood of the Lamb and the word of their testimony—not loving their lives even unto death—so too did the righteous in the Old Testament endure suffering for the sake of God.

It's a powerful through-line from ancient Israel's trust in God to the end-time saints' ultimate sacrifice, showing that faithfulness under fire has always been the mark of God's people.

THE REVELATION OF JESUS CHRIST REVEALS:

12:12 Therefore rejoice, you heavens, and you that dwell in them. Woe to the inhabiters of the earth and of the sea! for the devil is come down to you, having great wrath, because he knows that he has but a short time.

This verse marks a powerful pivot in the end times narrative. The heavenly realms erupt with rejoicing—not because the conflict is over, but because the enemy, the accuser, has finally been evicted from his place of access. No longer will Satan have the legal standing to accuse the brethren before God day and night. Heaven is cleansed. The air is cleared. A cosmic exhale.

But this heavenly celebration comes with a dire warning for earth: Woe. With Satan cast down, his focus shifts entirely to earth, unleashing his full fury. The third woe, introduced with the seventh trumpet (Revelation 11:14–15), now escalates through the bowl judgments (Revelation 15–16)—the final outpouring of God's wrath. This woe is not just atmospheric or geological; it is personal, spiritual, and violently demonic. No longer the prince of power of the air, Satan is now confined to earth. And he knows his time is short—only 3½ years remain before his final judgment.

His wrath is not only great—it is targeted. The woman, symbolic of Israel, becomes the object of his rage. This ushers in "the time of Jacob's trouble" (Jeremiah 30:7), a period of persecution and tribulation for the Jewish people unlike anything seen in history. The fury of the enemy will manifest through the Antichrist's rise, the implementation of the mark, and violent antisemitism that mirrors and exceeds historical atrocities.

This is why heaven rejoices—because the enemy has been stripped of his heavenly access. But earth groans, because Satan, in his desperation, turns the remaining time into a final, fiery assault. It is the countdown to Armageddon.

OLD TESTAMENT FORESHADOWS REVELATION:

And it shall come to pass in that day, that the LORD shall punish the host of the high ones that are on high, and the kings of the earth upon the earth. (Isaiah 24:21)

This verse, like Revelation 12:12, speaks of a time when heavenly beings (the host of the high ones) and earthly rulers (kings of the earth) face divine judgment. Revelation 12:12 reveals Satan being cast down to earth, and woe pronounced upon the earth and sea as judgment begins to fall. Isaiah 24:21 foreshadows this dual level judgment—both cosmic and earthly. The "high ones that are on high" can be understood as fallen spiritual beings—like Satan and his angels—who are punished along with rebellious human rulers in the end times.

THE REVELATION OF JESUS CHRIST REVEALS:

12:13 And when the dragon saw that he was cast to the earth, he persecuted the woman which brought forth the man Child.

This verse marks a dramatic turning point in the end-time narrative. With Satan (the dragon) permanently cast out of the heavenly realms, his access to accuse believers before God is revoked. Now confined to earth, his fury is unleashed—and it is targeted.

The dragon "persecuted the woman"—Israel. The woman, previously identified in Revelation 12:1 as clothed with the sun and crowned with twelve stars, is symbolic of the nation of Israel. She is the one who "brought forth the Man Child," a clear reference to Jesus Christ, the Messiah who came through the Jewish lineage. Now, with Christ ascended and the Church raptured, Satan's rage turns toward the earthly remnant of Israel, the nation from which the Savior came.

This persecution aligns with the prophetic "time of Jacob's trouble" (Jeremiah 30:7) and the final three and a half years of the Tribulation—the Great Tribulation. During this period, the dragon's focus shifts entirely to attempting to destroy the Jewish people—those who remain faithful to God and those who are awakening to their Messiah in the final days.

This verse echoes past attempts by Satan to destroy the Messianic line—such as Pharaoh's massacre of Hebrew infants (Exodus 1), Haman's plot in the Book of Esther, and Herod's slaughter of male children in Bethlehem (Matthew 2). But here in Revelation, this is Satan's final and most ferocious assault, knowing his time is short (Revelation 12:12).

OLD TESTAMENT FORESHADOWS REVELATION:

Alas! For that day is great, so that none is like it: it is even the time of Jacob's trouble; but he shall be saved out of it. (Jeremiah 30:7)

This verse prophesies a unique and severe time of tribulation—unlike anything Israel has faced before—directly aligning with Revelation 12:13, where the dragon (Satan) begins persecuting the woman (Israel) after being cast down to earth. The phrase "the time of Jacob's trouble" reinforces the ethnic and national identity of Israel in this prophetic context, and the promise "he shall be saved out of it" foreshadows the remnant that will be delivered (Revelation 12:14–17).

THE REVELATION OF JESUS CHRIST REVEALS:

[12:14] And to the woman were given two wings of a great eagle, that she might fly into the wilderness, into her place, where she is nourished for a time, and times, and half a time, from the face of the serpent.

This verse speaks to God's supernatural protection of Israel—symbolized by the woman—during the most intense phase of the Tribulation. The phrase "two wings of a great eagle" is not necessarily literal (as a plane or helicopter), but symbolic of divine deliverance swiftness. It echoes Old Testament imagery, such as Exodus 19:4, where God says to Israel, "I bare you on eagles' wings, and brought you unto Myself."

The "wilderness" represents a safe place of divine provision and protection, often associated with Petra in modern-day Jordan, which lies in the historical territory of ancient Edom. This location aligns with biblical geography and prophecies about Israel's end times flight and preservation (Isaiah 63:1; Hosea 2:14; Matthew 24:15–21).

This time designation "a time, and times, and half a time" is a Hebrew idiom for 3½ years, consistent with Daniel 7:25 and Daniel 12:7. This period refers to the last half of Daniel's 70th Week, also known as the Great Tribulation (Matthew 24:21). During this time, the Antichrist's betrayal of Israel reaches its peak, and Satan—cast down to earth—focuses his rage on the Jewish people.

The "serpent" is Satan, whose face Israel is protected from. Despite his pursuit (Revelation 12:15), God has prepared a place and provision for the faithful remnant. The term "nourished" implies supernatural sustenance, just as God provided manna in the wilderness during the Exodus. This protection mirrors God's unchanging nature—faithful to preserve His covenant people.

This verse encapsulates God's covenantal faithfulness and His strategic intervention during earth's darkest hour, ensuring that His redemptive plan for Israel continues to unfold—ultimately culminating in their national salvation and recognition of Jesus as Messiah (Zechariah 12:10).

OLD TESTAMENT FORESHADOWS REVELATION:

You have seen what I did unto the Egyptians, and how I bare you on eagles' wings, and brought you unto Myself. (Exodus 19:4)

This verse reflects God's protective deliverance of Israel during the Exodus—just as Revelation 12:14 describes God supernaturally aiding the woman (Israel) with "two wings of a great eagle" to flee into the wilderness and be nourished for a time, times, and half a time (3½ years) during the Great Tribulation. This prophetic imagery shows consistency in God's covenantal care—from the Exodus to the end times.

THE REVELATION OF JESUS CHRIST REVEALS:

12:15 And the serpent cast out of his mouth water as a flood after the woman, that he might cause her to be carried away of the flood.

This verse reveals Satan's furious pursuit of Israel (the woman) during the second half of the Tribulation. The imagery of the dragon casting out a flood is symbolic, not literal water—but an overwhelming force. In biblical symbolism, "floods" often represent invading armies or destructive multitudes (Jeremiah 46:7–8, 47:2; Daniel 9:26). These references consistently use the flood metaphor to depict powerful and consuming military invasions.

Here, the "flood" likely represents the Antichrist's armies unleashed to destroy the Jewish remnant fleeing into the wilderness—possibly to Petra, a place of divine refuge. This aligns with Jesus' warning in Matthew 24:15–22 for those in Judea to flee when the abomination of desolation occurs.

Yet, just as God parted the Red Sea for Israel during the Exodus, He will intervene again. Revelation 12:16 tells us "the earth helped the woman." This suggests a supernatural event—perhaps a literal earthquake or landslide—that swallows the advancing armies, halting their pursuit. It is a dramatic reminder of God's faithful protection over His covenant people, even during their most desperate hour.

OLD TESTAMENT FORESHADOWS REVELATION:

Who is this that comes up as a flood, whose waters are moved as the rivers? Egypt rises up like a flood, and his waters are moved like the rivers; and he says, I will go up, and will cover the earth; I will destroy the city and the inhabitants thereof. (Jeremiah 46:7–8)

This passage metaphorically describes Egypt's army as a rising flood—just as Revelation 12:15 uses the flood to represent a military force (likely the Antichrist's armies) pursuing Israel. The symbolic use of a flood as a destructive force aligns with both passages.

THE REVELATION OF JESUS CHRIST REVEALS:

12:16 And the earth helped the woman, and the earth opened her mouth, and swallowed up the flood which the dragon cast out of his mouth.

This verse highlights a divine intervention in the midst of Satan's wrath. The "woman," symbolizing Israel, is being pursued by the dragon (Satan), who unleashes a "flood" intended to destroy her. In this context, the "flood" likely refers to the Antichrist's armies pursuing Israel during the Great Tribulation.

But here, God steps in.

The earth itself "helps" the woman—a supernatural act of protection. This may be a literal geophysical event, like an earthquake, landslide, or opening of the ground, similar to Korah's rebellion in Numbers 16:31–33, where the earth opened and swallowed up the enemies of God. Symbolically, it speaks of God using creation as His agent of deliverance.

This rescue parallels God's historic pattern of preserving Israel—whether by parting the Red Sea, sending manna in the wilderness, or confusing enemy armies. He makes a way of escape in the wilderness (Isaiah 43:19).

The divine intervention also reflects the limits of the Antichrist's power. While Satan seeks to destroy the Jewish remnant, God distracts and diverts his efforts—possibly through uprisings from the east and north (Daniel 11:44). This deflection aligns with God's prophetic promise to preserve a remnant of Israel through the fire of Tribulation (Zechariah 13:8–9).

Ultimately, this verse reinforces that God is sovereign, even in the darkest times. He protects His covenant people, not just with angelic armies, but through creation itself. And in doing so, He demonstrates that no scheme of Satan can override the divine plan.

OLD TESTAMENT FORESHADOWS REVELATION:

And it came to pass, as he had made an end of speaking all these words, that the ground clave asunder that was under them: And the earth opened her mouth, and swallowed them up, and their houses, and all the men that belonged unto Korah, and all their goods. They, and all that belonged to them, went down alive into the pit, and the earth closed upon them: and they perished from among the congregation. (Numbers 16:31–33)

In both cases, the earth "opens its mouth" as a divine act of judgment and protection. In Numbers 16:31–33, God judges rebellion (Korah) and protects Moses and the faithful. In Revelation 12:16, God again uses the earth to protect the faithful remnant (Israel) by swallowing up the Antichrist's pursuing "flood" (symbolic of invading armies). This parallel powerfully reinforces the biblical theme: God commands creation to protect His people and to judge His enemies.

THE REVELATION OF JESUS CHRIST REVEALS:

[12:17] And the dragon was wroth with the woman, and went to make war with the remnant of her seed, which kept the commandments of God, and have the testimony of Jesus Christ.

Revelation 12:17 reveals the final burst of Satan's fury in the second half of the Tribulation, as the devil—symbolized by the dragon—turns his full wrath on the faithful remnant of Israel. This is not the Church, nor the Gentile believers converted by the 144,000 Jewish evangelists. This "remnant" is the surviving portion of Israel, a concept well established in Old Testament prophecy.

Who is the woman and her remnant?

- The "woman" in this passage is Israel, not Mary or the Church. She brought forth the Man Child (Christ), and the narrative has shown how she fled into the wilderness for divine protection (Revelation 12:6, 14).
- The "remnant of her seed" refers to the Jews who come to saving faith in Jesus during the second half of the Tribulation. These are those who now "keep the commandments of God and have the testimony of Jesus Christ."

The term "remnant" is consistently associated with Israel throughout the Old Testament:

- Isaiah 1:9—"Except the LORD of hosts had left unto us a very small remnant . . ."
- Isaiah 10:20—"The remnant of Israel . . . shall stay upon the LORD . . ."
- Joel 2:32—"In Mount Zion . . . shall be deliverance . . . in the remnant whom the LORD shall call."
- Zechariah 8:12—"I will cause the remnant of this people to possess all these things."

The Church is never called a remnant in Scripture. This terminology is used for the survivors of judgment within the house of Israel—those who come through Great Tribulation and are refined through suffering (Zechariah 13:8–9).

The Antichrist, under Satan's influence, is no longer focused on deceiving or recruiting but on destruction. The dragon is "wroth," meaning enraged. His target is now this repentant remnant of Jews who have finally recognized Jesus as Messiah. This fulfills Zechariah 12:10:

And I will pour upon the house of David, and upon the inhabitants of Jerusalem, the Spirit of grace and of supplications: and they shall look upon Me whom they pierced, and they shall mourn for Him, as one mourns for his only son, and shall be in grief for Him, as one that is in grief for his firstborn. (Zechariah 12:10)

This is "the time of Jacob's trouble" (Jeremiah 30:7), the most intense wave of antisemitism the world has ever known. God, however, preserves this remnant, who will inherit the promises made to Abraham, Isaac, and Jacob.

Revelation 12:17 paints a vivid picture of God's prophetic faithfulness and Satan's persistent rage. Despite the fury of the dragon, God's covenant with Israel stands. This remnant represents the climactic turning point for national Israel—finally embracing the Messiah and becoming a visible testimony of Christ in the darkest days of earth's history.

OLD TESTAMENT FORESHADOWS REVELATION:

And it shall come to pass in that day, that the remnant of Israel, and such as are escaped of the house of Jacob, shall no more again stay upon him that defeated them; but shall stay upon the LORD, the Holy One of Israel, in truth. The remnant shall return, even the remnant of Jacob, unto the Mighty God. For though your people Israel be as the sand of the sea, yet a remnant of them shall return: the consumption decreed shall overflow with righteousness. (Isaiah 10:20–22)

"Remnant of her seed" in Revelation 12:17 aligns directly with "remnant of Israel" in Isaiah 10:20–22. Both passages speak of a faithful remnant surviving tribulation and judgment, turning to God in truth. The dragon's war against this remnant in Revelation is consistent with Isaiah's vision of judgment and God's ultimate preservation of a faithful few. This Old Testament passage beautifully confirms that God has always planned to preserve a remnant of Israel, even in the midst of judgment and chaos—just as Revelation 12 affirms in the end times.

SUMMARY OF REVELATION 12

Revelation 12 unveils the spiritual battle behind world events, highlighting Israel's prophetic role, Satan's fury, and God's protective hand in the unfolding of end-time events. The chapter opens with a great sign in heaven—a woman clothed with the sun, the moon under her feet, and a crown of twelve stars (Revelation 12:1). She is pregnant and about to give birth, symbolizing Israel bringing forth the Messiah, the Man Child destined to rule all nations with a rod of iron (Revelation 12:5).

A second sign appears: a great red dragon, representing Satan, poised to devour the Child at birth (Revelation 12:3–4). The Child is caught up to God and His throne—pointing to Christ's ascension (Revelation 12:5), while the woman flees into the wilderness to a place prepared by God for 1,260 days, or 3½ years (Revelation 12:6).

War breaks out in heaven as Michael and his angels fight the dragon and his angels. Satan is defeated and cast down to earth, no longer having access to accuse the brethren before God (Revelation 12:7–9). A loud voice in heaven declares the arrival of salvation and the Kingdom of God, rejoicing in Satan's expulsion—but warning the earth of his wrath, knowing his time is short (Revelation 12:10–12).

Enraged, the dragon pursues the woman (Israel), but she is given two wings of a great eagle to escape into the wilderness, where she is nourished for a time, times, and half a time—another reference to 3½ years (Revelation 12:14). The dragon unleashes a flood to overtake her, symbolizing a great military assault, but the earth helps the woman by swallowing the flood (Revelation 12:15–16). Foiled again, the dragon turns his wrath against the remnant of her seed—those who keep God's commandments and hold the testimony of Jesus Christ (Revelation 12:17).

KEY TAKEAWAYS

- The Woman—Symbolizes Israel, the covenant people of God, central to redemptive history.
- The Man Child—Represents Jesus Christ, the Messiah, caught up to God's throne.
- The Dragon—Identifies Satan as the accuser and deceiver cast down to earth.
- The wilderness—God provides supernatural protection for Israel during the Great Tribulation.
- The remnant—Jewish believers who come to faith in Christ during the second half of Daniel's 70th Week.
- The war in heaven—Marks the midpoint of the Tribulation when Satan is cast out permanently.
- The Great Wrath—Satan's fury intensifies because he knows his time is limited.

Revelation 12 pulls back the curtain on the cosmic war between God and Satan, centered on Israel and the Messiah. It reminds believers that while the enemy may rage, God protects His people, and Christ has already secured the victory. This chapter is a prophetic anchor, linking past, present, and future in God's sovereign redemptive timeline.

Chapter 12

Revelation 13: Parenthetical—The Two Beasts: Antichrist and False Prophet

THE RISE OF THE UNHOLY TRINITY—Revelation 13 stands as one of the most pivotal and sobering chapters in all of prophetic Scripture. If Revelation 12 pulled back the veil to show us the spiritual war behind history—centered on Israel, the Messiah, and Satan—then Revelation 13 brings that conflict fully into the visible, physical world. Here, we witness the rise of what has been called the "unholy trinity": a demonic trio consisting of the dragon (Satan), the beast from the sea (the Antichrist), and the beast from the earth (the False Prophet). Together, they form a counterfeit trinity—mimicking the roles of the Father, the Son, and the Holy Spirit—but twisted with one goal: to usurp God's glory, deceive the nations, and destroy the saints.

The chapter begins with the first beast rising out of the sea—a symbol often representing the nations or the Gentile world. This beast is terrifying, with ten horns and seven heads, combining features of the beasts described in Daniel 7. He is not merely a man but a global empire and its leader—empowered directly by Satan. This is the Antichrist: the political and military figure who will dominate the world stage, demand worship, and persecute God's people during the final 3½ years of the Tribulation—called the Great Tribulation.

Next, a second beast arises—this one from the earth. He has two horns like a lamb but speaks like a dragon. He is deceptive in appearance, religious in tone, but satanic in power. This is the False Prophet, a spiritual leader who promotes the worship of the first beast. Under his influence, a global religious system emerges—blending politics, economics, and false worship into one final world order.

Together, these three form the most diabolical system the world has ever known. Revelation 13 is not merely a political forecast; it is a spiritual unveiling of Satan's last desperate attempt to counterfeit God's Kingdom. It is rebellion disguised as righteousness. It is the culmination of centuries of deception, now unleashed on a global scale.

And yet, even in the midst of this darkness, Revelation 13 is not without hope. The chapter draws a stark line between those who dwell on the earth and worship the beast—and those whose names are written in the Lamb's Book of Life. The faithful are called to endure. To see past the signs and wonders. To hold fast to the truth that even the greatest of satanic empires will fall before the returning King. Revelation 13 is a warning. It is a call to discernment. And above all, it is a reminder that the true King is coming—and the counterfeit will soon be crushed.

THE BEAST OUT OF THE SEA—UNVEILING THE ANTICHRIST

The identity of the Antichrist has sparked speculation for centuries. But Scripture makes one thing clear: the world will not know who he is until he confirms a seven-year covenant with Israel—a pivotal event described in Daniel 9:27. This covenant is the trigger that marks his rise to global power.

> And he shall confirm the covenant with many for one week: and in the midst of the week he shall cause the sacrifice and the oblation to cease, and for the overspreading of abominations he shall make it desolate, even until the consummation, and that determined shall be poured upon the desolate. (Daniel 9:27)

This "week" refers to a prophetic period of seven years. According to Daniel 9:27, the Antichrist will be revealed when he confirms a covenant with Israel—a treaty that marks the beginning of the Tribulation. Until that moment, his identity remains hidden.

The apostle Paul teaches in 2 Thessalonians 2 that that the Antichrist is currently being restrained and will not be revealed until the "Restrainer" is removed. Many Bible scholars believe this Restrainer refers to the Holy Spirit working through the Church. If so, this suggests that the Church will be taken out of the way—through the Rapture—before the Antichrist rises to global power.

> For the mystery of iniquity (lawlessness) is already at work: only He who now lets will let, until He be taken out of the way. And then shall that Wicked be

revealed, whom the Lord shall consume with the Spirit of His mouth, and shall destroy with the brightness of His coming. (2 Thessalonians 2:7–8)

Throughout history, many have speculated about the identity of the Antichrist—figures like Nero, Napoleon, Hitler, and even Henry Kissinger have been named. But Scripture is clear: he will not be revealed until *after* the Rapture and the signing of a peace covenant with Israel.

What We Know About the Antichrist

The identity of the Antichrist has long sparked speculation, but Scripture provides key insights into his rise and reign. He will not appear until a divinely appointed time—following the Rapture of the Church—and will be revealed through a deceptive peace covenant with Israel. Here's what the Bible reveals:

1. **He will not be revealed until after the Rapture**—According to 2 Thessalonians 2:6–8, the Antichrist is currently restrained from rising to power. That restraint will be lifted only after the Church is removed. Until then, his identity remains hidden.

2. **He will emerge as a global peacemaker**—In the wake of the Rapture—marked by global chaos, vanished billions, and economic collapse—the Antichrist will appear as a charismatic leader offering stability. He will broker a seven-year peace treaty with Israel, marking the official start of the Tribulation (Daniel 9:27).

3. **He will suffer a fatal wound—and be resurrected**—At some point during his reign, the Antichrist will be mortally wounded. Miraculously, he will recover—an event that the False Prophet will exploit to lead the world into worshiping him (Revelation 13:3, 14). This counterfeit resurrection will be Satan's imitation of Christ's victory over death.

4. **He will break the covenant at the midpoint**—After 3½ years of apparent peace, the Antichrist will betray Israel. He will end temple sacrifices, desecrate the holy place, and unleash fierce persecution—especially targeting the Jewish people (Daniel 9:27; Matthew 24:15–21).

5. **He will declare himself to be God**—In a climactic act of blasphemy, the Antichrist will set up an image of himself in the rebuilt Third Temple and demand worship as deity. Jesus foretold this moment when He warned:

I am come in My Father's name, and you receive Me not: if another shall come in his own name, him you will receive. (John 5:43)

6. **He will control politics, religion, and commerce**—During the Tribulation, the Antichrist will establish global dominance—politically, spiritually, and economically. No one will be able to buy or sell without taking his mark, symbolizing total allegiance (Revelation 13:16–17).

This "beast out of the sea" (Revelation 13:1) will rise from the turmoil of a world in ruins. He will promise peace but bring terror. He will demand worship but lead many to destruction. He will seem invincible—until the true King returns in glory and power to overthrow him forever.

Where Does the Antichrist Come From?

To trace the Antichrist's origin, we look beyond Revelation to the Book of Daniel. Together, these books reveal a prophetic timeline—from the rise of Gentile empires to the Second Coming of Christ.

Nebuchadnezzar's Dream—In Daniel 2, the prophet interprets King Nebuchadnezzar's dream of a towering statue made of various metals. Each section represents a successive Gentile empire:

- Head of gold—The Babylonian Empire (Daniel 2:38).
- Chest and arms of silver—The Medo-Persian Empire (Daniel 2:39).
- Belly and thighs of bronze—The Grecian Empire under Alexander the Great, later divided among four generals (Daniel 2:39).
- Legs of iron—The Roman Empire (Daniel 2:40), known for its crushing strength.
- Feet and toes of iron and clay—A modern reinterpretation of Rome's imperial legacy, embodied by America. Though never officially an empire, America has exercised global dominance through regime change, economic pressure, and military power—mirroring the reach of ancient Rome. According to Daniel 2:41–44, this fragile and divided kingdom sets the stage for the Antichrist, who rises from a ten-king coalition—likely supported, or even triggered—by America's decline or divine judgment. This final manifestation of the beast reveals America as the seventh head, and the Antichrist's alliance as the ten horns.

In the end, this entire structure is struck by a stone "cut without hands"—a clear symbol of Christ—who will crush every earthly kingdom and establish His eternal Kingdom (Daniel 2:44–45).

Daniel's Vision of the Beasts—Daniel 7 expands the prophetic timeline through a vision of four beasts rising from the sea. These creatures correspond to the empires in Nebuchadnezzar's statue (Daniel 2), but now emphasize their character and spiritual hostility:

- Lion with eagle's wings—Babylon (Daniel 7:4).
- Bear raised on one side—Medo-Persia (Daniel 7:5).
- Leopard with four wings and four heads—Greece (Daniel 7:6).
- Dreadful beast with ten horns—Rome, including its final phase: a divided, end-times kingdom marked by global influence, culminating in the rise of the Antichrist and his ten-king coalition (Daniel 7:7, 23–24).

Out of the ten horns comes a "little horn"—the Antichrist. He subdues three of the ten kings, speaks arrogant blasphemies against God, and wages war against the saints for three and a half years (Daniel 7:8, 24–25). Yet his reign is short. God intervenes, removes his dominion, and gives the everlasting Kingdom to the saints (Daniel 7:26–27).

Revelation and the Final Beast System

Revelation 13 does not describe the rise of a brand-new empire, but the emergence of a final ruler from the ruins of a collapsing world order. By this point, America—the seventh kingdom and modern face of Roman-style globalism—has already dominated the world stage for over two centuries. Though never officially an empire, America has mirrored imperial Rome through its military reach, regime changes, economic control, and cultural influence.

The Antichrist rises amid global chaos—after the Rapture of the Church and during the early stages of the Tribulation. He ascends through a ten-king coalition, not from the West, but from the Bible Lands. He does not build an empire from scratch; instead, he capitalizes on the weakening and eventual divine judgment of America.

As the Tribulation progresses, Revelation 17 and 18 reveal America as Mystery Babylon—a final end-times superpower, judged and removed just before Armageddon. Her fall clears the path for the Antichrist, the beast system, to assume global dominance through deception, crisis, and spiritual darkness.

But his reign is temporary. Empowered by Satan, he may deceive the nations, but he cannot outlast the Sovereign plan. Jesus Christ returns, destroys the beast system, and establishes His eternal Kingdom of righteousness and peace.

The Antichrist's Geographic Origin: A Middle Eastern Connection

The Bible provides several clues that point to the regional origin of the Antichrist, narrowing the focus to the territory once ruled by Alexander the Great and historically associated with ancient Assyria.

Daniel's Prophecies: The Grecian Empire and the "Little Horn"—In Daniel 8, the prophet sees a vision of a male goat (Greece) and a prominent horn (Alexander the Great). When that horn is broken, it is replaced by four notable horns—symbolizing the division of his empire among four generals.

- Daniel 8:9–11 describes a "little horn" emerging from one of these four divisions, specifically from the northern region, which historically includes modern-day Syria and parts of Turkey.
- This little horn grows in influence toward the south, east, and the "pleasant land"—a clear reference to Israel.
- Daniel 8:23 identifies him as "a king of fierce countenance" who arises in the latter days, speaking to the Antichrist's character and timing.

The King of the North—Later, in Daniel 11, this end-time ruler is portrayed as the "King of the North," opposing the King of the South (traditionally understood as Egypt). He launches military campaigns, invades Israel, and subdues many nations (Daniel 11:40–41). This further anchors his base of operations in the Middle Eastern region north of Israel.

Isaiah's Clues: The Assyrian Title—Several prophetic passages in Isaiah refer to the Antichrist symbolically as "the Assyrian."

- Isaiah 10:24, 27—"Be not afraid of the Assyrian . . . his burden shall be taken away from your shoulder."
- Isaiah 30:31—"For through the voice of the LORD shall the Assyrian be beaten down . . ."

The Assyrian title connects the Antichrist with northern Mesopotamia—a region encompassing parts of modern-day Iraq, Syria, Turkey, and Iran. This is consistent with the earlier prophetic frameworks in Daniel and reflects a Middle Eastern origin rather than a strictly Western one.

Does the Antichrist Have "No Regard for Women"?

Daniel 11:37 states that the Antichrist "shall have no regard for the desire of women." While this phrase has led to various interpretations, most scholars agree it likely does not indicate sexual perversion. Instead it could imply:

- A rejection of traditional family values or natural affection.
- A dismissal of the Messianic hope, since Jewish women longed to bear the Messiah.

- Or, according to some interpretations, a broader cultural alignment with ideologies—including certain religious or political systems—that do not prioritize or protect the rights and dignity of women.

Regardless of the exact meaning, the verse emphasizes the Antichrist's cold, self-exalting nature, and his rejection of anything or anyone that does not serve his ambition for absolute power.

The cumulative weight of Daniel and Isaiah's prophecies—combined with geographic and symbolic indicators—suggests that the Antichrist will emerge from the Middle East, specifically from the ancient Assyrian region. This aligns prophetically with the biblical emphasis on Israel and her neighbors as the focal point of end-time events.

The Imitator Will Fall

The Antichrist is not merely a rebel against God—he is a counterfeit of Christ. Scripture paints a chilling picture: this figure rises not just with political ambition, but with spiritual deception, mimicking the very Messiah he opposes. He will mirror Christ's mission, authority, even resurrection—but all in twisted form.

Why does he imitate?

Because Satan doesn't create—he corrupts. As a fallen archangel, Lucifer once stood in the courts of heaven. He beheld the majesty of God, the order of worship, the glory of righteousness. And in his rebellion, he didn't invent his own way—he hijacked heaven's pattern and warped it. The Antichrist is the culmination of that corruption: Satan's final attempt to duplicate God's plan and deceive the world.

> For there shall arise false Christs, and false prophets, and shall show great signs and wonders; insomuch that, if it were possible, they shall deceive the very elect. (Matthew 24:24)

That's why this deception will be so strong. But the more clearly we know the true Christ, the more easily we will spot the false one. This is the moment to be anchored in truth.

Make no mistake: the Antichrist is not Christ's opposite equal. He never was. He never will be. His power is temporary. His dominion is limited. His time is short. He may rise for a moment, but his fall is certain and final. Satan still seeks a throne. That ambition never died. But the Kingdom belongs to the Lord—and His reign has no rival.

God's eternal Kingdom cannot be fully established until the counterfeit kingdom is destroyed. Until then, in His sovereignty, God is allowing Satan's final rebellion to play out—for the whole world to witness the contrast between the deceiver's lies and the truth of Christ.

This is the battle of the ages. The entire earth will have a front-row seat:

- The Antichrist will be unmasked.
- The False Prophet will fall silent.
- Satan will be cast down.
- And Jesus Christ will return in glory to reign.

Then the world will finally declare:

Jehovah alone is God. And there is no one like Jesus.

The rebellion began long ago . . . before time began, Lucifer lifted his heart in pride and declared: "I will be like the Most High" (Isaiah 14:14). He led a third of the angels in a rebellion against God. Ever since, that rebellion has echoed across history—through empires, through lies, through false worship. But it won't echo forever. There's a day marked on heaven's calendar: the final day of Armageddon. On that day, this rebellion ends.

When Christ returns, He will not come alone. The redeemed—His Church—and His angels will return with Him. Clothed in glory. Riding on white horses. Safe in His presence. And we will witness what creation has groaned for:

- The defeat of Satan.
- The fall of the Antichrist.
- The silencing of the False Prophet.
- And the triumphant reign of Jesus Christ, the King of kings.

For the kingdom is the LORD's: and He is the governor among the nations. (Psalm 22:28)

History is winding down. Prophecies are unfolding. The final pieces are falling into place. And the King is coming.

So let me close with this: The Antichrist may imitate. He may deceive. But Jesus Christ—crucified, risen, and returning—is unmatched. Unshaken. Unchanging. There is no one like Him. And His Kingdom will never end.

"Ann, before we dive into Revelation 13:1–10 and the rise of the beast out of the sea, I think we need to pause for a moment. Let's step back and consider the broader context—Satan's empire hasn't emerged overnight. It's been developing throughout history strategically building toward this moment."

"Yes! And it's not random. Revelation 13:1 describes a beast with seven heads and ten horns—imagery packed with meaning. The seven heads symbolize seven world empires influenced by Satan, a truth confirmed in Revelation 17:9–10, which outlines these kingdoms across prophetic history."

> And here is the mind which has wisdom. The seven heads are seven mountains, on which the woman sits. And there are seven kings: five are fallen, and one is, and the other is not yet come; and when he comes, he must continue a short space. (Revelation 17:9–10)

"So, what are these seven heads? What do the seven super-kingdoms of Satan represent?"

"Let's walk through them—are you ready?"

Irene gave a quick nod. "Absolutely. Let's do it."

"First—Egypt. That's where it all began. Egypt enslaved God's people, trying to crush the covenant before it could take root. Remember Pharaoh? God raised up Moses to confront him."

"Exactly. Egypt tried to destroy the seed. Satan was aiming to abort Israel's destiny before it could be fulfilled."

"Second—Assyria. Ruthless and brutal. After the deaths of King David and his son Solomon, Israel split into two kingdoms: the northern kingdom consisting of ten tribes, and the southern kingdom of Judah and Benjamin. In 722 BC, the Assyrians conquered the northern kingdom and scattered the ten tribes throughout their empire. Once again, Satan struck at God's people—trying to erase the Abrahamic covenant promise before it could be fulfilled."

"And third?"

"Babylon. It wasn't just military conquest—it was spiritual seduction. Idolatry, sorcery, and paganism saturated the culture. They exiled Judah and defiled the temple."

"And Babylon becomes more than history—it's a prophetic symbol. Revelation's 'Mystery Babylon' picks up the thread of end-time deception."

"Exactly, Irene. Fourth—Persia. Though God used Persia to bring the Jews back home, Satan still moved behind the scenes. Remember Haman's plot in Esther?"

Irene nodded. "A satanic attempt at genocide. But once again, God intervened and preserved His covenant people."

"Fifth was Greece. Under Alexander the Great, the world was swept up in philosophy, culture, and human wisdom. Satan used it to elevate intellect over truth—subtly replacing God's revelation with prideful reasoning."

"And then comes Rome—number six."

"Yes. Rome was the iron empire. It ruled during Christ's First Coming—it crucified Jesus and persecuted the early Church with unrelenting force. Revelation 17:10 says:"

> And there are seven kings: five are fallen, and one is, and the other is not yet come; and when he comes, he must continue a short space. (Revelation 17:10)

"That 'one is'—that's Rome. John was living under its dominion when he wrote this."

Irene leaned forward. "That's six. What's number seven?"

I took a breath. "The seventh head . . . is America."

Irene blinked. "Seriously? I thought the Antichrist's empire would be based in the Middle East or Europe."

I nodded. "It will be—but that's part of the complexity. Revelation 17:10 says, 'five are fallen, one is, and the other is not yet come; and when he comes, he must continue a short space.' Rome was the sixth—John lived under it. The seventh is the next great superpower with global dominance."

Irene sat back. "And you think that's the United States?"

"Think about it. America may not be ancient like Egypt or Babylon, but her reach is global—militarily, economically, culturally. She has her tentacles in every continent, every conflict. She's the only empire in history with military bases in over 70 nations and the power to influence worldwide decisions."

Irene nodded slowly. "And only 250 years old."

"Exactly," I said. "Compared to the centuries of millennia of the other empires, America's dominance is brief—a 'short space,' just like Revelation says."

Irene furrowed her brow. "But where does the Antichrist fit into this? Isn't his power base in the Middle East?"

I smiled. "That's the twist. The Antichrist's empire—the ten-horn coalition—is a subset of the beast. It's likely formed from Middle Eastern and European regions, yes. But post-Rapture, after the sixth seal and the first four trumpets, the whole world changes."

Irene looked intrigued. "You mean geologically?"

"Exactly. The sixth seal causes a global earthquake—every mountain and island moved. That's followed by trumpet judgments that burn up a third of the earth, oceans, rivers, and sky. It's like God is reclaiming and reshaping the planet—burning away what doesn't belong."

Irene leaned forward again. "So you're saying the lower third of the old Pangaea landmass is destroyed, and the landmass is reoriented toward the Bible Lands?"

I nodded. "Yes. America remains geographically, but the world's attention and structure shift east. The Antichrist's kingdom will be centered around Israel—what the Bible calls the 'pleasant land'—but it will carry global authority. And America, having ruled as the seventh head, gives way to the final beast system."

Irene was quiet for a moment. "So America's rise wasn't random—it was strategic. A final empire before the real endgame begins."

I looked solemn. "She offers peace, security, even prosperity—but in the end, she's part of the beast system. She will fall before the King returns."

Irene tilted her head. "But wait—can we really call the Antichrist's empire a world empire? Doesn't he just make a covenant with Israel and a few nations at first?"

I nodded. "Exactly. That's what makes this so deceptive. For the first 3½ years of the Tribulation, his influence is mostly regional. Daniel 9:27 says he confirms a covenant with *many*, but not necessarily the whole world."

Irene leaned in. "So his kingdom doesn't start globally?"

I clarified, "No. It grows. He starts small, probably within a Middle Eastern or European alliance. But the global chaos after the Rapture creates a vacuum—and he fills it. That's why it's called a 'beast rising from the sea'—it rises from chaos."

Irene was thoughtful. "But it only lasts seven years."

I nodded. "Right. And compared to every major empire in history, seven years is nothing. That's why it's so striking—he has immense power, but it's brief. The Bible never says his rule is like the length or stability of Babylon or Rome."

Irene looked unsettled. "So then why is America so important in this?"

I hesitated. "Because America has acted like a global empire—without calling herself one. Think about it. She's overthrown governments, installed puppet leaders, and shaped entire regions through military, economic, and intelligence influence."

Irene blinked. "Regime changes."

I nodded. "Exactly. From Latin America to the Middle East. And in the vacuum left by her decline or judgment, the Antichrist steps into the space—offering the world a new hope, a new order. But it's a lie."

Irene was quiet. "So America is the last head . . . and the Antichrist is the final horn."

I looked her in the eye. "That's it. America is the seventh head of the beast. The Antichrist's ten-king coalition is the final phase—the beast's horns. It's not that he rules the entire globe immediately. He rules by deception, by proxy, and through crisis."

Irene nodded slowly. "And then it all crashes down"

I whispered, "Right before the King returns."

Irene furrowed her brow.

"So, Ann, let me recap: Egypt, Assyria, Babylon, Persia, Greece, Rome, and America. That's seven. But why do so many scholars still say the seventh kingdom is a revised or revived Rome?"

I nodded. "Good question. And honestly—it comes down to this: America functions like a revived Rome. Not geographically, but ideologically."

Irene tilted her head. "How so?"

"Think about it. Rome may have fallen in *form*, but not in *function*. Its core systems—law, government, military strategy, even infrastructure thinking—they didn't disappear. They morphed, migrated. And in the modern world, America has become the face of those systems."

Irene was quiet, processing.

"So . . . America is a kind of revived imperial power?"

I nodded. "Exactly. Just not with legions marching across Europe. America's dominance is economic, technological, military, and cultural. It's influence is global—Hollywood, Silicon Valley, Wall Street, D.C. That's not just power— that's empire."

Irene looked up.

"But it's not ruling by land conquest."

I smiled.

"Right. It's ruling by systems. America projects power through finance, media, tech, even moral ideology. That *is* a kind of imperialism. It's not borders— it's bandwidth. And that's why it fits Revelation 17:10: 'five have fallen, one is, the other has not yet come.'"

Irene leaned forward.

"So America is the 'one that has not yet come'—the seventh head."

I nodded. "Yes. The final form before the Antichrist's ten-king coalition rises. That's the beast's horn phase."

Irene shook her head slowly.

"Wow. So scholars aren't wrong to say it's 'revived Rome.' They're just missing *who* revived it."

I smiled.

"Exactly. Rome was the blueprint. America became the builder. And she only rules for a short space—just like Revelation said."

"Amen. And now, let's turn the page and meet the beast himself in Revelation 13:1–10."

———◆◆◆———

THE REVELATION OF JESUS CHRIST REVEALS:

^{13:1} And I stood upon the sand of the sea, and saw a beast rise up out of the sea, having seven heads and ten horns, and upon his horns ten crowns, and upon his heads the name of blasphemy.

"And I stood upon the sand of the sea, and saw a beast rise up out of the sea." This marks the unveiling of the first beast—the Antichrist—emerging from the chaotic sea of humanity. In Scripture, "the sea" often symbolizes more than water; it represents multitudes of people, nations in turmoil, and widespread political upheaval. Here, it captures the post-Rapture world: governments collapsing, economies failing, and societies unraveling. Out of this global chaos—this vacuum of leadership, order, and truth—rises the beast.

And John saw it. Picture him—exiled on the island of Patmos—standing on the shore, gazing into the future. From the sand beside the sea, he beholds a terrifying creature: not merely a political figure, but a spiritual one, animated by the forces of hell itself.

"Having seven heads." This beast is no ordinary power. The seven heads symbolize a composite authority—seven successive world empires that have risen throughout history to persecute God's people and resist His purposes. Each "head" represents both a kingdom and its king (Revelation 17:9–10), forming a satanic legacy of rebellion against God's redemptive plan.

These are the seven heads—empires that, for over 5,000 years, have stood in defiant opposition to God and His people:

1. **Egyptian Empire—The first great oppressor**. Egypt rose to power around 3100 BC, but it was during the New Kingdom (1550–1070 BC) that it enslaved Israel. Pharaoh defied the living God, and through Moses, God judged Egypt with plagues and parted the Red Sea— delivering His people and crushing the world's superpower in 1446 BC (1 Kings 6:1). Egypt remained a dominant force until its fall to Rome in 30 BC.

2. **Assyrian Empire—Ruthless and brutal**. After the division of Israel into northern and southern kingdoms, Assyria conquered the north and scattered the ten tribes in 722 BC (2 Kings 17). Satan, once again, attempted to erase the covenant by removing God's people from their land. The empire began to decline in the late 600s BC and ultimately fell to the Babylonians in 612 BC with the destruction of Nineveh.

3. **Babylon Empire—The empire of exile**. Babylon rose to dominate after Assyria's fall and conquered the southern kingdom of Judah in stages,

culminating in the destruction of Jerusalem and the Temple in 586 BC (2 Kings 25). It was Nebuchadnezzar who exiled Daniel and others, yet it was also in Babylon that God revealed to Daniel the prophetic timeline of all future kingdoms. The empire was known for its wealth, culture, and the famed hanging gardens. Babylon's dominance ended when it fell to the Medo-Persian Empire under Cyrus the Great in 539 BC.

4. **Medo-Persian Empire—The dual power**. Persia overthrew Babylon in 539 BC and allowed the Jews to return to Jerusalem and rebuild (Ezra 1:1–4). Though less overtly oppressive, the Persian era included plots like Haman's genocidal plan in the Book of Esther—yet God preserved His people. The empire became the largest empire of its time, stretching from India to Greece and Egypt. It lasted until 331 BC.

5. **Grecian Empire—Swift and shrewd**. Led by Alexander the Great, Greece conquered the Persian Empire around 331 BC. His empire later fractured into four parts, fulfilling Daniels prophecy (Daniel 8:8, 22). Under Greek rule, Antiochus IV Epiphanes desecrated the Temple—foreshadowing the Antichrist's future abomination of desolation.

Greek influence deeply shaped the world's culture, education, and religion—laying the intellectual and philosophical groundwork that the New Testament writers would later confront. Greece's dominance gradually faded as Rome rose to power, culminating in Rome's conquest of the Greek world by 146 BC.

6. **Roman Empire—The iron beast**. Rome conquered the known world and was in power during the time of Christ. It crucified the Messiah, destroyed the Second Temple in AD 70, and dispersed the Jewish people—ushering in a centuries-long diaspora. This places Rome at the heart of biblical prophecy and New Testament history.

Though the Western Roman Empire officially fell in AD 476, the Eastern Roman (Byzantine) Empire endured until AD 1453. Yet Rome's systems, laws, language, and culture never truly vanished. Its influence continued through Western civilization and modern governance. Many scholars believe Rome never fully disappeared but evolved—serving as a prophetic forerunner to modern global powers, particularly America, which many identify as the seventh kingdom in Revelation.

7. **American Empire—A modern reflection of Rome**. Though never officially labeled an "empire," America began its rise to global

prominence in the late 19th and early 20th centuries—especially after the Spanish-American War in 1898, when it acquired overseas territories like the Philippines, Guam, and Puerto Rico. Its true emergence as a world superpower followed World War II (1945), becoming dominant economically, militarily, and culturally.

America's global influence mirrors the imperial reach of ancient Rome—projected not through land conquest, but through military bases, intelligence networks, technology, media, and economic systems. It has often overthrown foreign governments, installed puppet regimes, and exported its ideologies worldwide, fulfilling the prophetic image of a kingdom that rules by influence rather than territory.

Biblically, many interpret America as the seventh kingdom in Revelation 17:10: "The other has not yet come; but when he does, he must remain for a little while." At just 250 years old, America's reign is brief compared to ancient empires. According to prophecy, her fall as Mystery Babylon (Revelation 17–18) comes near the end of the Tribulation—after the bowl judgments—just before the rise of the Antichrist's final push and the Battle of Armageddon.

"And ten horns, and upon his horns ten crowns." The ten horns represent ten kings or kingdoms—a confederation of nations that will come together in the end times to form the political base of the Antichrist. Crowns on these horns show that they possess real authority. But make no mistake—they will yield their power to the beast, a man energized by Satan himself.

"And upon his heads the name of blasphemy." And what is written on the heads of this beast? Blasphemy. Not just spoken, but branded. This beast defies God openly. He mocks heaven, desecrates truth, and demands worship. He will set himself up in the rebuilt Third Tempe of Jerusalem and declare himself to be God (2 Thessalonians 2:4). His entire empire is dripping in blasphemous rebellion—from the system, to the seat, to the soul of the man himself.

This is no myth. No allegory. This is prophetic reality. Just as Christ is the visible image of the invisible God, the Antichrist will be the visible face of the invisible dragon—Satan. He will be Satan's counterfeit messiah, stepping onto the world stage as a man of peace but swiftly revealing himself as a tyrant of hell.

He's not rising out of nowhere. He's rising out of the chaos. And chaos is coming. Planes will crash. Cars will pile up. Phones will ring unanswered. World leaders will vanish. The Rapture will leave the earth in disarray. And out of the smoke and confusion, a voice will rise: "I have the answers."

That voice will be smooth. Persuasive. Politically flawless. Economically brilliant. Charismatically unmatched. But hell-birthed. He won't appear as a monster. He'll appear as a savior to the broken, a leader for the lost, a solution for the shaken. But beneath that surface—he is the beast. Bearing crowns. Bearing heads. Bearing the name of blasphemy.

OLD TESTAMENT FORESHADOWS REVELATION:

Daniel spoke and said, I saw in my vision by night, and, behold, the four winds of the heaven strove upon the great sea. And four great beasts came up from the sea, diverse one from another. (Daniel 7:2–3)

Just as Daniel saw four beastly empires rising from the sea—symbolizing Gentile world powers—John sees a final beast rising from the sea, a culmination of all previous kingdoms. The sea in both passages represents the chaotic, unstable masses of humanity and political upheaval from which these tyrannical leaders emerge.

THE REVELATION OF JESUS CHRIST REVEALS:

13:2 And the beast which I saw was like to a leopard, and his feet were as the feet of a bear, and his mouth as the mouth of a lion: and the dragon gave him his power, and his seat, and great authority.

In this verse, John sees something terrifying—yet strangely familiar. This isn't a random creature of apocalyptic imagination. It's a prophetic composite, a fusion of beasts drawn directly from the Book of Daniel—written over 600 years earlier.

In Daniel 7, four world empires are symbolized by beasts:

1. Lion with eagle's wings—Babylon (Daniel 7:4)
2. Bear raised up on one side—Medo-Persia (Daniel 7:5)
3. Leopard with four wings and four heads—Greece (Daniel 7:6)
4. Dreadful beast with iron teeth and ten horns—Rome (Daniel 7:7)

Now in Revelation 13:2, notice what John sees:

- A leopard—swift and cunning (Greece)
- Feet like a bear—strong and crushing (Medo-Persia)
- Mouth like a lion—fierce and authoritative (Babylon)

But the order is reversed. Daniel looked forward through time. John, standing at the end, looks back—and sees the full culmination: a beast that embodies the worst of every Gentile empire that has ever opposed God and oppressed His people.

The phrase "And the dragon gave him his power, and his seat, and great authority" unveils the true source behind the Antichrist's dominion. The dragon—clearly identified in Revelation 12:9 as Satan—grants the beast his power, throne, and authority. This satanic transfer echoes the divine pattern seen in Christ's ministry: just as Jesus was empowered by the Holy Spirit to fulfill the Father's redemptive mission, the Antichrist is empowered by Satan to fulfill a counterfeit mission of deception, rebellion, and global domination.

This beast—symbolic of the final world ruler—is no ordinary political figure. He is a tyrant with the swiftness of a leopard (Greece), the brute strength of a bear (Medo-Persia), and the terrifying roar of a lion (Babylon). These traits, drawn from Daniel's vision (Daniel 7), depict a fusion of the most oppressive empires in history—now embodied in a single end-time figure.

Though he does not arise from peace or stability, the Antichrist seizes opportunity through global chaos, likely in the wake of the Rapture and early judgments of the Tribulation. His rise is not by merit, but by manipulation. His authority is not from men, but from the dragon. His ambition is not hidden—he openly blasphemes God and opposes His saints.

This composite beast represents the climax of human rebellion, spiritually empowered by Satan, and destined for judgment by the returning Christ.

OLD TESTAMENT FORESHADOWS REVELATION:

After this I beheld, and lo another, like a leopard, which had upon the back of it four wings of a fowl; the beast had also four heads; and dominion was given to it. After this I saw in the night visions, and behold a fourth beast, dreadful and terrible, and strong exceedingly; and it had great iron teeth: it devoured, and broke in pieces, and stamped the residue with the feet of it: and it was diverse from all the beasts that were before it; and it had ten horns. (Daniel 7:6–7)

Leopard (Daniel 7:6) parallels the swiftness and cunning of Greece in John's beast. Bear (Daniel 7:5, indirectly referenced through feet) reflects the brute force of Medo-Persia. Lion (Daniel 7:4, indirectly referenced through mouth) represents Babylon's boldness and dominion. These three elements are merged in Revelation 13:2, creating a composite beast—a symbolic representation of the final ruler, the Antichrist, empowered by Satan. This mirrors how John's vision in Revelation brings Daniel's prophecy to its ultimate fulfillment.

THE REVELATION OF JESUS CHRIST REVEALS:

[13:3] And I saw one of his heads as it were wounded to death; and his deadly wound was healed: and all the world wondered after the beast.

This verse marks a turning point in the rise of the Antichrist's global domination. The phrase "one of his heads as it were wounded to death" has captivated prophecy scholars and believers alike for centuries. It appears that the Antichrist—at some point during his ascent—suffers a fatal head wound. The wording "wounded to death" implies a mortal blow. But miraculously—or deceptively—"his deadly wound was healed."

The resurrection-like recovery leads the entire world to marvel and follow after the beast. This false resurrection is Satan's ultimate counterfeit of Christ's death and resurrection (Matthew 28:6). Just as Jesus was raised from the dead and declared with power to be the Son of God (Romans 1:4), the Antichrist will mimic this miracle to validate his false claim to divinity.

Revelation 13:13–14 reveals that the False Prophet is the one who performs great wonders to validate the Antichrist's resurrection, including calling fire from heaven and deceiving the masses through miracles:

> And deceives them that dwell on the earth, by the means of those miracles which he had power to do in the sight of the beast; saying to them that dwell on the earth, that they should make an image to the beast, which had the wound by a sword, and did live. (Revelation 13:14)

The parallel passage in 2 Thessalonians 2:9–12 provides further insight:

> Even him, whose coming is after the working of Satan with all power and signs and lying wonders. And with all deceivableness of unrighteousness in them that perish; because they received not the love of the truth, that they might be saved. And for this cause God shall send them strong delusion, that they should believe a lie. That they all might be damned who believed not the truth, but had pleasure in unrighteousness. (2 Thessalonians 2:9–12)

Satan cannot create life, but he is a master of deception. Whether the Antichrist's "resurrection" in Revelation 13:3 is literal or an elaborate illusion, the impact is undeniable—the world will believe it and worship the beast.

This moment raises key questions:

- Is the Antichrist truly resurrected? Or is this a staged miracle—what Scripture calls a "lying wonder" (2 Thessalonians 2:9)?
- Is it the False Prophet who performs this act? Or is it a direct display of Satan's power, now unrestrained?

These questions underscore Satan's limitations. He is not a life-giver—only God creates. But during the Great Tribulation, the restraining force (2 Thessalonians 2:6–7) is removed, and Satan is unleashed to deceive without limit. This apparent resurrection becomes his ultimate counterfeit—his imitation of Christ's victory over death.

In a world ravaged by the Rapture and divine judgments, the appearance of a man who seemingly conquers death will electrify the shaken masses. It will cement the Antichrist's status as a global savior—a false messiah. But for those who know the true Lamb, slain before the foundation of the world, this is nothing more than the serpent's final deception—desperate, blasphemous, and doomed to fail.

OLD TESTAMENT FORESHADOWS REVELATION:

Woe to the idol shepherd that leaves the flock! The sword shall be upon his arm, and upon his right eye: his arm shall be clean dried up, and his right eye shall be utterly darkened. (Zechariah 11:17)

Many scholars and prophecy teachers see the "idol shepherd" in this verse as a prophetic foreshadowing of the Antichrist—a false shepherd who abandons and misleads the flock, in stark contrast to Jesus, the Good Shepherd (John 10). The sword striking his arm and right eye suggests a violent, possibly fatal wound—echoing Revelation 13:3, which describes a deadly wound that is miraculously healed, astonishing the world and prompting worship of the beast.

Symbolically, the right arm often represents strength or authority, while the right eye conveys vision, discernment, or insight. The drying up of the arm and the darkening of the eye may signify both physical disfigurement and spiritual corruption or blindness.

Taken together, Zechariah 11:17 and Revelation 13:3 paint a chilling picture; a counterfeit resurrection, complete with visible, lasting scars. This grotesque mimicry of Christ's wounds may serve as a twisted "sign" to validate the Antichrist's satanic anointing—one last deception to captivate a world desperate for hope but blinded to truth.

THE REVELATION OF JESUS CHRIST REVEALS:

[13:4] And they worshiped the dragon which gave power to the beast: and they worshiped the beast, saying, Who is like to the beast? Who is able to make war with him?

This verse unveils one of the darkest spiritual deceptions in human history: global worship of Satan himself, masked behind the power and charisma of the Antichrist. The dragon here, as made plain in Revelation 12:9, is Satan—the ancient serpent, the deceiver of the whole world. His longing has always been worship. That was the heart of his rebellion in heaven (Isaiah 14:13–14), and in the wilderness, he even tempted Jesus to worship him (Luke 4:5–8). In Revelation 13:4, Satan finally gets what he craves—for a brief moment.

"And they worshiped the dragon which gave power to the beast." Mankind will willingly and blindly offer worship to Satan, not necessarily by name, but by exalting and idolizing the Antichrist, the man through whom Satan's power flows. This is unholy worship—the ultimate counterfeit to honoring Christ.

"And they worshiped the beast." The world will be enamored with the Antichrist—his charisma, authority, seemingly miraculous resurrection, and political dominance—that he will become an object of divine reverence. He will appear unstoppable, and people will not only admire him—they will revere him.

"Who is like unto the beast? Who is able to make war with him?" This echoes the kind of praise reserved only for God. Compare it to Exodus 15:11:

> Who is like unto You, O LORD, among the gods? Who is like You, glorious in holiness, fearful in praises, doing wonders? (Exodus 15:11)

This is blasphemous mimicry. The same language once used to glorify Jehovah (the God of Israel) is now misdirected to glorify the beast. It is a prophetic picture of what happens when humanity rejects God: they will worship power, fear domination, and bow before evil that promises peace.

And yet, the ultimate irony lies here: They ask, "Who is able to make war with him?" The answer is already written in Revelation 19:11–16—Jesus Christ, the Rider on the white horse, will make war—and He will win.

OLD TESTAMENT FORESHADOWS REVELATION:

> Yea, they sacrificed their sons and their daughters unto devils, And shed innocent blood, even the blood of their sons and of their daughters, whom they sacrificed unto idols of Canaan: and the land was polluted with blood. (Psalm 106:37–38)

In Psalm 106:37–38, we see demonic worship through idolatry and human sacrifice—a graphic picture of what happens when people turn from God to serve devils. In Revelation 13:4, that same dark spirit returns globally. But instead of pagan idols, the dragon (Satan) and the beast (the Antichrist) are exalted. The sacrifices may not be on altars, but they will be through allegiance, deception, and the shedding of innocent blood during the Great Tribulation.

This prophetic pattern—from ancient Canaan to the coming Tribulation—shows how mankind consistently trades the truth of God for the lies of demonic power. In Canaan, it was pagan idols and literal blood sacrifice. In Revelation 13, it is global worship of Satan's unholy trinity through allegiance to the beast. Canaan represents the battleground between God's covenant promises and Satan's seductive counterfeits. It's where truth confronts deception—and where every soul must choose.

THE REVELATION OF JESUS CHRIST REVEALS:

> 13:5 And there was given to him a mouth speaking great things and blasphemies; and power was given to him to continue forty and two months.

This verse is loaded with prophetic intensity. Don't miss the phrase: "and there was given to him." The Antichrist doesn't rise by sheer ambition. He doesn't claim power by force. He's granted it. It's permitted—not by Satan alone, but ultimately by God Himself. This is divine sovereignty in motion.

Even Satan's most powerful pawn can do nothing without God's allowance. Revelation 13:5 doesn't show a God who has lost control—but a God who is bringing His prophetic timeline to a close, on schedule, by design. This isn't chaos. It's judgment with precision. A global stage being set for the final confrontation between good and evil—because God said it would be so.

The Antichrist's "mouth speaking great things and blasphemies" parallels Daniel 7:8 and 7:25, where the "little horn" speaks pompous and arrogant words against the Most High. This is not just political rhetoric—it is outright defiance of heaven. The Antichrist will openly mock God, His people, and everything sacred.

Then we're told his power will last for forty-two months—3½ years, the second half of the Tribulation. That's the same time period repeatedly referenced throughout Daniel and Revelation (Revelation 11:2–3, 12:6, 14; Daniel 7:25). This is not symbolic—this is literal, prophetic precision.

But take comfort in this: His reign is limited. It's measured. It's temporary. God draws the line—not Satan. The Antichrist's blasphemies may be loud, and his influence vast, but it's all on a leash. And when the forty-two months are up, the Lion of the tribe of Judah will roar.

OLD TESTAMENT FORESHADOWS REVELATION:

And he shall speak great words against the Most High, and shall wear out the saints of the Most High, and think to change times and laws: and they shall be given into his hand until a time and times and the dividing of time. (Daniel 7:25)

Daniel's "time, times, and a dividing of time" equals 3½ years, the same as 42 months in Revelation 13:5. The Antichrist's blasphemies and temporary authority are foretold in Daniel 7:25 and fulfilled in Revelation. This reinforces the consistency between Old and New Testament prophecy—and highlights that God is in full control of the prophetic timeline.

THE REVELATION OF JESUS CHRIST REVEALS:

13:6 And he opened his mouth in blasphemy against God, to blaspheme His name, and His tabernacle, and them that dwell in heaven.

The Antichrist is more than just a political figure—he's the ultimate blasphemer. He launches a verbal assault against the very throne of God. This isn't just arrogance—it's warfare by words. His mouth becomes his greatest weapon—filled with pride, defiance, and deception.

This verse shows us that his hatred has three targets:

1. **God's Name**—He openly mocks God's character and identity.

2. **God's Tabernacle**—Likely a reference to heaven itself or even the rebuilt Third Temple. He despises everything holy.

3. **Those Who Dwell in Heaven**—He blasphemes the saints, angels, and possibly the raptured Church—those already with the Lord.

This is Satan's ultimate imitation of Christ—just as Jesus revealed the Father through truth, the Antichrist defames God through lies. He not only rejects God but dares to take His place. It's a calculated, full-scale blasphemy campaign from the pit of hell—permitted for a season, but destined for eternal judgment.

OLD TESTAMENT FORESHADOWS REVELATION:

And the king shall do according to his will; and he shall exalt himself, and magnify himself above every god, and shall speak marvelous things against the God of gods, and shall prosper till the indignation be accomplished: for that that is determined shall be done. (Daniel 11:36)

Daniel 11:36 offers a striking foreshadowing of the Antichrist described in Revelation. The verse speaks of a king who will exalt himself and speak blasphemies against the God of gods—directly paralleling Revelation 13:6, where the Antichrist opens his mouth in blasphemy against God, His name, His tabernacle, and those who dwell in heaven. This isn't just arrogance—it's calculated defiance. The Antichrist doesn't merely oppose truth; he positions himself as a false messiah, desecrating all that is holy.

But Daniel also makes it clear: this reign of terror is not limitless. It is permitted only "till the indignation be accomplished," aligning with Revelation's divinely set timeframe of forty-two months (Revelation 13:5). Together, these passages tie Old Testament prophecy to New Testament fulfillment, revealing a unified, sovereign plan—God's timeline for redemptive history, playing out exactly as foretold.

THE REVELATION OF JESUS CHRIST REVEALS:

13:7 And it was given to him to make war with the saints, and to overcome them: and power was given him over all kindreds, and tongues, and nations.

This verse represents one of the darkest moments in the Book of Revelation. Here, the Antichrist is granted authority—not by his own merit or power, but by divine permission—to wage war against the saints and temporarily overcome them.

"And it was given to him." This phrase reminds us of a powerful truth: even evil operates under God's sovereign permission. The Antichrist, like Satan himself, cannot move one inch outside the boundary of what God allows. Just as Jesus told Pilate, "You could have no power at all against Me, except it were given you from above" (John 19:11), we're reminded that God is always in control, even when it appears that evil is winning.

"To make war with the saints, and to overcome them." These "saints" refer specifically to those who come to faith during the Tribulation period—often called the Tribulation saints. The Church has already been raptured (1 Thessalonians 4:16–17), so these believers are converts post-Rapture. The Antichrist will relentlessly persecute them, and for a time, he will prevail—physically, but not spiritually. Their faith and martyrdom will testify against the wickedness of the beast system.

"And power was given him over all kindreds, and tongues, and nations." The Antichrist's influence is global. His control spans ethnic groups ("kindreds"), languages ("tongues"), and national borders ("nations")—this points to a worldwide dictatorship, something never before seen in human history. This isn't regional tyranny—it's a global system of political, religious, economic, and military control. God is not absent during this terrifying time. He is allowing Satan and the Antichrist a final stage to deceive and destroy—but only for a moment. This verse sets up the contrast between the Antichrist's temporary reign and Christ's eternal victory.

OLD TESTAMENT FORESHADOWS REVELATION:

And they that understand among the people shall instruct many: yet they shall fall by the sword, and by flame, by captivity, and by spoil, many days. (Daniel 11:33)

"They shall fall by the sword" corresponds with "it was given unto him to make war with the saints, and to overcome them." The phrase speaks of the persecution of the faithful during the rise of a wicked ruler—foreshadowing the Great Tribulation when saints will face intense global oppression.

THE REVELATION OF JESUS CHRIST REVEALS:

13:8 And all that dwell upon the earth will worship him, whose names are not written in the Book of Life of the Lamb slain from the foundation of the world.

This verse delivers one of the most sobering truths in the entire Book of Revelation. During the Great Tribulation, the entire unbelieving world—"all that dwell upon the earth"—will unite in worship of the beast, the Antichrist. But notice the dividing line: only those whose names are not written in the Book of Life will fall into this global deception. This "Book of Life" belongs to the Lamb, Jesus Christ, slain from the foundation of the world—a powerful reminder that the Cross was not an afterthought, but part of God's eternal redemptive plan.

Old Testament Echoes:

- Exodus 32:32—Moses appeals to God to blot him out of His Book if He would not forgive Israel.
- Daniel 12:1—Those "found written in the Book" shall be delivered.
- Isaiah 4:3—Refers to those who are "written among the living."

These foreshadow the "Book of Life," a divine registry of the redeemed.

New Testament Reinforcement:

- Luke 10:20—Jesus tells His disciples to rejoice because their names are written in heaven.
- 1 Peter 1:19–20—Christ, as the Lamb, was foreordained before the foundation of the world—again pointing to God's eternal plan.
- Philippians 4:3 and Revelation 3:5, 20:15—Further establish the reality and significance of the Book of Life.

Some scholars note that in the original Greek structure, the phrase "from the foundation of the world" may grammatically apply to the writing of names in the Book of Life rather than the timing of the Lamb's crucifixion. In other words, this may not only highlight the eternal nature of Christ's sacrifice, but also the foreknowledge of God, who has written the names of the redeemed long before history even began.

This verse draws a stark contrast: Those written in the Lamb's Book will resist the Antichrist, even at the cost of their lives. Those not written will worship the beast without question. It's a dividing line that stretches across eternity. Is your name written in the Book of Life? That's the most important question you'll ever answer.

OLD TESTAMENT FORESHADOWS REVELATION:

And it shall come to pass, that he that is left in Zion, and he that remains in Jerusalem, shall be called holy, even every one that is written among the living in Jerusalem. (Isaiah 4:3)

Isaiah 4:3 speaks prophetically of a preserved remnant, similar to those in Revelation whose names are written in the Lamb's Book of Life. The phrase "written among the living" is strikingly similar to the concept of the Book of Life, which records the names of those who belong to God and are spiritually alive. Just as Revelation 13:8 warns that all will worship the beast except those written in the Book, Isaiah 4:3 highlights the survivors in Jerusalem who are set apart—holy and written.

THE REVELATION OF JESUS CHRIST REVEALS:

13:9 If any man have an ear, let him hear.

This short verse is deceptively powerful. It's a universal call to pay attention—to not merely hear the words, but to understand and respond spiritually. This phrase echoes what Jesus said repeatedly to the seven churches in Revelation chapters 2–3. But here, something is noticeably absent: He does not say, "what the Spirit says unto the churches." That omission is striking.

Why? Because by this point in Revelation, the Church is no longer on the earth. This is the Tribulation. This warning is not directed to the Church, but to anyone still on earth, especially those facing the choice of whether to worship the beast or remain faithful to God.

It's a final appeal to pay attention, to perceive the truth, and to reject the deception of the Antichrist. It's also a reminder: spiritual discernment is critical in the days of great deception.

OLD TESTAMENT FORESHADOWS REVELATION:

And He said, Go, and tell this people, Hear you indeed, but understand not; and see you indeed, but perceive not. Make the heart of this people fat, and make their ears heavy, and shut their eyes; lest they see with their eyes, and hear with their ears, and understand with their heart, and convert, and be healed. (Isaiah 6:9–10)

In Isaiah, God is lamenting Israel's spiritual deafness and blindness—they hear but don't truly listen. Similarly, Revelation 13:9 is a call for spiritual discernment during a time of great deception. Those who refuse to "hear" the truth risk falling under the Antichrist's influence and judgment. Both passages emphasize the urgency of hearing with the heart, not just the ears.

THE REVELATION OF JESUS CHRIST REVEALS:

13:10 He that leads into captivity will go into captivity: he that kills with the sword must be killed with the sword. Here is the patience and the faith of the saints.

This verse is both a warning and a comfort—a divine declaration of justice in the midst of chaos.

"He that leads into captivity shall go into captivity." This is God's way of saying: what you sow, you will reap. Those who are imprisoning others—like the Antichrist and his regime—will themselves be imprisoned. Those who use coercion and bondage to dominate the world will not escape divine judgment.

"He that kills with the sword must be killed with the sword." The same sword used to shed the blood of the innocent will become the instrument of God's retribution. It echoes the ancient biblical principle found in Scripture.

Whoso sheds man's blood, by man shall his blood be shed; for in the image of God made He man. (Genesis 9:6)

To Me belongs vengeance, and recompence; their foot shall slide in due time: for the day of their calamity is at hand, and the things that shall come upon them make haste. (Deuteronomy 32:35)

Dearly beloved, avenge not yourselves, but rather give place unto wrath: for it is written, Vengeance is Mine; I will repay, says the Lord. (Romans 12:19)

Therefore if your enemy hunger, feed him; if he thirst, give him drink: for in so doing you shalt heap coals of fire on his head. Be not overcome of evil, but overcome evil with good. (Romans 12:20–21)

In short, vengeance belongs to God, not us. Even when evil seems unchecked—like the Antichrist persecuting the saints during the Great Tribulation—God's justice is never absent. He sees every wrong and promises to repay in His perfect timing. Our role isn't to retaliate but to trust Him, show mercy, and overcome evil with good, knowing that divine judgment will come—and when it does, it will be final.

"Here is the patience and the faith of the saints." This is the anchor verse for the persecuted believers during the Tribulation period. It's as if heaven is whispering to them: "Hold on. Trust God. The evil will not win. Keep your faith. Justice is coming." This moment demands endurance, not revenge. God is reminding His people that He is keeping score—and soon, the scales of justice will be perfectly balanced.

OLD TESTAMENT FORESHADOWS REVELATION:

And when He comes, He shall smite the land of Egypt, and deliver such as are for death to death; and such as for captivity to captivity; and such as are for the sword to the sword. (Jeremiah 43:11)

This verse in Jeremiah 43:11 offers a striking Old Testament parallel to the sobering prophecy found in Revelation 13:10, where the fate of individuals is sealed: those destined for captivity will go into captivity, and those appointed for the sword will fall by it. In Jeremiah's context, the prophet warns that judgment is coming upon Egypt—a land symbolizing refuge and false security for disobedient Israel. God declares through Jeremiah that no one will escape what has been decreed. Whether by sword, captivity, or death, judgment will come in exact measure to what is appointed.

In the Book of Revelation, this theme resurfaces during the Great Tribulation. It underscores an unsettling but vital truth: there comes a point in God's prophetic timeline when His patience gives way to justice. Just as Egypt could not escape divine judgment in Jeremiah's day, the world in Revelation 13 will face a final reckoning under the reign of the beast. Those who reject God's truth and align with the Antichrist will experience judgment according to their choices.

This parallel reinforces a recurring biblical principle: God's justice is not random but deliberate, righteous, and often pre-declared. It is a call to fear God, submit to His will, and understand that divine mercy has a window—but divine judgment has a certainty.

THE BEAST OUT OF THE EARTH—THE FALSE PROPHET

Before we step into verse 11, we must pause. Something dark is emerging—another key player in Satan's final rebellion against God. We've already seen the first beast rise from the sea: the Antichrist, a political tyrant who seizes the reins of power through chaos, diplomacy, and deception. But now, a second beast comes on the scene—and he is just as dangerous, if not more so.

This second beast doesn't rise out of turbulent waters but from the earth—a subtle, chilling contrast. The sea, throughout Scripture, symbolizes chaos, instability, and political unrest. The earth, however, can represent something more familiar, something that appears firm, calm, and even holy. Don't be deceived. The second beast is anything but holy.

The Most Grave Religious Deceiver in Human History

The Antichrist is a political dictator. But the second beast? He is a religious imposter. He appears like a lamb—gentle, pure, harmless. But when he speaks, his voice reveals the truth: it is the voice of a dragon. His words are venomous. He is no lamb; he is a serpent disguised in wool.

The man is the False Prophet, the spiritual mouthpiece of Satan's unholy trinity. He is the religious counterpart to the Antichrist. If the first beast seizes the nations by political power, the second beast seizes hearts and minds through religious deception.

Daniel, the Old Testament prophet, saw visions of the Antichrist. He saw the "little horn" and the four beasts rising from the sea in Daniel 7. But he never saw the False Prophet. This figure was not revealed to Daniel. He remained hidden in the shadows until the final book of the Bible—the Revelation of Jesus Christ—unveiled him to the apostle John.

John calls him "the False Prophet" three times:

1. **Revelation 16:13**—He is joined by the dragon (Satan) and the first beast (the Antichrist), spewing unclean spirits like frogs—symbols of deception and demonic influence.

2. **Revelation 19:20**—He performs miracles and deceives the world, leading multitudes into worship of the beast and marking them with the number of his name, 666.

3. **Revelation 20:10**—His final destination is the Lake of Fire, where he will be tormented day and night alongside the dragon and the Antichrist.

This isn't just a political regime or religious movement. This is demonic revival—a full-blown counterfeit of the Holy Trinity: Satan as the dragon, the Antichrist as the false messiah, and the False Prophet as the counterfeit Holy Spirit—make up the unholy trinity.

The False Prophet's Role in the End-Time Agenda

This beast from the earth is persuasive, cunning, and extraordinarily powerful. Revelation 13:12 tells us he exercises all the authority of the first beast. He is not a sidekick—he is the strategist behind global worship of the Antichrist. He is the enforcer. The miracle worker. The deceiver.

He performs signs and wonders, even calling fire down from heaven—just like Elijah. He builds an image of the Antichrist and demands worship. This is not symbolic idolatry. It is a literal, visible image—one that speaks and moves. It is either animated through demonic possession, technology, or false resurrection. And it comes with lethal consequences. Anyone who refuses to worship the image will be killed.

He institutes a global system of control—the mark of the beast. No one will be able to buy or sell without it. He controls the economy, society, and religious worship. Obey the beast—or be locked out, hunted, and eliminated. It will be the most coercive persecution system the world has ever known.

And this will be allowed to happen because the Church is gone. The Restrainer—the Holy Spirit in His role within the Church—is removed at the Rapture. What remains is a sliver of His saving power for those who repent, but not the full authority and power we experience today. The world will be without Spirit-filled believers, without godly leadership, and without moral restraint. Satan will have free rein.

Why We Must Understand the False Prophet

Of the two beasts, the False Prophet is arguably the most dangerous. Why? Because his deception is not brute force—it's seduction. It's spiritual. He won't look evil. He will appear as a man of peace, a man of compassion, a man of unity. But his mouth—his message—will be filled with dragon-speak: lies, blasphemy, and manipulation. He will blind the minds of millions. He will have near-total mind control over the earth's population.

He is the last great prophet of hell, leading the world into the worship of a man who will bring about humanity's final rebellion against God. The False Prophet will be a man possessed by Satan, performing miracles by demonic power, and leading a Christ-rejecting world into spiritual slavery under the Antichrist. We must understand him. We must expose him. We must be prepared.

Understanding God's Sovereign Permission

Before we meet the False Prophet in Revelation 13:11, we must pause to consider something profound—and sobering. Revelation 13 reveals not just the rise of two beasts but the unleashing of power—terrible, world-altering power. But don't miss this truth: every ounce of that power is permitted by God.

This chapter shows us, six different times, that Satan, the Antichrist, and the False Prophet only move within boundaries God allows. They are not gods. They are not sovereign. They are on a divine leash. And though that leash will be temporarily extended during the final 3½ years of the Tribulation, they still operate under God's sovereign timeline.

Let's walk through it:

1. **Power to Continue for Forty-Two Months**—"And there was given unto him a mouth speaking great things and blasphemies; and power was given unto him to continue forty two months" (Revelation 13:5). The Antichrist is not allowed to reign indefinitely. His time is limited to 42 months—the final half of the Tribulation, often called the Great Tribulation. The time has been measured. The days are numbered. Not a second more will be granted.

2. **Power to Make War on the Saints**—"And it was given unto him to make war with the saints, and to overcome them . . ." (Revelation 13:7). God allows the Antichrist to make war on the Tribulation saints and to prevail against them physically—but not spiritually. Their souls are sealed. Their eternity is secure. Their perseverance becomes a powerful testimony under pressure.

3. **Power Over All Nations**—". . . and power was given him over all kindreds, and tongues, and nations" (Revelation 13:7 continued). This is global dominion. The Antichrist will hold sway over every people group on earth. The system will be totalitarian, fueled by worship and enforced by fear. But this power is still borrowed—granted, not generated.

4. **Power to Perform Miracles**—"And deceives them that dwell on the earth, by the means of those miracles which he had power to do in the sight of the beast; saying to them that dwell on the earth, that they should make an image to the beast, which had the wound by a sword, and did live" (Revelation 13:14). The False Prophet will perform miraculous signs—including calling fire down from heaven. But this power is not divine. It is demonic. Satan, as the dragon, empowers this beast to deceive through counterfeit wonders.

5. **Power to Give Life to the Image**—"And he had power to give life unto the image of the beast, that the image of the beast should both speak, and cause that as many as would not worship the image of the beast should be killed" (Revelation 13:15). Whether this is technological sorcery, demonic animation, or literal deception, it is a permitted marvel. An image speaks. An image demands worship. And this "life" is another shocking display of power allowed during Satan's last stand.

6. **Power to Enforce the Mark**—"And he causes all, both small and great, rich and poor, free and bond, to receive a mark on their right hand, or on their foreheads" (Revelation 13:16). No one will be able to buy or sell without it. This is financial coercion on a global scale, enforced through a worship-based identification system. And again, the False Prophet has this power only because God allows it.

Why would God allow this?

Because it's the final chapter in Satan's rebellion. God allows the devil to pull out all the stops—to show his true nature. And in doing so, God separates the wheat from the tares (Matthew 13:24–30, 36–43). He forces the world to choose. And in the end, Satan will be exposed, defeated, and cast into the Lake of Fire forever. This is God's story—even when the enemy seems to take center stage.

COUNTERFEIT RELIGION

We all sense it. We feel it pressing in. If you are spiritually awake, you already know: the spirit of the Antichrist is alive and active in the world today. It's not hiding. It's not subtle anymore. It's bold. It's loud. And it's setting the stage. But what we don't talk about enough is this: the spirit of the False Prophet is also here. A counterfeit religion is rising. It may not have a name yet. It may not have an official spokesperson yet. But make no mistake—it is here, and it is working.

Just as the Antichrist's political spirit is infiltrating governments, economies, and systems, the False Prophet's religious spirit is infiltrating churches, pulpits, and platforms. It's softening the gospel. Diluting the Word. Eroding holiness.

Stripping away the power of the Cross, the blood, and the resurrection. It is a religion without Jesus. A gospel without repentance. A church without power.

A New Day, A New Theology

We're watching it happen in real-time. Christ is being quietly removed. Doctrine is being rewritten in the name of "relevance." And with every new cultural shift, we're told the Church must evolve again.

But listen to me—a new day brings a new theology, and new theology always brings a new morality. That's why we're seeing such confusion in the world today—sexual confusion, gender confusion, spiritual confusion. When the foundation shifts, everything else shakes with it.

This is not just about culture. This is about a counterfeit gospel sneaking in through the back door of the Church.

The Church Must Wake Up

Just as the world is preparing to receive the Antichrist, the religious world is preparing to receive the False Prophet. We are watching the erosion of the gospel that once healed the sick, saved the lost, and cast out demons.

Where is the power that once set captives free? Where is the fear of God in our gatherings? Where is the altar call that once demanded repentance?

I'll tell you where it's going: it's being slowly replaced by motivational speakers, life coaches, self-help sermons, and religious entertainment. And behind it all is a spirit—the spirit of the False Prophet—working to prepare hearts for a religion that will one day worship a beast.

Hold Fast to the Faith

So here's what I want to say before we turn the page. We must hold fast to the faith that was once delivered to the saints. We must cling to the gospel of Jesus Christ—His blood, His Cross, His resurrection, and the power of His Holy Spirit.

But if we don't . . . If we let that spirit sneak in unchallenged . . . If no one sounds the alarm . . . Then whole congregations will fall under a spiritual hypnosis, never realizing that they've traded truth for lies. They'll wake up one day and realize they lost the real Jesus while following a counterfeit gospel.

But not us. Not now. Not while we still have breath.

A Final Word Before We Meet the False Prophet

There is a religion coming. It's already here, disguised in light. It's the False Prophet's gospel: a religion with no Christ, no Cross, no Holy Spirit, and no power. It's all counterfeit.

But I'm telling you this because we're still here. And as long as we're here, we fight. We fight for truth. We fight for the real gospel. We fight for the presence and power of God in our lives, in our churches, and in this world.

So let the Church arise. And let us not be deceived. Because next . . . We meet the second beast. The False Prophet. And everything he brings with him.

"Ann, since Bible prophecy focuses on the Bible Lands, that would naturally include many Muslim nations, right? So what actually happened after the Prophet Muhammad died? I know Islam eventually split into Sunnis and Shiites—or Shia Muslims—but I am confused about what really separates them."

"Of course. After Muhammad died in AD 632, the Muslim community divided over who should succeed him. Sunnis believed leadership should go to a qualified companion—so they supported Abu Bakr, Muhammad's close friend. Shia Muslims, however, believed leadership should stay within the Prophet's bloodline and followed Ali, his cousin and son-in-law."

"So, it started as a political disagreement?"

"Exactly. But over time, it evolved into deep theological, legal, and cultural divisions. Today, Sunnis make up about 85–90 percent of the world's Muslims. Shia Muslims are about 10–15 percent, with Iran being their main stronghold."

"And Saudi Arabia is Sunni, right?"

"Yes. Saudi Arabia is considered the heart of Sunni Islam, while Iran leads the Shia world. The rivalry between these two has shaped regional politics for decades."

"That makes me wonder . . . If the Antichrist arises from the Middle East—say, from the Assyrian region mentioned in Isaiah—could the False Prophet emerge from the Sunni world, maybe even from Saudi Arabia?"

"That's a possibility some have considered. Though ethnic Assyrians today are mostly Christian, the term 'Assyrian' in prophecy may be geographical, not religious or ethnic. If the Antichrist arises from that region, possibly with Shia alignment, and the False Prophet comes from the Sunni sphere—like Saudi Arabia—it could represent a counterfeit reconciliation between the two major Islamic sects."

Irene nodded. "And since both Sunni and Shia Muslims claim the Dome of the Rock as sacred, a unified religious system centered in Jerusalem wouldn't be farfetched."

"Exactly. It would be Satan's masterpiece of deception—fusing political power and religious legitimacy. And as Revelation tells us, the whole world will marvel and follow the beast."

Irene, skeptical: "Ann, I'm still turning over what you said about the Sunni and Shia divide. It's always struck me as deep—irreconcilable even. But do you really think they could ever unite—especially in the end times?"

"That's a great question, Irene—and from a historical and theological perspective, their split is very real and very deep. But in the context of end-times prophecy, a temporary unification isn't just possible—it might be prophetically likely."

"Really? Even after centuries of disagreement?"

"Yes. What makes it possible is that both Sunni and Shia Muslims share a common apocalyptic expectation. They're both waiting for a messianic figure—someone who will bring justice, unite the Muslim world, and confront Israel and the West."

"So they're both looking for a savior-type figure?"

"Exactly. Sunnis expect the *Mahdi* to appear alongside Isa—what they call Jesus. Shias are waiting for the return of the Twelfth Imam, who they also call the *Mahdi*. The names and details vary, but both sects envision a powerful end-time leader who will revive Islam globally."

"That sounds like it could lay the groundwork for a false unity."

"It could—and I believe it will. In a world shaken by war, collapse, and the aftermath of the Rapture, the stage will be perfectly set for a charismatic figure—perhaps the Antichrist himself—to emerge and offer 'peace.' Under powerful satanic deception, he could unite both Sunni and Shia factions around a common cause."

"Like the destruction of Israel or opposition to the West?"

"Exactly. Both sects already share that desire in their end-time narratives. That common ground could become a powerful tool for unification—but it will be superficial and short-lived."

"Why short-lived?"

"Because it won't be based on truth. It'll be rooted in spiritual deception, political desperation, and false prophecy. As God's judgments unfold—like those described in Ezekiel 38–39 and Revelation 16–19—that fragile alliance will collapse. Their unity will be exposed for what it is: rebellion against God."

"So it's prophetically plausible, but destined to fall apart?"

"Exactly. Satan will use it to advance his agenda through the Antichrist and False Prophet, but God will have the final word. Every alliance forged in darkness will break under the weight of divine judgment."

"That's sobering—and clarifying. What looks like peace may be the setup for the greatest deception of all."

"Yes, and that's why we watch, pray, and stay rooted in the truth of God's Word. We need discernment now more than ever."

Irene, curious: "Ann, you mentioned the *Mahdi*—the Islamic messianic figure. It got me thinking . . . could this *Mahdi* actually be the Antichrist? And is there any chance he might be the Assyrian that the Bible talks about?"

"Great questions, Irene. You're definitely connecting some prophetic dots. Let's break this down, because it's both fascinating and theologically important. Yes, it's very possible—many prophecy scholars believe the *Mahdi* expected by Muslims may in fact be the Antichrist described in Scripture. And yes, he could very well be the Assyrian mentioned by prophets like Isaiah and Micah."

"Wow. So how does that even work? I thought the *Mahdi* was just an Islamic thing. How does he connect to biblical prophecy?"

"Islam's *Mahdi* and the Bible's Antichrist have eerily similar characteristics. Both are expected to rise during a time of global chaos. Both will be hailed as saviors. Both will establish a political and religious empire. Muslims believe the *Mahdi* will lead a global Islamic revival, defeat Israel, and bring in peace under Islamic law."

I continued. "But biblically, we know the Antichrist does the same things—only it's a deception. He brings false peace, persecutes God's people, and ultimately exalts himself as God."

Irene, pausing: "Okay, that's wild. But what about the Assyrian part? You've mentioned before that the Antichrist might actually be called 'the Assyrian.' What's that about?"

I nodded. "Multiple Old Testament verses refer to 'the Assyrian' as a future oppressor of Israel. Isaiah 10, Isaiah 14, and Micah 5 all describe this figure. It's not just a historical reference—it's prophetic. The ancient Assyrian empire covered what's now northern Iraq, northeastern Syria, and parts of Turkey. If the Antichrist comes from that region, it would match those prophecies."

"And get this," I continued. "That region plays a major role—not just in ancient biblical history, but also in modern Islamic end-times beliefs."

Irene nodded. "So, the *Mahdi*—who's supposed to save the Islamic world—could actually be the Antichrist, rising from the same region as the ancient Assyrians?"

I grew serious. "Exactly. It would be the ultimate satanic counterfeit. To Muslims, he'd appear as their long-awaited messiah. To the world, a man of peace. But in truth—he would be the beast of Revelation, rising out of the sea of chaos."

"And what about the False Prophet? Would he be Islamic too?"

"Likely, yes. The False Prophet is the second beast in Revelation 13—the religious leader who promotes worship of the first beast, the Antichrist. Now imagine if he came from an organization like the Muslim Brotherhood—which has enormous spiritual and political influence across Sunni nations and even ties to Shia leaders when convenient."

Irene, connecting the dots. "So what you're saying is . . . the *Mahdi* could rise from the Shia side—maybe even as Assyrian from Iran, Syria, or Turkey—and the False Prophet could emerge from the Sunni world, like Saudi Arabia or Egypt?"

"Yes. It would be the perfect deception. Sunni and Shia Muslims have been divided for 1,400 years. But both believe in an end-time Islamic savior figure. They just interpret him differently. If one man—this Antichrist—can fulfill both visions, and if a charismatic religious leader promotes him . . . it could create a temporary Sunni-Shia unity."

"And the Dome of the Rock?"

"Both Sunni and Shia claim it. It's the third holiest site in Islam. If the Antichrist and False Prophet promise peace, power, and Islamic dominance—including control of Jerusalem—they'll have religious and political leverage over the entire Muslim world."

"But that alliance won't last, would it?"

"No. Not at all. It would be superficial and short-lived. Built on lies, fear, and satanic power. Revelation and Ezekiel both show that this coalition will collapse in bloodshed and divine judgment. In the end, Satan's empire always devours itself."

Irene, sober. "It's all coming together, isn't it? Everything the world's religions are hoping for—and everything the Bible warns us about—happening all at once."

"Yes. But remember—God's people are not left in the dark. Scripture is our lamp. And this is why we study, watch, and remain faithful—because the deception will be strong. But the truth is stronger."

Irene, reflecting. "Ann, doesn't it all come back to Jerusalem? The Temple Mount? Isn't the Dome of the Rock the one thing standing in the way of the Third Temple?"

I nodded. "Absolutely. The Dome of the Rock is built right where many believe the Holy of Holies once stood—the heart of the ancient Jewish Temple. It's the third holiest site in Islam . . . but it's also the most sacred ground in Judaism. And that's what makes it the flashpoint of all end-time tensions."

"So . . . if anything were to happen to the Dome, or if someone negotiated some kind of shared access to the Temple Mount—could that trigger the prophecy in Daniel 9:27? The one where the Antichrist confirms a covenant with many?"

"Yes, Irene—and that's the exact verse to watch. Daniel 9:27 says, 'He shall confirm the covenant with many for one week'—which most scholars interpret as a seven-year peace treaty. It will look like a breakthrough—peace between Israel and her enemies. But it's a false peace. A setup. The bait before the trap is sprung."

Irene, wide-eyed. "And you think the Temple Mount is the key to all of this?"

"Without a doubt. Right now, Israel can't build the Third Temple because of the Dome of the Rock. But here's the shocking part: the Temple Institute in Jerusalem has already built the Third Temple—piece by piece. The blueprints are complete. The utensils, priestly garments, the altar—they're all ready. They just need the green light to assemble it on the Temple Mount."

"So it's not a matter of 'if,' but 'when.'"

Me, serious. "Exactly. All it would take is one charismatic world leader— someone with the influence to broker a deal between Israel and the Islamic nations. Someone who could calm tensions, propose a shared religious space, and present it as a win for everyone. And just like that, he earns the trust of 'many'— Israel, Arab nations, even the global community."

"That sounds exactly like the Antichrist."

"It is. He'll seem like a peacemaker. He might even invoke religious unity or tolerance. But midway through that seven-year treaty, he'll betray the agreement, enter the newly rebuilt Temple, and declare himself as God—that's the *abomination of desolation* Jesus warned about in Matthew 24:15–16."

> When you therefore shall see the abomination of desolation, spoken of by Daniel the prophet, stand in the holy place, (whoso reads, let him understand:) Then let them which be in Judea flee into the mountains. (Matthew 24:15–16)

Irene, processing. "So the Dome of the Rock isn't just a political hotspot— it's prophetic ground zero."

"Yes. It's both a symbol and a barrier. The peace treaty of Daniel 9:27 likely hinges on what happens at that exact spot. And the moment construction begins on the Temple Mount, we'll know we're not just reading prophecy—we're watching it unfold in real time."

Irene, softly. "And the world will cheer, thinking peace has finally come . . . not realizing it's only the quiet before the storm."

Me, gently. "That's why we stay awake—spiritually alert and grounded in Scripture. The Temple Mount may soon dominate headlines, but it already belongs to prophecy."

"Ann, something's still stirring in my spirit. The Tribulation won't center on America as the star of prophecy—it's focused on the Bible Lands. But America is undeniably in the spiritual crosshairs."

"Right. The focus of prophecy zeroes in on Israel, Jerusalem, and the surrounding nations—Babylon, Persia, Egypt, Syria. But the fallout? It touches everyone. Especially America. Don't forget, to the Muslim Brotherhood, America is the 'Great Satan,' and Israel is the 'Little Satan.'"

"That language has always struck me. 'Great Satan.' 'Little Satan.' It's not political. It's deeply spiritual. The enemy sees it for what it is: a cosmic war. Light versus darkness. Truth verses deception."

"And here's what's wild. If the Antichrist is of Shia influence—let's say from the Assyrian or Iranian line—and the False Prophet is of Sunni persuasion, say from Saudi Arabia, then you've got something the world has never seen: a united Islamic front. Shia and Sunni—historic enemies—suddenly aligned."

"Ann, that would be a global religious earthquake. And prophetically, it fits like a lock and key. Shia and Sunni united under the satanic counterfeit trinity—Satan, the Antichrist, and the False Prophet."

I nodded. "One World Religion. One world deception. Driven not by truth, but by fear, survival, and supernatural signs and lying wonders. The world will be seduced."

"And America?"

"She's not the bride in this story—she's the battlefield. A battleground of ideologies, identities, and loyalties. And I believe her fall—or her spiritual compromise—is just a domino in this unholy alliance."

"Ann . . . if what you're saying plays out—and I think it will—then the world stage is already set. We're not waiting for the curtain to rise. The actors are just waiting for the Church to exit."

Quietly. "Exactly. The Rapture removes the resistance. And what follows is a tidal wave of deception."

"Question: I've been reading headlines from just before the October 7, 2023 attacks. Is it true that Saudi Arabia and Israel were actually close to finalizing a peace agreement?"

"Yes, Irene, it's absolutely true. Just before those attacks, Saudi Arabia and Israel were deep in negotiations—very close to normalizing relations for the first time in history."

"Wait, like *actual peace* between them? Not just backchannel diplomacy?"

"Not just talk. Prime Minister Netanyahu even said at the UN on September 22 that they were 'at the cusp' of a historic agreement. And Saudi Crown Prince

Mohammad bin Salman confirmed they were 'getting closer.' The U.S. was heavily involved too—offering Saudi Arabia security guarantees and brokering the terms."

"That's huge. But then October 7 happened . . ."

"Exactly. The Hamas attacks shattered everything. The violence derailed the talks almost overnight. After that, Saudi Arabia paused the negotiations and publicly emphasized that Palestinian statehood would need to be addressed first before moving forward."

"So, the attacks weren't just about terror—they stopped a major prophetic shift."

"You could say that. Many believe it was spiritual sabotage. That moment, right before peace, could have changed the whole Middle East landscape. And then—chaos. War. Delay."

"And yet, it still feels like a setup. Like the stage is still being built for something . . . bigger."

"Oh, it is. The enemy hates peace. But prophecy is always on schedule."

Irene, thoughtful. "Ann, I still remember that moment in 2018—when the U.S. embassy officially opened in Jerusalem. It was May 14th, exactly seventy years to the day since Israel declared independence in 1948. That timing felt . . . prophetic."

I, nodding. "It was. But remember—it started months earlier. On December 6, 2017, President Donld Trump officially recognized Jerusalem as the capital of Israel, prompting other nations to follow suit. Then he announced that the U.S. embassy would be relocated from Tel Aviv to Jerusalem."

Irene, wide-eyed. "And no one else had done that, right? I mean, it had been talked about for years."

"Talked about, yes. But not acted on. The Jerusalem Embassy Act was passed in 1995, calling for the embassy to be relocated. But every president before Trump—Clinton, Bush, and Obama—signed waivers every six months to delay the move, always citing national security."

"But Trump followed through. He actually did it."

"He did. And the embassy officially opened on May 14, 2018—exactly seventy years after Israel became a nation. That wasn't political theater. That was a divine timestamp. Seventy is the number of completion, judgment, and restoration in the Bible. God was marking history."

Irene, quietly. "And many still don't realize how spiritually significant that moment was."

"But the remnant does. That move wasn't just bold—it was prophetic. And it set the stage for everything we're seeing unfold now."

Irene sighed. "And Trump was the one who did it."

"Yes," I said firmly. "Because he was appointed for that hour. Like Cyrus in the Old Testament—he didn't have to be perfect to be chosen. God isn't looking for spotless resumes; He's looking for willing vessels, even if they don't know they're being used. Cyrus was a Persian king—a Gentile—who wasn't part of Israel, yet God called him by name in Isaiah 44, more than a century before he was even born. God said to Cyrus:"

That says of Cyrus, He is My shepherd, and shall perform all My pleasure: even saying to Jerusalem, You shalt be built; and to the temple, Your foundation shall be laid. (Isaiah 44:28)

"And Cyrus did exactly that. After seventy years of Jewish captivity in Babylon—a judgment God ordained because Israel had failed to let the land rest every seventh year, known as the Sabbath year, totaling seventy missed Sabbaths—Cyrus conquered Babylon. He overthrew one of the most powerful empires the world had ever known. And instead of keeping the Jews enslaved, he issued a royal decree permitting them to return to their land and rebuild both Jerusalem and the Temple. That decree, issued in 538 BC, marked the end of Babylon's dominance and the beginning of Israel's restoration."

I paused, letting it sink in.

"And that's why so many have drawn the comparison between Cyrus and Trump. No, Trump isn't a perfect man—but neither was Cyrus. That's not the point. The point is that God used both of them to shift global history. Cyrus was used to restore Israel physically. Trump, I believe, was used to restore Jerusalem prophetically—bringing it back to the center of international recognition, just as God foretold."

Irene sighed. "Then came the Abraham Accords in 2020. That was huge—normalizing relations between Israel and several Arab nations."

"Yes. That was laying the groundwork for what's coming in Daniel 9:27—a peace deal that looks promising but leads to prophetic upheaval. The Abraham Accords weren't *the* covenant, but they were a forerunner. And Trump, again, was right in the middle of it."

Irene, quietly, "Then almost a year ago now . . . that assassination attempt in Butler, Pennsylvania. He nearly died."

"And he didn't. Because God said, 'Not yet.' That wasn't just political drama. That was divine delay. God paused the clock again. One final window before judgment. One last chance for repentance."

"Like Noah before the Flood. Like Lot before Sodom burned."

"Exactly, Irene. God always warns. And I believe Trump was—and still is—a divine appointee. People can argue, mock, reject him—but it doesn't change what God is doing. He's using Trump to set the stage."

"So did you believe he would win again in 2024?"

"He already had. Not just an election—he's won an assignment. And it's not just about cleaning up politics. Trump sees himself as a peacetime president, trying to fix the system. But I believe, God has other plans."

"What kind of plans?"

"A revealing. This isn't about restoration—it's about revelation. God is dragging wickedness into the light. Trump's presidency won't be about comfort—it'll be about confrontation. A wartime assignment in the spirit."

Irene, solemn. "Judgment begins at the house of God."

"And justice begins with exposure. This term will tear back the veil. The spiritual battle lines have never been clearer. America is standing at the threshold—and Trump, for all his flaws and fire, is standing in the gap."

"And the world watches. And waits."

I nodded. "Because the countdown hasn't stopped. The Tribulation clock is still ticking. But God, in His mercy, is still calling. Still shaking. And His eyes are still locked on Israel."

"Everything we're watching," I continued, "wars, politics, treaties, deception—it's all setting the stage. The first beast has risen . . ."

Irene leaned in, lowering her voice. "And now . . . the second one?"

I flipped the page slowly. "Yes. Revelation 13:11. Another beast. This one looks like a lamb—but speaks like a dragon."

———◆◆◆———

THE REVELATION OF JESUS CHRIST REVEALS:

13:11 And I beheld another beast coming up out of the earth; and he had two horns like a lamb, and he spoke as a dragon.

This verse marks the introduction of the second beast—commonly known as the False Prophet. While the first beast (Revelation 13:1) represents the Antichrist, a political leader rising from the sea of Gentile nations, this second beast comes "up out of the earth"—suggesting a very different kind of origin and role.

The imagery of the second beast "coming up out of the earth" is striking—and intentionally different from the first beast who rises "out of the sea." In prophetic language, the sea often represents the turbulent masses of Gentile nations (Daniel 7:2–3), pointing to a political or secular origin. But "the earth" suggests something stable, rooted—possibly religious or tied to Israel.

The earth is frequently symbolic of the land or people, often connected to religion, tradition, or spirituality. The second beast, unlike the blasphemous and warlike first beast, appears gentle and harmless—like a lamb. This lamb-like appearance is deeply deceptive, mimicking the imagery of Christ, the true Lamb of God (John 1:29). But this is no savior. Despite the appearance, he speaks like a dragon—his words are satanically inspired, aligned with the father of lies.

This contrast reveals the second beast's role: a religious deceiver. He does not conquer with brute force like the Antichrist, but with false doctrine, lying wonders, and spiritual manipulation. Many scholars and Bible teachers interpret this to mean he could be a false prophet, false messiah, or head of a global religion—one that supports and glorifies the Antichrist, leading the world into worship of the first beast.

Earth versus sea. Political verses religious.

- The first beast (the Antichrist)—political power, rising from the Gentile nations.
- The second beast (the False Prophet)—religious power, rising from "the earth," or possibly from within a religious system or region with deep spiritual roots (some suggest even the Middle East, or apostate Christianity).

Therefore "coming up out of the earth" hints at a religious or spiritual emergence, as opposed to political. The False Prophet masquerades as one who brings peace, morality, or religious truth—but his voice betrays him. He is a dragon in lamb's clothing, using religion to serve the agenda of the Antichrist and to prepare the world for the ultimate act of worship—devotion to Satan's counterfeit kingdom.

"And he had two horns like a lamb." The imagery is striking: he has the horns of a lamb—a picture of innocence, humility, gentleness. But he is a counterfeit. While Jesus is the true Lamb of God, this beast is pretending to be something he is not. He does not have power like the first beast; instead, he exercises it on behalf of the Antichrist (Revelation 13:12).

The two horns may represent religious authority or power, but without a crown, unlike the horns of the Antichrist, suggesting he operates under a different kind of influence—spiritual deception rather than military might.

"And he spoke as a dragon." Here's the real giveaway. His appearance is lamb-like, but his speech reveals his true nature. He speaks like a dragon—Satan. That's the same dragon from Revelation 12:9, "that old serpent, called the Devil."

Though his appearance is gentle, persuasive, and spiritual, his words are poisoned with blasphemy and deception. He is the ultimate wolf in sheep's clothing, a false prophet of satanic origin who uses religion as his platform to push worship of the Antichrist.

OLD TESTAMENT FORESHADOWS REVELATION:

If there arise among you a prophet, or a dreamer of dreams, and gives you a sign or a wonder, And the sign or the wonder come to pass, whereof he spoke unto you, saying, Let us go after other gods, which you have not known, and let us serve them; You shalt not listen unto the words of that prophet, or that dreamer of dreams: for the LORD your God proves you, to know whether you love the LORD your God with all your heart and with all our soul. (Deuteronomy 13:1–3)

The False Prophet in Revelation 13:11 performs miraculous signs and uses them to lead people into false worship—just like the false prophet in Deuteronomy 13:1–3. The warning in Deuteronomy matches the deception described in Revelation: miraculous signs do not always equal divine truth. God allows such a prophet to arise as a test of loyalty, which aligns with the Tribulation as a period of testing for those on earth.

THE REVELATION OF JESUS CHRIST REVEALS:

13:12 And he exercises all the power of the first beast before him, and causes the earth and them which dwell therein to worship the first beast, whose deadly wound was healed.

This verse introduces the False Prophet's full authority and his ultimate mission: to promote global worship of the Antichrist, the first beast whose "deadly wound was healed" (a reference to a miraculous, counterfeit resurrection in Revelation 13:3).

The False Prophet does not operate independently. He exercises "all the power of the first beast before him," meaning his authority and supernatural capabilities are entirely sourced from Satan through the Antichrist. He acts as a minister of propaganda, religious enforcement, and spiritual deception—convincing the world that the Antichrist is worthy of worship.

The phrase "causes the earth and them which dwell therein to worship" suggests compulsion, not mere persuasion. The False Prophet doesn't just suggest allegiance—he enforces it. This is the birth of a One World Religion, led by a deceptive miracle-worker who masquerades as a lamb but speaks like a dragon (verse 11).

"Whose deadly wound was healed." The healing of the beast's deadly wound is the centerpiece of his campaign. It mimics the death and resurrection of Jesus Christ. As Christ's resurrection is central to Christian faith, this false resurrection becomes the cornerstone of satanic worship. The False Prophet uses this miracle as proof of the beast's supposed divine nature.

OLD TESTAMENT FORESHADOWS REVELATION:

Then a herald cried aloud, To you it is commanded, O people, nations, and languages. That at what time you hear the sound of the cornet, flute, harp, sackbut, psaltery, dulcimer, and all kinds of music, you fall down and worship the golden image that Nebuchadnezzar the king has set up: And whoso falls not down and worships shall the same hour be cast into the midst of a burning fiery furnace. (Daniel 3:4–6)

Daniel 3:4–6 mirrors the global coercion of Revelation 13:12, where people from all nations, tribes, and tongues are commanded to worship an image of worldly power. Just as Nebuchadnezzar's image demanded worship on threat of death, the False Prophet compels worship of the beast under penalty of economic sanctions or execution (Revelation 13:15–17). Both events are driven by a centralized authority demanding loyalty to an image of power, not to God.

THE REVELATION OF JESUS CHRIST REVEALS:

[13:13] And he does great wonders, so that he makes fire come down from heaven on the earth in the sight of men.

This verse unveils the False Prophet's counterfeit power—a dazzling display of miraculous signs meant to deceive humanity. His ability to "make fire come down from heaven" is a direct imitation of Elijah (1 Kings 18:38), the revered prophet of God who called down fire to prove that the LORD is God. In doing so, the False Prophet attempts to borrow credibility by performing similar acts, fooling the masses into believing he is divine or divinely empowered.

"And he does great wonders." "Great wonders" translated from the Greek *megala semeia*, meaning mighty or spectacular signs. These are supernatural in appearance but demonic in origin.

"So that he makes fire comes down from heaven on the earth" was historically a signature of God's power (Elijah, Sodom, Pentecost tongues of fire). Now it is mimicked by Satan through the False Prophet.

"In the sight of men" emphasizes the public nature of the miracle. It's designed to be seen, admired, and believed, drawing the world into deception through spectacle.

Revelation 13:13 serves as a critical warning to discern miracles by their source. Not every sign is from God. In the last days, supernatural displays will increase, but many will be deceptive in nature, used to lead people into idolatry and away from the true gospel. The False Prophet will use spectacle to seduce the masses into worshiping the Antichrist.

OLD TESTAMENT FORESHADOWS REVELATION:

Then the fire of the LORD fell, and consumed the burnt sacrifice, and the wood, and the stones, and the dust, and licked up the water that was in the trench. (1 Kings 18:38)

This verse records Elijah's dramatic confrontation with the prophets of Baal on Mount Carmel. When Elijah called upon the LORD, fire came down from heaven—authenticating God's power and exposing the false prophets. In Revelation 13:13, the False Prophet performs a counterfeit version of this miracle, calling down fire "in the sight of men" to deceive them into worshiping the Antichrist. Just as fire from heaven validated Elijah's message as from God, the False Prophet's imitation miracle is designed to give false credibility to a satanic agenda—deception masquerading as divine power.

THE REVELATION OF JESUS CHRIST REVEALS:

[13:14] And deceives them that dwell on the earth by the means of those miracles which he had power to do in the sight of the beast; saying to them that dwell on the earth, that they should make an image to the beast, which had the wound by a sword, and did live.

This verse continues to unveil the terrifying influence of the False Prophet, the second beast. His primary tool is deception—not brute force, but counterfeit miracles that mimic divine power. These signs are not random parlor tricks—they are strategic, public, and persuasive. The phrase "in the sight of the beast" indicates that these acts are done in coordination with the Antichrist, serving his agenda and reinforcing his power.

These "miracles" aren't just to amaze people—they are means to an end. That end is idolatry. The False Prophet urges the world to construct an image of the beast, transforming political allegiance into religious worship. The call to "make an image" echoes ancient paganism, where physical idols were made to represent deities. But this one will likely be far more advanced—possibly technological, interactive, or AI-enhanced, making it all the more compelling in the eyes of a deceived humanity.

The reference to the beast's wound "by a sword" and miraculous survival again highlights the Antichrist's apparent resurrection—a satanic counterfeit of Christ's resurrection. This false resurrection is the emotional and spiritual catalyst that fuels mass worship and global submission.

Today's world is increasingly primed for such deception. In an age where miracles, technology, and spectacle blend into one, it won't take much to convince a world hungry for hope but detached from truth. The False Prophet taps into this hunger—offering spiritual excitement without salvation, and power without purity.

This verse reminds believers to test the spirits (1 John 4:1) and to measure "miracles" against the truth of Scripture. Not every sign is from God. Signs and wonders alone are not proof of truth. In fact, in the Great Tribulation, they will be the tools of the greatest religious deception the world has ever seen.

OLD TESTAMENT FORESHADOWS REVELATION:

And Moses and Aaron went in unto Pharaoh, and they did so as the LORD had commanded: and Aaron cast down his rod before Pharaoh, and before his servants, and it became a serpent. Then Pharaoh also called the wise men and the sorcerers: now the magicians of Egypt, they also did in like manner with their enchantments. For they cast down every man his rod, and they became serpents: but Aaron's rod swallowed up their rods. (Exodus 7:10–12)

Just as Pharaoh's magicians performed counterfeit wonders to imitate the divine, the False Prophet in Revelation deceives people with miraculous signs. Both scenes take place in the sight of men, displaying supernatural acts meant to persuade and manipulate. In Exodus 7:10–12, Aaron's rod swallows the others; in Revelation, Christ ultimately destroys the Antichrist and the False Prophet.

THE REVELATION OF JESUS CHRIST REVEALS:

[13:15] And he had power to give life to the image of the beast, that the image of the beast should both speak, and cause that as many as would not worship the image of the beast should be killed.

This verse reveals the terrifying culmination of counterfeit worship and deception in the Tribulation period. The False Prophet, empowered by Satan, takes deception to a chilling level—bringing life, or the appearance of life, to a manmade image of the Antichrist. This image, once lifeless, becomes animated and vocal, commanding both fear and allegiance.

This act is a satanic parody of God's creative power. Just as God breathed life into man, here the False Prophet "gives life" to an image—though it's likely through demonic power or technological manipulation. Many scholars debate whether this "life" is literal, demonic animation, or some form of artificial intelligence or illusion. Regardless of the mechanism, the deception is so strong that it results in worship—and in death for those who resist.

This moment echoes Nebuchadnezzar's golden image in Daniel 3. Just as the king demanded worship of an image under threat of death, so too will the False Prophet enforce idolatry with deadly consequences. The line is clearly drawn: worship the beast or die. There is no neutrality in the Tribulation—loyalty will either be to the Lamb or to the beast.

The speaking image symbolizes not only forced devotion but also total surveillance and control. It's not just about religion—it's about control, fear, allegiances, and execution. Anyone who refuses to comply with this final form of idolatry is sentenced to death. Martyrdom becomes the price for faithfulness to God during this dark hour.

Yet even in this horror, we're reminded: God is still sovereign. He has permitted this deception for a season, and He has already declared its end. The faithful who refuse to bow will reign with Christ, even if they lose their lives on earth.

OLD TESTAMENT FORESHADOWS REVELATION:

They that make a graven image are all of them vanity; and their delectable things shall not profit; and they are their own witnesses; they see not, nor know; that they may be ashamed. And the residue thereof he makes a god, even his graven image: he falls down unto it, and worships it, and prays unto it, and says, Deliver me; for you are my god. (Isaiah 44:9, 17)

In Isaiah 44:9, 17, the prophet condemns idol-making and the absurdity of worshiping manmade objects. In Revelation 13:15, the False Prophet animates a manmade image, making it appear alive, and demands worship—a direct inversion of God's truth and a final form of idolatry. Isaiah shows the futility of idols, while Revelation shows the danger of empowered, deceptive idols in the end times. The false worship of an image ties both passages together, contrasting God's warnings in the Old Testament with prophetic fulfillment in the New Testament.

THE REVELATION OF JESUS CHRIST REVEALS:

13:16 And he causes all, both small and great, rich and poor, free and bond, to receive a mark on their right hand, or on their foreheads.

This verse introduces one of the most sobering elements of end-times prophecy—the mark of the beast. The False Prophet, acting on behalf of the Antichrist, enforces a universal mandate that spans across every social and economic class: small and great, rich and poor, free and bond. This sweeping language indicates total societal control, leaving no one exempt.

The phrase "he causes all" reveals coercion and systematic enforcement. It's not optional. The False Prophet compels global compliance, functioning more like a totalitarian religious-political enforcer than a spiritual leader.

"Both small and great, rich and poor, free and bond." The reach of this mandate is absolute. It impacts the most powerful and the most vulnerable, the elite and the impoverished, the liberated and the enslaved. This is a deliberate echo of total economic, societal, and spiritual domination.

"To receive a mark." The Greek word for "mark" is *charagma*, referring to a stamp, brand, or engraving. This was often used in antiquity to signify ownership or allegiance, such as branding slaves or marking official documents. In this context, the mark becomes a symbol of loyalty to the Antichrist—a visible, irreversible sign of allegiance.

"On their right hand, or on their foreheads." The placement of the mark is deeply symbolic. The forehead represents the mind—the seat of belief, values, and identity. The right hand symbolizes action, work, and allegiance. In essence, the mark declares both mental and behavioral submission to the beast's authority. This is a direct counterfeit of God's seal on His servants (Revelation 7:3; Deuteronomy 6:8).

This verse reveals Satan's ultimate attempt to imitate God's covenant seal, demanding worship, loyalty, and control. Just as believers are sealed by the Holy Spirit (Ephesians 1:13), so the Antichrist will demand a counterfeit seal to mark his followers—those who have rejected the truth.

This mark is not just a financial mechanism (as we will see in verse 17), but a spiritual branding, marking people as participants in Satan's final rebellion.

OLD TESTAMENT FORESHADOWS REVELATION:

And these words, which I command you this day, shall be in your heart: And you shalt teach them diligently unto your children, and shalt talk of them when you sit in your house, and when you walk by the way, and when you lie down, and when you rise up. And you shalt bind them for a sign upon your hand, and they shall be as frontlets between your eyes. (Deuteronomy 6:6–8)

Just as God commanded His people to bind His Word to their hand and forehead—symbolizing their thoughts (forehead) and actions (hand)—the Antichrist, through the False Prophet, counterfeits this sacred practice by demanding his own mark of allegiance in the same locations. Revelation 13:16: ". . . to receive a mark on their right hand, or on their foreheads."

This is Satan's imitation of God's covenantal sign—twisting what was once holy into a symbol of rebellion. The mark of the beast represents not just economic submission, but spiritual betrayal, turning away from God's Word and choosing allegiance to the beast instead.

THE REVELATION OF JESUS CHRIST REVEALS:

[13:17] And that no man might buy or sell, except he that had the mark, or the name of the beast, or the number of his name.

This verse reveals a global economic control system orchestrated by the False Prophet and enforced through the mark of the beast. Under this satanic regime, economic participation—buying or selling—is restricted exclusively to those who pledge allegiance to the Antichrist through one of three identifiers:

1. The mark (a visible or embedded sign of loyalty, possibly technological).
2. The name of the beast (direct allegiance to his identity).
3. Or the number of his name (further explained in verse 18, famously associated with 666).

This passage isn't just about economics—it's about worship and allegiance. The ability to buy food, medicine, fuel, or shelter is now tied to who you worship. It is the ultimate test of faith for those living during the Great Tribulation.

This verse underscores the coming merger of religion, politics, and technology—a One World Government system with a digital economy where freedom is lost unless allegiance to the beast is given. It foreshadows the rise of a surveillance society, where digital ID systems or biometric verification could easily pave the way for such control.

OLD TESTAMENT FORESHADOWS REVELATION:

And when money failed in the land of Egypt, and in the land of Canaan, all the Egyptians came unto Joseph, and said, Give us bread: for why should we die in your presence? For the money fails. And Joseph said, Give your cattle; and I will give you for your cattle, if money fail. And they brought their cattle unto Joseph: and Joseph gave them bread in exchange for horses, and for the flocks, and for the cattle of the herds, and for the asses: and he fed them with bread for all their cattle for that year. (Genesis 47:15–17)

Economic control becomes centralized during a time of crisis. Survival becomes dependent on a single source (in Joseph's time, Egypt; in Revelation, the beast system). In both cases, the population surrenders autonomy to receive the ability to buy, sell, or survive. The difference is striking: Joseph's control brought life and preservation, while the beast's system brings idolatry and eternal consequence.

THE REVELATION OF JESUS CHRIST REVEALS:

13:18 Here is wisdom. Let him that has understanding count the number of the beast: for it is the number of a man; and his number is six hundred threescore and six.

This final verse in Revelation 13 isn't merely a cryptic warning—it's a summons. "Here is wisdom," it declares, signaling that what follows isn't for the casual reader or spiritually indifferent. The original Greek word for "count" is *psephizo*—to calculate, to discern, to reckon with intention. This verse demands more than curiosity; it demands spiritual insight. Like the wisdom literature of

Proverbs, it speaks to those who fear the LORD and walk in the knowledge of the Holy. Only those tuned to heaven's frequency will grasp what's truly at stake. Revelation 13:18 reminds us that end-time understanding doesn't come through intellect alone—it requires revelation. Divine insight, not just human analysis, will unlock what this number means and why it matters.

"For it is the number of a man." This is not just about numerology—it's about identity. The Antichrist will be a man, not a myth or demonic spirit alone. He will be possessed and empowered by Satan himself, but he will walk this earth in human flesh. His number links him to a man—fallen, godless, and corrupt. It is man exalting himself above God, echoing the pride of Lucifer who said, "I will be like the Most High" (Isaiah 14:14).

The infamous number—"six hundred threescore and six" (666)—has stirred fascination, fear, and speculation for centuries. The Bible calls it "the number of a man," symbolizing the Antichrist's connection to human limitation and imperfection. In contrast to the divine number 7, which represents God's completeness and perfection, the number 6 falls short—signifying rebellion and incompleteness. Repeated three times, 666 forms an unholy trinity, a satanic counterfeit of the Father, Son, and Holy Spirit.

Many scholars have tried to link 666 to historical or future figures using *gematria*—assigning numeric values to names in Hebrew or Greek. Nero, Caesar, Napoleon, and others have all been suggested. But Scripture is clear: 666 identifies the beast. Its true meaning will be fully recognized by those living in the Tribulation—likely the Tribulation saints—who will discern its connection to the Antichrist.

For those who remain during the Tribulation, the pressure to take this number will be immense. It will seem logical, even necessary—for commerce, safety, and survival. But to accept the mark and the number is to declare loyalty to the beast and reject the Lamb.

OLD TESTAMENT FORESHADOWS REVELATION:

Now the weight of gold that came to Solomon in one year was six hundred threescore and six talents of gold. (1 Kings 10:14)

The exact number 666 is used in connection with wealth, power, and worldly glory—all of which are mirrored in the Antichrist's reign and his economic control. Solomon, though wise, eventually fell into idolatry and foreign alliances—a type and shadow of the end-time apostasy. This amount of gold represents worldly wealth amassed without spiritual discernment, paralleling the economic grip of the beast system (Revelation 13:17–18).

◆◆◆

Irene, thoughtful. "Ann, as we wrap up our deep dive into Revelation 13, I feel like it's time we shift from commentary to clarity—from prophecy to present reality. Revelation isn't just a distant vision—it's becoming today's headlines. And we need to talk about that. Not with fear, but with focus."

I nodded. "Absolutely. I've been sensing it too. These aren't just ancient symbols or veiled metaphors. They're materializing. You can feel it. It's like prophecy is no longer waiting in the wings—it's stepping into center stage."

Irene, steady. "Exactly. The Lord showed John five specific political and spiritual agendas in Revelation 13 that will dominate the final phase of human history—right before Christ returns. And Ann, as I list them, I want people to understand: this isn't about politics. It's not left or right, red or blue. It's about kingdoms. The kingdom of light versus the kingdom of darkness."

Me, nodding with conviction. "Exactly, Irene. That's the truth we've got to hold onto—no matter what comes."

Irene continued:

1. A One World Leader
2. A One World Government
3. A One World Religion
4. A One World Monetary System
5. A One World Military Power

Irene, pausing. "These aren't just predictions—they're blueprints already in motion. Some elements will fully emerge during the Great Tribulation. But make no mistake: the infrastructure is being built now, right before our eyes."

I nodded slowly. "It's no longer subtle. World leaders are saying it. Religious leaders are embracing it. And freedoms? They're vanishing by design. Irene, the global stage is nearly complete—and the Antichrist is about to take center stage."

"Let's take these one at a time, Ann. Let's speak plainly and prophetically. And to those reading this—I want you to understand, we're not guessing. We're connecting dots that Scripture already laid out. Let's begin with the first one."

She continued:

"The rise of a *One World Leader*. Revelation 13:7–8 says the beast will have authority over 'every tribe, people, language, and nation.' That's global rulership. And I believe the spirit of that ruler is already at work."

I nodded. "I do too. You hear it in the calls for a 'Great Reset,' for global unity, for someone who can 'bring peace.' But it's not God's peace—it's a deceptive one. A counterfeit peacemaker. Just like Daniel 9:27 says, he'll make a covenant with Israel—but then he'll break it."

"Exactly," Irene said. "He'll rise from among the Gentile nations—likely the Middle East. Revelation says he comes from the sea, and Revelation 17:15 explains that the 'sea' represents the multitudes of peoples. And Ann, based on the prophecies and the signs—we're not waiting for him to be born. I believe he's alive right now."

"That gave me chills, Irene." I leaned in. "I believe it too. He may already be in a political or financial position. Maybe in the shadows. Maybe even in plain sight. But Scripture says he won't be revealed until the Restrainer—the Holy Spirit within the Church—is removed."

Irene nodded solemnly. "And that's why we keep sounding the alarm: be ready. Because when the Church is raptured, this man steps forward fully empowered. He'll look like a savior—but he'll be a serpent."

I continued:

"The rise of a *One World Government*. Irene, the idea of a One World Government used to sound like science fiction. Now? It feels like next week's breaking news."

"Yes," Irene said, nodding. "And Revelation 13:3 says it plainly: 'the whole world marveled' and 'gave allegiance to the beast.' That word *allegiance* isn't casual—it's total. It's unwavering loyalty to a global regime."

"And the whole world marveled . . ." I repeated. "That's such a loaded phrase. This won't be a slow political climb. It'll be sudden—triggered by crisis. Maybe even collapse. And in the chaos, people will welcome global control as the answer."

"You're absolutely right, Ann." Irene leaned forward. "We already saw a glimpse of it during the pandemic—how fast nations aligned. Borders blurred. Freedoms vanished—all in the name of safety. Global cooperation used to mean diplomacy. Now it means mandates."

I nodded. "I remember hearing world leaders talk about 'reimagining governance' and 'building back better.' But better for who? Because when you pull back the curtain, 'global governance' is just Bible prophecy wrapped in modern branding."

"Exactly." Irene's tone sharpened. "Globalism isn't a conspiracy theory—it's a prophetic certainty. The Bible might not say 'One World Government' word for word, but what it describes—total global control—is crystal clear."

"And people are being conditioned," I said. "They're told it's for peace, equality, safety. But it's all a setup. A trap. This government will demand worship, enforce economic control, and punish anyone who resists."

"Yes—and here's the good news," Irene added. "The Church won't be here to see its full power. What we're witnessing now are only shadows. But once the Rapture occurs, the system will snap into place overnight."

"And the infrastructure's already there," I said. "Technology, finance, surveillance, digital ID systems—it's all waiting. Waiting for the Antichrist to take the reins."

I continued:

"The rise of a *One World Religion*," I said quietly. "Irene, this is the part that really breaks my heart—the rise of a One World Religion. We're already watching the groundwork form: global unity movements, interfaith dialogues, the 'all paths lead to God' rhetoric. And churches that once stood on truth now sound like TED Talks. The doctrine's been diluted."

"It's subtle," Irene agreed, "but it's everywhere. Phrases like 'interfaith harmony' and 'global spirituality' sound peaceful—but they're spiritually deadly. They erase the exclusivity of the gospel and reduce Jesus to just one of many options."

"Exactly." I leaned forward. "They preach inclusion, but exclude Christ. They keep the language of faith—but strip out the Cross, the blood, repentance, and holiness. What's left is a hollow religion that Satan can easily fill."

Irene nodded soberly. "Revelation 13:12 and 15 tell us plainly: the second beast—this False Prophet—promotes the worship of the first beast, the Antichrist. It's not just a religious system that tolerates the Antichrist . . . it worships him. It celebrates him."

"And this isn't a far off fantasy anymore," I added. "Look at the Abrahamic Family House in Abu Dhabi—one compound, three buildings: a mosque, a synagogue, and a church. All positioned as equal. All interchangeable. But the gospel isn't interchangeable. Jesus said, 'I am the way, the truth, and the life. No one comes to the Father but by Me.'"

Irene's expression tightened. "They're building the infrastructure for a religion that includes everything—except the truth. And many believe this is the One World Religion. But here's the twist. It's not. Islam, especially traditional Islam, will never compromise on that level."

"Right," I replied. "The real One World Religion isn't built on unity—it's built on force. Revelation 13:15 is chilling. It says the image of the beast will be brought to life, and those who refuse to worship it will be killed. This isn't just deception—it's tyranny."

"And get this," Irene added, "the second beast has two horns like a lamb—but speaks like a dragon. Could those two horns represent Sunni and Shia Islam, coming together under deception? A spiritual fusion that no one saw coming?"

I paused. "That's possible. And terrifying. A false peace. A counterfeit unity. Not based on truth—but on submission. And imagine this: what if that 'image of the beast' is broadcast globally—like Times Square screens on every building, demanding allegiance five times a day, the way Islamic nations require public prayer?"

Irene shuddered. "It's so plausible. With AI, holograms, and global surveillance—it's all ready. And people won't just be persuaded. They'll be pressured. Worship . . . or die."

I nodded solemnly. "It's forced idolatry. This isn't about spiritual freedom—it's about total control. And here's the kicker: all of it is setting up a false trinity—Satan as the counterfeit Father, the Antichrist as the false Christ, and the False Prophet as the unholy Spirit."

"Ann, what about 666?" Irene asked, tilting her head. "Do you really think it's the number of a man's name?"

I smiled gently. "Not exactly. I believe Scripture should interpret Scripture. In 1 Kings 10:14, it says Solomon received 666 talents of gold in one year. That number isn't random—it links 666 to wealth, power, and man's pursuit of self-glory."

Irene raised an eyebrow. "Solomon started with wisdom."

"Exactly," I said. "But he drifted into compromise—idolatry, foreign alliances, and spiritual decline. His kingdom became a symbol of apostasy. That's what 666 really points to: man exalting himself without God."

Irene looked away. "It's all falling into place, isn't it?"

"Yes," I said softly. "But here's our hope: Jesus said, 'Upon this rock I will build My church, and the gates of hell shall not prevail against it.' The true Church—those who know Christ—won't be deceived. And we won't be here when the image speaks and demands worship. But we must warn while there's still time."

She continued:

"The rise of a *One World Economic System*," Irene began soberly. "Now, Ann, here's where it gets incredibly practical—and frankly, terrifying for those left behind. Revelation 13:16–17 lays it out: no one will be able to buy or sell unless they have the mark."

I nodded. "Exactly. That's the end of financial freedom. Cash? Useless. Credit cards? Obsolete. Your ability to eat, travel, even function in society—it'll all hinge on whether you comply with a global system of allegiance."

"And it's not just a currency shift—it's a control shift," Irene added. "Total surveillance. Total dependence. This system won't merely track your money—it will monitor your loyalty. If you don't worship the beast, you'll be shut out . . . and starved out."

I leaned forward. "And we've already had the dress rehearsal. COVID digitized everything overnight. Contactless payments, QR-code menus, stores refusing cash. It was a global test run—and the world passed with flying colors."

Irene nodded. "And then there's AI and biometrics, and digital ID systems. Microchips, palm scans, retina scans—these aren't science fiction anymore. They're already being implemented. And most people? They're embracing it in the name of convenience."

"But the Bible never said the mark would begin with force," I said carefully. "It may come dressed in comfort. Safety. Progress. 'Want to feed your family? Just take the scan.' It will sound reasonable—until it becomes irreversible."

Irene's voice lowered. "And that's the warning of Revelation 14. Once someone takes the mark, it's final. Eternal. There is no repentance, no reversal. It's not just an economic decision—it's a spiritual seal."

"Which is exactly why we speak now," I added. "This is why we preach and warn while there's still time. Because after the Rapture—once the Church is gone—there will be no global resistance. The mark will be mandated. Compliance will equal spiritual compromise."

Irene nodded, her eyes steady. "But praise God—He has not appointed us to wrath. The true Church will be gone before this reaches its full power. That's why now is the time to wake up. Now is the time to get right with Jesus."

She continued:

"The rise of a *One World Military Power*. This last political agenda ties everything together—because without enforcement, none of the others work. The One World Leader, the One World Government, the One World Religion, and the One World Economy all require military muscle to force compliance. Revelation 13:4 asks, 'Who is able to make war with the beast?' That implies a military so dominant, so overwhelming, that resistance is seen as impossible."

I nodded. "Exactly. And that question—'Who can make war with him?'— isn't rhetorical. It's prophetic. It reveals a terrifying truth: the Antichrist won't just persuade. He'll dominate. He'll enforce his rule through global might. Dissent won't be tolerated—it'll be eliminated."

Irene leaned forward. "We've already seen the foundations. Multinational military drills. NATO restructuring. New alliances forming. We're not just talking about boots on the ground anymore—we're talking drones, satellites, artificial intelligence, facial recognition, and cyberweapons. The next battlefield is everywhere."

I added: "And look at the global trend—disarm the people, empower the state. Strip away local defenses in the name of global peace. It's a setup. The more leaders talk about unity and safety, the more they erase national sovereignty."

"Exactly," Irene said. "This whole narrative of 'global security' is a Trojan horse. It sounds noble on the surface—but underneath, it's all about control. And the Bible already warned us this would happen."

I nodded soberly. "And once the mark is in place, there'll be no refuge. Revelation 13:15 says anyone who refuses to worship the image of the beast will be killed. This isn't just religious oppression—it's military enforcement. It's state-sponsored execution."

"And what's chilling," Irene added, "is how easily the world now accepts authoritarianism—as long as it comes wrapped in the language of 'safety.' COVID showed us that. Lockdowns. Compliance. Digital tracking. People didn't just tolerate control—they begged for it."

I sighed. "We're not waiting for Revelation 13 to start—we're watching its dress rehearsal. Global crises, silenced voices, suppression of truth, and the growing call for a New World Order. It's all happening—faster than most people realize."

Irene steadied her voice. "But here's the hope. All of this unfolds only after the Restrainer—the Holy Spirit operating through the Church—is removed. That's what 2 Thessalonians 2 tells us. The Rapture will clear the way for this beast system to rise. But until then, we warn. We preach. We stand."

I turned to the reader. "And if you're hearing this—it's not about fear. It's about urgency. The Antichrist's army won't arrive with sirens. It'll arrive with celebration—welcomed by a world already deceived."

Irene smiled faintly. "But don't forget what Revelation also says: *The Lamb wins*. Jesus isn't coming back as a Suffering Servant. He's returning as the conquering King—and he will crush every power that rises against Him."

SUMMARY OF REVELATION 13

Revelation 13 unveils Satan's final strategy to dominate the world through a counterfeit trinity: the dragon (Satan), the first beast (the Antichrist), and the second beast (the False Prophet).

John sees the first beast rise from the sea—symbolizing a political leader emerging from global chaos (Revelation 13:1). Empowered by the dragon, this Antichrist astonishes the world with a fatal wound that miraculously heals, leading many to worship him (Revelation 13:3–4). For 42 months, he blasphemes

God, persecutes the saints, and rules over all nations—except those written in the Lamb's Book of Life (Revelation 13:5–8).

Then comes a second beast from the earth—the False Prophet (Revelation 13:11). He appears gentle (like a lamb) but speaks with the voice of the dragon. Performing miracles, including calling fire from heaven, he deceives the world and commands worship of the Antichrist (Revelation 13:12–15).

The chapter climaxes with the mark of the beast—without it, no one can buy or sell (Revelation 13:16–17). The number tied to this global system is 666—"the number of a man" (Revelation 13:18), symbolizing the pinnacle of human rebellion against God.

KEY TAKEAWAYS

- The Antichrist's rise—Emerges from political turmoil with global influence and satanic power.
- Satanic empowerment permitted—God allows limited power for 42 months as part of His sovereign plan.
- The False Prophet's deception—A religious figure who uses miracles and mind control to enforce idolatry.
- Counterfeit resurrection and worship—The beast's wound is healed, leading the world to worship him in awe.
- The mark of the beast—A demonic economic system requiring allegiance through a physical mark.
- The number 666—Symbolizes ultimate humanism and rebellion; a counterfeit to divine perfection (777).

Revelation 13 is a chilling portrait of the final world system that will unite political, religious, economic, and military power under Satan's influence. Yet even as evil rises, this chapter underscores that all authority—even Satan's—is allowed by God for a season. It is a powerful warning to those left behind during the Tribulation, and a sobering reminder to today's believers: discern the times, resist deception, and cling to the true Lamb of God.

Chapter 13

Revelation 14:
Interlude—The
Harvest of Heaven and Hell

PREVIOUSLY IN TRUMPET I: Revelation 1–11—The Unveiling of Jesus Christ and the Prophetic Countdown to the End. The Book of Revelation opens with a striking promise—one no other book in Scripture offers so directly:

> Blessed is he that reads, and they that hear the words of this prophecy, and keep those things which are written therein: for the time is at hand. (Revelation 1:3)

This isn't just poetic language. It's a divine summons to watch, listen, and obey.

The Book of Revelation is not meant to confuse—it's meant to reveal. The very word *"revelation"* means unveiling or disclosure. And what is being unveiled? Jesus Christ Himself.

He is not just the main character—He is the Author of history, the righteous Judge of the nations, the Redeemer of mankind, and the soon-coming King of kings. From chapter 1 to chapter 13, the Book of Revelation lays out a clear and sobering prophetic timeline: the rise of global deception, the emergence of a false world order, the unveiling of the Antichrist, and the intensifying spiritual war between truth and delusion. Yet through every vision, every warning, and every unfolding event, the spotlight never leaves Jesus Christ. He stands at the center—sovereign over history, victorious over evil, and faithful to His promises. The Revelation is not merely about what is coming; it is about who is coming.

REVELATION 1: THE REVELATION OF JESUS CHRIST

In chapter 1, John sees the glorified Christ—not the humble teacher from Galilee, but the resurrected Lord, radiant in heavenly majesty. His hair is white like wool, His eyes blaze like fire, and His voice thunders like the sound of many waters. John, the same disciple who once leaned on Jesus' chest during the Last Supper, now falls at His feet as though dead. This vision sets the tone for the entire book: Revelation isn't primarily about beasts and bowls—it's about Jesus and His glory.

The Book of Revelation unfolds like a divine drama in three sweeping acts: past, present, and future. It's structure is not chaotic or mysterious, but follows a clear divine outline Jesus Himself gives John in Revelation 1:19:

> Write the things which you have seen, and the things which are, and the things which shall be hereafter. (Revelation 1:19)

This becomes a roadmap for the entire book:

- "The things which you have seen"—Christ revealed in glory (chapter 1)
- "The things which are"—Jesus' messages to the churches (chapters 2–3)
- "The things which shall be hereafter"—the prophetic future (chapters 4–22)

The outline or infographic below captures this progression—from the unveiling of Christ to His personal letters to the Church, and finally, to the climactic events that complete God's redemptive plan.

THE BOOK OF REVELATION

OUTLINE OF THE BOOK OF REVELATION

Revelation 1	Revelation 2-3	Rapture of the Church	Revelation 4-19	Second Coming of Jesus Christ	Revelation 20	Great White Throne Judgment	Revelation 21-22
Have Seen	Are Now		Will Happen		Will Happen		Will Happen
Vision	Church Age		Tribulation Age		Millennial Age		Eternal Age
AD 95	2000 Years		7 Years (3-1/2 + 3-1/2)		1000 Years		New Heaven, New Earth, New Jerusalem
	Rebirth of Israel 1948		7 Seals 7 Trumpets 7 Bowls				

Take a moment to study the structure—then let's return to the text, where Jesus begins speaking directly to His Church.

REVELATION 2–3: SEVEN MESSAGES TO SEVEN CHURCHES

Revelation chapters 2 and 3 deliver deeply personal messages to seven churches in Asia Minor (modern-day Turkey). These were real congregations in John's day, but they also represent spiritual conditions found throughout church history. Each message contains elements of commendation, correction, warning, and promise.

Taken together, these seven letters form a panoramic spiritual diagnosis of the Church from Pentecost to the present age. Many believe we are now living in the final Laodicean era—marked by lukewarm faith, self-reliance, and spiritual complacency. But even then, Jesus stands at the door and knocks, offering intimate fellowship to any who will hear His voice and open their hearts.

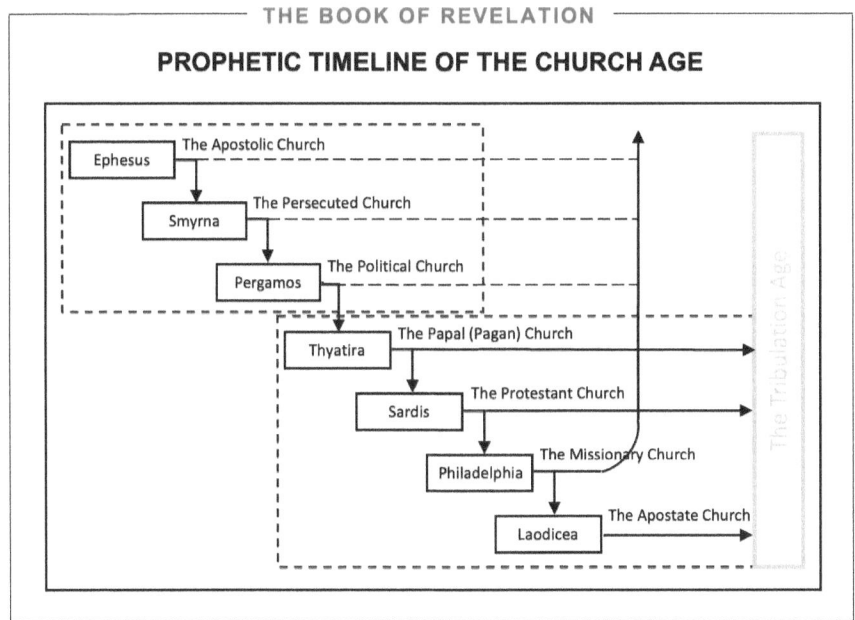

REVELATION 4: THE RAPTURE AND THE THRONE ROOM

Then something dramatic happens. In Revelation 4:1, John hears a voice like a trumpet saying, "Come up here." Instantly, he is caught up into heaven. This moment powerfully symbolizes the Rapture—when the Church will be "caught up . . . to meet the Lord in the air" (1 Thessalonians 4:16–17).

> For the Lord Himself shall descend from heaven with a shout, with the voice of the archangel, and with the trump of God: the dead in Christ shall rise first: Then we which are alive and remain shall be caught up together with them in the clouds, to meet the Lord in the air: and so shall we ever be with the Lord. (1 Thessalonians 4:16–17)

What John sees next is beyond breathtaking: the throne of God, surrounded by flashes of lightning and peals of thunder. Around the throne sit twenty-four elders, representing the redeemed saints clothed in white and crowned with gold. Before the throne burn seven lamps of fire—the seven Spirits of God. And closest to the throne, four living creatures cry out day and night, "Holy, holy, holy, is the Lord God Almighty, who was, and is, and is to come."

At this point in Revelation, the Church is no longer on earth. It is now in heaven—safe, victorious, and glorified—worshiping around the throne. What follows marks a dramatic shift in focus: from the Church Age to the Tribulation Age, as God's judgments begin to unfold upon a world that has rejected its Savior.

REVELATION 5: THE SCROLL AND THE LAMB

Then a crisis: a scroll appears, sealed with seven seals—the title deed to the earth. But no one in heaven or on earth is found worthy to open it. John begins to weep—until the Lion of the tribe of Judah, the Lamb who was slain, steps forward. Jesus alone is worthy. He takes the scroll, and heaven erupts in worship. The moment is pivotal: Christ is about to unleash the judgments that will redeem creation and complete God's redemptive plan.

But before turning to Revelation 6 and the breaking of the seals, we need to understand the prophetic framework behind the coming judgments: Daniel's 70th Week (Daniel 9:24–9:27). This remarkable prophecy outlines 70 "weeks" of years—490 years total—set apart for God's dealings with Israel and Jerusalem. Sixty-nine of those weeks (483 years) have already been fulfilled, ending with the crucifixion of the Messiah.

> Seventy weeks are determined upon your people and upon your Holy City, to finish the transgression, and to make an end of sins, and to make reconciliation for iniquity, and to bring in everlasting righteousness, and to seal up the vision and prophecy, and to anoint the Most Holy. (Daniel 9:24)

Daniel's 69 Weeks (483 Years)

> Know therefore and understand, that from the going forth of the commandment to restore and to build Jerusalem unto the Messiah the Prince shall be seven weeks, and threescore and two weeks: the streets shall be built again, and the wall, even in troublous times. (Daniel 9:25)

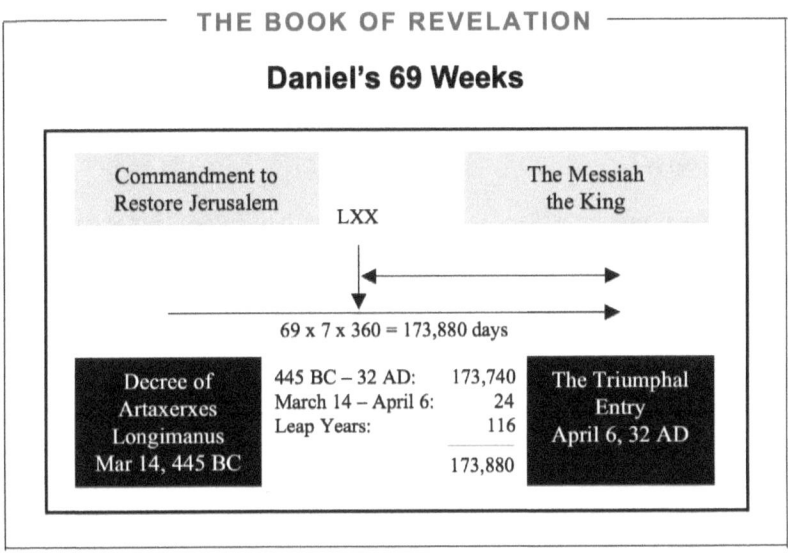

The Gap After the 69th Week

And after threescore and two weeks shall Messiah be cut off, but not for Himself: and the people of the prince that shall come shall destroy the city and the sanctuary; and the end thereof shall be with a flood, and unto the end of the war desolations are determined. (Daniel 9:26)

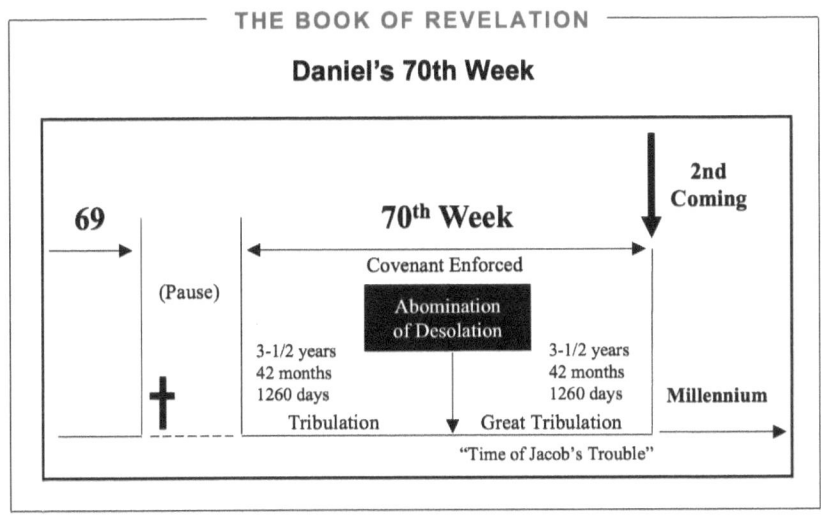

Daniel's 70th Week: The Tribulation Age (7 Years)

> And he (the Antichrist) shall confirm the covenant with many for one week: and in the midst of the week he shall cause the sacrifice and the oblation to cease, and for the overspreading of abominations he shall make it desolate, even until the consummation, and that determined shall be poured upon the desolate. (Daniel 9:27)

That leaves one final week—seven years—still to come. This is what we call the Tribulation Age, the final stretch in human history before Christ's Second Coming. Revelation chapters 6–19 detail what unfolds during this climactic period. The infographics above will help connect Daniel's prophecy with the events described in Revelation.

God gave Daniel a prophetic timeline of 70 "weeks" (70 x 7 years = 490 years) specifically for Israel and Jerusalem. The first 69 weeks (483 years) span from the decree to rebuild Jerusalem (Nehemiah 2) to the Messiah's First Coming—culminating in Jesus' triumphal entry and crucifixion. The Church Age—also known as the Gap—is a prophetic pause between the 69th and 70th week. The final seven-year period, known as Daniel's 70th Week, will begin after the Rapture and unfold during the Tribulation Age.

REVELATION 6–9: THE SEAL AND TRUMPET JUDGMENTS

Revelation 6 opens the scroll and unleashes the first six seal judgments:

1. **White Horse**—The Antichrist arrives, deceiving many with a false promise of peace.
2. **Red Horse**—Global war erupts, stripping peace from the earth.
3. **Black Horse**—Economic collapse and famine devastate nations.
4. **Pale Horse**—Death and Hades claim one-fourth of the world's population.
5. **Fifth Seal**—Martyrs cry out for justice from beneath the altar.
6. **Sixth Seal**—A cosmic upheaval shakes the heavens and the earth with earthquakes, darkness, and terror.

Revelation 7 interrupts the judgments with a powerful pause: God seals 144,000 Jewish evangelists to spread the gospel during the Tribulation. Through their witness, a great multitude from every nation is saved.

Revelation 8 unveils the seventh seal, which introduces the seven trumpet judgments:

1. **Trumpet 1**—Hail, fire, and blood burn a third of the earth's vegetation.
2. **Trumpet 2**—A fiery mountain plunges into the sea, destroying marine life and ships.

3. **Trumpet 3**—A star called Wormwood poisons a third of the freshwater.
4. **Trumpet 4**—The sun, moon, and stars are darkened by a third.
5. **Trumpet 5**—Demonic locusts rise from the abyss, tormenting those without God's seal for five months.
6. **Trumpet 6**—Four bound angels are released from the Euphrates River to lead an army that kills a third of mankind.

By Revelation 9, the earth is staggering under wave after wave of divine judgment—yet humanity still refuses to repent. The hardness of heart is astonishing. And though six trumpet blasts have already unleashed unimaginable devastation, the seventh trumpet has yet to sound—ushering in the final and fiercest wave of judgment: the bowl judgments (Revelation 15–16).

REVELATION 10: THE MIGHTY ANGEL AND THE LITTLE SCROLL

John sees a mighty angel descend from heaven, holding a small scroll. He is told to eat it—sweet as honey in his mouth, but bitter in his stomach—reflecting the dual nature of God's prophecy: joyful for the redeemed, but bitter for the rebellious. The angel declares that time is up—there will be no more delay. The final judgments are about to begin.

REVELATION 11: THE TWO WITNESSES AND THE FINAL TRUMPET

Two powerful prophets prophesy in Jerusalem for 1,260 days, performing miracles and calling the world to repentance. When they are killed, the world celebrates—until God raises them from the dead before all to see. Then the seventh trumpet sounds, signaling the final woe and the coming reign of Christ.

A TALE OF TWO HARVESTS: HEAVEN AND HELL

Before the final storm of divine wrath is unleashed through the seven bowl judgments, Revelation 14 offers a moment of prophetic pause—a heavenly interlude that reframes everything. It's as if God halts the chaos to lift the veil and declare: "This is where it's all headed."

This chapter is not structured chronologically like the rest—it's *thematic*. Think of it as a divine trailer reel for the seven-year Tribulation period, contrasting two eternal destinies:

- The faithful redeemed, standing victorious with the Lamb on Mount Zion.
- The beast worshipers, destined for eternal torment and judgment.

We witness two final harvests:

1. **A Harvest of Heaven**—The righteous who overcome the Tribulation—the Tribulation saints—sealed by God, refusing the mark of the beast.

2. **A Harvest of Hell**—The wicked, fully ripe for judgment, cast into the winepress of God's fury.

We hear the eternal gospel proclaimed one last time. We're shown the fall of Babylon. We witness God's blessing over those who remain faithful unto death. Revelation 14 is God drawing a final line in the sand—heaven or hell, Lamb or beast, life or wrath. There is no middle ground.

Here's a breakdown of Revelation 14:

1. **The Lamb on Mount Zion**—Christ stands triumphant on Mount Zion, surrounded by the 144,000 redeemed and sealed believers. These are heaven's elite—marked by the Father's name, untouched by compromise, and victorious through tribulation. They sing a new song only the redeemed can learn (Revelation 14:1–5).

2. **The Seven Angels**:

    o   The First Angel—Soaring across the skies, this angel declares the eternal gospel—God's final universal altar call. Every nation, tribe, tongue, and people hear it: "Fear God and give Him glory, for the hour of His judgment has come!" (Revelation 14:6–7). Even in wrath, God offers mercy.

    o   The Second Angel—This angel proclaims the collapse of Babylon, the great harlot—a symbol of corrupt spiritual, political, and economic systems. Many Bible scholars and prophecy teachers believe this represents America or a revived global empire. "Fallen, fallen is Babylon!" (Revelation 14:8).

    o   The Third Angel—A chilling warning to those who worship the beast or receive his mark: they will face the full, undiluted wrath of God. "He will be tormented with fire and brimstone . . . and the smoke of their torment ascends forever and ever" (Revelation 14:9–11). This is not metaphor—it is final, eternal judgment.

    o   Interlude—A brief but powerful pause (Revelation 14:12–13). Here, heaven speaks: "Blessed are the dead who die in the Lord from now on . . . their deeds will follow them." It's a reminder that God sees every sacrifice. The saints' endurance is not forgotten.

o The Fourth Angel—The heavenly harvest begins. The Son of Man, crowned in gold, reaps the righteous—those who overcame. "And He who sat on the cloud swung His sickle . . . and the earth was reaped" (Revelation 14:14–16). This is the final gathering of Tribulation saints into eternal rest.

o The Fifth, Sixth, and Seventh Angels—The final three angels announce and execute the harvest of wrath. Like overripe grapes crushed in a winepress, the wicked are gathered and judged. "The winepress was trampled . . . and blood came out . . . up to the horses' bridles" (Revelation 14:17–20). This is the preview of Armageddon—the coming crescendo of divine justice.

This chapter prepares us for what comes next: the unrestrained wrath of God poured out through the seven bowl judgments. But it also reminds us that God hasn't stopped calling, warning, and reaching. His gospel still echoes, even as the final pages of human history turn.

Now, let's step into Revelation 14:1.

THE REVELATION OF JESUS CHRIST REVEALS:

[14:1] And I looked, and, lo, a Lamb stood on the Mount Zion, and with Him a hundred forty and four thousand, having His Father's name written on their foreheads.

This verse is not a moment of warning or judgment—it's a snapshot of glory. The Lamb, Jesus Christ, is standing—not sitting, not retreating—on Mount Zion, the appointed throne of His earthly reign. This is a declaration of authority, fulfillment, and preservation.

The 144,000 who appear here are the same sealed servants introduced in Revelation 7—12,000 from each tribe of Israel. They have been divinely marked and preserved through the most chaotic, demon-infested period in human history: the Tribulation. Not 143,999—not one is missing. Just as Jesus prayed in John 17:12, "Those whom You gave Me I have kept; none of them is lost," their sealing is God's unbreakable signature of ownership and protection. God finishes what He starts—and not even the fury of hell can interrupt what He has ordained.

The seal—the Father's name written on their foreheads—stands in stark contrast to the mark of the beast in Revelation 13. This is a spiritual binary: you are either sealed by God or marked by the beast. There is no neutral ground. In the seven-year Tribulation, allegiance becomes visible, undeniable. But isn't that true even now? In the spiritual realm, every heart bears a mark. The question is: whose name is on yours?

Notice also the location: Mount Zion. This is the only place in Revelation that mentions it by name. While some interpret this as a heavenly Zion, others see it as a prophetic preview of Christ's future reign on earthly Jerusalem, where He will sit on the throne of David (Luke 1:32). Zion is not a random peak—it's the very hill God chose for His dwelling, where His King will rule (Psalm 2:6). It's not for the nations to decide—not the UN, not the Palestinians, not world leaders—but God Himself has appointed Zion for His Son's coronation.

This verse is also a prophetic anchor—a reassurance. While the Antichrist rages and the False Prophet deceives, God is still preserving His remnant. These 144,000 are not hiding. They're standing—with Jesus. They've passed through fire, like the three Hebrew boys in Daniel 3. Miraculously untouched. Supernaturally preserved. Just like them, these Jewish evangelists stood while the world bowed.

And what does this say to us? That Jesus is not looking for spectators—He's calling for those who will stand with Him, even when it's unpopular or unsafe. Even when the fire rages. Even when the crowd bows to the beast. These 144,000 are a picture of what bold, sealed, unashamed faith looks like.

OLD TESTAMENT FORESHADOWS REVELATION:

Yet have I set My King upon My holy hill of Zion. (Psalm 2:6)

This verse directly mirrors the image of Jesus (the Lamb) standing triumphantly on Mount Zion with the 144,000 in Revelation 14:1. It's a fulfillment of God's promise to enthrone His Son—not symbolically, but literally—on Zion, as King and Redeemer.

Irene leaned in, puzzled. "Ann, were the 144,000 only active during the trumpet judgments? Seeing them again in Revelation 14:1, standing with the Lamb on Mount Zion, makes it seem like their mission is finished."

I smiled gently. "That's a great question, Irene. The 144,000 first appear in Revelation 7, sealed by God before the seventh seal and trumpet judgments begin. They're Jewish evangelists—12,000 from each tribe of Israel—most likely active during those trumpet judgments."

Irene nodded. "So they're like God's frontline missionaries?"

"Exactly," I said. "They're described as virgins who follow the Lamb wherever He goes—fully devoted (Revelation 14:4). Then in Revelation 14, we see them again, victorious, standing with Jesus on Mount Zion."

She tilted her head. "Is that on earth or in heaven?"

"That's debated," I said. "Some scholars believe it refers to heavenly Mount Zion—especially since they sing before the throne (Revelation 14:3). That language suggests they've been taken up—like the Two Witnesses in Revelation 11—after completing their 3½-year mission during the first half of the Tribulation."

Irene's eyes widened. "So they don't go through the second half of the Tribulation?"

"Most likely not," I answered. "Revelation 14 seems to mark their 'mission accomplished' moment. They're never mentioned again, and their disappearance lines up with the start of the Great Tribulation—the final 42 months. It's a powerful picture of God's faithfulness: sealed, sent, and safely brought home."

"Wow," she said. "That really clears it up. I kept expecting them to reappear later in the book."

"A lot of people do," I said with a smile. "But their absence after chapter 14 speaks volumes. Not one is lost. They stand with the Lamb—proof that God finishes what He starts."

———◆◆◆———

THE REVELATION OF JESUS CHRIST REVEALS:

14:2 And I heard a voice from heaven, as the voice of many waters, and as the voice of a great thunder: and I heard the voice of harpers harping with their harps.

Heaven resounds with divine power and triumphant worship. The "voice from heaven" is thunderous and overwhelming—described as "many waters" and "great thunder"—echoing the majesty of the glorified Christ in Revelation 1:15. It's a voice that commands attention. Authority. Judgment. Glory.

And then—music. The sound of harpers harping with their harps cuts through the thunder like a melody of mercy. It's not chaos—it's a heavenly concert. Victory is being celebrated, not debated.

But who is making this sound? The context points us back to verse 1—the 144,000 sealed servants of God, standing with the Lamb on Mount Zion. These are the redeemed Jewish evangelists who have made it through the Tribulation without compromise. Now, they lift their voices in a new song (verse 3), and this moment in verse 2 sets the stage for it.

So here's the beautiful picture: the same 144,000 who once stood in the fire of Tribulation are now standing in the presence of the Lamb, and their worship reverberates through heaven like thunder and music combined. It's as if heaven itself is responding to their arrival—joining in a synchronized praise that testifies to their faithfulness and God's deliverance.

This verse is a collision of divine power and intimate worship. It reminds us that heaven is not shaken by earth's trials. Instead, it resounds with victory songs sung by those who overcame. And their praise becomes part of the very atmosphere of heaven.

OLD TESTAMENT FORESHADOWS REVELATION:

Hear attentively the noise of His voice, and the sound that goes out of His mouth. He directs it under the whole heaven, and His lightning unto the ends of the earth. After it a voice roars: He thunders with the voice of His excellency; and He will not stay them when His voice is heard. God thunders marvelously with His voice; great things does He, which we cannot comprehend. (Job 37:2–5)

In Revelation 14:2, John hears a voice like many waters, great thunder, and harps—a blend of majesty, power, and beauty. This echoes Job 37:2–5, where God's thunderous voice shows His authority over creation. In both books, the voice isn't just sound—it's divine command. In Job, it speaks to creation; in Revelation, it signals judgment and victory, marking the 144,000 with the Lamb.

THE REVELATION OF JESUS CHRIST REVEALS:

[14:3] And they sung as it were a new song before the throne, and before the four beasts, and the elders: and no man could learn that song but the hundred and forty and four thousand, which were redeemed from the earth.

This verse captures an intimate, exclusive moment in heaven. The 144,000—those sealed and preserved through the chaos of the Tribulation—now sing a "new song." It's not just any song. It's a heavenly anthem written from the ashes of earth's darkest hour and shaped by the suffering they endured for the Lamb.

It is sung "before the throne, and before the four beasts, and the elders." This means their song echoes in the very presence of the Godhead, the living creatures, and the twenty-four elders—those who represent the fullness of redeemed humanity. Heaven watches and listens as the 144,000 raise a melody only they can sing.

Why only them? Because this song isn't taught—it's lived. It is born from personal obedience, unparalleled perseverance, and a unique assignment: to evangelize during the most hostile time in human history. Theirs is the anthem of the sealed. The melody of the marked. The chorus of the conquerors.

This "new song" echoes the pattern seen elsewhere in Scripture. In Exodus 15, Israel sang a song of deliverance after crossing the Red Sea. In Revelation 5, the elders and living creatures sang a new song to the Lamb. But this song—this one—is exclusively theirs. It belongs to those "redeemed from the earth." Their lives have been a living sacrifice, and now their song is an eternal testimony.

This moment is not just a celebration. It's a prophetic declaration: God knows how to preserve His own. And when they stand before Him, they will not be silent.

OLD TESTAMENT FORESHADOWS REVELATION:

Sing unto Him a new song; play skillfully with a loud noise. (Psalm 33:3)

Psalm 33:3 sets the tone for Revelation 14:3, where the 144,000 sing a "new song" before the throne. It's a sacred anthem—learned through obedience, suffering, and loyalty to the Lamb. Their worship, like Psalm 33's "loud noise," echoes heaven's thunderous soundscape: water, thunder, and harps in perfect harmony.

THE REVELATION OF JESUS CHRIST REVEALS:

14:4 These are they which were not defiled with women; for they are virgins. These are they which follow the Lamb wheresoever He goes. These were redeemed from among men, being the firstfruits unto God and to the Lamb.

This verse offers one of the clearest windows in the character of the 144,000. These aren't just sealed survivors or bold evangelists—they are set apart, consecrated warriors of God. Their lives are marked by radical devotion, spiritual purity, and unwavering obedience.

"Not defiled with women; for they are virgins." This language has caused many to pause—is this literal or symbolic? Possibly both.

Literally, like the prophet Jeremiah—who, on the threshold of Babylonian judgment, was forbidden to marry (Jeremiah 16:1–4)—these 144,000 may have remained celibate as a sign of total dedication in a time of global corruption. Jesus also gave a sobering warning, implying that the Tribulation would be no time for domestic attachments:

Woe unto them that are with child and to them that give suck in those days. (Matthew 24:19)

But spiritually, the imagery runs deeper. In Scripture, idolatry is often portrayed as spiritual fornication (Ezekiel 16), and true worship as marital fidelity. Paul describes the Church as a "chaste virgin" presented to Christ (2 Corinthians 11:2), washed and set apart (Ephesians 5:26–27). In contrast, the Revelation reveals "Jezebel" and the harlot of Babylon—symbols of spiritual corruption and seduction. The 144,000, therefore, may be described as "virgins" in the sense that they have not bowed to the world's idolatry. They have kept themselves pure for the Lord alone.

"They follow the Lamb wheresoever He goes." This perhaps is the most compelling mark of all. These men are not followers in name only—they are followers in fire, obeying Christ with total allegiance. No fear. No compromise.

No hesitation. In a world gripped by deception, they walk in truth. While others worship the beast, they walk with the Lamb. Their footsteps trace His, even when the path leads through persecution, rejection, and death.

"Firstfruits unto God and to the Lamb." This phrase echoes the ancient practice in Israel of offering the very first and finest of the harvest to the Lord (Romans 11:15–16). These 144,000 are just that: the first and finest redeemed remnant of Israel—a down payment on a greater harvest yet to come. As "firstfruits," they signal a prophetic promise that more of Israel will turn to Messiah and be saved (Romans 11:25–26).

Their role may also parallel the "brethren" mentioned by Jesus in Matthew 25—the faithful Jewish remnant who endure the Tribulation and enter the Millennial Kingdom. Their place in God's prophetic timeline is not just as survivors, but as ambassadors of righteousness—a preview of Israel's restored destiny during Christ's thousand-year reign.

These 144,000 are the antithesis of Jezebel's seduction and Babylon's corruption. In a world prostituted to the beast, they are virgins of truth. In a world drunk with delusion, they are firstfruits of redemption. In a world led by lies, they are followers of the Lamb—unshaken, undefiled, and uncompromising.

And when the smoke clears, they are still standing—sealed, saved, and singing a song that only they can know.

OLD TESTAMENT FORESHADOWS REVELATION:

The word of the LORD came also unto me, saying, You shalt not take you a wife, neither shalt you have sons or daughters in this place. (Jeremiah 16:1–2)

This verse reflects the same calling to separation and purity as seen in the 144,000. Just as Jeremiah was instructed to abstain from marriage as a prophetic sign during a time of impending judgment, the 144,000 are described as virgins—set apart for an urgent, prophetic mission during the Tribulation. The purity is likely both literal and symbolic, mirroring Jeremiah's consecrated life.

THE REVELATION OF JESUS CHRIST REVEALS:

14:5 And in their mouth was found no guile: for they are without fault before the throne of God.

This closing description of the 144,000 seals their identity with unmatched integrity. "In their mouth was found no guile." That word "guile" means deceit, trickery, or hypocrisy. In a world swirling with lies, propaganda, and manipulation—where truth is traded for power—these men speak with clarity, truth, and sincerity. They are not influenced by the beast's system, nor do they twist their message to please men. Their words reflect the purity of their hearts, and their message is unmarred by compromise.

"For they are without fault before the throne of God." Not sinless—but blameless. In the eyes of heaven, they are pure. Set apart. Forgiven. Redeemed. Justified. Their standing comes not from their perfection but from their unwavering devotion to the Lamb. They didn't cave to pressure. They didn't bow to the beast. And now they stand faultless—not just before men, but before the throne of God Himself.

This final verse completes the portrait of the 144,000: bold in witness, pure in heart, truthful in speech, and radiant in holiness. They are God's special forces during the Tribulation—marked by heaven, untouched by compromise, and destined for eternal reward.

OLD TESTAMENT FORESHADOWS REVELATION:

The remnant of Israel shall not do iniquity, nor speak lies; neither shall a deceitful tongue be found in their mouth: for they shall feed and lie down, and none shall make them afraid. (Zephaniah 3:13)

This verse directly parallels Revelation 14:5 where the 144,000 are described as having "no guile" in their mouths. Zephaniah prophetically describes a purified remnant of Israel—morally upright, honest, and spiritually clean—just as Revelation portrays the 144,000 standing blameless before God.

THE REVELATION OF JESUS CHRIST REVEALS:

14:6 And I saw another angel fly in the midst of heaven, having the everlasting gospel to preach to them that dwell on the earth, and to every nation, and kindred, and tongue, and people.

The First Angel—Pre-Harvest Warning. This verse marks a stunning, supernatural turning point in the prophetic drama. Earth has descended into chaos. The Antichrist rules with iron and deception. The Church is gone. The 144,000 evangelists have finished their mission. The Two Witnesses have ascended to heaven. There are no churches, no pastors, no Christian media, no Gospel tracts being printed—just global darkness. But God, in His unmatched mercy, does not fall silent.

Instead, He sends an angel. A literal angel. Not just to watch or protect—but to preach. This angel flies "in the midst of heaven," meaning the atmospheric sky visible to people on earth. He's on a global mission—not bound by terrain, censorship, or fear. His voice thunders over nations, cultures, and languages. And what does he proclaim? The everlasting gospel—the unchanging, eternal message of redemption and worship directed to the one true Creator.

This refutes the idea that angels can't preach. In this unique moment of history, God appoints an indestructible heavenly messenger to shout the truth from the sky. Why? Because the gospel must go forth, even when the gates of hell try to shut it down.

He's proclaiming hope in the middle of horror. His message pierces the madness: "Fear God." "Give Him glory." "Worship the Creator." It's not the soft, seeker-friendly appeal of modern pulpits. It's urgent. Loud. Prophetic. Final.

The gospel message here is *not* a new gospel—it's the everlasting one. The same God who made heaven, earth, the sea, and the fountains of waters (verse 7) is now demanding attention before the final judgments fall. This is a last call to humanity. And it is divine grace in its most dramatic form.

This angel declares: judgment has arrived, yet mercy is still offered.

OLD TESTAMENT FORESHADOWS REVELATION:

The Spirit of the Lord GOD is upon me; because the LORD has anointed me to preach good tidings unto the meek; He has sent me to bind up the brokenhearted, to proclaim liberty to the captives, and the opening of the prison to them that are bound. (Isaiah 61:1)

Isaiah 61:1 foretells Christ proclaiming good news through divine anointing. Revelation 14:6 echoes this on a cosmic scale, where an angel preaches the everlasting gospel from the heavens. Both are God-ordained messages of salvation and warning before judgment falls.

THE REVELATION OF JESUS CHRIST REVEALS:

[14:7] Saying with a loud voice, Fear God, and give glory to Him; for the hour of His judgment is come: and worship Him that made heaven, and earth, and the sea, and the fountains of waters.

The angel's proclamation doesn't come in a whisper—it thunders "with a loud voice." Why? Because this is heaven's final warning. There's no more time for subtlety. The age of grace is closing. This is the last Gospel broadcast to a world that's chosen the beast over the Lamb.

"Fear God." This isn't the kind of fear preached in today's polished mega pulpits. It's not about reverence alone. It's holy trembling. It's the recognition that God is no longer winking at sin. The Antichrist demands worship. The False Prophet performs wonders. The dragon deceives. But now, heaven shouts back: "Worship the Creator!" "And give glory to Him"—not to technology, government, self, or Satan's counterfeit trinity. Glory belongs to God alone. And this isn't a suggestion. It's a command.

"For the hour of His judgment is come"—not *will* come, not *might* come. It has arrived. The bowls of wrath are about to be poured out. The door of mercy is still cracked open—but barely. The angel calls the world back to creation theology—a reminder that God made everything: "heaven, earth, sea, and the fountains of waters." This is direct rebuke against the Antichrist's counterfeit power, who claims to control the world but did not create it.

This verse is the anti-megachurch message—not because it lacks power, but because it confronts instead of comforts. In a generation where even the gospel has been watered down to suit itching ears, here's the raw, unfiltered truth: God is holy. Judgment is now. Choose wisely.

To the righteous remnant, this is good news—your vindication is near. To the rebellious earth dwellers, it's a wake-up call—and maybe your last.

OLD TESTAMENT FORESHADOWS REVELATION:

For the LORD is great, and greatly to be praised: He is to be feared above all gods. For all the gods of the nations are idols: but the LORD made the heavens . . . Give unto the LORD glory and strength . . . Give unto the Lord the glory due unto His name . . . Fear before Him, all the earth: say among the nations that the LORD reigns . . . He shall judge the people righteously. (Psalm 96:4–5, 7–10)

Just as Psalm 96 invites all nations to worship the Creator before His righteous judgment, Revelation 14:7 is a final global summons to fear, glorify, and worship the true God—before His judgments are poured out.

THE REVELATION OF JESUS CHRIST REVEALS:

^{14:8} And there followed another angel, saying, Babylon is fallen, is fallen, that great city, because she made all nations drink of the wine of the wrath of her fornication.

The Second Angel—Pre-Harvest Warning. The second angel steps onto the scene with a thunderous proclamation: "Babylon is fallen, is fallen." The repetition isn't redundancy—it's emphasis. Finality. Certainty. Heaven is announcing the irreversible collapse of the great harlot system that has seduced and corrupted the nations of the earth.

This is Babylon's first mention in Revelation, signaling the start of her fall—spiritually, politically, economically, and prophetically. She becomes the focus in Revelation 17 and 18.

The angel doesn't just declare Babylon's destruction—he reveals *why* she is judged: "Because she made all nations drink of the wine of the wrath of her fornication." This isn't just literal immorality. It's spiritual harlotry. Babylon has become the intoxicating force of false religion, economic greed, political corruption, and demonic deception. Her "wine" represents seduction, control, and wrath—she has intoxicated the nations with her lies, lured them into allegiance, and now must face divine wrath.

Historical and prophetic parallels:

- The term Babylon traces back to Genesis 10–11, where Nimrod built the Tower of Babel—a unified rebellion against God. From there, Babylon has symbolized man's attempt to rule without God, often through false religion and global control.
- Jeremiah 51:6–9 and Isaiah 13:19 both prophesy Babylon's destruction in language echoed here in Revelation.
- The Greek verb used for "is fallen" is *epesen*, which is in the aorist tense, signaling a completed, irreversible act, even if its full unfolding lies ahead. From heaven's vantage point: Babylon is already finished. It's as if God stamps her judgment in past tense—her fate is sealed.

Babylon is more than a city. She is a system—a fusion of corrupted religion, commerce, and power that has always opposed God. She's the fountainhead of every false doctrine, every twisted gospel, every idol that claims God's throne. And here's the provocative truth: Babylon has been Satan's headquarters since Genesis—and she is rising again.

In coming chapters (Revelation 17–18), we will expose Mystery Babylon—and present compelling evidence that she may well be America, a nation that began in covenant with God but now leads the world in moral compromise, spiritual apostasy, and global influence. The fornication is global—and so is the fallout.

The fall of Babylon is both judgment and a cleansing. It's God tearing down the scaffolding of Satan's empire to prepare the way for His Son's return. Before righteousness can reign, corruption must fall. So this is not just history—this is prophecy in motion. A warning. A promise. A foreshadowing of the final shaking before the King comes to reign. Are you ready for Babylon's fall? Because heaven already considers it done.

OLD TESTAMENT FORESHADOWS REVELATION:

Babylon has been a golden cup in the LORD's hand, that made all the earth drunken: the nations have drunken of her wine; therefore the nations are mad. Babylon is suddenly fallen and destroyed: howl for her; take balm for her pain, if so be she may be healed. (Jeremiah 51:7–8)

Both passages, Revelation 14:8 and Jeremiah 51:7–8, describe Babylon as intoxicating the nations with wine—a metaphor for corrupting influence. The "wine of her fornication" in Revelation echoes Jeremiah's imagery of a golden cup that made the earth drunk. The sudden and catastrophic fall of Babylon in both verses connects to God's decisive judgment on a system steeped in idolatry, deception, and rebellion.

This prophetic parallel underscores the continuity between the Old Testament judgment on historic Babylon and the future judgment on Mystery Babylon—a final global system of deception and immorality.

THE REVELATION OF JESUS CHRIST REVEALS:

[14:9] And the third angel followed them, saying with a loud voice, If any man worship the beast and his image, and receive his mark on his forehead, or on his hand.

The Third Angel—Pre-Harvest Warning. This is one of the most sobering warnings in all of Scripture. The third angel steps forward not with comfort—but with confrontation. His message is loud, direct, and crystal clear: do not worship the beast, do not receive his mark, and do not bow to his image. Why? Because to do so is to cross an eternal line.

The angel's tone is urgent. There's no whispering here—this is a loud voice from heaven, echoing across the chaos of earth. The world is in moral freefall, the Church has been raptured, the 144,000 are gone, and now even heaven's angels are warning mankind from the skies. And still—God is offering one final chance not to make the ultimate mistake. This is not symbolic language. This is prophetic truth: If you take the mark, you've chosen permanent allegiance to the beast—and permanent separation from God.

Worship and the mark are a package deal. Notice how the angel links the mark, the image, and worship together. These are not separate issues—they are intertwined. Taking the mark is not merely about survival or convenience—it is an act of worship. It's saying: "I reject Christ, and I embrace the Antichrist." Whether one realizes it or not, this act is spiritually binding.

Many may be tempted to rationalize: "I just need to feed my family . . ." "It's just a scan on my hand . . ." "God will understand . . ." But heaven's response is chilling: "Do not do it." Because to take the mark is to voluntarily seal your destiny in the Lake of Fire.

This is the unpardonable sin of the Tribulation. It's not a mistake you can walk back. It's not a lapse you can apologize for. This is the final spiritual contract—with Satan. That's why the warning is preemptive. This isn't about judgment falling yet—it's about preventing people from stepping into irreversible damnation. And remember: this is God's mercy on display. Even in wrath, He warns. Even in judgment, He pleads.

This angel's message also makes a grim but important comparison. Those who refuse the mark will likely die—beheaded, persecuted, starved. But their suffering is brief—and they will be with Christ forever. But those who take the mark? "The same shall drink of the wine of the wrath of God . . ." (verse 10) ". . . and the smoke of their torment ascends up forever and ever . . ." (verse 11). Eternal torment. No rest. No relief. No reversal. This is the great and terrifying contrast. A few moments of earthly ease in exchange for eternity in hell. Or a few moments of suffering on earth for eternal glory in heaven. The choice is yours. But the angel is pleading—don't choose wrong.

We live in a world that plays fast and loose with the truth. But in Revelation 14:9, there's no wiggle room. God draws a clear line in the sand. No neutral ground. No half-hearted faith. No passive resistance. You're either marked by God . . . or you're marked by the beast. Choose wisely. Eternity is at stake.

OLD TESTAMENT FORESHADOWS REVELATION:

Take heed to yourselves, that your heart be not deceived, and you turn aside, and serve other gods, and worship them; And then the LORD's wrath be kindled against you . . . Therefore shall you lay up these My Words in your heart and in your soul, and bind them for a sign upon your hand, that they may be as frontlets between your eyes. (Deuteronomy 11:16–18)

In Revelation 14:9, the warning is against worshiping the beast and receiving his mark on the forehead or hand—a satanic counterfeit of what God commanded in Deuteronomy: binding His Word on the hand and between the eyes as a sign of covenantal allegiance.

This contrast highlights a spiritual battle between two marks: God's mark—obedience, truth, and worship of the true God. The beast's mark—rebellion, deception, and worship of Satan's counterfeit system. In both passages, the issue is allegiance—either to the Creator or to the counterfeit.

THE REVELATION OF JESUS CHRIST REVEALS:

14:10 The same will drink of the wine of the wrath of God, which is poured out without mixture into the cup of His indignation; and he will be tormented with fire and brimstone in the presence of the holy angels, and in the presence of the Lamb.

This verse delivers one of Scripture's clearest and most sobering warnings— no symbolism, just the stark reality of divine judgment.

"The wine of the wrath of God." Wine in Scripture often symbolizes joy, celebration, or covenant. But here? It's the exact opposite. This wine is God's wrath, and it's not diluted. The phrase "poured out without mixture" means this judgment is undiluted—no mercy, no reprieve. In ancient times, wine was often mixed with water to soften its strength. But God's wrath in this moment? It's full strength, and it's just.

"The cup of His indignation." This echoes the prophetic imagery found in Jeremiah and Isaiah, where the nations are made to drink the cup of God's fury (Jeremiah 25:15–16; Isaiah 51:17). To drink from this cup is to fully absorb the consequences of rebellion against God. This isn't about a temporary punishment—it's eternal justice for those who reject grace and choose the mark of the beast.

"Tormented with fire and brimstone." The torment described is not symbolic—it is literal and eternal. Fire and brimstone are associated with the judgment of Sodom and Gomorrah, and throughout Scripture, they represent God's holy and consuming justice. This torment is conscious, continual, and inescapable.

"In the presence of the Lamb." This is especially striking. The torment doesn't occur in a dark corner of the universe—it happens before the very face of heaven. Why? Because divine justice is not hidden. God doesn't turn away from judgment; it is part of His holiness. The Lamb—Jesus Christ—who once offered mercy, now stands as Judge. The same Lamb who died to save mankind now witnesses the eternal fate of those who rejected His offer.

This verse demolishes the false gospel of universalism. It reminds us that rejecting God has consequences—eternal ones. The cup of wrath will be poured, and those who take the mark of the beast will drink it. This is not a scare tactic; it's a divine warning motivated by truth and love. It is far better to drink the cup of salvation today (Psalm 116:13), than the cup of wrath tomorrow.

OLD TESTAMENT FORESHADOWS REVELATION:

For in the hand of the LORD there is a cup, and the wine is red; it is full of mixture; and He pours out of the same: but the dregs thereof, all the wicked of the earth shall wring them out, and drink them. (Psalm 75:8)

Both passages speak of God's cup of wrath being poured out upon the wicked. Psalm 75:8 uses poetic imagery of a cup of judgment, red with wine, and warns that even the dregs—the most bitter and concentrated part—will be consumed by the unrepentant. Revelation 14:10 intensifies this with the phrase "without mixture," meaning full-strength fury. The progression from the Old Testament concept of a mixed cup to Revelation's undiluted wrath shows that the time for mercy has ended and judgment is now final.

THE REVELATION OF JESUS CHRIST REVEALS:

14:11 And the smoke of their torment ascends up forever and ever: and they have no rest day or night, who worship the beast and his image, and whosoever receives the mark of his name.

This is one of the most sobering verses in all of Scripture. It pulls no punches. There's no soft language here—no metaphor to cushion the blow. The phrase "smoke of their torment" rising forever is not symbolic hyperbole. It is a divine declaration of the eternal consequence of aligning with evil, of selling one's soul for temporary gain and rejecting the God of mercy and truth.

The wording "forever and ever" (Greek: *eis aionas aionon*) appears twelve times in Revelation. Eight of those refer to the glory and reign of God and Christ. Three describe the eternal punishment of Satan and his forces (Revelation 20:10). And this one? It's the only reference applied to people—those who willfully worship the beast and take his mark. That tells us just how serious this decision is. There's no rest. No reprieve. No second chance.

This verse hammers down the reality that hell is eternal. Jesus Himself, in Matthew 13:41–42, described the end for the wicked as a furnace of fire where there will be wailing and gnashing of teeth. That wasn't allegory—it was warning.

Some today want to sanitize hell, to rebrand it as symbolic or temporary. But Revelation 14:11 makes it unmistakably literal: torment that never ends. God is not cruel—He is holy. And in His holy love, He honors free will. Those who reject His truth and embrace deception seal their fate. It's not that God sends them to hell against their will—it's that they refuse heaven, even when angels are crying out from the skies.

Note the timing too: this warning comes before the bowl judgments. It's one last divine plea before wrath is poured out "without mixture" (verse 10). There's no grace blended in. The cup is full-strength judgment.

We may not like the idea of torment—but God's justice is as real as His mercy. And the time to settle this is now, not then. Because "then" is too late. Judgment will be final. The stakes are eternal.

OLD TESTAMENT FORESHADOWS REVELATION:

And the streams thereof shall be turned into pitch, and the dust thereof into brimstone, and the land thereof shall become burning pitch. It shall not be quenched night nor day; the smoke thereof shall go up forever: from generation to generation it shall lie waste; none shall pass through it forever and ever. (Isaiah 34:9–10)

This passage from Isaiah describes the judgment of Edom (modern-day southern Jordan)—a symbol of God's enemies—and serves as a prophetic foreshadowing of eternal punishment. Just like Revelation 14:11, it speaks of unceasing fire, rising smoke, and no rest—language that emphasizes the permanence and severity of divine judgment. Both verses emphasize smoke rising forever, a visual of ongoing torment; mention no relief, day or night; and reveal God's final and irreversible judgment on the wicked. This parallel strengthens the case that Revelation 14:11 is not symbolic, but deeply rooted in the biblical tradition of literal, everlasting judgment for those who rebel against God.

"Ann, I've been thinking a lot about what we covered in Revelation 14. The torment, the eternal fire . . . It's hard for people to accept that heaven and hell are real—*literal* places. It sounds too mythic, too abstract. I mean, where even *is* hell? Where *is* heaven?"

"I get it, Irene. Most people treat them like metaphors—just poetic symbols for good or evil, reward or regret. But the Bible never teaches them as allegories. They are real locations created by a real God who exists *outside* of time, space, and matter."

"Outside time, space, and matter? Like another dimension?"

I nodded. "Exactly. Think about Genesis 1:1—'In the beginning, God created the heavens and the earth.' That one verse captures time, space, and matter all in one breath. Time had a beginning. Space and matter came into being alongside it. But *God* wasn't born out of those elements. He spoke them into existence. So He had to exist *outside* of them."

Irene sighed. "So God operates in a higher realm—outside our universe. But that means heaven and hell would also exist in realms we can't reach with telescopes or rockets."

"Right. And yet, they are just as real—if not more real—than what we can touch. Just because something is unseen doesn't mean it's unreal. Remember, we live on a six-kilometer crust of Earth. Below that? It's literal fire and molten fury. Scientist estimate the inner core burns at over 6,000°C. You can't tell me that's coincidental."

"Wait—so are you saying hell could actually be *beneath* us?"

I nodded. "In part, yes. The Bible speaks of Hades, Tartarus, and the Abyss—all places that describe the underworld. And modern geology reveals layers that eerily mirror those biblical descriptions: the inner core (Abyss), outer core (Tartarus), inner mantle (Hades), and outer mantle (Paradise). Even paradise, which used to be in the underworld, before Christ emptied it."

"You mean the 'bosom of Abraham'—where the righteous dead went before Jesus came?"

"Exactly. Jesus said in Luke 16 that there was a great gulf fixed between paradise and the place of torment. And after the resurrection, Paul tells us Jesus 'led captivity captive'—He emptied paradise and took those saints with Him to heaven."

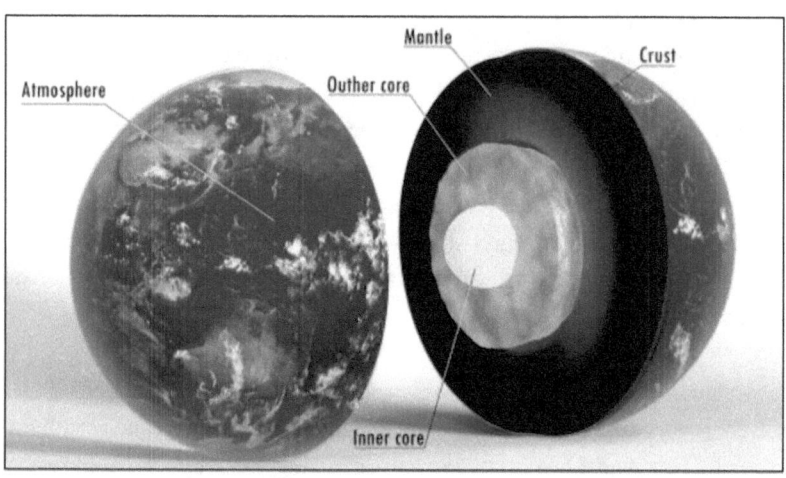

THE BOOK OF REVELATION

Layers of the Earth: A Visual Cross-Section

A stylized, cross-section of the Earth, depicting its internal structure—from the outer atmosphere to the crust, mantle, outer core, and inner core. This minimalist illustration captures the complexity of Earth's design, offering a timeless and universal representation of geologic order.

"So where is paradise now?"

"In the third heaven. Beyond this universe. Beyond the galaxies. Beyond even the 'observable universe' which scientists say spans 93 billion light years across. Heaven isn't on some cloud floating in space—it's in another dimension altogether, the throne room of God."

Irene in awe. "That gives me chills. And hell?"

"It's still below. But worse, it's not the end. Revelation tells us the final destination for the wicked is the Lake of Fire—what Scripture calls the *second death*. Right now, Hades is the *temporary holding cell*. The Lake of Fire is the *eternal prison*."

"I always thought the Lake of Fire in Revelation might be the *sun*. I mean, it's a burning place of judgment, right? But then in Revelation 21 and 22, it says there's no more sun. That confuses me."

I smiled kindly.

"That's a really good question, Irene. And you're not the only one who's thought that. Let's walk through it together. The Lake of Fire isn't the *sun*—it's actually something far more serious and eternal."

"Really? Then what exactly *is* it?"

"The Lake of Fire is mentioned clearly in Revelation 20. It's called the *second death*—the final destination after judgment. Not even hell escapes it. In fact, *hell itself* is thrown into it, along with death. 'And death and hell were cast into the Lake of Fire. This is the second death' (Revelation 20:14). So it's not just a physical location. It's a supernatural realm of eternal judgment."

"So it's not part of our universe?"

"Right. It's not like a planet or a star. It's something outside the natural order—a place God created for final judgment. Remember, *God lives outside of time, space, and matter*. He's not limited to what we can see."

"Okay, Ann, that helps. But what about the part in Revelation 21:23 that says there's no more sun?"

"Great observation, Irene. That verse says the New Jerusalem doesn't need the sun or moon to shine because the Lamb—Jesus—is the light. 'And the city had no need of the sun, neither of the moon . . . for the glory of God did lighten it' (Revelation 21:23). That doesn't necessarily mean the sun is destroyed—it just won't be needed anymore."

"So the sun could disappear . . . but it's irrelevant at that point?"

"Exactly. After the Great White Throne Judgment, the entire heaven and earth flee away (Revelation 20:11). God creates a new heaven and a new earth—and the old order passes away. That means no more oceans, no more night, and no more sun as we know it."

Irene sighed.

"Wow. That makes sense. So the Lake of Fire is still a real place—but it's not the sun. It's eternal. And Jesus becomes the light of everything."

"You nailed it. The Lake of Fire is the final, irreversible judgment. But for those who trust in Christ, there's no fear—only light, life, and eternity with Him."

"So both realms—heaven and hell—are waiting."

"Yes. Heaven for the redeemed. Hell for the rebellious. And the stakes couldn't be higher."

Irene sighed.

"It's sobering. We think this world is all there is, walking on this thin layer of crust, breathing in air as if it's permanent. But beneath us, there's fire. Above us, eternity. And we're caught in the middle."

"Caught . . . but not abandoned. God has given us His Word, His Son, and His Spirit. And the Bible gives startling accurate insights into realms we've never seen. That alone should convince us—heaven and hell aren't abstract concepts. They are divine destinations. The only question is . . . where are we headed?"

———— ◆◆◆ ————

THE REVELATION OF JESUS CHRIST REVEALS:

14:12 Here is the patience of the saints: here are they that keep the commandments of God, and the faith of Jesus.

This verse is a pause in the unfolding judgment—a spotlight on faithful warriors who endure without compromise.

"Here is the patience of the saints." The word "patience" here is better translated as perseverance or endurance. It's not passive waiting—it's active, courageous, and often costly faithfulness in the face of persecution, deception, and death. The saints are those who refuse to worship the beast, reject the mark, and stand firm in truth, even when it means martyrdom. This verse affirms that God sees their struggle and honors their resolve.

"They that keep the commandments of God." These are not lawless rebels. In the midst of a lawless age, they cling to God's Word. This isn't about legalism—it's about loyalty. They obey not out of fear, but out of love for the One true King.

"And the faith of Jesus." They are not just keeping religious traditions; they are anchored in faith in Christ. This phrase speaks of a deep, relational trust—a refusal to deny Him, no matter the cost. Their faith is not in governments, survival plans, or human strength—but in Jesus, the Lamb who reigns.

This verse stands in stark contrast to the previous verses, which describe the eternal torment of those who worship the beast. The patience of the saints is the counterpoint to the mark of the beast. While the world rushes to conform and survive, the saints resist to the end.

This isn't just about Tribulation saints—it's a timeless truth. In every generation, God's people are called to endure, to obey, and to keep the faith. Especially now, as global systems shift and deception increases, the patience of the saints is being tested. This verse reminds us: Hold the line. Stay faithful. Heaven sees you.

OLD TESTAMENT FORESHADOWS REVELATION:

Behold, his soul which is lifted up is not upright in him: but the just shall live by his faith. (Habakkuk 2:4)

Revelation 14:12 highlights the patience (endurance) of the saints, those who keep God's commandments and hold to the faith of Jesus. Habakkuk 2:4 introduces the enduring principle of living by faith, especially in the face of injustice, delay, and judgment.

This parallel draws attention to the fact that: From the Old Testament prophets to the end times saints, the mark of true righteousness is unwavering faith and obedience, even when evil seems to prevail. In both contexts, faithfulness becomes a form of spiritual resistance—anchoring the believer during times of great testing and turmoil. It's a timeless call to trust God's promises— even when His justice seems delayed.

Irene leaned back in her chair, Bible resting on her lap. "Ann, I've been thinking about something. A lot of people say the Ten Commandments don't really apply anymore. That in the New Testament, Jesus gave just two commandments: Love God and love your neighbor as yourself. So . . . are the Ten Commandments still something we're supposed to follow?"

I smiled gently. "That's a great question, Irene. And it's one that trips a lot of people up. But the truth is—yes, the Ten Commandments are still very much in effect. God doesn't change. His character is consistent from Genesis to Revelation."

Irene raised an eyebrow. "But didn't Jesus simplify it down to just two?"

I nodded. "He did. But He wasn't replacing the Ten Commandments—He was summarizing them."

I opened my Bible to Romans 13:8–10 and read aloud:

> Owe no man anything, but to love one another: for he that loves another has fulfilled the law. For this, You shalt not commit adultery, You shalt not kill, You shalt not steal, You shalt not bear false witness, You shalt not covet; and if there be any other commandment, it is briefly comprehended in this saying, namely, You shalt love your neighbor as yourself. Love works no ill to his neighbor: therefore love is the fulfilling of the law. (Romans 13:8–10)

I continued, "See that? Paul is explaining how love fulfills the law—because if you truly love someone, you won't lie to them, cheat them, or harm them. Love doesn't abolish the commandments—it lives them out."

Irene tilted her head. "So love is the foundation—but the commandments are still the structure?"

I nodded. "Exactly. The first four commandments teach us how to love God—don't worship idols, don't take His name in vain, keep the Sabbath. The last six teach us how to love people—honor your parents, don't steal, don't kill, don't lie."

Irene flipped back to Exodus. "Wow. So Jesus wasn't canceling the Ten Commandments—he was clarifying them."

I smiled. "That's right. God's moral law hasn't changed. Jesus even said in Matthew 5:17, 'I did not come to abolish the Law or the Prophets, but to fulfill them.' Love isn't a replacement—it's the perfect expression of God's law."

Irene nodded slowly, a new clarity forming in her eyes. "So loving God and loving people isn't about ignoring the Ten Commandments—it's about living them with purpose."

I whispered, "Exactly. Because when your heart is filled with love for the Lord, obedience becomes joy—not duty."

Irene glanced up from her Bible, a crease between her brows.

"Ann, I am reading Revelation 14:12 and it says, 'Here is the patience of the saints; here are they that keep the commandments of God, and the faith of Jesus.' That verse almost sounds like salvation is twofold. Not just believing in Jesus, but also keeping God's commandments?"

I smiled.

"You're catching something really important, Irene. That verse is often overlooked, but it shows that true, biblical faith isn't passive. It's a living, obedient faith. Revelation 14:12 isn't redefining salvation—it's revealing what it looks like when someone is truly part of God's Kingdom."

Irene nodded slowly.

"So it's more than just praying a prayer or saying we believe?"

I reached for my Bible.

"Exactly. James 2:19 says, 'Even the demons believe—and tremble!' And a few verses later, James writes, 'Faith without works is dead' (James 2:26). Faith in Jesus is essential—but if it doesn't produce fruit, something's missing."

Irene leaned in.

"So it's not just the Gospel of Salvation—it's the Gospel of the Kingdom?"

I beamed. "Yes! That's the shift we need to understand. The Gospel of Salvation is the doorway. But the Gospel of the Kingdom is the life we live after stepping through it. It's about surrender. Jesus didn't just say 'Believe in Me.' He said, 'Follow Me.'"

Irene tilted her head.

"So . . . entering the Kingdom means more than just believing?"

I nodded. "Yes. It's belief plus surrender. You believe in Jesus to be saved. But you enter the Kingdom by submitting to His rule. Revelation 14:12 shows us the saints—those who endure to the end—are both faithful to Jesus and obedient to God's commandments."

Irene blinked.

"So the commandments still matter?"

I gently said, "They do. Not as a means of earning salvation, but as evidence that you truly know the King. Jesus said, 'If you love Me, keep My commandments' (John 14:15). It's not either/or. It's both—and."

Irene looked down at her Bible, thoughtful. "So when Revelation says those saints keep the commandments *and* the faith of Jesus . . . it's describing a Kingdom people. Saved, surrendered, and standing firm."

I smiled. "Exactly. That's the Gospel of the Kingdom. It transforms people—and through them, entire nations and cultures. It's not just about being saved from something. It's about being saved for something—inheriting the Kingdom of God."

Irene sat back, wide-eyed. "So you're saying salvation isn't just about what we believe—but also how we live?"

I nodded thoughtfully. "Exactly. Jesus never said, 'Pray a prayer and live how you want.' He said, 'Deny yourself, take up your cross, and follow Me.' That's why He taught in parables—especially the ones about the hundredfold, sixtyfold, and thirtyfold harvests."

Irene tilted her head. "I always thought those were just about spiritual fruit. Like gifts or evangelism."

I smiled gently. "That's part of it. But it also points to levels of surrender. The hundredfold believer isn't just someone who believes in Jesus. They obey. They follow. They've passed through the refiner's fire. They've allowed Christ to strip away self and sin—and become His Bride."

Irene leaned forward. "Wait . . . so what about the sixtyfold and thirtyfold? They're still believers, right?"

I sighed. "They believe, yes. But belief alone isn't the full picture. The sixtyfold and thirtyfold may still be living for themselves—carnal, distracted, not bearing much fruit. Jesus is their Savior, but not their Lord. They haven't yet been refined. And here's the hard part, Irene: those not walking in obedience may be left behind after the Rapture."

Irene gasped. "You mean . . . like in the parable of the ten virgins?"

I nodded. "Exactly. Five were wise and ready. Five were foolish and unprepared. It's Russian Roulette with eternity. No one knows the day or the hour. You could get hit by a bus tomorrow. And if you're still walking in disobedience—still serving your flesh—you won't inherit the Kingdom."

Irene sat still, processing. "So believing in Jesus isn't the finish line—it's the starting point."

I smiled, "Well said. The finish line is becoming less like ourselves and more like Him. As John the Baptist said, 'He must increase, but I must decrease' (John 3:30). We're not just saved to escape hell—we're saved to become holy."

Irene looked down, solemn. "So if someone claims to love Jesus but doesn't follow His commandments . . ."

I gently finished her thought, "Then they're not living in the truth. Jesus said, 'If you love Me, keep My commandments.' Not suggestions. Commandments. And Revelation 14:12 links obedience and faith together for a reason. Again, it's not either/or—it's both."

Irene whispered, "It's a wake-up call."

I nodded. "It is. God's mercy is real—but so is His holiness. And the time to surrender is now. Not later. Not someday. Now."

THE REVELATION OF JESUS CHRIST REVEALS:

14:13 And I heard a voice from heaven saying to me (John), Write, Blessed are the dead which die in the Lord from henceforth: Yes, says the Spirit, that they may rest from their labors; and their works do follow them.

Voice from Heaven—This verse is a divine interruption—a voice from heaven breaking through the unfolding judgments to proclaim something astonishing: a blessing for the faithful dead. The timing is significant. We're in the Tribulation—the beast is rising, the mark is being enforced, and worship is demanded. Yet heaven declares, "Blessed are the dead who die in the Lord from henceforth."

"From henceforth"—Why this phrase? It marks a turning point. The first half of the Tribulation has passed. The Rapture is already behind us. The 144,000 Jewish evangelists have completed their mission. The Two Witnesses have been taken up to heaven. And now, anyone who chooses to follow Christ must do so at extreme personal cost—potentially martyrdom. Yet the Word from heaven is clear: there is a blessing even in death for those who remain faithful.

Who are "the dead which die in the Lord"? These are the Tribulation saints—those who refused to take the mark of the beast, who resisted the Antichrist's system, and who held on to faith even under the threat of death. Some were martyred; others may have died natural deaths. But all of them refused compromise. They are blessed, not because of how they died, but because of Whom they died for.

"That they may rest from their labors." The word "labors" here doesn't mean ordinary work—it speaks of exhausting toil, hardship, and suffering. These saints endured persecution, fear, hunger, and constant threats. Death becomes a relief—not in defeat, but in victory, for they are now at rest with Christ. Their war is over. Their burden is lifted.

"And their works do follow them." This is one of the most beautiful phrases in the Book of Revelation. Nothing done for Christ is ever forgotten. These believers may have died unknown on earth, uncelebrated by men—but heaven has recorded every act of faith, every refusal to bow, every stand for truth. Their works follow them, not to earn salvation—but to testify of it. Their lives become a trail of testimony, a fragrance of loyalty that echoes through eternity.

In a world drowning in fear, deception, and compromise, Revelation 14:13 reminds us that faithfulness to Jesus is always worth it—even unto death. This is heaven's perspective on martyrdom: not tragic loss, but eternal reward. And for those of us still living, it's a call to courage. The world may not see your sacrifice, but heaven does.

OLD TESTAMENT FORESHADOWS REVELATION:

The righteous perishes, and no man lays it to heart: and merciful men are taken away, none considering that the righteous is taken away from the evil to come. He shall enter into peace: they shall rest in their beds, each one walking in his uprightness. (Isaiah 57:1–2)

Just like Revelation 14:13 promises rest and reward to those who die in the Lord during the Tribulation, Isaiah 57:1–2 reveals that the righteous are often taken early—not as a curse, but as a divine act of mercy, removing them from greater evil to come. Both verses emphasize: Divine perspective on death—not loss, but relief and peace. Rest for the faithful—a cessation of labor and suffering. An eternal reward—"their works follow them" in Revelation, and "walking in uprightness" in Isaiah.

THE REVELATION OF JESUS CHRIST REVEALS:

14:14 And I looked, and behold a white cloud, and upon the cloud One sat like to the Son of Man, having on His head a golden crown, and in His hand a sharp sickle.

This verse unveils a striking vision of divine intervention—a heavenly harvest of the redeemed. John sees "a white cloud," symbolizing purity and divine presence. Seated on it is "One like the Son of Man"—a clear reference to Jesus, echoing Daniel 7:13 and His words in the Gospels. The title affirms Christ as both Judge and Kinsman-Redeemer.

The "golden crown" on His head signifies victory and kingship, not suffering or humiliation as in His First Coming. This is the exalted, reigning Christ—crowned and ready to act in sovereign power.

But in His hand is something deeply symbolic: a sharp sickle. This agricultural instrument was used to reap grain at harvest time. In Scripture, the sickle represents judgment and separation—the gathering of wheat (God's people) or the cutting down of tares (the wicked). Here, Jesus holds it not by accident, but with intent: He is about to reap the faithful who refused the mark of the beast, those who endured the Tribulation with unshakable faith.

This moment is sobering and hopeful all at once. The presence of the cloud and the crown reassure us—this harvest is not chaotic; it is royal, righteous, and deliberate. It is the fulfillment of divine justice and divine mercy, executed by the Lord Himself.

He doesn't delegate this task. He comes personally to oversee the gathering of His own. This is a hidden harvest—the believers who came to faith in the darkest days—the Tribulation—and now, at great cost, are being gathered home. This is the King reaping His remnant. Not one stalk of wheat will be overlooked. Not one tear-streaked saint will be left behind. The Lord of the harvest has arrived.

OLD TESTAMENT FORESHADOWS REVELATION:

Put you in the sickle, for the harvest is ripe: come, get you down; for the press is full, the vats overflow; for their wickedness is great. (Joel 3:13)

This verse mirrors the imagery of harvest and judgment in Revelation 14:14. Both passages speak of a divine harvest, not merely of crops but of people—either for salvation or judgment. The sickle in both Joel and Revelation is symbolic of final separation, a reaping of the righteous from the wicked, showing that God Himself is the Lord of the harvest. While Daniel 7 emphasizes the authority of the Son of Man, Joel 3 focuses on the urgency and severity of the harvest—a fitting echo of Revelation 14:14's sobering moment.

THE REVELATION OF JESUS CHRIST REVEALS:

14:15 And another angel came out of the temple, crying with a loud voice to Him that sat on the cloud, Thrust in Your sickle, and reap: for the time is come for You to reap; for the harvest of the earth is ripe.

The Fourth Angel—Grain Harvest (Heaven). This verse reveals a critical moment: the divine command to reap the earth. The angel emerges from the heavenly temple—the very presence of God—bearing a direct mandate from heaven. His voice is loud and authoritative because the time has arrived for a climactic act of judgment and redemption. This harvest isn't symbolic of routine ministry; this is the final reaping of the righteous—the "wheat"—those who, even in the darkest days of the Tribulation, have remained faithful to God and refused allegiance to the beast.

The one seated on the cloud, who receives this command, is none other than Christ Himself—described as "like the Son of Man" in the previous verse. He wears a golden crown, signaling royal authority, and holds a sharp sickle—an instrument of judgment and separation. The imagery here aligns with Jesus' own parables in Matthew 13, where He spoke of a time when angels would come and separate the wheat from the tares. That time is now.

The phrase "the harvest of the earth is ripe" in the Greek implies that the grain is fully matured—ready and even overripe. The window of grace is closing. This isn't the general call of evangelism. This is finality. This is divine intervention. The sowing is complete, the age is ending, and it's time for heaven to separate those who are His.

This harvest is different from the one that follows in verses 17–20 (the grape harvest, a picture of wrath). This is the gathering of the redeemed—those who've endured to the end, some of whom may have come to faith through the angelic proclamation (Revelation 14:6–7), others perhaps through the testimony of martyrs. Regardless of how they arrived, they represent the faithful of the entire Tribulation period—harvested by the Son of Man before the final outpouring of wrath begins.

The angel's timing is perfect because heaven's clock is precise. God's judgments do not fall early or late. They fall at the appointed time.

OLD TESTAMENT FORESHADOWS REVELATION:

> And it shall come to pass in that day, that the LORD shall beat off from the channel of the river unto the stream of Egypt, and you shall be gathered one by one, O you children of Israel. (Isaiah 27:12)

While more symbolic than Joel 3:13, this verse in Isaiah speaks of a divine harvest—a gathering by God Himself, one by one, of His people. The image is pastoral but prophetic, pointing to a future ingathering where God separates and redeems His chosen ones. Revelation 14:15 shows the Son of Man with a sickle, responding to an angelic call to begin the harvest of the earth. Isaiah 27:12 presents God personally gathering His people in the final days—a careful, deliberate harvest that mirrors the heavenly reaping.

THE REVELATION OF JESUS CHRIST REVEALS:

14:16 And He that sat on the cloud thrust in His sickle on the earth; and the earth was reaped.

This is the wheat harvest, the gathering of those who, even in the darkest era of human history, refused to bow to the beast or take his mark. These are believers who came to Christ after the Rapture, during the Tribulation, and paid dearly for their faith—many with their lives. Christ, personally, reaps this harvest. He doesn't delegate it. Why? Because He is the Shepherd of their souls, the One who died for them. Their loyalty to Him in a time of global apostasy is rewarded with His own hand ensuring not one is forgotten.

This act is intentional and full of compassion. It reminds us of John 10:14 where Jesus says, "I am the Good Shepherd, and know My sheep." In contrast to the later harvest of wrath—overseen by angels—this reaping is deeply personal. It reflects God's faithfulness to the faithful.

The word "reaped" signals finality. The righteous are gathered, sealed, and taken—perhaps martyred, but no longer vulnerable to the beast's cruelty. This reaping echoes the parable of the wheat and tares (Matthew 13:30), where Jesus said, "Let both grow together until the harvest." Now that time has come.

Even in the Tribulation, grace is at work, and Jesus is still Savior. His hand extends to those who turned to Him under persecution. This verse reveals that heaven does not forget its own, even when the world is at its darkest.

OLD TESTAMENT FORESHADOWS REVELATION:

For thus says the LORD of hosts, the God of Israel; the daughter of Babylon is like a threshing floor, it is time to thresh her: yet a little while, and the time of her harvest shall come. (Jeremiah 51:33)

This verse in Jeremiah 51:33 echoes Revelation 14:16—both use harvest as a metaphor for judgment. Just as Jeremiah foresaw Babylon's fall, Revelation shows the Son of Man reaping a ripe, rebellious earth. Together, they affirm God's perfect timing in both salvation and judgment.

THE REVELATION OF JESUS CHRIST REVEALS:

14:17 And another angel came out of the temple, which is in heaven, he also having a sharp sickle.

The Fifth Angel—Grape Harvest (Hell). This verse introduces a second harvester—another angel, emerging not from earth, but from the temple of heaven. The temple is the place of God's holy presence, so this angel comes with divine authorization. He does not act on his own but is commissioned by heaven to carry out judgment. The fact that this angel also carries a sharp sickle shows that he, like the Son of Man earlier (Revelation 14:14), has come to harvest—but this one is different.

Whereas Jesus reaped the first harvest—the righteous, the wheat—this second sickle is symbolic of the harvest of wrath. The next few verses (versus 18–20) confirm that this harvest is not about salvation but judgment. This angel does not reap the faithful; he gathers the grapes of the earth to be thrown into the great winepress of the wrath of God.

In agricultural terms, a grape harvest involves crushing. Spiritually, this signals an intense and crushing judgment about to be poured out on the unrepentant. That the angel comes out of the heavenly temple also affirms that this judgment is not arbitrary—it is sacred, sanctioned, and just.

This moment marks a turning point. The age of grace has come to its end. The Rapture has occurred. The Tribulation saints have been martyred or sealed. Now comes the grim reckoning for the rebellious—those who have taken the mark, worshiped the beast, and refused God's final call through angelic messengers.

This angel's sickle isn't just a harvesting tool; it is a symbol of the final severing—of separation, of justice, and of reckoning.

OLD TESTAMENT FORESHADOWS REVELATION:

For He comes, for He comes to judge the earth: He shall judge the world with righteousness, and the people with His truth. (Psalm 96:13)

This psalm looks forward to the coming of the Lord to Judge the earth, echoing the action initiated in Revelation 14:17, where the angel with the sharp sickle comes out from the heavenly temple—signaling divine judgment is about to be carried out. While Psalm 96:13 doesn't mention a sickle or harvest directly, it captures the righteous judgment upon the earth, the central theme of the final harvest scenes in Revelation 14. The psalm emphasizes that this judgment will be done in truth and righteousness, just as Revelation shows that God's wrath is precise, just, and holy.

THE REVELATION OF JESUS CHRIST REVEALS:

14:18 And another angel came out from the altar, which had power over fire; and cried with a loud cry to him that had the sharp sickle, saying, Thrust in your sharp sickle, and gather the clusters of the vine of the earth; for her grapes are fully ripe.

The Sixth Angel—Grape Harvest (Hell). This verse marks a powerful and sobering moment in the prophetic narrative of Revelation—a moment when heaven begins to answer the cries of the martyred and executes the long-awaited judgment of God upon a rebellious earth.

This angel does not come from the throne or the sky but from the altar—a direct reference to Revelation 6:9–11, where the souls of martyrs cry out for justice beneath the altar. The altar represents the place of sacrifice, prayer, and intercession. The fact that the angel emerges from it underscores that this moment of judgment is heaven's direct response to the blood of the saints and the injustice done to them.

Heaven remembers. Earth may forget, but heaven doesn't. Every cry, every injustice, every act of violence against God's people has reached the ears of the

Lord. Now, at the appointed time, divine vengeance begins to be poured out—not in chaos, but in perfect justice and timing.

"Power over fire"—the fire of judgment. This angel is given power over fire, symbolizing purification, judgment, and wrath. Fire in Scripture often signals God's holy response to sin—consuming everything that is impure or offensive in His sight. Just as fire consumed sacrifices on the altar in the Old Testament, now the fire of divine judgment will consume the wicked. This is not the fire of discipline. It is the fire of final judgment. This is not redemptive fire—it is retributive fire.

"Gather the clusters of the vine of the earth; for her grapes are fully ripe." The angel's command to gather the "clusters of the vine of the earth" is vivid. In contrast to the earlier harvest of the righteous (verses 14–16), this is a harvest of the wicked. The imagery of fully ripened grapes suggests that sin has reached its climax—there is no more room for repentance. The cup of iniquity is full. God does not act prematurely. He waits. He warns. But when the grapes of rebellion reach their fullness, He acts. And when He acts, He does so decisively.

"The grapes of wrath"—echoes of Joel and Isaiah. This grape harvest is no ordinary vintage—it is the "grapes of wrath." It points directly to Joel 3:3 and Isaiah 63:1–6, where God tramples the nations in His fury. This is a graphic, horrifying image, and it is meant to be. God's judgment on a rebellious world is not sanitized—it is blood-soaked and final. The contrast is striking: Jesus shed His blood to save, but these grapes are crushed in judgment because the wicked refused that blood. Now, they will shed their own.

This moment is a terrifying turning point. It shows that God's mercy, though abundant, has a limit. A day is coming when sin will reach its peak, and the world will face the winepress of the wrath of God. The harvest imagery is not just poetic—it is prophetic and literal. The angel from the altar signals that the cries of the righteous are not forgotten, and the time for God's vengeance—His holy, justified wrath—has arrived.

Let every reader take this seriously: what you choose today determines your harvest tomorrow. The wheat is gathered to safety; the grapes are cast into wrath. There is no neutral ground.

OLD TESTAMENT FORESHADOWS REVELATION:

Wherefore are You red in Your apparel, and Your garments like him that treads in the winepress? I have trodden the winepress alone; and of the people there was none with Me: for I will tread them in My anger, and trample them in My fury; and their blood shall be sprinkled upon My garments, and I will stain all My robes. For the day of vengeance is in My heart, and the year of My redeemed is come. (Isaiah 63:2–4)

When the angel in Revelation 14:18 cries out to thrust in the sharp sickle and gather the fully ripe grapes of the earth, it echoes the Messianic judgment scene in Isaiah 63:2–4. In both texts, the winepress is symbolic of God's wrath, and the staining of garments with blood highlights the severity of divine justice. The "day of vengeance" and "year of redemption" in Isaiah mirror the dual harvests of Revelation 14—one of the righteous (wheat) and one of the wicked (grapes).

THE REVELATION OF JESUS CHRIST REVEALS:

14:19 And the angel thrust in his sickle into the earth, and gathered the vine of the earth, and cast it into the great winepress of the wrath of God.

This verse describes the final execution of divine judgment upon the wicked of the earth. The angel, acting under God's authority, reaps the "vine of the earth"—a symbolic phrase representing the unredeemed, rebellious nations and peoples who have aligned themselves with the Antichrist and rejected the Gospel of Jesus Christ.

"The vine of the earth" contrasts with Jesus as the True Vine (John 15:1). Here, the vine is not rooted in heaven but in the world system that has become drunk with sin, pride, and idolatry. Its fruit—its "grapes"—are fully ripe, not for blessing but for wrath.

"The great winepress" is a powerful and terrifying metaphor for God's judgment. In ancient times, grapes were trampled underfoot in a winepress, their juice flowing out beneath the feet of the workers. Likewise, this image conveys the crushing and overflowing wrath of God poured out on the wicked during the final judgments of the Great Tribulation period.

Again, this winepress of divine fury echoes Isaiah 63:2–4, where the Messiah is seen trampling the winepress alone, and His garments are stained with the blood of the nations. It is a scene of holy vengeance, one not of cruelty, but of righteous retribution against those who have persecuted God's people, shed innocent blood, and worshiped the beast.

This moment in Revelation 14:19 stands as a prophetic prelude to the Battle of Armageddon, where God's wrath reaches its peak, and the wicked are crushed under His justice (Revelation 19:15–21).

OLD TESTAMENT FORESHADOWS REVELATION:

And it shall come to pass in that day, that the LORD shall punish the host of the high ones that are on high, and the kings of the earth upon the earth. And they shall be gathered together, as prisoners are gathered in the pit, and shall be shut up in the prison, and after many days shall they be visited. (Isaiah 24:21–22)

"Gathered together" mirrors "gathered the vine of the earth" in Revelation 14:19. Both passages refer to the final judgment of the wicked rulers and people of the earth. The wrath of God in Revelation is paralleled by the punishment from the LORD in Isaiah. The cosmic and judicial scope of Isaiah 24:21–22 aligns with the end-time harvest and wrath in Revelation 14.

THE REVELATION OF JESUS CHRIST REVEALS:

[14:20] And the winepress was trodden without the city, and blood came out of the winepress, even to the horse bridles, by the space of a thousand and six hundred furlongs.

The Seventh Angel—Execution of Hell's Harvest. (This angel is not named in this verse but executes or oversees the casting into the winepress of God's wrath.) This verse concludes the vision of the grape harvest of divine wrath, presenting one of the most graphic and sobering images of judgment in all of Scripture. The winepress, symbolizing God's wrath against unrepentant humanity, is now trodden "without the city"—a phrase with profound theological and prophetic implications.

"Without the city"—outside Jerusalem. The winepress is trodden outside the Holy City—a detail echoing the pattern of Jesus' own crucifixion, which occurred outside Jerusalem (Hebrews 13:12). It also aligns with prophetic geography, placing this judgment in the valley stretching from Megiddo to Bozrah—a distance of roughly 1,600 furlongs (about 180 miles). This exact region encompasses the Battle of Armageddon, the Valley of Jehoshaphat, and Bozrah in Edom (modern-day southern Jordan)—all sites mentioned in end-time war and judgment prophecies (Joel 3:2; Isaiah 63:1; Revelation 16:16).

"Blood came out of the winepress, even to the horse bridles"—a river of judgment. The text tells us blood flows up to the height of a horse's bridle—around four feet deep—for 180 miles. This is not hyperbole; it is a holy symbolism rooted in terrifying reality. While some interpret this literally, others see it symbolically reflecting the enormity of slaughter, the inescapable judgment, and the extent of divine retribution upon a Christ-rejecting world.

This is not mere poetic metaphor—it represents the culmination of rebellion, a world harvested in sin, finally meeting the wrath it has stored up for itself (Romans 2:5). Whether supernatural or literal, the magnitude of the carnage is meant to shock the conscience and drive home the seriousness of sin.

This is not a generic judgment—it is a judgment for apostasy. Jeremiah 30:7 calls it "the time of Jacob's trouble"—a period when Israel faces unprecedented peril for having turned away from the covenant of God, having rejected both the Old Testament prophecies and their fulfillment in Jesus the Messiah.

It is the just end for those who refuse the only remedy for sin: Jesus Christ. And we must not apologize for this truth. God is not cruel. He is just. And when mercy is rejected again and again, judgment is all that remains.

We often imagine mass death through the lens of modern warfare—nuclear weapons, missiles, and machine guns. But history proves otherwise. From bayonets to cannonballs, mankind has spilled rivers of blood without advanced technology. The Battle of Iwo Jima, the Civil War, and ancient conquests remind us: human depravity doesn't need nukes to destroy.

Though the threat of nuclear war—even the dreaded neutron bomb—looms large, it will not mark the end of humanity. Total extinction is not man's decision to make. Even if nuclear plants burn amid God's wrath, the final 3½ years must still unfold—because divine judgment and redemption remain on God's timeline. Man may trigger chaos, but God controls the conclusion. Amen!

Revelation 14 closes with this horrific imagery not as the final act—but as a prelude to the seven bowl judgments (Revelation 15–16), which intensify the outpouring of wrath upon the earth. If this is the prelude, how much more severe is what follows?

This verse serves as a dividing line: either one is under the blood of Christ, or under the blood of judgment. The time for choosing Christ is now. Because once the winepress is trodden—there is no turning back.

OLD TESTAMENT FORESHADOWS REVELATION:

The LORD has trodden under foot all my mighty men in the midst of me: He has called an assembly against me to crush my young men: the LORD has trodden the virgin, the daughter of Judah, as in a winepress. (Lamentations 1:15)

Lamentations 1:15 uses the winepress image to show God's judgment on Jerusalem for apostasy. Revelation 14:20 expands this from national to global scale—blood rising to the height of horse bridles over 180 miles. Both passages reveal the sobering reality of divine wrath: personal, bloody, and devastating for those who reject God's covenant and mercy.

Irene leaned in, eyes earnest. "Ann, we've gone over Revelation 14—the harvests, the sickles, the angels, and the judgments. But tell me, what's the real takeaway from the wheat and tares? What is Jesus really showing us with that metaphor?"

I met her gaze gently. "The lesson, Irene, is divine separation. A holy distinction. Everyone talks about discrimination—but this is the ultimate one. There's a day coming when God Himself will separate the righteous from the unrighteous. The wheat from the tares. The humble from the proud. And He'll use His angels to do it."

Irene's voice dropped. "So no one slips through?"

I shook my head. "No one." Jesus said:

> The enemy that sowed them is the devil; the harvest is the end of the world; and the reapers are the angels. (Matthew 13:39)

"They don't guess, Irene. They know who belongs to the Lamb and who doesn't. It's not chaos—it's precision. Every true believer will be gathered. And every counterfeit will be exposed and cast into fire."

Irene swallowed hard. "That's terrifying . . . but also comforting."

I nodded slowly. "It should be both. Here's what moved me most when I studied wheat and tares: When wheat ripens, it bows. Its head gets heavy with grain, and it leans low to the earth. But tares? When they ripen, they stay standing—erect, stiff, proud."

Irene's brow furrowed. "That's . . . symbolic."

"Exactly," I said. "Real Christians bow. As we mature, we bend lower. We worship deeper. We let go more. It's the fruit of surrender. But tares? They grow more self-reliant. More arrogant. Full of knowledge, titles, performance—but no yield. Still standing tall, even when they sing the songs."

Irene whispered, "So the sign of spiritual maturity isn't volume . . . it's humility."

"Yes," I said. "As we grow in Christ, we become less visible and more surrendered. Like wheat, we stop resisting. Our lives bow under the weight of the Spirit's fruit."

"And the tares?"

My tone sharpened. "They stay proud. They don't bow. They grip this world tighter. They're religious—but unchanged. And that's the difference."

Irene paused. "Wait—you said something once about wheat dying downward?"

I smiled softly. "Yes. As wheat ripens, its head bows, and its roots begin to wither. It loosens its grip on the earth. I call it 'the relaxing grasp.' The closer we get to heaven, the less we cling to this life. The old saints understood that. They talked about heaven constantly—not because they were morbid, but because their hearts were already there."

Irene's voice caught. "I saw that in my grandmother. In her last days, she spoke of Jesus more than anything. She was already leaning toward eternity."

"That's what wheat does," I said. "It yields. It ripens. It bows. The tares? They stand louder, angrier, more defiant. And right now—behind the scenes—the angels are gathering. The bundling has begun."

Irene's eyes welled. "Then I want to be wheat, Ann. Heavy with fruit. Bowed in worship. Loosening my hold on this world."

I reached over and gently took her hand. "Then keep growing. Keep bowing. Keep letting go. Because we are the harvest of the earth—and heaven is watching."

SUMMARY OF REVELATION 14

Revelation 14 is a prophetic chapter that stands in sharp contrast to the rising darkness of Revelation 13. While the previous chapter reveals the dragon (Satan), the two beasts—the Antichrist and the False Prophet—and the mark of rebellion, chapter 14 re-centers the vision on the Lamb, His faithful followers, and God's final messages of warning and judgment.

The chapter opens with John seeing the Lamb standing on Mount Zion with the 144,000 redeemed, who are sealed with the name of the Father on their foreheads (Revelation 14:1). These are those who have remained undefiled, who follow the Lamb wherever He goes, and who are described as "firstfruits unto God and to the Lamb" (Revelation 14:4).

John then witnesses three angels proclaiming urgent messages to the world. The *first angel* preaches the everlasting gospel to every nation, calling all to fear God and worship Him (Revelation 14:6–7). The *second angel* declares the fall of Babylon (America)—the corrupt world system that opposes God (Revelation 14:8). The *third angel* gives a grave warning: anyone who worships the beast or receives his mark will drink of the wine of God's wrath and suffer eternal torment (Revelation 14:9–11). This section affirms the endurance of the saints, who keep God's commandments and the faith of Jesus (Revelation 14:12–13).

The final section of Revelation 14 presents two dramatic and prophetic harvests—the harvest of heaven and the harvest of hell—symbolizing the final separation of the righteous and the wicked at the end of the age.

First, in Revelation 14:14–16, the Son of Man (Jesus Christ) appears, seated on a cloud, wearing a golden crown, and holding a sharp sickle. This is the grain harvest. And the *fourth angel* comes out of the temple and announces that the time has come, for the earth is ripe for reaping. In response to this divine signal, Christ swings His sickle and reaps the earth—a symbolic gathering of the righteous, often interpreted as the harvest of heaven.

Second, in verses 17–19, the *fifth angel* comes out of the temple in heaven also holding a sharp sickle. This begins the grape harvest, a symbol of God's wrath upon the wicked, often interpreted as the harvest of hell. Then, a *sixth angel* emerges from the altar—the same altar mentioned in Revelation 6:9–11, where the souls of the martyrs cried out for justice. This angel has power over fire, a sign of judgment, and commands the fifth angel to thrust in his sickle and gather the vine of the earth, for her grapes are fully ripe.

The *seventh* angel is not explicitly named, but is implied in verse 19, overseeing or executing the casting of the gathered grapes into the great winepress of the wrath of God. This winepress is trodden outside the city, and the result is catastrophic: blood flows as high as the horses' bridles, covering a distance of 1,600 furlongs—about 180 miles. This haunting image foreshadows the coming Battle of Armageddon, where judgment upon the rebellious world reaches its violent climax.

KEY TAKEAWAYS

- The Lamb and the 144,000—A vision of purity and loyalty in contrast to the beast marked followers of Revelation 13.
- Three angelic declarations—Final global warnings: worship God, Babylon (America) is fallen, judgment is coming for those who follow the beast.
- Eternal consequences—Those who reject Christ and take the mark face God's undiluted wrath.
- Two end-time harvests—One harvest gathers the righteous; the other gathers the wicked for judgment in the winepress of God's fury.
- The gathering of the tares—Foreshadows the Great and Terrible Day of the Lord, as angels begin the final separation and bundling.

Revelation 14 assures believers that God sees, seals, and stands with His own. It reminds the world that His patience will not last forever—judgment is not only coming, it has already been set in motion. This chapter is a call to repentance, endurance, and unwavering allegiance to the Lamb. As evil gathers for its final stand, the righteous are being bundled for the Kingdom. The harvest is near. The King is at the door.

Chapter 14

Revelation 15–16:
The Bowl Judgments
The Great Tribulation Age—
Daniel's 70th Week: Last 3½ Years

EARTH'S LAST DAYS UNLEASHED—As Revelation moves into chapters 15 and 16, the stage is set for the final and most intense wave of God's wrath: the seven bowl (or vial) judgments. These are not symbolic—they are the climactic outpouring of divine justice upon a rebellious, beast-worshiping world. They fall during the final half of Daniel's 70th Week—also called the Great Tribulation—a 3½-year period marked by unprecedented suffering, global deception, and divine retribution.

Revelation 15 serves as a heavenly prelude—a moment of solemn preparation. John sees seven angels holding the seven final plagues, called "last" because with them, God's wrath is completed (Revelation 15:1). Before him appears a sea of glass mingled with fire, beside which stand the victorious—those who refused the beast's mark—singing the song of Moses and the Lamb. Heaven readies itself for judgment, not with swords, but with bowls—each filled with righteous fury.

Then in Revelation 16, the bowls are poured out—swift, severe, and global. These judgments aren't symbolic; they are literal, physical, and catastrophic. The earth, sea, rivers, sun, throne of the beast, the Euphrates, and even the atmosphere—all come under divine assault. These plagues echo Egypt's, but far surpass them in scope and severity. They are heaven's direct response to the martyrs' cry beneath the altar (Revelation 6:10).

Unlike the seals and trumpets, these judgments come without restraint. No delay. No pause. No mercy. They are final. Irrevocable. And they prepare the stage for the earth's last rebellion—the Battle of Armageddon.

This is the end of man's defiance. The final grains of time are falling. The bowls are full . . . and now, they are poured.

THE REVELATION OF JESUS CHRIST REVEALS:

^{15:1} And I saw another sign in heaven, great and marvelous, seven angels having the seven last plagues; for in them is filled up the wrath of God.

Revelation 15:1 serves as a heavenly announcement, introducing the final and most intense series of judgments in the Book of Revelation—the seven bowl (or vial) judgments. This verse marks the transition from divine warning to the full and unrestrained execution of God's wrath.

"And I saw another sign in heaven, great and marvelous." The Greek word for "sign" here is *semeion*, which means a symbolic vision or miraculous sign pointing to a deeper spiritual truth. The word "another" (Greek: *allo semeion*) means another of the same kind—referring back to the signs in Revelation 12.

Revelation 15:1 is called "another sign" because it follows the first two heavenly signs mentioned in Revelation 12:1—the woman clothed with the sun (Israel)—and Revelation 12:3—the great red dragon (Satan). The Man Child (Christ) is a person in the Revelation 12 vision, not a separate *sign*. Now John witnesses a sign that is both great in scope and marvelous in nature—indicating that what is about to unfold is extraordinary, awe-inspiring, and terrifyingly final.

"Seven angels having the seven last plagues." These seven angels are God's appointed agents of judgment. Each holds one of the last plagues, indicating a completion—nothing more will follow. This is the end of divine restraint. These plagues are not symbolic; they are literal, devastating, and global in scope. They represent the culmination of God's response to sin, rebellion, and the unrepentant worship of the beast.

"For in them is filled up the wrath of God." The phrase "filled up" (Greek: *etelesthe*) means "completed" or "brought to an end." This is God's wrath in full strength, poured out without mixture (Revelation 14:10). The earlier seal and trumpet judgments were partial, with mercy still woven in. But now, with the bowls, there is no more delay, no more holding back. This is the end of God's longsuffering, and the beginning of His final, righteous vengeance.

This verse aligns with the final phase of Daniel's 70th Week—the last 3½ years of the Great Tribulation (Daniel 9:27; Matthew 24:15–21). It is the fulfillment of what the martyrs cried for in Revelation 6:10:

> And they cried with a loud voice, saying, How long, O Lord, holy and true, do you not judge and avenge our blood on them that dwell on the earth? (Revelation 6:10)

Now, the answer comes—wrath is filled, and judgment is released.

Revelation 15:1 reminds us that God's mercy has limits. He is patient and longsuffering, but not indifferent to sin. A day comes when the cup of iniquity is full—and the bowls of wrath must be poured out. This verse sets the tone for the final countdown to the Battle of Armageddon—a warning to the wicked, but a comfort to the righteous that justice will be done.

OLD TESTAMENT FORESHADOWS REVELATION:

> And if you walk contrary unto Me, and will not listen unto Me; I will bring seven times more plagues upon you according to your sins. (Leviticus 26:21)

Leviticus 26:21 warns, "I will bring seven times more plagues upon you according to your sins." This echoes in Revelation 15:1, where seven final plagues express God's complete wrath. In Leviticus, God disciplines Israel under the Old Covenant, escalating judgment in response to ongoing disobedience. Revelation, by contrast, applies this principle globally—judging a rebellious world.

Both passages highlight God's patience and offer space for repentance. But when sin reaches its fullness, judgment falls—not hastily, but righteously. God's mercy delays wrath, but His holiness demands it.

THE REVELATION OF JESUS CHRIST REVEALS:

> 15:2 And I saw as it were a sea of glass mingled with fire: and them that had gotten the victory over the beast, and over his image, and over his mark, and over the number of his name, stand on the sea of glass, having the harps of God.

This verse opens with one of the most awe-inspiring and mysterious images in Revelation—a sea of glass mingled with fire, standing before the throne of God in heaven. John had previously seen a similar sea in Revelation 4:6, described as "like unto crystal," representing purity, calm, and divine transcendence. But here in Revelation 15, the sea is "mingled with fire," indicating something new—judgment, purification, and the fiery trials of the saints who stand upon it.

"And I saw as it were a sea of glass mingled with fire." The fire mingled with the sea likely symbolizes the intense persecution and fiery tribulation these victorious saints have endured. These are the overcomers—the faithful remnant who did not worship the beast, refused his image, rejected his mark (666), and stood firm against the number of his name. They have come through great suffering, and the fire is a testament to what they have endured—and overcome.

This imagery resonates with 1 Peter 1:7, where believers are compared to gold that is refined by fire, and also with Isaiah 43:2, where God promises, "When you walk through the fire, you shalt not be burned."

"Stand on the sea of glass." Standing "on" the sea of glass conveys victory, stability, and peace, despite having passed through overwhelming trial. The sea is not turbulent, nor are the saints drowned in it—it is beneath their feet, a platform of triumph. They now stand, not fall; they worship, not weep. Their trials are behind them, and their reward is before them.

This is a scene of heavenly vindication—these saints stood against the world's greatest deception, and now they stand before the throne of God, harps in hand, ready to join in the eternal chorus of worship.

"Having the harps of God." The saints hold "harps of God," a powerful symbol of heavenly worship and celebration. Harps were also held by the twenty-four elders in Revelation 5:8. These instruments represent joy, music, praise, and restoration after suffering. Their song is not one of mourning—it is a song of victory.

These are the same faithful ones hinted at in Revelation 14—those who refused to bow to the beast or compromise their faith. Now, heaven acknowledges their perseverance with music and majesty.

Revelation 15:2 reminds us that the road to glory is often paved through fire. The overcomers are not those who escaped trouble, but those who stood faithful in the midst of it. The sea of glass mingled with fire teaches us that purity and suffering are often intertwined, and that true worship flows from tested faith.

In a world racing toward compromise and control, this verse assures us that God sees the faithful. The sea of glass is no longer still—it burns with fire. But those who endure, those who stand for Christ, will one day stand on that sea, harps in hand, and sing the song of the redeemed.

OLD TESTAMENT FORESHADOWS REVELATION:

He answered and said, Lo, I see four men loose, walking in the midst of the fire, and they have no hurt; and the form of the fourth is like the Son of God. (Daniel 3:25)

Just as the three Hebrew boys—Shadrach, Meshach, and Abednego—walked unharmed in the fiery furnace, so the saints in Revelation 15:2 stand victorious, having come through the fire of persecution and tribulation. In Daniel 3:25, the fourth man in the fire is a divine figure—"like the Son of God"—just as in Revelation, it is the Lamb who secures the victory for those who refuse the beast, his image, and his mark. The Hebrew men in Daniel refused to bow to Nebuchadnezzar's golden image; the saints in Revelation refuse to worship the beast or his image. Both accounts deal with defiance of idolatry under threat of death. In both cases, the faithful are delivered, vindicated, and ultimately honored for their steadfast allegiance to God.

THE REVELATION OF JESUS CHRIST REVEALS:

15:3 And they sing the song of Moses the servant of God, and the song of the Lamb, saying, Great and marvelous are Your works, LORD God Almighty; just and true are Your ways, You King of saints.

This verse reveals a powerful scene of victorious worship in heaven. The overcomers—those who refused the mark of the beast, resisted the Antichrist, and endured the fire of tribulation—are now seen standing on the sea of glass (Revelation 15:2), harps in hand, and songs in their mouths. Their triumph is not celebrated with shouts of self-glory but with a deep, reverent declaration of God's righteousness and majesty.

These worshipers are given "the harps of God" (Revelation 15:2), a phrase that reminds us of heaven's emphasis on musical worship. This is the third group in Revelation associated with harps:

1. **The twenty-four elders (Revelation 5:8)**—Representing the raptured Church.

2. **The 144,000 sealed servants (Revelation 14:2)**—Singing a new song no one else could learn.

3. **The Tribulation saints (Revelation 15:2)**—Those who endured fire and persecution and have come out victorious.

Harps signify joy, adoration, and victory. Heaven is not silent—it resounds with the song of the redeemed. And the music that fills the courts of glory is not about man, but about the Lamb.

"The song of Moses the servant of God, and the song of the Lamb." This verse is especially remarkable because it connects two great deliverances in Scripture:

- The Song of Moses—Exodus 15:1–21. Sung after Israel's miraculous deliverance through the Red Sea, when Pharaoh's armies were drowned. It is a song of triumph over enemies, a song of praise for God's power, wrath, and faithfulness.

- The Song of the Lamb—Revelation 5:9–12. Sung to the crucified and risen Christ, celebrating redemption by His blood, declaring Him worthy to open the scroll and fulfill God's final plan.

These overcomers in Revelation 15:3 sing both songs—because their experience reflects both deliverances. Like Moses and Israel, they've been brought through waters (the fire of tribulation). Like the saints in heaven, they've been redeemed by the Lamb. This dual song reflects the unity of the Testaments—the faithfulness of Yahweh (GOD the Father) in the Old Testament and the triumph of Jesus Christ (Yeshua; God the Son) in the New Testament.

"Great and marvelous are Your works, LORD God Almighty; just and true are Your ways, You King of saints." The lyrics of their song focus solely on God:

- "Great and marvelous are Your works"—a declaration of awe in response to God's acts of justice and power.
- "Just and true are Your ways"—heaven affirms that God's judgments are righteous, not cruel.
- "You King of saints"—He is sovereign over all people, all time, and all creation.

No mention is made of the saints' own endurance, strength, or achievements. Their victory song is Christocentric—focused completely on the glory, holiness, and justice of the LORD God Almighty.

Heaven's worship is deep, thoughtful, and centered on God. The overcomers don't celebrate their own survival—they celebrate the character of God who preserved and vindicated them. Their harps are not strummed to glorify man, but to exalt the Lamb. This reminds us that true victory worship is not self-congratulatory—it is filled with gratitude, humility, and reverence for God's greatness.

OLD TESTAMENT FORESHADOWS REVELATION:

Then sang Moses and the children of Israel this song unto the LORD, and spoke, saying, I will sing unto the LORD, for He has triumphed gloriously: the horse and his rider has He thrown into the sea. The LORD is my strength and song, and He is become my salvation: He is my God, and I will prepare Him a habitation; my father's God, and I will exalt Him. (Exodus 15:1–2)

Exodus 15:1–2 is the original "Song of Moses," sung after God miraculously delivered Israel by drowning Pharaoh's army in the Red Sea—just as Revelation 15:3 shows saints celebrating deliverance from the Antichrist and the Tribulation. Both songs focus not on the singers, but on God's mighty acts, His justice, and

His faithfulness. They both declare: "The Lord has triumphed!" and "Great and marvelous are Your works!"

Exodus 15:2 calls God "my strength and song," just as Revelation 15:3 calls Him "LORD God Almighty" whose ways are "just and true." Both songs exalt God's character, His judgments, and His rule over nations. The emphasis is not on man's endurance, but on God's glory.

THE REVELATION OF JESUS CHRIST REVEALS:

15:4 Who will not fear You, O Lord, and glorify Your name? For You only are holy: for all nations shall come and worship before You; for Your judgments are made manifest.

This verse is a crescendo of worship flowing from the victorious saints who overcame the beast and now stand before the throne of God. It's a declaration, a question, and a prophetic proclamation all in one—a call to fear, a revelation of holiness, and a vision of worldwide worship that is yet to come.

"Who will not fear you, O Lord, and glorify Your name?" This rhetorical question assumes its own answer: no one can rightfully deny God the reverence He is due. And yet, in our present age, we see a troubling decline in the fear of God—even among many professing believers. Reverential awe has been replaced by casual irreverence. The sacred is treated as common. The weight of God's holiness and judgment is rarely felt in a world numbed by pride, pleasure, and self-idolatry.

Psalm 33:8 reminds us:

Let all the earth fear the LORD: let all the inhabitants of the world stand in awe of Him. (Psalm 33:8)

But today, many mock what is holy and elevate what is evil. As Romans 3:18 declares:

There is no fear of God before their eyes. (Romans 3:18)

This verse in Revelation cuts through the noise and reminds us that God is still holy, and He will be feared.

"For You only are holy." This phrase is central: God alone is holy—not just in moral purity, but in absolute otherness, in majestic perfection, in righteous justice. His judgments are not merely deserved—they are the natural outflow of His holiness. This connects us back to the inner temple in Revelation 15:5–8, from which the angels and plagues emerge. God's judgment proceeds from the sanctuary—from the very heart of His holiness, not from anger or vengeance alone, but from righteousness.

Compare this to:

Oh let the wickedness of the wicked come to an end; but establish the just; for the righteous GOD tries the hearts and reins. (Psalm 7:9)

For the righteous LORD loves righteousness; His countenance does behold the upright. (Psalm 11:7)

"For all nations shall come and worship before You." This is prophetic and future tense—not yet fulfilled, but certain to come. Today, the nations rage (Psalm 2), but one day they will bow (Philippians 2:10–11). This global worship is a fulfillment of the Messianic inheritance promised in Psalm 2:8:

Ask of Me, and I shall give You the nations for Your inheritance, and the uttermost parts of the earth for Your possession. (Psalm 2:8)

It also echoes the prophetic hope in Zechariah 14:16 and Isaiah 66:23, where all nations will come to Jerusalem to worship the King during the millennial reign of Christ.

"For Your judgments are made manifest." In the context of Revelation, this is a direct reference to the bowl judgments about to be poured out. The world can no longer deny God's justice—it is visible, global, and unmistakable. What was once delayed is now manifest, or openly revealed.

This ties back to Revelation 11:18, at the seventh trumpet, where it was declared:

And the nations were angry, and Your wrath is come, and the time of the dead, that they should be judged, and that You should give reward unto Your servants the prophets, and to the saints, and them that fear Your name, small and great; and should destroy them which destroy the earth. (Revelation 11:18)

God's judgments aren't random acts—they are measured, holy responses to evil and injustice that have reached their appointed fullness.

Revelation 15:4 pulls back the veil and shows us the end of all things: God glorified, nations worshiping, and holiness revealed in justice. Though today we see rebellion, blasphemy, and moral decay, this verse assures us that the day is coming when every knee will bow, and the fear of the Lord will once again fill the earth.

Now is the time to return to reverence, to fear God not out of terror, but out of awe for His majesty, His mercy, and His holiness.

OLD TESTAMENT FORESHADOWS REVELATION:

All nations whom You have made shall come and worship before You, O LORD; and shall glorify Your name. For You are great, and do wondrous things: You are God alone. (Psalm 86:9–10)

Psalm 86:9–10 and Revelation 15:4 both declare a future moment when all nations will worship the one true God. In Psalm, David looks ahead prophetically, proclaiming that every nation God created will come and glorify His name, recognizing His greatness and uniqueness. Revelation 15:4 echoes this fulfillment, showing a heavenly scene where redeemed people from every nation worship God for His righteous acts.

Both passages highlight God's greatness, His exclusive divinity, and the global recognition of His glory. Psalm anticipates it; Revelation reveals its completion.

THE REVELATION OF JESUS CHRIST REVEALS:

[15:5] And after that I looked, and, behold, the temple of the tabernacle of the testimony in heaven was opened.

This verse opens a dramatic new scene in the Book of Revelation—the unveiling of the heavenly temple, referred to here as "the temple of the tabernacle of the testimony in heaven was opened." It signals a shift from heavenly worship to heavenly judgment, preparing the way for the seven angels to come forth with the bowl (vial) judgments.

John's vision confirms the existence of a literal temple in heaven—not symbolic or imagined, but a real sanctuary that exists in the heavenly realm. This heavenly temple is the original, the true tabernacle, of which the earthly tabernacle was only a shadow or pattern.

And look that you make them after their pattern, which was showed you in the mount. (Exodus 25:40)

Who serve unto the example and shadow of heavenly things, as Moses was admonished of God when he was about to make the tabernacle: for, See, says He, that you make all things according to the pattern showed to you in the mount. (Hebrews 8:5)

So when John says the temple in heaven was "opened," he is witnessing the true dwelling place of God—the center of divine justice, holiness, and glory.

"The tabernacle of the testimony." This title is significant. It echoes the Ark of the Covenant, which was housed in the Most Holy Place of the earthly tabernacle and was called the "Ark of the Testimony" because it held the Ten Commandments—the written testimony of God's covenant with Israel.

The phrase "tabernacle of the testimony" ties this vision directly to God's faithfulness to His covenant, His righteous laws, and His right to judge based on that testimony. It implies that judgment is not arbitrary—it is in accordance with God's revealed truth.

Unlike earlier visions (such as in Revelation 11:19, where the temple is opened and the ark is seen), this opening is not followed by worship—but by the emergence of the seven angels with the final plagues (Revelation 15:6). This is not a priestly moment—it is a judicial one. There is no mention of incense, mercy, or intercession here. This opening signals that the time for divine longsuffering has ended, and the time for full judgment has come.

It is worth noting that the temple is not mentioned in Revelation until after Revelation 4, which many believe represents the Rapture of the Church. From that point forward, the focus shifts to God's dealings with the nation of Israel and the tribulation world. Hebrews 9:23–24 makes the connection even clearer:

> It was therefore necessary that the patterns of things in the heavens should be purified with these; but the heavenly things themselves with better sacrifices than these. For Christ is not entered into the holy places made with hands, which are the figures of the true; but into heaven itself, now to appear in the presence of God for us. (Hebrews 9:23–24)

Revelation 15:5 is a sobering reminder that God's holiness and justice are not abstract—they are rooted in His heavenly reality. The heavenly temple is not a symbol—it is a functional center of worship and judgment, and it reveals that God sees, remembers, and responds to both covenant faithfulness and rebellion.

When the temple is opened here in Revelation 15:5, it is not to welcome intercession, but to initiate final judgment. The time for mercy has ended. What follows will be God's wrath poured out in full.

OLD TESTAMENT FORESHADOWS REVELATION:

> And he reared up the court round about the tabernacle and the altar, and set up the hanging of the court gate. So Moses finished the work. Then a cloud covered the tent of the congregation, and the glory of the LORD filled the tabernacle. (Exodus 40:33–34)

In Exodus 40:33–34, after Moses completed the tabernacle, God's glory filled it, and access was restricted—signifying His holy presence. In Revelation 15:5–8, the heavenly temple is opened, and smoke from God's glory fills it, with no one allowed to enter until the seven plagues are finished. Both scenes mark a completed work, a visible manifestation of God's presence, and a moment of transition—one into worship, the other into judgment.

THE REVELATION OF JESUS CHRIST REVEALS:

[15:6] And the seven angels came out of the temple, having the seven plagues, clothed in pure and white linen, and having their breasts girded with golden girdles.

As the heavenly temple is opened (Revelation 15:5), the vision now shifts from the worship of the overcomers to the formal procession of seven angels, emerging with divine authority and solemn purpose. These are no ordinary messengers—they are angelic ministers of judgment, uniquely dressed and divinely commissioned to unleash the final seven plagues upon the earth.

"And the seven angels came out of the temple, having the seven plagues." These seven angels carry the final seven plagues—the last expressions of God's wrath during the Great Tribulation. These are not random afflictions; they are measured, complete, and final.

> And I saw another sign in heaven, great and marvelous, seven angels having the seven last plagues; for in them is filled up the wrath of God. (Revelation 15:1).

This verse marks the beginning of the climactic phase of judgment, leading directly to Revelation 16, where each angel pours out his bowl (or vial) upon the earth.

These angels hold:

- Golden vials—shallow ceremonial bowls used in temple rituals, now used to symbolize sacred, deliberate judgment.
- The last plagues—after this, there will be no more plagues like these again. This is the end of God's wrath before the return of Christ.

"Clothed in pure and white linen." These angels are described in priestly attire—pure and white linen, symbolic of righteousness, purity, and divine service (Exodus 28:39–43; Leviticus 16:4). The linen garment was the standard attire for Levitical priests and especially the High Priest on the Day of Atonement. But here, they are not interceding—they are administering judgment.

The garments tell us:

- They serve in holy authority.
- Their actions are blameless and righteous.
- This is sacred duty, not chaos or wrath born of rage.

These angels are often referred to as "priestly angels," because they reflect the priestly order, not in function (sacrifice), but in purity and heavenly commission.

"Having their breasts girded with golden girdles." This detail echoes the description of Jesus in Revelation 1:13:

> And in the midst of the seven candlesticks One like unto the Son of Man, clothed with a garment down to the foot, and girded about the chest with a golden girdle. (Revelation 1:13)

The golden sash or girdle represents dignity and royalty, preparedness for service, and heavenly glory. The angels wear golden sashes to show that their authority comes from God Himself. They are not rogue agents—they are divinely commissioned with heaven's judgment.

While not detailed in this verse, Revelation 15:7 will tell us that one of the four living creatures (likely a cherubim, as described in Ezekiel 1 and 10) gives the angels the bowls. This highlights that even the angelic guardians of God's throne are involved in the release of judgment.

This moment is profoundly solemn. Heaven is silent. The temple is opened—not for intercession—but for execution of final justice. The purity of the angels' garments reminds us that God's wrath is not impulsive—it is holy, measured, and righteous. The scene teaches us that:

- Judgment is rooted in God's holiness.
- Service to God includes both mercy and justice.
- Every act of God—even wrath—is done in perfect righteousness.

OLD TESTAMENT FORESHADOWS REVELATION:

He shall put on the holy linen coat, and he shall have the linen breeches upon his flesh, and shall be girded with a linen girdle, and with the linen mitre shall he be attired: these are holy garments; therefore shall he wash his flesh in water, and so put them on. (Leviticus 16:4)

Leviticus 16:4 and Revelation 15:6 both emphasize the holiness and purity required to approach God's presence. In Leviticus, the high priest wears sacred linen garments and washes before entering the Holy of Holies on the Day of Atonement. This symbolizes reverence, purity, and preparation for a sacred task.

In Revelation 15:6, the seven angels who bring the final plagues are also dressed in pure, bright linen, symbolizing holiness and divine authority. Just as the priest prepared to intercede for sin, the angels are prepared to carry out God's final judgment. Both scenes involve sacred garments, cleansing, and a divine mission—one of mercy, the other of justice.

THE REVELATION OF JESUS CHRIST REVEALS:

[15:7] And one of the four beasts gave to the seven angels seven golden vials full of the wrath of God, who lives forever and ever.

This verse marks a solemn turning point in the Book of Revelation. The full weight of God's final wrath is now being formally handed over to the seven angels. It's not just the delivery of judgment—it is a ceremonial commissioning from the very heart of heaven's throne room.

"And one of the four beasts gave to the seven angels." These four "beasts" (Greek: *zoa*, meaning "living creatures") were introduced in Revelation 4:6–9. They are the cherubim—angelic beings who surround the throne of God, representing His majesty, holiness, and omniscience.

Their presence here is deeply significant:

- It tells us that this judgment originates from the throne of God.
- These living creatures act as heavenly attendants, bridging God's holiness and the angels of judgment.

So when one of the four cherubim gives the vials to the seven angels, we understand that what's about to unfold is directly authorized by God—not merely symbolic, but a real transference of divine wrath.

"Seven golden vials." The King James Version uses the word "vials," but the Greek word is *phiale*, which more accurately refers to:

- A shallow, broad bowl used in temple rituals.
- Symbolic of libation offerings, but here filled not with wine or oil—but the wrath of God.

This image is incredibly important: These are not deep vessels, slowly dripping judgment. They are shallow bowls, meant to be poured out quickly and completely—indicating the sudden, overwhelming outpouring of divine wrath. This matches the tone of Revelation 16, where each bowl is poured out in rapid succession with devastating, global consequences.

"Full of the wrath of God." This is not partial wrath. These bowls are full—symbolizing that God's patience has reached its end. These are the final judgments, completing what the seals and trumpets began.

As Revelation 15:1 declared: ". . . in them is filled up the wrath of God." This wrath is not impulsive or uncontrolled. It is measured, just, holy, and righteous—the final response to centuries of unrepentant sin, blasphemy, and rebellion.

"Who lives forever and ever." This phrase reminds us that God's eternal nature is not threatened by human rebellion. While the earth is reeling from the effects of sin, God remains sovereign, eternal, and unshaken.

- His judgments are not bound by time.
- His authority spans eternity past, present, and future.
- His justice is final because He is forever.

This echoes Daniel 4:34, where Nebuchadnezzar praises God:

His dominion is an everlasting dominion, and His Kingdom is from generation to generation. (Daniel 4:34)

And it echoes the very foundation of worship in heaven:

You are worthy, O Lord, to receive glory and honor and power: for You have created all things, and for Your pleasure they are and were created. (Revelation 4:11).

This is a holy moment in heaven. The angels do not grab the vials themselves. The cherubim do not throw them. Instead, with reverence and order, the heavenly throne room authorizes the release of final judgment. It reminds us that judgment is not manmade—it is God-ordained, and no force on earth can stop it once heaven decrees it.

OLD TESTAMENT FORESHADOWS REVELATION:

And Nadab and Abihu, the sons of Aaron, took either of them his censer, and put fire therein, and put incense thereon, and offered strange fire before the LORD, which He commanded them not. And there went out fire from the LORD, and devoured them, and they died before the LORD. (Leviticus 10:1–2)

Leviticus 10:1–2 shows Nadab and Abihu offering unauthorized fire, resulting in their death by God's judgment. In Revelation 15:7, angels receive golden bowls filled with God's wrath—authorized and holy. Both highlight God's holiness and the danger of disobedience. One reveals judgment for defiled worship; the other delivers judgment through obedient servants.

THE REVELATION OF JESUS CHRIST REVEALS:

15:8 And the temple was filled with smoke from the glory of God, and from His power; and no man was able to enter into the temple, till the seven plagues of the seven angels were fulfilled.

This verse marks a solemn turning point in heaven. After the seven angels receive the golden bowls filled with God's final wrath, the temple in heaven is filled with smoke—not from incense or sacrifice, but from God's glory and power. And then, for a time, heaven's inner sanctuary is closed—no one may enter until the final seven plagues have been poured out.

"And the temple was filled with smoke from the glory of God, and from His power." The imagery of smoke filling the temple is deeply rooted in Old Testament encounters with God's presence:

- Exodus 40:34–35—When Moses finished building the tabernacle, "the cloud covered the tent . . . and the glory of the LORD filled the tabernacle. And Moses was not able to enter . . . ."
- 1 Kings 8:10–11—At the dedication of Solomon's Temple, "the cloud filled the house of the LORD . . . for the glory of the LORD had filled the house."

- Isaiah 6:1–4—When Isaiah saw the LORD on His throne, "the house was filled with smoke."

In all these cases, smoke signifies the overwhelming weight of God's holiness—so intense that even the most righteous beings must step back.

Here in Revelation 15:8, the smoke represents the active, manifest glory and power of God in preparation for judgment. This is no longer the Shekinah glory inviting fellowship. This is holy fire, the visible sign that God Himself is present—and preparing to act.

"And no man was able to enter into the temple." This detail is extraordinary. Even in heaven, access to the temple is suspended. Why?

- Not because God is absent—but because He is fully engaged in judgment.
- Not because worship ceases—but because intercession is over.
- Not because mercy failed—but because grace has been exhausted.

Just as in the days of Noah, when "the LORD shut the door of the Ark" (Genesis 7:16), the door to grace is now shut for the world. These final judgments—poured from the seven bowls—are irrevocable and complete. This echoes Jesus' warning in Luke 13:25:

> When once the Master of the house is risen up, and has shut to the door, and you begin to stand outside, and to knock at the door, saying, 'Lord, Lord, open unto us'; and He shall answer and say unto you, 'I know you not, where you are from.' (Luke 13:25)

It also reflects the Day of Atonement (Leviticus 16), when the high priest entered the Holy of Holies in a cloud of smoke. But now, no priest enters—no one intercedes. Even the redeemed are denied access. The temple is sealed until judgment is finished.

"Till the seven plagues of the seven angels were fulfilled." This confirms the finality and severity of what is to come:

- These are the last judgments—not symbolic or partial.
- The wrath of God is full (Revelation 15:1).
- The temple remains closed until every drop of judgment is poured.

This underscores the truth that these plagues do not come from Satan, nor from mankind's sin alone. They come directly from God, out of His glory, power, and holiness.

This moment in heaven is sacred, terrifying, and awe-inspiring. The glory of God fills the temple, and no one—redeemed or angelic—may enter until the work of judgment is done.

It is a reminder:

- That God suffers alone the full weight of sin's horror.
- That mercy has a limit, and grace has a closing hour.
- That there comes a point when prayers stop, intercession ceases, and only judgment remains.

It is also a call for believers today to fear the Lord, to live soberly, and to urgently call others to repentance—before the door closes.

OLD TESTAMENT FORESHADOWS REVELATION:

And it came to pass, when the priests were come out of the holy place, that the cloud filled the house of the LORD, So that the priests could not stand to minister because of the cloud: for the glory of the LORD had filled the house of the LORD. (1 Kings 8:10–11)

1 Kings 8:10–11 and Revelation 15:8 both show God's glory filling the temple so completely that no one can enter. In 1 Kings, it halts worship; in Revelation, it delays access until judgment is complete. Both reveal God's overwhelming holiness—one in worship, the other in wrath.

"Ann, I've heard that term before—'Shekinah glory.' What exactly is it? What does it mean?"

"Ah, the Shekinah. That's a beautiful question, Irene. The word 'Shekinah' doesn't appear in the Bible word-for-word, but it's a Hebrew term meaning 'the dwelling' or 'the settling.' It refers to the visible, manifest presence of God—when God's glory would rest among His people."

"So it's like when the Israelites saw the pillar of cloud by day and the fire by night?"

"Exactly! That cloud, that fire—that was the Shekinah. In Exodus 40, when Moses finished building the tabernacle, the cloud filled it, and God's glory was so overwhelming that Moses couldn't even go inside. Later, in 1 Kings 8, the same thing happened at Solomon's Temple. The priests had to stop ministering because the glory cloud filled the house."

"And that's what's happening again in Revelation 15:8, isn't it? 'The temple was filled with smoke from the glory of God and from His power . . .'"

"Yes. But this time, the glory comes not for fellowship—but for judgment. That's why it's so solemn. No one can enter the heavenly temple—not even the redeemed—until the seven plagues are poured out."

"That feels so . . . final. Like the end of something sacred."

I nodded. "It is. That's the *smoke of glory*. A visible sign that God's overwhelming presence has filled His temple. And just like in the days of Noah, the door is shut. Remember Genesis 7:16? 'And the LORD shut him in.' Once the Ark was sealed, no one else could enter. The rain fell. The judgment began."

"So you're saying this is that same kind of moment?"

"Exactly. The temple sealing in Revelation is heaven's echo of the Ark's door. It means that grace has reached its limit. Intercession is over. Now judgment must run its full course."

"And those seven angels . . . they're not just bringing chaos—they're carrying out divine justice, aren't they?"

"Yes, Irene. These bowls aren't random punishments. They're not the work of Satan or natural disaster. These are holy, righteous judgments—poured out from the very throne of God. That's why they're delivered in golden bowls, just like the sacred offerings in the tabernacle. Even judgment is handled with purity and reverence."

"And yet . . . no one enters the temple. Not even angels?"

"No. And that's something that really humbles me. It shows us the loneliness of God in judgment. He alone bears the sorrow of what must be done. No intercessor steps in. No worship fills the sanctuary. It's as if heaven itself holds its breath while justice is released."

"It reminds me how serious sin really is . . . and how holy God is."

"Yes, Irene. And it reminds us of something else too—the urgency of the gospel. Because once that temple is filled with smoke and the door shuts . . . it's too late."

"Ann . . . I don't think I'll ever look at that verse the same again."

WHEN MERCY SHUTS ITS DOOR—Revelation 16 marks a solemn turning point in God's redemptive timeline. The bowls of wrath are not warnings—they are final. No more delay, no more calls to repent. Heaven's Temple stands filled with smoke, sealed off even from the redeemed, as God Himself personally presides over the outpouring of His righteous judgment.

This chapter reveals the full force of divine justice. The longsuffering mercy of God, offered through ages past, now gives way to retribution. These judgments are not arbitrary—they are holy, measured, and deserved. What follows is not chaos, but consequence.

These bowl judgments are not a new series but the final outpouring of wrath released under the seventh trumpet, which sounded back in Revelation 11 during

Trumpet I. That trumpet announced the coming of God's kingdom in power; the bowls now bring that reign into reality by dismantling the rebellious systems of the earth. What was once declared is now being executed—the trumpet has sounded, and the bowls are the response.

As we step into Revelation 16, we are witnessing the moment when mercy shuts its door, and justice takes the throne.

THE REVELATION OF JESUS CHRIST REVEALS:

16:1 And I heard a great voice out of the temple saying to the seven angels, Go your ways, and pour out the vials of the wrath of God upon the earth.

This verse marks the beginning of the end—the moment the long-anticipated bowl judgments commence. A "great voice"—likely the voice of God Himself—issues a command from within the Heavenly Temple. This voice does not echo from a court of angels, nor from a prophetic messenger. It comes from within the temple itself, the very place where no one was able to enter after the smoke of God's glory filled it (Revelation 15:8). This tells us that God alone now initiates what must come.

"And I heard a great voice out of the temple." The phrase "great voice" (Greek: *megale phone*) carries both authority and finality. This is not a suggestion, nor a warning—it is a command issued from the seat of divine sovereignty. Heaven has been silent, smoke-filled, and inaccessible since Revelation 15:8. Now, this single voice breaks that silence with power and purpose, signaling that the age of grace has ended, and the season of wrath has fully arrived.

This voice doesn't allow for delay or hesitation. The time of waiting, pleading, and patience is over. The command is urgent and absolute.

"Go your ways, and pour out the vials of the wrath of God." Each of the seven angels holds a golden bowl (*phiale*) filled to the brim with the wrath of God—not symbolic wrath, but real, divine, justified judgment. These are not mere annoyances or warnings. These are the final and complete judgments that will devastate the natural order, dismantle human systems, and expose the futility of rebellion against God.

The vials (better translated "bowls") are wide, shallow vessels used in temple service—originally for incense and worship (Revelation 5:8). Now, those same vessels are repurposed for judgment. What once carried the fragrance of prayer now carries the fury of justice.

These bowls will be poured out rapidly and sequentially—the judgments come in swift succession, leaving no time for response, recovery, or repentance. This pouring is not a trickle, but a complete dumping, signifying the full measure of divine indignation.

"Upon the earth." This detail reminds us of the target of these judgments: the rebellious world—those who have:

- Taken the mark of the beast.
- Worshiped his image.
- Blasphemed the name of God.
- Rejected every offer of grace.

These are not innocent bystanders—they are hardened rejectors of truth, fully aligned with the Antichrist's one world political, religious, economic, and military system, even after countless chances to repent.

Revelation 16:1 is a sobering verse, reminding us of three profound truths:

1. **God's patience has a limit**. He is longsuffering, not willing that any should perish (2 Peter 3:9), but there comes a day when grace gives way to judgment.

2. **Judgment is not chaos—it is divine order**. These bowls are not accidents of nature or symbolic myths. They are orchestrated acts of a holy and righteous God.

3. **There is a "too late."** The door to the Heavenly Temple is shut. The bowls are full. The voice has spoken. There is no further appeal.

OLD TESTAMENT FORESHADOWS REVELATION:

For thus says the Lord GOD of Israel unto me; Take the wine cup of this fury at My hand, and cause all the nations, to whom I send you, to drink it. And they shall drink, and be moved, and be mad, because of the sword that I will send among them. (Jeremiah 25:15–16)

Jeremiah 25:15–16 and Revelation 16:1 both show God commanding judgment on the nations. In Jeremiah, the cup of wrath is symbolic; in Revelation, the bowls are literal. One foreshadows judgment, the other unleashes it fully. Both reveal God's justice poured out by divine command.

THE REVELATION OF JESUS CHRIST REVEALS:

16:2 And the first went, and poured out his vial upon the earth; and there fell a noisome and grievous sore upon the men which had the mark of the beast, and upon them which worshiped his image.

The First Bowl Judgment—The first of the seven bowl (vial) judgments begins with a targeted affliction that brings severe physical torment, but it is not random or global. It is specific, judicious, and measured—poured out only on those who have taken the mark of the beast and worshiped his image.

This judgment marks the beginning of God's wrath being fully poured out under the seventh trumpet:

- In the earlier trumpet judgments, physical torment appeared symbolically—especially in the fifth trumpet (Revelation 9:1–11), where demonic locusts tormented those without the seal of God. Yet even then, the pain was temporary, and death was withheld.
- But now, in the first bowl (Revelation 16:2), the judgment is literal, immediate, and unrelenting—a grievous and painful sore afflicts all who bear the mark of the beast and worship his image. There is no delay, no restraint. The time of warning has passed. Under the final trumpet, divine justice begins its complete and righteous work.

"And there fell a noisome and grievous sore." The phrase "noisome and grievous sore" (Greek: *kakos kai poneros helkos*) refers to an ulcerated, festering wound that is extremely painful, malignant, and incurable. The Greek emphasizes something evil, destructive, and agonizing. It is not a light affliction, but a supernaturally inflicted plague, similar in severity and symbolism to the sixth plague in Egypt—the boils that fell upon Pharaoh and his people (Exodus 9:8–11).

This judgment directly touches the body, inflicting torment on those who had once looked to the mark of the beast as their seal of protection and prosperity. Instead of safety, they now bear a brand of pain. What they believed would save them from persecution now marks them for divine wrath.

"Upon the men which had the mark of the beast." This plague is not poured out indiscriminately—it is directed only toward those who have made a conscious decision to align themselves with the Antichrist system:

- They accepted the mark, fully aware of its significance.
- They worshiped the image of the beast, submitting to his counterfeit divinity.
- They rejected God, His Son, and the offer of salvation—even after multiple warnings.

This judgment is a direct response to their rebellion and serves as a visible, physical manifestation of the spiritual corruption they have chosen. What was once invisible allegiance is now painfully exposed on their flesh.

This judgment reminds us that allegiance matters. Those who chose the mark of the beast chose a master—and with it, they inherited that master's judgment. Their suffering is not just physical—it is spiritual exposure. The Antichrist could not protect them from God's wrath. His image could not shield them from holy judgment.

This verse is also a divine vindication of all those who refused the mark, even unto death. It reveals the truth behind the choice: loyalty to the beast leads to torment, but loyalty to the Lamb leads to eternal life.

OLD TESTAMENT FORESHADOWS REVELATION:

And the LORD said unto Moses and unto Aaron, Take to you handfuls of ashes of the furnace, and let Moses sprinkle it toward the heaven in the sight of Pharaoh. And it shall become small dust in all the land of Egypt, and shall be a boil breaking forth with blains upon man, and upon beast, throughout all the land of Egypt. And they took ashes of the furnace, and stood before Pharaoh; and Moses sprinkled it up toward heaven; and it became a boil breaking forth with blains upon man, and upon beast. And the magicians could not stand before Moses because of the boils; for the boil was upon the magicians, and upon all the Egyptians. (Exodus 9:8–11)

Both Revelation 16:2 and Exodus 9:8–11 describe physical afflictions of grievous sores or boils that cause great pain and discomfort. In both cases, these sores are supernaturally inflicted by God as acts of judgment against rebellion. Pharaoh hardened his heart, just as those in Revelation hardened theirs by worshiping the beast and taking his mark.

The boils in Egypt revealed God's power and the failure of false religion—the magicians of Egypt. In Revelation, the sores expose the spiritual corruption of those who aligned with the Antichrist. Just as the magicians couldn't escape the boils in Egypt, those who take the mark cannot escape the sores in Revelation. Both are judgments that touch the body as a sign of deeper spiritual decay.

THE REVELATION OF JESUS CHRIST REVEALS:

16:3 And the second angel poured out his vial upon the sea; and it became as the blood of a dead man: and every living soul died in the sea.

The Second Bowl Judgment—With the pouring out of the second bowl of God's wrath, judgment now strikes the salt waters of the earth—the seas and oceans. It is not symbolic or partial. This is total ecological collapse in one of the most expansive regions of the natural world. It is both terrifying and final.

This judgment brings the complete fulfillment of earlier warnings under the seventh trumpet:

- In the second trumpet judgment (Revelation 8:8), a burning mountain was cast into the sea, turning one-third of it to blood, and one-third of sea life died—a partial judgment meant to awaken repentance.

- But now, in the second bowl (Revelation 16:3), the devastation is total—the entire sea becomes as blood, and every living soul in it dies. Under the seventh trumpet, divine wrath is no longer restrained. What was once a warning has now become irreversible judgment.

"And the second angel poured out his vial upon the sea." Just as the first bowl struck the bodies of those who worshiped the beast, now the second bowl targets the seas, which cover more than 70 percent of the earth's surface. The sea, once teemed with life and wonder, is now transformed into a dead, rotting, crimson mass.

"And it became as the blood of a dead man." This vivid phrase is disturbing. The Greek implies blood that is thick, dark, and coagulated—not fresh or life-giving, but putrid, lifeless, and toxic. This isn't symbolic—it's describing a literal transformation of the oceans into a medium that resembles congealed, decaying blood.

Just as the Nile River was turned to blood in the first plague on Egypt (Exodus 7:20–21), here the oceans of the entire earth are struck, and the effect is irreversible. This plague is not merely an environmental crisis; it is a supernatural judgment revealing that God is undoing the natural order—the death of the sea means the death of global trade, fishing industries, oceanic travel, and weather systems.

"And every living soul died in the sea." There is no partiality here. Every form of sea life perishes—fish, whales, coral reefs, plankton, dolphins, seahorses, jellyfish—all of it. The seas are turned into a mass grave, uninhabitable and foul-smelling. The death of the oceans results in economic, ecological, and humanitarian disaster on a scale the world has never seen.

This is the environmental consequences of spiritual rebellion. Humanity's alignment with the Antichrist has not only corrupted the moral and spiritual order—it has triggered God's judgment upon creation itself.

When Adam sinned, it affected all of creation. As Romans 8:22 says:

> For we know that the whole creation groans and travails in pain together until now. (Romans 8:22)

The sea, like the rest of creation, has suffered the effects of man's rebellion. And now, in Revelation, the consequences reach their final stage.

Just as Adam was given dominion over creation and defiled it through sin, humanity—under the leadership of the beast—has once again corrupted the earth. The bowls of wrath represent God reclaiming what was His, even as He purges it through judgment.

This verse is not simply a record of ecological collapse—it is a moral reckoning. The death of the sea reminds us that sin has consequences not just for the soul, but for everything we touch. When humanity aligns with darkness, even creation itself mourns. And in the final hours of this age, God's patience has reached its end.

This judgment is not random. It is a measured and deliberate act by a holy God whose warnings have gone unheeded. Those who worshiped the beast chose rebellion over repentance, and now the result is not just spiritual death, but cosmic ruin.

OLD TESTAMENT FORESHADOWS REVELATION:

Wherefore, when I came, was there no man? When I called, was there none to answer? Is My hand shortened at all, that it cannot redeem? Or have I no power to deliver? Behold, at My rebuke I dry up the sea, I make the rivers a wilderness: their fish stinks, because there is no water, and dies for thirst. (Isaiah 50:2)

Isaiah 50:2 and Revelation 16:3 both reveal God's power to bring judgment through the waters. In Isaiah, God rebukes a faithless people, reminding them of His ability to dry up the sea and leave fish to rot—symbolizing devastation from divine intervention. In Revelation, the second bowl turns the sea into blood like a dead man, and every living creature in it dies. What was once a symbol of life becomes a scene of death.

Both passages show that God's control over nature is absolute, and when rejected, He can turn life-sustaining waters into instruments of judgment. Isaiah foreshadows it symbolically; Revelation fulfills it literally.

THE REVELATION OF JESUS CHRIST REVEALS:

[16:4] And the third angel poured out his vial upon the rivers and fountains of waters; and they became blood.

The Third Bowl Judgment—The third angel pours out his vial, and now judgment strikes not the sea, but the fresh waters—the rivers, streams, and underground springs—the very sources of life, agriculture, and sustenance. These are the waters we drink, the waters we irrigate with, the fountains that bubble up from the depths of God's creation.

This is no symbolic act. This is ecological collapse by divine decree. Just as God once turned the Nile to blood in Egypt to show Pharaoh that He alone was God, now the rivers of the earth are turned to blood as a final, undeniable act of judgment. Not red tide. Not chemical pollution. But blood. Literal or not, the message is the same: the world that refused the blood of Christ is now drowning in the consequences of rejecting it.

This judgment fulfills the warning first seen in the trumpet judgments, now completed under the seventh trumpet:

- In the third trumpet (Revelation 8:10–11), a star named Wormwood fell, turning a third of the rivers and springs bitter—a partial judgment meant to lead the world to repentance.
- But now, in the third bowl (Revelation 16:4), the judgment is total—all rivers and springs are turned to blood. Life-giving water is completely withdrawn. What was once symbolic and limited has become literal and global. God's patience has ended; justice flows without restraint.

This plague is a strike at the very lifeblood of human survival. It's a direct reversal of the water that flowed from Christ's side—a substitution rejected, now turned to wrath. While modern society proudly boasts of progress, engineering, and climate accords, the Creator of the ecosystem has the final say.

And notice: this judgment comes after centuries of pollution, greed, and disregard for God's creation. The rivers have already tasted oil spills, chemical waste, and the blood of martyrs. But now, under the righteous hand of God, the fresh water becomes undrinkable, unusable, and unmistakably supernatural.

This is not just judgment on water. It's a judgment on nations, on systems, on those who saw God's mercy and still refused to repent. It is as if the rivers themselves cry out for justice—and the blood they now carry is heaven's answer.

OLD TESTAMENT FORESHADOWS REVELATION:

And the LORD spoke unto Moses, Say unto Aaron, Take your rod, and stretch out your hand upon the waters of Egypt, upon their streams, upon their rivers, and upon their ponds, and upon all their pools of water, that they may become blood; and that there may be blood throughout all the land of Egypt, both in vessels of wood, and in vessels of stone. (Exodus 7:19)

Exodus 7:19 lists streams, rivers, ponds, pools, and even water stored in vessels; just as Revelation targets rivers and fountains. In both, the entire fresh water supply is struck, impacting both the natural environment and personal use. Judgment for rebellion—Pharaoh hardened his heart; the world in Revelation has done the same, and now the judgment is total. Both plagues invoke blood as a symbol of death, divine wrath, and the cost of rejecting God's command.

THE REVELATION OF JESUS CHRIST REVEALS:

[16:5] And I heard the angel of the waters say, You are righteous, O Lord, which are, and was, and shalt be, because You have judged thus.

The angel of the waters declares divine justice. In the middle of devastating judgment—where rivers and fountains have turned to blood—we hear a voice.

Not the voice of protest, but of praise. Not of complaint, but of holy affirmation. The angel of the waters—the divine being assigned over earth's rivers and springs—cries out: "You are righteous, O Lord!"

This is no random declaration. This is a holy verdict: that God's judgments are perfectly justified.

The Greek text omits "and shalt be," which normally appears in similar declarations (Revelation 1:8, 4:8). Why? Because there's no more "shalt be." The future has arrived. The moment of ultimate justice is here. This is the climax of rebellion, and now the righteous Judge of all the earth has stepped forward—not as Savior, but as Avenger.

The angel of the waters declares, "You are righteous, O Lord, which are, and was, and shalt be." This title reflects the eternal nature of God, and in this context, it is applied specifically to Jesus Christ—God the Son, the righteous Judge now executing divine wrath. Though the phrase echoes the divine name associated with Yahweh in the Old Testament, Revelation affirms that Yeshua—Jesus—shares fully in this eternal identity. He is no longer "the One who is to come," because He has come. Judgment is no longer a future warning—it is now unfolding in real time under His sovereign authority.

And what is this judgment? Blood for blood. The waters once offered refreshment and life, but now they offer only blood—a chilling echo of Exodus 7:20–21. The beast-worshipers, who spilled the blood of prophets and saints, now find nothing left to drink but their own sentence. They wanted no part in Christ's blood—now they drown in symbolic retribution. They mocked His sacrifice, and now they drink the cup of His wrath.

This verse reminds us: God's justice isn't emotional vengeance—it is holiness fulfilled. It is the inevitable outworking of a world that has refused mercy and rejected the Lamb. Now the Lion roars.

OLD TESTAMENT FORESHADOWS REVELATION:

He is the Rock, His work is perfect: for all His ways are justice: a God of truth and without injustice, just and right is He. (Deuteronomy 32:4)

Both verses exalt the righteousness of God's judgments. In both, God's perfection, truth, and justice are highlighted. Deuteronomy 32:4 is the Old Testament's national anthem of justice, just as Revelation 16:5 is its global counterpart of judgment. The angel of the waters in Revelation echoes Moses' declaration: God is always right, even in wrath.

THE REVELATION OF JESUS CHRIST REVEALS:

[16:6] For they have shed the blood of saints and prophets, and You have given them blood to drink; for they are worthy.

This verse is a thunderclap of divine retribution. It is God's courtroom verdict—delivered not with silence, but with the thunder of heavenly agreement. The ones who now suffer thirst and horror are not innocent victims. They are *guilty*. And heaven declares it: they are worthy of what they're receiving.

They've shed the blood of prophets. They've slaughtered the saints. From Abel to the martyrs under the altar in Revelation 6, the earth has been soaked in innocent blood. Kings, false religions, corrupt systems—have all silenced God's messengers with swords, prisons, and fire. And now? The blood they spilled becomes their only drink.

This is poetic justice. Heaven's irony. They reject the blood of Jesus, the only blood that could save them. Now they must drink the consequence—a chilling reversal of the communion cup.

Notice the phrase: "for they are worthy." It's one of the few times in Scripture when wickedness earns something. The same heaven that declared the Lamb worthy to receive blessing and glory (Revelation 5:12) now declares the wicked worthy to receive wrath.

The idea isn't vengeance out of rage—this is divine justice in perfect measure. God gives them exactly what they've earned, exactly what they've refused, and exactly what they've done to others. This moment in Revelation 16:6 is echoing back to Jesus' own words in Matthew 23:35:

That upon you may come all the righteous blood shed upon the earth, from the blood of righteous Abel unto the blood of Zacharias son of Barachias, whom you slew between the temple and the altar. (Matthew 23:35)

Their cup is full. Now God turns it upside down.

OLD TESTAMENT FORESHADOWS REVELATION:

And I will feed them that oppress you with their own flesh; and they shall be drunken with their own blood, as with sweet wine: and all flesh shall know that I the LORD am your Savior and your Redeemer, the Mighty One of Jacob. (Isaiah 49:26)

Isaiah 49:26 and Revelation 16:6 both portray a powerful image of divine justice expressed through blood. In Isaiah, God promises to make Israel's oppressors consume their own flesh and become drunk on their own blood—symbolizing total judgment and vindication for God's people. In Revelation 16:6, those who shed the blood of saints and prophets are now given blood to drink—a direct and just response to their crimes.

Both verses reveal the same truth: God repays blood with blood, showing that His justice is not only righteous but personal. What was done to His people, He returns in kind.

THE REVELATION OF JESUS CHRIST REVEALS:

16:7 And I heard another out of the altar say, Even so, LORD God Almighty, true and righteous are Your judgments.

In a moment that silences all arguments, the altar itself speaks. This is no ordinary altar. This is the very one seen in Revelation 6:9–11, where the souls of the martyrs—those slain for the Word of God and their testimony—cried out, "How long, O Lord, holy and true, do You not judge and avenge our blood?"

Now, that question is answered. He has judged. He has avenged. And the altar responds in agreement.

This declaration—"Even so, LORD God Almighty"—is heaven's thunderous "Amen." It is a holy echo confirming that God's wrath is not only deserved, it is righteous. The blood that cried for justice is now answered by justice.

The altar is where sacrifice is made, where blood was spilled in the Old Testament for atonement. But in this scene, it represents something even deeper. It is the Cross in shadow and type—the place where innocence was slain and mercy offered. Those who accepted Christ's sacrifice were covered by His blood. Those who rejected it now face the judgment their own sins have summoned.

This verse also echoes the old saying, "What goes around, comes around." But this is not karma—it is divine justice, flowing from the throne of the LORD God Almighty. His judgments are true, reflecting reality as it is, and righteous, perfectly aligned with moral truth.

OLD TESTAMENT FORESHADOWS REVELATION:

The fear of the LORD is clean, enduring forever: the judgments of the LORD are true and righteous altogether. (Psalm 19:9)

Both verses affirm the righteousness and truth of God's judgments. Psalm 19:9 praises God's law and judgments as pure and enduring, just as Revelation 16:7 does at the height of God's wrath. Both acknowledge that God's decisions are not arbitrary—they are holy, just, and trustworthy.

THE REVELATION OF JESUS CHRIST REVEALS:

16:8 And the fourth angel poured out his vial upon the sun; and power was given to him to scorch men with fire.

The Fourth Bowl Judgment—Here we witness something unthinkable: the very sun, the life-giver of earth, now becomes a tormentor. The fourth angel pours out his vial, not upon the earth, not upon the sea, but upon the sun—and it is given power to scorch men with fire.

This is the same sun that once warmed the earth and gave light to the crops. But now, under God's command, it becomes an agent of judgment. Where once its rays were life-sustaining, now they are deadly, searing, unbearable. This is not natural climate change. This is divine judgment dialed to full intensity.

This judgment brings to completion what was only partially seen in the trumpet judgments, now fulfilled under the seventh trumpet:

- In the fourth trumpet judgment (Revelation 8:12), a third of the sun, moon, and stars were struck, dimming light over the earth—a partial disruption meant to signal the fragility of creation under judgment.
- But now, in the fourth bowl judgment (Revelation 16:8–9), the sun's power is fully unleashed, not to darken but to scorch. The same source of light and life becomes an instrument of burning torment. There is no restraint—only righteous wrath. And yet, despite the severity, people blaspheme rather than repent (Revelation 16:9).

This plague touches the global climate. Imagine the chaos: widespread drought, scorched vegetation, crumbling infrastructure, collapsing power grids, unbearable heat. And worse, it directly afflicts human flesh—no sunscreen, no shelter, no escape.

It's a direct reversal of God's provision in the wilderness. In Exodus, the LORD gave His people a cloud by day to shield them from the desert sun. But now? No cloud. No covering. Just fire. Just judgment.

And this is toward the very end of the Great Tribulation—the final stretch. A moment when humanity's rebellion is so hardened, so unrepentant, that even fire from heaven won't move them to bow.

This isn't just environmental collapse—it's a heavenly response to spiritual rebellion. The same sun that rose on the just and the unjust is now used to separate the wheat from the chaff. The sun that once warmed the faithful now burns the rebellious. The light that once revealed truth now exposes sin. And the fire that could have refined has become the fire that consumes.

Take note: the first four bowl judgments mark the beginning of God's final, unrestrained wrath poured out on the earth and its inhabitants under the seventh trumpet. These are not random disasters but deliberate, targeted acts of divine justice—falling on those who bear the mark of the beast and refuse to repent. What the trumpet judgments only warned of, the bowls now fully deliver. These judgments expose hardened hearts and reveal the righteousness of God in real time.

As we move into the final three bowl judgments, the focus widens—from individuals to the systems that support global rebellion. These last plagues strike the spiritual, political, and military powers upholding the beast's empire. What began with personal affliction now culminates in the collapse of earthly thrones. God's justice is no longer just felt—it is seen dismantling the kingdom of darkness.

OLD TESTAMENT FORESHADOWS REVELATION:

For, behold, the day comes, that shall burn as an oven; and all the proud, yea, and all that do wickedly, shall be stubble: and the day that comes shall burn them up, says the LORD of hosts, that it shall leave them neither root nor branch. (Malachi 4:1)

Both verses depict a supernatural heat sent from heaven as a tool of divine wrath. In Malachi 4:1, it is "the proud and all that do wickedly" who are scorched; Revelation 16:8 parallels this by afflicting those who have rejected God and worshiped the beast. Malachi looks ahead to the Day of the Lord, just as Revelation reveals its final moments of fury.

THE REVELATION OF JESUS CHRIST REVEALS:

16:9 And men were scorched with great heat, and blasphemed the name of God, which has power over these plagues: and they repented not to give Him glory.

This is one of the most staggering verses in the entire Book of Revelation— not because of the intensity of judgment, but because of the unyielding condition of the human heart. The sun, once a symbol of warmth, life, and divine provision, is now transformed into a weapon of wrath. Scorching heat descends—not metaphorically, but physically—and mankind is afflicted with torment so severe it cannot be mistaken for coincidence.

And yet, the horror here is not in the heat. It is in the response. The people know the source. The passage explicitly states they "blasphemed the name of God, who has power over these plagues." This isn't ignorance. These are not atheists questioning if there is a God—these are men and women who know exactly who is sending the judgment—and hate Him for it.

This is the fulfillment of Romans 1:21:

Because that, when they knew God, they glorified Him not as God, neither were thankful; but became vain in their imaginations, and their foolish heart was darkened. (Romans 1:21)

This moment marks what theologians call "judicial hardening"—where repeated rebellion leads to divine confirmation of one's path. Just as Pharaoh's heart was hardened in the presence of ten unmistakable plagues in Egypt, so too the end-time rebels are sealed in their defiance. They have been given every opportunity to repent—through warnings, miracles, angelic proclamations, and even past judgments. But now, the door of mercy is shut.

This verse exposes a profound theological truth:

Judgment alone cannot produce repentance.

Only the grace of God, working through a humble, broken heart, leads to surrender. These people are not simply victims of wrath—they are participants in their own destruction. They blaspheme the One who could have saved them.

The sun—from worshiped to weapon—the irony runs deep. Once exalted as a deity in ancient paganism, the sun was first worshiped openly on the plains of Shinar under Nimrod (Genesis 10:8–10). Now, in Revelation, it becomes an agent of divine wrath. Nimrod—whose name means "to rebel"—laid the foundations of global rebellion against God. His empire birthed the Tower of Babel, the first great shrine to human defiance, and a possible origin point of sun worship. From there emerged systems like the Mazzaroth—the God-ordained celestial signs—later distorted into astrology, the zodiac, and global mythologies. What was once revered in darkness now becomes a tool of burning judgment from the true and living God.

- Deuteronomy 4:19 and 17:2–3 warn against worshiping the "host of heaven," especially the sun.
- 2 Kings 17:16–17 reveals that Israel eventually fell into this very sin.
- And now, in the final hour of judgment, the sun becomes God's instrument of vengeance.

This plague is not just physical—it's symbolic. It is God's divine response to millennia of sun worship and rebellion. The sun, once adored, now burns its worshipers.

- The sun reveals what's outside—but God's fire reveals what's inside.
- The same sun that once symbolized blessing now brings blistering curse.
- The proud heart would rather burn than bow.
- Those who once looked to the sun as a god now feel its heat as judgment.

Interestingly, the final global dictator, like Nimrod, may be an Assyrian (Micah 5:5–6 and Isaiah 10). The parallels between ancient rebellion and future tribulation underscore one theme: What began in defiance of God will end in the wrath of God.

OLD TESTAMENT FORESHADOWS REVELATION:

For the people turns not unto Him that smites them, neither do they seek the LORD of hosts. (Isaiah 9:13)

In both Revelation 16:9 and Isaiah 9:13, people are being judged by God—yet they do not turn back to Him. In Isaiah, the people understand that the affliction comes from "Him who smites them," just as Revelation states that they know God has "power over these plagues." Despite clear evidence of divine intervention and justice, there's a deep stubbornness in the hearts of the wicked. These verses both reveal a tragic truth: judgment does not always lead to repentance. Without humility, even the fire of heaven can harden the heart.

Irene looked puzzled.

"Ann, can I ask you something that's been on my mind? Isn't the zodiac what people use for horoscopes and astrology? I mean, I see it all over social media—'Mercury's in retrograde,' 'Check your star sign,' and all that. But . . . isn't that kind of stuff actually wrong, according to the Bible?"

Nodding thoughtfully. "Yes, Irene, you're right to question that. What we call the zodiac today is almost always tied to astrology, horoscopes, and fortune-telling—all of which are clearly forbidden in Scripture."

Irene interrupted. "Wait—does that include tarot cards too?"

"Yes, tarot cards are a form of fortune-telling or divination," I continued. "And the Bible clearly warns against all such practices—whether tarot, astrology, or palm reading. They're not harmless; they open doors to deception."

I leaned in. "In fact, these practices trace back to ancient sun worship and idolatry, rooted in Babylon and Nimrod's rebellion on the plains of Shinar."

Irene raised an eyebrow. "Wait . . . that was over 4,000 years ago?"

"Exactly," I said. "Genesis 10:8–10 introduces Nimrod, whose name means 'we will rebel.' He led the first organized defiance against God after the Flood—around 2348 BC. He established Babel, which later became Babylon, and likely introduced sun worship—possibly even building one of the earliest temples to the sun at a place known as Bab-El. It was there that the Mazzaroth—the original, God-given constellations (Job 38:32)—began to be corrupted into the zodiac and other counterfeit systems of divination."

Can you bring forth Mazzaroth in his season? Or can you guide Arcturus with his sons? (Job 38:32)

"So you're saying the constellations weren't originally bad?"

"Not at all," I said. "Psalm 19:1 tells us, 'The heavens declare the glory of God.' From the beginning, God placed signs in the sky)—Genesis 1:14 says they were for seasons, days, and years)—not for fortune-telling, but to reveal His appointed times, His redemptive story, and ultimately to point us to the Messiah."

I paused. "But like always, Satan took what God created for good—and twisted it."

"And now we've got horoscopes and fortune-tellers claiming the stars determine our destiny?"

Gently, I replied. "Yes, Irene—and that's exactly the problem. Deuteronomy 18:10–12 clearly warns against practices like sorcery, divination, astrology, and consulting mediums. These things don't just mislead people—they open the door to deception and pull hearts away from trusting God. The moment someone looks to the stars for answers instead of the Maker of the stars, they've stepped into real spiritual danger."

Irene, serious now. "Wow. I didn't realize it was that deep. So when people ask, 'What's your sign?'—they might be dabbling in something ancient and dark without even knowing it?"

I nodded. "Exactly. What seems like a harmless personality quiz is actually rooted in Babylonian rebellion and sun worship. It may look innocent on the surface, but it traces back to the same spirit of defiance that stood against God at Babel—and that same spirit will rise again in the end times through the Antichrist."

Irene, quietly. "So . . . the stars were meant to point us to God—but now people use them to replace Him."

I nodded. "Exactly. That's the deception. And it's why Revelation is so clear: the same sun people once worshiped will become their judgment. God will not be mocked. He placed signs in the heavens to declare His glory, not ours."

"Ann, I don't want to get too far off topic, but . . . I have to ask. Aren't the constellations—the ones God Himself placed in the sky—somehow a picture of the gospel? Like . . . from the beginning to the end, from Genesis to Revelation?"

Smiling warmly. "You're absolutely right, Irene—and that's not off-topic at all. It's actually at the very heart of God's revelation! Before there was ever a written Bible, God placed the gospel in the stars. In Job 38:32, the Bible calls it the Mazzaroth. These aren't the pagan zodiac signs used for fortune-telling—they're God-given constellations designed to tell the story of His Son: from the virgin birth to the Second Coming."

Irene's eyes widened. "Wait—are you saying the heavens literally preach the gospel?"

I smiled. "Yes! Psalm 19:1–4 says, 'The heavens declare the glory of God . . . their voice goes out into all the earth.' The constellations are like a celestial Bible. There are twelve major signs—often distorted by astrology—but originally designed by God to tell the story of His redemptive plan."

Irene leaned in. "I need to know more—can you walk me through them?"

I nodded, reaching for my binder.

"Absolutely. Here are some of my cliff notes."

The Mazzaroth: God's Gospel Story Written in the Heavens—Before there was a written Bible, there was a celestial one. In Job 38:32, God refers to the *Mazzaroth*—the divinely appointed constellations that move through their seasons. Psalm 19:1–4 declares, "The heavens declare the glory of God . . . their line is gone out through all the earth." These are not the zodiac signs twisted by astrology for fortune-telling, but twelve God-given constellations that proclaim the redemptive story of Jesus Christ—from His virgin birth to His triumphant return as King.

What follows is a journey through the heavens—a gospel written in the stars.

1. **Virgo (The Virgin)**—The Gospel Begins with a Virgin Birth. A woman holding a branch and a sheaf of wheat. Isaiah 7:14: "Behold, a virgin shall conceive, and bear a Son, and shall call His name Immanuel." Immanuel means *God with us*. Virgo represents Mary, who gave birth to the Messiah. Jesus is the Bread of Life and the Branch from David (Jeremiah 23:5).

2. **Libra (The Scales)**—The Price of Redemption Must Be Paid. A balanced scale representing judgment and atonement. Romans 3:23–24: "For all have sinned, and come short of the glory of God; Being justified freely by His grace through the redemption that is in Christ Jesus." Jesus paid the full price for our sin on the Cross.

3. **Scorpio (The Scorpion)**—The Sting of Death and Power of Sin. Symbolizes Satan's attack on the Seed of the Woman. 1 Corinthians 15:56: "The sting of death is sin; and the strength of sin is the law." Yet Jesus crushed the serpent's head (Genesis 3:15).

4. **Sagittarius (The Archer)**—The Victorious Warrior. A centaur aiming a sharp arrow. Psalm 45:5: "Your arrows are sharp in the heart of the King's enemies; whereby the people fall under You." Christ goes forth conquering and to conquer.

5. **Capricorn (The Sea-Goat)**—The Sin Offering and Sacrifice. A goat descending into the sea, symbolizing death and resurrection. Leviticus 16:22: "And the goat shall bear upon him all their iniquities unto a land not inhabited . . ." Christ bore our sins, descended into death, and rose again.

6. **Aquarius (The Water Bearer)**—The Pouring Out of the Spirit. A man pours water into the mouth of a fish. John 7:38: "He that believes on Me, as the Scripture has said, out of his belly shall flow rivers of living water." Jesus pours the Holy Spirit on believers.

7. **Pisces (The Fishes)**—The Redeemed Gathered into the Kingdom. Two fish bound together, swimming in different directions. Matthew 13:47: "The Kingdom of Heaven is like unto a net, that was cast into the sea, and gathered of every kind." Pisces represents the Church Age, the gathering of believers across the world.

8. **Aries (The Ram)**—The Lamb Slain and Raised to Reign. A ram lifting its head in triumph. Genesis 22:13: "And Abraham lifted up his eyes, and looked, and behold behind him a ram caught in a thicket by his horns . . ." John 1:29: "Behold the Lamb of God, which takes away the sin of the world."

9. **Taurus (The Bull)**—The Coming Judge and Ruler. A charging bull with powerful horns. Deuteronomy 33:17: "His glory is like a firstborn of his bull, and his horns are like the horns of unicorns . . ." Christ will return in strength and judgment.

10. **Gemini (The Twins)**—The Dual Nature of Christ. Two unified figures, symbolizing harmony. Hebrews 4:15: "He was in all points tempted like as we are, yet without sin." Jesus is both fully God and fully man—the Son of God and the Son of Man.

11. **Cancer (The Crab or Sheepfold)**—The Gathering and Security of the Saints. Historically depicted as a sheepfold or protective circle. John 10:28: "And I give unto them eternal life; and they shall never perish, neither shall any man pluck them out of My hand." Jesus keeps and protects His own.

12. **Leo (The Lion)**—The Triumphant Return of the King. A lion roaring in victory. Revelation 5:5: "Behold, the Lion of the tribe of Judah, the Root of David, has prevailed . . ." Jesus returns as King of kings and Lord of lords.

Irene, in awe. "That's amazing, Ann. The stars really do declare the glory of God—and they've been telling the Gospel story long before anyone ever opened a Bible!"

I nodded. "Exactly. But Satan couldn't leave that untouched. So he distorted the message through astrology, horoscopes, and sun worship—turning people's eyes away from the true Light of the world, Jesus Christ."

Irene leaned forward. "Now I understand why God told the prophets to warn against worshiping the sun and stars. It wasn't because the heavens were bad— it's because they were holy signposts, meant to point us to something far greater."

"To Someone greater," I said gently. And He's coming soon."

THE REVELATION OF JESUS CHRIST REVEALS:

16:10 And the fifth angel poured out his vial upon the seat of the beast; and his kingdom was full of darkness; and they gnawed their tongues for pain.

The Fifth Bowl Judgment—This verse reveals a direct strike against the very throne—the seat of authority—of the Antichrist. The fifth bowl of judgment doesn't merely affect the environment or humanity's physical well-being it targets the center of evil power itself, the seat of the beast, most likely referring to the political and spiritual stronghold of the Antichrist's rule.

This judgment is personal. God aims His wrath at the beast's dominion, disrupting the seat of global tyranny and plunging it into a supernatural darkness—not mere absence of light, but a palpable, tormenting darkness, echoing the ninth plague of Egypt:

And the LORD said unto Moses, Stretch out your hand toward heaven, that there may be darkness over the land of Egypt, even darkness which may be felt. And Moses stretched forth his hand toward heaven; and there was a thick darkness in all the land of Egypt three days: They saw not one another, neither rose any from his place for three days: but all the children of Israel had light in their dwellings. (Exodus 10:21–23)

Just as Pharaoh resisted God's hand until crushed by His judgment, so too does the Antichrist persist in rebellion—only to be met with God's terrifying response: a judgment of painful confusion, despair, and spiritual blindness. The kingdom of the beast—once illuminated by satanic influence and counterfeit miracles—is now blanketed in divine darkness.

The phrase "they gnawed their tongues for pain" conveys both excruciating physical torment and deep psychological anguish. This may suggest neurological distress caused by supernatural darkness, demonic oppression, or a despair so overwhelming that people inflict pain on themselves in sheer agony.

This echoes the torment Jesus described in outer darkness, where there is weeping and gnashing of teeth (Matthew 22:13, 25:30).

This is not symbolic alone—it is literal and supernatural. Just as God caused the sun to go dark in Exodus and on the day of Christ's crucifixion (Luke 23:44–45), this plague plunges the Antichrist's dominion into a miraculous, divine blackout. It's an act that exposes the utter impotence of Satan's counterfeit light.

This darkness is also spiritual in meaning—a cultural collapse, the implosion of moral clarity, and a final gasp of a world without God. As Isaiah said:

> For, behold, the darkness shall cover the earth, and gross darkness the people: but the LORD shall arise upon you, and His glory shall be seen upon you. (Isaiah 60:2)

Despite this unbearable darkness and pain, there is no repentance. Instead of crying out for mercy, they blaspheme God. This shows the deep, final hardening of hearts in the Great Tribulation. Their hatred for God outweighs their suffering.

OLD TESTAMENT FORESHADOWS REVELATION:

> But with an overrunning flood He will make an utter end of the place thereof, and darkness shall pursue His enemies. (Nahum 1:8)

The Book of Nahum is a prophecy of God's coming judgment on Nineveh, but its themes of divine wrath and inescapable judgment foreshadow the Great Tribulation in Revelation. The phrase "darkness shall pursue His enemies" aligns with Revelation 16:10, where darkness overtakes the seat of the beast—God's direct enemies at the end of the age. It conveys a vivid picture: darkness as a divine weapon—not simply the absence of light, but a symbol of judgment, confusion, and separation from God.

THE REVELATION OF JESUS CHRIST REVEALS:

> 16:11 And blasphemed the God of Heaven because of their pains and their sores, and repented not of their deeds.

This verse is one of the most chilling indictments of the unrepentant human heart in the face of divine judgment. Despite the grievous sores from the first bowl (Revelation 16:2), the scorching heat from the fourth bowl (Revelation 16:8), and the supernatural darkness from the fifth bowl (Revelation 16:10), people still refuse to repent. Instead, they blaspheme God—cursing the very One who alone holds the power to save them.

- The pain and sores here are not simply physical afflictions; they are compounding torments stacked upon one another, symbolizing the weight of God's just wrath.
- Instead of crying out for mercy, they curse God, continuing in rebellion even when judgment confirms His power and presence.

- This isn't ignorance—it's defiance. The text reveals they know it's God who is behind the plagues.

"And repented not of their deeds." This tragic phrase is repeated through Revelation (Revelation 9:20–21), showing a pattern of hardened hearts. These people have seen the hand of God in unmistakable ways, have heard prophetic warnings—through angels, judgments, and witnesses—yet refuse to change.

This echoes the condition of Pharaoh in Egypt, whose heart grew harder with each plague until destruction followed. It also mirrors Paul's warnings in Romans 1:21–32 about those who suppress the truth and are given over to depraved minds.

- These judgments reveal character more than they change it.
- God's justice is vindicated, because even under the heaviest judgment, the wicked prove their rebellion.
- This verse demonstrates that pain alone doesn't produce repentance—only humility before God does.

Revelation 16:11 is a sobering reminder of what happens when the human heart continually resists God. It is possible to be so hardened that even divine wrath only deepens rebellion instead of breaking pride. The time to repent is now, while grace is still extended—because there comes a day when judgment will fall, and the door will be shut.

OLD TESTAMENT FORESHADOWS REVELATION:

And when Pharaoh saw that the rain and the hail and the thunders were ceased, he sinned yet more, and hardened his heart, he and his servants. (Exodus 9:34)

In both passages, divine judgment falls—plagues in Egypt, and bowls of wrath in Revelation. Both Pharaoh and the end-time rebels experience visible, undeniable signs from God, yet they refuse to repent. Instead of humility, they harden their hearts further, just as the people in Revelation blaspheme the God of Heaven even while suffering from pains and sores. This is the pattern of what theologians call judicial hardening—when a person continually rejects God's mercy, their heart becomes resistant to truth and repentance.

This shows us that Revelation is not just a New Testament book of judgment—it mirrors the very character and justice of God shown in the Old Testament as well.

THE REVELATION OF JESUS CHRIST REVEALS:

16:12 And the sixth angel poured out his vial upon the great river Euphrates; and the water thereof was dried up, that the way of the kings of the east might be prepared.

The Sixth Bowl Judgment—This verse sets the stage for the final military campaign of human history—the Battle of Armageddon. Here, the sixth bowl judgment affects a significant geographical and prophetic location: the Euphrates River. This river has long served as a natural boundary between East and West—both politically and spiritually.

The Euphrates: more than a river:

- The Euphrates is mentioned 25 times in Scripture, often symbolizing the boundary between God's land and hostile nations (Genesis 15:18).
- In ancient times, it was the cradle of civilization—Babylon, Assyria, Sumer—and here becomes the grave of rebellion.
- The angel's act of drying up the Euphrates is a direct supernatural intervention, removing barriers for military advancement from the East.

Who are the kings of the East? The phrase "kings of the east" literally translates to "kings of the rising sun" (Greek: *Anatole heliou*). This may point toward modern eastern powers, such as China, which today fields the largest standing army in the world (over 2 million soldiers). Their movement across a dried Euphrates suggests a massive land invasion—likely on foot or with ground military vehicles, emphasizing scale and intent.

Though not mentioned in verse 12, the following verses (13–14) clarify that the real force gathering these armies is demonic. Three unclean spirits, like frogs, come from the mouths of the dragon (Satan), the beast (the Antichrist), and the False Prophet. These demonic spirits perform signs and seduce the kings of the world into assembling for a war they cannot win—against God Himself.

OLD TESTAMENT FORESHADOWS REVELATION:

And the LORD shall utterly destroy the tongue of the Egyptian sea; and with His mighty wind shall He shake His hand over the river, and shall strike it in the seven streams, and make men cross over dry-shod. And there shall be a highway for the remnant of His people, who will be left from Assyria, as it was for Israel in the day that he came up from the land of Egypt. (Isaiah 11:15–16)

Both passages describe a divine act of drying up a major waterway; in Isaiah, it's for Israel's deliverance; in Revelation, it's to prepare the way for judgment. Isaiah 11:15–16 speaks of God preparing a highway for His people's return. Revelation 16:12 speaks of the kings of the east being drawn into judgment via a supernaturally dried Euphrates. In both Isaiah and Revelation, God alters geography to fulfill His redemptive or judicial purpose.

THE REVELATION OF JESUS CHRIST REVEALS:

16:13 And I saw three unclean spirits like frogs come out of the mouth of the dragon, and out of the mouth of the beast, and out of the mouth of the false prophet.

This verse reveals one of the most disturbing supernatural moments in the Book of Revelation. As the sixth angel pours out his vial, John sees three unclean spirits "like frogs"—symbolic of impurity, deception, and plague—emerge from the mouths of the dragon (Satan), the beast (the Antichrist), and the False Prophet. These entities form an unholy trinity: a counterfeit of the holy trinity, the Father, the Son, and the Holy Spirit.

They are not literal frogs, but John likens their appearance or behavior to frogs—perhaps loud, unrelenting, and spiritually repulsive. Frogs, in Jewish culture, were considered ceremonially unclean (Leviticus 11:10), and in the second plague of Egypt (Exodus 8:1–15), frogs became a sign of judgment.

Verse 14 explains their purpose: "For they are the spirits of devils, working miracles, which go forth unto the kings of the earth and of the whole world." These demon spirits perform deceptive miracles—counterfeit signs—to influence world leaders and gather them for war. This is not human diplomacy or political strategy. This is supernatural manipulation. Evil spirits are the true force behind the global militarization and unification against Israel.

Just as God allowed a lying spirit to persuade Ahab through his false prophets (1 Kings 22:19–23), here too we see God permitting demonic spirits to fulfill His divine plan. This is a case of judicial deception—God giving people over to what they've already chosen (Romans 1:28, 2 Thessalonians 2:9–12).

These three unclean spirits go out "to the kings of the earth and of the whole world, to gather them to the battle of that great day of God Almighty" (Revelation 16:14). That battlefield will be Armageddon—a literal place in Israel (Revelation 16:16), specifically the Valley of Megiddo.

There will be no emails, no United Nations summits, no official invitations. The calling to war is spiritual and demonic. The leaders of the world—perhaps even unknowingly—are being drawn into a trap of divine judgment.

Why foot soldiers?

The presence of millions of foot soldiers (not merely missile strikes or drones) emphasizes that the goal is occupation—not annihilation. Armies will seek to possess Israel, likely to establish military control and governance. However, God Himself intervenes.

Isaiah's prophetic parallel: the winepress of wrath—Isaiah 63:1–6 offers a stunning parallel. The Messiah, returning in judgment, is described as coming from Edom and Bozrah, garments stained with blood from treading the winepress—a symbolic image used again in Revelation 14:19–20. (Edom is primarily located in what is now southern Jordan—especially the area south of the Dead Sea and around the mountainous region of Petra. Bozrah is widely believed to correspond to the modern town of Busaira—or Buseirah—in southern Jordan, not far from Petra.)

This shows that Jesus Himself personally executes vengeance on the nations gathered against Israel. He is the Warrior-King, coming not as the Lamb but as the Lion of Judah.

OLD TESTAMENT FORESHADOWS REVELATION:

And Aaron stretched out his hand over the waters of Egypt; and the frogs came up, and covered the land of Egypt. And the magicians did so with their enchantments, and brought up frogs upon the land of Egypt. (Exodus 8:6–7)

The frogs in Exodus invaded every part of Egyptian life, making clear that no corner of rebellion is safe from judgment. In Revelation, the unclean spirits like frogs invaded global leadership, preparing the world for its final rebellion—the Battle of Armageddon. This is a profound echo that what began in Egypt's resistance to God ends in the world's final stand against Him.

THE REVELATION OF JESUS CHRIST REVEALS:

16:14 For they are the spirits of devils, working miracles, which go forth to the kings of the earth and of the whole world, to gather them to the battle of that great day of God Almighty.

This verse reveals a terrifying truth—that miracle-working demons will be released in the end times, sent on a global mission to deceive the rulers of the earth. These spirits are not merely symbolic. They are literal demonic agents that proceed from the mouths of the unholy trinity: the dragon (Satan), the beast (the Antichrist), and the False Prophet.

And what is their purpose?

To gather the world for war—not just any war, but "the battle of that great day of God Almighty." The showdown at Armageddon.

Satan has always sought to counterfeit the miraculous to lead people away from the truth (2 Thessalonians 2:9). From Pharaoh's magicians mimicking Moses to the sorcerers of Acts, deception has always followed lying wonders. But in Revelation, the deception is at a cosmic level—rulers, nations, generals, and kings all fall prey.

Today, we are already witnessing the foreshadowing of this deception. You can see it in:

- The rise of global antisemitism.

- The godless leaders who blaspheme truth, jail believers, legislate evil.
- Even in churches that once preached holiness but now tolerate compromise. Yes—even some professing Christians are under the influence of a spirit that resists repentance. They are becoming accustomed to hardening their hearts, resisting conviction, and treating prophetic warnings as noise.

Just as God allowed a lying spirit to persuade Ahab in 1 Kings 22, He will again allow unclean spirits to draw the rebellious into judgment. These kings and armies won't be dragged by force. They will come willingly, passionately, under the belief that they are finally going to solve the Middle East problem—and eliminate Israel once and for all. That is the great deception.

- There is a spiritual summons happening right now. The world is being postured. The spirits are already whispering. The hatred of Israel is no accident—it is prophetic.
- The stage is set. Even before the Rapture, we can feel the winds of Revelation 16 rising.
- This isn't just a future warning—it's a current call. If you can't respond to the Holy Spirit now, what makes you think you would later?

Just as these devils call the kings to war, the Holy Spirit is calling the Church to worship, to repentance, to readiness. Will you listen to the Holy Spirit—or will you ignore His voice until it's too late?

OLD TESTAMENT FORESHADOWS REVELATION:

And there came forth a spirit, and stood before the LORD, and said, I will persuade him. And the LORD said unto him, Wherewith? And he said, I will go forth, and I will be a lying spirit in the mouth of all his prophets. And He said, You shalt persuade him, and prevail also: go forth, and do so. Now therefore, behold, the LORD has put a lying spirit in the mouth of all. These your prophets, and the LORD has spoken evil concerning you. (1 Kings 22:21–23)

Just as lying spirits persuaded King Ahab to enter a fatal battle, unclean spirits in Revelation deceive the kings of the world. In both accounts, God permits the spirits to carry out their mission to bring judgment. Ahab thought he would win, but it lead to his death. Likewise, the kings of Revelation are led into the trap of Armageddon by deceptive signs and false promises.

THE REVELATION OF JESUS CHRIST REVEALS:

16:15 Behold, I come as a thief. Blessed is he that watches, and keeps his garments, lest he walk naked, and they see his shame.

In the midst of catastrophic judgments and global rebellion, Jesus suddenly interjects this urgent warning. It's a personal appeal, a flash of grace in a chapter dominated by wrath. These are red-letter words—the voice of Christ Himself cutting through the chaos, reminding the reader: "I am still coming. Don't be caught unaware."

The phrase "I come as a thief" echoes earlier New Testament teachings (Matthew 24:42–44; 1 Thessalonians 5:2) where the unexpectedness of His return is emphasized. A thief doesn't send a notice. He comes when people least expect it. This does not imply Jesus is a thief, but rather that His coming will be sudden, unannounced, and will catch many unprepared.

The blessing is pronounced: "Blessed is he that watches." This speaks of spiritual vigilance. A heart that is not lulled to sleep by compromise or wearied by the delay. To watch is to stay awake, alert, and sensitive to the Spirit's leading—especially in dark and deceiving times.

"And keeps his garments." In Revelation, garments symbolize righteousness (Revelation 3:4–5, 19:8). To keep one's garments means to guard your spiritual integrity, to walk in purity, repentance, and readiness. It is the opposite of carelessness or defilement.

"Lest he walk naked, and they see his shame." This is not about physical nakedness, but spiritual exposure. In the Day of Judgment, all will be revealed. Those who have not stayed clothed in Christ's righteousness will be exposed in their shame—stripped of every excuse, left uncovered before a holy God.

Jesus places this sobering verse right between demonic deception (verse 14) and the gathering for Armageddon (verse 16)—as if to say: "Even now, there's still time to wake up. Even in the darkest moment, the light of repentance can shine." This is an altar call in the middle of a war zone. A plea of mercy in the valley of judgment.

OLD TESTAMENT FORESHADOWS REVELATION:

And the eyes of them both were opened, and they knew that they were naked; and they sewed fig leaves together, and made themselves aprons. And they heard the voice of the Lord GOD, walking in the garden in the cool of the day: and Adam and his wife hid themselves from the presence of the Lord GOD amongst the trees of the garden. And the Lord GOD called unto Adam, and said unto him, Where are you? And he said, I heard Your voice in the garden, and I was afraid, because I was naked; and I hid myself. And He said, Who told you that you were naked? Have you eaten of the tree, whereof I commanded you that you should not eat? (Genesis 3:7–11)

Revelation 16:15 echoes Eden. Just as Adam and Eve lost their covering through disobedience, so can believers who cease to remain spiritually alert. To "keep one's garments" means to stay clothed in Christ's righteousness, walking in holiness and readiness. In Genesis 3:7–11, shame led to hiding. In Revelation, the warning is clear: don't be found spiritually naked when Christ returns. Fig leaves of self-effort won't cover us—only His grace will. The question remains: Are we watching? Are we clothed? Will we be ready?

THE REVELATION OF JESUS CHRIST REVEALS:

16:16 And He gathered them together into a place called in the Hebrew tongue Armageddon.

This single verse carries a weight of history, prophecy, and finality that reverberates throughout all of Scripture. Armageddon is not merely a location— it is a divine rendezvous point for the final confrontation between the forces of evil and the King of kings.

This verse reveals the culmination of demonic persuasion (verses 13–14), where the dragon (Satan), the beast (the Antichrist), and the False Prophet send out unclean spirits to stir up world leaders. Their armies are summoned not by military orders or political treaties—but by demonic deception. Yet, despite this rebellion, it is ultimately God who allows this gathering. The phrase "He gathered them" shows divine sovereignty over even the rebellious acts of men.

What is Armageddon?

"Armageddon" comes from the Hebrew *Har-Megiddo*, meaning "mountain of Megiddo." Though there is no specific mountain by that name. Megiddo is a strategic and storied location in Israel's history, located about 60 miles north of Jerusalem near the Jezreel Valley—a natural battleground that has hosted more conflicts than nearly any place on earth.

This region has witnessed pivotal military confrontations:

- Judges 4–5—Deborah and Barak defeated Sisera and his 900 iron chariots at the river Kishon near Megiddo.
- Judges 7—Gideon's 300 defeated the Midianites, Amalekites, and "the children of the east."
- 1 Samuel 31—King Saul was slain by the Philistines on nearby Mount Gilboa.
- 2 Kings 9:27—Ahaziah, king of Judah, was fatally wounded by Jehu near Megiddo.
- 2 Kings 23:29–30—The godly King Josiah was killed by Pharaoh Necho at Megiddo.
- In more modern history, Napoleon Bonaparte said the Jezreel Valley was the most natural battlefield he'd ever seen.

This land soaked with blood, victory, and judgment will serve as the final stage for the most climactic confrontation in world history.

Armageddon is the final exposure of human pride, religious deception, and political rebellion. The nations gather thinking they are launching war against Israel or each other—but ultimately, they are rising up against the Lamb (Revelation 17:14). Their doom is certain.

This is not just a political war—it is spiritual warfare manifesting physically, where Christ returns as Judge and King to destroy the armies of the beast.

OLD TESTAMENT FORESHADOWS REVELATION:

Therefore wait you upon Me, says the LORD, until the day that I rise up to the prey: for My determination is to gather the nations, that I may assemble the kingdoms, to pour upon them My indignation, even all My fierce anger; for all the earth shall be devoured with the fire of My jealousy. (Zephaniah 3:8)

In both verses, God is the One gathering the nations—this is no accidental conflict; it is a divinely orchestrated judgment. Zephaniah 3:8 says, "all the earth shall be devoured," and Revelation 16:16 confirms this is a worldwide conflict drawn into one fateful battlefield. Both passages focus on the fury, jealousy, and wrath of God being unleashed in a final showdown between righteousness and rebellion.

THE REVELATION OF JESUS CHRIST REVEALS:

16:17 And the seventh angel poured out his vial into the air; and there came a great voice out of the temple of heaven, from the throne, saying, It is done.

The Seventh Bowl Judgment—This verse marks the climactic moment of God's final series of judgments—the seventh bowl poured out into the air, targeting the very atmosphere that surrounds all creation. It is the last and most sweeping act of divine wrath in the Great Tribulation.

"And the seventh angel poured out his vial into the air." This final bowl targets the very atmosphere enveloping the planet—completing God's judgment not only on individuals or systems, but on creation itself. Though Satan was once called "the prince of the power of the air" (Ephesians 2:2), during the bowl judgments—the final 3 ½ years of Daniel's 70th Week—he has already been cast down to earth (Revelation 12:9). This climactic act declares that no realm is exempt from God's wrath: earth, sea, rivers, sun, darkness—and now the very air itself—fall under His judgment. The devastation is total. The kingdom of the beast collapses. Heaven thunders, "It is done."

"And there came a great voice out of the temple of heaven, from the throne." This is no ordinary voice—this is the voice of God Himself, speaking from His heavenly throne. It is final. It is absolute. And it echoes back to Jesus' words on the Cross:

> When Jesus therefore had received the vinegar, He said, It is finished: and He bowed His head, and gave up the ghost. (John 19:30)

But whereas Jesus' cry on the Cross declared the completion of redemption, this cry—"It is done"—declares the completion of judgment.

"Saying, It is done." Three of the most sobering words in all of Scripture. No more bowls. No more chances. The cup of God's wrath has been poured to the last drop. Every offer of grace has now been refused. Every trumpet has sounded. Every seal has been broken. And now, God's justice has run its full course.

This is the final reference to the Heavenly Temple in Revelation. It has served as the launching point for divine judgments (Revelation 11:19, 15:5–8), but now, with the declaration "It is done," the temple is no longer the center of activity—God's justice has been executed. The era of mercy has closed, and the final acts of wrath are unfolding.

OLD TESTAMENT FORESHADOWS REVELATION:

> Behold, it is come, and it is done, says the Lord GOD; this is the day whereof I have spoken. (Ezekiel 39:8)

Both verses emphasize finality, divine authority, and completion of God's predetermined judgment. In Ezekiel 39:8, the prophecy refers to the destruction of Gog and his armies—a climactic judgment against the enemies of Israel. In Revelation 16:17, the seventh bowl marks the last outpouring of God's wrath before the return of Christ. The language in both is strikingly similar: "It is done" in Revelation and "It is come, and it is done" in Ezekiel. These declarations signal the fulfillment of long-awaited prophetic events, where God's sovereignty and justice are dramatically and unmistakably displayed for all the world to witness.

THE REVELATION OF JESUS CHRIST REVEALS:

> 16:18 And there were voices, and thunders, and lightnings; and there was a great earthquake, such as was not since men were upon the earth, so mighty an earthquake, and so great.

This verse signals one of the most terrifying and awe-inspiring climaxes in all of the Book of Revelation. It comes immediately after the seventh and final bowl is poured out. When the voice from heaven declares, "It is done" (verse 17), verse 18 unleashes a cataclysmic reaction—an unprecedented shaking of both heaven and earth. This is not merely poetic language; it marks a literal, divine upheaval of creation itself, underscoring the finality and force of God's judgment.

This trio—"voices, and thunders, and lightnings"—has appeared repeatedly throughout Revelation as a hallmark of divine judgment and the majesty of God's throne (see Revelation 4:5, 8:5, 11:19). These are not random noises—they are heaven's alarm bells, signaling that God Himself is intervening. They mark transitions of judgment and divine activity, reminding us that heaven is not passive. God is not silent. His throne speaks with power, and His presence now shakes creation to its core.

"And there was a great earthquake . . . so mighty an earthquake, and so great." This is not a localized tremor—it is global, cataclysmic, and without precedent. The repetition intensifies the description, leaving no doubt about its severity. Scripture itself underscores the uniqueness: "such as was not since men were upon the earth." This is the final and most violent shaking in human history—surpassing every natural disaster ever recorded. It is the physical unraveling of a world in rebellion, signaling that the kingdom of man is collapsing under the weight of divine judgment.

This earthquake:

- Splits cities (Revelation 16:19).
- Reshapes the earth (Revelation 16:20).
- Signals the end of the present world order—physically, politically, and spiritually.

It's the culmination of wrath—the final, physical consequence before the appearance of Christ at His Second Coming (Revelation 19).

The shaking in Revelation 16:18 is more than geological—it's spiritual, political, and cosmic. God is dismantling the old order in preparation for the Kingdom of His Son. The throne of the beast is broken. The systems of Mystery Babylon (America) begin to fall (Revelation 17–18). What God starts with thunder, He ends with a quake. This is not just judgment—it is a final call to recognize that only what is unshakable will remain (Hebrews 12:27).

> And this word, yet once more, signifies the removing of those things that are shaken, as of things that are made, that those things which cannot be shaken may remain. (Hebrews 12:27)

OLD TESTAMENT FORESHADOWS REVELATION:

> For thus says the LORD of hosts; Yet once, it is a little while, and I will shake the heavens, and the earth, and the sea, and the dry land; And I will shake all nations, and the desire of all nations shall come: and I will fill this house with glory, says the LORD of hosts. (Haggai 2:6–7)

"I will shake the heavens and the earth" directly parallels the unprecedented earthquake in Revelation 16:18. The shaking of all nations aligns with the global scope of the final bowl judgment. Haggai 2:6–7 links this shaking to the coming of the "desire of all nations"—a messianic reference to Jesus Christ, foreshadowing His Second Coming. Revelation 16:18 is the immediate precursor to the return of Christ in Revelation 19.

THE REVELATION OF JESUS CHRIST REVEALS:

16:19 And the great city was divided into three parts, and the cities of the nations fell: and great Babylon came in remembrance before God, to give to her the cup of the wine of the fierceness of His wrath.

This verse marks a climactic moment in God's final judgment—a massive, literal upheaval that fractures the great city, causes the cities of the nations to collapse, and brings Babylon—America (Revelation 17–18)—to remembrance before God. It is not just geological; it is judicial. The physical shaking reflects the fall of global systems that have long defied the Lord. Babylon—representing the apex of rebellion and idolatry—is now called to drink the full cup of divine wrath. What humanity built in pride, God now tears down in justice.

"And the great city was divided into three parts." Bible scholars often debate the identity of this "great city." Some suggest Jerusalem, others see it as Babylon, either literal or symbolic. Regardless, the division into three parts may represent total disruption, fragmentation, and collapse of what was once unified—politically, religiously, or economically. God is unraveling the pride and false unity of a world built in rebellion to Him.

"And the cities of the nations fell." This isn't just one city—it's global. Every city, every monument to human pride and self-sufficiency, crumbles under the weight of divine wrath. Skyscrapers, capitals, financial centers—all are reduced to rubble. Revelation 16:18 speaks of an earthquake "such as was not since men were upon the earth," and this is its effect: a worldwide collapse of civilization as we know it. It's as though the entire infrastructure of human power is being dismantled to make way for the Kingdom of Christ.

"And great Babylon came in remembrance before God." God never forgets righteousness—and He never overlooks wickedness. Babylon here represents the culmination of human rebellion, false religion, and corrupt power. "Came in remembrance" doesn't mean God had forgotten her—it means her judgment was now fully due. The time of patience is over. Her sins have reached heaven (Revelation 18:5), and now God pours the cup of His fierce wrath upon her.

"To give her the cup of the wine of the fierceness of His wrath." This is a direct reversal of what Babylon offers the world. She gave nations her intoxicating cup of immorality and spiritual adultery (Revelation 17:2). Now she must drink God's cup—not of pleasure, but of punishment. The imagery of wine in a cup represents something overflowing and inescapable. Babylon will drink every last drop of the judgment she stored up over the centuries.

- This verse is not just about structures falling—it's about systems collapsing. Economic, political, and spiritual empires that defy God will not stand.
- No city is too great to fall. The fall of Babylon warns us that human achievement apart from God is destined for destruction.
- What the world builds without God, God will shake apart. What He builds, no man can destroy.

OLD TESTAMENT FORESHADOWS REVELATION:

And Babylon, the glory of kingdoms, the beauty of the Chaldees' excellency, shall be as when God overthrew Sodom and Gomorrah. (Isaiah 13:19)

Both verses speak of Babylon's fall as a deliberate act of divine judgment. Revelation 16:19 emphasizes God remembering Babylon—meaning her sins have reached full measure. Isaiah 13:19 compares her fate to Sodom and Gomorrah, cities destroyed by fire and brimstone in divine wrath.

This connection shows how the end times judgment of Babylon is not new—it's a recurring theme in Scripture that underscores God's justice and the final fall of rebellious world systems.

THE REVELATION OF JESUS CHRIST REVEALS:

16:20 And every island fled away, and the mountains were not found.

This verse follows the pouring out of the seventh bowl of God's wrath, marking the final wave of catastrophic judgment upon the earth. What we see here is not merely poetic exaggeration—it is geological upheaval on a global scale, unlike anything humanity has ever witnessed.

The text tells us that:

- "Every island fled away"—This suggests that islands, often isolated and serene, will be submerged, scattered, or violently shifted by the earth's final and greatest quake.
- "And the mountains were not found"—Mountains, symbols of strength and permanence, will crumble or flatten, possibly swallowed by shifting tectonic plates or reduced by supernatural force.

This is not merely a natural disaster—it is a supernatural dismantling of creation itself. The shaking of the earth signals not just seismic upheaval but divine uncreation, a deliberate tearing down of the old world in preparation for the new heaven and new earth (Revelation 21:1). The scale of destruction is beyond comprehension: earthquakes of this magnitude would unleash global tsunamis, perhaps explaining why entire islands "flee." Mountains crumble, topography is rewritten, and with it, the very framework of civilization collapses. This is the end of the old order—and the world as we know it.

This verse signifies more than just an earthquake—it marks the collapse of every manmade and natural symbol of stability. Mountains vanish, islands flee, and the illusion of earthly security is shattered. What remains is not geography, but God's throne and His unshakable Kingdom. It is a final reminder: everything built by human hands will fall, but only God endures forever.

OLD TESTAMENT FORESHADOWS REVELATION:

The hills melted like wax at the presence of the LORD, at the presence of the LORD of the whole earth. (Psalm 97:5)

This verse captures the raw, unstoppable force of God's presence—a presence so holy and consuming that even the mightiest mountains dissolve like wax. Psalm 97:5 is a perfect Old Testament parallel to Revelation 16:20, where "every island fled away, and the mountains were not found." The imagery reinforces that when God rises to judge the earth, nothing—not even the most immovable parts of creation—can stand in His way.

THE REVELATION OF JESUS CHRIST REVEALS:

16:21 And there fell upon men a great hail out of heaven, every stone about the weight of a talent: and men blasphemed God because of the plague of the hail; for the plague thereof was exceeding great.

This verse closes the final bowl judgments with one of the most terrifying natural phenomena described in all of Scripture—a storm of hailstones, each weighing approximately a talent (about 100 to 150 pounds), falling from the sky. This isn't symbolic—it's literal, physical devastation from heaven. Hailstones of this magnitude would be capable of obliterating buildings, smashing vehicles, and crushing people under their massive weight.

Throughout the Bible, hail has been used as a weapon of divine judgment:

- Exodus 9:23–24—Hail plagued Egypt in one of the ten judgments.
- Joshua 10:11—God rained down hail on the enemies of Israel.
- Isaiah 28:17—"Hail shall sweep away the refuge of lies."

Yet here in Revelation 16:21, it is not just regional—it's global and final. It underscores that nature itself, under divine command, becomes the tool of judgment against hardened humanity.

But what's most sobering is the reaction.

Rather than fall to their knees in repentance, "men blasphemed God." Even in the face of catastrophic wrath, their hearts remain defiant. This is a devastating portrayal of judicial hardening—where, after so many chances to repent, the human heart chooses cursing over contrition.

God is not unjust in this judgment. These are those who have:

- Rejected His Son.
- Murdered His saints.
- Worshiped the beast.
- Blasphemed His name.
- Refused every warning.

And now the cup of wrath is full.

OLD TESTAMENT FORESHADOWS REVELATION:

And it came to pass, as they fled from before Israel, and were in the going down to Bethhoron, that the LORD cast down great stones from heaven upon them unto Azekah, and they died: they were more which died with hailstones than they whom the children of Israel slew with the sword. (Joshua 10:11)

In both Joshua 10:11 and Revelation 16:21, hailstones are used by God as direct instruments of judgment from heaven. In Joshua's time, it was a regional act of divine warfare to defend His covenant people. In Revelation, it is a global act of final wrath upon a rebellious world that has rejected Christ and blasphemed His name. This connection shows the consistency of God's justice across Scripture—He uses nature to execute judgment when human rebellion reaches its fullest.

Irene looked shaken. "Ann . . . I can't stop thinking about what you said earlier. After the seal and trumpet judgments, the population drops to about 3 billion. But that doesn't even include the 1.5 billion Tribulation martyrs—or the losses during the bowl judgments. So . . . where does that leave us?"

I nodded solemnly. "You're right. Let's break it down. We start with 8 billion people worldwide. The Rapture takes many—perhaps several hundred million. Then war, famine, pestilence, natural disasters, and the trumpet judgments reduce the population to roughly 3 billion."

Irene leaned in. "And then another 1.5 billion are martyred?"

"Exactly," I said. "Faithful Tribulation saints who die for Christ's name. That would leave about 1.5 billion."

She exhaled. "And then come the bowls."

"Yes," I said softly. "Here's the key difference: the seals and trumpets impacted one-third, one-fourth, or specific portions of the earth. But the bowl judgments? They're total. No fractions. No restraint. No pause. It's God's full wrath—poured out without mixture."

"So how many survive?" she whispered.

"Very few," I replied. "If we're estimating conservatively, perhaps 200 to 400 million make it to the end—maybe even less."

Her eyes widened. "That's like the current U.S. population. Out of 8 billion?"

"Exactly," I said. "From 8 billion to a remnant. Isaiah said, 'Few men are left' (Isaiah 24:6). Zechariah wrote that two-thirds would perish, and only one-third would remain to be refined (Zechariah 13:8–9)."

Irene looked down, then back at me. "So after the Rapture . . . seals and trumpets bring us to 3 billion. Then we subtract 1.5 billion martyrs. And the bowls possibly reduce us to less than 5 percent of the original population."

"That's the picture Revelation gives," I said. "Jesus warned us in Matthew 24:22, 'Except those days should be shortened, there should no flesh be saved.'"

Tears welled in her eyes. "I'm stunned. The numbers, the scale, the suffering—it's hard to grasp. And yet . . . I'm overwhelmed by the grace that anyone is saved at all."

I nodded. "That's what keeps me going. God has extended mercy again and again. But there comes a point when the window closes."

Her voice was soft. "Ann . . . this makes me want to pray harder. Warn louder. Love deeper. We're still in the age of grace, right?"

"We are," I said. "And this is our moment. Because when those bowls are poured out—it's too late."

———◆◆◆———

SUMMARY OF REVELATION 15–16

Revelation 15 and 16 present the final, climactic expression of God's wrath poured out upon the unrepentant world. These chapters mark the end of divine patience and the full unveiling of righteous judgment on those who have persistently rejected God's mercy.

Chapter 15 begins with John seeing seven angels with seven last plagues— "for in them is filled up the wrath of God" (Revelation 15:1). Before the plagues are unleashed, John beholds a victorious group of saints standing on a sea of glass mingled with fire (Revelation 15:2). These are the overcomers—those who refused the mark of the beast and remained faithful. They sing the song of Moses and the song of the Lamb (Revelation 15:3–4), symbolizing the unity of the Old and New Covenants, and declaring God's power, justice, and holiness.

Next, the temple in heaven is opened, revealing the tabernacle of testimony (Revelation 15:5). Seven angels emerge, clothed in pure white linen with golden sashes, ready to administer judgment. One of the four living creatures gives them golden bowls filled with the wrath of God (Revelation 15:6–7). The temple fills with smoke from the glory and power of God, and no one can enter until the judgments are complete (Revelation 15:8)—a striking sign that intercession is over, and judgment has begun.

In chapter 16, the seven angels unleash swift, devastating judgments.

1. **First Bowl**—Grievous sores (Revelation 16:2).
2. **Second Bowl**—Sea becomes blood (Revelation 16:3).
3. **Third Bowl**—Freshwaters become blood (Revelation 16:4).
4. **Fourth Bowl**—Scorching heat (Revelation 16:8).
5. **Fifth Bowl**—Darkness on the beast's kingdom (Revelation 16:10).
6. **Sixth Bowl**—Euphrates River dries up (Revelation 16:12–16).
7. **Seventh Bowl**—Global earthquake and hail (Revelation 16:17–21).

KEY TAKEAWAYS

- The wrath of God is final and righteous—These judgments are not arbitrary but are the just consequence of humanity's rebellion and persecution of God's people.
- Mercy has a deadline—The course of the Heavenly Temple (Revelation 15:8) signifies the end of intercession. Time has run out.
- The hardened heart will not repent—Even under extreme suffering, humanity curses God rather than turning to Him.
- Spiritual deception is real and powerful—Unclean spirits lead the nations to Armageddon, showing the world's final, unified rebellion.
- God remains sovereign—Despite chaos on earth, everything unfolds according to God's divine timetable. The declaration "It is done" (Revelation 16:17) parallels Jesus' words on the Cross—showing that just as redemption was finished, so too now is judgment.

Revelation 15 and 16 are sobering chapters that remind us of both God's longsuffering mercy and His ultimate justice. They affirm that the time of grace will end and judgment is certain, but even amid wrath, the overcomers stand victorious, praising the Lamb. These chapters are both a warning and a comfort: a warning to the rebellious and a comfort to the faithful, assuring us that evil will not go unpunished, and that God's Kingdom will prevail.

Chapter 15

Revelation 17: Interlude— Religious Babylon Riding Political Power

MYSTERY BABYLON REVEALED—The Spiritual Harlot Behind Global Dominion. Revelation 17 unveils one of the most haunting figures in all of prophecy—Mystery Babylon the Great, "the mother of harlots and abominations of the earth" (Revelation 17:5). This chapter is not merely symbolic; it prophetically exposes a corrupt global religious system that seduces nations, manipulates rulers, and spreads spiritual corruption across the earth.

John is carried by the Spirit into the wilderness and shown a woman seated on a scarlet beast covered in blasphemous names. She's clothed in purple and scarlet, adorned with gold, precious stones, and pearls, holding a golden cup brimming with abominations. Her appearance is extravagant—yet deeply disturbing. This vision is meant to be understood, not dismissed. It reveals a spiritual system that allies itself with political power, exalts false worship, and deceives the world—until her final judgment comes.

THE RISE AND FALL OF A GLOBAL SUPERPOWER: AMERICA

For generations, interpreters have pointed to ancient Rome or a revived European empire as the identity of the mysterious woman in Revelation 17. Others have looked to Babylon in modern-day Iraq. But in light of current global realities and prophetic fingerprints, a growing number of scholars and watchmen are reconsidering that conclusion. Instead of an ancient city, many now see a modern empire cloaked in wealth, influence, and spiritual seduction: the United States of America.

To be clear: when we speak of "America," in this context, we mean the United States—not the broader North America continent that includes Canada, Mexico, and Greenland. The U.S. alone matches the full spectrum of prophetic traits described in Revelation 17–18: the economic superpower, the cultural exporter, the political seductress, and the spiritual deceiver.

America in the Theater of Bible Prophecy

While the United States is not geographically within the original "Bible Lands," one often-overlooked hypothesis brings her directly into the end-time stage. Revelation 6:12–14 describes a cataclysm so great that it may reshape the very structure of the earth. Some believe this global upheaval could return the planet to a single landmass—just as it was in the beginning (Genesis 1:9–10, 2:10–14).

Should the continents be restored to a pre-divided landmass, North America could become physically linked to Eurasia and the Middle East—positioning the U.S. directly within the prophetic stage foretold in Scripture (see map, page 15).

Following the sixth seal, the trumpet judgments devastate one-third of the earth, possibly affecting the southern hemisphere. What remains? A dominant northern supercontinent—anchored by Eurasia and America. In this scenario, the United States not only survives—it ascends as the final global superpower.

A Superpower Unmasked

If this prophetic scenario proves true, it redefines how we understand Babylon's final emergence. America would stand uniquely positioned to fulfill the role of Mystery Babylon—the woman who rides the beast. She is rich, powerful, and deeply influential. She is drunk with the blood of the saints. Her reach encircles the earth. And her fall will send shockwaves across nations.

Revelation 17 focuses on the political dimension of this end-time empire. The woman rides the beast—symbolizing governmental dominion driven by spiritual compromise. She is not the beast herself, but she controls it . . . for a time.

This is the unholy fusion of political power and religious deception—global dominance rooted in rebellion. It's the story of a nation that once revered God but now uses its influence to seduce, dominate, and deceive.

John writes that she "sits on many waters," a phrase later defined in Revelation 17:15 as "peoples, multitudes, nations, and tongues." This is not a localized kingdom—it is a global empire, veiled in liberty but spiritually bankrupt. A land that persecutes the righteous while promoting rebellion in the name of progress. Eventually, the beast turns on her. Revelation 17:16 reveals that the Antichrist will despise the woman, strip her bare, and burn her with fire. The empire that once ruled is betrayed by the very system it helped create.

Prophetic Clues From Isaiah and Jeremiah

Though America is never named in Scripture, the prophetic characteristics found in Isaiah 18 and Jeremiah 50–51 are too specific to ignore. These passages describe a dominant, prideful nation across the seas—rich in treasure, mingled with many peoples, and destined for judgment. The clues are embedded not in names, but in unmistakable traits.

Let's begin with Isaiah 18:1–2:

> Woe to the land shadowing with wings, which is beyond the rivers of Ethiopia: That sends ambassadors by the sea, even in vessels of bulrushes upon the waters, saying, Go, you swift messengers, to a nation scattered and peeled, to a people terrible from their beginning onward; a nation meted out and trodden down, whose land the rivers have spoiled! (Isaiah 18:1–2)

Key traits:

- "Shadowing with wings"—America's national symbol is the bald eagle.
- "Beyond the rivers of Ethiopia"—From Israel's vantage, this points west, across the Atlantic.
- "Scattered and peeled"—America spans from coasts and time zones.
- "Meted out and trodden down"—A land divided into states, counties, and districts.
- "Whose land the rivers have spoiled"—A nation whose rivers bear the marks of industrial exploitation.

Now, consider Jeremiah 50–51:

> Your mother shall be sore confounded; she that bare you shall be ashamed: behold, the hindermost (youngest) of the nations shall be a wilderness, a dry land, and a desert. (Jeremiah 50:12)

> A sword is upon their horses, and upon their chariots, and upon all the mingled people that are in the midst of her; and they shall become as women: a sword is upon her treasures; and they shall be robbed. (Jeremiah 50:37)

> O you that dwell upon many waters, abundant in treasures, your end is come, and the measure of your covetousness. (Jeremiah 51:13)

> Though Babylon should mount up to heaven, and though she should fortify the height of her strength, yet from Me shall spoilers come unto her, says the LORD. (Jeremiah 51:53)

More clues:

- "Your mother shall be sore confounded"—America's founding mother is Great Britain.
- "Hindermost of the nations"—The U.S. is one of the youngest empires in prophetic scope.
- "Mingled people"—A tapestry of ethnic and cultural diversity unmatched in history.
- "Abundant in treasures"—The most materially prosperous nation on earth.
- "Dwelling on many waters"—Positioned between the Atlantic and Pacific, bordering lakes and rivers.
- "Mount up to heaven"—First to the moon. Now aiming for Mars.

Together, these fingerprints paint a mosaic that fits no ancient empire—but mirrors the modern United States. This Babylon does not rise from the ruins of Rome or the sands of Iraq. She rises from the power centers of today: Wall Street, Hollywood, Silicon Valley, and Washington, D.C.

WHY GOD PAUSES FOR BABYLON

Revelation 17 and 18 are not chronological progressions—they're parenthetical interludes. These chapters zoom in to highlight Babylon's fall, first announced in Revelation 14:8 and again in Revelation 16:19. Before we witness the return of Christ in Revelation 19—before the final Battle of Armageddon—God pauses to judge Babylon.

Why the pause?

Because Babylon is the hinge point of the end-time world system. Her spiritual pride, global deception, moral rebellion, and seductive influence has touched every nation, every throne, every soul. She is not just a corrupt city—she is the mother of spiritual harlotry, the source of global seduction. Everything flows from her: false religion, economic excess, political manipulation, and the persecution of the saints.

So God gives her special attention.

The seventh bowl has just been poured out. Earthquakes have shattered cities. Islands have disappeared. Mountains have crumbled. And in that moment of global collapse, Babylon comes into remembrance before God (Revelation 16:19). Not as an afterthought. But as the climax of divine justice.

Revelation 17 exposes her spiritual and political corruption—her alliances with kings and her fornication with the beast. Revelation 18 then unveils her commercial power and material seduction—the merchants, the gold, the luxury, the idolatry of wealth. Together, these chapters don't just present a metaphor. They reveal a real-world empire—unveiling Mystery Babylon—not merely as a symbol of sin, but as a real-world empire. Once blessed, now fallen. Once a beacon, now a harlot.

And God pauses. Because her judgment is essential. She is the final expression of the world's rebellion. And she is remembered—for wrath, for reckoning, for justice.

The atmosphere was quieter than usual—still, weighty. A sense of spiritual heaviness lingered as Irene closed her Bible, her fingers resting on the edge of Revelation 17. The words hung in the air, refusing to be dismissed. She finally broke the silence.

"Ann, can I ask you something that's been sitting heavy on my heart?"

Her voice was soft, but laced with urgency.

"I've been digging into Revelation 17—and I can't shake the thought . . . what if this is us? America. I mean, the Middle East calls us 'The Great Satan.' Even Israel gets labeled 'Little Satan.'"

"You're not the only one asking that, Irene. The woman in Revelation 17 isn't just symbolic—she's powerful, global, and deadly. She's drunk with the blood of the saints. She deceives nations. That doesn't sound like ancient Rome anymore. Honestly? I sounds a lot like modern America."

"But weren't we founded as a Christian nation? And Israel—aren't they God's chosen people?"

"Yes, but being chosen doesn't mean being innocent. God chose Israel, but He judged her every time she turned away. And America? We began with prayer in Congress, Scripture engraved in stone, and a vision rooted in biblical values. But we've fallen far. Now we export war, hypersexual culture, gender confusion, media propaganda—and we call it freedom."

"Still, with platforms like X.com and these independent podcasts—aren't people starting to wake up?"

I nodded. "Some are. The truth is surfacing. I've heard podcasters uncover corruption in both America and Israel—deep-state agendas, covert military operations, even false flags that never make the headlines. And have you noticed? USAID always seems to show up wherever there's chaos. None of this is accidental?"

Irene rubbed her temples. "So you think America's behind all of it?"

I gave a measured nod. "Let's just say . . . her fingerprints are everywhere. Think about it."

- Wars in the Middle East?
- Coups in South America?
- Color revolutions in Europe?
- Biological research and experimentation in Africa and Asia?

I leaned in. "And who funds the unrest?"

Irene exhaled. "Dark money. Global NGOs. Shell corporations. Billionaires with savior complexes."

My voice was firm. "Exactly. It's not elected—it's entrenched. That's what Revelation reveals. The woman rides the beast. She isn't the beast—but she controls it. She steers it. That's Political Babylon: the seductress behind the systems, the corruption behind every throne."

Irene sighed. "So what happens to her?"

I replied softly. "Revelation says: 'The beast will hate the woman, make her desolate and naked, and burn her with fire.' Eventually, God lets the system consume itself. That's the fate of Political Babylon: collapse. Reckoning."

Irene's voice dropped. "And if that's America . . . are we close?"

I looked away, then met her eyes. "I think we're already in it. The fault lines are cracking—morally, spiritually, economically. And just like ancient Babylon, when pride replaces repentance, judgment isn't far behind."

Irene nodded slowly. "Then may we be found watching—not asleep at the wheel."

My voice was steady. "Amen. Revelation isn't just a warning—it's an invitation. An invitation to come out of her, cling to Christ, and stand on truth— no matter how loud the lies become."

THE ANCIENT SPIRIT BEHIND MYSTERY BABYLON

Mystery Babylon's fall in Revelation is not the beginning of her story—it is the culmination of a rebellion that began in the ancient world. Her roots trace all the way back to Babel, Babylon, and the idol worship that emerged through figures like Semiramis and Tammuz. The prophets Jeremiah and Ezekiel were among the first to confront this counterfeit religious system.

Jeremiah: The Weeping Prophet Against the Queen of Heaven

In Jeremiah's day, Israel had turned from covenant loyalty to cultic worship. In Jeremiah 7:18, he exposes the tragic scene: entire families participating in idolatry— gathering wood, baking cakes, and offering drink offers to the "queen of heaven."

The children gather wood, and the fathers kindle the fire, and the women knead their dough, to make cakes to the queen of heaven, and to pour out drink offerings unto other gods, that they may provoke Me to anger. (Jeremiah 7:18)

This queen is none other than Semiramis, the self-proclaimed goddess and wife of Nimrod. In Jeremiah 44:17, the people openly reject God's warnings, choosing instead to trust in their pagan worship:

But we will certainly do whatsoever thing goes forth out of our own mouth, to burn incense unto the queen of heaven, and to pour out drink offerings unto her, as we have done, we, and our fathers, our kings, and our princes, in the cities of Judah, and in the streets of Jerusalem: for then had we plenty of victuals (food), and were well, and saw no evil. (Jeremiah 44:17)

They attributed their prosperity not to God—but to the goddess they created. It was a complete inversion of truth.

Ezekiel: The Prophet Who Peered Into the Temple

In Ezekiel 8, God pulls back the curtain to show the spiritual adultery taking place—not in Babylon, but inside His own temple in Jerusalem. What Ezekiel sees is devastating:

- Idols carved into sacred walls
- Elders worshiping in secret
- Women weeping for Tammuz
- Priests turning their backs to God to worship the sun

Then he brought me to the door of the gate of the LORD's house which was toward the north; and, behold, there sat women weeping for Tammuz. (Ezekiel 8:14)

These were Israel's own leaders, embracing Babylonian idolatry inside the holy courts of God.

The Birth of a False Religion

The foundation of Mystery Babylon was laid in Genesis 10–11, when Nimrod, Noah's rebellious great-grandson, established Babel and its infamous tower. Nimrod's wife, Semiramis, claimed divinity and gave birth to a son, Tammuz, who she said was miraculously conceived by a sunbeam. He was hailed as a messianic figure—a false Christ

When Tammuz died, mythology claimed he was resurrected after forty days of mourning. From this arose the mother-child cult, a pagan archetype that spread through empires.

- Ishtar and Tammuz (Assyria)
- Astarte and Baal (Phoenicia)
- Isis and Horus (Egypt)
- Aphrodite and Eros (Greece)
- Venus and Cupid (Rome)

These cults practiced:

- Temple prostitution
- Virgin dedications
- Cake and incense offerings to the goddess
- Forty-day mourning seasons
- Fertility rites with eggs and rabbits

Modern echoes of these rituals remain today—evidence of a global system rooted in Babel.

The Prophets' Final Stand

God's prophets stood alone against this seductive system. Their message was clear:

> Howbeit I sent unto you all My servants the prophets, rising early and sending them, saying, Oh, do not this abominable thing that I hate. (Jeremiah 44:4)

But the people refused to listen. When warnings were ignored, judgment followed. That pattern plays out throughout Scripture—and it reaches its peak in Revelation 17. The harlot riding the beast is not a new entity. She is the same ancient spirit, now fully global, adorned in luxury, drunk with the blood of saints, and seated atop a world government. She has always existed. Now, in the final hour, God exposes her and prepares to destroy her once and for all.

A JEALOUS GOD AND A FINAL WARNING

It's no coincidence that the first two commandments directly confront the spirit of Babylon:

> You shalt have no other gods before Me. You shalt not make unto you any graven image, or any likeness of anything that is in heaven above, or that is in the earth beneath, or that is in the water under the earth: You shalt not bow down yourself to them, nor serve them: for I the LORD your God am a jealous God, visiting the iniquity of the fathers upon the children unto the third and fourth generation of them that hate Me. (Exodus 20:3–5)

From the very beginning, God has rejected goddess worship and all distortions of His truth. He alone is to be worshiped. There is no biblical support for exalting Mary—or any female figure—as divine. Mary was a faithful servant and disciple, honored but never deified. After Acts 1:14, she fades from the biblical narrative. There is no throne, no crown—only Christ is exalted.

Yet mother-and-child worship lies at the heart of spiritual harlotry. It is the root of Mystery Babylon—an ancient, global deception repackaged in empire after empire. When John sees the woman riding the beast, he marvels—not because she is unfamiliar, but because she is all too familiar. Her seductive spirit has persisted for millennia.

A Final Word on Religious Babylon

Revelation 17 unveils a shocking image: a seductive woman, Mystery Babylon, seated on a scarlet beast. She embodies a global religious system—deceptive, powerful, and spiritually corrupt—one that manipulates governments and intoxicates nations.

But her reign is temporary. The beast she rides—the Antichrist himself—turns on her, strips her, devours her, and burns her with fire. The alliance of politics and religion collapse. Judgment is swift.

This isn't just apocalyptic imagery—it's divine prophecy. A spiritual system built on compromise, falsehood, and control will not survive. Revelation 17 doesn't just warn about the past or future—it speaks to our moment.

Mystery Babylon is rising—but she will fall. And her fall is a final call to turn from deception and cling to the one true God.

Irene spoke, more to herself than anyone else.

"Ann, something's been gnawing at me. I remember that golden statue unveiled in early 2023—on top of the Manhattan Appellate Courthouse. They called it *NOW*. A female figure with braided hair shaped like horns, a lace collar like Ruth Bader Ginsburg's. But it didn't feel like a tribute. It felt like a statement."

She paused, unsettled.

"Like it was saying: 'Move over Moses, there's a new Lawgiver in town.' I know that's not what it literally says, but honestly—doesn't that send chills down your spine?"

I nodded slowly. "Oh, I saw it. And no—you're not imagining things. That statue made headlines for a reason. It wasn't just public art; it was a spiritual statement. And not a good one."

I leaned forward.

"Almost certainly modeled after *Inanna*—also known as *Ishtar*—the ancient Mesopotamian goddess of sex, war, fertility, and domination. Later, she appeared as *Astarte*, *Ashtoreth*, even *Semiramis*. Different names. Same deception."

"The braided horns, the confrontational stance—it all fits," I continued. "This wasn't about justice. It was about spiritual rebellion—an ancient idol reintroduced under the guise of progress."

Irene blinked. "Wait—so *Ishtar*, *Astarte*, and *Semiramis* . . . they're all the same? And now she's showing up—on a courthouse in America?"

I nodded. "Exactly. Same goddess, different mask. That's the spiritual harlotry Revelation 17 exposes—now parading as progressive art."

"Remember Jeremiah? He warned Israel about baking cakes to the queen of heaven. Ezekiel saw women weeping for *Tammuz* inside God's Temple. And now? We're exalting the same ancient goddess on our public buildings—and calling it *empowerment*."

Irene interrupted. "I even read about a similar statue installed in Texas—part of the same series by Pakistani-American artist Shahzia Sikander. It wasn't an exact replica of *NOW*, but the spiritual vibe was the same—defiant, crowned with twisted braids, that same unsettling power. This one was called *WITNESS*. First displayed in Madison Square Park, then relocated to the University of Houston's Cullen Family Plaza in February 2024."

"And not long after it was installed in Houston, a massive storm swept through—and knocked the head clean off. I mean . . . if that's not a sign, what is?"

I nodded slowly. "Yes—and that felt like a divine echo of Exodus: 'You shall have no other gods before Me.' These aren't coincidences, Irene. They're prophetic warnings. Revelation 17 calls her the 'mother of harlots'—clothed in purple and scarlet, dripping in gold, pearls, and seduction. Mystery Babylon is alive and flaunting herself in plain sight."

"And we call it modern! But it's just ancient paganism with better lighting."

I nodded. "Exactly. We've exchanged the fear of God for idols wrapped in feminism, sexual freedom, and 'artistic expression.' But underneath it all, it's the same old lie from Genesis 11. Babel never really fell—it just learned how to brand itself better."

"It's so clear now. Revelation 17 isn't just about spiritual seduction—it's political, cultural, and global. We're not watching history. We're watching prophecy unfold."

I sighed. "Exactly. When God showed John the New Jerusalem, He took him to a high mountain. But when He revealed the harlot riding the beast, He led him into the wilderness. That contrast says it all. One is heaven-bound. The other? Spiritually barren."

Irene shivered. "That gives me chills. We've glamorized rebellion. Branded it. Marketed it. Turned it into a movement. But this isn't just bad politics—it's spiritual warfare."

"And that's why Revelation 16:15 warns us: 'Behold, I come as a thief. Blessed is he that watches, and keeps his garments, lest he walk naked, and they see his shame.' Babylon's seduction is strong . . . but the remnant is stronger."

Irene, softly: "Amen, Ann. Amen."

"Before we wrap this up, Ann—can we just talk about NASA for a second? Jeremiah 51:53 says, 'Though Babylon should mount up to heaven . . .' That screams space program to me. I mean, we claimed the moon! Planted a flag like we owned it. It was this colossal moment of pride and progress."

"It was. But have you ever noticed—we haven't gone back? Not in over fifty years. In an age where we advance tech faster than ever, shouldn't we have moon colonies by now?"

"So . . . are you saying we never went?"

I shook my head. "Not exactly. But I *am* saying this: even if we did, I question the motive. It wasn't just science—it was spectacle. It was about making a name for ourselves. Just like Babel. Genesis 11:4 says, 'Let us build a tower . . . and make a name.' Same spirit. Different century."

"So you think there are spiritual limits—even in space?"

"Yes. Psalm 115:16 says, 'The heaven, even the heavens, are the Lord's: but the earth He has given to the children of men.' God sets boundaries. The Tower of Babel wasn't just about height—it was a rebellion. A declaration of independence from God."

"Wow. So NASA is like Babylon's Tower 2.0?"

Smiling. "Something like that. Rockets instead of bricks. But the same message: 'Let us ascend . . . let us make a name.' It's pride disguised as progress. And Revelation 17 pulls the curtain back—showing the harlotry for what it really is. Global. Defiant. Headed for judgment."

Irene stared at me, still shaken.

"Wow. Babylon's pride. NASA's Tower. It really is all connected."

I, smirking. "And don't even get me started on alien talk . . ."

Irene's eyes widened. "Oh no—you're going there?"

"I kind of have to. Have you noticed how mainstream it's becoming? UAP hearings in Congress . . . military pilots going on record . . . even NASA launching a panel to 'study anomalies.' But here's the thing, Irene—it's not what it looks like.

"So . . . you don't believe in aliens?"

"Not in the green-men-from-Alpha-Centauri kind of way. But I do believe something's happening—just not from another galaxy. The Bible talks about *lying signs and wonders*, spiritual wickedness in high places. I think it's demonic deception dressed up in cosmic clothes."

"Like a smokescreen?"

"Exactly. What if the whole alien narrative is a setup? A way to explain away the Rapture? Or unite the world under a false external threat? Even Reagan hinted in a speech that the nations of the earth would unite if we faced an alien invasion."

Irene, quietly. "Uniting the world . . . just like Babylon tried to do."

"Yep. Globalism. False unity. Spiritual deception. Same agenda. And NASA? Maybe they're not inventing it—but they're sure helping normalize it. Astrobiology, habitable zones, the search for intelligent life—it's all part of the narrative arc."

"But what about the videos? The pilot testimonies?"

"Oh, I believe they're seeing something. But not *extraterrestrial—extra-dimensional*. Demonic manifestations meant to deceive. Paul warned about doctrines of demons. Revelation talks about frogs-like spirits deceiving kings. This isn't fantasy—it's prophecy."

Irene whispered, "That makes my stomach turn . . . but it explains so much. The obsession. The timing. The sudden 'transparency.'"

"Exactly. And here's the scariest part: people are more willing to believe in aliens than in God. They'll reject Jesus—but prep for little green men."

"So what do we do?"

"We stay grounded in truth. We don't get swept up in the spectacle. We remember Ephesians 6:12:"

For we wrestle not against flesh and blood, but against principalities, against powers, against the rulers of the darkness of this world, against spiritual wickedness in high places. (Ephesians 6:12)

"And we keep our eyes on the sky—not for UFOs, but for our returning King."

Irene smiled through the weight of it all.

"Now that's a headline you'll never see on CNN."

I grinned.

"But you'll see it in the clouds. One day soon."

———◆◆◆———

THE REVELATION OF JESUS CHRIST REVEALS:

[17:1] And there came one of the seven angels which had the seven vials, and talked with me, saying unto me, Come hither; I will show to you the judgment of the great whore that sits upon many waters.

This verse transitions us into one of the most sobering unveilings in the entire Book of Revelation. One of the seven angels who had just poured out the final bowl judgments (Revelation 16) now calls John forward with an invitation: "Come hither . . ." It is both intimate and intense. Heaven wants John—and us—to see something clearly. Not just for theological curiosity, but for spiritual urgency.

This "great whore" is not merely a woman—it is a symbolic personification of a global, seductive system. The Greek word for "whore" (*porne*) indicates more than immorality—it conveys unfaithfulness, seduction, and spiritual prostitution. This is a direct contrast to the purity of the Bride of Christ in Revelation 19. Where the Bride is clothed in righteousness, this woman is clothed in false religion, political power, and global deceit.

Throughout Scripture, spiritual unfaithfulness is often likened to prostitution or adultery (Jeremiah 3:6–9; Ezekiel 16; Hosea 1–3). Here, we see the full maturity of that spiritual harlotry in the last days—a system that began at Babel, flourished in Babylon, and now culminates in Mystery Babylon: a worldwide, seductive power masquerading as truth.

"Sits upon many waters." The imagery of sitting on "many waters" speaks to the scope of her influence. Thankfully, we don't have to guess what it means. Revelation 17:15 interprets it for us: "The waters . . . are peoples, and multitudes, and nations, and tongues." In other words, this harlot reigns over a global empire. She is not confined to one location. She influences cultures, languages, governments, and religions. This is the global system of deception—driven by spiritual compromise and fueled by wealth, luxury, and idolatry.

The word "sits" implies control, authority, and arrogance. She doesn't merely exist among the waters—she dominates them. This is the image of a false religious and commercial system enthroned over the world, seducing the nations with her counterfeit light.

The angel does not say, "I will show you the harlot." He says, "I will show you the judgment of the harlot." From the start, the focus is not merely on what she is—but on what is coming to her. Her power is great, but it is temporary. Her seduction is global, but her sentence is sure. God is about to expose, strip, and destroy this counterfeit system once and for all.

OLD TESTAMENT FORESHADOWS REVELATION:

O you that dwell upon many waters, abundant in treasures, your end is come, and the measure of your covetousness. (Jeremiah 51:13)

This is a direct link to the language of Revelation 17:1. It speaks of Babylon, the city "dwelling on many waters," paralleling the "great whore that sits upon many waters." The "many waters" here refer both to geographical rivers (Babylon sat on the Euphrates) and to the symbolic dominance over many peoples and nations—just as Revelation 17:15 explains.

THE REVELATION OF JESUS CHRIST REVEALS:

17:2 With whom the kings of the earth have committed fornication, and the inhabitants of the earth have been made drunk with the wine of her fornication.

This verse unveils the scope and seduction of Mystery Babylon's influence—reaching both global leaders and everyday people. "With whom the kings of the earth have committed fornication." This is not about literal immorality but a spiritual and political unfaithfulness. In Scripture, fornication often symbolizes idolatry, spiritual compromise, and alliances with ungodly powers.

- These "kings" are political leaders who have partnered with Babylon—not just economically, but ideologically and spiritually.
- They trade truth for influence, righteousness for riches, and divine allegiance for temporal power.
- Like Israel in the Old Testament who formed unholy alliances with Egypt, Assyria, or Babylon (Hosea 7:11; Isaiah 30:1–3), these kings have sold their nations' integrity to the harlot system for wealth, comfort, and control.

"And the inhabitants of the earth have been made drunk." The language of intoxication is critical here. The harlot doesn't merely influence global leaders—she seduces the masses. To be "drunk" in this context speaks of deception, moral confusion, and spiritual stupor. Just as literal wine dulls the senses, Babylon's influence numbs consciences, clouds judgment, and blinds hearts to truth. The world drinks deeply from her cup—false religion, consumerism, sexual perversion, media manipulation, and material luxury—and it relishes every drop. But what Babylon offers is pleasurable poison: sweet and enticing in the moment, yet deadly in its end. It's a system that intoxicates with comfort and convenience—only to lead its followers to destruction.

This verse warns us: Babylon isn't just an ancient empire or future system—it's a spiritual pattern present even now. It shows up when churches compromise the gospel to stay culturally relevant. When politicians trade conviction for power.

When societies abandon truth in pursuit of indulgence. Wherever there is seduction, corruption, or rebellion—Babylon is there.

This is the hour to be sober-minded. Paul said, "And be not drunk with wine, wherein is excess; but be filled with the Spirit" (Ephesians 5:18). Babylon's wine may be sweet to the world, but it is poison to the soul.

OLD TESTAMENT FORESHADOWS REVELATION:

Stay yourselves, and wonder; cry you out, and cry: they are drunken, but not with wine; they stagger, but not with strong drink. For the LORD has poured out upon you the spirit of deep sleep, and has closed your eyes: the prophets and your rulers, the seers has he covered. (Isaiah 29:9–10)

This passage reveals the mystery of spiritual intoxication—a divine judgment where people are so resistant to truth that God allows them to be spiritually dazed, stumbling in delusion. It mirrors Revelation 17:2, where Mystery Babylon has seduced the kings and deceived the inhabitants of the earth through her intoxicating influence.

THE REVELATION OF JESUS CHRIST REVEALS:

17:3 So he carried me away in the spirit into the wilderness: and I saw a woman sit upon a scarlet-colored beast, full of names of blasphemy, having seven heads and ten horns.

This is no ordinary scene—it is a divine unveiling. John, exiled on Patmos, is now spiritually transported into the wilderness—a symbolic landscape of desolation, confusion, and spiritual barrenness. This setting is critical. In Scripture, the wilderness is often a place of testing, rebellion, or judgment (Hosea 2:14; Matthew 4:1). Here, it foreshadows the spiritual ruin left in the wake of Babylon's deception.

"So he carried me away into the wilderness." Wherever there is harlotry, there is confusion. There is barrenness. There is moral and spiritual desolation. The wilderness here isn't just a geographical location—it is a symbol of a world system devoid of truth. Just as ancient Israel turned from God and became spiritually adulterous (Jeremiah 3:6–9; Ezekiel 16:32), so too does Mystery Babylon reflect false devotion, feigned intimacy, and pretended affection—but only to gain favors and control.

"And I saw a woman sit upon a scarlet-colored beast." John sees a woman riding a scarlet-colored beast—not walking beside it, not resisting it, but controlling it. The color scarlet points to royalty, sin (Isaiah 1:18), and even blood. The beast is "full of names of blasphemy"—suggesting not just casual rebellion, but an institutionalized defiance against God.

"Having seven heads and ten horns." The seven heads and ten horns mirror the description of the beast (the Antichrist) in Revelation 13 and Daniel 7, symbolizing political power, kingdoms, and alliances. The woman sits on this beast, implying a temporary dominance—yet her end is foretold: the very beast she rides will turn and devour her (Revelation 17:16).

This is the image of religious harlotry riding on political power. When religion is hijacked by worldly ambition, when state and false worship merge, the result is coercion, corruption, and counterfeit spirituality. Lenin cynically declared that "religion is the opiate of the people." In the case of Mystery Babylon, he wasn't entirely wrong—but it is not true faith that intoxicates—it's the harlot's religion, the systematized perversion of worship, that drugs the masses.

America's own slow drift toward state-sponsored paganism—through schools, media, and courts—is eerily in line with this prophetic picture. It is not secularism that rises unchecked, but spiritual deception clothed in cultural acceptability.

This is not just an apocalyptic vision—it's a warning. The church must discern the difference between true devotion and religious seduction. The harlot wears gold, speaks smooth words, and flatters the kings of the earth—but her end is judgment. The wilderness reveals what the city hides: a system of rebellion cloaked in religious garb.

Who is Lenin?

Vladimir Ilyich Ulyanov (1870–1924)—he later adopted "Lenin" as a revolutionary alias—was a Russian revolutionary, political theorist, and the founder of the Soviet Union. He was the leader of the Bolshevik Party, which seized power during the Russian Revolution of 1917, overthrowing the Russian monarchy (Tsar Nicholas II) and establishing a communist government.

Why he's relevant to Revelation 17 and 18:

Lenin's views, especially his hostility toward religion and his embrace of state control over every aspect of life, echo the beast system described in Revelation. The merging of ideology, economics, and religion (or anti-religion) into a global power is a hallmark of Mystery Babylon—and Lenin's regime was a preview of that in many ways.

OLD TESTAMENT FORESHADOWS REVELATION:

The burden of the desert of the sea. As whirlwinds in the south pass through; so it comes from the desert, from a terrible land. . . . And, behold, here comes a chariot of men, with a couple of horsemen. And he answered and said, Babylon is fallen, is fallen; and all the graven images of her gods He has broken unto the ground. (Isaiah 21:1, 9)

This is a prophetic vision about the fall of Babylon, seen from the wilderness. It mirrors John's vision in Revelation 17:3, where the woman—Mystery Babylon—is shown in the wilderness just before her destruction is revealed. Both passages use apocalyptic symbolism to describe judgment on a corrupt world system.

THE REVELATION OF JESUS CHRIST REVEALS:

[17:4] And the woman was arrayed in purple and scarlet-color, and decked with gold and precious stones and pearls, having a golden cup in her hand full of abominations and filthiness of her fornication.

This verse offers one of the most vivid symbolic descriptions in Revelation. Every word and image in this verse is deeply prophetic and theological, designed to reveal the spiritual seduction and corruption of Mystery Babylon—the woman riding the beast (the Antichrist).

"And the woman was arrayed in purple and scarlet-color." These two colors are rich in symbolism. Purple, the royal hue of the Roman Empire, was worn by senators, consuls, and most notably the emperor himself. It represented power, wealth, and imperial authority. Scarlet, or bright red, carries dual meanings: biblically, it is a color of sin and bloodshed (as in Isaiah 1:18), yet historically, it also holds strong religious connotations—worn prominently by Roman Catholic clergy, especially cardinals. When combined, purple and scarlet reflect a fusion of political and religious influence—a system dressed in grandeur and prestige, yet inwardly corrupted by pride, sin, and bloodguilt. This is no ordinary attire— it's the uniform of global seduction.

"And decked with gold and precious stones and pearls." This vivid imagery intentionally echoes the sacred vestments of the Old Testament high priest (Exodus 28:17–20), yet here it is tragically distorted. Instead of symbolizing holiness and divine service, the adornment reflects worldly opulence, pride, and seduction. What was once set apart for worship has been twisted into a display of excess and spiritual corruption. Much like the Laodicean church in Revelation 3:17, this woman believes herself to be rich, adorned, and lacking nothing, but in the eyes of God, she is wretched, blind, and spiritually bankrupt. The lavish display is not a sign of blessing—it is an indictment.

"Having a golden cup in her hand." This striking image draws directly from Jeremiah 51:7, which declares:

Babylon has been a golden cup in the Lord's hand, that made all the earth drunken: the nations have drunken of her wine; therefore the nations are mad. (Jeremiah 51:7)

The cup itself glitters with deceptive beauty—it appears holy, prestigious, even divine—but its contents betray its appearance. Inside is filth: spiritual corruption, falsehood, and moral decay. This golden cup is not just an accessory—it is a tool of seduction, used to intoxicate the nations, to lure them away from the truth through false religion, spiritual compromise, and perverse indulgence. What looks sacred is, in reality, a vessel of destruction, cloaking evil in the illusion of splendor.

"Full of abominations and filthiness of her fornication." This phrase exposes the moral and spiritual decay hidden within the golden cup. In the Old Testament, "abominations" are repeatedly linked to idolatry, child sacrifice, sexual immorality, and pagan worship (Isaiah 44:19; 2 Kings 23:13; Ezekiel 8). These were not just cultural offenses—they were spiritual betrayals that provoked God's wrath. The word "fornication" here speaks to spiritual adultery: a betrayal of covenant faithfulness to the one true God. Instead of devotion, the woman aligns herself with false religious systems and corrupt political powers. Her religion is not pure; it is a toxic blend of deception, mixing truth with error, grace with works, and light with darkness. It's seductive—but it leads souls away from God and into judgment.

This verse illustrates how false religion can look beautiful on the outside while being deeply offensive to God on the inside. Like the Pharisees, she is a "whitewashed tomb" (Matthew 23:27), ornate and decorated, but full of decay.

Many see this as a reference to apostate religious systems, especially those that merge spiritual language with political control or religious ceremony with idolatry. It warns of any system—religious or institutional—that claims to represent Christ while denying His finished work on the Cross (Hebrews 10:10–14). As mentioned in Ephesians 2:8–9:

> For by grace are you saved through faith; and that not of yourselves: it is the gift of God: Not of works, lest any man should boast. (Ephesians 2:8–9)

To say otherwise is blasphemy. This is why adding to the gospel (Galatians 1:6–9) is not just error—it is spiritual fornication and blasphemy.

OLD TESTAMENT FORESHADOWS REVELATION:

> For the lips of a strange woman drop as a honeycomb, and her mouth is smoother than oil: But her end is bitter as wormwood, sharp as a twoedged sword. (Proverbs 5:3–4)

In Proverbs, wisdom literature warns against the seductive power of deception, comparing it to a harlot whose words are sweet like honey but whose path leads to death. This directly parallels the woman in Revelation 17:4—glorious in appearance, dressed in royal colors, adorned with gold, and holding a golden cup. But that cup is not filled with blessing—it holds abominations and filthiness. What looks divine is actually poisonous, and the wormwood mentioned in Proverbs 5:3–4—symbolizing bitterness, judgment, and death—is echoed again in Revelation 8:11. The Bible consistently warns us: deception often wears beauty, but its end is always destruction.

THE REVELATION OF JESUS CHRIST REVEALS:

17:5 And upon her forehead was a name written, MYSTERY, BABYLON THE GREAT, THE MOTHER OF HARLOTS AND ABOMINATIONS OF THE EARTH.

This verse is one of the most chilling and revealing declarations in the Book of Revelation. What John sees here is not just a powerful figure—but a religious system so influential, so deeply entrenched in global politics, that she is labeled the "mother" of spiritual prostitution and abomination.

"And upon her forehead was a name written." In biblical times, a harlot might wear her name on her forehead, identifying her trade. Here, God unmasks this religious-political system for what it truly is: a global spiritual counterfeit. Her identity is no longer hidden—it's written plainly, for John (and us) to see.

Contrast this with the seal of God on the foreheads of His 144,000 servants (Revelation 7:3, 14:1). While the saints are marked by devotion and truth, this woman is marked by deception and corruption.

"MYSTERY, BABYLON THE GREAT." The word "Mystery" signals that this is not literal Babylon, the ancient city on the Euphrates, but a spiritual Babylon—a continuation of the religious rebellion that began at the Tower of Babel (Genesis 11). This system is cloaked in religious language, rituals, and ceremony, but its core is idolatry, syncretism, and seduction.

She is Babylon revived, not geographically, but spiritually—influencing empires, churches, and cultures through a counterfeit form of worship that replaces the simplicity of the gospel with ceremony, wealth, and power.

"THE MOTHER OF HARLOTS AND ABOMINATIONS OF THE EARTH." She is not just a harlot herself—she is the origin of many others. This suggests a system that gives birth to many false religious expressions. Could this include institutionalized religion, cults, apostate denominations, or any movement that exalts tradition above truth and blends paganism with Christian language? This echoes Isaiah 1:21, where Jerusalem is called a harlot for abandoning the LORD. And in Nahum 3:4, Nineveh is condemned for its "whoredoms" and "witchcrafts."

In Scripture, "Mystery" is used to describe profound spiritual truths once hidden but now revealed. The apostle Paul speaks of the "great mystery" concerning Christ and His Bride—the Church (Ephesians 5:31–32), and again in Ephesians 3:1–9, where the Church is unveiled as part of God's eternal plan, hidden from ages past but now made known through Christ.

> For this cause shall a man leave his father and mother, and shall be joined unto his wife, and they two shall be one flesh. This is a great mystery: but I speak concerning Christ and the church. (Ephesians 5:31–32)

But in Revelation 17, we encounter a rival "mystery"—a spiritual counterfeit. Instead of a pure Bride clothed in white linen (Revelation 19:8), we see a woman adorned in purple and scarlet, dripping with gold and seduction. Instead of walking in faithful devotion, she is drunk with the blood of the saints.

This is not the Bride of Christ.

This is the bride of Antichrist—a false religious system that mimics the outward beauty of holiness but is inwardly corrupt. She is a perversion of the true Church, seducing the nations and aligning with the beast. Her mystery is not one of redemption, but of rebellion. This system, "Babylon the Great," is not just immoral—it is idolatrous and global. It offers the appearance of godliness but denies its power (2 Timothy 3:5). It claims spiritual authority, yet leads people into spiritual slavery. And its judgment is coming swiftly.

OLD TESTAMENT FORESHADOWS REVELATION:

> The LORD said also unto me in the days of Josiah the king, Have you seen that which backsliding Israel has done? She is gone up upon every high mountain and under every green tree, and there has played the harlot. . . . And I saw, when for all the causes whereby backsliding Israel committed adultery I had put her away, and given her a bill of divorce; yet her treacherous sister Judah feared not, but went and played the harlot also. And it came to pass through the lightness of her whoredom, that she defiled the land, and committed adultery with stones and with stocks. (Jeremiah 3:6, 8–9)

Jeremiah 3:6 and verses 8–9 captures the spiritual adultery of Israel—God's chosen people chasing after idols, defiling the land, and abandoning their covenant. Just as Revelation 17:5 describes Mystery Babylon as the mother of harlots, Jeremiah reveals Israel's descent into systemic religious corruption and idolatrous imitation. Where Revelation exposes a future global harlot, Jeremiah grieves over a national harlot in Israel—both using the language of spiritual prostitution to reveal how far God's people had fallen.

THE REVELATION OF JESUS CHRIST REVEALS:

> [17:6] And I saw the woman drunken with the blood of the saints, and with the blood of the martyrs of Jesus: and when I saw her, I wondered with great admiration.

This verse marks the emotional and spiritual climax of John's vision. The harlot, already revealed as a global, religious-political system of deception and idolatry, is now shown to be *drunk*—not with wine, but with the blood of God's people. This is not mere persecution—it is a ravenous appetite for destruction. She is intoxicated by martyrdom.

John's reaction is telling. He does not marvel at the Antichrist. He does not marvel at the beast from the earth or the sea. But here, when he sees this religious system, dressed in opulence and claiming moral authority—yet drenched in the blood of the saints—he is stunned. The word translated as "admiration" (*thauma mega*) in the KJV is more accurately rendered "great astonishment" or *horrified awe*. John is not impressed—he is aghast.

This is the spiritual betrayal that wounds deepest: a religious system that claims to serve God—yet persecutes His people. The harlot of Revelation 17 is not secular. She is religious, but rooted in false worship. Her legacy stretches back through history: from Old Testament idolatry, to the rejection and murder of God's prophets, to Rome's brutal persecution of early Christians. She reemerged in the inquisitions, crusades, and religious wars—often turning not against heresy, but against the true followers of Christ.

Foxe's *Book of Martyrs* and numerous historical accounts estimate over fifty million Christians have been executed—not by pagans, but by corrupt religious systems wielding political power. From Rome to inquisitions, torture chambers, and execution racks—this harlot has filled her golden cup with the blood of those who dared to follow Christ outside her rule.

Horrified, we realize this sobering truth: the most dangerous enemy of truth is not atheism—it is religious hypocrisy masked as righteousness. It is Babylon, offering communion with one hand and a dagger with the other. This is why God's judgment is not just justified—it is fierce. He remembers the blood of every martyr, and He hears the cry of every saint. Now, the day of reckoning has come.

This verse is a sobering reminder: not all that claims the name of Christ serves Him. When religion merges with empire, when truth is sacrificed for control, and when the Bride is replaced by a harlot—God intervenes. Babylon may look regal, but she is drunk with guilt. Her day of judgment is at hand.

OLD TESTAMENT FORESHADOWS REVELATION:

Why trims you your way to seek love? Therefore have you also taught the wicked ones your ways. Also in your skirts is found the blood of the souls of the poor innocents: I have not found it by secret search, but upon all these. (Jeremiah 2:33–34)

In Jeremiah 2:33–34, God exposes religious corruption in His own city, accusing Israel of dressing like a harlot to seduce and murdering the innocent. The image of blood on the skirts mirrors the blood-soaked harlot of Revelation 17:6. It is not hidden. It is open. God says, "I didn't need to look hard. The blood is everywhere." Like the harlot of Revelation, Jerusalem became unfaithful—not through secular rebellion, but through false religion, manipulating people, killing the prophets (Matthew 23:37), and shedding the blood of the innocent.

THE REVELATION OF JESUS CHRIST REVEALS:

17:7 And the angel said to me, Wherefore did you marvel? I will tell you the mystery of the woman, and of the beast that carries her, which has the seven heads and ten horns.

After the shocking vision of the woman—arrayed in purple and scarlet, drunken with the blood of saints—John is left speechless, stunned in awe and horror. The angel immediately responds to John's astonishment with a rhetorical question: "Why did you marvel?" As if to say: "This should not surprise you. Let me explain."

The angel proceeds to unveil the mystery. This moment is pivotal. What had appeared as a symbolic spectacle—rich, regal, seductive—now demands spiritual interpretation. The vision wasn't simply about a seductive woman. It was about a system: religious and political. Spiritual adultery wedded to civil authority.

John, a man familiar with persecution from pagan Rome, would not have been surprised to see pagan rulers persecute believers. What stunned him was the *religious garb* of the persecutor. This wasn't a Roman general or an atheist empire. It was a religious system—a "church"—dressed in wealth and royalty, yet drunk on the blood of those it claimed to represent.

The woman rides the beast, meaning she's not just partnered with worldly power—she controls it, steers it. The Church was never called to ride the beast of politics. She was called to bear her cross. When religion climbs onto the back of government for control, influence, or prestige, it ceases to represent the crucified Christ and begins to resemble the scarlet harlot.

The angel promises to decode the vision. The mystery of the woman—and of the beast—is about to be unveiled. This prepares us for the verses ahead, where symbols become systems, and prophecy intersects with geopolitics and apostate religion.

The great marvel of Revelation 17:7 isn't that persecution exists—it's who is doing the persecuting. A woman pretending to love Christ, while betraying Him. This is not the love of the Bride, but the feigned affection of a harlot—one who flatters, seduces, and kills to keep her power.

OLD TESTAMENT FORESHADOWS REVELATION:

Son of man, cause Jerusalem to know her abominations, And say, Thus says the Lord GOD unto Jerusalem; Your birth and your nativity is of the land of Canaan; your father was an Amorite, and your mother a Hittite. . . . But you did trust in your own beauty, and played the harlot because of your fame, and poured out your harlotry on every one that passed by; his it was. Ezekiel 16:2–3, 15)

Ezekiel was shown the harlotry of Jerusalem—not merely political sin, but deep religious unfaithfulness. God uses the language of marriage to describe His covenant relationship with His people, and their betrayal is portrayed as spiritual adultery. This image foreshadows the harlot in Revelation 17:7, who appears outwardly religious but is inwardly unfaithful—choosing to align with worldly powers instead of remaining loyal to God.

THE REVELATION OF JESUS CHRIST REVEALS:

[17:8] The beast that you saw was, and is not; and will ascend out of the bottomless pit, and go into perdition: and they that dwell on the earth will wonder, whose names were not written in the Book of Life from the foundation of the world, when they behold the beast that was, and is not, and yet is.

"The beast that you saw was, and is not; and will ascend out of the bottomless pit." This phrase echoes the mystery of the Antichrist and mirrors the language of Revelation 13:3, where John sees a beast with a mortal wound that was healed—prompting the whole world to marvel.

- The "bottomless pit" (Greek: *abussos*) is mentioned multiple times in Revelation (Revelation 9:1–2, 11, 11:7, 20:1, 3). It is a realm of demonic confinement—not merely symbolic, but literal and supernatural in nature.
- This suggests the beast's rise is not merely political or natural, but spiritual and demonic in origin. It's not just a revival of a past empire—it is energized by hell itself.
- Many scholars believe this represents a resurrected or reincarnated world leader, a counterfeit of Christ's death and resurrection—a blasphemous parody of the true gospel.

"And go into perdition." This points directly to the final destiny of the beast: utter destruction. The same word "perdition" is used in 2 Thessalonians 2:3 describing "the son of perdition"—a title for the Antichrist. Despite his momentary rise and global influence, his end is predetermined. God allows the beast to fulfill prophecy, but his doom is certain.

"And they that dwell on the earth will wonder." This is a recurring phrase in Revelation used to describe the unsaved masses (Revelation 3:10, 13:8). These are people fully given over to the beast, amazed and enthralled by his power and counterfeit miracles (2 Thessalonians 2:9–10).

"Whose names were not written in the Book of Life from the foundation of the world." This is one of the clearest dividing lines in all of Scripture. Two groups exist in the end times:

1. Those whose names are in the Lamb's Book of Life—the redeemed.
2. Those who marvel after the beast—the unredeemed.

This Book of Life is referenced multiple times (Revelation 3:5, 13:8, 20:12, 15). It represents divine foreknowledge and eternal security for those truly saved.

- From the foundation of the world—emphasizes God's sovereignty. Before creation, God already knew who would be His.
- Those who worship the beast do so because they are not in the Book of Life—not the other way around.

"When they behold the beast that was, and is not, and yet is." This phrase is a mockery of God's eternal name. In Revelation 1:8, Christ is proclaimed as the One "who was, and is, and is to come"—a declaration of divine sovereignty, timelessness, and certainty. In contrast, the beast is described as "was, is not, and yet is"—a parody of true deity, unstable and deceptive.

This reflects the broader theme of the counterfeit trinity: Satan, the Antichrist, and the False Prophet—a demonic imitation of the Father, Son, and Holy Spirit. The beast's apparent death and resurrection will be a false miracle, designed to deceive the ungrounded, drawing worship through spectacle rather than truth.

The world's spiritual blindness in the last days will not be accidental. According to Romans 1:18–32, it stems from willful rebellion and results in divine judgment. The refusal to love the truth will open the door to strong delusion (2 Thessalonians 2:9–12). What looks like power will in fact be deception—a final test of allegiance.

OLD TESTAMENT FORESHADOWS REVELATION:

I beheld then because of the voice of the great words which the horn (little horn) spoke: I beheld even till the beast was slain, and his body destroyed, and given to the burning flame. As concerning the rest of the beasts, they had their dominion taken away: yet their lives were prolonged for a season and time. (Daniel 7:11–12)

The "little horn" in Daniel 7:11–12 is a type of the Antichrist, just as the beast is in Revelation 17:8. Both texts describe a blasphemous world leader who rises to power but is ultimately destroyed by divine judgment—a direct parallel to "go into perdition." The beasts in Daniel and Revelation mirror each other in symbolism—beasts representing empires or systems controlled by demonic forces. Just as in Revelation, the world marvels at this leader's power and presence until God brings it to an end.

Irene leaned in, brow furrowed.

"Ann, can I ask you something? I've been turning this over in my mind. Revelation keeps talking about names written in the Book of Life. And we just read that some names were written there before the foundation of the world. If that is true . . . does that mean the wicked are just . . . doomed? That they never had a chance?"

I exhaled slowly, then nodded.

"Yes, it's true. Revelation 13:8 and 17:8 both say that those who worship the beast don't have their names written in the Lamb's Book of Life—from the foundation of the world. And Ephesians 1:4 says God chose us in Christ before the world began."

Irene's voice softened. "So . . . were our fates sealed before we were born?"

I shook my head gently. "Not exactly. God's foreknowledge is perfect—He sees the end from the beginning. But that doesn't mean He forces anyone's hand. Scripture also says He desires all to be saved (1 Timothy 2:4), and He's patient, not wanting anyone to perish (2 Peter 3:9). The invitation is real."

Irene frowned. "But if the names were already written—or not written—is there even a chance for the wicked to repent?"

I leaned forward. "There's always a chance—until it's too late. Exodus 32:33 and Revelation 3:5 both talk about names being *blotted out*. That means they were there to begin with. People can walk away from the truth. But they can also return."

Irene nodded slowly. "So rebellion can harden a heart . . . but repentance can still change the story?"

I smiled. "Exactly. Paul said in 2 Thessalonians 2:11 that God sends a strong delusion—*after* people reject the truth. It's not predestined damnation. It's judgment that follows persistent refusal. But until that line is crossed, the Gospel still calls."

Irene whispered. "It's all so sobering. But also . . . kind of beautiful. That God still calls. Still waits."

I looked her in the eye. "That's why Revelation isn't just about wrath—it's about mercy. About warning. And about hope." Jesus said:

> All that the Father gives Me shall come to Me; and him that comes to Me I will in no wise cast out. (John 6:37)

I continued. "The Lamb's Book of Life reminds us that God knows us fully—and still invites us freely."

Irene sat back, letting it sink in. "That's grace. And a reason to keep watching, praying . . . and reaching people."

I nodded. "Exactly. Because until that final trumpet sounds—there's still time."

Irene leaned forward, puzzled.

"Ann, that verse—'Whoever comes to Me I will never cast out'—I've always loved it. But I've also wondered . . . is that it? Just come to Him once and you're in? What about obedience? What about making Him Lord, not just Savior?"

I nodded. "You're asking the right question. Coming to Jesus isn't a one-time handshake—it's a life handed over. Yes, salvation begins when we repent and believe. But the proof we meant it? That shows up in how we live. Not perfectly—but faithfully."

Irene sat back, processing.

"So salvation isn't earned, but it is revealed?"

"Exactly." I paused.

"When Jesus says He won't cast out anyone who comes to Him, He's not promising to bless lip service. He's talking about real surrender—hearts that come broken, humble, and hungry for Him. He receives those. He transforms those."

"So we don't work for salvation, but real salvation produces good works?"

"Right." I opened my Bible. "Ephesians 2:8–9 says we're saved by grace through faith, not by works—but the very next verse says we're created in Christ for good works. If there's no fruit, something's wrong with the root."

Irene smiled faintly. "That makes sense. And it also explains why Jesus said:"

And why call you Me, Lord, Lord, and do not the things which I say? (Luke 6:46)

I nodded. "It's not about being perfect. It's about direction. When He's truly Lord, our hearts turn toward Him. We grow. We repent. We keep going."

Irene looked down, reflective.

"You know, I think a lot of us came to Him for salvation . . . but we're just now learning what it means to make Him Lord."

I smiled. "And that's okay. That's part of the journey. He doesn't cast us out when we're slow to learn. He walks with us. But He won't let us stay half-hearted either. He's full of grace—and full of truth."

Irene whispered. "That's the Jesus I want to follow."

"Then keep coming to Him," I said gently. "And don't stop."

◆◆◆

THE REVELATION OF JESUS CHRIST REVEALS:

¹⁷⁹ And here is the mind which has wisdom. The seven heads are seven mountains, on which the woman sits.

This verse serves as a key interpretive moment in Revelation 17. The angel invites the reader to use wisdom—this isn't just surface-level information. Spiritual discernment and a knowledge of Scripture and history are required to understand the symbolism.

The phrase "seven mountains" has traditionally been interpreted as a reference to Rome, famously known as "the city on seven hills." In ancient times, Rome was described by poets and historians as being built upon seven literal hills—Aventine, Caelian, Capitoline, Esquiline, Palatine, Quirinal, and Viminal. Therefore, many believe this points to Rome as the geographic and spiritual seat of the harlot, lending weight to the view that Mystery Babylon is tied to Roman ecclesiastical power—particularly in connection to the Roman Catholic Church and its historical influence over kings, nations, and religious systems.

But the text goes further: "And here is the mind which has wisdom." This phrase suggests that more is going on beneath the surface. The mountains may represent not only a geographical location but also seven kings or kingdoms, as verse 10 will clarify. This reflects composite symbolism—Rome may be the historical type, but it points forward to a global religious and political system in the end times.

This verse echoes the language of Revelation 13:18—"Here is wisdom." That earlier chapter dealt with identifying the number of the beast (666). Now, it's about identifying the city and system behind the woman who rides the beast.

This system:

- Looks religious (symbolized by the woman)
- Is politically powerful (rides the beast)
- Has historical roots in Rome
- Will culminate in the final global rebellion against God

OLD TESTAMENT FORESHADOWS REVELATION:

Behold, I am against you, O destroying mountain, says the LORD, which destroys all the earth: and I will stretch out My hand upon you, and roll you down from the rocks, and will make you a burnt mountain. (Jeremiah 51:25)

Both verses speak symbolically of mountains, not just as geographical features, but as emblems of power and dominion. In Revelation 17:9, the "seven mountains" refer to the scope and seat of the woman's influence. In Jeremiah 51:25, the "destroying mountain" is symbolic of Babylon, which—like the woman in Revelation—wields power to corrupt and destroy the earth. God's judgment in both cases is directed not just at a location, but at a system of domination, pride, and false worship.

THE REVELATION OF JESUS CHRIST REVEALS:

[17:10] And there are seven kings: five are fallen, and one is, and the other is not yet come; and when he comes, he must continue a short space.

This verse continues the angel's explanation of the symbolic seven heads, now clarified to also represent seven kings or kingdoms—world empires throughout history that have ruled in opposition to God and His people.

"And there are seven kings: five are fallen." The phrase is widely interpreted as referring to five historic world empires that have already risen and fallen by the time of John's writing in the first century AD.

These kingdoms—Egypt, Assyria, Babylon, Medo-Persia, and Greece—each played significant roles in biblical history and in their oppression of God's people. From Egypt's enslavement of Israel to Babylon's destruction of Jerusalem, these empires were not merely political powers; they embodied systems of rebellion against God. By Revelation's account, they had already fallen, setting the stage for what was present in John's day—and what was still to come.

"One is." This refers to the sixth empire, present in John's day—Rome. Rome ruled over Jerusalem, crucified Christ, and was actively persecuting the Church at the time John wrote Revelation.

"And the other is not yet come; and when he comes, he must continue a short space." This seventh king—or kingdom—is still future from John's perspective. It will rise for a brief and decisive moment in history, representing a revived expression of imperial world dominance. In our view, this is America. Though influential, the United States is relatively young—just 250 years old—especially when compared to the long-standing reigns of previous world empires. Yet despite her youth, she emerges with unparalleled global influence.

This passage is both historical and prophetic—it outlines the flow of global kingdoms that lead to the final showdown between Christ and the beast. The phrase "continue a short space" implies a temporary reign—a warning that though the final empire may appear powerful, its time is limited by God's sovereignty.

"Here is the mind which has wisdom" (verse 9). The symbolism here isn't meant to be casual—it requires spiritual discernment and prophetic insight. John is being shown a heavenly overview of how earthly kingdoms rise, fall, and culminate in the final rebellion before Christ returns.

OLD TESTAMENT FORESHADOWS REVELATION:

And in the days of these kings shall the God of Heaven set up a Kingdom, which shall never be destroyed: and the Kingdom shall not be left to other people, but it shall break in pieces and consume all these kingdoms, and it shall stand forever. (Daniel 2:44)

Daniel 2:44, that's Christ's Millennial Kingdom—the Rock cut without hands that smashes all other kingdoms and stands forever. It shows Gentile world empires in statue form—culminating in Christ's eternal reign. Revelation 17:10 interprets these empires as seven kings, five of which had already fallen in John's day. Both passages anticipate a final empire (the seventh kingdom), followed by the Kingdom of Christ.

THE REVELATION OF JESUS CHRIST REVEALS:

[17:11] And the beast that was, and is not, even he is the eighth, and is of the seven, and goes into perdition.

This verse presents a profound paradox—introducing a final ruler or kingdom described as the eighth, yet "of the seven."

"And the beast that was, and is not." This echoes Revelation 17:8 and refers to a kingdom or ruler that once existed, vanished—likely through a fatal wound—and then reemerges in a counterfeit resurrection. This mirrors the Antichrist in Revelation 13:3, whose apparent death and miraculous revival astonish the world.

"Even he is the eighth." Though seemingly new, this final form is not truly separate. It is the culmination of all previous empires—an intensified, climactic manifestation of satanic rebellion. The Antichrist's empire appears distinct, but it is deeply rooted in the legacy of those that came before.

"And is of the seven." This beast draws from the spiritual DNA of earlier empires: the pride of Babylon, the absolutism of Persia, the intellectual brilliance of Greece, and the iron strength of Rome. It is a fusion of everything that defied God, now embodied in one global, end-time regime.

"And goes into perdition." Despite its terrifying rise, the beast's end is guaranteed—eternal ruin. "Predition" speaks to utter destruction, confirmed in Revelation 19:20, when the beast is cast into the Lake of Fire.

Together with verses 9–10, this passage ties the seven heads to seven kingdoms— Egypt, Assyria, Babylon, Medo-Persia, Greece, Rome, and America. The eighth represents the final Antichrist system—revived, deceptive, spiritually corrupt, and doomed. It underscores the cyclical nature of rebellion throughout history, climaxing in one final empire. But it also affirms a greater truth: no matter how powerful evil becomes, its judgment is certain, and Christ's victory is assured.

OLD TESTAMENT FORESHADOWS REVELATION:

Thus he said, The fourth beast shall be the fourth kingdom upon earth, which shall be diverse from all kingdoms, and shall devour the whole earth, and shall tread it down, and break it in pieces. And the ten horns out of this kingdom are ten kings that shall arise: and another shall rise after them; and he shall be diverse from the first, and he shall subdue three kings. (Daniel 7:23–24)

This prophecy in Daniel 7:23–24 parallels Revelation 17:11, where we witness the rise of a final empire—one that evolves from the legacy of previous global powers, yet takes on a new and more sinister form. The "eighth" beast in Revelation closely mirrors the "little horn" of Daniel 7: a ruler who arises from among established nations, yet proves uniquely powerful, blasphemous, and ultimately doomed. Both passages emphasize more than political transitions— they reveal a supernatural counterfeit kingdom marked by deception, domination, and defiance against God. And both affirm that while these powers may appear unstoppable, divine judgment will prevail.

THE REVELATION OF JESUS CHRIST REVEALS:

17:12 And the ten horns which you saw are ten kings, which have received no kingdom as yet; but receive power as kings one hour with the beast.

This verse introduces ten future rulers, identified as "horns"—a prophetic symbol of power and authority (Daniel 7:24). Unlike historical monarchs, these kings have not yet received their kingdoms at the time of John's vision. Instead, they will emerge in the end times as part of a ten-nation coalition or global alliance, distinct from any past empire.

The phrase "received no kingdom as yet" emphasizes that these rulers are part of a future prophetic fulfillment, likely a revived form of Roman-style global governance—possibly an international body or union of elite world powers.

They will receive their authority "for one hour with the beast," indicating a brief but divinely appointed window of influence. This is not an accident of history, but a strategic moment in God's timeline. Their purpose is singular: to unite under the Antichrist's leadership during the final phase of human rebellion.

This vision corresponds directly with Daniel 7:24, which also describes ten kings arising from the fourth beast. These ten kings likely represent global elites— whether political, economic, or military—who will relinquish their individual sovereignty to serve a common agenda.

Yet, despite their apparent power and unity, their reign is short-lived and doomed. It is a counterfeit kingdom permitted for a season but destined for destruction. Their authority is not earned, but granted, and strictly limited by God's sovereign hand.

OLD TESTAMENT FORESHADOWS REVELATION:

And whereas you saw the feet and toes, partly of potter's clay, and part of iron, the kingdom shall be divided; but there shall be in it of the strength of the iron, forasmuch as you saw the iron mixed with miry clay. And as the toes of the feet were partly of iron, and partly of clay, so the kingdom shall be partly strong, and partly broken. And whereas you saw iron mixed with miry clay, they shall mingle themselves with the seed of men: but they shall not cleave one to another, even as iron does not mix with clay. (Daniel 2:41–43)

Daniel 2:41–43 describes the final stage of world empires as a kingdom divided—symbolized by feet and toes made of iron and clay. This fragile, unstable mix reflects both strength and weakness. The "ten toes" correspond prophetically with the "ten horns" in Revelation 17:12, representing ten end-time rulers. These ten kings will not have received kingdoms yet, but will rise briefly with the Antichrist, sharing power for "one hour." Just as iron and clay do not hold together, this final alliance will be marked by division and internal instability. The parallel between Daniel's statue and Revelation's beast reveals a unified biblical picture of a final, fragile global order that will ultimately fall to the unshakable Kingdom of Christ (Daniel 2:44).

THE REVELATION OF JESUS CHRIST REVEALS:

[17:13] These have one mind, and will give their power and strength to the beast.

This verse reveals the coordinated allegiance of the ten kings to the Antichrist. Though distinct rulers, they are unified in purpose—sharing "one mind." This unity isn't natural; it is spiritually driven, part of Satan's strategy to centralize global power under the beast.

Their surrender is complete: they give their authority and strength to the beast, voluntarily becoming instruments of his final empire. This recalls the rebellion at Babel (Genesis 11:1), where humanity's unified defiance led to divine judgment. Now, that same rebellious spirit reemerges on a global scale.

In contrast to the Church—united by the Holy Spirit in truth—these kings are united by deception and destruction. Their short-lived alliance paves the way for swift judgment (Revelation 17:16–17), showing that unity apart from God leads only to ruin.

OLD TESTAMENT FORESHADOWS REVELATION:

For they have consulted together with one consent: they are confederate against You. (Psalm 83:5)

In Revelation 17:13, the ten kings "have one mind" and unite to give their authority to the beast—a picture of global consensus and alliance for evil. In

Psalm 83:5, a coalition of nations conspires together "with one consent" against God's people, forming a military and political confederacy. Both passages describe a unified alliance of rulers or nations with a common agenda—ultimately opposing God and His purposes.

THE REVELATION OF JESUS CHRIST REVEALS:

[17:14] These will make war with the Lamb, and the Lamb will overcome them: for He is Lord of lords, and King of kings: and they that are with Him are called, and chosen, and faithful.

This verse signals the climax of earth's final rebellion—a direct confrontation between the kingdom of darkness and the Kingdom of Christ. Though the ten kings and the beast unite in war against the Lamb, the outcome is never in doubt: the Lamb triumphs.

"These will make war with the Lamb." The "these" refers to the ten kings of verse 13—leaders aligned with the beast, empowered by Satan, and committed to resisting Christ. This points to the future Battle of Armageddon (Revelation 19:19), where global forces gather in open defiance of the returning King.

"And the Lamb will overcome them." In stunning contrast to the world's might, Christ appears as the Lamb—gentle, yet all-powerful. His victory isn't just military; it's divine. The word "overcome" (Greek *nikao*) echoes John's themes of spiritual victory (John 16:33; 1 John 5:4–5). Christ's identity as the Lamb underscores that he conquers not by force alone, but by sacrificial authority.

"For He is Lord of lords, and King of kings." This exalted title affirms Christ's absolute supremacy. Earthly rulers may boast of power, but their thrones are dust compared to His. This echoes Deuteronomy 10:17 and 1 Timothy 6:15, where God is praised as the highest authority in heaven and earth.

"And they that are with Him are called, and chosen, and faithful." These are Christ's followers—those who responded to His call (Romans 8:30), were chosen by grace (Ephesians 1:4), and remained faithful even unto death (Revelation 2:10). At His return, they ride with Him, clothed in white (Revelation 19:14), sharing in His glory and triumph.

This verse is a sober yet hope-filled reminder: no matter how vast the opposition, no worldly empire can defeat the Lamb. His victory is certain. And those who walk with Him—called, chosen, and faithful—will reign with Him. In the end, it's not about political might or military strength. It's about allegiance to the King who cannot be defeated.

OLD TESTAMENT FORESHADOWS REVELATION:

The noise of a multitude in the mountains, like as of a great people; a tumultuous noise of the kingdoms of nations gathered together: the LORD of hosts musters the host of the battle. They come from a far country, from the end of heaven, even the LORD, and the weapons of His indignation, to destroy the whole land. (Isaiah 13:4–5)

In Revelation 17:14, ten kings join forces with the beast to make war against the Lamb. Yet, Christ—the Lord of lords and King of kings—overcomes them, leading an army of the *called, chosen,* and *faithful.* Likewise, Isaiah 13:4–5 depicts the Lord Himself mustering an army—His weapons of indignation—to bring judgment on rebellious nations. Both passages present a prophetic picture of divine confrontation: nations assemble in defiance, a great clash looms, and heaven responds with sovereign fury. The imagery of global multitudes, military tumult, and God's appointed wrath reveals the futility of human rebellion and the certainty of Christ's ultimate victory.

THE REVELATION OF JESUS CHRIST REVEALS:

17:15 And he says to me, The waters which you saw, where the whore sits, are peoples, and multitudes, and nations, and tongues.

This verse serves as an interpretive key: the angel explains that the "waters" mentioned earlier (Revelation 17:1) symbolize global populations—not literal seas. The phrase "peoples, multitudes, nations, and tongues" underscores the vast, worldwide scope of the harlot's influence. Mystery Babylon is not confined to a single region—it is global, spanning cultures, nations, and civilizations.

This language mirrors Genesis 11 and the Tower of Babel, where humanity was once unified in rebellion until God scattered them by language. In the end times, that scattered world reunites—not in godly harmony, but in universal apostasy, orchestrated by this counterfeit spiritual system.

Mystery Babylon is a transnational and transcultural power—a religious and ideological force that seduces and dominates the world through deception, false worship, and spiritual fornication. Her position "upon the waters" indicates influence over the masses—governing, manipulating, and corrupting nations through her appeal.

OLD TESTAMENT FORESHADOWS REVELATION:

Now therefore, behold, the LORD brings up upon them the waters of the river, strong and many, even the king of Assyria, and all his glory: and he shall come up over all his channels, and go over all his banks. (Isaiah 8:7)

In Isaiah 8:7, "the waters of the river" metaphorically represent a powerful invading force, in this case, the Assyrian empire. The imagery of raging, overflowing waters is used throughout the Old Testament as a symbol of invading peoples, powerful nations, or overwhelming political and military force. This matches Revelation 17:15, where "waters" are explicitly interpreted as "peoples, and multitudes, and nations, and tongues." This parallel helps illustrate how biblical prophecy often uses water imagery to symbolize large-scale geopolitical movement and control—a theme echoed powerfully in Revelation's unveiling of Mystery Babylon's global dominion.

THE REVELATION OF JESUS CHRIST REVEALS:

17:16 And the ten horns which you saw upon the beast, these will hate the whore, and will make her desolate and naked, and will eat her flesh, and burn her with fire.

This verse unveils a stunning reversal: the same political powers (symbolized by the ten horns) that once upheld Mystery Babylon—the corrupt religious-political system—will ultimately destroy her. Though they cooperated with her for a time, their allegiance was only temporary.

"They will hate the whore"—a sharp turn from alliance to animosity. Once Babylon has served her purpose, the beast and his kings reject her. "Make her desolate and naked" speaks to the stripping away of her wealth, influence, and pretense. "Eat her flesh" is graphic imagery of complete devouring, possibly from within, while "burn her with fire" reflects the severity and finality of divine judgment—echoing Old Testament penalties for harlotry (Leviticus 21:9).

This is not just human betrayal but a fulfillment of God's sovereign plan. The very powers she once seduced become instruments of her ruin. Her end reminds us: worldly alliances rooted in corruption are unstable and doomed. Babylon's downfall is a warning to all systems built on compromise and spiritual infidelity—used, exposed, and finally judged.

OLD TESTAMENT FORESHADOWS REVELATION:

Behold, I am against you, says the LORD of hosts; and I will discover your skirts upon your face, and I will show the nations your nakedness, and the kingdoms your shame. And I will cast abominable filth upon you, and make you vile, and will set you as a gazing stock. And it shall come to pass, that all they that look upon you shall flee from you, and say, Nineveh is laid waste: Who will bemoan her? Where shall I seek comforters for you? (Nahum 3:5–7)

This vivid passage from Nahum mirrors the judgment described in Revelation 17:6 and 17:16, where Mystery Babylon, the symbolic harlot, is exposed, disgraced, and ultimately destroyed. Just as Nineveh—the once-glorious harlot city—is stripped bare and made a public spectacle, Babylon too is "made desolate and naked" and burned with fire.

In both cases, the Lord Himself initiates the judgment, lifting the veil of false glory and revealing the filth beneath. The imagery is stark: exposure, humiliation, rejection. The nations that once admired these cities now recoil in horror and abandon them. The parallel is unmistakable—what begins as seduction ends in shame. The harlot who once ruled the nations becomes a desolate ruin, judged by God and scorned by those who once benefited from her influence.

Nahum's prophecy against Nineveh serves as a chilling prophetic echo of Babylon's fall in Revelation. It reinforces the consistent biblical theme: God will not be mocked by systems that parade sin in the guise of power. What is built on pride, oppression, and spiritual infidelity will fall.

Irene, pointing to her open Bible and the U.S. map spread across the table, said gravely, "Ann, that verse you just read—Nahum 3:5–7—it wasn't just about Nineveh. It speaks to Mystery Babylon—and it feels like a warning aimed straight at America. This isn't symbolism anymore. It's happening right in front of us. Have you looked at how the 2017 and 2024 total solar eclipses intersect over the U.S.?"

I nodded. "Yes. The 2017 eclipse—called the 'Great American Eclipse'— swept from Oregon to South Carolina. The 2024 one traced a path from Texas to Maine. Together, they form a perfect 'X' over the heart of the nation—or maybe a Cross. And where they intersect? *Carbondale, Illinois*. They call it the 'Crossroads of America.' If that's not prophetic, I don't know what is."

Irene leaned in. "It feels like God Himself drew an 'X' across the land—as if to say, 'Time's up.'"

"I added, "And it gets even more sobering. That 2024 eclipse didn't just trace a path across the nation—it passed over seven towns named *Nineveh*. That's no coincidence. That's a harbinger . . . a divine warning."

Irene, flipping through her notes, read aloud: "Nineveh, Texas. Missouri. Indiana. Ohio. Pennsylvania. Virginia. New York. Seven towns. And in Scripture, seven always points to completion—divine fulfillment. Could this be *our* Jonah moment?"

I, thoughtful: "Jonah's message was simple—'Yet forty days, and Nineveh shall be overthrown' (Jonah 3:4). It was a countdown. They repented, and judgment was withheld. But a century later, Nahum came—and this time, there was no warning, no invitation to turn back. Only judgment."

Irene whispered, "It's like we're living in the space between Jonah and Nahum. That 'X' across the nation? Maybe it was a seven-year warning—2017 to 2024. And now, we could be in a final four-year window—2024 to 2028—a last breath of mercy before judgment falls."

I leaned in. "And right in the middle of that timeline? Trump re-emerges—survives two assassination attempts, one involving a head wound. It's impossible not to think of the head wound imagery in Revelation 13:3, 12 and 14."

Irene, nodding: "Exactly. Whether people love him or hate him, I believe God has given Trump an assignment. He wants to be a peace president, but everything is pointing to him becoming a wartime president. And Elon Musk? His goals with Neuralink might sound noble—but they're laying the technological groundwork for the mark of the beast system."

I agreed. "Right. Trump's push for digital currency seems innovative—until you realize it opens the door to total control. It's not about demonizing them. It's about understanding that God is allowing the infrastructure to be built—one the Antichrist will ultimately seize and weaponize."

Irene nodded solemnly. "They're tools—pawns in a larger prophetic picture. And America? Spiritually, we're in Nineveh's shoes. But the question is: which Nineveh are we? The city that repented—or the one Nahum declared judgment upon?"

I replied, "Nahum 3:5–7 exposes Nineveh—stripped bare, publicly shamed. It's the same imagery in Revelation 17:16, where Mystery Babylon is devoured and burned by the very kings she once seduced. It's a recurring pattern."

Irene whispered, "A prophetic echo."

I said, "And the shame is isn't hidden—it's public. This isn't just divine judgment; it's exposure. America, once a beacon of light to the nations, now exports corruption and mocks the God who blessed her."

Irene, eyes welling with tears, whispered, "That's why those seven towns named Nineveh beneath the eclipse feel like a final harbinger—a divine warning we can't ignore. Jonah gave Nineveh forty days. What if we've been given four years, from 2024 to 2028? Forty days—4 + 0 equals 4. And in Scripture, four often represents the earth, the created world . . . even finality."

I continued, "God told us to look up. He gave the sun, moon, and stars as signs—not just for seasons, but to mark prophetic times. What if these eclipses aren't just cosmic events, but heaven's trumpet call?"

Irene's eyes widened. "And what about the Shemitah cycle? Every seven years, God gives nations a reset. The next one ends in 2028."

I nodded. "Which could align with the Rapture. But here's what most people miss—our calendar isn't God's calendar. The Jewish civil year begins in Tishrei, around September, and the religious new year starts in Nisan, around March. So, 2028 overlaps with 2029 on God's timetable."

Irene, barely above a whisper: "So we're not watching dates—we're crossing prophetic thresholds."

I, resolute. "That's why I wrote *The Vanishing: The Day Will Begin Like Any Other—Until the Rapture Silences the World*. I want people to see how the biblical feasts, the Shemitah cycles, and God's calendar all converge—and how little time we may truly have left."

Irene, trembling, "Then what do we do?"

I answered softly: "We watch. We warn. We weep. And we remain faithful. Jonah's message still echoes—repent or perish. But if Nahum's shadow is falling over us, then our urgency has never been greater."

Irene, voice breaking, "Then we pray like never before—and speak the truth, no matter the cost."

I took her hand and said gently: "Amen. Whether America repents or falls, we must stand like Jonah in the city and Nahum on the wall. Truth-tellers. Watchmen. Messengers of mercy—while there's still time."

THE REVELATION OF JESUS CHRIST REVEALS:

17:17 For God has put in their hearts to fulfill His will, and to agree, and give their kingdom to the beast, until the words of God shall be fulfilled.

This verse unveils a profound truth behind the chaos of end times: God is sovereign—even over evil alliances.

"For God has put in their hearts to fulfill His will, and to agree." The ten kings and the beast may appear as independent agents of rebellion, but they are not operating outside God's authority. As with Pharaoh in Exodus or Babylon in Jeremiah 25:9, God can use even the wicked to accomplish His divine purposes. He implants unity in their hearts, not for righteousness, but as part of His judgment against the harlot system.

"And give their kingdom to the beast." This refers to the transfer of global authority to the Antichrist. The ten kings voluntarily relinquish their power, forming a unified world government. But their submission is temporary—a part of God's plan, not their triumph.

"Until the words of God shall be fulfilled." Every prophetic word, every decree spoken through Scripture, will come to pass. This line draws the curtain back on heaven's master plan: nothing is random. Every twist in history, every political shift, is moving toward the fulfillment of God's unshakable Word.

Revelation 17:17 is not a statement of despair but a reassurance of divine orchestration. What may seem like chaos is, in fact, part of a larger, sovereign design. Even the Antichrist and his kingdom are instruments in God's hands—

used for a time, then judged in perfect justice. This verse anchors us in confidence: God is not reacting—He is reigning.

OLD TESTAMENT FORESHADOWS REVELATION:

The king's heart is in the hand of the LORD, as the rivers of water: He turns it withersoever He will. (Proverbs 21:1)

Proverbs 21:1 affirms God's control over rulers—even when they act for evil. In Revelation 17:17, God places it in the hearts of ten kings to hand their kingdoms to the beast, fulfilling His will. Though their actions seem rebellious, they serve God's larger purpose. Just as He steered Pharaoh or Babylon, He directs end-time events to fulfill prophecy and bring about Christ's return.

THE REVELATION OF JESUS CHRIST REVEALS:

[17:18] And the woman which you saw is that great city, which reigns over the kings of the earth.

This final verse of Revelation 17 strips away the last layer of symbolism and delivers a startling truth: the woman—the harlot riding the beast—is not just a religious entity or abstract metaphor. She is a literal city, a centralized power with global reach and influence. This city reigns over the kings of the earth, meaning she holds sway over the world's political systems, economic engines, and spiritual climate. Her authority is not confined to the spiritual realm—it extends to presidents, monarchs, prime ministers, and international coalitions.

In John's time, that city was unmistakably Rome, the capital of an empire that dominated the known world. But this prophetic vision stretches beyond first-century Rome. It anticipates a New World Order—an end-time Babylon—where a singular city embodies the convergence of spiritual deception, political manipulation, and economic control. Whether this "great city" is a literal rebuilt Babylon, a future version of Rome, or a modern global capital such as New York, Washington D.C., Brussels, or another metropolis, the point remains clear: she is the nexus of corrupted power and influence.

This woman, Mystery Babylon, is not a passive victim but an active manipulator—a mother of harlots. She gives birth to systems of false religion, apostasy, and immorality that infiltrate and contaminate the nations. Her influence is intoxicating, seductive, and deadly. She thrives on power, wealth, and deception, and her throne is established upon the waters—meaning the masses of people, languages, and nations she dominates.

The phrase "reigns over the kings of the earth" speaks to the merger of church and state, where spiritual corruption and political ambition feed each other. This harlot city wields immense control, not merely by force, but through seduction, ideology, and economic enticement. Her reach is universal, her strategies are subtle, and her downfall is certain.

Revelation 17:18 is not just a conclusion—it is a key. It unlocks the identity of the woman, exposes the foundation of her influence, and prepares the reader for what comes next. Revelation 18 will reveal her sudden and violent destruction. What the world sees as a majestic city, Scripture unveils as a harlot drunk with the blood of the saints, destined to be judged by the very kings she once ruled.

This verse is a divine indictment—a reminder that any power, city, or system that exalts itself against God and exploits others for gain will ultimately face the wrath of a righteous King. Mystery Babylon may seem untouchable, but her fall is inevitable, swift, and complete.

OLD TESTAMENT FORESHADOWS REVELATION:

> Sit you silent, and get you into darkness, O daughter of the Chaldeans: for you shalt no more be called, The lady of kingdoms. (Isaiah 47:5)

Isaiah 47:5 portrays Babylon as the proud "Lady of Kingdoms," once exalted but destined for shame and ruin. Revelation 17:18 mirrors this, revealing the woman as "that great city" ruling over earthly kings. Both represent dominate, corrupt powers brought low by divine judgment. The connection between Isaiah and Revelation underscores how ancient Babylon's fall foreshadows the final collapse of Mystery Babylon—spiritual, global, and doomed.

SUMMARY OF REVELATION 17

Revelation 17 introduces one of the most provocative and symbolic figures in Bible prophecy—Mystery Babylon the Great, described as "the mother of harlots and abominations of the earth" (Revelation 17:5). John is carried away in the Spirit into the wilderness, where he sees a woman seated upon a scarlet-colored beast with seven heads and ten horns (Revelation 17:3). She is clothed in purple and scarlet, adorned with gold, precious stones, and pearls, and holds a golden cup filled with abominations (Revelation 17:4). Her wealth and appearance suggest religious grandeur, but her identity reveals spiritual corruption.

The beast she rides represents political power—resurrected empires and future kingdoms under the Antichrist. The woman, meanwhile, is a counterfeit religious system that aligns with political leaders, deceives nations, and persecutes the saints. John marvels at this vision—not because of the beast, but because the Church he had known was persecuted and poor. Yet here stands a religious system that is rich, influential, and drunk with the blood of the martyrs (Revelation 17:6).

The angel explains that the seven heads symbolize both seven mountains and seven kings—representing a sequence of dominant world empires: Egypt, Assyria, Babylon, Medo-Persia, Greece, Rome, and a seventh, widely interpreted as modern America (Revelation 17:9–10). These kingdoms rise and fall in succession, leading to an eighth—embodying the final Antichrist system. This eighth kingdom is deceptive, spiritually corrupt, and destined for destruction. It is described as the beast "that was, and is not, and yet is"—a chilling reference to a revived empire under satanic influence (Revelation 17:8, 11). The ten horns signify ten kings who will emerge in the end times. Though their rule is brief, they will receive authority together and give their allegiance fully to the beast. (Revelation 17:12–13).

Shockingly, the very kings who once empowered the woman will ultimately betray her, turning violently against her and leaving her desolate (Revelation 17:16). This dramatic reversal isn't random—it's divinely orchestrated. God uses their rebellion to execute His judgment on the false religious system she represents. The chapter concludes by identifying the woman as "that great city, which reigns over the kings of the earth" (Revelation 17:18). Many interpret this as a prophetic symbol of a revived Roman or Babylonian-style global power—often associated with modern America due to its unparalleled political, economic, and cultural influence.

KEY TAKEAWAYS

- Mystery Babylon revealed—Symbolizes a global religious system corrupted by wealth, power, and compromise.
- The woman and the beast—Represents the alliance between false religion and political power.
- Spiritual adultery and persecution—The woman is drunk with the blood of the saints, highlighting centuries of religious persecution.
- Seven mountains and ten kings—Allude to historical empires and future leaders united under the Antichrist.
- God's sovereignty over judgment—God allows this system to rise, but He also orchestrates its downfall through the very kings who once empowered it.

Revelation 17 is a sobering unveiling of false religion's rise and fall. It reminds believers that not all that appears spiritual is righteous, and that ultimate allegiance must be to Christ, not institutions. While the world is seduced by Mystery Babylon's influence, God's people are called to discernment, purity, and endurance. The woman rides for now—but the Lamb will reign forever.

Chapter 16

Revelation 18: Interlude— Commercial Babylon Influencing Global Politics

AMERICA'S FINAL HOUR—The Fall of Commercial and Religious Babylon. Revelation 18 shifts the lens. Where Revelation 17 revealed Religious Babylon—the spiritual harlot seducing kings and riding the beast—Revelation 18 exposes Commercial Babylon, the global marketplace of greed, luxury, and corruption. Yet both are faces of the same end-time entity: Mystery Babylon, a system as old as Babel, now grown into full maturity and destined for divine collapse.

A mighty angel descends with the holy authority, declaring, "Babylon the great is fallen, is fallen!" (Revelation 18:2). This is more than the fall of an empire—it's the unraveling of a civilization. The sins of this system have piled to heaven like another tower of Babel, provoking God's final judgment.

What dazzled the world with prosperity and influence becomes desolate in an instant. Kings are shaken. Merchants weep. The pillars of the global economy tremble. And at the center of it all stands a nation long seen as a beacon of liberty and blessing—America. Once a land of covenant and consecration, she now exports immorality, mocks truth, and shelters demonic ideologies. The great city that once launched missionaries now manufactures rebellion.

But this judgment is not without mercy. Even in wrath, God issues a final invitation: "Come out of her, My people, that you be not partakers of her sins, and that you receive not of her plagues" (Revelation 18:4). This is more than a call to geographical relocation—it's a call to spiritual separation. A warning to disentangle from the comforts of compromise, from the luxuries of a fallen culture, and from the false gospel of tolerance without truth.

Revelation 18 is not just a forecast of economic collapse. It is a divine ultimatum. A final trumpet blast to the faithful. A closing chapter for a nation once consecrated—and now corrupted.

One last call.

One final call.

And a decision for every believer: Will you remain entangled—or will you come out before the fire falls.

FROM COVENANT TO CORRUPTION: AMERICA'S DECLINE

America did not begin as Babylon—she began in covenant with God. From the windswept shores of Plymouth Rock, our forefathers consecrated this land to the glory of God and the advancement of the Gospel of Jesus Christ. The Mayflower Compact was not just a civil document—it was a sacred vow, a declaration that this new nation would honor the God of the Bible.

In 1789, on the very ground that would later become Ground Zero, America's first Congress gathered at Federal Hall in New York City. After George Washington took the oath of office, they walked in unity to St. Paul's Chapel, where they committed the infant nation to God in solemn prayer. That same chapel—small, stone, and unshaken—would miraculously survive the collapse of the Twin Towers centuries later, standing as a silent witness to both America's consecration and her warning.

Our founding documents bore the fingerprints of faith. The Declaration of Independence appealed to "Nature's God," "the Creator," and "the Supreme Judge of the world." The U.S. Constitution, penned by men deeply shaped by Scripture, reflected a reverence for moral law, personal liberty, and divine accountability. Courtrooms displayed the Ten Commandments. Currency carried the confession: "In God We Trust." America's legal and cultural framework was built on a Judeo-Christian ethic—a foundation of religious, moral, and ethical values drawn from both Judaism and Christianity, emphasizing justice, human dignity, and moral responsibility.

But somewhere along the way, we broke the covenant.

- We removed prayer from our schools.
- We legalized the slaughter of the unborn—over 60 million lives lost.
- Even after *Roe v. Wade* was overturned, abortion remains legal—and celebrated—in many states, often up to the moment of birth.

- We exalt pride over repentance, perversion over purity, and tolerance over truth.
- We've redefined marriage, dismantled gender, and taught children ideologies that war against God's design for family.

The spirit of Babylon has crept into our education systems, media, government, and even our pulpits. We no longer blush—we boast. We glorify what God calls an abomination. We platform perversion and persecute righteousness. Like ancient Israel, we now call evil good and good evil.

And still—God warns.

September 11 was more than a tragedy. It was a harbinger. A divine wake-up call. But rather than repent, we responded with defiance. Our leaders stood on national platforms and quoted Isaiah 9:10, not realizing that this verse was not a promise of hope—but a prophecy of rebellion and judgment.

> The bricks are fallen down, but we will build with hewn stones: the sycamores are cut down, but we will change them into cedars. (Isaiah 9:10)

Revelation 18 shows us the destination of a nation that began in covenant and ends in corruption. America, once a shining city on a hill, now teeters on the brink of divine judgment—not because God has abandoned her, but because she has forsaken God.

Still, the voice from heaven cries out: "Come out of her, My People" (Revelation 18:4). The time to repent is now. The hour to return to covenant is now. The question remains: Will we be remembered among the righteous—or forgotten among the ruins as Babylon falls?

"Wow, Ann . . ." Irene whispered, leaning back with wide eyes. "When you really step back and look at it all—the covenants, the Scriptures etched in stone, the prayers, the dedication to God—it's stunning. We were a nation founded in faith. And now—look how far we've fallen."

"It is stunning," I said softly, my voice steady. "But it's also sobering. Because most people don't see it. They don't realize how prophetic our national journey has been. We began in reverence—on our knees. Now we flirt with rebellion, celebrate sin, and call it freedom. And worst of all—we've forgotten the very One who gave us that freedom."

"Do you think we'll even make it to our 250th birthday in 2026?"

I looked at her solemnly. "Honestly? Only if there's repentance. Not political theater or a surge of patriotism. I'm talking about true repentance—a return to the God of our fathers. A national awakening. Without that . . . Revelation 18 shows us exactly what happens when a nation collapses beneath the weight of its own iniquity."

"And yet," Irene said softly, "we were born with such purpose. That phrase—'a city on a hill'—that wasn't just poetic, was it?"

I shook my head. "No, Irene. It was prophetic. John Winthrop spoke those words even before the Pilgrims stepped off the boat. America was meant to be a light—a witness to the nations. But when light is dimmed by compromise, it becomes darkness."

Irene sat forward. "Okay, Ann. Can we shift gears for a moment? Help me trace the journey—from Plymouth Rock to New York City to Washington, D.C. I want to follow the timeline."

"Absolutely!" I smiled. "It's a story of divine direction guided by practical steps. Here's the basic outline:"

1.   Plymouth Rock (1620)

"This was the spiritual foundation of America. The Pilgrims landed seeking religious freedom, and they signed the Mayflower Compact—not just a political agreement, but a covenant to honor God in this new land. Long before the thirteen colonies existed, there was a prayerful beginning."

2.   New York City—Federal Hall (1789)

"By then, the colonies had declared independence and ratified the U.S. Constitution. George Washington took the first presidential oath at Federal Hall on Wall Street. That same day, Congress walked to nearby St. Paul's Chapel and dedicated the new nation to God in prayer. Remarkably, that very chapel—small and historic—stood untouched amid the ruins of 9/11. A silent witness to both our consecration and our warning."

3.   Washington, D.C. (1800)

"Eventually, the capital was moved to a more central, neutral location. John Adams became the first president to occupy the White House. His prayer still echoes: 'May none but honest and wise men rule under this roof.' Tragically, that prayer has not always been heeded."

4.   From 13 to 50 States

"After independence, America began to grow. Between 1791 and 1796, three new states were added—Vermont, Kentucky, and Tennessee. From 1803 to 1821, states like Ohio, Indiana, and Missouri joined, marking early westward expansion. Between 1836 and 1848, Arkansas through Wisconsin entered the Union. The

Gold Rush brought California in 1850, and by 1859, Oregon had secured Pacific access."

"Despite the Civil War, the nation continued expanding—Kansas to Colorado entered from 1861 to 1876. A surge of western states followed from 1889 to 1896—North Dakota through Utah. By 1912, with Arizona and New Mexico, the 'Lower 48' were complete. Finally, in 1959, America reached her current 50 states with the additions of Alaska and Hawaii."

I paused, then added, "From those humble beginnings, the nation stretched from sea to shining sea. But no matter how large we've become, the question still remains: will we stay true to the God who blessed our beginning?"

"It's amazing," Irene whispered. "Those weren't just political milestones—they were spiritual markers. Symbolic ones."

"Exactly," I nodded. "From the windswept shores of Massachusetts to the steps of the Capitol, God was written into our national story from the very beginning. But now . . . we've pushed Him to the margins."

"And Revelation 18," Irene said, her voice soft, "it feels like the final chapter . . . unless we return."

I looked at her, my voice barely audible. "Unless we return."

"Wait a second, Ann—" Irene leaned in.

"Didn't Christopher Columbus discover America in the 1400s. But then you mentioned the Pilgrims in the 1600s. I'm confused. Who actually *founded* America? And why did they leave their homes in the first place?"

I smiled gently. "That's a great question, Irene—and honestly, you're not alone. Everyone remembers the rhyme, 'In 1492, Columbus sailed the ocean blue.' Yes, he sailed under the Spanish flag and opened the door to the New World. But he didn't *found* America. He mostly landed in the Caribbean and parts of Central and South America."

"So he didn't start America as a Christian nation?"

"No, that came over a century later. The covenant story begins in 1620, when the Pilgrims arrived on the shores of what would become Massachusetts."

"Right, right—Plymouth Rock!" Irene nodded. "So why did they come here, really?"

"They were fleeing religious persecution," I explained. "They were English Separatists—Christians who broke away from the Church of England. The state church had become corrupt, tightly bound to political power, and hostile toward biblical preaching."

I continued. "At first, they fled to the Netherlands—cities like Leiden. But even there, they feared for their children's future. Dutch culture was highly secular, and they saw it eroding their spiritual foundations. So they prayed—and God opened the door for a daring voyage across the Atlantic."

"That's so brave," Irene said quietly. "They left everything behind?"

"Everything. These weren't political rebels—they were people of *covenant*. They longed to build a community where they could worship God freely, raise godly families, and govern themselves under the authority of Scripture. That's why they wrote the Mayflower Compact. It literally begins with the words: 'In the name of God, Amen.'"

"So the root of America isn't just exploration—it's consecration."

"Exactly," I nodded. "Columbus opened a map. The Pilgrims opened a covenant. They weren't chasing gold or empire—they were pursuing freedom to follow Jesus Christ without fear. That's why we call them the *spiritual* forefathers of America."

"And Great Britain wouldn't allow them that freedom?"

"No. The Crown and the Church of England were deeply entangled. If you didn't conform to the state religion, you risked prison, fines—even death. These believers finally said, 'Enough. We must go where Christ is Lord—not the king, not the pope.'"

Irene exhaled slowly. "So America wasn't born out of rebellion—it was born out of revival."

"Exactly," I said. "Our beginnings weren't perfect, but they were intentional. These were people who believed that God's Word should rule hearts more than any king's sword could rule hands."

Irene leaned back thoughtfully. "So, why do people say America is 250 years old in 2026? Weren't the Pilgrims here way before that?"

I nodded. "They were—1620 at Plymouth Rock. But 1776 is when America officially declared independence from Britain. That's when we became a nation."

"Ah," Irene said, "so 1776 is like our national birthday?"

"Exactly," I smiled. "The Declaration of Independence was our birth certificate. Everything before that was preparation—spiritual foundation, covenant beginnings—but 1776 is when we said, 'We're a sovereign nation under God.'"

Irene nodded slowly. "So we're not just turning 250—we're standing at a crossroads."

"Right," I said gently. "It's more than a celebration. It's a call to remember where we started—and who we're supposed to be."

———◆◆◆———

GUARDIANS AGAINST HARLOT RELIGION: THE FINAL WARNING

Revelation 18 does not unveil a new adversary—it pronounces a final judgment on a spiritual system God has warned about for millennia. What was once whispered by the prophets is now declared by a mighty angel: Mystery Babylon's time is up. Her seduction is exposed. Her sentence is sealed.

This chapter brings full clarity to what Jeremiah, Ezekiel, and others saw only in pieces—the rise and reign of a harlot system that began at Babel, wove its way through empires and temples, and now dominates global civilization. The so-called *queen of heaven*, the mother of false religion and spiritual corruption, has reached her final hour. And heaven does not grieve—heaven rejoices (Revelation 18:20).

Throughout history, God raised up prophets to confront her. They stood in the gap, calling out idolatry disguised as tradition, sensuality dressed in religious robes, and compromise labeled as peace. Many were mocked. Many were martyred. But they spoke truth. And now, the system they warned about no longer hides—it defines the culture.

Revelation 18 reveals that the harlot spirit now reigns openly. It markets rebellion as righteousness, turns worship into commerce, and celebrates a counterfeit "sacred mother and child" while denying the true Son. This isn't religion—it's spiritual rebellion dressed in the garments of reverence.

Her sins have reached unto heaven, and God has remembered her iniquities. (Revelation 18:5)

This is why the voice from heaven urgently cries, "Come out of her, My people" (Revelation 18:4). The line is drawn. The harlot church will not merge with the Bride of Christ. Light has no fellowship with darkness. False worship cannot coexist with truth.

What began with subtle compromise ends in full exposure and judgment. Babylon's idols may carry new names—tolerance, inclusivity, feminism, mysticism—but the spirit behind them is ancient. They exalt self, deify the feminine, and marginalize Christ. This is the heart of Babylon's religion. And Revelation 18 shows the consequence of embracing it.

This isn't just paganism—it's apostasy. Not innocent ignorance, but willful deception. Not just misguided people, but a spiritual empire drunk with the blood of saints and saturated with demonic influence (Revelation 18:2, 24). And in the end, God does not merely expose it—He destroys it. He collapses the architecture of false worship, dismantles the marketplace of spiritual corruption, and executes justice on the empire built on blasphemy.

The prophets warned. The Scriptures confirmed. Now, the Judge speaks.

Final Word: The Hour Has Come

Revelation 18 isn't just an account of Babylon's collapse—it's a final call to every nation, church, and soul caught in her web. The judgment it describes is not symbolic—it is swift, fiery, and absolute. This is God's verdict on a civilization that once walked in covenant and now dines in darkness.

America's story mirrors Babylon's: from dedication to desecration, from shining city to spiritual ruin. But still—mercy calls. "Come out of her, My people." That call still echoes. It is the thread of mercy woven into the pages of wrath. The hour is late. The fire is near. And the choice remains: Will we remain entangled—or will we come out of her?

THE REVELATION OF JESUS CHRIST REVEALS:

[18:1] And after these things I saw another angel come down from heaven, having great power; and the earth was lightened with his glory.

This verse marks a dramatic shift—a heavenly interruption in the unfolding judgment. After witnessing the harlot's rise and fall in Revelation 17, John now sees "another angel" descending from heaven—not just any angel, but one with great authority, whose radiant glory lights up the entire earth.

This brilliance stands in stark contrast to Babylon's darkness. The world, steeped in deception and spiritual corruption, is suddenly illuminated—symbolizing divine revelation, exposure, and the pronouncement of judgment. It echoes Ezekiel 43:2, where the glory of the LORD fills the temple, and Isaiah 60:1–2, where God's light shines while deep darkness covers the earth.

The phrase "after these things" links this moment to Revelation 17 but signals a new phase of divine action. This is no longer just the spiritual fall of Babylon—it is the collapse of an entire global system: religious, economic, and political. The angel's descent declares heaven's final verdict and carries heaven's authority to execute it.

As with past warnings—whether in Sodom (Genesis 19) or Nineveh (Jonah 3)—God sends messengers before judgment falls. And here, the angel's glory foreshadows the brilliance of Christ Himself, who will soon replace Babylon's counterfeit light with the true Light of the World.

OLD TESTAMENT FORESHADOWS REVELATION:

And, behold, the glory of the God of Israel came from the way of the east: and His voice was like a noise of many waters: and the earth shined with His glory. (Ezekiel 43:2)

Both Revelation 18:1 and Ezekiel 43:2 describe a heavenly being arriving with glory so radiant that it illuminates the earth. The "glory of God" shining across the earth in Ezekiel directly parallels the angel of great power whose descent lights the earth in Revelation. The imagery of light, heavenly descent, and global impact are clear prophetic markers in both texts, emphasizing divine authority and impending action.

THE REVELATION OF JESUS CHRIST REVEALS:

18:2 And he cried mightily with a strong voice, saying, Babylon the great is fallen, is fallen, and is become the habitation of devils, and the hold of every foul spirit, and a cage of every unclean and hateful bird.

This verse is one of the most thunderous declarations in all of Scripture—a divine indictment against the final world system known as "Mystery Babylon." The angel's voice is not soft or symbolic. It is mighty, unignorable, echoing like a trumpet blast of judgment across the earth. His cry signals the irreversible collapse of a once-dominant spiritual and political empire: "Babylon the great is fallen, is fallen."

"Is fallen, is fallen"—finality and fulfillment. The repetition isn't poetic embellishment—it emphasizes certainty and finality. This echoes Isaiah 21:9: where Babylon's fall is similarly declared with absolute assurance:

And, behold, here comes a chariot of men, with a couple of horsemen. And he answered and said, Babylon is fallen, is fallen; and all the graven images of her gods He has broken unto the ground. (Isaiah 21:9)

It also confirms the earlier warning in Revelation 14:8, now fulfilled. Babylon's fall is no longer a prophecy—it's a present reality.

"And is become the habitation of devils." The word "*become*" is crucial. Babylon wasn't always a stronghold of evil. It *devolved*—through rebellion, compromise, and apostasy. This transformation serves as a warning: when truth is rejected and God is abandoned, spiritual deterioration is inevitable. What began as powerful or prosperous becomes a magnet for demonic activity. Babylon is now a dwelling place for devils, a haven of foul spirits, and a cage for spiritual corruption.

This mirrors the prophetic imagery of Isaiah 13:19–22, where Babylon's fall results in desolation inhabited by wild, unclean creatures: "It shall never be inhabited . . . and their houses shall be full of doleful creatures."

"And the hold of every foul spirit, and a cage of every unclean and hateful bird." Unclean birds, in prophetic literature, symbolize false doctrines, deceptive spirits, and demonic interference. This parallels Jesus' parable in Matthew 13:4, 19, where birds snatch away the seed—representing Satan's efforts to prevent truth from taking root. Babylon has not only corrupted government and commerce but also ensnared the world through spiritual darkness.

This is not just ancient prophecy—it's a present-day wake-up call. Babylon's descent into demonic habitation wasn't sudden; it was the result of sustained rebellion and rejection of truth. And the pattern is repeating. America, like Babylon, was once shaped by covenant and conviction—but now flirts with the same spiritual decline. Revelation 18:2 doesn't just reveal Babylon's fate; it warns every nation standing at the edge of compromise. The threshold of judgment is real. But so is the opportunity for mercy. While there is still time, let us repent. Let us return. Before the darkness falls completely, may we once again be lit by the glory of God.

OLD TESTAMENT FORESHADOWS REVELATION:

And Babylon, the glory of kingdoms, the beauty of the Chaldeans' excellency, shall be as when God overthrew Sodom and Gomorrah. It shall never be inhabited, neither shall it be dwelt in from generation to generation: neither shall the Arabian pitch tent there; neither shall the shepherds make their sheepfold there. But wild beasts of the desert shall lie there; and their houses shall be full of doleful creatures; and owls shall dwell there, and satyrs shall dance there. (Isaiah 13:19–21)

Both passages speak of the fall of Babylon as an act of divine judgment. Isaiah's prophecy refers to ancient Babylon's total desolation, filled with wild, unclean creatures—matching Revelation's image of a city turned into a "habitation of devils" and "unclean birds." The unclean animals represent demonic presence and spiritual corruption, emphasizing God's total rejection of the place. Revelation draws from this imagery to portray Mystery Babylon—a future global spiritual and commercial power—falling under the same kind of irreversible judgment as the literal Babylon of the Old Testament.

THE REVELATION OF JESUS CHRIST REVEALS:

[18:3] For all nations have drunk of the wine of the wrath of her fornication, and the kings of the earth have committed fornication with her, and the merchants of the earth are waxed rich through the abundance of her delicacies.

This verse gives us a sobering picture of the global influence and corruption of Mystery Babylon. It highlights three key groups impacted by Babylon's fall: the nations, the kings, and the merchants—each entangled in her web of wealth, idolatry, and spiritual seduction.

"For all nations have drunk of the wine of the wrath of her fornication"— global seduction. The metaphor of wine signifies intoxication—not with literal alcohol, but with spiritual compromise, materialism, and rebellion against God.

This verse suggests that the entire world has willingly participated in Babylon's sins. Her "fornication" represents idolatry, false religion, and unholy alliances—a mixing of what is sacred with what is profane. This is more than just religious compromise—it's spiritual adultery on a global scale. Nations have not merely tolerated Babylon; they've become drunk with her influence, losing clarity and moral discernment.

"And the kings of the earth have committed fornication with her"—political complicity. The kings—political leaders and rulers—are said to have entered into fornication with Babylon. This indicates alliances built on greed, corruption, and power plays, rather than on righteousness or justice. These are governments and regimes that have profited from, protected, or been seduced by Babylon's wealth and influence. They're not innocent observers—they're active participants in her idolatrous system.

"And the merchants of the earth are waxed rich through the abundance of her delicacies"—commercial prosperity. This portion zeroes in on the economic arm of Babylon. The merchants—global businesspeople, corporations, and traders—have grown wealthy through Babylon's luxuries and consumerism. The word "delicacies" (Greek: *strenos*) implies luxurious living, sensual indulgence, and excess. The merchants have exploited the demand for luxury, vanity, and pleasure, growing rich through Babylon's obsession with self-indulgence.

For example:

- America's vast economic engine has fed global supply chains, from fashion and entertainment to military and tech industries.
- Foreign aid, reconstruction efforts, and trade deals have helped other nations become prosperous—but often at the cost of spiritual compromise and alignment with Babylon's corrupt systems.

This mirrors modern globalization: powerful economies seduce nations into economic dependence, and in exchange, those nations often adopt the values and worldview of the power they depend on.

This verse isn't just a critique of wealth—it's a warning against wealth that flows from rebellion against God. It calls out the false peace and prosperity that blinds nations, leaders, and businesses to their spiritual bankruptcy. When Babylon falls, everything built on her false promises collapses with her.

Babylon's fall is not just a financial collapse—it is a moral and spiritual reckoning. The entire world will feel the impact, especially those who have benefited from her wickedness. As believers, we are reminded to remain separate from the world's systems (Revelation 18:4) and store up treasures not on earth—but in heaven (Matthew 6:19–21).

OLD TESTAMENT FORESHADOWS REVELATION:

When your wares went forth out of the seas, you filled many people; you did enrich the kings of the earth with the multitude of your riches and of your merchandise. (Ezekiel 27:33)

In Ezekiel 27:33, Tyre, like Babylon in Revelation, was a wealthy maritime trade empire, and its merchants and kings grew rich through commerce and luxury. Tyre's fall is depicted as a tragedy for the nations that traded with her—mirroring the lament of the merchants in Revelation 18:11–19. The language of riches, delicacies, and international influence aligns with Revelation 18:3, where Babylon's corruption and wealth have intoxicated nations and rulers alike. Both passages emphasize the judgment of God upon economic idolatry and spiritual fornication through wealth and commerce.

THE REVELATION OF JESUS CHRIST REVEALS:

18:4 And I heard another voice from heaven, saying, Come out of her, My people, that you be not partakers of her sins, and that you receive not of her plagues.

This verse marks one of the most powerful and compassionate turning points in Revelation 18. While the chapter unfolds the dramatic judgment of Babylon—the global spiritual and economic empire—verse 4 issues a divine warning and a merciful invitation: "Come out of her, My people."

"Come out of her, My people, that you be not partakers of her sins." This call echoes the Old Testament pattern of deliverance before destruction—just as God called Lot out of Sodom (Genesis 19:12–17), and called Israel out of Egypt (Exodus 5:1), so now He pleads with His people to exit Babylon before judgment falls. "Let My people go, that they may serve Me."—Exodus 5:1.

The voice from heaven is urgent and clear: Separation is survival. God's people are not meant to cozy up to Babylon's system of greed, pride, immorality, and false religion. To remain in her is to risk being judged with her.

Who are "My people"? While some interpret this call as directed primarily toward believing Jews—especially given Babylon's historical Jewish population and America's modern parallel—the phrase undeniably encompasses all who truly belong to God. Jew and Gentile alike are included in this divine summons. Revelation 18:4 is a clarion call to the remnant, the faithful, and even the spiritually slumbering. It urges repentance, discernment, and a decisive break—both spiritual and, where necessary, physical—from Babylon's seductive grip. This is not merely a geographic command, but a heart-level call to come out of compromise and align wholly with the holiness of God.

"And that you receive not of her plagues." God's mercy is revealed in the warning itself. Before the hammer falls, the voice from heaven gives time to escape. This is reminiscent of Lot's rescue from Sodom (Genesis 19:12–17) and Rahab's deliverance from Jericho (Joshua 2)—both examples where divine warnings preceded destruction, and obedience marked the path to salvation.

Ultimately, we are reminded once again that spiritual Babylon is not merely a symbol—it's a system. A seductive blend of religion, politics, and commerce. And Revelation 18:4 is God's final altar call to anyone still entangled. If judgment is near, the time to come out is now.

OLD TESTAMENT FORESHADOWS REVELATION:

Depart you, depart you, go you out from there, touch no unclean thing; go you out of the midst of her; be you clean, that bear the vessels of the LORD. (Isaiah 52:11)

Both verses are a divine call to separate from a corrupt or defiled system. In Isaiah 52:11, the command is to leave Babylon—literal and spiritual—and remain pure, especially for those who are carrying out God's holy purposes. In Revelation 18:4, God's people are likewise warned to come out of spiritual Babylon to avoid sharing in her sins and her judgment.

THE REVELATION OF JESUS CHRIST REVEALS:

[18:5] For her sins have reached to heaven, and God has remembered her iniquities.

This verse stands as a divine indictment—one steeped in the language of final judgment. Babylon's sins, like bricks in a tower, have been stacked so high they symbolically breach the heavens themselves. This is no coincidence—it recalls Genesis 11, where humanity arrogantly attempted to build the Tower of Babel "whose top may reach unto heaven." What began as architectural defiance has evolved into spiritual rebellion. Babylon's descendants have indeed reached heaven—not with stone and mortar, but with iniquity.

"God has remembered her iniquities." The phrase is chilling. It does not imply that God had forgotten—it means that His divine patience has run its course. Babylon's guilt has ripened to the point of no return. For a time, it appeared she was escaping consequences: living in luxury, seducing nations, and committing spiritual adultery. But now, the time of judgment has come. What was once tolerated is now being judged. Her sin is no longer hidden—it's full, flagrant, and festering before God's throne.

Note the progression:

1. Judgment has already begun. The earth has reeled under the 21 judgments—seals, trumpets, and bowls—each one escalating heaven's response to unrepentant sin.

2.   But before Christ's return—before Armageddon and the marriage supper of the Lamb—God pauses the prophetic timeline. Why? To deal decisively with Babylon. This is not a footnote judgment—it is a centerpiece of divine justice.

3.   Why such a dramatic interruption? Because Babylon has defiled the world. Her influence is global—polluting governments, seducing economies, corrupting religion, and perverting moral truth.

This is no ordinary empire. Babylon is a spiritual contagion—a system that traffics in both goods and souls. Her wealth intoxicates. Her influence deceives. Her religion mocks God while mimicking holiness. Revelation 18:5 marks the tipping point. God's forbearance ends. Justice descends.

"God has remembered." That is not just a statement—it's a sentence. Judgment is no longer delayed. The divine scales tip, and Babylon's sins now demand reckoning.

OLD TESTAMENT FORESHADOWS REVELATION:

And the LORD said, because the cry of Sodom and Gomorrah is great, and because their sin is very grievous; I will go down now, and see whether they have done altogether according to the cry of it, which is come unto Me; and if not, I will know. (Genesis 18:20–21)

Genesis 18:20–21 describes how the sin of Sodom and Gomorrah cried out to God, prompting His judgment. Likewise, in Revelation 18:5, Babylon's sins have "reached to heaven," signaling that God's patience has run out. Both accounts highlight a key truth: persistent, unrepentant sin eventually demands a holy response. When iniquity reaches its fullness, mercy gives way to judgment. The time for reckoning comes—and God, in His justice, acts.

THE REVELATION OF JESUS CHRIST REVEALS:

[18:6] Reward her even as she rewarded you, and double unto her double according to her works: in the cup which she has filled fill to her double.

This verse initiates Babylon's divine sentencing. The command, "reward her even as she rewarded you," reflects the principle of divine justice—what she did to others is now returned upon her own head. As Obadiah 1:15 declares: "As you have done, it shall be done unto you; your reward shall return upon your own head."

"And double unto her double according to her works"—double judgment for double sin. This is not vindictive revenge—it is righteous and proportional. In the Old Testament, double restitution was sometimes required for theft and fraud (Exodus 22:4, 7). Here, Babylon's offenses are so severe that her judgment is doubled. She poured out a cup of greed, idolatry, immorality, persecution, and deception. Now, God fills her cup with wrath—twice over.

"In the cup which she has filled fill to her double"—judgment that fits the crime. Babylon deceived nations, seduced kings, and corrupted commerce. Now, her empire collapses under the weight of its sin. As in Jeremiah 25:15–16, where God made the nations drink the cup of His fury, Babylon must drink deeply of the judgment she earned.

God's justice is both deliberate and multiplied. Babylon had every opportunity to repent, but she refused. Now, the time has come: the cup of iniquity has overflowed—and she receives back not only what she gave, but double.

OLD TESTAMENT FORESHADOWS REVELATION:

> Call together the archers against Babylon: all you that bend the bow, camp against it round about; let none thereof escape: recompense her according to her work; according to all that she has done, do unto her; for she has been proud against the LORD, against the Holy One of Israel. (Jeremiah 50:29)

Jeremiah 50:29 parallels Revelation 18:6 by declaring that Babylon will be repaid according to all she has done—because of her pride against the LORD. Both passages emphasize God's justice: what Babylon inflicted on others will be returned to her, doubly so. The core message is that divine retribution is proportional, rooted in God's holiness, and carried out by Him—not man. Pride and rebellion are the root offenses, and judgment is the inevitable result.

THE REVELATION OF JESUS CHRIST REVEALS:

> [18:7] How much she has glorified herself, and lived deliciously, so much torment and sorrow give her: for she says in her heart, I sit as a queen, and am no widow, and shall see no sorrow.

This verse exposes the pride, delusion, and false security of end-times Babylon. Her self-glorification and indulgent lifestyle are not just signs of wealth—they are evidence of deep spiritual corruption.

"How much she has glorified herself, and lived deliciously." The Greek word translated "lived deliciously" (*streniao*) implies reckless luxury and wanton indulgence—a self-centered abundance without accountability. Babylon exalts herself in opulence, living like royalty, but with no fear of God. Her materialism fuels her arrogance.

"I sit as a queen, and am no widow, and shall see no sorrow." This boast is chilling. It reflects the mindset of invincibility—of one who believes she is above judgment. This exact language echoes ancient Babylon's pride in Isaiah 47:7–8, where she declared herself eternal and untouchable. But such arrogance is the seed of her downfall.

This "queen" refuses to acknowledge that judgment is coming. She mocks the idea of loss, widowhood, or grief. It's a strange boast, especially in biblical language, where widowhood often symbolizes spiritual loss—as in:

- Lamentations 1:1—"How does the city sit solitary, that was full of people! How is she become as a widow!"
- Isaiah 54:4–5—Israel is called a widow whom the LORD will redeem.
- Leviticus 21:14—A widow is forbidden to be the wife of a high priest—symbolizing defilement or unfitness for holy union.

Biblically, widowhood is often a metaphor for loss, vulnerability, or spiritual abandonment. Babylon claims immunity from sorrow and judgment, believing her wealth insulates her from divine wrath. Yet this false confidence mirrors the Laodicean church in Revelation 3:17, which believed it was "rich and in need of nothing," but was, in God's eyes, "wretched, miserable, poor, blind, and naked."

Babylon is not a pure bride awaiting her groom—she is a harlot pretending to be a queen. Her pride will be answered with proportional punishment: "so much torment and sorrow give her." This reflects God's justice throughout Scripture—"Pride goes before destruction" (Proverbs 16:18). As she lifted herself up, so she will be brought down.

In the end, Babylon symbolizes a world system built on self-idolatry, sensuality, and rebellion. Its outward beauty conceals inner rot. Revelation 18:7 is both a prophecy and a warning: wealth without repentance leads to ruin, and pride—no matter how regal—always precedes the fall.

OLD TESTAMENT FORESHADOWS REVELATION:

And you said, I shall be a lady forever: so that you did not lay these things to your heart, neither did remember the latter end of it. Therefore hear now this, you that are given to pleasures, that dwell carelessly, that says in your heart, I am, and none else beside me; I shall not sit as a widow, neither shall I know the loss of children: But these two things shall come to you in a moment in one day, the loss of children, and widowhood: they shall come upon you in their perfection for the multitude of your sorceries, and for the great abundance of your enchantments. (Isaiah 47:7–9)

Isaiah 47:7–9 offers a striking parallel to Revelation 18:7. Both portray a proud, self-exalting power—Babylon in Isaiah and Babylon in Revelation—declaring, "I shall be a lady forever" and "I am no widow." These boastful claims reflect a dangerous delusion of permanence and immunity from judgment. In both cases, the figure lives in pleasure, denies sorrow, and insists, "I am, and none else beside me." Yet God declares that loss and widowhood will strike suddenly, exposing the arrogance rooted in sorcery, enchantments, and rebellion. Isaiah's literal Babylon and Revelation's end-times Babylon share the same spirit of pride, luxury, and idolatry—and both face swift, divine judgment.

THE REVELATION OF JESUS CHRIST REVEALS:

18:8 Therefore shall her plagues come in one day, death, and mourning, and famine; and she shall be utterly burned with fire: for strong is the Lord GOD who judges her.

This verse delivers a climactic declaration of divine judgment. Babylon's sins—stacked high like a tower—now demand swift and irreversible consequences. The phrase "in one day" underscores the suddenness and shock of her collapse. What once appeared unshakable will fall instantly, with no time for repentance or retreat.

This mirrors the plagues of Egypt in Exodus 9:14, where God's judgments were not mere natural events but direct confrontations with false gods and national pride. Like Egypt, Babylon trusted in her wealth, idolatry, and self-glorification—and now faces divine retribution.

The trio of plagues—death, mourning, and famine—signals total unraveling:

- Death claims the people.
- Mourning grips the survivors.
- Famine breaks the illusion of prosperity.

The phrase "utterly burned with fire" conveys not just destruction but purification. Fire in Scripture often symbolizes God's holy judgment and consuming presence (Malachi 4:1), revealing the spiritual rot hidden beneath Babylon's outward splendor.

The final line reminds us who is in control: "For strong is the Lord GOD who judges her." This is not chaotic collapse but sovereign justice. Babylon's judgment is righteous, final, and unstoppable—executed by a God whose strength far surpasses her counterfeit power.

OLD TESTAMENT FORESHADOWS REVELATION:

Babylon is suddenly fallen and destroyed: howl for her; take balm for her pain, if so be she may be healed. We would have healed Babylon, but she is not healed: forsake her, and let us go every one into his own country: for her judgment reaches unto heaven, and is lifted up even to the skies. (Jeremiah 51:8–9)

Just like Revelation 18:8 says Babylon's plagues come "in one day," Jeremiah 51:8 says she is "suddenly fallen and destroyed." Both passages reveal that Babylon's sins have reached a point of no return—her judgment is final and irreversible. Jeremiah 51:9 says her judgment has "reached unto heaven," echoing Revelation 18:5 and reinforcing the divine source of the wrath. The plea to "let us go every one into his own country" mirrors Revelation 18:4: "Come out of her, My people." These verses together underscore the completeness and divine certainty of Babylon's fall—both as a literal empire in Jeremiah's day and as a future global system in Revelation.

THE REVELATION OF JESUS CHRIST REVEALS:

18:9 And the kings of the earth, who have committed fornication and lived deliciously with her, will bewail her, and lament for her, when they will see the smoke of her burning.

Revelation 18:9 paints a vivid picture of worldwide grief—not over righteousness lost, but over luxury destroyed. This verse reveals the deep political and economic entanglement that global leaders had with Mystery Babylon. The word "fornication" here is symbolic, representing spiritual and economic unfaithfulness. These kings—world rulers—benefited from her excesses and wealth, aligning with her corrupt systems and material indulgences.

The phrase "lived deliciously" suggest a lifestyle of opulence, indulgence, and self-gratification. These world leaders did not just tolerate Babylon; they were partners in her decadence, willingly complicit in her idolatry, moral compromise, and economic exploitation.

But now, her downfall is visible—"the smoke of her burning" is a dramatic image, indicating catastrophic judgment. This could be symbolic of complete destruction, or even hint at literal fire—perhaps referencing war, divine wrath, or events like nuclear fire or divine calamity. Either way, Babylon's fall is not private—it's public and shocking. Her allies look on, stunned and devastated, because her fall means their downfall is near. She was the source of their wealth, and now that foundation is gone.

The lamentation of these kings is not repentance—it's grief over lost profit. They don't mourn her sins, only her ruin. This reflects the coldness of global politics and economics—where alliances are transactional, and morality is often sacrificed for wealth and power.

This imagery is consistent with Jeremiah 50–51, which foretells the destruction of literal Babylon with similar language of fire, lamentation, and judgment. And Isaiah 47:7–8 reveals Babylon's arrogance: "I shall be a lady forever . . . I shall not sit as a widow," which echoes Revelation 18:7–9.

This judgment is not just poetic, it is prophetic. It reminds us that God will ultimately judge every corrupt system—whether political, religious, or economic—that sets itself up in defiance of His righteousness. Babylon's fall is a warning for all nations: what seems immovable can fall in an instant.

OLD TESTAMENT FORESHADOWS REVELATION:

Who has taken this counsel against Tyre, the crowning city, whose merchants are princes, whose traffickers are the honorable of the earth? The LORD of hosts has purposed it, to stain the pride of all glory, and to bring into contempt all the honorable of the earth. (Isaiah 23:8–9)

In Isaiah 23:8–9, Tyre, like Babylon in Revelation 18, was a powerful maritime and trade city. Her "merchants" and "traffickers" were honored by nations—just like the kings and merchants who prospered through Babylon. When Tyre fell, the surrounding nations lamented because their economic ties were severed—mirroring the weeping of kings in Revelation 18:9. God Himself declares the purpose: to bring down pride and worldly glory—exactly what He does to end-time Babylon.

THE REVELATION OF JESUS CHRIST REVEALS:

[18:10] Standing afar off for the fear of her torment, saying, Alas, alas, that great city Babylon, that mighty city! For in one hour is your judgment come.

This verse portrays a moment of global shock and horror as the judgment of end-time Babylon unfolds. The "kings of the earth" (Revelation 18:9)—political leaders who once benefited from Babylon's power, wealth, and immorality—now stand afar off, terrified by her torment, yet unwilling or unable to intervene. They cry out in astonishment: "Alas, alas!"—a mournful dirge repeated for emphasis, signaling deep lament and disbelief.

The emphasis on "one hour" is significant and repeated throughout the chapter (verses 10, 17, 19). It reveals the speed and completeness of God's judgment—swift, decisive, and inescapable. This is not a slow economic decline or gradual fall from grace. It's an instant collapse, leaving no time to prepare, no time to react, and no time to escape.

This mirrors God's judgment on Egypt through the death of the firstborn—sudden, terrifying, and final (Exodus 12). Just as Pharaoh had ignored repeated warnings, Babylon receives sudden destruction after years of defiance, pride, and seduction of the nations.

The phrase "that great city Babylon, that mighty city" underscores Babylon's global prominence. She is the heartbeat of world commerce and finance—the Wall Street of the world. Her downfall shakes the political and economic foundations of the earth. When she falls, it isn't just a city that collapses—it's the system behind it: trade, luxury, debt, and global control. But God's justice always meets pride with humbling. The greater the sin, the greater the judgment.

Kings (Revelation 18:9–10), merchants (Revelation 18:11–17), and sea captains (Revelation 18:17–19)—three categories of global elites—are each described as watching from a distance, mourning, not because of righteousness, but because they lost their source of wealth and security. This signals not repentance, but grief over economic collapse. Their cries reveal just how deeply entwined they were with Babylon's corrupt system.

For the believer, this verse is a sobering warning: do not place your trust in systems, cities, or economies. What seems mighty today can fall in a moment. This verse reminds us of the call in Revelation 18:4: "Come out of her, My people." God's people are called to spiritual separation before the collapse comes.

OLD TESTAMENT FORESHADOWS REVELATION:

But these two things shall come to you in a moment in one day, the loss of children, and widowhood: they shall come upon you in their perfection for the multitude of your sorceries, and for the great abundance of your enchantments. For you have trusted in your wickedness: you have said, None sees me. Your wisdom and your knowledge, it has perverted you; and you have said in your heart, I am, and none else beside me. Therefore shall evil come upon you; you shalt not know from where it rises: and mischief shall fall upon you; you shalt not be able to put it off: and desolation shall come upon you suddenly, which you shalt not know. (Isaiah 47:9–11)

Both Isaiah 47:9–11 and Revelation emphasize "in one day" or "in one hour," stressing the swiftness and surprise of divine justice. Babylon—both historical and prophetic—is described as mighty, self-reliant, and proud, but destined for a swift fall. The surrounding nations stand in shock, just as in Isaiah, where judgment comes with desolation no one can escape. This passage in Isaiah forms a prophetic backdrop to Revelation 18:10, portraying God's timeless pattern: judgment for pride, sorcery, luxury, and defiance.

THE REVELATION OF JESUS CHRIST REVEALS:

[18:11] And the merchants of the earth will weep and mourn over her; for no man buys their merchandise any more.

This verse highlights the economic collapse of the Babylonian system—interpreted by many as a prophetic picture of a global commercial empire. Here, merchants, not kings or religious leaders, express profound grief. Why? Because the foundation of their wealth—the luxurious lifestyle and insatiable consumption associated with Babylon—has been destroyed in an instant.

Who are the merchants? In context, "merchants" refers to global business tycoons, international traders, importers, exporters, and corporate powerhouses. These are the engines of the world's economy—the CEOs, magnates, and industries that profited off the excesses of a fallen system.

Their mourning isn't spiritual—it's economic. They weep not for Babylon's sins, but because "no man buys their merchandise anymore." Their profits vanish. The markets collapse. The system that once guaranteed endless consumption and wealth is gone.

This verse also foreshadows the economic stranglehold of the beast system. Earlier in Revelation (13:16–17), we're told that no one will be able to buy or sell without the mark of the beast. This shows how commerce, control, and worship are intertwined in the final empire. But now, the very commercial Babylon that enforced the beast system is judged. The world that once celebrated economic power is reduced to ashes, and its merchants are powerless to stop it.

This verse also highlights the global interdependence of nations. Just as today's countries are linked through trade, finance, and supply chains, the collapse of one "great city" sends economic shockwaves across the world. Babylon's fall disrupts commerce—imports halt, supply chains disintegrate, and financial towers crumble. This exposes the idolatry of materialism, where luxury and trade have become false gods—and now God brings that system to an end.

This moment parallels Ezekiel 27, where Tyre, the ancient trading hub, is judged by God. Merchants weep, ships mourn, and commerce vanishes. Revelation 18 presents this same pattern—magnified globally. The mourning of merchants in verse 11 isn't out of repentance, but out of grief over lost profit.

It is a sobering reminder: any economy or system built on greed, exploitation, and luxury without righteousness will ultimately fall under the justice of God.

OLD TESTAMENT FORESHADOWS REVELATION:

The merchants among the people shall hiss at you; you shalt be a terror, and never shalt be any more. (Ezekiel 27:36)

Ezekiel 27 is a lamentation over the fall of Tyre, a powerful trading city like Babylon in Revelation. Verse 36 shows merchants reacting in shock and dismay—just like the Revelation 18:11 merchants. It captures the emotional and economic devastation when a global trade center collapses. The phrase "never shalt be any more" mirrors the finality of Babylon's fall in Revelation 18. This verse offers a pointed and poetic reflection of the sorrow and silence that follows when a once-thriving economic empire is judged by God.

THE REVELATION OF JESUS CHRIST REVEALS:

18:12 The merchandise of gold, and silver, and precious stones, and of pearls, and fine linen, and purple, and silk, and scarlet, and all thyine wood, and all manner vessels of ivory, and all manner's vessels of most precious wood, and of brass, and iron, and marble.

This verse opens one of the most sobering and prophetic passages in Revelation. In the context of Babylon's fall, we are shown a list—an inventory of luxury and wealth—detailing the economic lifeblood of a corrupt global system. But this is no ordinary trade report. It is a divine expose.

Revelation 18:12–13 enumerates 28 specific commodities, beginning with gold and ending with the souls of men. This is no coincidence. The structure of the list forms a theological statement: it reveals the descent of a civilization that once valued prosperity and dignity but devolved into spiritual depravity and human exploitation.

- "The merchandise of gold, and silver, and precious stones . . ." These first items are markers of legitimate commerce, beauty, craftsmanship, and prosperity. They represent the beginnings of a flourishing society— an echo of ancient Israel's temple treasury, Solomon's wealth, or the splendor of Eden's resources.
- But as the list continues, the nature of the merchandise shifts. Luxury becomes obsession. Trade becomes exploitation. The items listed move from external wealth to internal corruption—culminating in the trafficking of bodies and souls.

This divine order is a spiritual diagnosis. It's a reminder that when wealth becomes a god, people become commodities. What starts as the blessing of commerce ends in the curse of corruption. And Babylon—the symbolic system of end-times greed, sensuality, and rebellion—embodies this fall completely.

This isn't just about ancient Babylon—it's a mirror held up to our world today. The same spirit lives on in modern systems that still profit from human bondage. Human trafficking and child exploitation are rampant. Pornography has become a global industry of soul-destruction. Forced labor hides behind cheap goods. Addiction industries—whether chemical, digital, or emotional—enslave countless lives. Even our privacy is commodified, sold by tech giants in exchange for power and profit. The soul itself has become merchandise. What Revelation exposed, we now experience. And God's justice will not remain silent forever.

God's warning is clear: any nation or system that descends from honoring God to exploiting humanity is on a path to judgment. Revelation 18:12–13 is not just a shopping list—it's a litmus test. It challenges us to evaluate the systems we support, the values we promote, and the spiritual price we're willing to pay for comfort or convenience.

Jesus warned in Mark 8:36:

> For what shall it profit a man, if he shall gain the whole world, and lose his own soul? (Mark 8:36)

That's the tragic arc of Babylon. But for the believer, the trajectory must be reversed: we value souls above silver, and truth above treasure. Let us not be deceived by Babylon's glitter. The world's riches fade, but the soul endures. May we walk in truth, uphold justice, and cling to Christ—lest we too find ourselves complicit in a system destined for destruction.

OLD TESTAMENT FORESHADOWS REVELATION:

Tarshish was your merchant by reason of the multitude of all kind of riches; with silver, iron, tin, and lead, they traded in your fairs. Javan, Tubal, and Meshech, they were your merchants: they traded the persons of men and vessels of brass in your market . . . Syria was your merchant by reason of the multitude of the wares of your making: they occupied in your fairs with emeralds, purple, and broidered work, and fine linen, and coral, and agate . . . (Ezekiel 27:12–22)

Ezekiel 27 is a prophetic lamentation over Tyre—a city that glorified in its wealth and global influence through trade, yet was ultimately judged by God for its pride and spiritual corruption. Revelation 18 revisits that imagery and applies it to end-time Babylon, showing that the same spiritual system persists throughout history. Revelation 18:12–13 and Ezekiel 27:12–22 are directly connected by theme, imagery, and divine message: *History repeats itself when sin remains unchecked.* Babylon is Tyre reborn—a global economic and spiritual empire that builds itself on the commodification of everything—even souls—and is destined for God's righteous judgment.

THE REVELATION OF JESUS CHRIST REVEALS:

[18:13] And cinnamon, and odors, and ointments, and frankincense, and wine, and oil, and fine flour, and wheat, and beasts, and sheep, and horses, and chariots, and slaves, and souls of men.

This verse completes the inventory of Babylon's merchandise, exposing how deeply commerce, sensuality, and spiritual deception are intertwined. Unlike verse 12's focus on luxury goods, verse 13 emphasizes indulgence, idolatry, and the commodification of life.

Aromatics like cinnamon, ointments, and frankincense symbolize more than wealth—they represent sensuality, religious mimicry, and emotional manipulation. Babylon doesn't erase worship; it commercializes it. Even frankincense, once used for holy purposes, is not part of the market—worship repackaged as product.

Items like wine, oil, flour, and livestock reflect an empire driven by appetite excess. These goods aren't necessities—they're signs of overconsumption and elitist lifestyles. Babylon's economy thrives on indulgence, not need. It is gluttony disguised as prosperity.

But the climax is chilling: "slaves, and souls of men." The trade descends from fragrances to food to flesh. Babylon commodifies human life—physically and spiritually. The Greek word for "souls" (*psychas*) refers to the inner life, the very essence of a person. Babylon not only traffics bodies—it seeks control over identity, mind, and spirit.

Where do we see Babylon in today's world?

- In churches that sell the gospel.
- In corporations that addict for profit.
- In governments that trade in human suffering.
- In a world where nothing is sacred—not even the soul.

Let us not be numb to the warning of Revelation 18:13. This is not just a list of goods—it is a catalog of corruption. It's a prophetic autopsy of a fallen world system. The question we must ask is: Are we trading the sacred for the sensual? Are we selling out the soul for the sake of status? Because Revelation makes one thing clear: Babylon falls. And when it does, every soul it tried to enslave will either be freed by Christ or judged with the system.

OLD TESTAMENT FORESHADOWS REVELATION:

Judah, and the land of Israel, they were your merchants: they traded in your market wheat of Minnith, and Pannag, and honey, and oil, and balm. Damascus was your merchant in the multitude of the wares of your making . . . with wine of Helbon, and white wool. Dan also and Javan going to and fro occupied in your fairs: bright iron, cassia, and calamus were in your market. (Ezekiel 27:17–25)

Just like Revelation 18, Ezekiel 27 reveals a world system obsessed with luxury and profit, even at the expense of human life and sacred values. Tyre was a symbol of economic pride, and its fall was a warning to every future empire—including Babylon in Revelation 18—that God will judge those who enrich themselves through oppression, idolatry, and corruption.

The thing that has been, it is that which shall be; and that which is done is that which shall be done: and there is no new thing under the sun. (Ecclesiastes 1:9)

Revelation 18:13 parallels Ezekiel 27:17–25, forming a prophetic echo that spans the Testaments: Both portray empires built on luxury goods and sensual indulgence. Both expose a perverse economic system that trades in human beings and their souls. Both end in sudden, divine judgment.

THE REVELATION OF JESUS CHRIST REVEALS:

[18:14] And the fruits that your soul lusted after are departed from you, and all things which were dainty and goodly are departed from you, and you will find them no more at all.

Revelation 18:14 continues the mournful cry over the fall of Mystery Babylon, the end-times system of global corruption. This economic and religious political power captivated the world by offering wealth, status, indulgence, and control. But here, we see its total collapse—not only materially, but spiritually. The verse delivers a sobering pronouncement: everything the world once lusted after is gone.

The Scripture says, "And the fruits that your soul lusted after are departed from you." The Greek word for "lusted after" (*epithumia*) carries the meaning of intense craving, longing, or passion. It's not casual desire—it's the kind of inner hunger that defines one's identity and purpose. Babylon wasn't built on trade alone. It was built on humanity's addiction to beauty, luxury, and excess. It wasn't just about food or fashion—it was about comfort, control, identity, and the illusion of superiority. And tragically, the world bought in—completely.

But now? It's all gone—suddenly. The fruits are gone. The dainties are gone. The fashion and finery are gone. The illusion of sophistication and security is gone. And the Holy Spirit delivers a final blow: "You will find them no more at all." In Greek, this is an emphatic phrase meaning "not ever again—absolutely never." This is a total and permanent judgment.

The verse prophetically envisions the collapse of the global luxury economy. High fashion—the prestige of places like Fifth Avenue—turns to ashes. The fine foods, exotic imports, and culinary status symbols vanish forever. Entire economic systems—Wall Street, international supply chains, luxury brands—crumble in an instant. This isn't symbolic; it's a real-world inventory of everything Babylon built and everything God brings to ruin.

And yes—slavery still exists today. Not always in the traditional sense, but economically and psychologically. Modern Babylon thrives on debt bondage, corporate dependence, crushing taxation, and mass consumption. People live paycheck to paycheck, burdened by credit cards, dependent on subsidies, and tied to monthly subscriptions. What the world calls "freedom" is often cleverly disguised bondage.

The commodities of comfort—food, fashion, fragrance, entertainment—become chains. They keep people plugged into Babylon's web, sedated and distracted from eternal things. Revelation 18:12–13 lists 28 commodities, from gold to garments, from spices to slaves. These are literal—not symbolic—divided into four groups of seven. In biblical numerology, four represents the world, and seven represents completion. When these vanish, God is making a final, full declaration: "Enough."

Babylon isn't just falling. It's being erased. And this verse is more than a judgment on a city or nation—it is a call to the Church. Revelation 18:4 calls out,

"Come out of her, My people." This is a wake-up cry. Are we lusting after the fruits of the world? Are we attached to what God is about to strip away? Are we entangled in systems that enslave us and numb our spiritual senses?

If it can be taken from us, it was never eternal. Revelation 18:14 is the obituary of a world that chased luxury and lost its soul. It is a haunting reminder that what we call desirable today may be detestable tomorrow—especially when God judges it. Let us not cling to dainties destined for dust.

Instead, let us fix our eyes on a Kingdom that cannot be shaken (Hebrews 12:28), and store up treasures that will never perish, spoil, or fade (1 Peter 1:4). This is our call—not to blend in with Babylon, but to come out of it. Not to crave what the world adores, but to hunger for what is eternal.

OLD TESTAMENT FORESHADOWS REVELATION:

> When your wares went forth out of the seas, you filled many people; you did enrich the kings of the earth with the multitude of your riches and of your merchandise. In the time when you shalt be broken by the seas in the depths of the waters your merchandise and all your company in the midst of you shall fall. All the inhabitants of the isles shall be astonished at you . . . you are become a terror, and never shalt be any more. (Ezekiel 27:33–36)

Revelation 18:14 echoes Ezekiel 27:33–36 most directly—a judgment against a luxurious, trade-driven city that put its trust in riches. Both passages proclaim a permanent loss: what was once lusted after, celebrated, and enjoyed will never be found again. The wealth you trusted—gone. The pleasures you craved—vanished. Forever.

THE REVELATION OF JESUS CHRIST REVEALS:

18:15 The merchants of these things, which were made rich by her, shall stand afar off for the fear of her torment, weeping and wailing.

This verse captures the emotional collapse of Babylon's economic elite—the merchants who profited most from her global trade empire. Their reaction is not one of repentance—but shock, sorrow, and self-pity. Why? Because everything they trusted in—their wealth, their power, their partnerships with Babylon—is destroyed in an instant.

They "shall stand afar off." This phrase repeats throughout Revelation 18 (versus 10, 15, 17) and reveals something important: They distance themselves from the judgment, but not from the system. They were close enough to profit, but now they're far off to protect themselves. It shows a cowardly detachment—they mourn the loss, but not the sin. These merchants were once close to her, tangled in the web of Babylon's luxury and corruption. Now they retreat in fear, unwilling to suffer with her but unable to forget what they've lost.

"Which were made rich by her." Their grief isn't over righteousness—it's over revenue. They're not crying because Babylon was sinful, but because she was profitable. Their riches were tied to her corruption, and her fall signals their financial ruin. This is a sobering warning to every modern economic system that builds itself on moral compromise, human exploitation, and ungodly alliances. Wealth without God becomes a snare, and when the system collapses, so does the identity and security of those who depended on it.

"For the fear of her torment." This is not compassion—this is terror. They're not afraid of her; they're afraid because of her punishment. It's a fear that says: "If it happened to her . . . it could happen to us." This torment is mental, emotional, and spiritual—they're not in physical flames, but they are in psychological panic. The judgment came suddenly—so severe, so final—it sent a shockwave throughout the world. Babylon's fall wasn't just an economic collapse. It was the unraveling of the seventh world kingdom, just as Revelation foretold.

"Weeping and wailing." The Greek implies loud lamentation—public displays of anguish. These are the cries of regret, not repentance. They are weeping not for the souls lost, but for the lifestyle gone. The dainties, the riches, the comforts—everything they thought was permanent—gone in a day. It mirrors the kind of emotional collapse described in Proverbs 1:26–27, when sudden destruction comes and no remedy remains.

Revelation 18:15 reveals the merchant's selfish sorrow as they mourn Babylon's fall—not out of repentance, but fear and financial loss. They stand at a distance, unwilling to share in her judgment yet devastated by the collapse of the system that made them rich. Their weeping reflects regret over lost luxury, not guilt over sin. It's a sobering picture of how deeply tied their identity was to wealth and comfort. Babylon's fall wasn't just economic—it was the unraveling of the seventh world kingdom, shaking the foundations of those who trusted in it.

OLD TESTAMENT FORESHADOWS REVELATION:

I also will laugh at your calamity; I will mock when your fear comes; when your fear comes as desolation, and your destruction comes as a whirlwind; when distress and anguish comes upon you. (Proverbs 1:26–27)

In Proverbs 1:26–27, wisdom is personified and cries out to the foolish, offering truth and protection. But when she is rejected, the consequences arrive swiftly and shockingly. The laughter of wisdom isn't cruel—it's the divine irony of people who had every chance to turn but refused to listen.

Likewise, in Revelation 18:15, the merchants had grown rich off Babylon's system. They ignored the warnings, profited from corruption, and placed trust in a world that was destined to fall. When judgment comes, they are emotionally and mentally unprepared—just like those in Proverbs. Proverbs 1 is the spiritual root. Revelation 18 is the prophetic fruit.

THE REVELATION OF JESUS CHRIST REVEALS:

^{18:16} And saying, Alas, alas, that great city, that was clothed in fine linen, and purple, and scarlet, and decked with gold, and precious stones, and pearls!

This verse continues the lament over Babylon's sudden fall—this time with a focus on the outer appearance of her wealth and glory. Those who once benefited from her luxury now mourn her destruction, not out of repentance, but because of what they've lost. The grief of merchants, kings, and shipmasters is centered on the collapse of a system that made them rich. Their sorrow reveals a heart tethered to treasure rather than truth.

The description of Babylon's attire—"clothed in fine linen, and purple, and scarlet, and decked with gold, and precious stones, and pearls"—mirrors the imagery of the harlot in Revelation 17:4. This repetition connects Religious Babylon and Commercial Babylon as two manifestations of the same corrupt system: one spiritual, the other economic. Purple and scarlet are colors of royalty and religious authority. Fine linen suggests refinement and false purity. Gold and jewels symbolize extravagant wealth and worldly allure. Altogether, they represent a seductive blend of power, prosperity, and pretense.

Babylon was more than a city; it was a global influence—a system that blended commerce with corruption, wealth with idolatry. The mourners call her "that great city," highlighting her prominence on the world stage. But the greatness was deceptive. Beneath the surface was pride, greed, and spiritual decay. She dazzled the nations with promises of abundance, but lured them into compromise and dependency. Like a harlot, Babylon dressed to impress, but her beauty masked betrayal.

The repeated cry of "Alas, alas" echoes ancient judgments—like those against Tyre in Ezekiel 27 and Nineveh in Nahum 3. These are not cries of repentance but shock and loss. The world weeps not because Babylon was wicked, but because she was profitable. Her riches fed their indulgence. Her fall ends their lifestyle.

Now, her luxury is stripped, her splendor reduced to smoke. Her collapse is not only economic—it is prophetic. It signals the unraveling of the seventh world kingdom, long foretold in Revelation. This empire—whether symbolically or literally tied to a present-day power like America—falls under divine judgment. Her wealth, once envied, becomes her shame. Her glittering facade was built on sand.

The fall of Babylon exposes the heart of a system that idolized prosperity and rejected God. It reveals the danger of tying identity to materialism and success. What looked glorious was in fact rotten. What was celebrated is now condemned. Revelation 18:16 is more than a record of destruction—it is a warning: Do not be seduced by Babylon's sparkle. What dazzles the flesh can destroy the soul. Instead, invest in a Kingdom that cannot be shaken—eternal, holy, and built by God alone.

OLD TESTAMENT FORESHADOWS REVELATION:

You have been in Eden the Garden of God; every precious stone was your covering, the sardius, topaz, and the diamond, the beryl, the onyx, and the jasper, the sapphire, the emerald, and the carbuncle, and gold: the workmanship of your tabrets and of your pipes was prepared in you in the day that you were created. (Ezekiel 28:13)

Ezekiel 28:13, though addressed to the king of Tyre, clearly points beyond a human ruler to Satan himself—glorious in Eden, adorned in beauty, and ultimately corrupted by pride. This dual-layered prophecy reveals both a historical figure and the spiritual force behind him.

The same imagery reappears in Revelation 18:16, where Babylon is described as clothed in gold, jewels, and fine linen. Like Tyre, Babylon dazzled the world with wealth and influence, but beneath the surface lay deep spiritual corruption. Both were economic powerhouses driven by pride and rebellion—and both fell under God's judgment.

Ezekiel 28 foreshadows Revelation 18, revealing that the spirit of Satan—self-exaltation, deception, and idolatry—has powered worldly empires from Eden to Babylon, from Genesis to Revelation. Their beauty was a mask, their wealth a snare, and their fall a divine warning.

THE REVELATION OF JESUS CHRIST REVEALS:

[18:17] For in one hour so great riches is come to nought. And every shipmaster, and all the company in ships, and sailors, and as many as trade by sea, stood afar off.

This verse doesn't whisper—it thunders. It proclaims the sudden collapse of a global economic empire once thought invincible. "In one hour"—a phrase repeated in verses 10, 17, and 19—underscores how rapid, shocking, and irreversible Babylon's fall will be. This isn't a slow decline. It's catastrophic. Instant. Divine. "So great riches is come to nought." What the world considered untouchable is reduced to nothing. This is more than a stock market crash. More than a recession. It is supernatural judgment against a Satanic system disguised as prosperity.

The verse then draws our attention to the seafarers—the shipmasters, sailors, and merchants who once fueled Babylon's wealth. These are the agents of international trade, and now they stand at a distance, watching helplessly as ports close, merchandise halts, and oceanic commerce collapses. Revelation 18:18 says they "saw the smoke of her burning"—a literal, visible destruction, massive enough to be seen from the sea. This suggests a real, identifiable city.

"What city is like unto this great city?" (Revelation 18:18). This is not symbolic language. It describes a global trade center—rich, admired, and deeply interconnected with the world's economy. Some scholars have suggested this points to New York City: home of Wall Street, the United Nations, luxury trade, fashion, finance, media, and culture. A coastal city, visible by sea. A symbol of economic might and, increasingly, moral decline.

Could this city represent more than New York—perhaps even America as a whole? Possibly. But Revelation's emphasis is on a city, one so powerful that its fall sends economic shockwaves around the globe.

The fall of Babylon teaches us three urgent truths:

1. **No system is too big to fall before God**—When judgment comes it is swift, complete, and public.

2. **Economic prosperity can be deceptive**—The world mourns not for truth or justice—but for lost luxury.

3. **God is calling His people to come out**—"Come out of her, My people . . ." (Revelation 18:4) is a divine command, not a suggestion.

Revelation 18:17 is not just about financial ruin—it is a divine warning to a world that has built without God. In one hour, God will prove who truly reigns. Don't anchor your life to Babylon. Don't invest in what God has already decreed will burn. Instead, build on a Kingdom that cannot be shaken (Hebrews 12:28)—one that is eternal, holy, and unbreakable.

OLD TESTAMENT FORESHADOWS REVELATION:

Your riches, and your fairs, your merchandise, your mariners, and your pilots, your calkers, and the occupiers of your merchandise . . . shall fall into the midst of the seas in the day of your ruin. The suburbs shall shake at the sound of the cry of your pilots. And all that handle the oar, the mariners, and all the pilots of the sea, shall come down from their ships . . . and shall cry bitterly . . . (Ezekiel 27:27–30)

Revelation 18:17 closely parallels Ezekiel 27:27–30, highlighting: The collapse of wealth. The devastation of trade. The mourning of maritime merchants. The global ripple effect of God's judgment on commercial empires.

Babylon is the modern Tyre—clothed in riches, commanding the seas, admired by nations—but destined to fall in one hour.

THE REVELATION OF JESUS CHRIST REVEALS:

18:18 And cried when they saw the smoke of her burning, saying, What city is like to this great city!

This verse paints a powerful visual scene: global maritime traders—shipmasters, sailors, and merchants—stand afar off (Revelation 18:17), gazing at black pillars of smoke rising from the once-great city of Babylon. They weep, wail, and wonder, "What city is like unto this great city?" Babylon is utterly burned with fire (Revelation 18:8), a symbol throughout Scripture of God's righteous, consuming judgment.

This one verse, combined with the broader chapter, points to multiple layers of catastrophe:

- Fire (Revelation 18:8, 18)—Possibly missile strikes, bombs, or nuclear war—as referenced in Jeremiah 50:32.
- Earthquake (Revelation 16:18–19)—"So great an earthquake, and so mighty"—God shakes the very foundations.
- Tidal waves (Jeremiah 51:42)—"The sea is come up upon Babylon." A global trade center near the coast, drowned in waves.
- Power grid failure (Isaiah 47:5)—"Get you into darkness." EMP? Solar flares? The lights go out—literally and spiritually.

This is not symbolic only—it speaks of a real-world city, devastated by multiple natural and supernatural forces, in such a way that no one on earth can help or rebuild it.

"What city is like unto this great city!"—This is the voice of shock and admiration—now turned to horror. These merchants once worshiped Babylon's wealth, her trade routes, her innovation, her luxury. Now, they weep not for her righteousness—but for their loss. This phrase becomes a mockery of Babylon's former pride. Like Lucifer in Isaiah 14:16–17—"Is this the one who shook kingdoms?"—the world stands in stunned disbelief at the downfall of what once seemed untouchable. "What city is like this great city?" (Revelation 18:18) is both a lament and a wake-up call.

What kind of city fits such a description today?

- A global center of wealth and influence.
- Admired by all nations for its power and innovation.
- A leader in culture, fashion, finance, and media.
- A city visible from the sea, crowned with towering skyscrapers.

Cities like New York City, Chicago, and Los Angeles often come to mind, embodying many of these prophetic traits. While interpretations vary, the profile Revelation paints is striking—and sobering.

Babylon's burning is not merely the end of a city—it is God's final verdict on a world system built apart from Him. The smoke rising is more than physical destruction; it is the funeral pyre of a fallen world order—commercial, political, and spiritual.

We are not called to weep over Babylon—we are called to come out of her (Revelation 18:4). Let her smoke be a warning. Let her judgment be the turning point. In a world intoxicated with Babylon's dazzle, may we be found sober, set apart, and standing on the unshakable foundation of God's Word.

OLD TESTAMENT FORESHADOWS REVELATION:

And Moses stretched forth his rod toward heaven: and the LORD sent thunder and hail, and the fire ran along upon the ground; and the LORD rained hail upon the land of Egypt. So there was hail, and fire mingled with the hail, very grievous, such as there was none like it in all the land of Egypt since it became a nation. (Exodus 9:23–24)

The fire and hail that fell on Egypt in Exodus 9:23–24 foreshadow the fiery judgment of Babylon in Revelation 18:18. Both are not just acts of destruction, but visible signs of God's wrath against systems that resist Him. Egypt's fire came as a judgment on a hardened nation; Babylon's burning represents the fall of a corrupt, global empire. In both cases, fire falls from heaven, destruction is sudden, and the world watches in fear. What was once powerful and admired is reduced to smoke. Let Babylon's fall be a warning: don't build your life in a world God plans to judge. Build on the eternal Kingdom that will never fall.

Irene, quietly flipping through her Bible.

"Ann . . . we've been sitting with Revelation 18 all day. And I just keep thinking—this feels familiar. Like we've seen God do this before. Judging a proud empire, a wealthy superpower, a nation drowning in idolatry."

Nodding slowly. "You're right, Irene. Revelation 18 isn't just prophecy—it's precedent. God has always judged empires that exalt themselves above Him."

I pulled out my notes.

- Noah's Flood—2348 BC—God's first global judgment, cleansing a corrupt world system not with fire, but with water.
- Sodom, around 2000 BC—burned for its wickedness.
- Egypt, judged in 1446 BC with plagues and parted seas.

- Assyria fell when Nineveh was destroyed in 612 BC.
- Tyre—a proud trading empire, often under Assyrian control—was besieged by Babylon and later crushed by Alexander in 332 BC.
- Babylon, collapsed in 539 BC, the night Belshazzar drank from the sacred vessels.
- Medo-Persia, 539–331 BC—rose under Cyrus, later judged and conquered by Greece.
- Greece, brought under Roman control by 146 BC.
- Rome—the Western Empire fell in AD 476, and the Eastern (Byzantium) in 1453 AD.

Irene nodded. "These aren't just historical accidents—they're divine patterns. When nations grow drunk on their own power, when they exploit and exalt themselves, when they forget the God who gave them breath—judgment follows. Every time."

"Exactly. Take Egypt for example. The same kind of spiritual power that drove Egypt's rise in pride is the same that fueled Mystery Babylon's fall. Ancient principalities don't die—they migrate. They wear new names. They find new hosts. Egypt had its gods—Apis the bull, Baal, Osiris—all symbols of livestock, wealth, and economic dominance. But when God judged Egypt through the plagues—especially the fifth plague—He struck at the core of their economy. The cattle, the horses, their agricultural strength—gone. God wasn't just dismantling a government; He was overthrowing a demonic system."

Irene, wide-eyed. "That's right! Egypt worshiped the bull—and so does America! The 'bull market' isn't just financial jargon. It's spiritual. It's symbolic. And when God judged Egypt, He crushed their cattle. Didn't touch Israel's livestock—but Egypt's? Gone."

I nodded, eyes narrowed. "Exactly. And today, America's bull economy—Wall Street, the dollar, the relentless pursuit of more—is being shaken. Inflation, national debt, the rise of digital currency . . . It's no accident. God is doing what He's always done: stripping idols. Shaking foundations. Because wealth has become worship."

Irene, softly. "And what about the horses . . . the military might?"

Nodding, deeply reflective. "That too. In Egypt, horses represented strength and status—the pride of their chariots. In America, it's our military: unmatched power, global dominance, defense budgets bigger than entire nations. But like Egypt, America has forgotten who gave her that strength. And when God judges, He goes straight for what a nation treasures most."

Irene, her voice trembling. "It's happening again, isn't it? The pattern. Sodom . . . Egypt . . . Tyre . . . ancient Babylon . . . and now—us?"

"Yes. It's the same spiritual cycle. The Lord is confronting territorial powers—those ancient spirits that empower nations to exalt themselves against Him. Revelation 18 isn't just poetic—it's prophetic. It shows how God judges systems, economies, and ideologies that defy His sovereignty. The Tower of Babel, ancient Babylon, and Mystery Babylon—they're not separate stories. They're chapters in the same rebellion. And America—if she refuses to repent— will follow the same path."

Irene, eyes wide with realization. "And the command—'Come out of her, My people'—it sounds just like, 'Let My people go.' It's not just about geography, is it? It's about spiritual alignment."

I nodded. "Exactly. God isn't relocating His people— he's separating them. Out of compromise. Out of corruption. Whether it's Egypt or Babylon, the call is the same: Come out. Be set apart. In Egypt, the plagues were physical. In Revelation, they're both physical and spiritual. But the purpose hasn't changed— deliverance, separation, and purification."

Irene, wiping away a tear. "And America . . . we've been warned, haven't we?"

"Over and over again. The Twin Towers on 9/11. Two total solar eclipses, seven years apart, tracing an 'X' across the heart of America—passing directly over seven towns named Nineveh. That's not coincidence. That's mercy. A Jonah moment. A final warning before the storm. Because God always sends a word before He sends a sword."

Irene sighed. "And just like in Egypt, God is confronting the gods—the false systems, the idols of commerce and pride."

"Exactly. Egypt lost its firstborn, its wealth, its military might. Babylon falls in one hour—suddenly, completely. What God judged in Egypt, He's judging again in Revelation. It's the same spiritual rebellion—just dressed in modern clothing."

Irene, quiet and resolute. "And just like then . . . the people of God must be ready—set apart, surrendered, alert."

I nodded. "Absolutely. We need to be like Moses, Jeremiah, Jonah—willing to speak truth, willing to weep over sin, and willing to wait for the Lord's timing. The hour is late. The signs are here. The call is urgent."

"Then let's pray, Ann," Irene whispered.

"Let's cry out for mercy. Let's wake up the Church—before Revelation 18 stops being prophecy and starts becoming our obituary."

I leaned in, eyes steady. "Amen. Because the same God who judged Egypt and Babylon is the same God who redeems. If we repent, He restores. But if we rebel—He removes. And right now, America stands at the crossroads."

THE REVELATION OF JESUS CHRIST REVEALS:

18:19 And they cast dust on their heads, and cried, weeping and wailing, saying, Alas, alas, that great city, wherein were made rich all that had ships in the sea by reason of her costliness! For in one hour is she made desolate.

"And they cast dust on their heads, and cried, weeping and wailing." This scene captures global mourning—not repentance. Casting dust on one's head was a visible sign of deep grief in the ancient world, often used during moments of devastation (Job 2:12; Lamentations 2:10). But the mourners here aren't saints lamenting sin—they're merchants, mourning profit. They weep not over judgment, but over the collapse of a system that enriched them.

"For in one hour is she made desolate." The phrase "in one hour" is thundered three times (verses 10, 17, 19), highlighting the speed and finality of Babylon's fall. This isn't poetic exaggeration—it's prophetic precision. The Lord is emphasizing that no matter how powerful or prosperous, a world system can collapse in a moment under divine judgment.

Those crying out—shipmasters, merchants, sea traders—represent the global economy. Babylon was their golden goose:

- "By reason of her costliness"—Her luxury made others rich.
- "That great city"—She wasn't just admired; she was idolized.

But now that same extravagance has become her downfall. The empire that promised prosperity has burned up, and those who profited from her stand at a distance, watching the smoke rise, unable to stop her collapse.

This verse reminds us of a deeper truth: worldly riches are temporary, and no empire is too big to fall. Those who are invested in Babylon will grieve when she falls. But those who belong to Christ will not mourn—they will rejoice. Revelation 18:4 calls, "Come out of her, My people." Don't attach your heart to what God has marked for destruction. Instead, anchor your life in the Kingdom that cannot be shaken.

OLD TESTAMENT FORESHADOWS REVELATION:

And shall cause their voice to be heard against you, and shall cry bitterly, and shall cast up dust upon their heads, they shall wallow themselves in the ashes. And they shall make themselves utterly bald for you, and gird them with sackcloth, and they shall weep for you with bitterness of heart and bitter wailing. And in their wailing they shall take up a lamentation for you, and lament over you, saying, What city is like Tyre, like the destroyed in the midst of the sea? (Ezekiel 27:30–32)

Revelation 18:19 closely parallels Ezekiel 27:30–32, highlighting a prophetic pattern: what God once did to Tyre, He will do again to end-time Mystery Babylon. The casting of dust on their heads is a traditional expression of deep mourning in the ancient world—an outward sign of inward devastation. The cry, "What city is like unto this great city?" (Revelation 18:18), echoes the lament over Tyre, a once-glorious maritime empire whose sudden fall shocked the world. In the same way, Mystery Babylon will be mourned—not for her righteousness, but for her riches. She is the Tyre of the end times: glorified, enriched, admired—and suddenly, irreversibly—gone.

THE REVELATION OF JESUS CHRIST REVEALS:

^{18:20} Rejoice over her, you heaven, and you holy apostles and prophets; for God has avenged you on her.

While the kings of the earth weep, the merchants wail, and the sailors mourn (Revelation 18:9, 11, 17), heaven is told to rejoice. Why? Because God's justice has finally prevailed. Proverbs 14:34 reminds us, "Righteousness exalts a nation: but sin is a reproach to any people." This is the first direct command to rejoice in the Book of Revelation, and it comes at the fall of Mystery Babylon.

Heaven rejoices because:

- Wickedness has ended.
- The Antichrist system is collapsing.
- God's people are avenged.
- Righteousness is vindicated.

The martyrs—God's apostles and prophets who were persecuted, silenced, and killed—are honored here. Their cries from Revelation 6:10, "How long, O Lord . . .?", are answered in Revelation 18:20 with a divine response of justice. This isn't a moment of revenge—it's a celebration of God's righteousness and faithfulness.

Mystery Babylon represents far more than a single city. It symbolizes a global infrastructure of rebellion against God. Its foundations are corrupt religion (Revelation 17), greedy economics (Revelation 18), arrogant politics (Revelation 13, 18), and a prideful, self-indulgent culture (Isaiah 47:7–9). This system has intoxicated nations and persecuted the faithful—but in Revelation 18, God brings it to a sudden and final end.

Now, all of it falls. This is heaven's final break with everything that stood in defiance of Christ. And this rejoicing points forward—to the marriage supper of the Lamb (Revelation 19), to Christ's return, and to the Kingdom of God made visible. "The kingdoms of this world are become the kingdoms of our Lord, and of His Christ" (Revelation 11:15).

"Rejoice over her, you heaven." This isn't merely a call to celebrate Babylon's fall. It's a call to examine our hearts. Are we grieving over the world's collapse—or celebrating heaven's justice? Do we mourn luxury's loss—or rejoice in righteousness restored? Are we clinging to Babylon's treasures—or longing for Christ's return?

Babylon has fallen. Rejoice—not because the world is burning, but because the King is coming. Fix your eyes not on the smoke—but on the sky.

OLD TESTAMENT FORESHADOWS REVELATION:

Rejoice, O you nations, with His people: for He will avenge the blood of His servants, and will render vengeance to His adversaries, and will be merciful unto His land, and to His people. (Deuteronomy 32:43)

This link between Revelation 18:20 and Deuteronomy 32:43 shows the continuity of God's justice—from Moses' hope to John's fulfillment. What was once a promise is now a reality: the prophets' blood cried out, and now heaven rejoices. God's enemies fall, and His people rise.

THE REVELATION OF JESUS CHRIST REVEALS:

18:21 And a mighty angel took up a stone like a great millstone, and cast it into the sea, saying, Thus with violence will that great city Babylon be thrown down, and will be found no more at all.

This powerful scene marks the absolute, irreversible fall of Babylon—the world system of political corruption, economic greed, religious deception, and spiritual rebellion. A mighty angel—representing divine authority—hurls a millstone into the sea to declare that Babylon is forever destroyed.

Millstones in the Bible were massive and heavy, used to grind grain. Once cast into the sea, they cannot be retrieved. The imagery is final—Babylon will never rise again. This isn't symbolic shaking; it's total annihilation.

"Thus with violence will that great city Babylon be thrown down." Babylon's fall is sudden, not gradual. It is not negotiated—it's violent. This is divine judgment against a satanic empire that deceived nations, trafficked souls, and glorified itself above God. The repeated phrase "found no more at all" (verses 22–23) underscores the permanence of this destruction. No more music, no more craftsmen, no more life. The system is gone.

In Revelation, the sea often symbolizes multitudes and nations (Revelation 17:15). So Babylon's plunge into the sea may also suggest that the nations will witness her downfall and absorb the shock of her collapse.

Babylon's destruction reveals several timeless truths:

1. **God's judgment is certain**—What man glorifies, God can erase.

2. **Pride precedes a fall**—Babylon said, "I sit as a queen" (Revelation 18:7), but she is violently cast down.

3. **No system stands against God**—Babylon's power—economic, political, and spiritual—vanished in one hour.

4. **This marks the end of an age**—With Babylon destroyed, the world system collapses, making way for Christ's return.

God doesn't just reform Babylon—He removes her. What the world called indestructible, God declares will be "found no more at all." So let us not build on the foundations of Babylon, but on the Kingdom that cannot be shaken (Hebrews 12:28). Her fall is not just a warning—it's a turning point. Don't anchor your life in what God has marked for destruction.

OLD TESTAMENT FORESHADOWS REVELATION:

And it shall be, when you have made an end of reading this book, that you shalt bind a stone to it, and cast it into the midst of Euphrates: And you shalt say, Thus shall Babylon sink, and shall not rise from the evil that I will bring upon her: and they shall be weary. Thus far are the words of Jeremiah. (Jeremiah 51:63–64)

Jeremiah 51:63–64 is the clearest Old Testament parallel to Revelation 18:21, and it emphasizes a sobering truth: When God judges, it is decisive. Mystery Babylon's fate is sealed, not softened. This is a prophetic call to the Church today—come out of Babylon (Revelation 18:4), for her judgment is certain, and her end has already been written.

THE REVELATION OF JESUS CHRIST REVEALS:

18:22 And the voice of harpers, and musicians, and of pipers, and trumpeters, will be heard no more at all in you; and no craftsman, of whatsoever craft he be, will be found any more in you; and the sound of a millstone will be heard no more at all in you.

This verse is a vivid and solemn funeral dirge for Babylon. It's not just that Babylon has fallen—it's that life as it was known has ceased. The music stops. Industry stops. The hum of productivity and creativity is gone. Factories close. Lights are off. It's all over. What was once a vibrant hub of culture, economy, and entertainment is now a desolate shell, silenced by judgment.

"And the voice of harpers, and musicians, and of pipers, and trumpeters, will be heard no more at all in you." The arts were once celebrated and elevated in Babylon. Music, entertainment, performances, and festivals filled the streets. This city was a cultural powerhouse, much like modern cities such as New York, Los Angeles, or Paris. But now, no more music. No concerts. No celebrations. No more distractions for the truth. The silence represents not only loss, but finality.

"And no craftsman, of whatsoever craft he be, will be found any more in you." This speaks to the collapse of industry and innovation. The economy doesn't just slow down—it ceases altogether. Skilled labor is gone. Factories are abandoned. Inventions stop. There are no jobs to return to, no trades to practice. The creative, innovative spirit of man—once driven by Babylon's systems—is now cut off.

"And the sound of a millstone will be heard no more at all in you." In biblical times, the sound of a millstone grinding grain was a symbol of daily life, food supply, and community rhythm. To say the millstone is silent is to say: There is no more production. No more bread. No more normal. The hum of agriculture, economy, and sustenance is now a ghostly memory. Babylon is not just judged—it is abandoned.

Revelation 18:22 underscores a total shutdown of society:

- No entertainment—cultural silence.
- No industry—economic collapse.
- No food production—social disintegration.
- No revival—irreversible judgment.

This verse should awaken modern society to the sobering truth: the systems we idolize are fragile, and the day will come when the stage goes silent, the assembly lines stop, and the power grid fails—not by accident, but by decree.

The message is clear: Don't build your life in Babylon. Her music may seem sweet now, her economy strong, her arts flourishing—but a day is coming when all of it will stop. "Come out of her, My people." (Revelation 18:4). The silence of Babylon will be deafening. But those who listen to God's voice today will never be silenced in eternity.

OLD TESTAMENT FORESHADOWS REVELATION:

Moreover I will take from them the voice of mirth, and the voice of gladness, the voice of the bridegroom, and the voice of the bride, the sound of the millstones, and the light of the candle. (Jeremiah 25:10)

Jeremiah 25:10 describes God's judgment on ancient Babylon—and in Revelation 18:22, we see a prophetic repeat of that judgment on end-time Mystery Babylon, the world's final rebellious system. Both passages emphasize a complete removal of joy, industry, celebration, and normal life. The music stops, the light goes out, and society collapses—not due to war alone, but by the hand of God's final decree.

THE REVELATION OF JESUS CHRIST REVEALS:

[18:23] And the light of a candle shall shine no more at all in you; and the voice of the bridegroom and of the bride will be heard no more at all in you: for your merchants were the great men of the earth; for by your sorceries were all nations deceived.

This verse begins with a chilling image: "And the light of a candle shall shine no more at all in you." Light in Scripture symbolizes truth, life, guidance, and the presence of God (John 1:4–5). Its removal from Mystery Babylon means complete spiritual blackout. Not only is there physical desolation, but also a moral and spiritual void. The city that once glittered with lights, towers, and innovation now lies in eternal shadow, abandoned and judged. This judgment is final—"no more at all" is repeated emphatically to stress that Babylon's influence and existence will never return.

"And the voice of the bridegroom and of the bride will be heard no more at all in you." The "voice of the bridegroom and of the bride" symbolizes life continuing, new beginnings, family, and community joy. The end of weddings is the end of hope for tomorrow. Babylon's fall interrupts even the most personal human celebrations. It tells us that this is not a temporary collapse—it is a permanent cutoff from normal human life and future generations. This echoes Jeremiah 7:34 and Jeremiah 25:10, where God removes joy, marriage, and mirth from Jerusalem and Babylon due to their unrepentant sin.

"For your merchants were the great men of the earth." Babylon's economy was built on the exaltation of the marketplace. Her merchants—dealmakers, billionaires, corporate moguls—were global influencers. They shaped nations, controlled commerce, and dictated culture. The world worshiped wealth, and Babylon was its sanctuary. But these "great men" were not great in righteousness, only in power and profit. They were complicit in deception, and their wealth became a weapon against truth.

"For by your sorceries were all nations deceived." Perhaps the most sobering line: "by your sorceries were all nations deceived." The Greek word for "sorceries" is (*pharmakeia*), which refers to witchcraft, drug use, enchantments, and manipulative control. This implies:

- Babylon seduced the world with spiritual deception.
- She offered counterfeit wisdom, power, and pleasure.
- Her influence was not just commercial—it was occultic, psychological, and systemic.

Nations weren't just fooled by luxury—they were enchanted by lies, and they chose illusion over truth.

Revelation 18:23 is a summary of why Babylon falls:

- She promoted darkness instead of light.
- She silenced love and joy with corruption.
- She exalted greed over grace.
- She deceived the entire world with spiritual seduction.

This verse reveals the heart of Babylon—not just a city or empire, but a system of rebellion, cloaked in wealth and masked with glamour. It seduces, blinds, and controls. And in the end, God turns out the lights.

Babylon is a warning to every generation: If you build your life on prosperity without purity, power without prayer, or entertainment without eternity, you may gain the world and still fall with Babylon. *The candle has gone out. The wedding bells are silenced. The merchants are exposed. And the spell is broken. Babylon is no more.*

OLD TESTAMENT FORESHADOWS REVELATION:

Then will I cause to cease from the cities of Judah, and from the streets of Jerusalem, the voice of mirth, and the voice of gladness, the voice of the bridegroom, and the voice of the bride: for the land shall be desolate. (Jeremiah 7:34)

Both verses depict a God-ordained desolation—the celebration of life is brought to a halt. The sounds of joy and union—weddings—are cut off, marking a complete and irreversible judgment. In Jeremiah, it is national; in Revelation, it is global. This connection strengthens the case that Revelation 18:23 is drawing heavily from Old Testament prophetic language, especially in Jeremiah 7:34, to frame the fall of end-time Mystery Babylon.

THE REVELATION OF JESUS CHRIST REVEALS:

18:24 And in her was found the blood of prophets, and of saints, and of all that were slain upon the earth.

This verse delivers the final and most damning indictment against Mystery Babylon. Beneath her gold and luxury, behind her music, markets, and global influence—there was blood. The beauty of Babylon masked brutality. Her hands are stained with the blood of God's people—prophets, saints, and all the righteous slain throughout history. This isn't just about economic corruption or cultural decadence. It's about spiritual murder—the silencing, persecuting, and killing of those who stood for truth.

Mystery Babylon is not only a city or a system—it is the manifestation of the world's hatred for holiness. Throughout the Bible, Babylon represents any society, empire, or system that exalts itself against God and persecutes His people.

- She rejected the voice of the prophets.
- She shed the blood of the saints.
- She led the world into rebellion, and now the guilt of the world is upon her.

Jesus echoed this same theme in Matthew 23:35, accusing the religious elite of carrying the guilt of righteous blood—from Abel to Zechariah. Revelation 18:24 extends that indictment to Mystery Babylon. This is the divine reasons for her total destruction: not merely her sins, but her war against the holy.

Verse 24 is the divine justification for Babylon's complete destruction. All the prior verses showed what would happen to Babylon—this verse shows why. God's justice is not random—it is righteous. The cry of the martyrs in Revelation 6:10—"How long, O Lord, until You avenge our blood?"—finds its answer in Revelation 18:24. The blood speaks. And God has heard.

Babylon was admired by the world . . . but hated by heaven. Behind the bright lights was deep darkness. Behind the luxury was a long trail of tears, prisons, executions, and silenced preachers. You can hide corruption behind candles, but you can't hide blood from God. This is not just the end of a city-nation—it is the end of an era, the closure of a long war between heaven and earth. With Mystery Babylon's fall, the stage is now set for the return of the King and the reign of righteousness.

OLD TESTAMENT FORESHADOWS REVELATION:

As Babylon has caused the slain of Israel to fall, so at Babylon shall fall the slain of all the earth. (Jeremiah 51:49)

Jeremiah 51:49 prophesies judgment on ancient Babylon, but its language reaches beyond its immediate historical context. It also foreshadows the judgment of end-time Mystery Babylon described in Revelation 18:24. In both cases, Babylon is portrayed not only as a center of idolatry and greed, but more gravely, as the persecutor of God's people.

This connection reveals a spiritual pattern: Babylon, in every age, becomes the embodiment of human rebellion—where worldly power, false religion, and violence against the righteous converge. The blood of the prophets, saints, and all the righteous slain—from Abel (Genesis 4) to the martyrs of Revelation—is spiritually attributed to Babylon's system. It is a city in spirit more than in geography, a symbol of all that exalts itself against God and suppresses truth.

Thus, Jeremiah's warning is not just a historical record—it is a prophetic shadow of a coming global reckoning. The fall of Babylon, then and in the future, is a testimony: God sees every drop of innocent blood, and he will repay.

SUMMARY OF REVELATION 18

Revelation 18 is a solemn and climactic chapter that portrays the sudden and total destruction of Babylon the Great—the symbolic center of the world's economic, political, and spiritual corruption. Following the judgment of Religious Babylon in Revelation 17, this chapter focuses on the fall of Commercial Babylon, a system that has enriched the elite, deceived the nations, and persecuted God's people.

This chapter begins with a mighty angel announcing Babylon's collapse, declaring her habitation now desolate and filled with demons and unclean spirits (Revelation 18:2). Her sins have reached to heaven, and God has remembered her iniquities (Revelation 18:5). A voice from heaven calls God's people to "Come out of her, My people" (Revelation 18:4), urging separation from her sins and warning of shared judgment if they remain. Babylon, once the pinnacle of wealth and power, is repaid double for her arrogance and idolatry (Revelation 18:6–8).

Her destruction is swift—"in one hour"—a phrase repeated throughout the chapter to emphasize the suddenness of her fall (Revelation 18:10, 17, 19). The kings of the earth mourn her, the merchants weep over lost riches, and shipmasters grieve the end of trade (Revelation 18:9–19). Yet in stark contrast, heaven is called to rejoice (Revelation 18:20), for God has avenged the blood of His prophets and saints.

A mighty angel enacts a symbolic judgment by casting a great millstone into the sea, declaring that Babylon will be found no more at all (Revelation 18:21). The chapter ends with silence—the sounds of music, marriage, and industry cease (Revelation 18:22–23). Her merchants, the great men of the earth, had deceived nations through sorcery. Now, exposed and destroyed, her legacy is one of blood—the blood of the prophets, saints, and all who were slain on the earth (Revelation 18:24).

KEY TAKEAWAYS

- Babylon's judgment is final—The world's corrupt system of greed, pride, and idolatry collapses suddenly and irreversibly.
- Call to come out—God commands His people to separate from Babylon to avoid sharing in her sins and plagues.
- Global shock and heaven's rejoicing—Earth mourns the fall of its greatest empire, while heaven celebrates divine justice.

- Silence and desolation—Babylon's destruction leads to the end of music, marriage, work, and life—everything stops.
- Deception and bloodshed exposed—The true source of Babylon's power was sorcery and blood—the persecution of the righteous.

Revelation 18 reveals that God will not allow rebellion, corruption, and deception to stand forever. The wealth and glamour of Babylon were a facade for deep spiritual wickedness. This chapter is a call to discernment and separation, reminding believers to set their hope not on the systems of this world, but on the Kingdom of Christ. Mystery Babylon may glitter, but she is destined for fire. The fall of Babylon clears the way for the return of the King and the reign of righteousness.

Chapter 17

Revelation 19:
The Return of the King
The Great Tribulation Age—
Daniel's 70th Week: Last 3½ Years

THE CROWNED KING RETURNS—After the fall of Mystery Babylon in Revelation 18, the scene shifts from earth's judgment to heaven's celebration. Revelation 19 is the climax of divine justice and the triumphant unveiling of Christ—not as the Lamb slain, but as the conquering King of kings and Lord of lords. The chapter opens with the roar of heavenly praise, rejoicing over the righteousness of God's judgments and the long-awaited marriage supper of the Lamb.

This chapter marks the close of the Great Tribulation—the final half of Daniel's 70th week (Daniel 9:27)—and ushers in the Second Coming of Christ. Here, Jesus returns not in humility, but in glory, power, and vengeance, leading heaven's armies to strike down the nations and establish His Millennial Kingdom.

Revelation 19 is the moment the world has waited for since Eden—when the rightful King returns to reclaim the earth. Every crown, every kingdom, and every knee will now bow before Him.

WHY BIBLE PROPHECY MATTERS

Before we open Revelation 19 and witness the glorious return of Christ, we must remember: this is not myth or metaphor. This is prophecy—divinely inspired and historically accurate. The Bible contains more than 2,500 prophetic statements, and over 2,100 of them have already been fulfilled with stunning precision. These were not vague predictions or poetic metaphors. They were specific. Verifiable. Supernatural.

Why such precision? Because these prophecies were given by the God who "declares the end from the beginning" (Isaiah 46:10). The past accuracy of prophecy gives us unwavering confidence in what remains—especially Revelation 19 through 22.

There are more than 400 references in Scripture to the Second Coming of Christ. For every prophecy about His First Coming, there are eight about His return. This is not a fringe idea. This is the hope of the Church. The King is coming—and heaven takes it seriously. So must we.

A Prophetic Perspective: The 200 Million

To grasp the weight of biblical prophecy, consider this: Nearly 2,000 years ago, John saw an army numbering 200 million (Revelation 9:16). In his day, the world's total population likely numbered around 150–175 million—making such a vision seemingly impossible.

However, the army in Revelation 9 is not human. It is demonic—riders on supernatural horses that breathe fire and brimstone, unleashed during the sixth trumpet judgment. This terrifying force is a spiritual judgment, not a geopolitical invasion.

Later, in Revelation 16:12, we see a very different army—the kings of the East crossing the dried-up Euphrates, preparing for Armageddon. Many scholars believe this refers to a massive human coalition, possibly involving modern nations such as China, which today claims the potential to mobilize over 200 million people. What once seemed implausible now aligns with global military capabilities.

So we ask: If 2,100+ prophecies have come to pass exactly as foretold, why doubt the rest? Why dismiss the return of the King, the judgment of nations, and the establishment of the Kingdom?

Bible prophecy is history written in advance—and we are now living in the pages that lead to Revelation 19.

WHY THE THRONE OF DAVID STILL MATTERS

The return of the King is not symbolic. This is not allegory. This is Jesus Christ—bodily, visibly, and gloriously—returning to earth with His saints and angels to establish His rightful throne.

But to understand Revelation 19, we must ask: What throne is He returning to?

In Luke 1:31–33, the angel Gabriel made a stunning promise to Mary:

> And, behold, you shalt conceive in your womb, and bring forth a Son, and shalt call His name Jesus. He shall be great, and shall be called the Son of the Highest: and the Lord GOD shall give unto Him the throne of His father David: And He shall reign over the house of Jacob forever; and of His Kingdom there shall be no end. (Luke 1:31–33).

Let that sink in: The throne of David.

Not a heavenly throne—Jesus was already seated at the right hand of the Father. This is something else. This is a Davidic, political, earthly throne—one that was never occupied during His First Coming, and remains unfulfilled to this day.

God's Covenant with David—A Kingdom Forever

The foundation of Revelation 19 lies not only in future prophecy, but in ancient promise. God made an unbreakable covenant with David in 2 Samuel 7:11–16:

- He would give David a royal dynasty (Isaiah 7:13).
- He would establish an eternal throne (2 Samuel 7:13, 16; 1 Chronicles 17:12; Isaiah 55:3).
- He would build a political kingdom (Genesis 17:2–8), confirmed by oath (Psalm 89:3–4, 34; Psalm 132:11).

These promises have never been revoked—and they've never been spiritualized away. The Church cannot fulfill them. In fact, God made it crystal clear in Ezekiel 37:21–28 that Israel will be regathered, David will be king, and God's sanctuary will dwell in their midst forever.

The First Church Council Affirmed It

Even the early Church took these promises literally. At the Jerusalem Council (Acts 15:16–18), James quoted Amos 9:11–12 to declare that after the Gentiles are called out (the Church Age), God will "return and rebuild the tabernacle of David." This isn't just spiritual revival. It's the restoration of a literal kingdom on earth.

> After this I will return, and will build again the tabernacle of David, which is fallen down; and I will build again the ruins thereof, and I will set it up: That the residue of men might seek after the LORD, and all the Gentiles, upon whom My name is called, says the LORD, who does all these things. Known unto God are all His works from the beginning of the world. (Acts 15:16–18)

> In that day will I raise up the tabernacle of David that is fallen, and close up the breaches thereof; and I will raise up his ruins, and I will build it as in the days of

old: That they may possess the remnant of Edom (modern-day southern Jordan), and of all the nations, which are called by My name, says the LORD that does this. (Amos 9:11–12)

Enoch Saw It Before the Flood

The anticipation goes back further than David—further than Abraham or Moses. It stretches all the way to Enoch, who lived before the Flood.

In Jude 1:14–15, we read the oldest recorded prophecy from a prophet:

And Enoch also, the seventh from Adam, prophesied of these, saying, Behold, the Lord comes with ten thousands of His saints, to execute judgment upon all, and to convince all that are ungodly among them of all their ungodly deeds which they have ungodly committed, and of all their hard speeches which ungodly sinners have spoken against Him. (Jude 1:14–15)

Though Enoch lived around 3467–3013 BC, over 3,000 years before Christ's First Coming, he saw the Second Coming in glory. His prophecy is strikingly New Testament in tone—describing the Lord's visible return with His saints in judgment. It reveals the ancient hope embedded in early humanity: that God would one day return—not only to judge the wicked, but to vindicate the righteous.

Revelation 19: The Fulfillment Begins

Now, at last, that moment arrives:

- Heaven rejoices. Babylon has fallen. The false systems of religion, politics, and commerce are destroyed.
- The marriage supper of the Lamb is announced (Revelation 19:7–9). The Bride—the Church—has made herself ready.
- And then, the heavens open (Revelation 19:11), and the Faithful and True rides forth on a white horse. His name is *The Word of God*. He wears many crowns, and His robe is dipped in blood.
- Armies follow Him—clothed in fine linen, riding on white horses. This is not just judgment—it's a royal procession. The King reclaiming His territory.
- The Antichrist and the False Prophet are captured and thrown alive into the Lake of Fire (Revelation 19:20). The armies of the earth are struck down.
- And the stage is now set for Revelation 20: the millennial reign, where Christ rules the earth for 1,000 years, fulfilling every promise made to David, to Israel, and to the saints.

What Does This Mean for Us?

Revelation 19 is both a sobering wake-up call and a glorious reassurance. The same Jesus who came in humility will return in power. The King who wore a crown of thorns will now wear many crowns, and the Lamb who was slain is now revealed as the Lion of Judah, roaring in righteousness. This vision demands a response from us. Do we take this promise seriously? Because God does. Heaven does. The Bride is ready. The King is returning. And this is not the end—it is the beginning of the Kingdom.

THE REVELATION OF JESUS CHRIST REVEALS:

^{19:1} And after these things I heard a great voice of many people in heaven, saying, Alleluia; Salvation, and glory, and honor, and power, unto the Lord our God.

The First Hallelujah—"And after these things"—marks a clear chronological transition, as it does in Revelation 4:1, 7:1, and 18:1. Heaven now turns its focus from the judgment of Babylon to the joyful fulfillment of God's redemptive plan. The fall of Mystery Babylon—both religious (Revelation 17) and commercial (Revelation 18)—has shaken the earth. Now, the response in heaven is thunderous praise.

"I heard a great voice of many people in heaven." This is not a single cry, but a unified roar of praise. A heavenly multitude—likely including the Church (the Bride), angels, and redeemed saints—erupts in triumphant celebration. Their voices declare that the time has come: judgment has fallen, justice has been served, and Christ is ready to reign.

"Saying, Alleluia." This is the first and only time the word "Alleluia" appears in the New Testament—and it appears four times in this chapter (verses 1, 3, 4, 6). Derived from the Hebrew *Hallelu Yah* ("Praise the LORD"), it forms the opening anthem of eternity's final song.

In the Old Testament, particularly in Psalms 146–150, "Hallelujah" is sung in moments of great deliverance and worship. Now, in Revelation 19, the same word is sung just before Christ returns—not just as Savior, but as King and Judge.

"Salvation, and glory, and honor, and power, unto the Lord our God." Each word in this phrase is packed with theological weight, forming a doxology of divine attributes:

- Salvation (*soteria*)—Complete and final deliverance—not only personal but cosmic. God is bringing the story of redemption to its climax.
- Glory (*doxa*)—The radiance, majesty, and perfection of God are now fully revealed.

- Honor (*time*)—The reverence that the world refused to give is now offered in full by heaven.
- Power (*dynamis*)—God's omnipotence is now on full display—righteous, awesome, and unstoppable.

This divine chorus proclaims not only who God is—but what He has done.

This eruption of praise follows the collapse of Mystery Babylon—the corrupt, global system that persecuted the saints and promoted deception (Revelation 17–18). The celebration is more than relief—it's vindication. The martyrs' cries from Revelation 6:10—"How long, O Lord . . . until You judge and avenge our blood?"—have been answered.

And with this, a dramatic shift in Christ's role begins to unfold:

- First, He came as the Prophet—revealing the Father:

The LORD your God will raise up unto you a Prophet from the midst of you, of your brethren, like unto me; unto Him you shall hear. (Deuteronomy 18:15).

- Now, He serves as our High Priest—interceding on our behalf:

Seeing then that we have a great High Priest, that is passed into the heavens, Jesus the Son of God, let us hold fast our confession. For we have not an High Priest which cannot be touched with the feeling of our infirmities; but was in all points tempted like as we are, yet without sin. (Hebrews 4:14–16).

- And soon, He will return as King of kings and Lord of lords—executing judgment and reigning in righteousness (Revelation 19:16).

The first *Hallelujah* is more than a sound—it's a summons. A glimpse of future joy, and a present challenge to the Church. In a world stained by injustice, compromise, and delay, Revelation 19:1 declares: Justice is coming. Every corrupt system will fall. Every martyr will be vindicated. Every crown will be cast before the Lamb.

So ask yourself: Will you meet this moment with weariness or with worship? Will your voice rise to join heaven's multitude when the King returns? Because heaven already knows—The intercessor is rising, the delay is over, and the King is coming.

OLD TESTAMENT FORESHADOWS REVELATION:

Honor and majesty are before Him: strength and beauty are in His sanctuary. Give unto the LORD, O you kindreds of the people, give unto the LORD glory and strength. (Psalm 96:6–7)

Psalm 96:6–7 calls the nations to glorify God for His strength, majesty, and coming judgment. Revelation 19:1 fulfills that call as heaven erupts in praise, declaring His salvation, glory, honor, and power. What began as a prophetic invitation in the Psalms becomes a heavenly reality. The fall of Babylon confirms God's justice, and the same themes of glory and strength resound—uniting Old Testament worship with the final victory of Christ.

THE REVELATION OF JESUS CHRIST REVEALS:

[19:2] For true and righteous are His judgments: for He has judged the great whore, which did corrupt the earth with her fornication, and has avenged the blood of His servants at her hand.

"For true and righteous are His judgments." This declaration affirms that God's judgments are always perfect, without error, bias, or injustice. In a world where justice is often delayed or denied, heaven affirms that God alone is the righteous Judge. He sees the hidden corruption, the systemic evil, and the suffering of His people—and He judges accordingly, with truth and righteousness (Psalm 19:9; Daniel 4:37).

"For He has judged the great whore." This phrase refers back to Mystery Babylon, portrayed in Revelation 17–18 as the great harlot who sits upon many waters. She represents a false religious system—seductive, idolatrous, and spiritually corrupt—intertwined with political power and wealth. Her fornication is symbolic of unfaithfulness to God through spiritual adultery, false doctrine, and global deception. Her fall is final. Her influence is broken. What she corrupted for centuries is now judged.

"Which did corrupt the earth with her fornication." The scope of her evil is global—she "corrupted the earth." This is more doctrinal error; it's a worldwide spiritual defilement that fueled rebellion, persecuted the righteous, and polluted truth. Her influence was not passive—it was aggressively anti-God and anti-Christ.

"And has avenged the blood of His servants at her hand." This statement ties directly to Revelation 6:9–10, where the souls of the martyrs cry out, "How long, O Lord, holy and true, do you not judge and avenge our blood on them that dwell on the earth?" Now, the answer has come. God has personally avenged their blood—not out of vengeance, but out of divine justice. Romans 12:19 reminds us: "Vengeance is Mine; I will repay, says the Lord." Believers are forbidden from seeking revenge—but here, God Himself answers the cry of the persecuted Church by executing final judgment.

Revelation 18:20 issued the command to "Rejoice over her, O Heaven." Revelation 19:2 is the response to that call—heaven's celebration of justice finally served. This is not cruel rejoicing, but a righteous celebration that evil has been overthrown and the blood of the faithful has been honored.

Revelation 19:2 is a powerful reminder that God sees every injustice, hears every cry, and will act at the appointed time. For the persecuted, martyred, and oppressed, this verse is both a comfort and a promise. Justice will come—not by our hand, but by His. And when it does, heaven will erupt in praise, declaring His judgments are true and righteous.

OLD TESTAMENT FORESHADOWS REVELATION:

To proclaim the acceptable year of the LORD, and the day of vengeance of our God; to comfort all that mourn. (Isaiah 61:2)

Isaiah 61:2 foretells two phases of Christ's mission—His First Coming to proclaim grace ("the acceptable year") and His Second Coming to execute justice ("the day of vengeance"). Revelation 19:2 fulfills the second half, as heaven praises God for judging the great harlot and avenging His saints. Together, these verses bridge the mercy of the Gospel and the righteousness of God's final judgment.

THE REVELATION OF JESUS CHRIST REVEALS:

19:3 And again they said, Alleluia. And her smoke rose up forever and ever.

The Second Hallelujah—"And again they said, Alleluia." This verse marks the second "Alleluia"—a renewed cry of worship in heaven. It's repetition emphasizes the fullness and permanence of God's judgment. This is not praise for destruction itself, but a celebration that justice has been fully served. The heavenly hosts—redeemed saints, angels, and elders—rejoice because evil's reign has come to a definitive and irreversible end.

"And her smoke rose up forever and ever" is a vivid image of total destruction. This language echoes Revelation 14:10–11, where the smoke of torment rises eternally, and harkens back to Genesis 19:28, where smoke marked God's judgment on Sodom and Gomorrah. Here, it symbolizes the finality of Babylon's fall:

- "Forever and ever" means just that—there will be no recovery or resurrection of this corrupt world system.
- Both the religious deception of Revelation 17 and the economic seduction of Revelation 18 are permanently judged.
- Babylon represents not just a city, but every false system, empire, or ideology that has opposed Christ and led people away from truth.

This verse is also a sobering theological truth: God's judgment is not temporary or symbolic. Just as His Kingdom is eternal (Revelation 11:15, 22:5), so too is His justice upon the wicked (Revelation 14:11). The phrase "forever and ever" is not poetic exaggeration—it is a terrifying reality for those who reject the mercy of Christ. Once divine judgment is executed, there is no appeal, no second chance, no reopening of the door (Luke 13:25).

This moment also reflects a shift in Christ's role. The altar once symbolized mercy and intercession. Now, from that same place, justice flows. The Lamb who once pleaded now reigns. The time for grace has passed; now comes recompense.

Revelation 19:3 stands as one of the most sobering verses in all of Scripture. Heaven's second "Alleluia" is not a cry of cruelty—it's a declaration of relief, vindication, and holy justice. For believers, it becomes a call to worship the God who judges righteously. For unbelievers, it sounds an urgent final warning: *forever means forever*. There will be no reversal, no retrial, and no mercy once the judgment is passed. The time to repent is now. The time to proclaim the gospel is now. For once the door is shut—it will not open again.

OLD TESTAMENT FORESHADOWS REVELATION:

It shall not be quenched night nor day; the smoke thereof shall go up forever: from generation to generation it shall lie waste; none shall pass through it forever and ever. (Isaiah 34:10)

Isaiah 34:10 is a prophecy of divine judgment against Edom, but symbolically it represents the judgment of all nations who oppose God. Just like in Revelation 19:3, Isaiah describes smoke rising forever, emphasizing total, irreversible destruction. Both verses use "forever and ever" language to express that God's judgment is eternal and final—there's no restoration for the wicked system once it falls. The imagery of smoke signifies the visible, ongoing consequence of divine judgment—an eternal memorial of God's justice.

THE REVELATION OF JESUS CHRIST REVEALS:

[19:4] And the four and twenty elders and the four beasts fell down and worshiped God that sat on the throne, saying, Amen; Alleluia.

The Third Hallelujah—Revelation 19:4 brings the final appearance of the twenty-four elders and the four living creatures—heavenly representatives who surround God's throne in Revelation 4–5. The elders likely represent the redeemed of all time: twelve tribes of Israel and twelve apostles, symbolizing Old and New Testament saints. The living creatures (cherubim) are high-ranking angelic beings, perpetually declaring God's holiness. Here, they join in united, reverent worship, affirming God's judgment on Babylon and anticipating Christ's reign.

They "fell down and worshiped" God—not casually, but with solemnity and surrender. Their posture shows heaven's unanimous agreement with what God has done and what He's about to do. His throne—the symbol of sovereign authority—is now the focus of all attention as the heavens prepare for the earth's true King.

Their declaration, "Amen; Alleluia," is heaven's seal and song. *Amen*—"Let it be so"—ratifies God's justice. *Alleluia*—"Praise Yahweh"—erupts in joy. This third Hallelujah parallels Psalm 72:19, where the millennial glory of Christ is praised: "Blessed be His glorious name forever . . . Amen and Amen." Just as Psalm 72 ends with worship, so too does the role of the elders—as they affirm the close of one age and the dawn of another.

Some scholars note this is the final mention of the twenty-four elders. Their silence from this point on may suggest a shift—from heavenly intercessors to the ready Bride, returning with Christ (Revelation 19:7–14). Their last words aren't words at all—they're worship.

This verse calls us to join heaven in agreement. "Amen" is our declaration of faith. "Alleluia" is our response of praise. Together, they proclaim: Let evil fall. Let justice rise. Let the King return. And let the Church worship with one voice—because the throne is not empty, and the reign is near.

OLD TESTAMENT FORESHADOWS REVELATION:

And blessed be His glorious name forever: and let the whole earth be filled with His glory; Amen, and Amen. (Psalm 72:19)

Both verses feature a heavenly declaration of praise directed toward God's glory and sovereign rule. "Amen" is spoken in both contexts as a sacred ratification—a seal of unshakable truth and agreement with God's revealed will. The twenty-four elders and four living creatures in Revelation 19:4 worship just as the psalmist does—affirming that God's Kingdom will fill the earth with His glory. Psalm 72:19 is messianic and millennial in tone, pointing to the reign of the righteous King, while Revelation 19:4 occurs just before the Second Coming of Christ, as heaven prepares for His millennial rule.

THE REVELATION OF JESUS CHRIST REVEALS:

[19:5] And a voice came out of the throne, saying, Praise our God, all you His servants, and you that fear Him, both small and great.

This verse introduces a divine summons that echoes from the very heart of heaven: "Praise our God, all you His servants, and you that fear Him, both small and great." This is not a distant call—it proceeds from the throne itself, underscoring its supreme authority and sacred origin. Whether from an angel or from Christ, the voice carries the weight of God's own heart, initiating a final, unified chorus of praise before Christ visibly returns.

The command to "Praise our God" is deeply personal. It doesn't just say "Praise God"—but "Praise our God." This reflects the covenant intimacy shared between the redeemed and their Lord. Worship here is not just a duty—it's a response to belonging. It includes every servant, every saint, every soul who has ever feared God, whether small or great. Status doesn't matter. Title doesn't matter. What matters is faithfulness.

This moment in heaven gathers the Church, the heavenly host, and all who have honored God—inviting them to exalt Him together. It's a direct echo of Psalm 115:13: "He will bless them that fear the LORD, both small and great." The scene shifts now from the sobering judgment of Babylon to an atmosphere of triumphant anticipation—ushering in the final "Hallelujah" in verse 6.

Revelation 19:5 stands at a divine threshold:

- From judgment to joy.
- From man's rule to Christ's reign.
- From silence to song.

It reminds us that praise is not a passive act—it's a response to God's unfolding majesty. And whether hidden or known, every believer is called to join in. Because at the climax of history, when the King is ready to return, heaven doesn't just observe—it erupts in worship.

OLD TESTAMENT FORESHADOWS REVELATION:

He will bless them that fear the LORD, both small and grèat. (Psalm 115:13)

Both verses address those who fear the Lord, regardless of status—"small and great." Psalm 115:13 speaks of God's blessing, and Revelation 19:5 calls for those blessed servants to respond in praise. This parallel affirms that God's relationship with His people is not based on rank or recognition—but on reverence and faithful service. In both passages, the fear of the Lord is the great equalizer—it unites the entire body of believers in blessing and worship.

THE REVELATION OF JESUS CHRIST REVEALS:

[19:6] And I heard as it were the voice of a great multitude, and as the voice of many waters, and as the voice of mighty thunderings, saying, Alleluia: for the Lord GOD omnipotent reigns.

The Fourth Hallelujah—"And I heard as it were the voice of a great multitude." Revelation 19:6 unveils the crescendo of heaven's praise: "And I heard as it were the voice of a great multitude, and as the voice of many waters, and as the voice of mighty thunderings, saying, Alleluia: for the Lord GOD omnipotent reigns." This is no whisper—it's a cosmic roar. John hears a united cry from a vast heavenly host, echoing the call to worship from verse 5. It is likely the sound of the Church, angels, Tribulation martyrs, and Old Testament saints—each one proclaiming the sovereignty of God.

The voice is like "many waters" and "mighty thunderings"—imagery that evokes unstoppable power and awe, much like the voice of God Himself (Ezekiel 43:2; Revelation 1:15). It's thunderous, majestic, and unmistakable: heaven is declaring a truth that shakes creation.

This is the fourth and final "Alleluia" in Scripture—a climactic shout of triumph. No longer focused on Babylon's fall, this Hallelujah proclaims that "the Lord GOD omnipotent reigns." The Greek term *Pantokrator* emphasizes God's total, unrivaled authority. And the verb "reigns" is in the present tense: His rule is no longer hidden—it is about to be revealed in glory. This marks the turning point where the kingdoms of this world give way to the reign of Christ in the Millennial Kingdom (Revelation 20).

Revelation 19:6 is more than a victory song—it is the thunderous soundtrack of history's climax. Heaven is not whispering. It is celebrating. The King is not just coming—He is reigning. And we are invited, even now, to join the anthem.

No matter how loud the chaos on earth becomes, one truth will thunder over it all: "The Lord GOD omnipotent reigns!"

OLD TESTAMENT FORESHADOWS REVELATION:

The LORD reigns, He is clothed with majesty; the LORD is clothed with strength, wherewith He has girded Himself: the world also is established, that it cannot be moved. (Psalm 93:1)

Both verses declare that "The LORD reigns"—a triumphant proclamation of His sovereign kingship. In Psalm 93:1, the LORD is clothed in majesty and strength, just as in Revelation 19:6 He is celebrated as the Omnipotent (all-powerful) ruler. Psalm 93 continues (verse 4) with language that mirrors Revelation 19:6: "The Lord on high is mightier than the noise of many waters, yea, than the mighty waves of the sea."—which parallels John's description of the voice of praise being like many waters and mighty thunderings.

THE REVELATION OF JESUS CHRIST REVEALS:

19:7 Let us be glad and rejoice, and give honor to Him: for the marriage of the Lamb is come, and His wife has made herself ready.

This verse opens with a joyful triad: "Be glad"—a deep, sacred delight; "rejoice"—a shared celebration among heaven's hosts; and "give honor"—the full praise due to God for bringing His redemptive plan to completion. Unlike the prior hallelujahs praising God for judgment, this one celebrates fulfillment—the long-awaited union of Christ and His Bride. The seven-year engagement is over. The wedding day has arrived.

"For the marriage of the Lamb is come." This marks the climactic fulfillment of Christ's covenant promise, echoing His words at the Last Supper:

> But I say unto you, I will not drink henceforth of this fruit of the vine, until that day when I drink it new with you in my Father's kingdom. (Matthew 26:29)

Now, in heaven, the Lamb—Christ, who gave His life for His Bride—joins her in final union. This moment follows the Bema Seat Judgment (2 Corinthians 5:10), where believers are rewarded and purified, and precedes the marriage supper of the Lamb (Revelation 19:9), where invited guests—Old Testament and Tribulation saints—celebrate the occasion.

"And His wife has made herself ready." The Bride is now called "wife," signaling that the union is complete. Her readiness doesn't come from her own strength but from the Spirit's sanctifying work and her faithful obedience. Her garments, described in verse 8, represent the righteous acts of the saints—a testimony to grace, endurance, and spiritual preparation.

This fulfills Paul's words in Ephesians 5:27:

> That He might present it to Himself a glorious Church, not having spot, or wrinkle, or any such thing; but that it should be holy and without blemish. (Ephesians 5:27)

Revelation 19:7 gives us a preview of the wedding of eternity—the Church, once betrothed at the Cross and refined through time, is now gloriously united with Christ forever. It is not merely an escape from Tribulation, but a consummation of joy, where Jesus fulfills His promise to dine again with us in His Father's Kingdom.

And if you are in Christ, you already hold the invitation.

OLD TESTAMENT FORESHADOWS REVELATION:

> I will greatly rejoice in the LORD, my soul shall be joyful in my God; for He has clothed me with the garments of salvation, He has covered me with the robe of righteousness, as a bridegroom decks himself with ornaments, and as a bride adorns herself with her jewels. (Isaiah 61:10)

Isaiah speaks of rejoicing and giving honor to God—exactly as Revelation 19:7 begins: "Let us be glad and rejoice, and give honor to Him." The Bride—the Church—is depicted as adorned, clothed in garments of salvation and righteousness—paralleling Revelation 19:8, where the Bride is given fine linen, clean and white, symbolizing the righteous acts of the saints. Isaiah 61:10 is a messianic prophecy, fulfilled ultimately in the person and work of Christ—and here in Revelation 19, we see the climax of that prophecy, when the redeemed Church is fully united with her Bridegroom.

THE REVELATION OF JESUS CHRIST REVEALS:

[19:8] And to her was granted that she should be arrayed in fine linen, clean and white: for the fine linen is the righteousness of saints.

This verse unveils the Bride's preparation for her divine wedding. The phase "to her was granted" highlights that the bride's garment is a gift, not something she earned. It is the grace of God that clothes her—just as Psalm 45:13–14 portrays a royal bride brought before the King in glorious attire, not of her own making.

The "fine linen, clean and white," symbolizes purity and victory. It's more than Christ's imputed righteousness—it reflects the transformed life of the saints. Revelation clarifies: "For the fine linen is the righteousness of saints." The Greek word *dikaiomata* refers not to salvation itself, but to the visible, Spirit-enabled deeds that follow it—acts of faith, obedience, service, and love.

At the Bema Seat of Christ (1 Corinthians 3:12–15), believers are judged—not for sin, but for the quality of their works. Gold, silver, and precious stones survive the fire and become part of the Bride's radiant adornment. The Church doesn't just arrive forgiven—she arrives gloriously prepared.

This stands in sharp contrast to the harlot of Revelation 17, clothed in worldly splendor but stained with rebellion. The Bride wears righteousness. Her beauty is divine, eternal, and reflective of her faithfulness to the Bridegroom.

In the end, Revelation 19:8 is a powerful reminder: we are saved by grace, but rewarded for obedience. The wedding garments are granted—but their brilliance comes from lives that honored Christ. May we live today in a way that prepares us for that glorious moment—when heaven celebrates the Bride who made herself ready.

OLD TESTAMENT FORESHADOWS REVELATION:

Let your priests be clothed with righteousness; and let your saints shout for joy. (Psalm 132:9)

Just as the Bride in Revelation is arrayed in fine linen, which is the righteousness of the saints, Psalm 132:9 speaks of God's priests—symbolic of His people—being clothed with righteousness. The idea of wearing righteousness as spiritual clothing is consistent in both verses, emphasizing a life of holiness and consecration before God. Revelation 19:8 is set in the context of the marriage of the Lamb, a time of great joy—Psalm 132 likewise ends with the saints shouting for joy, linking both celebration and righteousness.

THE REVELATION OF JESUS CHRIST REVEALS:

^{19:9} And he says to me, Write, Blessed are they which are called unto the marriage supper of the Lamb. And he says to me, These are the true sayings of God.

This is the fourth of seven beatitudes in Revelation (1:3, 14:13, 16:15, 20:6, 22:7, 14). Here, a profound blessing is pronounced—not upon the Bride—but upon those "invited" to the marriage supper of the Lamb. This supper is not the wedding ceremony itself, but the celebratory banquet that follows, much like ancient Jewish weddings: the private ceremony came first, followed by a public feast with honored guests.

Who is the Bride? Who are the Guests?

- The Bride is the Church—redeemed by the blood of Jesus (Ephesians 5:25–27; 2 Corinthians 11:2). She is betrothed to Christ now and awaits her full union with Him in heaven.
- The Guests are not the Bride—You don't invite the bride to her own wedding supper. The invited include Old Testament saints, Tribulation martyrs, and others redeemed outside the Church Age. They are honored participants, but not the Bride. Even John the Baptist referred to himself as a "friend of the Bridegroom" (John 3:29).

What About Israel?

In the Old Testament, Israel is portrayed as the covenant wife of Yahweh—often unfaithful, yet never forgotten (Isaiah 54:5; Hosea 2). Though she was temporarily set aside due to unbelief (Romans 11:25), her full restoration is central to God's redemptive plan and will unfold during the Tribulation and into the Millennial Kingdom. In contrast, the Church—the Bride of Christ—is not reformed Israel, but a distinct New Covenant body, formed of both Jew and Gentile united in Christ. This new creation was a mystery hidden in ages past but now revealed (Ephesians 3:6), demonstrating God's grace and wisdom.

That the Gentiles should be fellow heirs, and of the same body, and partakers of His promise in Christ by the gospel. (Ephesians 3:6)

"These are the true sayings of God." John is commanded to write these words down—not as metaphor or poetic flourish, but as absolute, divinely authoritative truth. This stands in stark contrast to the lies of Mystery Babylon, who claimed, "I sit as a queen" (Revelation 18:7), only to be judged and destroyed. Unlike the harlot, the true Bride is pure, prepared, and forever united with her Bridegroom.

Revelation 19:7–9 is not merely a poetic celebration—it is a prophetic fulfillment. This moment in heaven reflects the structure and symbolism of an ancient Jewish wedding, offering profound insight into Christ's relationship with

His Church. Each step in the traditional ceremony corresponds to a key redemptive event.

1. **Betrothal (*Ketubah*)**—"For you are bought with a price . . ." (1 Corinthians 6:20). The Church was legally and spiritually pledged to Christ at Calvary. This betrothal was sealed with the blood of the Bridegroom, much like the bride price paid in ancient Israel.

2. **Groom's Departure**—". . . I go to prepare a place for you . . ." (John 14:1–3). Just as the Jewish groom would return to his father's house to build a dwelling for his bride, Christ ascended to heaven to prepare an eternal home for His Church.

3. **Surprise Gathering (The Rapture)**—"For the Lord Himself shall descend . . . we shall be caught up . . ." (1 Thessalonians 4:16–17). ". . . the Bridegroom came, and they that were ready went in with Him to the marriage: and the door was shut." (Matthew 25:10). In Jewish tradition, the groom would return unexpectedly for his bride—often at night with a trumpet call. This foreshadows the Rapture, when Christ comes to gather His Bride to Himself, suddenly and gloriously.

4. **Marriage Ceremony**—". . . the marriage of the Lamb is come, and His wife has made herself ready." (Revelation 19:7). This heavenly union represents the formal completion of Christ's covenant with His Bride. The Bride has been purified, rewarded, and now presented in glory.

5. **Marriage Supper**—"Blessed are they which are called unto the marriage supper of the Lamb." (Revelation 19:9). The grand celebration includes not just the Bride (the Church), but also invited guests—faithful saints from other dispensations (Old Testament and Tribulation believers). It marks the joyous beginning of the Kingdom Age.

This divine wedding narrative isn't just prophetic—it's deeply personal. It tells the story of a pursuing Bridegroom, a prepared Bride, and a coming Kingdom where love, holiness, and joy converge eternally.

We are living in the courtship stage now—called to remain faithful, consecrated, and expectant. Soon, the trumpet will sound, and the Bride will be with her Bridegroom forever.

OLD TESTAMENT FORESHADOWS REVELATION:

And in this mountain shall the LORD of hosts make unto all people a feast of fat things, a feast of wines on the lees, of fat things full of marrow, of wines on the lees well refined. (Isaiah 25:6)

The "marriage supper of the Lamb" in Revelation 19:9 is the fulfillment of this prophesied messianic banquet in Isaiah 25:6. The imagery of a lavish, celebratory feast prepared by the LORD aligns perfectly with the wedding supper, where Christ and His Bride (the Church) are united and the invited guests rejoice. In Jewish eschatology, Isaiah 25 was seen as a kingdom banquet of the righteous, and Jesus Himself alludes to this concept in Luke 22:16 and Matthew 26:29 when He promises to eat again with His disciples in the Kingdom.

Irene leaned forward, eyes wide with curiosity, as I flipped through my notes with practiced ease.

"Ann, the more I read Revelation 19:7–9, the more fascinated I become—not just with end-time events, but with how God mirrored His eternal plan in something as detailed and beautiful as the Jewish wedding!" Her voice brimmed with awe. "The symbolism, the sequence—it's almost cinematic. Why did no one ever teach us this growing up?"

I smiled. "Because we were busy looking at wedding photos instead of the wedding blueprints in the Bible." Then I nodded, "But yes, Irene—it's all there. God's covenant love is etched into every stage. Are you thinking of Revelation 19:9?"

"Exactly! 'Blessed are they which are called unto the marriage supper of the Lamb.' It's regal and intimate," she said, her voice softening. "But I want to go deeper. Can we walk through them, the five stages of the Jewish wedding? I want to understand how each part maps onto our salvation story."

Without hesitation, I turned to the section of my notes. "Let's do it. This is the wedding that changes everything."

1. **The Ketubah—The Betrothal**—Christ's First Coming.

I sighed gently. "This is where it all begins. In Jewish tradition, the groom would leave his father's house and pay the bride price to establish a covenant—*the ketubah*. That's the engagement. It wasn't casual—it was legal, binding."

I looked up and met Irene's gaze. "That's exactly what Jesus did. He left heaven, came to earth, and paid the price for us with His blood. First Corinthians 6:19–20 says, 'You were bought with a price.'"

"So the Cross—that was our betrothal?" Irene asked softly.

"Yes," I nodded. "Just like in Jewish culture, the covenant was sealed before the marriage ceremony. That's why Paul calls the Church a 'chaste virgin' in 2 Corinthians 11:2. We're already spoken for. Already His. We're just waiting for the Groom to come back and complete the promise."

2. The Groom Returns to the Father's House—A 2,000-Year Wait.

"This is the part that stirs my heart, Ann," Irene said, eyes shining. "The groom goes back to prepare a place for his bride. That's what Jesus was talking about in John 14:2–3, right? 'In My Father's house are many mansions . . . I go to prepare a place for you. And if I go and prepare a place, I will come again, and receive you unto Myself.'"

I nodded. "Exactly. That's the tradition. After the betrothal, the groom returns to his father's house to build a home for his bride. And for the past 2,000 years, that's what Christ has been doing—preparing our dwelling place in heaven."

"I read that Jesus was crucified around AD 30," Irene continued thoughtfully. "And Hosea 6:2 says, 'After two days He will revive us.' If a day is like a thousand years, as 2 Peter 3:8 suggests, then could His return possibly be around 2030?"

I smiled. "We're not setting dates—but we *are* watching patterns. God doesn't move randomly. He honors His appointed times—through feasts, sabbaths, even wedding traditions. Nothing is accidental in the divine timetable."

3. The Surprise Gathering—The Rapture.

Irene smiled, eyes twinkling. "This is my favorite part. The groom returns at midnight, a shout goes out, and the bride is gathered by torchlight to the groom's house for the huppah."

I nodded. "Exactly. That's the Rapture of the Church—1 Thessalonians 4:16–17: 'For the Lord Himself shall descend from heaven with a shout . . . and the dead in Christ shall rise first. Then we who are alive and remain shall be caught up together with them.' Just like the groom came suddenly and without warning in the Jewish tradition, Christ will come unexpectedly to gather His Bride.

"The Church is swept into the bridal chamber," Irene whispered, "not just for seven literal days like in the Jewish tradition, but for seven prophetic years—while the Tribulation unfolds on earth."

"Right," I said softly. "While the world undergoes judgment, the Bride remains hidden—protected and cherished—just like in the Jewish wedding tradition. That image of the bridal is so powerful. It reminds us that we are not appointed to wrath, but to joy, safety, and union with our Bridegroom."

4. The Marriage Ceremony (Private)—Seven Years in Heaven.

I nodded. "This is where we come to the Judgment Seat of Christ—2 Corinthians 5:10 and 1 Corinthians 3:11–15. It's a private moment in heaven where the Bride is both purified and rewarded."

"So when Revelation 19:7 says, 'the Bride has made herself ready,' that's through the refining of the Judgment Seat? Her works—gold, silver, precious stones—become her adornment?"

"Exactly. The fine linen is granted, but it also reflects the righteous acts of the saints—Revelation 19:8. Crowns, jewels, garments that radiate glory. And this isn't about gender—both men and women are the Bride. It's about spiritual union, not earthly roles."

5. **The Marriage Supper (Public)**—Christ's Second Coming.

"And now we're at Revelation 19:9—the marriage supper of the Lamb. The moment it all becomes public. A royal banquet. And it says, 'Blessed are those who are called to the marriage supper of the Lamb.'"

"Yes, Irene. The Bride isn't a guest—she's the honored one. The invited guests are likely the Old Testament saints, Tribulation martyrs, and possibly even angels. This is heaven's celebration of the union. The ultimate wedding feast, foreshadowed in Isaiah 25:6."

"So just to clarify—it's the Rapture first, then the Judgment Seat of Christ, followed by the private marriage ceremony, then the marriage supper of the Lamb—all in heaven—and after that, the Second Coming?"

"Exactly. And all of this begins before the scroll with seven seals is opened in Revelation 6. By then, the Bride is safely in heaven."

Irene's voice trembled. "Ann . . . the detail God built into this is incredible. It's more than symbolic. It's personal. We're not just studying prophecy—we're reading our wedding invitation."

Smiling, I nodded. "And that's why the angel says, 'These are the true sayings of God.' Because this isn't just doctrine—it's destiny."

"That's so rich. So we'll have the Bema Seat, the marriage ceremony, and then a grand celebration—with the entire redemptive family of God gathered to honor the Lamb. It's like a prophetic convergence of love, justice, and joy."

I nodded. "It really is. And it shows how precise God's plan is. The Church isn't just saved—we're betrothed (engaged). Right now, we're being prepared as a spotless Bride. That's why the Bema Seat matters. It's not just about reward; it's part of our adornment."

"And all of this happens while the earth is enduring the Tribulation. What a striking contrast—judgment and chaos below, joy and union above."

"That contrast is no accident. Just like Noah was lifted in the ark before the Flood, the Church will be lifted in the Rapture before God's wrath falls. And then comes the marriage—the moment we've been waiting for."

"So beautiful. It's more than theology—it's a love story."

"Exactly. And we're living in the courting period right now," I said softly, my eyes shining with conviction. "Courting is the intentional pursuit of a committed relationship—it's that sacred season of invitation, pursuit, and choosing love freely. It comes before the formal engagement. Right now, Jesus is calling us, preparing us, drawing us closer. And soon . . . He'll come to take us home."

Irene nodded, her voice barely above a whisper.

"It really is a love story, isn't it?"

I whispered back, "The greatest one ever written."

THE REVELATION OF JESUS CHRIST REVEALS:

^{19:10} And I fell at his feet to worship him. And he said to me, See you do it not: I am your fellow-servant, and of your brethren that have the testimony of Jesus: worship God: for the testimony of Jesus is the spirit of prophecy.

"And I fell at his feet to worship him." John overwhelmed by the glory of what he had just seen—the marriage supper of the Lamb and heaven's majestic rejoicing—John instinctively falls at the angel's feet in worship. It wasn't idolatry in rebellion, but awe misdirected in a moment of holy wonder. Yet heaven does not permit even sincere misplacement of worship.

The angel responds with a firm rebuke: "See you do it not!" In the Greek, *Hora me!*—stop it immediately. His words underscore a key truth: even the most majestic angels are not to be worshiped. They, like us, are servants of the same King. As Hebrews 1:14 reminds us, angels are "ministering spirits," and as fellow servants, they always point upward—to God alone.

The angel further clarifies, "I am your fellow-servant, and of your brethren that have the testimony of Jesus." He aligns himself not with heavenly hierarchy, but with all who remain faithful to Christ. This mirrors Revelation 12:17, where the dragon makes war on those who "keep the commandments of God and have the testimony of Jesus." The true bond among God's servants—angelic or human—is their devotion to the Lamb.

Then comes the command: "Worship God!" Not man. Not angels. Not saints. Worship is reserved for the Lord alone. Throughout Scripture, only Jesus receives worship rightly:

- Thomas declared, "My Lord and my God" (John 20:28).
- Peter fell at Jesus' knees (Luke 5:8).
- Joshua bowed before the Commander of the Lord's army—likely a pre-incarnate Christ (Joshua 5:13–15).

Even angels, radiant and powerful as they are, never receive glory. They redirect it to the One on the throne.

The angel concludes: "For the testimony of Jesus is the spirit of prophecy." This profound statement reveals the purpose of all true prophecy: to point to Jesus. From Genesis to Revelation, Christ is the centerpiece. The prophets spoke of Him, the Gospels revealed Him, the Epistles teach Him, and Revelation crowns Him. Every vision, every word of judgment or promise, finds its fulfillment in Him.

This moment also marks a transition—from the Lamb of the Supper to the Lion of Judgment. The next verse (Revelation 19:11) will reveal Christ, not as the Suffering Servant, but as the conquering King. Eyes like fire. Many crowns. A robe dipped in blood. And an army following—not to fight, but to witness His triumph.

OLD TESTAMENT FORESHADOWS REVELATION:

Then said I, Lo, I come: in the volume of the book it is written of me, I delight to do Your will, O my God: yea, Your law is within my heart. (Psalm 40:7–8)

Psalm 40:7–8 points to Christ as the central figure of all Scripture. Revelation 19:10 echoes it: "The testimony of Jesus is the spirit of prophecy." Every prophetic symbol and promise leads to Him. Jesus confirms this in Hebrews 10:7—He came to fulfill what was written. From beginning to end, the Bible is His story.

THE REVELATION OF JESUS CHRIST REVEALS:

[19:11] And I saw heaven opened, and behold a white horse; and He that sat upon him was called Faithful and True, and in righteousness He does judge and make war.

"And I saw heaven opened." Heaven opens for the second time in connection to Jesus—not in humility, but in majesty. At His baptism, heaven opened to declare Him the beloved Son (Luke 3:21–22), launching His earthly mission as the Lamb. But now, the skies split open to reveal the conquering King. This is no longer the Suffering Servant; this is the righteous Judge, riding forth as the Lion of Judah and Commander of heaven's armies.

"And behold a white horse." The white horse is a symbol of royal triumph and victory. Roman generals rode white horses after conquest—but this is no imitation. The true King appears, fulfilling every prophecy of righteous war and divine judgment. In contrast to the counterfeit rider in Revelation 6:2—the Antichrist—this Rider is not bringing false peace. He is the Prince of Peace, returning to overthrow rebellion and establish His Kingdom (Zechariah 14:3–5).

"And He that sat upon him was called Faithful and True." These names speak to His unchanging character:

- Faithful—He keeps every promise, including His return (Acts 1:11).
- True—He is the embodiment of truth itself (John 14:6), in a world saturated with deception.

This title echoes Revelation 3:7 and Revelation 1:5, reinforcing His identity as the faithful witness. At His First Coming, Jesus read Isaiah 61:1–2 but paused before "the day of vengeance of our God." Now, in Revelation 19:11, He resumes that unfinished verse—the time of vengeance has arrived.

"And in righteousness He does judge and make war." This is the only truly just war in history. His judgment is perfect. His warfare is holy. Isaiah 11:4–5 foretells this moment: He will strike the earth with the rod of His mouth and slay the wicked. Isaiah 63:3 paints Him alone treading the winepress, His garments stained in wrath. This is not the gentle Jesus of Palm Sunday, but the King of Glory—no longer humiliated, but exalted. The one who was spat upon and crucified now returns crowned in majesty, leading heaven's armies.

This verse fulfills the second part of Isaiah 61:2, and marks the climactic return of Christ—not to offer salvation, but to execute justice. His enemies will fall. His Bride will reign with Him. His Kingdom will be established on earth.

This is not a metaphor. This is the future. Heaven has opened. The King is riding. And His name is Faithful and True.

Even so, come, Lord Jesus (Revelation 22:20).

OLD TESTAMENT FORESHADOWS REVELATION:

But with righteousness shall He judge the poor, and reprove with equity for the meek of the earth: and He shall smite the earth with the rod of His mouth, and with the breath of His lips shall He slay the wicked. And righteousness shall be the girdle of His loins, and faithfulness the girdle of His reins. (Isaiah 11:4–5)

Isaiah 11:4–5 foretells a Messianic Judge who rules with perfect justice. The phrases "with righteousness shall He judge" and "He shall smite the earth with the rod of His mouth" directly foreshadow Revelation 19:11, where Christ returns to judge and make war in righteousness.

Even the titles "Faithful and True" in Revelation echo Isaiah's description of the coming King, whose rule is girded in righteousness and faithfulness. This is not symbolic only—it is a prophetic mirror confirming that the Judge of the nations has always been Christ.

THE REVELATION OF JESUS CHRIST REVEALS:

19:12 His eyes were as a flame of fire, and on His head were many crowns; and He had a name written, that no man knew, but He Himself.

"His eyes were as a flame of fire." This image, first introduced in Revelation 1:14, speaks of Christ's piercing, all-knowing gaze. His eyes don't just shine—they burn with truth, exposing every hidden thing.

> Neither is there any creature that is not manifest in His sight: but all things are naked and opened unto the eyes of Him to whom we must give account. (Hebrews 4:13)

> The eyes of the LORD are in every place, beholding the evil and the good. (Proverbs 15:3)

Christ's gaze is not passive—it consumes falsehood, exposes motives, and penetrates to the soul. As He rides into battle, He does so as the righteous Judge who sees not as man sees, but according to truth.

"And on His head were many crowns." These are not *stephanos* crowns of victory, but *diademata*—royal crowns symbolizing dominion. Unlike the deceiver of Revelation 6:2, who wears one crown, Christ wears many. He does not merely win—He reigns.

- Psalm 24:10 calls Him "The King of glory."
- Isaiah 9:6–7 proclaims the endless increase of His government and peace.
- Revelation 11:15 thunders, "The kingdoms of this world are become the kingdoms of our LORD, and of His Christ; and He shall reign forever and ever."

Every crown speaks of territory won, justice upheld, and power unchallenged. They symbolize His absolute rule over heaven, earth, Israel, the Church, and the nations. No enemy can strip them. No rival can claim them. He is the King of kings and Lord of lords.

"And he had a name written, that no man knew, but He Himself." Even in all we know of Christ—Jesus, Yeshua, Messiah, Son of God, Alpha and Omega—this verse declares there is more. There is a name so holy, so transcendent, that only He understands it.

- Like God's reply in Exodus 3:14: "I AM THAT I AM."
- Like Philippians 2:9 says, "God has given Him a name above every name."
- Like the angel in Judges 13:18 who said, "Why do you ask My name, seeing it is secret?"

This secret name isn't for display. It's not for preaching or printing. It belongs to Him alone—etched in eternity, worn in glory, and revealing depths of deity beyond human grasp.

Revelation 19:12 reveals Christ, not in humility, but in unveiled majesty: His eyes blaze with divine discernment, penetrating every heart and motive with holy fire. The crowns upon His head proclaim universal kingship—He alone holds supreme authority over every realm. And the mysterious name He bears, known only to Himself, underscores the infinite depth of His divine identity. This is not the Jesus of Sunday School stories or stained-glass windows. This is the returning King, the righteous Judge, the eternal Word—coming to reclaim what is His and to rule with absolute power and glory.

When He appears, there will be no more debate. No more doubt. Only worship, awe, and the cry: "He is Lord."

OLD TESTAMENT FORESHADOWS REVELATION:

Who is this that comes from Edom, with dyed garments from Bozrah? This that is glorious in His apparel, traveling in the greatness of His strength? I that speak in righteousness, mighty to save. Wherefore are You red in Your apparel, and Your garments like him that treads in the wine fat? I have trodden the winepress alone; and of the people there was none with Me: for I will tread them in My anger, and trample them in My fury; and their blood shall be sprinkled upon My garments, and I will stain all My raiment. (Isaiah 63:1–3)

Isaiah 63:1–3 offers a vivid preview of Christ's return in Revelation 19:12. The figure "glorious in His apparel" parallels the many crowns on Christ's head, both portraying divine royalty. "I that speak in righteousness" echoes the title "Faithful and True," who judges with holy fire in His eyes. The mystery of "Who is this?" aligns with the hidden name known only to Christ. Finally, the warrior treading the winepress alone in Isaiah directly foreshadows Revelation 19:15, where Christ executes judgment in righteous fury. Together, these passages unveil the Messiah as both Savior and Judge.

THE REVELATION OF JESUS CHRIST REVEALS:

19:13 And He was clothed with a vesture dipped in blood: and His name is called The Word of God.

"And He was clothed with a vesture dipped in blood." This powerful image echoes Isaiah 63:3, where the Messiah declares, "I have trodden the winepress alone . . . their blood shall be sprinkled upon My garments." This is not the blood of Christ's sacrifice at Calvary, but the blood of His enemies—signifying the justice He brings as the Warrior-King. It anticipates His righteous vengeance at

Armageddon (Revelation 19:15). This is no longer the suffering Lamb—but the conquering Lion of Judah.

"And His name is called The Word of God." This name identifies Jesus as the eternal Logos, the perfect expression of God's nature and will. John 1:1–3 affirms: "In the beginning was the Word . . . and the Word was God." Jesus is both the message and the Messenger, God's final and fullest revelation (Hebrews 1:1–3). This connects His earthly ministry with His heavenly return—He is the Word who once spoke peace and now declares judgment.

Gospel portraits converge in Revelation:

- Matthew reveals Him as King of kings.
- Mark presents Him as the faithful Servant.
- Luke portrays Him as the Son of Man.
- John declares Him the eternal Word of God.

Now in Revelation, these facets unite: crowned in majesty, eyes of fire, garments stained in righteous wrath. He is the same voice that spoke creation into existence (Genesis 1:3) and now speaks destruction upon the wicked.

In verse 12, Jesus bears a name known only to Himself—perhaps the new name of Revelation 3:12—underscoring His divine mystery. Yet in verse 13, we are told what we *can* know: He is *The Word of God*. Even in full glory, Christ remains beyond full comprehension—ever worthy of worship, ever deeper than we can fathom.

Revelation 19:13 unveils Jesus as the righteous Judge and divine Word—His blood-stained robe signaling judgment, His name proclaiming deity, and His hidden identity reminding us of the eternal wonder of who He is. This is not the humble Savior on a donkey—but the reigning Word on a white horse, finishing what He began.

OLD TESTAMENT FORESHADOWS REVELATION:

Gird your sword upon Your thigh, O Most Mighty, with Your glory and Your majesty. And in Your majesty ride prosperously because of truth and humility and righteousness; and Your right hand shall teach You awesome things. The King's daughter is all glorious within: her clothing is of wrought gold. She shall be brought unto the King in raiment of needlework: the virgins her companions that follow her shall be brought to You. (Psalm 45:3–4, 13–14)

Psalm 45 offers a poetic and prophetic glimpse into what Revelation reveals in full splendor. It reminds us: Christ is not only Savior, but Warrior-King. The Church is not just a follower, but His prepared and radiant Bride. And the wedding supper is not merely symbolic—it is the culmination of covenant love, fulfilled in heaven. As Psalm 45 opens with majesty and ends in marriage, it leads us prophetically to the great celebration in Revelation 19, where the Word of God, riding in glory, receives His Bride at last.

THE REVELATION OF JESUS CHRIST REVEALS:

19:14 And the armies which were in heaven followed Him upon white horses, clothed in fine linen, white and clean.

"And the armies which were in heaven followed Him." This verse unveils a majestic moment: Jesus does not return alone—He is accompanied by the armies of heaven. While this heavenly host includes angelic beings (Matthew 25:31), it also features the glorified saints—the redeemed Church, the Bride of Christ—now returning in triumph alongside the King of kings and Lord of lords.

"Clothed in fine linen, white and clean." The fine linen, white and clean, echoes Revelation 19:8, symbolizing the righteousness of the saints. These followers do not carry weapons—they come not to fight, but to *witness* the Kings' final victory. Their presence is celebratory and symbolic, not combative. This scene is the final act of the marriage celebration in heaven: the Bride, purified and glorified, now rides in royal procession behind her Bridegroom.

Numerous passages support this glorious return:

- Zechariah 14:5—"And the LORD my God shall come, and all the saints with you."
- Jude 1:14—"Behold, the Lord comes with ten thousands of His saints."
- 1 Thessalonians 3:13—". . . at the coming of our Lord Jesus Christ with all His saints."
- 2 Thessalonians 1:7, 10—". . . revealed from heaven with His mighty angels . . . glorified in His saints."
- Matthew 25:31—". . . and all the holy angels with Him . . ."
- Colossians 3:4—"When Christ . . . shall appear, then shall you also appear with Him in glory."

These passages confirm: the angels and the Church—raptured and rewarded—returns with Christ to reign. This is not their battle—it is Christ's. But they share in His triumph.

Symbolism: white horses and fine linen:

- White horses signify victory, purity, and kingly authority. Roman generals rode white horses in triumphal parades—now Christ rides as the Victor of all victors, with His saints in formation behind Him.
- Fine linen speaks to righteousness, purity, and glory. It is not self-earned but Christ-bestowed, given to those who have been made ready (Revelation 19:8).

This is not the humble Jesus of the manger, nor the Suffering Servant of the Cross. This is the conquering Word of God, leading a holy procession in righteousness and splendor. His Bride follows—not in battle gear, but in glory. No swords are needed. The victory is His alone.

What a scene it will be: heaven opened, white horses galloping, saints and angels thundering across the skies. This is the fulfillment of our blessed hope— the King returns, the Church rides in triumph, and the world witnesses the glory of God revealed in Christ.

OLD TESTAMENT FORESHADOWS REVELATION:

The chariots of God are twenty thousand, even thousands of angels: the LORD is among them, as in Sinai, in the holy place. (Psalm 68:17)

Psalm 68:17 describes a heavenly procession of divine chariots and angelic hosts, which mirrors the armies of heaven following Christ in Revelation 19:14. Just as the LORD descended on Mount Sinai with a mighty display of power and presence, so He returns in Revelation 19 with an army of saints and angels behind Him—symbolic of judgment, authority, and the establishment of His Kingdom. The imagery of "twenty thousand chariots" and "thousands of angels" parallels the white horses and righteous linen in Revelation, showing majesty, might, and divine righteousness.

THE REVELATION OF JESUS CHRIST REVEALS:

19:15 And out of His mouth goes a sharp sword, that with it He should smite the nations: and He shall rule them with a rod of iron: and He treads the winepress of the fierceness and wrath of Almighty God.

"And out of His mouth goes a sharp sword." This is not a literal blade, but a vivid symbol of Christ's all-powerful spoken Word. The same voice that spoke the universe into being in Genesis 1 now unleashes judgment on the nations. His Word is alive, active, and sharper than any two-edged sword (Hebrews 4:12). At His return, Jesus needs no human weaponry—He speaks, and His enemies fall. Isaiah 11:4 foretells this: "He shall smite the earth with rod of His mouth," and Revelation 1:16 reinforces it—"out of His mouth went a sharp two-edged sword." His Word is not a metaphor—it is decisive, final, and irresistible.

"That with it He should smite the nations." The nations that once rallied under the Antichrist's banner now face their Judge. Those who mocked and asked, "Who is able to make war with the beast?" (Revelation 13:4), are swiftly silenced. This is the Battle of Armageddon, but it's not a battle in the traditional sense— there's no struggle, no back and forth. Christ speaks, and the rebellion is crushed. As Exodus 15:3 declares, "The LORD is a man of war: the LORD is His name."

"And He shall rule them with a rod of iron." This phrase echoes Psalm 2:9, a messianic prophecy: "You shalt break them with a rod of iron." It reveals that Christ's reign during the Millennial Kingdom will not be soft or symbolic. It will be strong, unbending, and global. His authority will no longer be questioned or ignored. Revelation 2:27 and 12:5 confirm that this iron rule is part of His promised dominion—justice without delay, mercy no longer deferred.

"And He treads the winepress of the fierceness and wrath of Almighty God." This intense imagery comes from Isaiah 63:3: "I have trodden the winepress alone . . . their blood is sprinkled upon My garments." Just as grapes are crushed in a winepress, so too are the enemies of God crushed beneath His righteous anger. This is no symbolic act—it is the full outpouring of divine wrath. The blood-stained garment mentioned in Revelation 19:13 is not from Calvary, but from conquest.

Revelation 19:15 is not the comforting promise of the Rapture, when Christ comes *for* His Church. This is His *Revelation*—when He comes *with* His saints to conquer, cleanse, and claim the earth. The Lamb has become the Lion. The silent Servant has become the sovereign Judge. He is Faithful and True, the Word of God, the King of kings—and His return will leave no room for debate, delay, or defiance. The battle belongs to the Lord, and the victory is already written.

OLD TESTAMENT FORESHADOWS REVELATION:

If I whet My glittering sword, and My hand takes hold on judgment; I will render vengeance to My enemies, and will reward them that hate Me. I will make My arrows drunk with blood, and My sword shall devour flesh; and that with the blood of the slain and of the captives, from the beginning of revenges upon the enemy. (Deuteronomy 32:41–42)

This excerpt from the Song of Moses—Deuteronomy 32:41–42—powerfully foreshadows Revelation 19. The "sword" devouring flesh parallels the sharp sword from Christ's mouth (Revelation 19:15) used to strike the nations. The vivid imagery of vengeance, blood, and divine judgment anticipates the winepress of God's wrath that Jesus treads alone at His return. Revelation completes what Moses began—the final, holy justice of the conquering King.

THE REVELATION OF JESUS CHRIST REVEALS:

$^{19:16}$ And He has on His vesture and on His thigh a name written, KING OF KINGS, AND LORD OF LORDS.

This verse unveils the final and supreme declaration of Jesus Christ's authority. As He rides forth on the white horse, He bears a visible and royal title— "KING OF KINGS, AND LORD OF LORDS"—written on His vesture and thigh.

This is not merely a name; it is a proclamation of ultimate dominion over every earthly and spiritual authority.

The vesture likely refers to the flowing outer garment draped across His chest and possibly down His leg, symbolizing royal attire. The thigh is biblically symbolic of strength and authority (Genesis 32:25, where Jacob wrestled with the angel and was touched on the thigh). Kings in ancient times would also carry seals or swords at their thighs, representing their right to rule and judge.

The title "King of kings, and Lord of lords" declares that there is no power above Christ—no Caesar, no emperor, no principality, no beast, no ruler—only One supreme King. This fulfills Deuteronomy 10:17, where God is called "God of gods, and Lord of lords." It echoes the apocalyptic vision of Daniel 2:47, where even pagan kings acknowledge that the God of Heaven rules over all.

In 1 Timothy 6:15, Paul says Jesus will be revealed in due time as "the blessed and only Potentate, the King of kings, and Lord of lords," reinforcing that this title is uniquely His.

As Christ returns in glory and righteous judgment, He no longer appears as the Suffering Servant but as the sovereign Warrior-King, putting down rebellion, judging the nations, and establishing His millennial reign on earth.

OLD TESTAMENT FORESHADOWS REVELATION:

For the LORD your God is God of gods, and Lord of lords, a great God, a mighty, and a terrible, which regards not persons, nor takes reward. (Deuteronomy 10:17)

This title, first given to Yahweh in Deuteronomy 10:17, reappears in Revelation 19:16—now inscribed on Christ's robe as He returns in glory. What was once proclaimed of GOD in the Law is now fulfilled in Jesus—revealing Him as the divine King of kings and Lord of lords, who comes to reign forever.

THE REVELATION OF JESUS CHRIST REVEALS:

[19:17] And I saw an angel standing in the sun; and he cried with a loud voice, saying to all the fowls that fly in the midst of heaven, Come and gather yourselves together to the supper of the great God.

This verse marks a dramatic and solemn turning point in the vision of Christ's return. After the triumphant declaration of Jesus as King of kings and Lord of lords in verse 16, Revelation 19:17 shifts to depict the gathering of divine judgment upon the armies of the Antichrist at Armageddon.

An angel—"standing in the sun"—symbolizes one who is fully visible, exposed in brilliance and authority, acting under divine commission. The sun, which gives light to all the earth, implies that this declaration is public and universal, visible to all. The angel cries with a loud voice, announcing a grotesque yet prophetic invitation: a call to birds of prey to gather for "the supper of the great God."

This is a grim contrast to the marriage supper of the Lamb in verse 9. There, the redeemed feast in joy; here, God's enemies becomes the feast—devoured by the birds of the air. This echoes Ezekiel 39:17–20, where the LORD calls the birds and beasts to a great sacrificial feast upon His defeated enemies. It underscores God's justice: those who rebel against Him will not go unpunished.

This "supper" is not metaphorical—it is a literal cleanup operation after the Battle of Armageddon. The carnage of fallen kings, generals, and warriors will be so massive that scavenging birds are summoned to dispose of the dead. It's a picture of divine wrath and complete victory.

The contrast is sobering: either one attends the wedding supper of the Lamb, or becomes the feast at the supper of the great God. This stark reality magnifies the mercy of salvation and the gravity of rejecting Christ.

OLD TESTAMENT FORESHADOWS REVELATION:

And, you son of man, thus says the Lord GOD; Speak unto every feathered fowl, and to every beast of the field, Assemble yourselves, and come; gather yourselves on every side to My sacrifice that I do sacrifice for you, even a great sacrifice upon the mountains of Israel, that you may eat flesh, and drink blood. You shall eat the flesh of the mighty, and drink the blood of the princes of the earth. (Ezekiel 39:17–18)

In Ezekiel 39:17–18, God summons birds and beasts to feast on the fallen— a "great sacrifice" following the defeat of His enemies. This mirrors Revelation 19:17–18, where an angel calls birds to "the supper of the great God" after the Battle of Armageddon. Both scenes portray the aftermath of divine judgment, where the wicked are overthrown and creation itself is summoned to consume the evidence. Ezekiel's vision follows Gog and Magog's defeat; Revelation marks the fall of the beast (the Antichrist) and the False Prophet. The graphic imagery underscores the severity and finality of God's wrath.

THE REVELATION OF JESUS CHRIST REVEALS:

[19:18] That you may eat the flesh of kings, and the flesh of captains, and the flesh of mighty men, and the flesh of horses, and of them that sit on them, and the flesh of all men, both free and bond, both small and great.

This verse continues the sobering call from the previous verse to the "fowls that fly in the midst of heaven," summoned to participate in the "supper of the great God." This is not a celebration but a massive divine judgment scene. It is a ghastly reversal: those who were powerful, prideful, and elevated in earthly stature now become food for the scavengers of the air. Six times the word "flesh" is used in this paragraph, emphasizing the frailty and mortality of man when opposed to God's righteousness.

The verse is a direct parallel to Ezekiel 39:17–20, where the LORD calls birds and beasts to a great sacrificial feast of the fallen enemies of Israel. It also echoes Revelation 14:14–20 and 16:13–16, leading into the Battle of Armageddon, when the armies of the Antichrist are slaughtered by Christ Himself at His Second Coming.

It's important to contrast this scene with the "marriage supper of the Lamb" (Revelation 19:9). There are two suppers described in this chapter—one of grace (for the Bride of Christ) and one of wrath (for the enemies of God). Every soul will attend one or the other.

Jesus alludes to this judgment in Luke 17:37 and Matthew 24:28, saying, "Wheresoever the body is, thither will the eagles be gathered together," suggesting a gathering of birds around the dead—a vivid allusion to judgment following Christ's return.

OLD TESTAMENT FORESHADOWS REVELATION:

And the slain of the LORD shall be at that day from one end of the earth even unto the other end of the earth: they shall not be lamented, neither gathered, nor buried; they shall be dung upon the ground. (Jeremiah 25:33)

Like Revelation 19:18, Jeremiah 25:33 paints a picture of widespread judgment at the end of days. The dead span all social ranks—"from one end of the earth to the other"—echoing Revelation's reference to kings, captains, mighty men . . . bond and free, small and great. In both verses, there is no burial, no mourning, no honor—only desolation and exposure, emphasizing the finality of divine wrath. Revelation 19:18 shows the fowls consuming the flesh; Jeremiah 25:33 says they are left like refuse, both evoking God's contempt for the rebellion of mankind.

THE REVELATION OF JESUS CHRIST REVEALS:

[19:19] And I saw the beast, and the kings of the earth, and their armies, gathered together to make war against Him that sat on the horse, and against His army.

This verse captures one of the most staggering moments in all of Scripture: the collective rebellion of humanity's most powerful leaders—under the Antichrist—against Jesus Christ Himself. The beast, the kings of the earth, and their armies unite in a final confrontation, intending to wage war against the One riding the white horse and His heavenly army of glorified saints and angels.

But what appears to be a climactic battle isn't a battle at all. There is no real contest. The power imbalance is infinite—finite beings attempting to overthrow the Infinite One. The entire scene borders on the absurd, a tragic satire of human pride thinking it can dethrone its Creator.

This moment draws together numerous prophetic strands:

- Psalm 2:1–9 asks, "Why do the nations rage . . . against the LORD and against His Anointed?" God's response is not alarm but laughter—a divine scoff at human arrogance. Verse 9 declares, "You shall break them with a rod of iron," directly fulfilled in Revelation 19:15.
- 2 Thessalonians 2:8 declares, "The Lord shall consume (the Antichrist) with the spirit of His mouth, and shall destroy with the brightness of His coming." Christ's mere presence is enough to obliterate the opposition.
- Daniel 11:44–45 and Joel 2 foresee this massing of armies in the Middle East, particularly around the Valley of Megiddo, with the Antichrist's headquarters set in Jerusalem.
- Hosea 5:15 offers a key insight: Christ does not return until the Jewish remnant cries out in national repentance. This fulfills Matthew 23:39— "You shall not see Me hereafter, till you shall say, 'Blessed is He that comes in the name of the Lord.'"

Even the imagery in this scene is foreshadowed:

- Nahum 2:3 describes red shields, symbolic of bloodshed.
- Nahum 3:2 refers to the "rattling of wheels" and war machines—perhaps even suggesting modern mechanized warfare.

This moment represents the culmination of humanity's rebellion—a final, futile attempt to resist divine authority. And yet, heaven does not scramble. Christ does not fight with conventional weapons. He simply speaks. And the war ends before it begins.

There is no drawn-out battle. No back-and-forth. No question of the outcome. The Antichrist and the kings of the earth are confronted by the Word of God, the sword proceeding from Christ's mouth (Revelation 19:15). Judgment falls swiftly. The King returns—and His dominion is uncontested.

OLD TESTAMENT FORESHADOWS REVELATION:

Proclaim you this among the Gentiles; Prepare war, wake up the mighty men, let all the men of war draw near; let them come up: Beat your plowshares into swords, and your pruninghooks into spears: let the weak say, I am strong. Assemble yourselves, and come, all you nations, and gather yourselves together round about: cause your mighty ones to come down, O Lord. (Joel 3:9–11)

Just like Revelation 19:19, Joel 3:9–11 depicts a global call to war, where the nations are deliberately gathering to fight, not realizing they're marching to their own judgment. Joel describes the mobilization of all nations for battle—mirroring the gathering of the beast, kings of the earth, and their armies against Christ in Revelation. The call for warriors to assemble is met by God's "mighty ones" coming down—a veiled reference to the armies of heaven accompanying the Messiah. Joel 3 continues into the imagery of the winepress of God's wrath (Joel 3:13), which is also seen in Revelation 19:15.

Irene leaned in, her brow furrowed with concern.

"Ann, I've been reading about the Battle of Armageddon and the Gog and Magog war, and honestly . . ."—she paused—". . . I'm confused. Are they the same event? And where exactly does the Valley of Megiddo fit into all of this?"

I smiled warmly, sensing the weight behind her question.

"You're not alone, Irene. These prophetic events can be tricky, especially because the names sometimes overlap and the details are spread across different books of the Bible. But you're asking *exactly* the right questions. Let's break it down—one step at a time."

I flipped open my Bible and turned to Ezekiel.

"Let's start with Gog and Magog in Ezekiel 38 and 39," I said, running my finger along the verses.

"Many Bible scholars believe this invasion happens before the seven-year Tribulation officially begins. It's often seen as a pre-Tribulation war—a kind of trigger event that sets the stage for Daniel's 70th Week."

"So this war happens before the Rapture?"

I shook my head thoughtfully. "Not necessarily before the Rapture—but most scholars place it either just before or right at the start of the Tribulation. Ezekiel 38 and 39 describe a dramatic, sudden invasion of Israel led by a figure called Gog from the land of Magog. He leads a powerful coalition of nations against Israel—but God Himself intervenes in a miraculous and unmistakable way."

Irene leaned forward. "And who are those nations exactly?"

I nodded and turned to Ezekiel 38:1–6.

"These are the nations Ezekiel lists, many of which scholars link to modern regions," I explained.

- Magog—believed to be from the far north, often associated with areas near the Black and Caspian Seas—many connect it with Russia.
- Rosh—some translations read this as 'chief prince,' but others take it as a proper noun—possibly Russia, though that's debated.
- Meshech and Tubal—likely located in modern-day Turkey.

- Persia—that one's clear: it's modern-day Iran.
- Cush—thought to be parts of Sudan or Ethiopia.
- Put—generally linked to Libya or North Africa.
- Gomer—possibly Eastern Europe or parts of Turkey.
- Togarmah—often identified with Armenia or the Caucasus region.

I looked up. "So it's a pretty broad coalition, mostly from the north, east, and parts of Africa—all converging on Israel."

"Wow," Irene said, eyes wide. "That's a serious coalition."

I nodded. "It really is. But here's the thing—God steps in supernaturally. We're talking massive earthquakes, torrential rain, hailstones, fire from heaven, and even confusion among the invading forces. It's divine judgment on full display."

I paused and looked at her, flipping to Ezekiel 38:19–20.

> And it shall come to pass at the same time when Gog shall come against the land of Israel, says the Lord GOD, that My fury shall come up in My face. For in My jealousy and in My fire of My wrath have I spoken, Surely in that day there shall be a great shaking in the land of Israel; So that the fishes of the sea, and the fowls of the heaven, and the beasts of the field, and all creeping things that creep upon the earth, and all the men that are upon the face of the earth, shall shake at My presence, and the mountains shall be thrown down, and the steep places shall fall, and every wall shall fall to the ground. (Ezekiel 38:18–20)

"No one will be able to claim Israel defended herself. The victory will be undeniably God's. The whole world will see—it was the Lord who rose up and fought for His people."

"And that sets the stage for the rise of the Antichrist?"

I nodded. "Exactly. After God supernaturally defeats Israel's enemies, the nation will likely experience a surge of confidence—a false sense of peace. That's when the Antichrist steps in, offering a covenant of protection that seems like the answer to everything. But it's a trap—the calm before the storm."

"A deceptive calm," Irene murmured.

"Yes," I said. "Whether Israel's sense of 'peace and safety' stems from a treaty brokered by the Antichrist at the very beginning of the Tribulation, or—as some scholars argue—it reflects an illusion of security during the first half of the Tribulation, the effect is the same. Ezekiel 38:11 captures that moment of perceived safety—just before the Gog and Magog invasion. Meanwhile, Ezekiel 38:18–20 portrays the cataclysmic response of divine judgment."

> And you shalt say, I will go up to the land of unwalled villages; I will go to them that are at rest, that dwell safely, all of them dwelling without walls, and having neither bars nor gates. (Ezekiel 38:11)

Irene leaned closer. "And isn't there something in Ezekiel about the weapons being burned for seven years?"

I nodded. "Yes—Ezekiel 39:9 spells it out clearly. After the invasion is crushed, the people of Israel won't just bury the weapons—they'll repurpose them. The detail about the duration is significant."

> And they that dwell in the cities of Israel shall go forth, and shall set on fire and burn the weapons, both the shields and the bucklers, the bows and the arrows, and the hand staves, and the spears, and they shall burn them with fire seven years. (Ezekiel 39:9)

"So much weaponry left behind," I added. "And Israel doesn't just discard it—they use it as fuel. That seven-year detail isn't a throwaway line—it has prophetic weight. It suggests the war must happen early enough in the prophetic timeline—likely before or near the beginning of the Tribulation—to allow that full period to unfold before Christ's return at Armageddon."

Irene nodded slowly. "That's another clue it happens before or at the start of the Tribulation. If it were Armageddon—at the very end—there wouldn't be seven years left to burn anything."

"And does God use the birds for clean up here too?"

"Yes," I nodded. "According to Ezekiel 39:17–20, God summons the birds—carrion feeders—for a great sacrificial feast after this Gog and Magog war. They're called to devour the flesh of the slain, from mighty men to horses. It's graphic, but intentional. It's God's way of showing that this wasn't just a military defeat—it was divine judgment."

I flipped to the passage and read aloud:

> And, you son of man, thus says the Lord GOD; Speak unto every feathered fowl, and to every beast of the field, Assemble yourselves, and come; gather yourselves on every side to My sacrifice that I do sacrifice for you, even a great sacrifice upon the mountains of Israel, that you may eat flesh, and drink blood. You shall eat the flesh of the mighty, and drink the blood of the princes of the earth, of rams, of lambs, and of goats, of bulls, all of them fatlings (symbols of strength and abundance) of Bashan (a land of plenty, located in what is today southern Syria). And you shall eat fat till you be full, and drink blood till you be drunken, of My sacrifice which I have sacrificed for you. Thus you shall be filled at My table with horses and chariots, with mighty men, and with all men of war, says the Lord GOD. (Ezekiel 39:17–20)

"That's similar to Revelation 19, isn't it?" Irene asked.

"Exactly. Revelation 19:17–18, describes something nearly identical after the Battle of Armageddon. The angel calls the birds to the 'supper of the great God.'

Many scholars see this as a deliberate parallel—Ezekiel's bird feast foreshadows the greater judgment at Christ's Second Coming."

I continued, "But after the *final* Gog and Magog war in Revelation 20:7–10—after the Millennium—there's no mention of birds at all. Why? Because that battle ends instantly. There's no long drawn-out conflict. Fire falls from heaven and consumes the enemies. Judgment is swift and complete."

"So," Irene said slowly, "you're saying the birds are summoned in both Gog and Magog and Armageddon?"

"Yes," I confirmed. "But they're different events. Ezekiel's feast follows the first Gog and Magog war—before or early in the Tribulation timeline. Revelation's feast follows Armageddon—at the Second Coming. Both are vivid, symbolic declarations that when God moves in judgment, it is final, overwhelming, and unmistakably divine. Even the birds bear witness."

Irene shivered. "That gives me chills. It's almost poetic in a terrifying way."

"It is," I said gently. "Biblical judgment often carries a kind of solemn beauty—it's God's justice on full display. Majestic, but sobering."

Her brow furrowed. "Okay, now where does Armageddon come in?"

I smiled. "That's a great question. Armageddon is the climactic military showdown—it marks the end of the Tribulation, closing out Daniel's 70th Week. Revelation 16:16 says the kings of the earth are gathered to a place called Armageddon—that's the valley region near Megiddo, in northern Israel."

"So . . . is it one big battle?"

I shook my head. "Not quite. Think of it less as a single clash and more as a final military campaign. The Antichrist's forces are mobilized across multiple nations, gathering for war. It's global in scope. But it culminates in a single, dramatic moment: Christ's return."

She leaned in. "That's when Jesus rides in on the white horse?"

"Exactly," I said, flipping to Revelation 19. "The bowl judgments have devastated the earth. Babylon—America—has fallen. By this time, Earth's population is dramatically reduced—possibly down to 200 to 400 million. What remains of the world's armies gathers under the Antichrist to launch a final assault on Jerusalem."

"And then?"

"And then . . . the sky opens. Jesus returns—Faithful and True—riding on a white horse, followed by the armies of heaven clothed in fine linen, white and clean. It's not even a battle in the traditional sense. His Word—symbolized as the sword from His mouth—strikes the nations. The Antichrist and False Prophet are captured and thrown alive into the Lake of Fire. The rest? Slain by the breath of His mouth. It's swift. Unstoppable. Righteous."

Irene nodded slowly. "That's Revelation 19:19–21, right? Where Christ defeats the Antichrist and his armies?"

"Exactly. That's the climax of Armageddon—the moment the rebellion of mankind meets the wrath of the Lamb."

I flipped a few pages back. "And it's not isolated to Revelation. Zechariah 14:2–4 says the Lord will gather all nations to battle against Jerusalem, then He Himself will descend—His feet standing on the Mount of Olives, which splits in two. That's not poetic imagery. That's a literal, earth-shaking return."

Irene leaned in. "And Joel talks about this too?"

"Absolutely. Joel 3 expands the picture. God says He'll gather the nations to the Valley of Jehoshaphat to judge them for how they treated His people Israel. Joel 3:2 and 3:12 describe this vividly. Many scholars identify this valley with the Kidron Valley, located between the Temple Mount and the Mount of Olives in Jerusalem."

"So not the same as the Valley of Megiddo?"

"Right. Megiddo is in the Jezreel Valley, about 60 miles north of Jerusalem. Think of it this way: Megiddo is the battlefield—Armageddon's military staging ground. Jehoshaphat is the courtroom—God's place of judgment."

Irene's eyes widened. "And that judgment—could it be the Sheep and Goat Judgment that Jesus describes in Matthew 25?"

I nodded. "Very possibly. In Matthew 25:31–46, Jesus says when the Son of Man returns in glory, He'll sit on His glorious throne and separate the nations like a shepherd divides the sheep from the goats. The Sheep are welcomed into the Millennial Kingdom. The Goats? Sent into everlasting fire prepared for the devil and his angels."

Irene paused, then smiled. "Wow. So to recap, the timeline looks like this:"

1. **Gog and Magog** *(Ezekiel 38–39)*—Likely pre-Tribulation.

2. **Tribulation** *(Revelation 6–18)*—Begins after the Rapture.

3. **Armageddon** *(Revelation 16:16; 19:19–21)*—Ends the Tribulation.

4. **Gog and Magog** *(Revelation 20:7–9)*—Happens after the Millennium.

I nodded. "Perfect summary, Irene. And here's the key takeaway: Jesus wins. Every war—every rebellion—ends the same way: with Christ victorious, the enemy defeated, and God's justice perfectly fulfilled."

Irene's eyes shimmered. "That's what I love most. We're not just tracing prophecy—we're watching the last chapters unfold. And the Bride?"

I smiled. "She's already safe in the arms of the Groom."

Irene leaned in. "Ann, can we keep going? I'm trying to understand—what happens the moment Jesus returns? When He touches down on the Mount of Olives—is *that* the Battle of Armageddon? Is *that* when the Mount splits in two?"

I nodded. "Yes, it's one of the most dramatic prophetic moments in all of Scripture. Zechariah 14:4 tells us that Jesus returns to the very place He ascended from nearly 2,000 years ago—the Mount of Olives. And when His feet touch down? A massive earthquake splits the mountain in two, forming a great valley running east to west. This isn't symbolic—it's a literal, seismic event."

I paused and flipped to the passage.

> Then shall the LORD go forth, and fight against those nations, as when He fought in the day of battle. And His feet shall stand in that day upon the Mount of Olives, which is before Jerusalem on the east, and the Mount of Olives shall cleave in the midst thereof toward the east and toward the west, and there shall be a very great valley; and half of the mountain shall remove toward the north, and half of it toward the south. (Zechariah 14:3–4)

"This moment marks the climax of the Tribulation—the very end of Daniel's 70th Week. It coincides with the final conflict we call Armageddon. The armies of the world have gathered against Jerusalem, but they're no match for the King of kings. When Jesus returns, He comes in glory, power, and justice—splitting the mountain and shattering the rebellion with just His Word."

Irene tilted her head. "But is *that* where Armageddon takes place? Is the Mount of Olives the same as the Valley of Megiddo?"

I smiled. "Great question—and one a lot of people wonder about. No, they're not the same place. The Mount of Olives is in Jerusalem, just east of the Old City. That's where Jesus physically returns, and it's where the mountain splits in two—*that's* localized. But the Valley of Megiddo, often called Armageddon, is about 60 to 70 miles north of Jerusalem in the Jezreel Valley. Two very different locations, both crucial to end-times prophecy."

I flipped to Revelation. "Revelation 16:16 says the kings of the earth are *gathered* by demonic spirits to a place called Armageddon. It's the staging ground—a global military campaign with a central base in the Valley of Megiddo. But the final confrontation happens when Jesus descends to Jerusalem and strikes down His enemies. So Megiddo is the military rally point, while the Mount of Olives is the site of Christ's return and victory."

Irene leaned forward. "So Armageddon is where the final battle is launched?"

I nodded. "Exactly. The armies of the world gather in the Valley of Megiddo, but battle doesn't stay there. As Christ descends, the campaign shifts south toward

Jerusalem. That's where He intervenes directly—setting foot on the Mount of Olives. And when His feet touch down, Zechariah 14:4 tells us the mountain splits in two. That miraculous split opens a valley of escape for the Jewish remnant trapped in the city."

"They flee to the rose-red mountains of Petra, right?"

> And you shall flee to the valley of the mountains; for the valley of the mountains shall reach unto Azal: yea, you shall flee, like as you fled from before the earthquake in the days of Uzziah king of Judah: and the Lord my God shall come, and all the saints with You. (Zechariah 14:5)

"Exactly. Many Bible scholars believe Petra—or Bozrah, as referenced in Isaiah 63—is the place of refuge prepared by God. It fits the prophetic picture perfectly. It's remote, fortified by natural rock walls, and historically tied to Edom and Moab—regions in southern and central Jordan. Revelation 12:6 even hints at a wilderness refuge, a place God protects for 1,260 days, which aligns with the last half of the Tribulation."

Irene sighed. "So Zechariah 14 and Revelation 16 are describing related but distinct events. Jesus touches down in Jerusalem, the Mount of Olives splits, the remnant escapes, and then the actual confrontation happens in Megiddo. Right?"

"Close," I said with a smile. "They're absolutely connected—but the confrontation starts in Megiddo and climaxes in Jerusalem. Revelation 16:16 tells us the kings of the earth are *gathered* to Armageddon—the Valley of Megiddo. That's the staging ground. But Zechariah 14 picks up the action in Jerusalem, where Jesus Himself returns, stands on the Mount of Olives, and initiates divine intervention. The mountain splits in two, providing a miraculous escape route for the Jewish remnant hiding in the city."

I flipped the pages of my Bible and continued, "And this isn't just symbolic imagery. The Valley of Megiddo is a real place—a wide, fertile plain in northern Israel, also known as the Jezreel Valley. Historically, it's one of the most contested battlefields in the world. Think about it—Deborah and Barak defeated Sisera there in Judges 4–5, Gideon faced the Midianites nearby in Judges 6–7. King Saul died in that region. Even General Allenby's World War I victory in 1918 was called the *Battle of Megiddo*. It's as if that ground has been preparing for this final confrontation for millennia."

"That gives me chills. So when Jesus returns, Revelation 19 says He's on a white horse, and behind Him are the armies of heaven—saints and angels."

I nodded. "Exactly. And He doesn't fight with conventional weapons. His victory comes by the sword that proceeds from His mouth—His Word. Revelation 19:15 says, 'Now out of His mouth goes a sharp sword, that with it He should strike the nations.' One word from Christ is enough to end the rebellion."

Irene's eyes widened. "And that connects to Revelation 14, doesn't it? That chilling image of the blood rising up to a horse's bridle?"

"Yes," I said solemnly. "Revelation 14:20 is part of a prophetic preview. It speaks of the winepress of God's wrath—symbolic of the massive judgment that culminates at Armageddon. The verse says the blood flows for 1,600 furlongs—that's roughly 180 miles. Some scholars interpret it literally, others symbolically, but either way, the message is clear: the judgment is vast, final, and devastating."

I paused.

"That passage, paired with the vision in Revelation 19, paints a sobering picture. When Christ returns, it isn't to negotiate. It's to judge. The armies of the Antichrist don't stand a chance. He speaks—and it's over."

Irene's voice lowered. "And those who are killed at Armageddon . . . they're the armies of the Antichrist, right? Revelation 19:21 says, 'the remnant were slain with the sword of Him who sat on the horse,' and the birds were 'filled with their flesh.' That's the 'supper of the great God.' It's gruesome."

"It is," I said gently. "Revelation doesn't sugarcoat judgment. These are the ones who took the mark, worshiped the beast, and raised weapons against the returning King. There's no ambiguity—they die in open rebellion against Christ. It's final. Their souls are sent to Hades, awaiting the Great White Throne Judgment in Revelation 20:11–15."

Irene paused, then asked, "So is the *supper of the great God* just in the Valley of Megiddo?"

I shook my head. "No, it's not limited to Megiddo. The *supper of the great God* isn't about a single location—it's the global aftermath of Jesus' return and His swift judgment. It's almost like a grim counterpart to the *marriage supper of the Lamb*. One is a celebration of covenant and life; the other is a declaration of judgment and death."

I opened to Revelation 19:17–18.

"In this passage, an angel cries out to the birds of the air, summoning them to a great feast. It's graphic—flesh of kings, commanders, mighty men, horses and their riders. It paints the scene of a battlefield strewn with the fallen. But what it really shows is the completeness of Christ's victory. There are no survivors among those who oppose Him."

I continued, softer now. "And it parallels Ezekiel 39:17–20—after the Gog and Magog battle, God tells the birds and beasts to gather for a great sacrificial feast. It's a divine cleanup, yes—but also a public, visible sign that evil has been crushed. The enemies of God don't just fall—they're consumed, utterly undone."

Irene furrowed her brow. "And the Antichrist and the False Prophet? Revelation 19:20 says they're cast alive into the Lake of Fire."

I nodded. "Correct, Irene. That's actually the first mention in all of Scripture of *anyone* being thrown into the Lake of Fire. There's no trial. No appeal. No delay. Just instant, eternal judgment. And here's the remarkable part—when Satan is thrown in a thousand years later in Revelation 20:10, it says the Antichrist and the False Prophet are still there. It's not annihilation. It's eternal torment."

She blinked. "So after Armageddon, the rebellion is crushed. Earthly kingdoms fall. Jesus begins His reign. And the next thing we see is Satan being bound for a thousand years in Revelation 20:1–3. Wow."

I nodded again. "Exactly. Revelation 19 ends with a complete divine triumph. Human rebellion is shattered. The kings of the earth fall. The beast and his prophet are judged. The stage is cleared for Christ to establish His Kingdom."

She leaned back, taking it in.

"Then Revelation 20 opens with the dragon in chains. But before we even go there . . . I feel like we need to pause. The wrath, the justice, the return of the King—it's overwhelming. Sobering. And glorious."

I smiled gently.

"It really is. Armageddon isn't just the final war. It's the ultimate unveiling of Jesus as Judge, King, and Warrior. It's where the 'Faithful and True' rides forth—not in humility like at His First Coming, but in majesty and power. It's not just the end of an age. It's the beginning of forever."

Irene leaned forward, counting off on her fingers.

"Okay, let me see if I've got this straight:"

1. Armageddon begins as a campaign—the kings of the earth gather their armies in the Valley of Megiddo, the Jezreel Valley in northern Israel. *(Revelation 16:16)*
2. The battle shifts south toward Jerusalem—as Jesus descends from heaven, mounted on a white horse, with the armies of heaven behind Him. *(Revelation 19:11–14)*
3. Jesus lands on the Mount of Olives, and it splits in two—creating a way of escape for the Jewish remnant. *(Zechariah 14:4)*
4. The Jewish remnant flees through the new valley—likely toward Petra—while Jesus strikes down the beast's armies. *(Zechariah 14:5; Joel 3; Revelation 19:15)*
5. The Antichrist and the False Prophet are captured and thrown alive into the Lake of Fire—no delay, no trial, eternal judgment. *(Revelation 19:20)*
6. The 'supper of the great God' follows—birds feast on the flesh of kings, captains, and warriors. *(Revelation 19:17–18, 21; Ezekiel 39:17–20)*

7.   Satan is bound in the abyss for 1,000 years—unable to deceive the nations during Christ's reign. *(Revelation 20:1–3)*

8.   The Sheep and Goat Judgment—Jesus judges the nations, likely in the Valley of Jehoshaphat, based on how they treated His brethren (Israel and the saints). *(Matthew 25:31–46; Joel 3:2)*

9.   First Resurrection—the resurrection of the righteous, completed with the Tribulation martyrs and likely the Old Testament saints. *(Revelation 20:4–6; Daniel 12:2; Isaiah 26:19)*

10. The Millennial Kingdom begins—Christ rules from Jerusalem for 1,000 years. *(Revelation 20:4–6)*

I smiled. "Beautifully summarized, Irene. These aren't vague symbols or mystical ideas—they're concrete prophetic milestones. God's calendar is perfect. Every event is deliberate."

Irene nodded, eyes misting. "And it all ends with Jesus reigning in glory."

I leaned in, voice soft. "Every time. Every knee will bow. Every nation will see. And we—His Bride—will reign with Him."

THE REVELATION OF JESUS CHRIST REVEALS:

^{19:20} And the Beast was taken, and with him the False Prophet that wrought miracles before him, with which he deceived them that had received the mark of the beast, and them that worshiped his image. These both were cast alive into a Lake of Fire burning with brimstone.

This verse records one of the most decisive and terrifying moments of divine judgment in Scripture—the immediate capture and condemnation of two of the most notorious figures in end-times prophecy: the beast (the Antichrist) and the False Prophet. There is no trial, no debate, no escape—just divine justice, executed instantly and publicly.

"And the Beast was taken." This beast is none other than the Antichrist, the satanically empowered world leader who rose to dominate global politics, economics, and religion (Revelation 13:1–8). His reign of terror culminated in the Battle of Armageddon, where he dared to challenge Christ directly. But the outcome is not a drawn-out conflict. Jesus takes him—sovereignly and effortlessly.

"And with him the False Prophet." This second figure is the deceptive religious leader who performed counterfeit miracles, including calling fire from heaven, to deceive multitudes into worshiping the beast and receiving his mark

(Revelation 13:11–15). While the Antichrist ruled by force, the False Prophet ruled by persuasion—coercing millions into spiritual adultery and eternal ruin.

"These both were cast alive into a Lake of Fire burning with brimstone." This is a shocking and unique judgment. Rather than dying first and awaiting judgment like all others, these two are cast alive into the Lake of Fire—a conscious, eternal judgment. This introduces us to Gehenna, the final hell described in Scripture, distinct from Hades (the temporary realm of the dead). Their eternal sentence begins immediately.

This is the first explicit mention of the Lake of Fire in the Bible, a place of burning brimstone and unending torment. A thousand years later, in Revelation 20:10, we learn that they are still there—undestroyed, still suffering. This confirms the torment is not symbolic or temporary, but eternal, as Jesus also warned in Matthew 25:46.

> And these shall go away into everlasting punishment: but the righteous into life eternal. (Matthew 25:46)

The beast (the Antichrist) and the False Prophet once appeared invincible to the world. Their power, deception, and supernatural displays caused the world to marvel and ask: "Who is like the beast? Who can make war with him?" (Revelation 13:4). But Christ does not engage in a struggle—He simply acts. They are seized and condemned in a single breath of divine authority.

This marks the end of the satanic counterfeit trinity:

- The dragon (Satan),
- The beast (the Antichrist),
- The False Prophet (the deceiving spirit of false religion).

With two-thirds now judged, only Satan remains to be bound in the abyss (Revelation 20:1–3), preparing the way for Christ's millennial reign on earth.

The contrast here is profound. These two are cast alive into eternal damnation. In contrast, in Revelation 11:11–12, two faithful witnesses—often understood to be Moses and Elijah—were taken alive into heaven. One group ascends in victory; the other descends in judgment.

Those who stand with Christ are rewarded with life and glory. Those who oppose Him face a judgment that is swift, public, and everlasting.

OLD TESTAMENT FORESHADOWS REVELATION:

> For Tophet is ordained of old; yea, for the king it is prepared; he has made it deep and large: the pile thereof is fire and much wood; the breath of the LORD, like a stream of brimstone, do kindle it. (Isaiah 30:33)

Tophet, historically a place of burning judgment, foreshadows the Lake of Fire in Revelation 19:20. Isaiah says it's "prepared for the king"—a prophetic glimpse of the Antichrist, who leads the kings of the earth and is cast alive into the Lake of Fire. The "stream of brimstone" links directly to Revelation's fiery judgment. This verse reveals that God ordained eternal judgment long before Revelation. Tophet's imagery confirms the continuity of prophecy: from Isaiah to John, God's justice is sure, fiery, and final.

THE REVELATION OF JESUS CHRIST REVEALS:

19:21 And the remnant were slain with the sword of Him that sat upon the horse, which sword proceeded out of His mouth: and all the fowls were filled with their flesh.

This final verse of Revelation 19 presents the sobering conclusion to the Battle of Armageddon. Following the dramatic judgment of the beast (the Antichrist) and the False Prophet—who are both cast alive into the Lake of Fire (verse 20)—the "remnant" refers to the remaining human forces allied with them. These are the deceived armies of the world who have joined Satan's unholy coalition to wage war against Christ at His Second Coming.

The "sword" that slays them is not a literal weapon in Christ's hand but the sword that proceeds from His mouth—a symbol of His divine authority and righteous judgment through His Word (Hebrews 4:12; 2 Thessalonians 2:8). With a single spoken command, He executes swift justice, showing that Christ needs no physical army or weapons to conquer. His Word is enough.

For the Word of God is quick, and powerful, and sharper than any two-edged sword, piercing even to the dividing asunder of soul and spirit, and of the joints and marrow, and is a discerner of the thoughts and intents of the heart. (Hebrews 4:12)

The imagery closes with the graphic and prophetic fulfillment of God's invitation to the birds of the air (verse 17): "All the fowls were filled with their flesh." This brutal end highlights the absolute and final defeat of evil. It's a grim contrast to the marriage supper of the Lamb earlier in the chapter—while the saints are celebrating with the Lord, the wicked become the supper in judgment.

With all opposition vanquished, Jesus now takes His rightful place on the Throne of David, fulfilling messianic prophecies from Isaiah 9:6–7 and Luke 1:32–33. This signals the beginning of the Millennial Kingdom, where Christ will reign in justice, righteousness, and peace.

As Zechariah 14:3–4 foretold, He will set foot on the Mount of Olives and establish His rule from Jerusalem. The kingdoms of this world have become the

Kingdom of our LORD and of His Christ, and He shall reign forever and ever (Revelation 11:15).

OLD TESTAMENT FORESHADOWS REVELATION:

For, behold, the LORD will come with fire, and with His chariots like a whirlwind, to render His anger with fury, and His rebuke with flames of fire. For by fire and by His sword will the LORD plead with all flesh: and the slain of the LORD shall be many. (Isaiah 66:15–16)

Isaiah's vivid prophecy foreshadows the apocalyptic imagery of Revelation 19. The Lord arriving "with fire" and "chariots like a whirlwind" reflects divine wrath unleashed in overwhelming force. His "sword" as a tool of judgment parallels the sharp sword proceeding from Christ's mouth in Revelation 19:21—symbolizing the power of His spoken word and unchallengeable authority.

The statement that "the slain of the LORD shall be many" anticipates the magnitude of destruction seen at the Battle of Armageddon. In both texts, judgment is neither metaphorical nor partial—it is complete and righteous.

Isaiah 66:15–16 affirms a central truth echoed in Revelation: when Christ returns, He comes not only to reign, but to execute final justice. The same God who pleads with all flesh by mercy also pleads by sword, ensuring the ultimate triumph of righteousness.

SUMMARY OF REVELATION 19

Revelation 19 is a climactic and victorious chapter that follows the fall of Babylon in Revelation 18 and ushers in the triumphant return of Jesus Christ as King of kings. The scene begins in heaven with loud, resounding praises—four hallelujahs—celebrating God's righteous judgment against the great harlot who corrupted the earth (Revelation 19:1–3). The twenty-four elders and four living creatures respond with a solemn "Amen; Alleluia," affirming the justice of God's actions (Revelation 19:4).

A voice from the throne summons all God's servants to praise Him, and the heavenly response crescendos into a thunderous multitude declaring, "Alleluia: for the Lord GOD omnipotent reigns" (Revelation 19:6). The moment all of heaven has anticipated arrives—the marriage of the Lamb—as the Bride, the Church, has made herself ready, clothed in fine linen, symbolizing the righteousness of the saints (Revelation 19:7–8). A blessing is pronounced upon those invited to the marriage supper of the Lamb (Revelation 19:9), confirming the truth of these prophetic events.

Overcome by glory, John attempts to worship the angel delivering the message but is corrected: worship belongs to God alone, for "the testimony of Jesus is the spirit of prophecy" (Revelation 19:10).

Suddenly, heaven opens, and Christ appears on a white horse—Faithful and True, wearing many crowns, with eyes like flames of fire (Revelation 19:11–12). His robe is dipped in blood, and His name is called The Word of God (Revelation 19:13). The armies of heaven follow Him on white horses, clothed in clean, white linen (Revelation 19:14). From His mouth comes a sharp sword to strike the nations, and He rules them with a rod of iron, fulfilling the fierce wrath of Almighty God (Revelation 19:15).

On His robe and thigh is written His title: KING OF KINGS, AND LORD OF LORDS (Revelation 19:16).

An angel summons the birds of the air to feast on the corpses of those slain in the final battle—the supper of the great God (Revelation 19:17–18). The Beast (the Antichrist) and the False Prophet, who deceived the world through miracles and the mark of the beast, are seized and cast alive into the Lake of Fire (Revelation 19:20). The rest of their armies are slain by the sword from Christ's mouth, and the birds gorge themselves on their flesh (Revelation 19:21).

KEY TAKEAWAYS

- Four hallelujahs in heaven—Heaven rejoices over the final judgment of Babylon and the arrival of Christ's reign.
- Marriage of the Lamb—The Church, as the Bride of Christ, is gloriously united with Him in heaven before the Second Coming.
- Christ's Second Coming—Jesus returns as a conquering King, riding on a white horse, leading the armies of heaven.
- Judgment of the Antichrist and False Prophet—The Antichrist and False Prophet are cast into the Lake of Fire, never to rise again.
- Victory over evil—The armies of the earth are defeated, and Jesus establishes His kingship, transitioning to the millennial reign.

Revelation 19 marks the turning point of human history. Jesus, no longer seen as the suffering Lamb, now rides forth as the conquering King. His Second Coming ends the reign of evil and ushers in a new era of righteousness, justice, and peace. The scene is both sobering and thrilling—reminding believers of the certainty of Christ's return and the call to be part of His victorious Bride.

Chapter 18

Revelation 20:
The Millennial Kingdom

THE MILLENNIAL REIGN OF CHRIST—Revelation 20 stands as one of the most significant chapters in all of Scripture, marking a turning point not only in prophecy but in the history of the cosmos. It bridges the dramatic Second Coming of Jesus Christ in Revelation 19 with the breathtaking unveiling of the new heaven and new earth in Revelation 21. At its core, Revelation 20 announces the dawn of a new era—one in which Jesus Christ reigns bodily on the earth for 1,000 years in what is known as the Millennial Kingdom.

The chapter is a theological masterpiece. It details the binding and the final defeat of Satan, the glorious resurrection and vindication of the righteous, and the fulfillment of God's long-standing covenant promises to Israel and to the redeemed. Far from being merely symbolic, this 1,000-year reign is presented as a literal period of time—a golden age of peace, righteousness, and divine governance under the supreme authority of Jesus Christ the King of kings.

The vision begins with striking imagery: an angel from heaven descends with the key to the bottomless pit and a heavy chain. Satan, identified as the dragon, the ancient serpent, and the devil himself, is seized, bound, and cast into the abyss for a thousand years (Revelation 20:1–3). This is a singular moment in human history—when the tempter of the nations is rendered powerless, unable to deceive or destroy. The removal of Satan's influence paves the way for Christ to rule unopposed, establishing an era that reflects the justice and holiness of heaven itself.

THOSE WHO REIGN WITH CHRIST

One of the most beautiful truths found in Revelation 20 is the identity and destiny of those who reign with Christ during the Millennium. Scripture declares that "they lived and reigned with Christ for a thousand years" (Revelation 20:4). But who are "they"?

1. **Church Age Believers**—These are the saints who have lived and died from Pentecost until the Rapture. According to 1 Thessalonians 4:16–17, they are raised and glorified at the Rapture—caught up to meet the Lord in the air. Philippians 1:23 and 2 Corinthians 5:8 confirm that believers go immediately into Christ's presence upon death. At His return, they accompany Him, clothed in white linen, symbolic of purity and righteousness (Revelation 19:14).

2. **Old Testament Saints**—Though not explicitly named in Revelation 20, their resurrection is repeatedly promised in the Old Testament. Daniel 12:2 speaks of those who "sleep in the dust of the earth" awakening to everlasting life. Isaiah 26:19 declares, "Your dead shall live; together with my dead body they shall arise." These promises culminate in their participation in the Millennial reign.

3. **Tribulation Martyrs**—Specifically mentioned in Revelation 20:4–6, these believers suffered martyrdom during the Tribulation because they refused to worship the beast or receive his mark. Though they paid the ultimate price, their reward is exalted—resurrected, honored, and enthroned with Christ.

These comprise the First Resurrection—a resurrection unto life, joy, and authority in Christ's Kingdom.

RESURRECTION TIMELINE: EXPLAINED

The Bible presents the doctrine of resurrection with clarity and intentional sequence. Revelation 20 offers key insights into the timeline of future resurrections, distinguishing between the righteous and the unrighteous.

1. **The Church Returns with Christ**—Already Glorified.

The resurrection of the Church—the Rapture—occurs prior to the Tribulation. As described in 1 Thessalonians 4:13–17 and 1 Corinthians 15:51–

52, believers are raised and transformed, meeting the Lord in the air. This glorious event happens before the wrath of God is poured out upon the earth. Revelation 4:1 symbolizes this heavenly calling. Paul affirms in Philippians 1:23 and 2 Corinthians 5:8 that believers who die are immediately with the Lord. These glorified saints return with Jesus in Revelation 19:14 and Jude 14–15.

By the time Christ returns at the end of the Tribulation (Revelation 19:11–16), the Church is already with Him—riding in His heavenly army. This proves that the saints have already been resurrected and glorified, now returning in triumph alongside their King.

2. **The First Resurrection**—The Righteous Are Raised to Reign.

Revelation 20:4–6 presents the First Resurrection—a resurrection exclusively for the righteous. This includes the Tribulation martyrs, and by implication, the Old Testament saints. Although the Old Testament saints are not named here, their resurrection is clearly taught in Daniel 12:1–2, Isaiah 26:19, and Job 19:25–27. This resurrection occurs at the beginning of the Millennium.

Three Phases of the First Resurrection:

- Christ the Firstfruits (1 Corinthians 15:20–23).
- The Church at the Rapture (1 Thessalonians 4:13–17).
- Tribulation Martyrs and Old Testament Saints (Revelation 20:4–6).

This sequence honors the unique roles of God's people throughout redemptive history while underscoring their shared inheritance in the Kingdom.

3. **The Second Resurrection**—Judgment of the Unrighteous.

The Second Resurrection is reserved for the unrighteous—those who rejected God's offer of salvation. Revelation 20:5, 11–15 describes this event, which occurs after the Millennium.

At the Great White Throne Judgment, the dead are raised to stand before the Lord. The Book of Life is opened, but tragically, their names are not found in it. Instead, they are judged according to their deeds and cast into the Lake of Fire. This is the second death—eternal separation from God.

THE NATURE OF THE MILLENNIAL KINGDOM

The Millennial Kingdom is not a metaphor—it is the literal fulfillment of numerous promises made throughout the Old Testament. Isaiah 11, Zechariah 14, and Psalm 2 are replete with visions of a righteous King ruling from Jerusalem, of peace flowing like a river, and of the wolf lying down with the lamb.

In this age:

- War will cease, and nations will beat their swords into plowshares (Isaiah 2:4).
- The knowledge of the Lord will cover the earth as the waters cover the sea (Isaiah 11:9).
- Righteousness and justice will define governance (Psalm 72).

Jesus will reign as King, not just spiritually over hearts, but physically over nations. The curse of Eden will be reversed, creation will flourish, and humanity will live in harmony with its Creator. Every promise made to Abraham, David, and the prophets finds its fulfillment here.

THE FINAL REBELLION AND SATAN'S END

Astonishingly, even after 1,000 years of Christ's perfect rule, humanity's heart remains susceptible to deception. When Satan is released for a short season (Revelation 20:7–8), he immediately sets out to deceive the nations. He gathers a vast multitude—likened to Gog and Magog—for one last attempt to overthrow God's Kingdom.

But it is hopeless. Fire rains down from heaven and devours the rebels. Satan, their instigator, is cast into the Lake of Fire, where the Antichrist and the False Prophet have already been tormented for a thousand years (Revelation 20:9–10). This is the final and eternal judgment—a permanent end to Satan's influence and presence.

THE GREAT WHITE THRONE JUDGMENT

Now comes the most solemn moment in history. Revelation 20:11–15 introduces the Great White Throne Judgment—a courtroom of unspeakable finality.

Heaven and earth flee from God's presence. Every soul that rejected Christ stands before Him. The books are opened—records of every thought, word, and action. Another book, the Book of Life, is opened. Those not found in it are judged by their deeds and sentenced to the Lake of Fire.

Even Death and Hades—the last enemies—are thrown into the fire, signifying their complete defeat. The second resurrection ends in the second death. This is not annihilation, but eternal separation from God's presence—a sobering reminder of the weight of human choice.

THE FINAL WORD: HOPE AND TRIUMPH

Revelation 20 is not merely a chapter of judgment—it is one of completion and glory. It affirms that evil will not have the final word. Satan will be silenced.

Death will be destroyed. And those who are Christ's will reign with Him forever and ever.

This chapter fulfills the longing of every faithful heart: to see justice done, righteousness prevail, and the promises of God fulfilled without delay. It assures the believer that their labor is not in vain and that their future is secure.

Revelation 20 ends the story of rebellion and opens the door to eternity— Revelation 21 and 22 unveil a new creation where God dwells with His people forever.

Irene furrowed her brow.

"Ann, "I've been thinking—why is there even a Millennium? I mean, in Revelation 20, it really hit me: God sets aside a literal 1,000-year reign of Christ on earth. That's so specific. What's the purpose of that time? What's He trying to show us?"

I nodded. "That's a great question, Irene—and the Bible gives us clear insight when we zoom out and take in the bigger picture. One of the most vivid scenes comes from Zechariah 14:3–9. It describes Jesus physically returning, standing on the Mount of Olives, and that mountain splitting in two. It's a dramatic moment—His Second Coming made visible and undeniable."

Irene nodded. "Right—and it even talks about a continuous day, where the light doesn't fade, even in the evening. It's like the natural cycle of day and night is somehow changed."

> And it shall come to pass in that day, that the light shall not be clear, nor dark: But it shall be one day which shall be known to the LORD, not day, nor night: but it shall come to pass, that at evening time it shall be light. (Zechariah 14:6–7)

I smiled. "Exactly. The verse even says, 'Only the Lord knows how this can happen.' That never-ending light represents something profound—God's unfiltered presence dwelling on earth. Zechariah also describes living waters flowing out from Jerusalem—one stream to the Dead Sea, the other to the Mediterranean. It's not just spiritual—it's a literal transformation of geography and government, all centered on Jesus Christ the King of kings ruling from Zion."

> And it shall be in that day, that living waters shall go out from Jerusalem; half of them toward the former sea, and half of them toward the hinder sea: in summer and in winter shall it be. And the LORD shall be King over all the earth: in that day shall there be one LORD, and His name one. (Zechariah 14:8–9)

Irene leaned in. "So . . . it's not just a symbolic reign? It's literal?"

I nodded. "Absolutely. The Millennial Kingdom is a real, physical, earthly reign. Psalm 2:8 says the Father promised Jesus the nations as His inheritance— and He's going to rule from the very ground He once walked. That brings us to the first major purpose of the Millennium."

1. To Establish Christ's Kingdom on Earth and Reward the Faithful.

Irene's eyes widened. "So . . . we actually rule with Him?"

I smiled. "Yes! Daniel 7—verses 18, 21–22, and 27—says that the saints of the Most High will be *given* the Kingdom, and they'll reign with Him forever. Paul echoes this in 1 Corinthians 6:2–3, where he reminds believers that we'll judge the world—and even angels. This life? It's preparation. A proving ground for eternal leadership."

> Do you not know that the saints shall judge the world? And if the world shall be judged by you, are you unworthy to judge the smallest matters? Know you not that we shall judge angels? How much more things that pertain to this life? (1 Corinthians 6:2–3)

Irene leaned back, amazed. "I always thought of heaven as the end of the story—but this Millennium is an entire phase of reward and reigning."

I nodded. "Exactly. Jesus said some will rule over ten cities, other five— based on how faithful they were with their God-given gifts in this life. That's Luke 19. Like someone once said: 'This is training time for reigning time.'"

Irene smiled. "That's powerful. So . . . what's the second purpose?"

2. To Fulfill the Biblical Covenants.

I continued. "The second purpose is to fulfil the biblical covenants. God made four covenants with Israel: the Abrahamic covenant, the Davidic covenant, the Land covenant, and the New Covenant. None of these have been fully fulfilled— yet. But during the Millennium, they will be."

Irene leaned in. "So Jesus—the Son of David—will actually reign from a real throne in Jerusalem?"

I nodded. "Yes. He'll literally sit on David's throne. Luke 1:32–33 says Jesus will reign over the house of Jacob forever. That hasn't happened yet. Jerusalem won't just be Israel's capital—it will be the capital of the entire earth. And that's why Jesus must return—to fulfill God's promises, physically and completely."

> He shall be great, and shall be called the Son of the Highest: and the Lord God shall give unto Him the throne of His father David: And He shall reign over the house of Jacob forever; and of His kingdom there shall be no end. (Luke 1:32–33)

Irene's voice grew quiet with awe. "That's incredible. So . . . what's the third reason?"

3. To Fulfill Old Testament Prophecies.

I continued. "The third purpose is to fulfill Old Testament prophecy. Passages like 2 Samuel 7:12–13, Psalms 72:7–11, and Isaiah 9:7 describe a future reign marked by peace, justice, and global prosperity—things the world has never fully experienced. But during the Millennium, those promises will come to life."

> Of the increase of His government and peace there shall be no end, upon the throne of David, and upon His kingdom, to order it, and to establish it with judgment and with justice from henceforth even forever. The zeal of the LORD of hosts will perform this. (Isaiah 9:7)

I smiled. "Isaiah 11 paints an Eden-like vision: animals living in harmony, children playing safely near once-deadly snakes, and the whole earth filled with the knowledge of the Lord. It's not symbolic—it's prophetic."

Irene's eyes widened. "So that means . . . the curse is lifted?"

I nodded. "Yes—and that brings us to the fourth and final purpose."

4. To Restore the Earth to God's Original Design.

I continued. "The fourth and final purpose is to restore the earth to God's original design. When Adam sinned, five curses were issued—on the serpent, on Satan, on the woman, on the man, and on the ground itself. That's Genesis 3. But in the Millennium, those curses begin to reverse."

Irene leaned in. "What does that look like?"

I smiled. "Isaiah 35 says the desert will blossom like a rose. Isaiah 11 tells us animals will return to plant-based diets—no more violence in nature. Even the land will yield abundantly. The whole earth will respond to the presence of its Creator."

> The wilderness and the solitary place shall be glad for them; and the desert shall rejoice, and blossom as the rose. It shall blossom abundantly, and rejoice even with joy and singing: the glory of Lebanon shall be given unto it, the excellency of Carmel and Sharon, they shall see the glory of the LORD, and the excellency of our God. (Isaiah 35:1–2)

> The wolf also shall dwell with the lamb, and the leopard shall lie down with the kid; and the calf and the young lion and the fatling together; and a little child shall lead them. And the cow and the bear shall feed; their young ones shall lie down together: and the lion shall eat straw like the ox. (Isaiah 11:6–7)

"So the Millennium is Eden revisited . . . a restored global garden of Eden."

I nodded. "Exactly. That's why Paul called Jesus the 'second Adam' in 1 Corinthians 15. Where the first Adam failed, Christ succeeds. The Millennium is part of that full-circle redemption—restoring what was lost, step by step."

Irene's voice softened. "I see it now. The Millennium isn't just a pause before eternity—it's part of the redemption process."

I agreed. "Right. And as 2 Peter 3:13–15 says, we're looking forward to a new heaven and a new earth filled with righteousness. But while we wait, we're called to live pure and blameless lives—because God is giving the world time to repent and be saved."

Irene looked down, thoughtful. "Ann . . . I feel convicted. Are we living like we're preparing to rule? Like citizens of that coming Kingdom?"

My voice was gentle but firm. "That's the question, Irene. Because this isn't just prophecy—it's our destiny."

Irene looked puzzled.

"Ann, you've identified *who* will reign with Christ— but *what* does that actually mean? What does it *look* like to rule and reign with Him during the Millennium? Are we talking about literal thrones? Assignments? Territories? Or is it more symbolic?"

I smiled. "Great question, Irene. The Bible is actually very clear: after Jesus returns, He'll rule from a literal throne in Jerusalem. Not symbolically— *physically* and *literally* from Israel. Jerusalem will be the capital city of the entire world during the Millennium."

Irene leaned in. "So then . . . what does it really mean for *us* to reign with Him?"

I nodded thoughtfully. "Paul gives us a glimpse in 2 Timothy 2:11–13—he says, 'if we endure, we will also reign with Him.' And in 1 Corinthians 6:2–3, he reminds us that believers will judge the world—even angels. That tells us we're being prepared for a kind of divine government."

I paused. "Our faithfulness *now*—how we treat people, navigate problems, steward ministry, and guard our hearts—actually shapes what we'll be entrusted with *then*. In the Millennium, we don't just observe Christ's reign—we participate in it."

Irene's brow furrowed slightly. "That's amazing . . . but also kind of intimidating. So it's not about earning salvation—it's about being prepared for reward and responsibility?"

I nodded. "Exactly, Irene. Salvation is already secured—sealed at the Rapture for those who are in Christ. But after that comes the Judgment Seat of Christ, also known as the *Bema Judgment*. That's not about punishment—it's where our works are tested."

I continued. "Not for *salvation*, but for *reward*—for assignments and responsibilities in the Millennium. How we served God here—our faithfulness, our humility, our obedience—determines what we'll be entrusted to steward there."

Irene smiled slowly. "So this life *really* is training time for reigning time."

I nodded. "That's right! Jesus made it clear in Luke 19—some will be put in charge of ten cities, others five. It's not metaphorical; it's literal leadership in His Kingdom. There will be a divine government with real structure and real roles."

I paused, then added with a smile. "But unlike the world, God doesn't promote based on status, success, or resumes. He promotes based on humility, faithfulness, and quiet obedience. It's not about being impressive—it's about being trustworthy."

Irene tilted her head. "So . . . our hearts matter just as much as our hands?"

I nodded gently. "Even more so. In 2 Timothy 2, Paul urges Timothy to be a good worker—someone who rightly handles the Word of truth, avoids foolish arguments, and lives with integrity. But he's not just talking about *actions*."

I paused. "Our *motives* matter too. God doesn't just see what we do—He sees why we do it. The Judgment Seat of Christ isn't just about our visible service— it's about the heart behind it."

Irene sat back, thoughtful. "That really puts everything into perspective. It's not just about waiting for heaven—it's about preparing to lead in Christ's Kingdom."

I nodded. "Absolutely. And John 3:30 captures the heart of it: 'He must increase, I must decrease.' Everything we do now should point to His glory—not our own. When we stand before Him, it won't be about fame or flash. It'll be about faithfulness."

Irene smiled. "Thank you, Ann. That really helps me understand what it means to rule and reign with Christ. It's a call to live intentionally—and humbly— *now*, because it's all preparing us for what's *next*."

My voice softened. "Exactly, Irene. The Millennium isn't just a prophecy to admire—it's a position to prepare for. Let's live like we believe it. Now that we've explored both the purpose of the Millennium and the meaning behind reigning with Christ, let's walk through Revelation 20 together—verse by verse."

THE REVELATION OF JESUS CHRIST REVEALS:

20:1 And I saw an angel come down from heaven, having the key of the bottomless pit and a great chain in his hand.

This verse marks a dramatic turning point in the divine timeline: the binding of Satan. After the cataclysmic events of the Battle of Armageddon (Revelation

19), John now sees a heavenly emissary—not Christ Himself, but simply "an angel"—descend with divine authority to take control of the adversary of souls.

The angel is described as coming down from heaven, signifying divine mission and authority. He carries two crucial items:

1. **The key to the bottomless pit (Greek: *abussos*)**—the same pit referenced in Revelation 9:1, where demonic locusts emerging during the fifth trumpet judgment. Possessing the key symbolizes delegated authority from God to open or seal this spiritual prison.

2. **A great chain**—not physical as in steel, but spiritual and supernatural, capable of restraining a fallen spirit. It's a chain forged by God's power, not by man's hands, capable of binding the prince of darkness himself.

The bottomless pit, or abyss, is not the same as hell (Gehenna). Rather, it is a temporary holding place for certain demonic beings—an underworld prison reserved for especially dangerous entities (Luke 8:31; Revelation 9:1–11).

At Christ's return, Satan is not yet cast into the Lake of Fire (which is the final place of eternal torment—Gehenna—prepared for the devil and his angels, Matthew 25:41). Instead, he is bound and imprisoned in the abyss for 1,000 years, so that he can no longer deceive the nations during Christ's millennial reign.

This action fulfills earlier promises: the crushing of Satan's power (Genesis 3:15), the answer to the cry of the martyrs (Revelation 6:10), and the beginning of God's direct kingdom rule on earth.

It is profound that Jesus doesn't even bind Satan Himself—He sends an angel, a mere servant of God. This is a powerful statement: Satan is no equal to God. Despite his rebellion and chaos, the devil's defeat requires no effort on the part of the Almighty. An unnamed angel, armed with divine authority, is more than sufficient.

From Revelation 12, we know Satan was cast down to earth with great fury, knowing his time is short (Revelation 12:12–13). His access to heaven was revoked, and he has since raged against the remnant of Israel—especially during the Great Tribulation. This final step, the binding in the bottomless pit, follows his complete defeat at Armageddon and ends his reign of deception for a thousand years.

OLD TESTAMENT FORESHADOWS REVELATION:

By His Spirit He has garnished (adorned) the heavens; His hand has formed (pierced) the crooked (fleeing) serpent. (Job 26:13)

The "crooked serpent" in Job 26:13 is an ancient title for Satan, also known as the dragon (Revelation 20:2). This verse attributes God's authority and power over that serpent—just as Revelation 20:1 shows an angel from heaven, under divine authority, binding Satan and casting him into the bottomless pit. The use of "his hand" forming or controlling the serpent reflects the complete sovereignty and dominion of God over Satan—even to the point of appointing a single angel to arrest him.

THE REVELATION OF JESUS CHRIST REVEALS:

20:2 And he laid hold on the dragon, that old serpent, which is the Devil, and Satan, and bound him a thousand years.

"And he laid hold on the dragon." The word "dragon" recalls Satan's fierce and destructive nature as portrayed earlier in Revelation (12:3–9). The angel from heaven, armed with the authority of God (verse 1), now seizes this ancient enemy without a fight. There is no struggle, no celestial war here—just an angel arresting the most feared adversary in human history. This signifies Satan's utter powerlessness before divine authority.

"That old serpent, which is the Devil, and Satan." Four titles are used here to leave no doubt about who is being bound:

1. **Dragon**—His ferocious and fearsome persona.

2. **Old Serpent**—A direct reference to his role in Genesis 3, where he deceived Eve in the garden of Eden.

3. **Devil**—The accuser or slanderer of the saints.

4. **Satan**—The adversary of God and mankind.

This comprehensive identification makes it clear that this is not symbolic evil or a vague spiritual enemy. This is Satan himself—real, personal, and finally restrained.

"And bound him a thousand years." Here begins the Millennium, a literal 1,000-year reign of Christ on earth, mentioned six times in Revelation 20 (verses 2–7). The fact that Satan is bound during this period means:

- He cannot deceive the nations (verse 3).
- He cannot tempt or accuse.
- The earth enters an era of peace, righteousness, and justice—a return to Edenic conditions.

This verse assures us that Satan is not a co-equal with God. His power is permitted for a time, but in this moment, that time ends. A single angel binds him, emphasizing that God does not need to lift a finger—His word is final, and His will is done.

Satan's binding marks the beginning of God's earthly reign through Christ, a season of peace and restoration long promised in the prophets (Isaiah 11, Micah 4, and Zechariah 14). It's a glorious reminder that the power of evil is limited, and the Kingdom of Christ is eternal.

OLD TESTAMENT FORESHADOWS REVELATION:

And I will put enmity between you and the woman, and between your seed and her seed; it shall bruise your head, and you shalt bruise his heel. (Genesis 3:15)

In Genesis 3:15, we see the first prophetic mention of the coming defeat of Satan, who is referred to as the serpent—the same "old serpent" named in Revelation 20:2. This verse introduces the spiritual battle between Satan and the "seed of the woman" (ultimately fulfilled in Christ). The promise that the serpent's head would be crushed is ultimately fulfilled in stages—first at the Cross, then the Second Coming, and now in Revelation 20:2, where Satan is seized and bound, no longer able to deceive the nations.

THE REVELATION OF JESUS CHRIST REVEALS:

20:3 And cast him into the bottomless pit, and shut him up, and set a seal upon him, that he should deceive the nations no more, till the thousand years should be fulfilled: and after that he must be loosed a little season.

This verse continues the dramatic judgment against Satan following the return of Christ in Revelation 19. After centuries of deception and destruction, Satan is physically restrained, sealed, and imprisoned for a definite, divine period of 1,000 years—the length of Christ's millennial reign.

"And cast him into the bottomless pit." The bottomless pit (Greek: *abussos*, "abyss") is a special place of spiritual imprisonment, distinct from both Hades—temporary abode of the dead—and the final Lake of Fire. It is the same abyss from which demonic locusts were released in Revelation 9. In Luke 8:31, the demons begged Jesus not to send them into "the abyss," indicating its use as a holding cell for rebellious spirits. Here, Satan is forcibly cast into this pit, reinforcing that this is not a symbolic binding, but a real act of divine restraint.

"And shut him up, and set a seal upon him." This is a triple-lock: bound with a chain (verse 2), cast into the abyss (verse 3), and shut in and sealed (verse 3). The seal shows divine authority and finality. Just as the tomb of Jesus was sealed by Rome (Matthew 27:66), this seal declares the inescapable confinement of Satan. But unlike Christ, who broke the seal in resurrection victory, Satan cannot break the seal; he is fully subject to God's authority.

"That he should deceive the nations no more." This reveals Satan's primary weapon: deception. From the garden of Eden (Genesis 3:1–5) to the Tribulation

(Revelation 12:9, 13:14), deception has been his chief strategy. His removal allows for a millennium of peace and truth, where nations are no longer blinded by lies, nor manipulated by spiritual darkness.

"Till the thousand years should be fulfilled." Here begins the millennial reign—a literal 1,000-year period where Christ rules from Jerusalem with righteousness and peace (Isaiah 2:2–4; Zechariah 14; Revelation 20:4–6). During this time: Satan is imprisoned, Jesus rules as King of kings, the saints reign with Him, and the earth experiences Edenic restoration.

"And after that he must be loosed a little season." This is perhaps the most jarring phrase in the verse. Why release him at all? The word "must" indicates divine necessity—part of God's sovereign plan.

Reasons for this "little season":

- To test the hearts of those born during the Millennium.
- To prove that even in a perfect world, with Satan removed, man's heart still needs redemption.
- To prepare the world for the final judgment at the Great White Throne (Revelation 20:11–15).

OLD TESTAMENT FORESHADOWS REVELATION:

You break the heads of leviathan in pieces, and gave him to be meat to the people inhabiting the wilderness. (Psalm 74:14)

Leviathan in this verse is a symbolic representation of chaotic evil or Satan himself—often depicted as a great sea serpent or dragon, just as Satan is called "that old serpent" in Revelation. In Revelation 20:3, God binds and seals Satan in the bottomless pit so he can no longer deceive the nations for 1,000 years. Similarly, Psalm 74:14 shows God's power in defeating and subduing Leviathan, prefiguring Christ's authority over Satan at the beginning of the millennial reign. This psalm is a poetic celebration of God's victory over cosmic evil, foreshadowing the final judgment and restraint of Satan in the end times.

Irene leaned in. "Okay, Ann, can we go back to something I've been wondering about? After Armageddon—when Jesus returns and defeats the Antichrist—there's still another judgment, right? Not the Great White Throne, but something else that happens before the Millennium starts?"

I nodded. "Yes! You're thinking of the Sheep and Goat Judgment—that's found in Matthew 25:31–46. It takes place after Christ's Second Coming, but before the Millennial Kingdom begins. It's when Jesus judges the surviving nations, based on how they treated 'His brethren'—which many believe refers to the Jewish people and Tribulation saints."

Irene frowned. "So this isn't about the Church or the resurrected saints?"

I nodded. "Exactly. This is a judgment of the nations—of living people who survived the Tribulation. They're not part of the raptured Church or the resurrected saints. These are actual men and women who lived through the twenty-one judgments and witnessed Christ's return. They now stand before Him—not to be resurrected, but to be separated: sheep to enter the Millennial Kingdom, goats to face judgment."

Irene leaned in. "And how does Jesus judge them? What's the standard?"

"He separates them like a shepherd does with sheep and goats—just as He describes in Matthew 25:32. The standard isn't church membership or theology—it's how they treated His 'brethren' during the Tribulation."

Irene blinked. "His brethren?"

I nodded. "Most scholars believe that refers to faithful Jewish believers or Tribulation saints—those who stood for Christ in a time of global deception and persecution. The sheep are those who showed compassion, even risking their lives to help. The goats are the ones who ignored, betrayed, or opposed them. In doing so, they were rejecting Christ Himself."

"So this is more about actions revealing the condition of their heart?"

I nodded. "Exactly. Their actions didn't save them—salvation is always by grace through faith. But how they treated God's people during the Tribulation revealed what was truly in their hearts. It was the evidence of their faith or unbelief."

I continued, "The sheep showed compassion to Christ's 'brethren'—likely the Jewish remnant or faithful believers under persecution—which proved their alignment with God. The goats, on the other hand, rejected them, and in doing so, rejected Christ Himself."

Irene exhaled slowly. "And the outcome?"

I said softly, "The sheep inherit the Kingdom—'Come, you blessed of My Father'—and they enter the Millennial Kingdom in their natural, earthly bodies. But the goats are cast into everlasting fire, prepared for the devil and his angels. It's a sobering division based on their response to Christ—through His people—in the darkest time in human history."

Irene leaned back. "Wow. So it's a kind of 'entrance judgment' into the Millennial Kingdom?"

I smiled. "That's a great way to put it. After Jesus returns, He defeats the Antichrist, casts him and the False Prophet into the Lake of Fire, binds Satan in the abyss, and then conducts this judgment of the nations—those who physically survived the Tribulation."

I continued, "It's not the Great White Throne—that comes later. This is a unique judgment: the Sheep and Goat Judgment. Jesus separates the righteous from the unrighteous based on how they treated His brethren during the Tribulation. Those whose actions reflected true faith are welcomed into the 1,000-year reign of Christ. The rest? They're cut off—cast into eternal fire."

Irene furrowed her brow. "And this isn't the same as the Great White Throne Judgment in Revelation 20?"

I shook my head. "Nope. The Great White Throne Judgment happens *after* the Millennium. It's the final judgment for all the unbelieving dead from every era—those who never placed their faith in God. They're resurrected for judgment, and their names aren't found in the Book of Life. It's a resurrection to condemnation."

I continued, "The Sheep and Goat Judgment, on the other hand, is *before* the Millennium. It's for the living nations—those who survived the Tribulation. Jesus judges them based on how they treated His brethren during those terrible years. It's not about earning salvation—it's about their actions revealing their allegiance."

Irene let out a breath. "Whew! Okay, that clears things up. I love how Jesus ends all the confusion—He judges rightly, rewards faithfully, and sets everything in order."

THE REVELATION OF JESUS CHRIST REVEALS:

20:4 And I saw thrones, and they sat upon them, and judgment was given to them: and I saw the souls of them that were beheaded for the witness of Jesus, and for the Word of God, and which had not worshiped the beast, neither his image, neither had received his mark upon their foreheads, or on their hands; and they lived and reigned with Christ a thousand years.

"And I saw thrones, and they sat upon them, and judgment was given unto them." John sees thrones, symbolic of authority and rulership. Those who "sat upon them" are like the Raptured saints, including the Church, who return with Christ at His Second Coming (Revelation 19:14). These thrones echo Daniel 7:9 and Matthew 19:28, where Jesus promised His followers they would sit on thrones judging the nations. These saints are delegated authority to govern during the Millennium, co-reigning with Christ.

"And I saw the souls of them that were beheaded for the witness of Jesus, and for the Word of God." This refers specifically to the Tribulation martyrs—those who came to faith during the Tribulation and were executed (many by beheading) for refusing to deny Christ. Their "witness" and allegiance to the Word of God are underscored, highlighting their faithfulness unto death.

"And which had not worshiped the beast, neither his image, neither had received his mark upon their foreheads, or on their hands." This confirms that these individuals resisted the Antichrist during his reign, refusing the mark of the beast (Revelation 13:16–17) and any form of idolatrous submission. Despite intense pressure, they chose loyalty to Christ over survival in a hostile world system.

"And they lived and reigned with Christ a thousand years." This passage refers to the resurrection of the Tribulation martyrs, who are resurrected and granted glorified bodies to reign alongside Christ during His Millennial Kingdom. This event is also called the first resurrection (verse 5), which represents the resurrection of the righteous—a category that includes not only Tribulation martyrs but also, most likely, the Old Testament saints (Daniel 12:2; Isaiah 26:19). Though Jesus brought the souls of the righteous dead into heaven after His resurrection (Ephesians 4:8), their glorified bodies are given at this stage, just prior to the Millennium.

This thousand-year reign is literal, not symbolic, fulfilling Old Testament prophecies of the Messiah's physical reign on earth—see Isaiah 11 (a restored Eden-like earth), Zechariah 14 (His reign from Jerusalem), and Psalm 2 (Messiah ruling the nations with a rod of iron).

Together, these resurrected saints—Church Age believers, Tribulation martyrs, and Old Testament saints—reign alongside Christ in glorified bodies, showcasing the fulfillment of God's redemptive plan.

OLD TESTAMENT FORESHADOWS REVELATION:

And the Kingdom and dominion, and the greatness of the Kingdom under the whole heaven, shall be given to the people of the saints of the Most High, whose Kingdom is an everlasting Kingdom, and all dominions shall serve and obey him. (Daniel 7:27)

Daniel 7:27 directly parallels Revelation 20:4, where the Tribulation martyrs are resurrected and reign with Christ for 1,000 years. Daniel foresaw the day when God's faithful people—even those who suffered and were martyred—would be vindicated and enthroned, sharing in Christ's Kingdom authority.

THE REVELATION OF JESUS CHRIST REVEALS:

[20:5] But the rest of the dead lived not again until the thousand years were finished. This is the first resurrection.

This verse draws a sharp, sobering line between two resurrections.

The First Resurrection—This is the resurrection of the righteous, described in verses 4 and earlier throughout Scripture. It includes:

- The Raptured Church (Revelation 4:1; 1 Thessalonians 4:16–17).
- The Old Testament Saints (Daniel 12:2; Isaiah 26:19).
- The Tribulation Martyrs (Revelation 20:4).

They reign with Christ during the Millennium. These are those who belong to the "first resurrection"—blessed and holy are they (Revelation 20:6). This is a resurrection to life, glorified life, eternal life. It happens in stages, but it's all part of the same resurrection category—for the saved.

The Second Resurrection—who are they? These are the unbelievers, the Christ-rejecters, the ones who never repented, never turned to God, never received the gift of salvation.

- They are not resurrected at the Second Coming.
- They remain in Hades (a temporary holding place for the souls of the lost) until after the 1,000-year reign of Christ.
- Their bodies remain in the grave, their souls in torment.

When are they raised? At the second resurrection, 1,000 years later—for judgment. They will stand before the Great White Throne (Revelation 20:11–15) to be judged according to their works. This is a resurrection unto damnation (John 5:29).

Two resurrections, two destinies—first resurrection means life with Christ. Second resurrection means judgment before the throne. There is no third category. Everyone will be in one of these two. You don't want to be in the second.

This verse reminds us of the gravity of eternity. There is a resurrection day coming for everyone. The question is not if you will be raised—but when. Will it be to reign or to be judged?

OLD TESTAMENT FORESHADOWS REVELATION:

And many of them that sleep in the dust of the earth shall awake, some to everlasting life, and some to shame and everlasting contempt. (Daniel 12:2)

Revelation 20:5 describes two resurrections. The first resurrection—of the righteous, who live and reign with Christ. The second resurrection—of the wicked, who are judged after the Millennium. Daniel 12:2 reflects the same dual outcome. Some awaken to everlasting life (first resurrection). Others to shame and everlasting contempt (second resurrection). Both passages clearly distinguish between the destiny of the righteous and the wicked at the time of resurrection.

Daniel gives the prophetic foundation; Revelation unveils the precise timeline and fulfillment.

THE REVELATION OF JESUS CHRIST REVEALS:

20:6 Blessed and holy is he that has part in the first resurrection: on such the second death has no power, but they will be priests of God and of Christ, and shall reign with Him a thousand years.

"Blessed and holy is he that has part in the first resurrection." This is one of the seven beatitudes found in the Book of Revelation, and it pronounces divine favor and sanctification upon those who take part in the first resurrection—the resurrection of the righteous. These are the redeemed: the Church raptured before the Tribulation (1 Thessalonians 4:16–17), the Old Testament saints (Daniel 12:2), and the Tribulation martyrs (Revelation 20:4). They are set apart—holy—and are declared blessed, meaning eternally favored and joyful in God's presence.

"On such the second death has no power." The "second death" is later defined in Revelation 20:14 as being cast into the Lake of Fire—eternal separation from God. But those who are part of the first resurrection are completely exempt from this fate. Their names are written in the Book of Life (Revelation 20:15). They've already passed from death into life (John 5:24) and are eternally secure in Christ.

"But they will be priests of God and of Christ." These resurrected saints will serve in priestly roles, not just in worship and intercession, but as mediators of divine truth, rulers of righteousness, and stewards of God's glory during the Millennial Kingdom. This is a fulfillment of promises made to believers (Exodus 19:6; 1 Peter 2:9; Revelation 1:6) that they would be a royal priesthood.

"And shall reign with Him a thousand years." This confirms the literal millennial reign of Christ on earth—1,000-year period of peace, justice, and righteousness (Isaiah 11, Zechariah 14, Psalm 2). Those who belong to Christ will co-reign with Him, sharing in His authority and governing in their glorified bodies, distinct from the mortal population that enters the Millennium.

OLD TESTAMENT FORESHADOWS REVELATION:

But the saints of the Most High shall take the Kingdom, and possess the Kingdom forever, even forever and ever. (Daniel 7:18)

This pairing brings full circle the promise God made through Daniel centuries before John's Revelation. In Daniel 7:18, the saints are not just participants in the kingdom—they possess it forever. In Revelation 20:6, this promise is fulfilled as those who are part of the first resurrection—including Old Testament saints, the raptured Church, and Tribulation martyrs—reign with Christ in His Millennial Kingdom and are immune to the second death.

Irene blinked in disbelief and threw up her hands.

"Wait—hold on a second. We just finished reading Revelation 20, and . . . Ann, are you serious? It barely says *anything* about the actual 1,000-year reign! The first few verses are all about Satan being bound, and then it jumps to the resurrection of the Tribulation martyrs and Old Testament saints. But the Millennium itself? There's practically *nothing*! And then by verse 7, it's already talking about what happens *after* the thousand years are over? I don't get it—why doesn't it say more about the Millennium *itself*?"

I smiled knowingly. "I know—it surprises a lot of people. You'd expect chapters filled with details about Christ's 1,000-year reign. But Revelation 20 is more like a divine headline reel. It marks the timeline with precision—six mentions of 'a thousand years'—but it's not meant to give the whole story. The actual description of what happens during the Millennium? That's scattered like gold dust throughout the Old and New Testaments."

Irene raised an eyebrow. "Wait, seriously? So Revelation 20 just headlines it—but there's actually a lot more about the Millennium hidden in the rest of the Bible?"

I nodded. "Exactly. Think of Revelation 20 as the timestamp—God's way of anchoring the timeline with six direct references to 'a thousand years.' But the real beauty? It's like a divine treasure map. The full picture of what unfolds during that reign is revealed piece by piece across Scripture, just waiting to be discovered."

Irene exhaled slowly, her curiosity piqued. "Okay . . . I'm listening. Where do we even being?"

I leaned in slightly. "Let's start with the Old Testament. Take Isaiah 2:2–3— it paints this breathtaking image of all the nations streaming to Jerusalem. Not for tourism—for truth. The Lord Himself will be there, teaching His ways, settling disputes, and establishing justice."

> And it shall come to pass in the latter days, that the mountain of the LORD's house shall be established in the top of the mountains, and shall be exalted above the hills; and all nations shall flow unto it. And many people shall go and say, Come you, and let us go up to the mountain of the LORD, to the house of the God of Jacob; and He will teach us of His ways, and we will walk in His paths: for out of Zion shall go forth the law, and the word of the LORD from Jerusalem. (Isaiah 2:2-3)

I paused, then continued. "And then there's Isaiah 11:6–9. Picture this: wolves lying down with lambs, toddlers playing near cobra dens without a hint of danger. It's not just poetic—it's Eden restored. The world finally at peace, just as God intended."

Irene's eyes widened. "Whoa . . . so that's not just poetic fluff? You're saying that's literal prophecy—about the actual Kingdom?"

I nodded, my tone warm but firm. "Absolutely. Isaiah wasn't painting metaphors—he was describing what the world will actually look like under Christ's reign. And Isaiah 65:17–25 takes it even further. People will live for centuries again, like in the days before the Flood. A hundred-year-old will be considered a youth."

I leaned in. "And then there's Ezekiel 40 through 48. It's mind-blowing. Nine whole chapters detailing the Millennial Temple—it's architecture, the restored priesthood, the tribal boundaries. It's not symbolic—it's blueprints. Literal, physical, and enormous."

Irene tilted her head, absorbing it. "So the Millennium is basically the ultimate reset—God's will finally done on earth as it is in heaven."

My face lit up. "Exactly! Daniel saw it too. In Daniel 2:44, he describes God's Kingdom as one that crushes all earthly empires—and it never gets overthrown. It stands forever."

I continued with growing excitement. "Then in Daniel 7:13–14 and verse 27, he sees the Son of Man receiving dominion, and the saints of the Most High inheriting that Kingdom. This isn't just symbolic language—it's describing a literal reign, with real people, in a real geographical kingdom. This is the fulfillment of every promise of justice and peace God has ever made."

Irene leaned forward. "Okay, but what about the New Testament? Does Jesus even talk about the Millennium?"

I nodded immediately. "All over the place. In Matthew 19:28, Jesus tells the disciples they'll sit on twelve thrones, judging the twelve tribes of Israel. That's not some distant heavenly vision—that's the Millennial Kingdom, right here on earth."

And Jesus said unto them, Verily I say unto you, That you which have followed Me, in the regeneration when the Son of Man shall sit in the throne of His glory, you also shall sit upon twelve thrones, judging the twelve tribes of Israel. (Matthew 19:28)

I paused, then added, "And in Luke 1:32–33, the angel tells Mary that Jesus will sit on the throne of His father David and reign forever. That's not symbolic. That's a literal throne in Jerusalem."

Irene blinked. "Wait—like, physical geography?"

"Exactly," I said. "Then you've got Acts 3:20–21, where Peter talks about the 'restoration of all things,' just like the prophets foretold. That's Millennium language—God's order restored on earth."

> And He shall send Jesus Christ, which before was preached unto you: Whom the heaven must receive until the times of restitution of all things, which God has spoken by the mouth of all His holy prophets since the world began. (Acts 3:20–21)

Irene looked thoughtful. "What about Paul?"

I smiled. "Oh, definitely. In 1 Corinthians 15:24–28, Paul lays it out: Christ must reign until every enemy is under His feet—including death. That reign he's talking about? That's the Millennium in action—Jesus ruling until the final victory."

Irene sat back, stunned. "Wow, Ann . . . So Revelation 20 gives us the bones—and the rest of Scripture? It breathes in the flesh and spirit."

I smiled gently. "Exactly. It's one of the most stunning harmonies in all of Scripture. Revelation *declares* it. The prophets *describe* it. The Gospels *confirm* it. The apostles *affirm* it. God's plan isn't scattered—it's intricately and perfectly woven."

Irene's voice dropped to a whisper. "So when we pray, 'Your Kingdom come,' we're literally asking for the Millennium to arrive?"

I nodded. "Yes! And one day soon, we won't just witness it—we'll walk into that Kingdom as co-heirs, co-rulers with Christ. It's not just prophecy—it's our future destiny."

Irene looked thoughtful.

"With all these resurrected saints—Old Testament believers, Tribulation martyrs, the raptured Church—and then those who survived the Tribulation in their natural bodies . . . the population must be enormous by now."

I nodded. "Exactly. And that's part of why God had to cleanse the earth during the seal, trumpet, and bowl judgments. It wasn't just about wrath—it was preparation. The land needed to be purified and renewed. But it's not gone—it's still here. Just . . . restored. Like it was in the beginning—a single, unified landmass, the way it was during Creation."

Irene furrowed her brow. "So when we talk about all that fire and judgment—the forests burning, the cities collapsing—isn't that total destruction?"

I shook my head gently. "Not necessarily. In both Scripture and nature, fire doesn't just destroy—it refines. It clears the way for something new. Burned land isn't the end of the story. In fact, it often becomes richer, more fertile—ready for life to flourish again."

Irene leaned in. "How so?"

I smiled. "After a fire, the ash left behind actually enriches the soil. It's full of nutrients—like potassium and phosphorous—that feed new growth. And some plants, like certain pine trees and wildflowers, *need* fire to reproduce. Their seeds are locked inside cones or pods that only open under intense heat. It's called serotiny. Fire doesn't just destroy—it awakens the next generation."

Irene blinked. "That's wild. So even fire has a purpose?"

"Absolutely," I said. "It clears out dead vegetation—things that choke the soil—and makes space for fresh life to emerge. Over time, entire ecosystems regenerate. It's nature's reset button."

Irene's voice softened. "And spiritually?"

My expression grew more reflective. "In Scripture, fire is almost always connected to purification, not just punishment. It's part of God's pattern—judgment, then renewal. Look at Joel 2:25: 'I will restore to you the years that the locust has eaten.' And Isaiah 61:3: 'To give them beauty for ashes.' God doesn't just tear down—He rebuilds. He judges sin, yes, but His heart is always set on restoration."

Irene blinked, processing. "So . . . the judgments weren't just about wrath—they were restoration in motion?"

I nodded. "Exactly. God wasn't just punishing—He was reclaiming His land. Isaiah 35:1 says, 'The desert shall rejoice and blossom as the rose.' Even the Dead Sea will be full of life again. During the Millennial reign, the earth will be transformed—like Eden restored. No more pollution, no more poisons, no more curse—just creation, healed and thriving."

> Then said he unto me, These waters issue out toward the east country, and go down into the desert, and go into the sea; which being brought forth into the sea, the waters shall be healed. And it shall come to pass, that everything that lives, which moves, wheresoever the rivers shall come, shall live: and there shall be a very great multitude of fish, because these waters shall come to that place: for they shall be healed; and everything shall live wherever the river comes. And it shall come to pass, that the fishers shall stand upon it from En Gedi (western shore of the Dead Sea) even unto En Eglaim (northern end of the Dead Sea); they shall be a place to spread forth nets; their fish shall be according to their kinds, as the fish of the great sea, exceeding many. (Ezekiel 47:8–10)

Irene's voice was quiet, almost reverent. "So in the Millennium, we're not walking through some post-apocalyptic wasteland—we're walking on a redeemed earth?"

I smiled, my words gentle but full of certainty. "Yes. A scorched earth, healed. A world made new. That's the wonder of what God does. What looks like devastation now becomes the soil of restoration. The Millennium is the ultimate portrait of His mercy—taking the ashes of judgment and rewriting them into flourishing, radiant glory.'"

Irene nodded slowly, eyes glistening. "Wow. Beauty for ashes, indeed."

Irene tilted her head, curious.

"But, Ann—if the earth is going to be repopulated during the Millennium, is there even enough room for everyone? I mean, won't it start feeling crowded?"

I smiled. "Great question. But here's the thing—most people don't realize just how much open land there actually is. The earth's total surface area is about 510 million square kilometers, but only about 29 percent of that is land—that's roughly 149 million square kilometers."

Irene raised an eyebrow. "Okay, so less than a third is land . . . but surely by now we're living all over it, right?"

I chuckled. "Not even close. Only about 10 percent of earth's land is densely populated—cities, urban sprawl, the crowded places we think of. Maybe another 10 to 15 percent is moderately populated—small towns, suburbs, farmlands. That means roughly 75 percent of the land is still wild, untouched, or barely inhabited."

Irene blinked. "Seriously? Then what's taking up all that empty space?"

I gestured as I listed it out. "Deserts, for starters—like the Sahara and the Gobi. Just those two alone make up about 33 million square kilometers. Then you've got mountain ranges, tundras, glaciers, deep jungles, and massive boreal forests—places that are either too dry, too cold, or too wild for comfortable living. And don't forget all the protected lands—national parks, wildlife reserves, entire wilderness regions."

Irene shook her head slowly. "Wow . . . I had no idea there was that much uninhabited land."

My eyes lit up. "Exactly. And that's what makes the Millennium so extraordinary. With Jesus reigning, Satan bound, no more war, no more famine—and a truly righteous government? The earth will thrive. Regions once deemed unlivable will blossom again. The land won't just be occupied—it'll be renewed."

Irene's eyes widened. "So there's more than enough space for the resurrected saints and the survivors to multiply over a thousand years?"

I nodded. "More than enough. With a renewed earth—restored like Eden—and people living longer again, like in the days of Noah, we're talking about a vast, global population by the end of the Millennium. But this time, everything is under perfect leadership."

Irene's voice grew soft. "That gives me chills. It really brings to life what it means to pray, 'Thy Kingdom come.'"

I smiled. "Amen, Irene. The scorched earth will bloom again—and in God's Kingdom, there's room for everyone."

Irene's voice was filled with awe.

"Ann, I was rereading Isaiah 11—the wolf living with the lamb, the leopard lying down with the goat, children playing safely near vipers . . . It's like a return back in Eden. Can you even imagine that kind of peace?"

My eyes lit up. "Yes! It's one of the most powerful glimpses we have of the Millennial Kingdom. Edenic harmony, fully restored. No violence in nature, no fear—just perfect peace. Isaiah 11:6–9 isn't just poetic imagery—it's prophetic truth. A real picture of what's coming."

Irene leaned back, thinking. "You know, it reminded me of the sixth day of Creation. God filled the earth with life—beasts, animals, creeping things, everything that moves. And then, last of all, He created Adam and Eve to care for it all. There's an order to it—He restores first, and then He fills."

I nodded. "Exactly. That's a divine pattern woven through everything God does. He always restores before He fills. It's how salvation works—first He cleanses the sinner through the blood of Jesus, then He fills them with the Holy Spirit. And in judgment, it's the same. The Tribulation burns away the corruption. Then comes the Millennium, when He fills the earth again—this time with righteousness."

Irene's eyes lit up. "Oh wow—just like how fire renews the land. I was reading Psalm 104:24 the other day: 'O Lord, how manifold are Your works! In wisdom have You made them all. The earth is full of Your riches.' It even mentions the beasts of the forest creeping out at night, lions roaring—every creature seeking its food from God. Everything has a rhythm. A purpose. A place."

> He appointed the moon for seasons: the sun knows his going down. You make darkness, and it is night: wherein all the beasts of the forest do creep forth. The young lions roar after their prey, and seek their meat from God. The sun arises, they gather themselves together, and lay them down in their dens. Man goes forth unto his work and to his labor until the evening. (Psalm 104:19–23)

I smiled thoughtfully. "It really does, Irene. And that actually leads us into something most people don't talk about—dinosaurs and dragons."

Irene raised an eyebrow "Wait—dragons? You mean like actual fire-breathing dragons?"

I nodded. "Yes—really. Not fantasy—Bible. In Genesis 1:24–25, God created 'beasts of the earth'—distinct from 'cattle' and 'creeping things.' That category includes massive, now-extinct creatures—what we would recognize today as dinosaurs. The word 'dinosaur' wasn't coined until the 1800s. Before that, people just called them dragons or serpents. Ancient cultures didn't make this stuff up—they were describing what they saw."

Irene leaned in, intrigued. "So dinosaurs were real—and they actually lived alongside people?"

I nodded. "Absolutely. Look at Job 40. God describes a creature called *Behemoth*. It eats grass like an ox, has immense strength, bones like bronze, and a tail like a cedar tree. That's not an elephant or a hippo—neither of those have tails like that. It sounds much more like a sauropod dinosaur—one of those massive, long-necked giants."

Irene shivered. "That gives me chills. It's like history and prophecy are woven together into one continuous thread. Even the old dragon stories—maybe those fairy tales have roots in something real, don't they?"

I nodded. "Exactly. In Job 41, God talks about *Leviathan*—a massive sea creature that breathes fire and smoke. Its breath kindles coals, and flames shoot from its mouth. That's not mythology—that sounds like the original fire-breathing dragon."

Irene's eyes widened. "You mean there were *actual* fire-breathing dragons—before the Flood?"

I nodded. "Yes. Psalm 74 and Isaiah 27 both speak of God defeating *Leviathan*—the twisted, piercing serpent of the sea. It's a theme woven all throughout the Old Testament. But after the Flood, everything changed. God wiped out most of the earth—including those ancient beasts. Only the creatures preserved on the ark survived. That's why we find millions of fossilized remains around the world—buried rapidly, catastrophically, just like the Bible describes."

Irene leaned forward. "So in the Millennium . . . are you saying those kinds of beasts might be restored too?"

I smiled. "That's entirely up to God—but honestly, I wouldn't be surprised. Isaiah 11:9 says, 'the earth shall be full of the knowledge of the Lord,' and we know the whole ecosystem returns to Edenic balance. Even the fiercest animals become gentle. The curse on creation will be lifted. Who's to say some of those ancient creatures—redeemed, tamed—won't walk among us again?"

Irene's voice was hushed. "That would be . . . majestic. Honestly, I never thought I'd be this excited about the animal kingdom."

I laughed softly. "Me neither! But it reveals something so beautiful about God's heart—He doesn't just restore us. He restores the land, the animals, the very atmosphere. All of creation has been groaning for redemption . . . and in the Millennium, it finally gets to sing again."

Irene looked thoughtful.

"Ann, something's been stirring in me. I've been thinking about the sea—the oceans, the rivers, the fish. If the Millennium is really a return to something Eden-like, does that mean those are gone? I know Revelation 21 says there's 'no more sea'—but isn't that after the thousand years? Are we really going without oceans for a whole millennium?"

I smiled. "That's such a great question, Irene. And yes, you're exactly right to draw that distinction. The 'no more sea' reference in Revelation 21 is tied to the new heaven and new earth—*after* the Millennium. It doesn't apply to Christ's 1,000-year reign. During the Millennium, earth is still earth—restored, yes, but still very physical. That includes oceans, lakes, rivers . . . and yes, fish."

Irene let out a breath of relief. "Whew, I thought so. I mean—didn't Jesus eat broiled fish after His resurrection?"

I nodded. "He did. Luke 24:42–43 says they gave Him a piece of broiled fish and some honeycomb, and He ate it—in His glorified body. That moment tells us so much. Glorified humans and natural humans will still engage with a very real, physical creation—complete with food, water, and shared experiences."

> And they gave Him a piece of a broiled fish, and of an honeycomb. And He took it, and did eat before them. (Luke 24:42–43)

Irene's eyes lit up. "So the oceans—are still teeming with life?"

I nodded. "Yes. In fact, Ezekiel 47 gives us a stunning prophecy. A river will flow from the Millennial Temple, and when it reaches the Dead Sea, it heals it. Suddenly, that lifeless body of water becomes vibrant—filled with fish. The passage even says, 'a great multitude of fish.' That's not metaphor. That's literal restoration—God reviving what was once dead."

> Afterward he brought me again unto the door of the house (Millennial Temple); and, behold, waters issued out from under the threshold of the Temple eastward: for the forefront of the house stood toward the east, and the waters came down from under from the right side of the Temple, at the south side of the altar. Then brought he me out of the way of the gate northward, and led me about the way without unto the outer gate by the way that looks eastward; and, behold, there ran out waters on the rights side. (Ezekiel 47:1–2)

Irene smiled. "I love that. Water being healed, land being healed . . . it's really is like Eden 2.0. And it makes total sense when you think about how God created everything back in Genesis."

My eyes lit up. "Exactly! The six days of Creation are like a divine blueprint—and God always follows His patterns. First, He separates. Then, He fills. He brings order, and then abundance. That's what the Millennium is all about. He's not destroying the earth—He's restoring it. Purifying it for His glory."

Irene nodded slowly. "That's so powerful. *Day One*, God made the waters. *Day Two*, He separated them. *Day Three*, He gathered them together to form the oceans, rivers, and lakes, and brought forth dry land. So it's not just the land He's restoring—it's the waters, too."

I smiled. "Exactly. And on *Day Four*, He set the sun, moon, and stars in place—to mark seasons, days, and years. That shows His intention for order, rhythm, and light. Then *Day Five* came—the fish, the great sea creatures, and the birds. He told them to 'be fruitful and multiply.' That wasn't just poetic—it was prophetic. God's design was for the skies and seas to teem with life."

Irene leaned in. "And *Day Six*—He created the animals on the land, and then finally, humans. Adam and Eve were placed last, not because they were an afterthought, but because they were meant to steward it all."

I nodded. "Yes! In Genesis, God first shaped the environment—light, land, seas, vegetation—*then* He created animals and people to inhabit it. That same divine pattern is at work in the Millennium. He's restoring creation before fully repopulating it with resurrected Tribulation and Old Testament saints. Just like in Genesis, He's bringing order out of chaos—redeeming what was broken."

Irene smiled softly. "And *Day Seven* . . . He rested."

My voice grew quiet. "Exactly. The seventh day was holy—God's Sabbath. The seventh Millennium is like a cosmic *Day Seven*: a thousand-year rest, a time of peace, justice, and restoration. Everything He made, He called 'very good.' And in the Millennium, we'll finally see that goodness unveiled again."

Irene grinned. "So . . . the dolphins stay?"

I laughed. "Yes! Dolphins, whales, coral reefs, rainbow fish—all restored, all thriving. Even in His judgment, God's nature is always restoration. Remember Joel 2:25? 'I will restore the years that the locust has eaten.' That promise isn't just for people—it's for creation itself. Even the oceans get redeemed."

Irene's tone softened, reflective. "It makes me think of Psalm 104 again: 'O LORD, how manifold are Your works! In wisdom You have made them all. The earth is full of Your riches.' He doesn't throw away His creation—He restores it."

I nodded. "Absolutely. That's the heart of it. Revelation 21 comes later— *after* the Great White Throne Judgment, when God creates a new heaven and a new earth. That's when there's *no more sea*. But during the 1,000-year reign? That's Eden, revived. Rivers will flow. Fruit trees will bloom. And yes—I believe the oceans will sing again."

Irene smiled. "That's beautiful. So the Millennium isn't about removal—it's about restoration."

I nodded. "Exactly. Christ reigns. Creation rejoices. The land is healed, the seas are teeming with life, and even the animals live in peace. Isaiah 11 paints the picture: 'The wolf shall dwell with the lamb . . . and the earth shall be full of the knowledge of the Lord as the waters cover the sea.' So yes—I believe the sea remains until that final renewal."

Irene's voice was soft but certain. "So do I. Eden 2.0 isn't about a reset—it's about a redemption. Everything God once called 'very good' . . . He's making good again."

Irene tilted her head, a thoughtful crease forming between her brows.

"Ann, I've been studying the Feasts of the Lord again—Passover, Unleavened Bread, Firstfruits, Pentecost, Trumpets, Atonement, and Tabernacles. They're so rich with meaning. But it got me wondering . . . will these feasts still be observed in the Millennium?"

I nodded, a thoughtful smile forming. "Great question, Irene. And actually, the Bible gives us a clear 'yes'—at least for one of them: the Feast of Tabernacles, also known as *Sukkot*. In Zechariah 14, it says that after Christ returns, all nations will go up to Jerusalem year after year to worship the King and celebrate the Feast of Tabernacles. It becomes a global appointment with the King."

> And it shall come to pass, that every one that is left of all the nations which came against Jerusalem shall even go up from year to year to worship the King, the LORD of hosts, and to keep the Feast of Tabernacles. (Zechariah 14:16)

"Jesus is the fulfillment of each feast:"

1. **Passover**—Christ's crucifixion.
2. **Unleavened Bread**—His sinlessness.
3. **Firstfruits**—His resurrection
4. **Pentecost**—The Holy Spirit arrival.
5. **Trumpets, Atonement, Tabernacles**—Yet future, tied to His return.

> Let no man therefore judge you in meat, or in drink, or of the new moon, or of the sabbath days: Which are a shadow of things to come; but the body is of Christ. (Colossians 2:16–17)

Irene blinked. "Wait—so Christians will observe Jewish feasts?"

"Yes, but not under the Old Covenant law," I explained. "These feasts point to Jesus—they're prophetic celebrations. In the future, as Zechariah 14 shows, even Gentile nations will joyfully honor them during the Messiah's reign. It's not about obligation—it's about worship in light of fulfillment. Jesus didn't abolish the Law; He fulfilled it. Now we see these feasts through Him."

Irene's eyes lit up with recognition. "Right! I read that somewhere. It's fascinating. The Feast of Tabernacles is the one that celebrates God *dwelling* with His people, isn't it?"

I nodded. "Exactly. Tabernacles is all about *presence*—God making His home with His people. And in the Millennium, that promise will be literally fulfilled. Jesus will dwell among us, reigning from Jerusalem."

I leaned in, my voice warming. "So the Feast of Tabernacles won't just be a shadow or a symbol anymore—it will become a living, global celebration of His kingship. Year after year, nations will gather—not out of ritual, but out of awe and joy."

Irene leaned forward, her curiosity deepening. "So what about the others—like Passover and Pentecost? Will we continue observing those too?"

I met her gaze and offered a gentle shake of the head. "Not in the same way, no. Jesus has already fulfilled them."

I paused, giving the moment weight.

"He *is* our Passover Lamb—the perfect sacrifice once for all. He's the Unleavened Bread, sinless and broken for us. He rose as the Firstfruits of the resurrection. And Pentecost—well, that marked the outpouring of the Holy Spirit, the birth of the Church."

I smiled softly. "Those feasts were prophetic shadows, and in Christ, they've reached their fullness. We honor their meaning, but we don't repeat what's already been fulfilled. The emphasis shifts from rehearsal to remembrance—and worship rooted in completion."

Irene tilted her head, her brow furrowed in thought. "So . . . they're not 'done away with'—they're fulfilled?"

I nodded, a gentle smile forming. "Exactly. *Fulfilled*, not forgotten."

I let the words settle, then continued. "I believe we'll still commemorate their meaning—just in a new light. It's like the Sabbath rest. According to Isaiah 66:23, that rhythm of worship will continue into the age to come."

And it shall come to pass, that from one new moon to another, and from one sabbath to another, shall all flesh come to worship before Me, says the Lord. (Isaiah 66:23)

I looked back at Irene. "It's no longer about ritual—it's about reverence. Worship won't be law-driven—it'll be love-driven. Every gathering will reflect the fullness we now have in Christ."

Irene's brow furrowed as she reflected. "And maybe the Feast of Trumpets and the Day of Atonement will still hold some future significance? I mean, Trumpets points to His return, and Atonement to Israel's national repentance."

I met her gaze, my voice calm and steady. "That's very possible. Many scholars believe these feasts may be honored in a memorial way—a sacred remembrance of what God has accomplished through Christ."

I paused, considering the wonder of it all. "Especially for those still living in natural bodies during the Millennium, these annual observances could become powerful moments of reflection—reminders of grace, judgment, and redemption. Not as a requirement, but as a reverent echo of fulfilled prophecy."

Irene nodded slowly, her voice laced with wonder. "That makes sense. And the Feast of Tabernacles really does feel like the great annual celebration. It's joyful, it's inclusive, and it showcases the Kingdom in all its beauty."

I raised a finger, leaning in slightly. "Exactly—and here's the thing: it won't be optional."

Her eyebrows lifted.

"Zechariah makes that crystal clear," I continued. "Any nation that refuses to come up to Jerusalem to worship the King and celebrate the Feast of Tabernacles—well, no rain for them. That's Zechariah 14:17."

> And it shall be, that whoso will not come up of all the families of the earth unto Jerusalem to worship the King, the LORD of hosts, even upon them shall be no rain. (Zechariah 14:17)

"Obedience will still matter—even in the Millennium. Not out of fear, but out of rightful reverence for the King who reigns."

Irene's eyes widened, her voice barely above a whisper. "Whoa—so obedience will still matter? Even with Christ physically reigning on the earth?"

I nodded solemnly. "Absolutely. Christ's reign will be righteous and visible—but free will won't be erased."

I paused, letting that truth settle.

"People who survive into the Millennium in their natural, unresurrected bodies will still have the capacity to choose. That's why the Millennium, though filled with peace and restoration, will also be a proving ground—a final age of testing before the Great White Throne Judgment."

Irene smiled, her eyes shining with wonder. "So in the end, these feasts aren't just ancient rituals—they're prophetic previews of God's entire redemptive plan."

I nodded slowly, the weight of truth lingering in the moment. "Exactly. They were never just about the past—they point forward to what's still unfolding."

I leaned back slightly, a quiet joy stirring in my chest. "And the Millennium gives us a front-row seat to watch that plan fulfilled—not just in symbols, but in reality. Christ, dwelling among us. Ruling from Jerusalem. The nations gathered in joyful worship."

I looked at her, eyes bright. "Just like He promised."

Her voice dropped to a whisper, full of awe. "I think the Feast of Tabernacles might end up being my favorite holiday."

I smiled, a soft chuckle escaping. "Mine too, Irene. Mine too."

Irene's brow furrowed, her voice tinged with concern.

"Ann, I came across something in Isaiah 65:20 that really shook me. It says if someone dies at one hundred, they're considered a child—and it also says the sinner at one hundred will be accursed. Wait . . . there's *death* in the Millennium? And *sinners*? I thought it was going to be paradise on earth—with Jesus reigning!"

> There shall be no more thence an infant of days, nor an old man that has not filled his days: for the child shall die one hundred years old; but the sinner being one hundred years old shall be accursed. (Isaiah 65:20)

I nodded slowly, my expression reflective.

"That's a really important—and often overlooked—detail, Irene. Yes, there *will* be death during the Millennium, but not the way we understand it now."

I leaned in slightly. "The people who die during that time won't be the glorified saints like us. They'll be mortals—those who survived the Tribulation and entered Christ's Kingdom in their natural, unresurrected bodies."

Irene leaned in, her eyes wide with concern. "So . . . those who make it through the Tribulation—but aren't raptured or resurrected—they're the ones who can still die?"

I nodded. "Exactly. These survivors will enter the Millennial Kingdom in their natural, mortal bodies."

I paused for emphasis.

"They'll repopulate the earth during Christ's thousand-year reign. And their children—just like us in this present age—will have free will. They'll need to make their *own* decision to follow Christ. Salvation won't be inherited—it will still come through personal faith and obedience."

She furrowed her brow, struggling to reconcile it. "But . . . isn't the Millenium supposed to be paradise? Why would death still be possible?"

"That's the twist," I said gently. "It *will* be a time of peace and restoration—but not perfection yet. That comes later, in the new heaven and new earth."

I paused, then added, "During the Millennium, lifespans will be dramatically extended—restored to what they were before the Flood. Think about Methuselah, Noah's grandfather—he lived 969 years."

Irene's eyes widened slightly.

"So in that context," I continued, "someone dying at one hundred would be like a child dying today. Isaiah 65:20 says such a death would be considered a curse—because the expectation under Christ's reign is a long, full life. Early death would signal rebellion, not blessing."

Irene's brows drew together, her voice barely above a whisper. "That's . . . wild. But what about the part that says, 'the sinner being accursed'? That sounds really harsh."

I nodded soberly. "It does—at first. But when you look closer, it reveals something important."

I paused, choosing my words carefully.

"Even with Satan bound and Jesus physically reigning from Jerusalem, sin will still exist—not in the glorified saints, but in the hearts of those born during the Millennium. It's a sobering reminder: the root of sin isn't just external—it's in the human heart. The capacity to rebel won't be gone."

She looked stunned, her voice hushed. "So . . . paradise doesn't mean perfection?"

"Exactly," I said gently. "It means righteousness enforced."

I gave her a moment to absorb that before continuing.

"Jesus will rule with a rod of iron—just like Psalm 2 says: He will break the nations like a potter's vessel. No more delayed judgment like we see today. In the Millennium, sin will be confronted swiftly and justly."

I softened my tone. "Grace will still be present—but so will accountability. Under Christ's reign, justice and mercy will walk hand in hand."

Irene hesitated, her voice barely above a whisper. "So . . . it's not the Age of Grace anymore?"

I met her eyes and shook my head gently. "Not in the same way."

I let the words settle, then continued. "Grace will still be present—Jesus never stops being merciful. But during the Millennium, grace won't be the primary atmosphere like it is now."

I leaned in slightly. This is the *Kingdom Age*—ruled by righteousness and justice. Jesus will reign not just as Savior, but as King. And in His Kingdom, holiness won't just be invited—it will be expected."

She looked troubled, her brow creased. "So . . . no one gets away with anything?"

"Exactly," I said gently. "That's why Isaiah says the sinner will be accursed."

I let the truth settle before continuing.

"In a world ruled by the perfect King, rebellion won't be hidden—it will be exposed and judged. Even in near-Eden conditions, the human heart can still choose sin. And in that age, justice won't be delayed—it will be swift."

I looked at her with quiet conviction. "It's not cruelty—it's clarity. A holy King cannot turn a blind eye to defiance. His justice is part of His love."

Irene's expression darkened, her voice soft. "That's . . . honestly kind of heavy. We always talk about the lion and the lamb, the peace of the Millennium . . . but not *this* part."

I nodded gently. "Because it's not easy to talk about—but it is real."

I paused for a moment, then continued.

"The Millennium isn't heaven. It's a glimpse—a thousand-year preview of what the world could look like under the perfect rule of Christ. Peace, prosperity, righteousness . . . and yet, even then, the human heart will still have the freedom to choose rebellion."

Her eyes searched mine, full of sorrow. "Even after everything God has done?"

I exhaled, the weight of it pressing on my heart. "Yes."

I paused, my voice low. "That's why Revelation ends with one final uprising—when Satan is released after a thousand years. It's God's ultimate proof: that without a changed heart, even paradise isn't enough."

I looked at her gently. "The problem was never the world, Irene. It's the will."

Irene exhaled slowly, her eyes distant with reflection. "That really puts things into perspective. It's like . . . even in the perfect environment, you still need transformation. You still need Jesus."

I nodded, my voice quiet. "Exactly. And that's why the Millennium matters."

I paused, then added, "It proves the problem was never the world around us—it's always been the heart within us."

She leaned back, thoughtful. "So in a way, the Millennium shows that only Christ can truly change us—from the inside out, for eternity."

I smiled softly. "Exactly."

I let the moment linger, then continued.

"And that brings us to the final chapter—when God makes *all things new*: a new heaven, a new earth, and the New Jerusalem. No more death. No more curse. No more sin."

I looked at her, eyes shining with quiet hope. "That's the forever our hearts were made for."

Irene tilted her head, a curious frown forming.

"Ann, I've still been thinking a lot about the Millennium, and something's been bugging me. If we're getting glorified bodies, does that mean we'll all look about the same age? Like . . . would I end up looking the same as my great-grandmother?"

I chuckled softly, the question bringing a smile. "That's such a great question, Irene—and honestly, yes! A lot of Bible scholars believe our glorified bodies will reflect the prime of human life."

I leaned in slightly. "Most suggest we'll look about the age Jesus was when He rose from the dead—so somewhere around 33 or 33½. Not just in appearance, but in strength, vitality, and wholeness."

Irene's eyes lit up, her voice filled with wonder. "So we'll all look young and radiant? That sounds amazing! But . . . what about recognizing people? Will I still know my mom—or my kids?"

I nodded, offering a reassuring smile. "Absolutely. Remember, after Jesus was resurrected, His followers *did* recognize Him—even if it took a moment. And when Moses and Elijah appeared with Him on the Mount of Transfiguration, they were recognized instantly."

I leaned in gently. We'll still know each other—but even better than we do now. In a deeper, purer way—free from pain, free from the limits of earthly roles or age. No confusion. No loss. Just perfect, eternal fellowship."

Irene chuckled, eyes twinkling. "Wow . . . so no more aging—and no more 'Listen to your elders' speeches!"

I laughed with her. "Exactly. Just perfect unity and love in Christ."

Then I softened, my tone more reflective. "But here's the beautiful part—even though we'll recognize and cherish our loved ones, our truest identity—both in the Millennium and in eternity—will be found in Jesus."

I met her gaze gently. "That's what makes everything so pure . . . so whole."

Irene leaned in, a playful seriousness in her voice. "Okay, but what about marriage? Like . . . if I was married more than once—who am I with?"

I smiled gently, understanding the weight behind the question. "Jesus actually addressed that directly in Matthew 22:30. He said that in the resurrection, people 'neither marry nor are given in marriage, but are like the angels in heaven.'"

> For in the resurrection they neither marry, nor are given in marriage, but are as the angels of God in heaven. (Matthew 22:30)

I glanced at her warmly. "In our glorified state, human marriage won't be needed. Our deepest fulfillment will be in Christ Himself—complete, eternal, and perfect."

Irene's eyebrows lifted, her voice soft with surprise. "So . . . no marriage at all?"

I nodded gently. "Right. Marriage as we know it ends when we receive our glorified bodies."

I paused, then added with quiet reverence, "In eternity, our deepest and most complete union will be with Christ Himself. He's the Bridegroom—and we, His redeemed people, are the Bride."

Irene tilted her head, her brows gently furrowed. "So . . . no spouses in the glorified sense?"

I smiled softly, compassion in my voice. "Not in the earthly, romantic sense."

I let the moment breathe, then continued.

"But here's the beauty—we'll all be united in a love that far surpasses even the deepest connection we've ever known. It's not a loss—it's a gain. Not something lesser, but something far greater. More fulfilling. More complete. Perfect love, without the pain or limits of this world."

Irene leaned in, curiosity sparking in her eyes. "And what about children? Will we have kids during the Millennium?"

I shook my head gently. "Not for those of us with glorified bodies—there won't be marriage or children in that state."

I paused, then added, "But for those who survive the Tribulation and enter the Millennium in their natural, mortal bodies? Yes. They'll marry, have children, and live incredibly long lives—much like the pre-Flood era."

I smiled softly. "Remember what Isaiah 65 says—someone who dies at one hundred will still be considered a child. Under Christ's reign and a restored earth, life expectancy will stretch dramatically."

Irene's eyes widened. "Wait—so people can *die* during the Millennium?"

I nodded. "Yes—but it's very different from what we're used to."

I continued gently, "Isaiah 65 says that if someone dies at one hundred, they'll be considered a child. That implies lifespans will be dramatically extended—likely restored to what we saw before the Flood in Genesis."

I paused, then added, "So natural humans—those who survived the Tribulation—will still experience aging and death, just on a much slower scale."

A soft smile formed. "But glorified saints? We'll be immortal. No death. No decay. Just everlasting life in glorified bodies."

Irene leaned forward, curiosity shining in her eyes. "What about the kids born during that time? Will they still grow up like we did?"

I nodded. "Yes—they'll grow up and mature much like we do today, probably reaching adulthood around twenty or thirty. But with extended lifespans, they'll live far longer than we do now."

I paused, then added, "And just like every generation before them, they'll need to make their *own* decision to follow Christ. Salvation won't be automatic. Free will still applies—eternity will still hinge on personal faith."

Irene's voice softened, a hint of awe beneath her words. "So . . . it's a time of restoration—but also a time of testing?"

I nodded gently. "Exactly. The curse will be lifted, the earth will flourish, and righteousness will reign. But even in that beauty, the human heart must still choose."

I paused, then added, "The Millennium will be like a final, glorious classroom—where the world is given one last opportunity to learn obedience, experience truth, and prepare for eternity."

Her eyes welled with quiet tears. "This is so much bigger than I imagined. And more beautiful."

I smiled warmly. "It is, Irene."

I paused, my voice tender. "And here's the best part—everything broken now—our bodies, our relationships, even time itself—will be redeemed in His Kingdom. The best is truly yet to come."

Irene tilted her head, her expression thoughtful. "Ann, I've been thinking about something . . . and it's kind of heavy."

I gave her a gentle smile. "Go ahead, Irene. I'm listening."

Irene hesitated, then asked, "What happens to children who are aborted? I mean . . . I believe their spirits go to heaven, right? But what happens to them there? Do they grow up? Do they become adults? And—would their parents ever be reunited with them?"

I nodded slowly, my voice soft. "That's a tender question, Irene. And yes—most Bible scholars believe that children who die in the womb or in infancy—including those aborted—go immediately into the presence of God."

Irene's eyes glistened. "Really?"

The burden of the word of the LORD for Israel, says the LORD, which stretches forth the heavens, and lays the foundation of the earth, and forms the spirit of man within him. (Zechariah 12:1)

As you know not what is the way of the spirit, nor how the bones do grow in the womb of her that is with child: even so you know not the works of God who makes all. (Ecclesiastes 11:5)

Then shall the dust return to the earth as it was: and the spirit shall return unto God who gave it. (Ecclesiastes 12:7)

Before I formed you in the belly I knew you; and before you came forth out of the womb I sanctified you, and I ordained you a prophet unto the nations. (Jeremiah 1:5)

I continued, "Absolutely. Psalm 139 says God knits us together in the womb. He sees our unformed substance and writes all our days in His book before one of them begins. And remember what Jesus said: 'Let the little children come to Me, for the kingdom of heaven belongs to such as these.'"

For you have possessed my reins: you have covered me in my mother's womb. I will praise You; for I am fearfully and wonderfully made: marvelous are Your works; and that my soul knows right well. My substance was not hid from You, when I was made in secret, and curiously wrought in the lowest parts of the earth. Your eyes did see my substance, yet being unperfect; and in Your book all my members were written, which in continuance were fashioned, when as yet there was none of them. (Psalm 139:13–16)

Irene nodded slowly. "So . . . even though their life on earth was cut short, their *eternal* life continues?"

I smiled. "Yes. Their spirit doesn't die—it returns to the One who gave it."

Irene leaned in, her voice dropping to a whisper. "Will the parents who chose abortion be able to see those children again?"

I paused, my voice full of compassion. "If they've repented and received Christ's forgiveness? Yes. God's mercy covers *every* sin at the Cross—including abortion. There is no condemnation for those who are in Christ Jesus. In His grace, I believe God can restore even that relationship."

Irene's voice cracked. "That's so merciful . . ."

I nodded. "It is. But it doesn't remove the weight of what abortion is. It's the ending of a life that God created. And for decades, our nation legally protected it."

Irene's expression darkened. "You're talking about *Roe v. Wade*, right?"

I nodded. "Yes. That decision came down on January 22, 1973, and for over 49 years, it legalized abortion in all fifty states. But then—something historic happened."

Irene leaned forward. "I remember! President Trump appointed three Supreme Court justices who helped shift the balance of the Court."

I smiled. "Exactly. And on June 24, 2022, the Supreme Court overturned *Roe v. Wade* in the *Dobbs v. Jackson Women's Health Organization* case. They ruled that abortion is not a constitutional right, and they sent the decision back to the individual states."

Irene breathed out. "That was huge."

I nodded, "It was. A turning point in history. A nation can't be blessed while shedding innocent blood. And that was a moment of national mercy."

Irene blinked away a tear. "Do you think aborted children grow up in heaven?"

I nodded. "I believe they do. Whether instantly—like Adam and Eve—or gradually, I think God completes the lives that were never lived on earth. Some scholars, like Randy Alcorn, believe they may grow and learn in heaven—becoming the full person God intended."

Irene looked off. "And one day, we'll see them?"

I smiled. "We will. And I believe they'll be radiant, whole, and filled with joy. Not angry, not bitter—just complete in Christ."

Irene tilted her head. "Do you think we'll all look the same age?"

I chuckled. "Maybe! A lot of scholars suggest our glorified bodies will reflect the 'prime' of life—like Jesus when He rose from the dead, around 33. Not just appearance, but vitality, wholeness, and immortality."

Irene raised an eyebrow. "So no children in heaven?"

I shook my head gently. "Not in the glorified state. Jesus said in Matthew 22:30 that in the resurrection, we neither marry nor are given in marriage—we'll be like the angels. That means no new births, no parenting as we know it. Everyone will be perfectly whole and mature—unified in Christ."

Irene's voice softened. "So, even children will be transformed?"

I nodded. "Yes. Earthly relationships will be transformed too. Our deepest identity won't be as parents, or children, or spouses—it will be as the redeemed Bride of Christ."

Irene exhaled. "That's . . . a lot. But it's also so beautiful."

I leaned in, my voice warm. "It is. And here's the best part—everything broken now . . . our bodies, our relationships, even time itself—will be redeemed in His Kingdom. The best is truly yet to come."

Irene furrowed her brow, deep in thought.

"Ann, I was reading Isaiah 65 again, I'm still trying to wrap my head around something. It says we'll build houses and live in them, plant vineyards and eat the fruit. Does that mean . . . we'll actually be working during the Millennium?"

I smiled reassuringly. "Yes, Irene—but not the kind of work we're used to. It won't be burdensome or exhausting. It'll be deeply fulfilling."

I paused, then added, "Remember, the curse from Genesis 3—the thorns and thistles, the sweat of the brow just to survive? In the Millennium, that curse will be lifted. Labor will be joyful again, like it was meant to be in Eden. Everything we do will carry purpose, beauty, and lasting fruit."

Irene's eyes widened, a wave of relief washing over her face.

"So . . . no more burnout? No more work stress?"

I nodded warmly. "Exactly. Isaiah 65:21–22 says, 'They shall not build and another inhabit.' That's a powerful reversal of injustice."

And they shall build houses, and inhabit them; and they shall plant vineyards, and eat the fruit of them. They shall not build, and another inhabit; they shall not plant, and another eat: for as the days of a tree are the days of My people, and My elect shall long enjoy the work of their hands. (Isaiah 65:21–22)

I leaned in slightly. "In this life, people pour their hearts into building something—only to see it lost to war, stolen by corruption, or buried in broken systems. But in the Kingdom, that won't happen."

I smiled. "What you build, you'll enjoy. What you plant, you'll harvest. No fear of loss, no systems of exploitation—just peace, justice, and lasting joy in the work of your hands."

Irene furrowed her brow. "I read something that said justice will be immediate in the Kingdom—like if someone commits a crime, they're dealt with on the spot. That sounds . . . intense. Even harsh. But I guess I understand. Sin won't be allowed to take root, right?"

I nodded slowly. "Exactly. The Millennium is the age of righteousness."

I paused, then added, "Jesus will rule with a rod of iron—swift, perfect justice. People born during that time in natural bodies will still have a sin nature, the ability to rebel. But rebellion won't be allowed to spread or fester. That's how peace is preserved."

I looked at her gently. "Justice won't be delayed. There will be no loopholes, no corruption. Righteousness will be the law of the land—because the King Himself will be on the throne."

Irene blinked, absorbing the weight of it. "So . . . basically, if someone starts a war—they're gone?"

I gave a solemn nod. "Exactly. The moment someone stirs up violence or acts with deception, it's dealt with swiftly and righteously."

I paused for emphasis. "It may sound severe from our current perspective, where justice is often delayed or distorted. But in a world still inhabited by mortals, swift justice is what preserves global peace."

I met her gaze. "Remember, glorified saints like us won't sin—we've already passed through judgment. But the nations? They'll still need governance. And it won't be through leniency. It will be through perfect justice—because righteousness will rule the earth."

Irene smiled softly, her voice full of wonder. "It says, 'the days of My people shall be like the days of a tree.' That's beautiful—long life, deep roots."

I nodded, moved by the thought. "Yes—and the verse continues: 'they shall long enjoy the work of their hands.'"

I paused, letting the imagery breathe.

"Just imagine . . . planting a vineyard and savoring its fruit, not just for years—but for centuries. No more wasted effort. No more futility or frustration."

I looked at her warmly. "In the Kingdom, everything you do will have meaning—rich, enduring purpose that echoes through time."

Irene's voice trembled, emotion rising in her throat. "Verse 23 really got to me: 'They shall not labor in vain or bear children for calamity.' That hit me hard."

They shall not labor in vain, nor bring forth for trouble; for they are the seed of the blessed of the LORD, and their offspring with them. (Isaiah 65:23)

"So . . . no more children born into war, abuse, or poverty?"

I met her eyes and gave a steady nod. "Right. In the Kingdom, every child born will grow up in a world governed by peace and righteousness."

I paused, letting the truth settle.

"Why? Because any threat—any hint of calamity—is removed swiftly. There will be no corrupt leaders exploiting the weak. No predators hiding in the shadows. No war. No abuse. No fear."

I smiled softly. "The world will finally be safe . . . safe for children to grow, to laugh, to flourish. Just as God always intended."

Irene leaned back slowly, her expression softening with awe. "I think I'm starting to see . . . this isn't just a pause before eternity. It's the redemption of everything earth was meant to be."

I smiled gently. "Exactly."

I opened my Bible and added, "And listen to this—Isaiah 65:24 says, 'Before they call, I will answer; and while they are still speaking, I will hear.'"

> And it shall come to pass, that before they call, I will answer; and while they are yet speaking, I will hear. (Isaiah 65:24)

I looked at her, eyes shining. "Can you imagine that kind of closeness with God? Communion so deep, so uninterrupted, that your prayer doesn't even need to finish—He's already responding."

I leaned in. "It's Eden, restored. Eden 2.0. But this time, Jesus isn't walking in the garden occasionally—He's physically present. Reining in righteousness. From Jerusalem."

Irene leaned in, her voice hushed with wonder.

"So Ann, what about us—glorified believers? What will we actually *do* during the Millennium?"

I smiled, a spark of anticipation lighting my voice.

"That's a great question. Revelation 20 says we will 'reign with Christ for a thousand years.'"

I paused meaningfully. "We'll help administer His justice, govern cities and regions, mentor others, and teach the nations the ways of God. It'll be leadership rooted in wisdom and love."

I added thoughtfully, "Some scholars even believe we might participate in rebuilding—restoring ecosystems, reviving architecture, maybe even redeeming music, art, and cultural expressions that were lost or distorted. Imagine co-laboring with Christ to bring beauty and truth back into every sphere of life."

Irene's eyes lit up with wonder. "Like being sent to a part of the world to help it flourish—and actually watching it thrive this time?"

I nodded, my voice warm. "Exactly. No more failed systems. No more red tape or corruption. Just Spirit-led assignments that bear real fruit. Whatever He entrusts to us will be meaningful, lasting—and filled with joy."

Irene's eyes sparkled. "That sounds incredible—like we'll be Kingdom ambassadors."

I nodded with a smile. "Exactly. And here's the amazing part—every ounce of faithfulness you're living out right now—every whispered prayer, every quiet act of love, every moment you chose to forgive instead of retaliate—it's all preparing you. This life? It's training ground. That one? It's where we reign."

A quiet awe softened Irene's features. "Ann, I don't think I've ever looked forward to the Millennium more than I do now."

I smiled, my heart full. "Me too, Irene. The best is truly yet to come—and we've only just begun to glimpse it."

Irene leaned forward, curiosity dancing in her eyes.

"Ann, I've been wondering . . . what do you think worship and education will look like during the Millennium? I mean, we know Jesus will be reigning from Jerusalem, but what about daily life—how will people learn and worship?"

I smiled, touched by the depth of her question.

"I'm so glad you asked that. It's going to be breathtaking. Worship in the Millennium won't look anything like our current experiences. For one, Zechariah 14 tells us that all the nations will be required to go up to Jerusalem each year to worship Jesus Christ the King of kings and celebrate the Feast of Tabernacles."

Irene blinked in surprise. "Wait—a literal, physical journey to Jerusalem? From every nation on earth?"

I nodded, my voice calm but firm. "Exactly. That's what Zechariah 14 says. And here is the sobering part—verse 17 makes it clear that if any nation refuses to go, God will withhold rain from them. No worship, no water. In that day, worship won't be optional. It will be expected—enforced even—because Jesus Christ the King of kings will be physically reigning from Jerusalem.

And it shall be, that whoso will not come up of all the families of the earth unto Jerusalem to worship the King, the LORD of hosts, even upon them shall be no rain. (Zechariah 14:17)

Irene tilted her head, clearly pondering the logistics.

"But Ann, if people are expected to travel to Jerusalem every year—what about those living thousands of miles away? Are we talking about airplanes? Cars? I mean . . . probably not, right? Maybe horses? But even that sounds like such a burdensome journey."

I smiled, sensing both her curiosity and concern.

"You're right to wonder about that. Scripture doesn't give us every detail—but it does give us some important clues. First, it's true that Jesus wouldn't impose anything oppressive or unjust. Remember, He said His yoke is easy and His burden is light. So whatever system of travel exists, it will align with His character—merciful, efficient, and just."

Irene's brows lifted. "So . . . how do scholars think we'll get around?"

I leaned in slightly.

Well, for glorified believers like us—those raptured or resurrected—it's very possible that our travel will be supernatural. After His resurrection, Jesus appeared and disappeared at will. He walked through locked doors. He vanished from Emmaus and reappeared in Jerusalem. Some scholars believe we may have that same ability—to move at the speed of thought, unhindered by time or terrain."

And their eyes were opened, and they knew Him; and He vanished out of their sight. (Luke 24:31)

Then the same day at evening, being the first day of the week, when the doors were shut where the disciples were assembled for fear of the Jews, came Jesus and stood in the midst, and says unto them, Peace be unto you. (John 20:19)

Irene's eyes widened in awe. "Wow. So, like . . . teleportation?"

I chuckled softly. "Something like that. And for those in natural bodies—the ones who survive the Tribulation and live through the Millennium—it may still involve traditional or renewed forms of transportation. Maybe a mix of restored creation travel—like caravans or swift animals—or even something totally new God designs for that age. We don't know exactly—but we can trust it won't be unjust or overly burdensome."

Irene nodded slowly. "That makes sense. If Jesus is ruling, even the travel will reflect His wisdom and kindness."

Irene's eyes widened. "That's wild. But people can still choose to disobey?"

I gave a sober nod. "They can—but there are immediate consequences. Unlike today, where judgment is delayed, in the Millennium it's swift and just. And here's the incredible part—Jesus won't just be reigning; He'll be teaching. Isaiah 2 says people from every nation will say, 'Come, let us go up to the mountain of the Lord . . . that He may teach us His ways.'"

Irene laughed softly. "Jesus, the Teacher! I love that. But what about schools? Colleges? Will we have those too?"

I smiled. "Absolutely—but with one major difference: they'll teach truth. Can you imagine universities where every curriculum is grounded in Scripture? No false ideologies. No distortion of science. No moral confusion. Just pure, life-giving knowledge."

Irene's eyebrows rose. "So the world will still be learning—but learning truth."

I nodded firmly. "No more competing ideologies. No more half-truths or false religions. Isaiah 2:3 says, 'Out of Zion shall go forth the law, and the word of the Lord from Jerusalem.' Education won't vanish—it'll just be perfected. The nations will learn Torah—God's law—as it was meant to be taught. Jesus Himself will teach, and we, the glorified saints, will serve as instructors, guides, and mentors."

Irene blinked in amazement. "That's . . . incredible. Like the whole world attending the same Bible school—with Jesus as the Headmaster!"

I laughed. "Yes! That's actually a perfect picture. Micah 4:2 echoes Isaiah, saying nations will say, 'Come, let us go up to the mountain of the LORD, to the house of the God of Jacob, that He may teach us His ways.' Pilgrimages of hungry-hearted people will come to Jerusalem—not as tourists, but as disciples."

> And many nations shall come, and say, Come, and let us go up to the mountain of the LORD, and to the house of the God of Jacob; and He will teach us of His ways, and we will walk in His paths: for the law shall go forth of Zion, and the word of the LORD from Jerusalem. (Micah 4:2)

Irene tilted her head. "So . . . would kids still go to school, too?"

I nodded. "Absolutely—but what they'll learn will be different. Children will be raised in righteousness. They'll learn God's laws, the truth of creation, history without distortion, and even languages like Hebrew might be commonly taught again. Zephaniah 3:9 even suggests God will 'restore a pure language' so that everyone may call on Him with one voice."

> Therefore wait you upon Me, says the LORD, until the day that I rise up to the prey: for My determination is to gather the nations, that I may assemble the kingdoms, to pour upon them My indignation, even all My fierce anger: for all the earth shall be devoured with the fire of My jealousy. For then will I turn to the people a pure language, that they may all call upon the name of the LORD, to serve Him with one consent. (Zephaniah 3:8–9)

Irene's eyes lit up. "So language won't divide us anymore . . . and truth will be the curriculum. That sounds like heaven on earth."

I smiled. "That's exactly what it will be. A world finally governed and taught by truth Himself—Yeshua HaMashiach (Jesus the Messiah), ruling in righteousness, with His people helping carry out His will."

Irene leaned back, eyes reflecting wonder. "So worship and learning won't be compartmentalized. They'll go hand in hand—everywhere, all the time."

I nodded, sensing the weight of that truth. "Exactly. No more 'sacred versus secular.' Everything will be sacred. Every classroom, every subject—whether it's music, science, architecture, math, or history—it will all reflect God's glory. Finally, the world will operate the way it was meant to."

Irene's voice softened, filled with hope. "Ann, this gives me so much hope. The Millennium isn't just a pause before eternity—it's a restoration. A preview of everything we've longed for."

I nodded, my words echoing the truth I've held close. "Exactly. It's the Kingdom Age. And we won't be spectators—we'll be participants. Leaders. Teachers. Worshipers. Builders. Lovers of truth."

Irene leaned forward, her eyes filled with quiet wonder.

"Ann, I've been thinking . . . We always talk about what Jesus will be doing during the Millennium, but what about the people—Jews and Christians? Will we finally be united? Or are we still somehow separate?"

I smiled warmly. "That's such a beautiful question, Irene. And yes—absolutely, we will be united—one in the Kingdom. But it's not a flattening of identity. God still honors His covenants with Israel. The Church doesn't replace Israel. Instead, we're joined together, each with unique callings, but under one King."

Irene tilted her head thoughtfully. "So, we're not all just merged into one category of believer?"

I shook my head. "Nope. Think of it like this: Ephesians 2 tells us Jesus broke down the dividing wall between Jew and Gentile, making 'one new man' from the two. That spiritual truth will be fully visible during the Kingdom Age. We'll be one body, one family—but with God-given distinctions still intact."

> For He is our peace, who has made both one, and has broken down the middle wall of partition between us. Having abolished in His flesh the enmity, even the law of commandments contained in ordinances; for to make in Himself of two one new man, so making peace. And that He might reconcile both unto God in one body by the Cross, having slain the enmity thereby. (Ephesians 2:14–16)

Irene raised her eyebrows. "One new man . . . That's a powerful picture. And that's from Paul, right?"

I nodded. "Yes, from Ephesians 2. And Romans 11 builds on that with Paul's olive tree analogy. Gentiles were grafted into the promises given to Israel. The roots are Jewish. And Paul warns not to boast against the natural branches. God hasn't abandoned Israel—He's fulfilling His promises to her."

> And if some of the branches be broken off, and you, being a wild olive tree, were grafted in among them, and with them partake of the root and fatness of the olive tree, boast not against the branches. But if you boast, you support not the root, but the root supports you. (Romans 11:17–18)

And they also, if they abide not still in unbelief, shall be grafted in: for God is able to graft them in again. For if you were cut out of the olive tree which is wild by nature, and were grafted contrary to nature into a good olive tree: how much more shall these, which be the natural branches, be grafted into their own olive tree? (Romans 11:23–24)

Irene smiled gently.

"So that 'grafted in' idea isn't just poetic—it's prophetic."

I leaned in. "Exactly."

"Romans 11 even says, 'All Israel will be saved.' During the Millennium, many Jews will recognize Jesus—Yeshua—as their long-awaited Messiah. That restoration is part of the beauty of the Messianic Age."

Irene paused, her voice soft. "So Jews and Gentiles, side by side . . . worshiping together?"

My eyes lit up.

"Yes! Zechariah 14 says all nations will go up to Jerusalem each year to worship Jesus Christ the King of kings and celebrate the Feast of Tabernacles. That includes Jews and Gentiles. It's a picture of worship rooted in Jewish heritage but expanded to include the whole world."

Irene leaned back in awe.

"That's amazing. Like a worldwide festival led by Jesus."

I chuckled. "Exactly. And Isaiah 2 and Micah 4 tell us that people from every nation will come to Jerusalem to learn God's ways. It'll be one global classroom—and Jesus will be the Teacher. There'll be no confusion, no clashing ideologies. Just truth."

Irene nodded slowly.

"And no more misunderstandings between Jews and Christians?"

I met her eyes.

"That's right. Jesus will heal the wounds of history—centuries of division, pain, even persecution. In the Kingdom, He brings reconciliation. And the New Jerusalem in Revelation shows both identities honored: twelve gates for the tribes of Israel, twelve foundations for the apostles. It's symbolic unity—eternal, beautiful, and intentional."

Irene blinked, visibly moved.

"Ann . . . that gives me hope. Real hope. Not just for the world—but for the story of God's people. It all fits."

I nodded softly. "It does. The Millennium won't erase our stories. It'll weave them together into one masterpiece—with Jesus, the Jewish Messiah and Savior of the world, at the center."

———◆◆◆———

THE REVELATION OF JESUS CHRIST REVEALS:

^{20:7} And when the thousand years are expired, Satan will be loosed out of his prison.

This brief but profound verse marks a dramatic shift in redemptive history. After a thousand years of peace, prosperity, and the visible reign of Christ from Jerusalem—known as the Millennial Kingdom—Satan is released from the abyss where he had been bound since Revelation 20:1–3.

During the Millennium, Christ reigns with the glorified saints (Revelation 20:4–6), the curse is reversed (Isaiah 11), and righteousness is enforced (Isaiah 2:2–4; Zechariah 14:16–19). But at the close of this golden age, Satan is released for one final rebellion.

Why? Because even under perfect external conditions, the hearts of unregenerate people can still be deceived. This confirms the truth of Jeremiah 17:9: "The heart is deceitful above all things, and desperately wicked: who can know it?" This rebellion highlights a theological truth: The environment alone doesn't save people—only the blood of Christ does.

In verse 8, Satan deceives "the nations in the four corners of the earth, Gog and Magog," gathering them for battle. This reference echoes Ezekiel 38–39, where a similar uprising is described. However, this is not a direct repetition of Ezekiel's war—it is a final, global rebellion. Gog and Magog are symbolic names here, representing nations at enmity with God. This shows that despite 1,000 years of peace and the direct reign of Jesus, some mortals will still choose to follow Satan when given the chance.

Revelation 20:10 is the end of Satan's story. Not annihilation. Not retirement. Eternal torment. Jesus Himself warned of this in Matthew 25:41: "Depart from Me, you cursed, into everlasting fire, prepared for the devil and his angels." The Lake of Fire is the final destination for Satan, the Antichrist, and the False Prophet (Revelation 19:20), and ultimately for Death and Hades themselves (Revelation 20:14). It is a place of conscious, eternal punishment.

This verse (Revelation 20:7) sets in motion the final separation of good and evil. It reveals the justice of God, giving people every chance—even a utopia—yet proving the necessity of heart transformation. And it sets the stage for the Great White Throne Judgment and the arrival of the new heaven and new earth in Revelation 21.

OLD TESTAMENT FORESHADOWS REVELATION:

Son of man, set your face against Gog, the land of Magog, the chief prince of Meshech and Tubal, and prophesy against him. And say, Thus says the Lord GOD; Behold, I am against you, O Gog, the chief prince of Meshech and Tubal:

And I will turn you back, and put hooks into your jaws, and I will bring you forth, and all your army, horses and horsemen, all of them clothed with all sorts of armor, even a great company with bucklers and shields, all of them handling swords. (Ezekiel 38:2–4)

Gog and Magog are mentioned in both passages—but in different end times contexts. Ezekiel 38–39 describes a massive attack against Israel, which some scholars view as a type of foreshadowing of the final rebellion in Revelation 20. Revelation 20:7 reuses these names symbolically to describe the global rebellion led by Satan after the 1,000 years. So while Ezekiel's Gog and Magog may refer to a specific prophetic war before the Millennium, Revelation uses them more symbolically to represent the final war against God's people after the Millennium—bookending the age of rebellion.

THE REVELATION OF JESUS CHRIST REVEALS:

20:8 And will go out to deceive the nations which are in the four quarters of the earth, Gog and Magog, to gather them together to battle: the number of whom is as the sand of the sea.

After being bound for a thousand years (verse 7), Satan is released for one final act of rebellion. This moment underscores a crucial truth: even after a perfect world governed by Jesus Christ Himself for 1,000 years, some human hearts will still choose rebellion. This reveals the depth of human depravity and the necessity of eternal transformation, not just external conditions.

"And will go out to deceive the nations which are in the four quarters of the earth." This phrase emphasizes the global scale of this deception. Even in a world where peace, justice, and truth have reigned, Satan's release allows him to once again infiltrate the nations, proving that true loyalty to God must come from the heart, not merely from ideal circumstances.

"Gog and Magog." These names are symbolic representations of all the rebellious nations of the earth. While originally mentioned in Ezekiel 38–39 as specific enemies of Israel, here they represent the archetypal enemies of God in the final rebellion. This is not the same battle as Ezekiel's war (which is likely pre-Millennial), but a separate, end of Millennium rebellion, using the names to signify a universal uprising.

"To gather them together to battle." This mirrors Satan's tactics throughout Scripture—to unite the wicked against the righteous (Psalm 2:1–3). But this isn't merely a military campaign; it's a spiritual revolt against God's final authority, a desperate, doomed attempt to overthrow His eternal Kingdom.

"The number of whom is as the sand of the sea." This echoes Genesis 22:17— God's promise to Abraham—and shows the tragic irony: just as God promised an innumerable host of faithful descendants, here we see an innumerable army of rebels—proof that without true inward transformation, multitudes can still fall prey to deception.

Even after 1,000 years of peace, free will remains, and the choice to follow Christ must be personal and real. Satan's deception proves that external righteousness—millennial law and order—doesn't equal internal righteousness. Gog and Magog are symbolic of human rebellion united under Satan's final push—ultimately setting the stage for God's final act of justice. The enormity of this rebellion highlights the necessity of the new heaven and new earth in Revelation 21—where sin and Satan will never rise again.

OLD TESTAMENT FORESHADOWS REVELATION:

And you shalt come up against My people of Israel, as a cloud to cover the land; it shall be in the latter days, and I will bring you against My land, that the nations may know Me, when I shall be sanctified in you, O Gog, before their eyes. (Ezekiel 38:16)

Both verses described a massive gathering of rebellious nations. Gog is the symbolic or literal leader of an anti-God coalition, used by God to demonstrate His power and holiness. In both scenarios, God allows the rebellion to rise for a purpose: to judge the wicked and glorify Himself in victory. While Ezekiel 38:16 likely refers to a pre-Millennial battle, Revelation 20:8 uses the names "Gog and Magog" again to signal a final global rebellion.

THE REVELATION OF JESUS CHRIST REVEALS:

20:9 And they went up on the breadth of the earth, and compassed the camp of the saints about, and the beloved city: and fire came down from God out of heaven, and devoured them.

This dramatic moment marks the final rebellion in all of human history. After a thousand years of Christ's righteous and visible reign on earth—a period marked by peace, justice, and prosperity—Satan is released (verse 7) and once again deceives the nations. What's shocking is not just Satan's activity, but how many people choose to follow him, even after experiencing the perfection of Christ's rule.

"And they went up on the breadth of the earth, and compassed the camp of the saints about, and the beloved city." The "camp of the saints" and the "beloved city" almost certainly refer to Jerusalem, the millennial capital of Christ's government (Isaiah 2:2–4; Zechariah 14:9–17). This is the location of Christ's throne and His glorified saints who rule with Him (Revelation 20:4–6). The imagery of being "compassed about" suggests an overwhelming military force, similar to Gog's description in Ezekiel 38:9—"you shalt come like a storm . . ."

"And fire came down from God out of heaven, and devoured them." God's response is instant and decisive: fire comes down from heaven and devours the enemies. This parallels 2 Kings 1:10–12, where Elijah calls down fire from heaven, and also Genesis 19:24, when Sodom is judged. No battle is fought. There is no resistance by the saints, no armies mobilized. God Himself steps in, bringing final judgment.

Despite 1,000 years of ideal conditions, humanity still rebels—proving that:

- External righteousness cannot transform an internal heart.
- Environment is not the issue. The issue is sin.

This verse testifies that man's sinful nature is not cured by better laws, leaders, or circumstances. Only a new heart, given through the New Covenant in Christ, can truly save and transform.

This verse underscores total depravity—the doctrine that the human heart, without Christ, is incapable of righteousness. It also proves that justice and truth, even when perfectly displayed, do not eliminate sin. Only the Cross can do that. The Millennial Kingdom serves as God's final demonstration to the world: even in the best possible world, man will choose rebellion if not born again.

OLD TESTAMENT FORESHADOWS REVELATION:

And I will plead against him with pestilence and with blood; and I will rain upon him, and upon his bands, and upon the many people that are with him, an overflowing rain, and great hailstones, fire, and brimstone. (Ezekiel 38:22)

This passage is part of the Gog and Magog prophecy in Ezekiel 38–39, which closely mirrors the end-time rebellion described in Revelation 20:8–9. In both accounts: Gog and Magog gather nations for war. They surround the people of God. God Himself intervenes with fire from heaven. The result is total destruction of the enemies.

THE REVELATION OF JESUS CHRIST REVEALS:

20:10 And the devil that deceived them was cast into the Lake of Fire and brimstone, where the beast and the false prophet are, and will be tormented day and night forever and ever.

This verse marks the final and irreversible defeat of Satan. After being bound for 1,000 years (Revelation 20:1–3) and briefly released to deceive the nations one last time (Revelation 20:7–9), Satan now meets his eternal fate: the Lake of Fire—the ultimate destination of judgment prepared for the devil and his angels (Matthew 25:41).

Notable truths:

- The Beast and the False Prophet are still there—They were cast into the Lake of Fire a thousand years earlier in Revelation 19:20. This directly refutes the doctrine of annihilation—the belief that the wicked cease to exist after judgment. Their ongoing torment proves that hell is eternal.
- "Tormented day and night forever and ever"—The Greek phrase "*eis tous aionas ton ainonon*" is used consistently to describe eternal duration—the same phrase applied to God's eternal nature (Revelation 4:9–10, 11:15). It implies unending, conscious punishment.
- No parole. No escape. No rest. This is the final judgment for Satan—the great deceiver of humanity, the enemy of God's people, and the corrupter of nations. His influence ends, but his punishment continues eternally.
- Justice is fulfilled—God's justice is not merely corrective; it is also retributive. The same enemy who sought to destroy God's creation is now completely and eternally defeated. He never rises again. The Lake of Fire is not symbolic—it is the final reality for those who rebel against the Most High.

OLD TESTAMENT FORESHADOWS REVELATION:

You have defiled your sanctuaries by the multitude of your iniquities, by the iniquity of your traffic; therefore will I bring forth a fire from the midst of you, it shall devour you, and I will bring you to ashes upon the earth in the sight of all them that behold you. And they that know you among the people shall be astonished at you: you shalt be a terror, and never shalt you be any more. (Ezekiel 28:18–19)

Though addressed to the "King of Tyre," the chapter is often seen as referring to Satan behind the earthly ruler—similar to how Revelation layers symbolic and literal meanings. Like Revelation 20:10, this passage speaks of fire as the means of God's judgment. While Ezekiel's wording emphasizes shame and annihilation-like imagery—"never shalt you be any more"—Revelation clarifies that the punishment is not annihilation, but eternal torment. The Ezekiel passage thus foreshadows the severity and finality of God's judgment on Satan.

THE REVELATION OF JESUS CHRIST REVEALS:

20:11 And I saw a Great White Throne, and Him that sat on it, from whose face the earth and the heaven fled away; and there was found no place for them.

This powerful verse marks the beginning of what is known as the Great White Throne Judgment—the final courtroom of divine justice (Daniel 7:9–10). John the Revelator opens this passage with a striking vision: a "Great White Throne"—

"great" in power and authority, "white" in purity and righteousness. The One seated on it is none other than Christ Himself, as affirmed in John 5:22: "For the Father judges no man, but has committed all judgment unto the Son."

What makes this scene terrifying is not only the judgment itself but the reaction of creation: "the earth and the heaven fled away." This echoes 2 Peter 3:10–12, which prophesies the dissolution of the current heavens and earth by fire. In the face of absolute holiness and perfect justice, the material universe as we know it cannot stand. There is no place left to hide. No appeal. No excuse. Just the unfiltered presence of Divine Judgment.

> But the Day of the Lord will come as a thief in the night; in the which the heavens shall pass away with a great noise, and the elements shall melt with fervent heat, the earth also and the works that are therein shall be burned up. Seeing then that all these things shall be dissolved, what manner of persons ought you to be in all holy conversation and godliness. Looking for and hastening unto the coming of the Day of God, wherein the heavens being on fire shall be dissolved, and the elements shall melt with fervent heat? (2 Peter 3:10–12)

This is not the Bema Seat Judgment for believers (2 Corinthians 5:10). That occurs earlier and is a judgment of rewards. This is the judgment of the unsaved dead—those who rejected Christ, those who were never born again.

The phrase "there was found no place for them" is haunting. It implies complete exclusion—no mercy remains. These souls have nowhere left to go except toward the judgment that leads to the second death. Heaven is closed to them, earth has fled, and eternity stretches ahead with only one destination: the Lake of Fire.

This verse introduces the most solemn moment in human history. It confirms that God's justice is final, His verdicts unchallengeable, and His holiness unapproachable by the unredeemed.

OLD TESTAMENT FORESHADOWS REVELATION:

> Of old have You laid the foundation of the earth: and the heavens are the work of Your hands. They shall perish, but You shalt endure: yea, all of them shall wax old like a garment; as a vesture shalt You change them, and they shall be changed. (Psalm 102:25–26)

Revelation 20:11 says "the earth and the heaven fled away; and there was found no place for them," describing their removal before final judgment. Psalm 102:25–26 prophesies the perishing and transformation of the heavens and the earth—clearly indicating their temporary nature in contrast to the eternal nature of God. Both passages point toward cosmic upheaval preceding the final age— the Millennial Kingdom Age—of judgment and restoration.

———◆◆◆———

Irene furrowed her brow, eyes scanning the passage.

"Ann . . . looking at Revelation 20:11–15, I'm wondering—verses 12 through 15, the Great White Throne Judgment—are those almost like a separate scene? Like an interlude between verse 11, where heaven and earth flee, and Revelation 21:1, where the new heaven and new earth appear?"

I nodded slowly. "Yes, that's exactly how many Bible scholars understand it. Revelation 20:12–15 is often seen as a distinct judicial moment—a kind of solemn pause in the divine timeline. It's as if the courtroom of eternity opens up after the old creation vanishes in verse 11, and just before the new creation is unveiled in Revelation 21."

Irene leaned in, her voice hushed. "So you're saying there's a gap in reality between the old and the new . . . and in that gap, the final judgment takes place?"

I nodded. "Exactly. Revelation 20:11 says the earth and the heaven fled from His presence—meaning they're no longer the backdrop for what happens next. It's as if the entire created order is rolled away to make room for this divine courtroom. The old creation is gone—but the new hasn't begun yet. What remains is pure, eternal justice."

Irene's brow furrowed. "So then where exactly does the judgment take place? If there's no earth or heaven, what's the setting?"

I answered gently. "It's often understood as a kind of cosmic courtroom—outside time and space as we know it. The old creation has fled, and the new one hasn't appeared yet. In that in-between moment, God deals with sin once and for all. That's what makes the Great White Throne Judgment so weighty. It doesn't take place on earth. It's not in heaven. It's in the unfiltered presence of God alone."

Irene leaned in, her voice hushed with intensity. "Okay . . . but here's my big question—where are *we*? I mean, if we're glorified saints and both earth and heaven are gone, where are *we* during the Great White Throne Judgment?"

I smiled gently. "I love that question—and honestly, it's one a lot of believers ask. First, remember this: the Great White Throne Judgment isn't for us. That moment is reserved for the wicked dead—those who rejected Christ."

Irene nodded slowly, her brow still furrowed. "Right. So . . . we're not there?"

I shook my head with gentle reassurance. "Exactly. Romans 8:1 couldn't be clearer: 'There is therefore now no condemnation for those who are in Christ Jesus.' That means we won't be in trial—not as the judged, and not even as the jury. We're with Christ, fully secure, beyond judgment."

Irene's eyes softened. "So then where are we, physically? I mean, if the old heaven and earth are gone?"

I smiled. "Most scholars believe we're either in what Paul described as the third heaven—the very presence of God—or perhaps in a transcendent realm that exists outside our normal understanding of time and space. We're not suspended in limbo—we're with the Lord. And during that final moment of judgment, our role is simply to rest in His victory."

Irene's voice was hushed with wonder. "Wow. So since we'll have glorified bodies like Jesus did after His resurrection, we're not bound by earth, space, or even time anymore?"

I smiled, nodding. "Exactly. Think about how Jesus, after His resurrection, could suddenly appear in locked rooms, walk alongside disciples without being recognized, and then vanish or ascend into the clouds. That wasn't metaphor—that was *preview*. Our glorified bodies will be like His—physical yet not limited, eternal yet fully human."

Irene's eyes widened. "So we'll be alive and free—completely unhindered."

I nodded again. "Fully alive. Fully free. We'll be with Christ, beyond the reach of judgment or decay. While we may *witness* the Great White Throne Judgment as part of the heavenly host, we won't be part of it."

Irene exhaled slowly, her voice solemn. "That makes sense. So when the books are opened and the dead are judged, it's really the final declaration of God's justice on all who rejected His offer of grace."

I nodded, my voice soft but resolute. "That's exactly it. It's not a trial with deliberation—it's a verdict. Every deed, every rejection, every opportunity ignored—it's all accounted for. No one at the Great White Throne can claim ignorance or innocence. It's the righteous conclusion of God's longsuffering mercy."

Irene sat in silence, absorbing the weight of it. "And after that?"

I smiled gently. "After that comes glory. Revelation 21 begins with the most breathtaking hope: a new heaven and a new earth. The old order of things—the curse, sorrow, pain, death—is gone. Eternity begins. No more sin. No more tears. Just the fullness of God's presence—and the restoration of all things."

Irene's voice was hushed with reverence. "Wow. So Revelation 20:12–15 is its own event—a final, eternal declaration that every soul matters, and that every decision about Christ has everlasting consequence."

I nodded, the weight of it settling between us.

"Exactly, Irene. Those verses form a solemn and standalone moment—Revelation's great reckoning. It's a deliberate pause in time, a cosmic courtroom outside of space and history where God delivers final justice. It's the last word on sin, rebellion, and unbelief—before Revelation 21 unveils the eternal order."

"Amen and Amen," Irene said.

Irene leaned forward, eyes wide.

"So, Ann . . . looking at Revelation 20:11 again, it really startled me when it said, 'the earth and the heaven fled away; and there was found no place for them.' What does that even mean? Does it mean the whole world is destroyed before judgment?"

I nodded thoughtfully. "That's a great question, Irene. And you're right to pause there—it's one of the most dramatic, sobering verses in all of Scripture. Most Bible scholars agree this isn't symbolic. It's describing a literal event: the dissolution of the current heaven and earth. In that moment, creation as we know it vanishes—making way for the final judgment and the new creation to follow."

Irene's eyes widened. "Wait—so the whole earth and sky . . . gone? Just like that?"

I nodded, my voice solemn. "Yes. Revelation 20:11 describes something far greater than natural disaster or symbolic language. Many Bible scholars believe it's a moment of cosmic 'uncreation.' The present heaven and earth aren't just destroyed—they flee from the face of God. They're erased to make way for something entirely new. And it's distinct from the judgments during the Tribulation. This is even bigger—this is the end of the old order of creation itself."

Irene leaned forward, brows furrowed. "That sounds a lot like 2 Peter 3:10, right?"

I nodded. "Exactly. Peter describes the same cataclysmic event. In 2 Peter 3:10–14, he says:"

> But the *Day of the Lord* will come as a thief in the night; in the which the heavens shall pass away with a great noise, and the elements shall melt with fervent heat, the earth also and the works that are therein shall be burned up. Seeing then that all these things shall be dissolved, what manner of persons ought you to be in all holy conversation and godliness. Looking for and hastening unto the coming of the *Day of God*, wherein the heavens begin on fire shall be dissolved, and the elements shall melt with fervent heat? Nevertheless we, according to His promise, look for new heavens and a new earth, wherein dwells righteousness. Wherefore, beloved, seeing that you look for such things, be diligent that you may be found of him in peace, without spot, and blameless. (2 Peter 3:10–14)

"It's not poetic metaphor, Irene—it's prophetic certainty. God will dissolve this present creation down to its atomic structure. The 'heavens'—meaning the first and second heavens, our atmosphere and the cosmos—will be completely burned up. But the third heaven, the place where God dwells, remains untouched. That eternal realm is not part of the created order—it's the dwelling of the uncreated God."

Irene's eyes widened. "That phrase 'fled away' almost sounds like even creation itself doesn't want to stand before God."

I nodded slowly. "That's a powerful way to see it. It's as if the old, cursed creation recoils in the presence of absolute holiness. There's nowhere left for the fallen world to hide when the full weight of divine justice arrives. God removes every trace of the old order before the final judgment unfolds. It's like heaven's courtroom requires a cleansed, uncontaminated space—a blank slate—before the eternal verdict is pronounced on the wicked dead."

Irene leaned in, brows furrowed. "That lines up with what the prophets foresaw too. Didn't they say the *Day of the Lord* would be a time of darkness and judgment?"

I nodded, my tone growing sober. "Exactly. Joel, Isaiah, Zephaniah—they all spoke of the *Day of the Lord* as a time of deep darkness, trembling, and divine reckoning. And the apostle Peter connects that prophetic thread to the ultimate conclusion of time. The *Day of the Lord* is not just about judgment in the Tribulation—though that's part of it, like Revelation 6:17 says: 'the great day of His wrath has come, and who is able to stand?' But it culminates again after the Millennium in Revelation 20:11–15. That's the final wave—when sin is dealt with permanently and personally."

Irene tilted her head. "I always thought the *Day of the Lord* and the *Day of God* were the same thing. But they're not?"

I shook my head gently. "Not quite. The *Day of the Lord* is God's dramatic intervention in human history—His judgment against sin and the cleansing of creation. It includes events like the Tribulation, the Second Coming, and even the final judgment after the Millennium."

I paused, letting the weight of it settle before continuing.

"But the *Day of God* points to what comes after. It's the eternal state—the moment everything is fully renewed. No more death. No more sin. Satan is gone. It's when time gives way to eternity, and as Paul says in 1 Corinthians 15:28, 'God will be all in all.' That's the glorious beginning of forever."

Irene's voice was quiet. "So the Great White Throne Judgment happens *after* the earth and sky flee—but *before* the new heaven and new earth are created?"

I nodded solemnly. "Yes. And that timing is powerful. It means there's no place left to hide. Revelation 20:11 doesn't use poetic imagery—it's a literal, sobering truth. When it says, 'there was found no place for them,' it underscores this: everything familiar—every refuge—is gone. Creation itself flees before God's holiness."

I paused, letting the weight of the words linger. "There's no courtroom on earth, no scenery in the sky—only the throne of God and every soul, standing exposed before Him. It's the final reckoning. Every excuse is silenced. Every secret is seen. It's the ultimate moment of divine justice."

Irene's voice dropped to a whisper. "And who's sitting on that throne?"

"Jesus," I said. "John 5:22 says, 'The Father judges no one, but has given all judgment to the Son.' Jesus is uniquely qualified—He's both the Son of God and the Son of Man. He walked among us, bore our sin, rose from the dead, and now is seated as the righteous Judge over creation. That's why the Father has entrusted all judgment to Him."

I paused. "It's the final moment of accountability. And what makes it so staggering is this: every person standing before Him once had the chance to receive His mercy. He's not just Judge—He's the One who died to save them."

Irene's voice trembled. "That hits hard. I mean, we usually talk about Jesus as Savior, Redeemer, and Friend—but here, He's the Judge. There's no second chance at this point, is there?"

I shook my head solemnly. "No. This is the second resurrection—the resurrection of the unbelieving dead. They're not raised to receive reward, but to face judgment. It's the final reckoning."

I paused, letting the weight of it sink in. "That's why Revelation 20 is so sobering. Verse 11 isn't just a transitional moment—it's the line between time and eternity. The end of sin, death, and rebellion. But also . . . the beginning of final separation. Once that throne is revealed, there's no turning back."

Irene leaned forward, eyes scanning her open Bible.

"And then Revelation 21:1 says, 'I saw a new heaven and a new earth: for the first heaven and the first earth were passed away.' So that confirms it, doesn't it? The old creation is gone before the new one appears."

I nodded with quiet certainty. "Exactly. God doesn't patch up the old world— He replaces it completely. Revelation 20:11 is the turning point. It marks the end of one age—the Millennial Kingdom—and the dawn of another—the Eternal Kingdom. The old is passed away. The new has come."

Irene's voice dropped to a whisper. "Wow. It gives new weight to that phrase, 'heaven and earth shall pass away.' That's not just poetic—it's literal."

I nodded. "Exactly. It's not metaphor—it's the reality of a holy God cleansing everything that was tainted by sin. If even the heavens and earth flee from His presence, what hope does unrepentant sin have? This is the moment Paul spoke of—when every knee bows, and every tongue confesses that Jesus Christ is Lord."

Irene whispered, her eyes wide.

"So we either bow now in love . . . or then in fear."

I nodded slowly. "Exactly. That's the heart of grace—Jesus invites us to bow now, freely, lovingly. Because once that throne is set, and the earth and heaven are gone, all that remains is the Book of Life . . . and whether your name is written in it."

THE REVELATION OF JESUS CHRIST REVEALS:

20:12 And I saw the dead, small and great, stand before God; and the books were opened: and another book was opened, which is the Book of Life: and the dead were judged out of those things which were written in the books, according to their works.

This is one of the most sobering verses in all of Scripture—the unveiling of the Great White Throne Judgment, where no believer is present, only the unsaved dead from all of human history. Rank, wealth, status, or obscurity makes no difference—both "small and great" stand equally before God.

"And the books were opened." This phrase reveals a heavenly record. Plural "books" refer to the detailed documentation of every individual's life—their thoughts, words, deeds, motives, even secret sins. These are the divine audit logs. Jesus said in Matthew 12:36 that people will give account for every idle word. Ecclesiastes 12:14 affirms that "God will bring every deed into judgment, including every hidden thing."

"And another book was opened, which is the Book of Life." The Book of Life is the singular book of the redeemed. Those not found written in this book (Revelation 20:15) will be cast into the Lake of Fire. This confirms that salvation is by grace, not works. If your name is in this Book, your sins were judged at the Cross—you will not face this judgment.

"And the dead were judged out of those things which were written in the books, according to their works." Their works do not determine whether they're saved, but rather the degree of their punishment. Jesus said in Luke 12:47–48 that some will receive "many stripes," others "few"—indicating levels of accountability. In other words, works can mitigate punishment, but never save.

The word "dead" appears seven times in verses 12–14—emphasizing that these are spiritually dead souls, separated from God, now standing in resurrected bodies before the Judge. This is the second resurrection (Revelation 20:5)—the resurrection unto damnation (John 5:29).

This is not a trial to determine guilt—guilt is assumed. It's a sentencing hearing. The only way to avoid this judgment is through Jesus Christ. If your name is not written in the Book of Life, you face this judgment alone.

Before God ushers in the new heaven and the new earth (Revelation 21), He must finally and fully deal with sin. The Great White Throne Judgment is that final act of divine justice. But here's the good news:

If any man sin, we have an Advocate with the Father, Jesus Christ the righteous. (1 John 2:1)

OLD TESTAMENT FORESHADOWS REVELATION:

For God shall bring every work into judgment, with every secret thing, whether it be good, or whether it be evil. (Ecclesiastes 12:14)

"Every work into judgment" matches Revelation 20:12 where the dead are judged "according to their works." "Every secret thing" aligns with the idea that nothing escapes God's books—He sees all, and every hidden thing will be accounted for. It reflects the moral and eternal accountability that Revelation 20:12 describes so vividly. This verse reinforces the biblical truth that God's final judgment is thorough, fair, and absolute—nothing is overlooked, and every deed will be weighed. It's a fitting Old Testament lens for viewing the Great White Throne Judgment.

THE REVELATION OF JESUS CHRIST REVEALS:

[20:13] And the sea gave up the dead which were in it; and Death and Hell delivered up the dead which were in them: and they were judged every man according to their works.

This verse describes the moment all remaining dead—those who were never part of the first resurrection—are brought forth to stand before the Great White Throne of Judgment. These are not believers. These are the spiritually lost—those who rejected God's grace. This is the second resurrection—the resurrection of condemnation (John 5:29).

"And the sea gave up the dead which were in it." This detail shows us that no one is forgotten. Whether a person died in a shipwreck, was cremated, lost at sea, or buried in the most obscure place on earth—God will reassemble every molecule of every person. As Creator, He knows their DNA, their soul, and their record. The God who formed Adam from the dust can reassemble every life form ever created. All will rise and be judged. There will be nowhere to hide. There is no escape from this final reckoning.

"And Death and Hell delivered up the dead which were in them." This refers to the intermediate state—the holding cell, if you will, of the spiritually lost. "Death" speaks of the grave, and "Hell" (Greek: *Hades*) speaks of the place of torment where souls are kept until judgment. It's not the final hell yet—that's the Lake of Fire. This is the holding cell, and it's being emptied for court.

"And they were judged every man according to their works." Let this sink in: they were judged by works—not by grace. At this point, there is no blood of Jesus, no mercy, no Cross, no intercessor, no hope. Only the cold record of what they did. Every deed, word, motive, thought—it's all recorded in God's books (Ecclesiastes 12:14; Matthew 12:36). The standard? Perfection.

And no one can meet it.

This judgment is inescapable and eternal. There is no appeal. No second chance. No purgatory. No reincarnation. This is not a courtroom—it's a sentencing. The books will be opened. The facts will be laid bare. The verdict is final. But here's the hope: no Jew or Christian will be here. Those who put their faith in Jesus Christ are already judged at Calvary. Their names are written in the Lamb's Book of Life, and their sins are remembered no more (Hebrews 8:12).

Bottom line? If you don't know Jesus, this verse should fill you with urgency. The time to repent is now—because this judgment is final.

OLD TESTAMENT FORESHADOWS REVELATION:

If I ascend up into heaven, You are there: if I make my bed in hell, behold, You are there. (Psalm 139:8)

Psalm 139:8 reveals that no place, not even the depths of Sheol (translated here as hell), is beyond God's reach. This concept undergirds Revelation 20:13's dramatic truth: even Death and Hell (Sheol/Hades) must yield the dead to stand before God's throne. David's psalm affirms that all are known by God, no matter where they are. Revelation shows the moment of reckoning for those who once hid in death or the sea.

THE REVELATION OF JESUS CHRIST REVEALS:

20:14 And Death and Hell were cast into the Lake of Fire. This is the second death.

This verse marks one of the most final and sobering declarations in all of Scripture: death itself dies. Here, "death" and "hell" (Greek: *Hades*; Hebrew equivalent: *Sheol*) are personified and then destroyed. This signals the complete and irreversible end of sin's dominion and the final defeat of every enemy of God.

The "Lake of Fire" is introduced in Revelation as the final, eternal place judgment—what Jesus often referred to as Gehenna (Matthew 5:22, 10:28; Mark 9:43–48). It differs from Hades, which is a temporary holding place for the souls of the unsaved dead. At this point in the prophetic timeline, even Hades has fulfilled its purpose and is discarded forever.

The "second death" stands in contrast to the first death, which is physical. All humans die once (Hebrews 9:27), but those who reject Christ experience this second, eternal separation from God. It is called "death," but it is not annihilation. Instead, it is conscious, eternal torment—forever cut off from the presence and mercy of God. This is the death of death itself—a phrase made famous by theologian John Owen. With Death and Hell thrown into the Lake of Fire, the last enemy is fully and finally destroyed (1 Corinthians 15:26). There will be no more dying, no more graves, no more fear. This verse is the cosmic reset—ushering in eternity where God reigns and all enemies are subdued.

OLD TESTAMENT FORESHADOWS REVELATION:

Like sheep they are laid in the grave; death shall feed on them; and the upright shall have dominion over them in the morning; and their beauty shall consume in the grave from their dwelling. (Psalm 49:14)

Psalm 49:14 presents a poetic but sobering image of death's temporary reign—the grave (Sheol) consumes the wicked, but it's not the end. The righteous will rise and rule "in the morning," symbolizing resurrection and final dominion. This anticipates the abolition of death's dominion and the final triumph of God's justice, which we see completed in Revelation 20:14 when Death and Hell are destroyed forever in the Lake of Fire—the second death. This psalm echoes the contrast between temporary judgment and eternal outcome.

THE REVELATION OF JESUS CHRIST REVEALS:

[20:15] And whosoever was not found written in the Book of Life was cast into the Lake of Fire.

This verse delivers the final, sobering conclusion of the Great White Throne Judgment. After all the books have been opened, after every thought, deed, and motive has been laid bare, there remains only one deciding factor: Is your name in the Book of Life?

Scripture refers to this sacred record in several places:

- Exodus 32:32–33—Moses pleads for Israel, saying, "Blot me out of your book."
- Psalm 69:28—The wicked are blotted out of the book of the living.
- Philippians 4:3—Paul mentions fellow laborers "whose names are in the Book of Life."
- Revelation 13:8, 17:8, 21:27—Only those written in the Lamb's Book of Life will escape judgment and enter the New Jerusalem.

It is Christ's Book. Those whose names are written in it are those who have been redeemed by the blood of the Lamb (Revelation 13:8). This is not about our merit, but about our relationship with Jesus.

Although the books of deeds are opened (Revelation 20:12), and every action is evaluated, it is not our works that save us. Works confirm the sentence, but it is the absence of one's name in the Book of Life that determines eternal separation from God. If you rely on your works, you are judged by them. And no one can stand justified before a holy God based on human effort (Romans 3:20; Titus 3:5).

This is the final destination of all who rejected Christ. It is the "second death" (Revelation 20:14), eternal separation from God in conscious torment—originally prepared for the devil and his angels (Matthew 25:41).

As noted, Hades (temporary hell) and Death (the grave) are emptied and absorbed into this eternal reality. It is the ultimate consolidation of judgment. All who stood at the Great White Throne Judgment and were not found in the Book of Life are cast into this place. No appeals. No escape.

Some ask, "Why would a loving God send anyone to hell?" The answer is found in John 3:16–21: God doesn't send people to hell—they choose it by rejecting the only provision for salvation: Jesus Christ. Hell is not just a consequence; it is a witness to God's righteousness, His justice, and man's responsibility. If we saw sin the way God sees sin, we would understand why a place like hell must exist.

This verse is a divine warning and a gracious call. It reminds us that eternal judgment is real, and that God keeps perfect records. But it also offers hope: If you know Jesus, your name is written in the Lamb's Book of Life. If you don't, now is the time to come to Him—not with excuses, but with repentance and faith. Because when you stand before the throne, again, it's not what you know—it's who you know.

OLD TESTAMENT FORESHADOWS REVELATION:

Then they that feared the LORD spoke often one to another: and the LORD listened, and heard it, and a book of remembrance was written before Him for them that feared the LORD, and that thought upon His name. (Malachi 3:16)

"A Book of Remembrance" in Malachi reflects God's careful recordkeeping of those who belong to Him, just as Revelation 20:15 refers to the Book of Life. Those in Malachi's "book" are spared and treasured, while in Revelation, those not found in the Book of Life are cast into the Lake of Fire. This supports the biblical theme of divine records that testify to one's eternal fate—whether for reward or judgment.

SUMMARY OF REVELATION 20

Revelation 20 is a monumental chapter that unveils the final stages of God's redemptive plan, highlighting Christ's 1,000-year reign and the ultimate judgment of evil. The chapter begins with an angel descending from heaven, binding Satan with a great chain and casting him into the bottomless pit for a thousand years—preventing him from deceiving the nations during this time (Revelation 20:1–3).

Next, John sees thrones and those seated upon them, given authority to judge. He sees the souls of the Old Testament saints and the souls of the Tribulation martyrs—those who refused the mark of the beast—resurrected to reign with Christ for 1,000 years (Revelation 20:4). This is called the first resurrection, and those who partake in it are declared blessed and holy, immune to the second death

(Revelation 20:5–6). This Millennium marks a time of peace, justice, and global righteousness under Christ's literal rule on earth.

When the thousand years are completed, Satan is released and deceives the nations once more, gathering them for battle—referred to as Gog and Magog—against the saints and the beloved city (Revelation 20:7–8). But fire comes down from heaven and devours them, and Satan is cast into the Lake of Fire, joining the Antichrist and the False Prophet in eternal torment (Revelation 20:9–10).

The final and sobering scene is the Great White Throne Judgment. John sees heaven and earth flee from the presence of Him who sits on the throne (Revelation 20:11). The dead, great and small, stand before God. Books are opened, including the Book of Life, and all are judged according to their works (Revelation 20:12). Even the sea, Death, and Hades give up their dead. Then, Death and Hades themselves are cast into the Lake of Fire—this is the second death (Revelation 20:13–14). Finally, anyone not found written in the Book of Life is also cast into the Lake of Fire (Revelation 20:15).

KEY TAKEAWAYS

- The binding of Satan—Satan is imprisoned for 1,000 years to allow Christ's reign without deception.
- The First Resurrection—A resurrection unto life for the righteous who will never face the second death.
- The Millennial Kingdom—Believers reign with Christ in a literal kingdom marked by peace and righteousness.
- The final rebellion—Even after 1,000 years of perfection, humanity's sin nature is revealed once more.
- The Lake of Fire—Satan, the Antichrist, the False Prophet, and all unbelievers face eternal separation from God.
- The Great White Throne Judgment—A solemn judgment for the unbelieving dead, judged by their works.
- The Book of Life—Only those whose names are written in the Lamb's Book of Life escape the second death.

Revelation 20 reminds us of the sovereignty of Christ, the certainty of final justice, and the necessity of redemption. It reveals that even a perfect environment cannot change the human heart—only Christ can. This chapter stands as both a comfort to the faithful and a warning to the rebellious, urging us to be ready for the day when God will make all things new. The One who reigns for a thousand years is the same One who will judge all the earth with righteousness.

Chapter 19

Revelation 21: The New Heaven, New Earth, and New Jerusalem

THE END THAT BEGINS EVERYTHING—Revelation 21 marks one of the most breathtaking turning points in all of Scripture—the moment where time dissolves into eternity. After the sobering finality of the Great White Throne Judgment in Revelation 20, the apostle John is given a vision so radiant, so saturated with majesty, that human language strains to describe it: a new heaven and a new earth, untouched by sin, sorrow, or death. This is not a cosmetic renovation, but a completely new creation—the full realization of God's promise to "make all things new" (Revelation 21:5).

To appreciate the glory of Revelation 21, we must first look back. Revelation 19 revealed the victorious return of Christ at Armageddon. Revelation 20 walked us through His 1,000-year reign—the Millennial Kingdom—followed by Satan's final rebellion, his eternal judgment in the Lake of Fire, and the chilling scene of the Great White Throne. By the end of Revelation 20, every unredeemed soul has faced divine justice, and death itself has been destroyed. The drama of redemptive history has reached its climax.

Now, the spotlight shifts. With sin judged, Satan defeated, and the old creation dismantled, God unveils a new reality—a place where righteousness dwells (2 Peter 3:13). The darkest night has ended, and Revelation 21 opens like a sunrise breaking over a brand-new world.

> Nevertheless we, according to His promise, look for new heavens and a new
> earth, wherein dwells righteousness. (2 Peter 3:13)

The Sea Is No More: Symbolism and Substance

The detail in Revelation 21:1—"there was no more sea" may seem small, but it
carries profound symbolic weight. In ancient Jewish thought, the sea often
represented chaos, evil, and separation. It was the realm of the unknown and the
uncontrollable. Its removal signals more than a geographical change; it represents
the eradication of all that divides and destabilizes. The fear, danger, and distance
once associated with the sea are forever gone. What remains is unbroken peace
and unity—God's creation in perfect order.

From Final Judgment to Eternal Glory

Revelation 21 follows the fire, fury, and final reckoning of Revelation 20 like
dawn after the longest night. Just moments earlier in the vision, John witnessed
the most sobering courtroom in history—the Great What Throne—where the
Book of Life was opened, and every soul not found in it faced eternal separation
from God.

But now, a divine reversal. The cosmos turns a page. Sin has been dealt with.
The curse has been lifted. Satan is gone. And God, who once walked with man in
Eden, now tabernacles with His people—forever.

The Long-Awaited City

John's vision doesn't merely reveal a new earth—it presents a new city. The New
Jerusalem, radiant with God's glory, descends from heaven like a bride adorned
for her husband (Revelation 21:2). This is not a metaphor, but a literal, eternal
reality—a city built on apostolic foundations, guarded by gates named after
Israel's tribes, and welcoming to all nations.

It is the fulfillment of a promise made long ago. Abraham searched for this
city—"whose architect and builder is God" (Hebrews 11:10). The faithful of
every generation longed for it. And now, at last, the vision becomes reality.

> For he looked for a city which has foundations, whose builder and maker is God.
> (Hebrews 11:10)

Revelation 21 is more than a prophecy; it is the crescendo of redemption, the
inheritance of the saints, and the eternal home of those whose names are written
in the Lamb's Book of Life. It marks the final answer to every tear, every pain,
and every unfulfilled hope. Here, eternity begins—with God's presence, His
purified people, and the perfection of His promise.

A NEW HEAVEN, A NEW EARTH . . . AND NO MORE SEA?

When John opens Revelation 21 with the words, "And I saw a new heaven and a new earth: for the first heaven and the first earth were passed away; and there was no more sea," he isn't speaking in parables or poetry. He's recording a literal transformation of the cosmos. The former creation—scarred by sin, tainted by the curse—is gone. And in its place, something unimaginable: a new universe, untouched by darkness and decay.

The Greek word translated "passed away" is *parerchomai*. It doesn't imply annihilation in the absolute sense, but a transition—one state giving way to another. Think of it not as total destruction, but as a profound and glorious metamorphosis. The older order has served its purpose. The new has come.

And There Was No More Sea

Then comes a striking detail: "and there was no more sea." To modern ears, that may sound disappointing—after all, so many of us cherish oceans, beaches, and the mystery of the deep. But in biblical language, the sea often symbolizes chaos, danger, separation, and death. It was the home of *Leviathan* (Psalm 104:26), the origin of the beast (Revelation 13:1), and the place of restless darkness. In the ancient world, the sea was feared—unpredictable, untamable, a barrier between lands and people.

> There go the ships: there is that Leviathan, whom you have made to play therein.
> (Psalm 104:26)

So what does its absence mean in Revelation 21? It means chaos is gone. Fear is gone. Separation is gone. This is a new world governed by peace, order, and unity. The sea, as the symbol of the old world's turbulence and division, has no place in eternity. God's final creation is one of unbroken wholeness—nothing left to divide us from Him or from each other.

THREE HEAVENS: WHAT EXACTLY GETS MADE NEW?

John says he saw "a new heaven," and to understand what that means, we need to recognize that Scripture speaks of three distinct "heavens."

1. **The First Heaven**—The Atmospheric Heaven.

This is the sky—the visible atmosphere where clouds form, birds fly, and weather takes place. Created in Genesis 1:8, it's part of the physical world that's currently groaning under the weight of sin (Romans 8:22). But it will be made new—refreshed and purified by God's hand. No more storms. No more lightning strikes or tempests. Just crystal skies and beauty untainted.

For we know that the whole creation groans and travails in pain together until now. (Romans 8:22)

2. **The Second Heaven**—The Celestial Realm.

This refers to outer space—the sun, moon, stars, and galaxies. It's the majestic canvas of the cosmos, vast and awe-inspiring. Yet even this realm is not untouched by sin's reach. Ephesian 2:2 calls Satan "the prince of the power of the air," and Ephesians 6:12 reveals that spiritual warfare takes place in the heavenly realms. This second heaven is defiled, but it too will be swept clean—purged of every demonic presence. When God renews the heavens, He will evict darkness from the cosmos once and for all.

The heavens declare the glory of God; and the firmament shows His handywork. (Psalm 19:1)

If the fallen skies still reflect His beauty, imagine how they will shine once restored in perfect righteousness.

3. **The Third Heaven**—God's Dwelling Place.

This is the eternal abode of God, beyond time and space. Paul referred to being "caught up to the third heaven" (2 Corinthians 12:2), a realm distinct from the created heavens. It is the throne room of the Almighty. This heaven is not subject to judgment or re-creation—it is timeless, holy, and unshaken.

I knew a man in Christ above fourteen years ago, (whether in the body, I cannot tell; or whether out of the body, I cannot tell: God knows), such as one caught up to the third heaven. (2 Corinthians 12:2)

And here's the astonishing truth: one day, the third heaven comes down to earth. Revelation 21:3 says, "Behold, the tabernacle of God is with men." The New Jerusalem, descending from heaven, becomes the eternal capital of the new creation—where God dwells with His people face to face.

A NEW EARTH: PARADISE REGAINED

John not only sees a new heaven—he sees a new earth. And just like with the heavens, this isn't an annihilation but a divine transformation. The earth, originally designed to be God's dwelling place with man, is renewed to fulfill that purpose. The curse is reversed. Eden is restored—only better.

This new earth is where righteousness dwells (2 Peter 3:13). It's a world where glorified saints will live forever in glorified bodies, worshiping, reigning, serving, and fellowshipping with God. There will be cities, nations, beauty, purpose, and joy beyond imagination.

This is the home we've been waiting for. Not a cloud in the sky or a ghostly afterlife, but a real, redeemed, resurrected creation. One that satisfies the soul and glorifies the Savior.

A CITY LIKE NO OTHER

The New Jerusalem—heaven comes home. After the new heaven and new earth appear, John's eyes are drawn to something dazzling and definitive. "And I, John, saw the Holy City, New Jerusalem, coming down from God out of heaven, prepared as a bride adorned for her husband" (Revelation 21:2).

This isn't allegory. It isn't a vision of floating clouds or vague spiritual ideals. This is a real city—God's eternal capital, designed for a new creation, descending not just with splendor but with purpose. It is the moment when heaven and earth are no longer divided. God moves in.

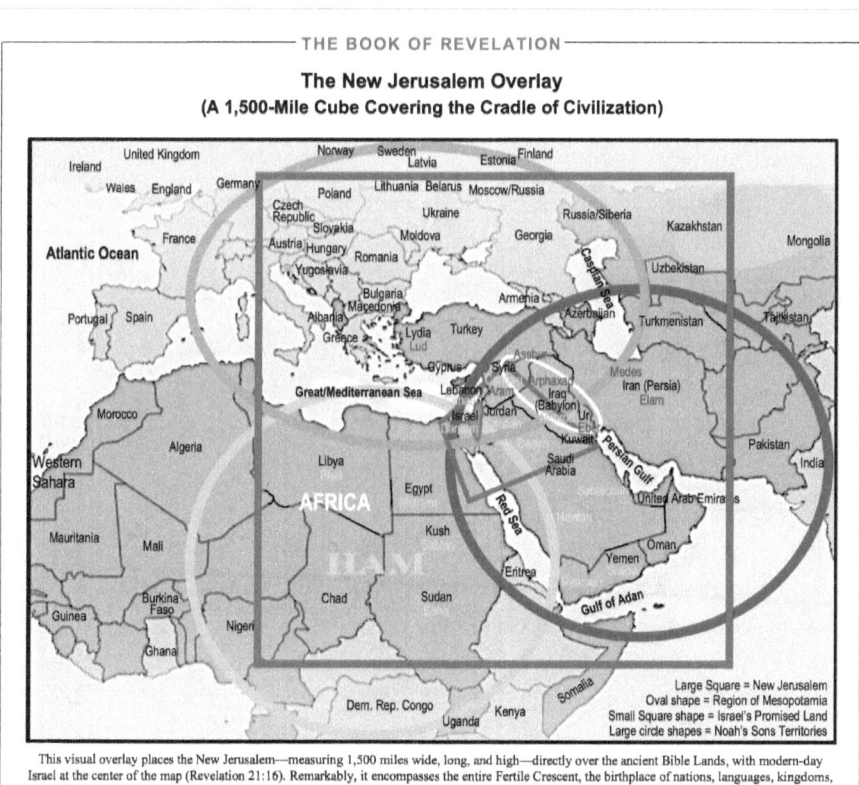

THE BOOK OF REVELATION

The New Jerusalem Overlay
(A 1,500-Mile Cube Covering the Cradle of Civilization)

This visual overlay places the New Jerusalem—measuring 1,500 miles wide, long, and high—directly over the ancient Bible Lands, with modern-day Israel at the center of the map (Revelation 21:16). Remarkably, it encompasses the entire Fertile Crescent, the birthplace of nations, languages, kingdoms, and Scripture. It is here, in this divinely selected region, that God's eternal city will descend—bringing redemption full circle, from Eden to eternity.

The city is not heaven alone—it's heaven made tangible. It is the convergence of two realms: divine glory and redeemed humanity. The tabernacle of God is now with men (Revelation 21:3). No more temple. No more evil. Just the presence of God—face-to-face, forever.

Architectural Wonder: The Shape of the Sacred

John describes the New Jerusalem as a perfect cube, measuring approximately 1,500 miles in length, width, and height (Revelation 21:16). This is a structure beyond comprehension—towering past the edge of earth's atmosphere, if taken literally. But even more than its scale is its shape.

Why a cube? The only other cube in Scripture is the Holy of Holies—the innermost sanctuary of the tabernacle and the temple, where God's presence rested above the mercy seat. In the New Jerusalem, the Holy of Holies expands to become an entire city. Each inch is sacred. Every stone radiates divine glory. The veil is gone. Access is granted.

Unity in Stone: The Foundations and Gates

The city bears names—etched into its very structure:

- Twelve gates, each named after one of the tribes of Israel (Revelation 21:12).
- Twelve foundations, each inscribed with the names of the apostles of the Lamb (Revelation 21:14).

This is not accidental design. This is theology in architecture.

- The gates represent the Old Covenant—the patriarchs, the promises, the journey of Israel.
- The foundations declare the New Covenant—the gospel preached to the nations through the apostles.

Together, they form one dwelling, one people, one redemptive plan. What Paul envisioned in Ephesians 2—where the dividing wall between Jew and Gentile is shattered in Christ—is now carved into the walls of eternity. Salvation was never either/or. It was always both.

Materials of Majesty: Nothing Common Here

The New Jerusalem is made of precious things, each detail echoing divine purpose:

- Gates of pearl—each gate carved from a single pearl (Revelation 21:21). Pearls are formed through irritation, pressure, and time. These gates whisper of the suffering that opened the way: Christ's wounds became our welcome.

- Foundations adorned with jewels (Revelation 21:19–20)—reminiscent of the high priest's breastplate in Exodus, which bore the names of the tribes of Israel. The city's foundation testifies: God keeps His covenant.
- Streets of transparent gold—so pure they shine like glass. In this city, even what we walk on is a reflection of God's unfiltered glory.

This is no utilitarian build. It is worship in structure—beauty that preaches.

Light and Life: The Eden We Were Always Meant For

John goes on to say there is no need for sun or moon in the New Jerusalem, "For the glory of God gives it light, and its lamp is the Lamb" (Revelation 21:23). The original light of Genesis 1 returns—not created light, but the light of the Creator Himself.

And in the very center of the city, flowing from the throne, is the River of Life (Revelation 22:1). On its banks grows the Tree of Life, now accessible once more, its leaves bringing healing to the nations (Revelation 22:2). This is Eden restored—no longer a garden lost, but a kingdom gained. Not just regional, but global and eternal.

The Lamb's Bride and Our Eternal Home

The New Jerusalem is not just a city—it is a bride adorned for her husband (Revelation 21:2). It is God's people made beautiful by grace, and the place where they will dwell with Him forever.

This is the city Abraham longed for—"whose architect and builder is God" (Hebrews 11:10). This is the inheritance of the saints. This is the home we were made fore. No more sorrow. No more separation. Only light, life, and the face of God.

RENOVATION OR ANNIHILATION?

When John writes in Revelation 21:1, "And I saw a new heaven and a new earth: for the first heaven and the first earth were passed away," the question naturally follows: Does this mean creation is obliterated? Or is it gloriously reborn? The answer matters—because it shapes our hope.

Not Erased, But Transformed

The language of Scripture consistently points toward renovation, not annihilation. The Greek word translated "passed away" in Revelation 21:1 is *parerchomai*. It doesn't mean obliteration. It means transition. Think of it like a ship sailing over the horizon—it passes from one place to another. It's not gone; it's simply no longer what it was. Jesus used this very word in Matthew 24:35:

> Heaven and earth shall pass away, but My words shall not pass away. (Matthew 24:35)

His point wasn't about destruction, but permanence—His words endure beyond a world that is changing form. The same transformation imagery shows up in 2 Peter 3:10–13. Peter says the elements will "melt with fervent heat." But this isn't cosmic evaporation—it's refinement. Just as gold is purified in fire, the created order will be purged and perfected.

> But the *Day of the Lord* will come as a thief in the night; in the which the heavens shall pass away with a great noise, and the elements shall melt with fervent heat, the earth also and the works that are therein shall be burned up. Seeing then that all these things shall be dissolved, what manner of persons ought you to be in all holy conversation and godliness. Looking for and hastening unto the coming of the *Day of God*, wherein the heavens begin on fire shall be dissolved, and the elements shall melt with fervent heat? Nevertheless we, according to His promise, look for new heavens and a new earth, wherein dwells righteousness. (2 Peter 3:10–13)

Fire Like the Flood—Judgment with Purpose

Peter even gives us a precedent. In 2 Peter 3:6, he compares the coming fiery judgment to the Flood of Noah's day. That Flood devastated the world, but it didn't erase the planet. It cleansed it. Reshaped it. In the same way, the fire to come is not annihilation—it is purification. The cosmos will be judged, yes—but not discarded.

> Whereby the world that then was, being overflowed with water, perished. But the heavens and the earth, which are now, by the same word are kept in store, reserved unto fire against the day of judgment and perdition of ungodly men. (2 Peter 3:6–7)

> Seeing then that all these things shall be dissolved, what manner of persons ought you to be in all holy conversation and godliness. (2 Peter 3:11)

This becomes even clearer in 2 Peter 3:11, where he says the heavens shall be "dissolved." That's not destruction in the modern sense—it's a word that speaks of disassembly and renewal. Like an architect tearing down a ruined facade to rebuild a better structure, God is preparing creation for eternity.

Greek Words, Eternal Truths

To understand this cosmic renovation, it helps to note that the New Testament uses three different Greek words for "world."

1. **Ge**—The physical earth or land. This is the ground beneath our feet—the soil, the mountains, the terrain.

2. **Kosmos**—The ordered system, often the world's moral or societal structure. This is where we get "cosmos."

3. **Aion**—An age or era of time. When Jesus says, "I am with you always, even unto the end of the world" (Matthew 28:20), He's using aion, meaning the end of a time period, not the destruction of the globe.

The point? Scripture is precise. When it speaks of the *world passing away*, it often means an age ending, a system being replaced, or a form being transformed—not obliteration.

Resurrection: The Model for Renewal

The clearest example of this principle is our own resurrection. Paul says in 1 Corinthians 15:52, "We shall be changed." Not replaced. Changed. The same body—transformed. In 2 Corinthians 5:1, Paul calls our mortal bodies a "tent," which will be replaced by a heavenly "building." Not annihilated—but upgraded.

And just as our bodies will be raised incorruptible, so too the earth and heavens will be changed—not discarded as junk, but reborn in glory.

The Earth Is Your Inheritance

Jesus said, "The meek shall inherit the earth" (Matthew 5:5). Psalm 37:11 echoes it. This isn't spiritual abstraction. It's a promise.

Blessed are the meek: for they shall inherit the earth. (Matthew 5:5)

But the meek shall inherit the earth; and shall delight themselves in the abundance of peace. (Psalm 37:11)

If the earth is utterly annihilated, what is left to inherit? The logic is inescapable: The earth will endure—but transformed, purified, and made worthy of the saints. God isn't throwing away His creation. He's redeeming it. The same Creator who called it "very good" in Genesis 1 is not preparing it for eternal perfection in Revelation 21.

A World Purged, Prepared, and Made Perfect

So when John writes that the first heaven and earth "passed away," he's describing a sweeping, cosmic transition—from a sin-stained world to one fit for God's dwelling.

- Not a blank slate, but a renewed creation.

- Not annihilation, but transfiguration.
- Not the end of the world, but the beginning of forever.

Like our resurrection bodies, the world itself will be cleansed, glorified, and made new. And this newly remade creation will become the eternal home of God and His people. Revelation 21:1 isn't the end. It's the grand reveal of a new beginning—a beginning that will never end.

ETERNITY BEGINS WITH GOD

The final chapter of sin—the first chapter of forever. At the very center of eternity—before the jewels, the gates, or even the new creation—is God Himself. Revelation 21:3–4 delivers the triumphant climax of the entire redemptive narrative: "Behold, the tabernacle of God is with men . . . and God shall wipe away all tears from their eyes."

This is the moment Abraham yearned for—the city "whose architect and builder is God" (Hebrews 11:10). It's the inheritance of the saints. It's the fulfillment of every promise, the consummation of every covenant, the healing of every wound. This is not just the end of time. It is the beginning of eternity. A forever shaped not by chronology—but by the presence of God.

Theological Fulfillment: A Dwelling Made of Glory

Revelation 21 doesn't just describe a place—it reveals a Person. The ultimate reward of the redeemed is not golden streets or jeweled walls, but unbroken communion with God Himself.

The New Jerusalem, described in verses 2 and 10–27, is more than a city—it is a dwelling place. And more than a dwelling—it is a Bride, prepared in beauty, honor, and intimacy. This is not a metaphor floating in mystery. It is heaven come home—God's manifest presence descending to earth.

The tabernacle is no longer behind a curtain. The temple is no longer a building. "God Himself will be with them, and be their God" (Revelation 21:3). This is Eden redeemed. Creation restored. Relationship resurrected.

As Revelation 21 begins, sin is gone. Death is no more. Satan is cast down. The old has passed, and everything is new. And God—not merely nearby, but dwelling among His people—is the crowning joy of it all. Eternity begins not with an event, but with a Person.

A cozy living room with Bibles open, cups of tea steaming, and the sun beginning to set through the window. Irene leans forward, her brows furrowed in curiosity.

"So, Ann," she begins, her voice tinged with wonder, "just to make sure I'm tracking—from where we've been to where we're headed. The Millennium shows us what earth could look like under Christ's rule. And the Eternal Age? That's when heaven and earth finally become one."

I nod, my expression softening.

"Beautifully put. The Millennium is the promise honored. The Eternal Age is the promise fulfilled."

Irene's eyes narrow thoughtfully as she turns another page in her Bible.

"Then what exactly is the difference between the people who live in the New Jerusalem and those who live on the new earth? Scripture paints a picture of perfection—but it feels like there are layers to it."

I smile knowingly, my fingers resting on Revelation 19.

"Oh, absolutely. There are layers. This is one of those breathtaking truths that often gets overlooked. The New Jerusalem is the eternal home of the Bride—those who didn't just believe, but made themselves ready. Not by striving or earning salvation, but by joyfully surrendering and letting Christ live through them."

I tap gently on the page. "Revelation 19:7 says it plainly: 'The Bride has made herself ready.' That readiness wasn't self-made effort—it was love lived out. Obedience flowing from devotion."

Irene leans in closer, her voice hushed in awe.

"So these are the hundredfold believers? The ones raptured before the Tribulation?"

I nod slowly, the warmth in my eyes matching the weight of my words.

"Exactly. They are the raptured Church—the ones who didn't just believe in Jesus, but lived as overcomers. Their obedience wasn't about earning salvation—it was the evidence of it. They chose intimacy over comfort, surrender over self. And in doing so, they bore fruit that brought honor to the Bridegroom."

I glance toward the heavens as if glimpsing what waits beyond the veil.

"These are the ones who dwell in the New Jerusalem—the radiant city descending from heaven, prepared like a Bride adorned for her Husband."

I continued, my voice soft with reverence. "When Jesus said, 'I go to prepare a place for you,' this may well be that very place—the dwelling where the Bride was with Him during the seven years of Tribulation. Hidden in heaven, safe and secure, she remained by His side while wrath was poured out on the earth."

Let not your heart be troubled: you believe in God, believe also in Me. In My Father's house are many mansions (dwelling places): if it were not so, I would have told you. I go to prepare a place for you. And if I go and prepare a place for you, I will come again, and receive you unto Myself; that where I am, there you may be also. And where I go you know, and the way you know. (John 14:1–4)

"And now," I add, "after a thousand years of reigning with Christ during the Millennium among the nations, her eternal home descends—out of the third heaven, onto the newly restored earth."

I paused, letting the weight of the words settle. "It's not just a destination. It's her home. The reward of a love story written before time began."

"That makes so much sense now," Irene said, her eyes wide with wonder. "Our *dwelling place* doesn't change—just its *location* does."

"Beautifully said, Irene," I replied with a smile. "That's the brilliance of God's design. It's the same city Jesus promised. The one the saints of old longed for. The one the Bride has already been dwelling in—hidden with Him. When eternity begins, it simply moves—from heaven to the new earth."

"So we're not waiting for construction," she laughed, "we're just waiting for *move-in* day!"

I laughed with her. "Exactly! And the best part? No packing. No moving truck. Just glorified bodies and eternal joy."

She leaned back with a sigh, her fingers tapping the edge of her Bible. "Hebrews 12:22 . . . John 14:2 . . . Revelation 21:2 . . . it's all connected."

I nodded, my heart full. "It's all *His* story. And we get to live in the very city He designed—where the light never fades, and our Bridegroom is right there with us. Forever."

A pause settles between us, the kind that invites deeper questions.

Irene's brow furrows again, curiosity still dancing in her eyes.

"And what about the others?" she asks softly. "The thirtyfold and sixtyfold you've mentioned before?"

I smiled gently, grateful for her hunger to understand.

"Those who believe in Jesus as the Son of God—and are willing to follow Him—even if they didn't bear the full fruit of transformation in this life . . . they are still His. They're still saved."

I placed a hand over my heart, feeling the weight of grace.

"Jesus is merciful. He honors faith."

"They too will receive glorified bodies," I continued, "but their eternal dwelling will be different. These are the ones who will live on the new earth—not inside the New Jerusalem, but as part of the nations who walk in its light."

I flip to Revelation 21:24 and tap the page with reverence.

"It says, 'The nations of those who are saved shall walk in its light.' They're not the residents of the city itself—but they are welcomed into its radiance."

Irene leans back, pondering. "So the Bride and the guests—both are part of God's family, but their roles differ?"

"Exactly," I say with a nod. "Just like any wedding—there's the Bride, and then there are honored guests."

I pause, then add gently, "God the Father has His covenant people, Israel—His wife. Jesus, the Son, has His Bride—the Church."

"And the redeemed of all ages?" Irene prompts.

"They dwell together—united in glory—each in their appointed place," I reply. "God isn't a respecter of persons, but He *is* a God of order, reward, and preparation. Merit in His Kingdom doesn't come from striving—it comes by grace, through surrender."

Irene's voice drops, almost a whisper. "That's so profound. And the Tribulation? That's the refining fire?"

I nod, the weight of it resting in my chest. "Yes. The Tribulation is not just wrath—it's also mercy. It shakes the earth, but it also wakes the sleepers."

I lean in slightly. "When the hundredfold Bride is raptured, that very event triggers the Tribulation. And in the chaos that follows, multitudes will cry out to Jesus. Many will seal their faith with their blood . . ."

I pause, reverently. ". . . but they will rise. At Christ's Second Coming, they will be resurrected—alongside the faithful saints of the Old Testament—and together, they will reign with Him."

Irene nodded slowly, her voice quiet with conviction. "So our entrance into the marriage of the Lamb isn't about recognition—it's about readiness. Faithfulness. Living a transformed life."

"Amen," I said, the truth settling between us like a warm light. "Our good works aren't the currency of salvation—but they *are* the garments of the Bride. Revelation tells us she's clothed in fine linen—'the righteous acts of the saints.' Not perfection, but fruit. Visible evidence of inward surrender."

Irene's eyes glistened as she whispered, "And one day, we'll see those gates swing open . . ."

I nodded with joy. "Yes—and those whose names are written in the Lamb's Book of Life will enter in. No more waiting. No more veil. Just His presence."

She smiled. "Until then, we keep living in joyful obedience—not to earn His love, but to reflect it."

"Exactly, Irene. We're not just saved *from* something—we're saved *for* something. The new earth will be filled with the redeemed of the Lord—but the Bride? She will dwell with Him, in the city He prepared, in the New Jerusalem . . . face-to-face, forever."

Irene leaned forward, Bible open in her lap, a thoughtful crease on her brow.

"Ann, I was reading Hebrews 12:22 again—"

But you are come unto Mount Zion, and unto the city of the living God, the heavenly Jerusalem, and to an innumerable company of angels. (Hebrews 12:22)

"—and I just had this moment where I thought: wait a second . . . does that mean the angels live in the New Jerusalem too?"

I smiled, warmed by the depth of her question. "That's such a beautiful observation, Irene. And yes—I believe it's absolutely possible."

I tapped the passage gently.

"The phrase 'you are come unto' doesn't just suggest a passing visit—it implies arrival, even residence. And 'an innumerable company of angels'? That's not just a few messengers fluttering in for announcements. That's multitudes—living, serving, worshiping."

I met her gaze with quiet certainty.

"I think you're right. They dwell there. And in that city, they serve the King—side by side with the redeemed."

Irene's eyes lit up with another spark of insight.

"And then my next thought was . . . maybe that explains why the New Jerusalem is 1,500 miles high. Not just wide and long like a regular city. I mean, that's massive! Could it be layered—like dimensions upon dimensions—for glorified saints *and* angelic hosts?"

A grin tugged at the corners of my mouth.

"I love that thought, Irene! Think about what Jesus said in John 14:2: 'In My Father's house are many dwelling places.'"

I paused, letting the gravity settle.

"He wasn't just preparing rooms for us—maybe He was preparing space for the divine administration too. Saints, angels, possibly even other celestial beings we don't yet know. The New Jerusalem isn't just a city. It's a cosmic sanctuary. A throne-room and a home."

She leaned back, awe softening her features.

"It's beyond anything we've ever imagined."

Irene nodded thoughtfully. "I'm starting to see the cube not just as a shape—but as a symbol of completeness. Height, width, depth. Heaven's design for eternal community."

I smiled. "Amen. Whether it's 1,500 miles high to house multitudes of glorified saints and angels—or simply to display the infinite majesty of God—it will be utterly breathtaking."

Irene grinned. "And I'll take a room with a view, please. Preferably near the Tree of Life."

I laughed softly. "You and me both, Irene. I've heard the light there never fades."

Irene leaned forward again, her voice hushed with reverence.

"Now, here's the other thing I've been pondering . . . what about God's wife? Israel. Are *they* included in the city as well? Is it just the Church—the Bride of Christ—or does the faithful remnant of Israel have a place inside those gates?"

I smiled gently, sensing the weight of the question.

"That's a powerful and important question, Irene. And I believe the answer is yes—at least for the faithful remnant, those who are part of the hundredfold. Just like among the Gentiles, not every Israelite will dwell in the city. But those who embraced Jesus as Messiah, who lived in covenant faith and surrender, will."

I flipped to Romans 11 and tapped on the verse.

And so all Israel shall be saved: as it is written, There shall come out of Zion the Deliverer, and shall turn away ungodliness from Jacob. (Romans 11:26)

"Paul says in verse 26, 'And so all Israel will be saved.' But the context here matters—it's about the believing remnant. The ones grafted back in through faith in Christ."

Irene leaned back in her chair, eyes narrowing in thought.

"Ann, I was reading the Parable of the Sower again (Matthew 13:3–9, 18–23; Mark 4:3–9, 13–20; Luke 8:4–8, 11–15)—the part about some bearing fruit thirtyfold, sixtyfold, and a hundredfold—and it struck me. Jesus didn't say that just about Gentiles. He was speaking to Jews. The same standard applies across the board, doesn't it?"

I smiled, nodding. "Exactly. Jesus was Jewish, speaking to a Jewish audience. Before the Cross, there were only Jews. But His words were timeless. That parable wasn't about ethnicity—it was about the condition of the heart. Jew or Gentile, we're all measured by the same response to the Word."

Irene flipped to Mark 4 and pointed. "So the hundredfold—that's the Bride. The ones who fully surrendered. Sixtyfold and thirtyfold—still saved, but with different levels of fruit."

I rested my hand over the page. "Yes. It's about depth of surrender, not bloodline. Romans says there's no difference—Jew and Gentile alike are justified by faith. And here, Jesus shows that our fruitfulness—how we let the Word transform us—is what marks our place in the Kingdom."

Irene tilted her head, wonder lacing her voice.

"So then the New Jerusalem becomes this beautiful, multi-dimensional home. The Bride, the angels, and the faithful of Israel—Gods covenant people—all present?"

I nodded, smiling with quiet awe. "Exactly. It's not just a city—it's a testimony. Revelation 21:12 says the twelve gates are named after the twelve tribes of Israel. That means Israel isn't only honored—they're woven into the very architecture of eternity."

I tapped her Bible gently.

"And the twelve foundations of the city's wall? They bear the names of the twelve apostles—representing the Church. Jew and Gentile, Old Covenant and New, all brought together. It's the complete story of redemption, carved into stone."

Irene leaned back, eyes wide with dawning understanding.

"So it's both. Israel and the Church. The city itself reflects that union—God's covenant fulfillment in both Testaments."

I smiled, the truth settling like sunlight on my heart.

"Yes! The New Jerusalem isn't just a city—it's a living testimony. A masterpiece of redemption. Jew and Gentile. Heaven and earth. Angels and saints. All dwelling together in perfect harmony under the reign of the Lamb."

I paused, letting the wonder sink in.

"It's the fulfillment of every promise, etched into the very walls and gates of eternity."

Irene spoke softly, the weight of realization in her tone. "So it's both. Israel and the Church. The city itself reflects that union—God's covenant fulfilled in both Testaments."

I nodded, heart full. "Yes! The New Jerusalem isn't just a destination—it's a declaration. A living, radiant testimony of God's entire redemptive story. Jew and Gentile. Heaven and earth. Angels and saints. All together, dwelling in perfect harmony under the Lamb."

A pause. A breath. The sacredness of it all hung in the air. "It's the ultimate fulfillment—not just of prophecy, but of promise. A love story, fully told.

THE REVELATION OF JESUS CHRIST REVEALS:

²¹˙¹ And I saw a new heaven and a new earth: for the first heaven and the first earth were passed away; and there was no more sea.

This verse opens one of the most awe-inspiring transitions in the entire Bible. It is the moment when the old, corrupted creation gives way to a new, eternal order—a new heaven and a new earth. The apostle John, writing from exile on the island of Patmos, sees this staggering vision unfold after the final judgment has taken place (Revelation 20:11–15). Now that sin has been judged and death has been defeated, a new creation emerges.

There are two prevailing theological views regarding what happens to the current heaven and earth:

1. **Annihilation View**—This interpretation holds that the present heaven and earth will be completely destroyed, erased from existence, and replaced by a brand-new creation.

2. **Renovation View**—Others believe the current heaven and earth will be purified and transformed—not eliminated, but redeemed. Like gold refined by fire or a body resurrected in glory, the earth is purged by fire (2 Peter 3:10–13), remade into something incorruptible.

The Greek word translated "passed away" (*parerchomai*) does not necessitate annihilation. It can imply a transformation or a transition, much like how Paul describes the resurrection body in 1 Corinthians 15—changed, not discarded. Just as our bodies are not replaced, but glorified, so the earth and sky may likewise be renovated rather than destroyed.

This new creation is necessary because the old world, though beautiful, has been marred by sin, curse, and demonic defilement. The heavens have been the arena of spiritual warfare (Ephesians 6:12), and the earth groans under the weight of decay (Romans 8:22). After Christ's 1,000-year reign on earth—when Satan is released and ultimately judged—the stage is set for an eternal, sinless realm. Paradise is not only regained; it is eternally secured.

One of the most surprising statements in this verse is: "and there was no more sea." This detail holds deep symbolic and practical meaning:

- In John's day, the sea represented chaos, danger, separation, and the unknown. As a prisoner on Patmos, the sea physically separated him from the people he loved.
- In Scripture, the sea often symbolizes rebellion and evil: The beast rises from the sea (Revelation 13:1). Demons entered swine and rushed into the sea (Matthew 8:30–32). Ancient Jewish thought saw the sea as a place of deep, dark forces (Job 26:5–6; Isaiah 27:1).

In the new creation, the sea—both literally and symbolically—will no longer serve its purpose of cleansing, dividing, or representing danger. The earth will no longer need its antiseptic salinity or stormy chaos to maintain balance. All is at peace.

This new earth is not just Eden restored—it's Eden perfected. There will be no more curse, no more decay, and no more sorrow. It is the fulfillment of Jesus' promise: "Heaven and earth shall pass away, but My words shall not pass away"

(Matthew 24:35). It also answers the prayer Jesus taught: "Thy Kingdom come, Thy will be done, on earth as it is in heaven" (Matthew 6:10).

Peter saw it coming (2 Peter 3:10–13). Isaiah foretold it (Isaiah 65:17, 66:22). Jesus alluded to it (Matthew 19:28). And now John sees it with his own eyes: a new heaven and a new earth.

The new creation is not some distant, ethereal dream. It is the eternal home of the redeemed, brought forth by the same power that raised Christ from the dead. The universe, once groaning under sin, will be liberated in glorious re-creation. And the Holy City—the New Jerusalem—will descend upon this purified earth as the eternal capital of God's Kingdom (Revelation 21:2).

OLD TESTAMENT FORESHADOWS REVELATION:

For, behold, I create new heavens and a new earth: and the former shall not be remembered, nor come into mind. (Isaiah 65:17)

This verse aligns beautifully with Revelation 21:1, where John declares the vision of a new heaven and new earth, signifying God's ultimate act of re-creation and restoration. Isaiah 65:17 speaks of a time when the old, broken world is not only replaced but completely overshadowed by the glory of the new. This prophetic declaration in Isaiah is echoed and fulfilled in the vision John receives in Revelation, establishing a consistent biblical pattern of hope, restoration, and permanence in God's eternal plan.

Irene leaned forward, curiosity sparkling in her eyes.

"Ann, if there's no sea in the new earth, then I guess no ships either? And probably no aircraft, right? I mean, if the New Jerusalem is 1,500 miles high, air traffic would be kind of pointless. Commercial jets cruise at what—30,000 to 40,000 feet? That's only about 5.7 to 7.6 miles up? Compared to 1,500 miles, that barely scratches the surface! That's over 200 times higher!"

I grinned. "Totally pointless—and probably impossible in that new reality! Who needs airplanes when you can travel by thought? No TSA lines, no jet lag, no turbulence, no middle seat. Just pure, glorified, instantaneous movement. I'd take that over a boarding pass any day."

Irene laughed. "Ha! Finally, a world without flight delays! But seriously— the more I think about it, the more beautiful it sounds. No buzzing engines in the sky. No pollution. And the birds? They'll finally get to fly without fear."

I nodded, my smile warm. "Exactly, Irene. I've always felt a bit sad watching birds get startled—or worse, struck—by airplanes. But in the new heaven and new earth, creation will be at peace. The skies will belong to them again. No more noise, no more danger. Just freedom to soar under God's light-filled skies."

"Just imagine the quiet. The stillness. The sound of wind through trees, wings in flight, and the music of creation—undisturbed. The Eternal Age is going to be breathtaking, Ann."

I smiled, my voice soft with certainty. "And absolutely safe. Nothing harmful, nothing defiling, nothing to disrupt God's perfect harmony. Just pure peace—between people, with creation, and most of all, with Him."

Irene whispered, eyes wide with wonder.

"And to think—we've only just begun to understand it. Whatever we can imagine now . . . it's going to be so much better."

I nodded, my voice full of quiet joy.

"Amen. As Scripture says, 'No eye has seen, no ear has heard, no mind has conceived what God has prepared for those who love Him'—but through His Spirit, He gives us glimpses. Just enough to stir our hearts with hope."

> But as it is written, Eye has not seen, nor ear heard, neither have entered into the heart of man, the things which God has prepared for them that love Him. (1 Corinthians 2:9)

THE REVELATION OF JESUS CHRIST REVEALS:

²¹˸² And I John saw the Holy City, New Jerusalem, coming down from God out of heaven, prepared as a bride adorned for her husband.

Revelation 21:2 introduces us to one of the most awe-inspiring visions in all of Scripture: the New Jerusalem, the Holy City, descending from heaven—God's eternal gift for His redeemed people. This verse continues the prophetic flow of Revelation 21:1, now shifting the focus from the re-creation of the cosmos to the culmination of God's redemptive plan: the eternal dwelling place of God with humanity.

The New Jerusalem is not just any city—it is holy, heavenly, and prepared by God. It is described as coming down "from God out of heaven," showing its divine origin. This isn't a city built by human hands but one architected and crafted by God Himself (Hebrews 11:10). Unlike the corrupted cities of this fallen world, the New Jerusalem is untouched by sin and time—it is pure, perfect, and prepared in love.

John writes that the city was "prepared as a bride adorned for her husband." This is deeply symbolic and theological. The city is both a place and a people—a metaphor for the Bride of Christ, the Church, clothed in righteousness and beauty

(Ephesians 5:25–27). Just as a bride prepares with joy and splendor for her wedding day, so has this city been prepared by God for the eternal union of Christ and His people. It is the place where God's promises find their final fulfillment.

Notice the direction: "coming down"—this is heaven coming to earth, not humanity escaping earth. This affirms a central biblical truth: God's ultimate goal is not to take us away from the world but to restore and dwell with us in it. The New Jerusalem doesn't rise—it descends, just as Jesus came down in His incarnation. It is the final answer to the Lord's Prayer: "Thy Kingdom come, Thy will be done in earth, as it is in heaven" (Matthew 6:10).

Revelation 21:3 (immediately following) underscores this by declaring that the tabernacle of God is with men—God will dwell with His people forever. This is the consummation of the covenant: "I will be their God, and they shall be My people." (Ezekiel 37:27; 2 Corinthians 6:16). The throne of God, as Revelation 22 confirms, will be in the city, not in some far-off spiritual realm.

Many believers assume they'll spend eternity floating in heaven, but Scripture consistently points to a renewed earth as our eternal home. Verses like Psalm 37:9, 11, 29 and Matthew 5:5 promise the righteous will inherit the earth, not abandon it. The New Jerusalem represents heaven on earth, a place where eternity and material creation merge perfectly under Christ's reign.

Revelation 21:2 is more than poetic—it's the beginning of eternity as it was always meant to be. Heaven isn't just where we go—it's coming here, to a new earth, with a new city, where we will live in the unfiltered glory of God, forever.

OLD TESTAMENT FORESHADOWS REVELATION:

Awake, awake; put on your strength, O Zion; put on your beautiful garments, O Jerusalem, the Holy City: for henceforth there shall no more come into you the uncircumcised and the unclean. (Isaiah 52:1)

Isaiah 52:1 foretells a glorified Jerusalem—clothed in beauty and holiness—mirroring John's vision in Revelation 21:2. The imagery of Jerusalem as the Holy City, being adorned and restored, directly echoes John's description of the New Jerusalem as "prepared as a bride adorned for her husband."

Irene leaned in, flipping back to Revelation 21.

"Ann, I've been thinking. People keep debating whether the New Jerusalem actually touches the new earth or just hovers above it. But honestly, I don't get it. If it's a city—with streets, gates, foundations—doesn't that imply it lands?"

I smiled, encouraged by the question. "You're asking a great one, Irene. And I think you're right to be puzzled by the hovering theory. Some people connect the idea to the Shekinah glory—how God the Father's presence hovered over the Holy of Holies in the Old Testament."

Irene raised a brow. "But that was the presence of God. A cloud. A glory manifestation. Not a whole city!"

I nodded firmly. "Exactly. The Shekinah was God alone, revealing Himself in a limited, powerful way. But the New Jerusalem is something else entirely. It's a city—massive, radiant, physical. Revelation gives it exact dimensions: 1,500 miles in every direction. That's not a symbolic cloud. That's real construction."

Irene pointed to verse 12. "And it has gates! Twelve gates that stay open. It talks about nations walking in and out, and those glorified saints bringing their glory into it. That doesn't sound like something floating above the sky."

My tone softened with conviction. "No, it doesn't. The whole structure—the foundations, the walls, the open access—it all suggests it lands on the new earth. The idea that it hovers might come from tradition or poetic interpretation, but Revelation never actually says it doesn't land. It says it comes down out of heaven, but never that it stops in mid-air."

Irene tapped her Bible. "And it's not just God's throne that's there. It's the Bride. The remnant of Israel. The angels. It's the full, eternal dwelling place of God—with His people. The text says, 'Behold, the tabernacle of God is with men' (Revelation 12:3). Not *above* man."

I leaned back, thoughtful. "That's the heart of it, isn't it? We're not just talking about the Holy of Holies anymore—we're talking about the capital city of eternity. And the beauty is that it brings together all of God's redemptive work. Jew and Gentile. The Bride and the nations. Heaven and earth."

Irene smiled. "So it's not a satellite—it's home."

I chuckled. "Well said. And whatever floor plan God chooses, we'll be exactly where we're meant to be."

THE REVELATION OF JESUS CHRIST REVEALS:

21:3 And I heard a great voice out of heaven saying, Behold, the tabernacle of God is with men, and He will dwell with them, and they will be His people, and God Himself will be with them, and be their God.

This verse marks one of the most climactic moments in the entire Bible—the full and final restoration of God's presence with humanity. What began in Eden, where God walked with Adam in the cool of the day, and was tragically broken by sin, is now completely and eternally restored. God doesn't just visit; He dwells with His people forever.

"Behold, the tabernacle of God is with men." The word "tabernacle" recalls God's dwelling place with Israel in the wilderness (Exodus 40:34) and later in Solomon's Temple (1 Kings 8:10–11), where His glory would fill the sanctuary. Now, in Revelation 21:3, the "tabernacle" is not a tent or temple—but the very presence of God Himself. John uses this word to evoke the idea that God will now permanently dwell among His redeemed, no longer hidden, no longer distant.

John 1:14 says, "The Word became flesh and dwelt (tabernacled) among us." That was His First Coming. Here in Revelation 21, the dwelling becomes eternal, the final fulfillment of God's redemptive purpose.

"And He will dwell with them, and they will be His people." The Greek word here for "dwell" (*skenosei*) is the same root as "tabernacle." It suggests a permanent, settled relationship—an unbroken intimacy between God and His people. This fulfills the repeated covenant promise throughout Scripture: "I will be their God, and they shall be My people" (Leviticus 26:11–12; Jeremiah 31:33; Ezekiel 37:27).

This promise also echoes Jesus' own words in John 14:2–3, "I go to prepare a place for you . . . that where I am, there you may be also." Now, the place is prepared. The people are gathered. The presence of God is fully manifested.

"And God Himself will be with them, and be their God." There is great tenderness here. Not only is God with His people—He is their God. This phrase expresses belonging, relationship, and covenantal fulfillment. God's presence is no longer mediated through priests, sacrifices, or distant worship—but is direct, relational, and permanent.

This verse captures the ultimate goal of redemption: Emmanuel—God with us—forever. Not in part, not in shadow, not behind a veil, but in full glory. The separation caused by sin has been erased, and the New Jerusalem becomes the everlasting meeting place of God and His people. This is the true joy of heaven—not just golden streets or pearly gates—but the undiminished presence of God Himself, dwelling forever with those He has redeemed.

OLD TESTAMENT FORESHADOWS REVELATION:

And I will set My tabernacle among you: and My soul shall not abhor you. And I will walk among you, and will be your God, and you shall be My people. (Leviticus 26:11–12)

Revelation 21:3 is the full realization of what God promised in Leviticus. What was once symbolized in the physical tabernacle in the wilderness—God's presence with Israel—is now eternally fulfilled in the New Jerusalem. There's no more tent or temple needed. God Himself becomes the dwelling place, and His people live in uninterrupted, intimate fellowship with Him forever.

THE REVELATION OF JESUS CHRIST REVEALS:

[21:4] And God will wipe away all tears from their eyes; and there will be no more death, neither sorrow, nor crying, neither will there be any more pain: for the former things are passed away.

This verse is one of the most hope-filled and comforting promises in all of Scripture. It captures the heart of God's redemptive plan: not just the removal of sin, but the complete healing of every effect sin ever caused.

"And God will wipe away all tears from their eyes." This is deeply personal. It doesn't say tears will stop or fade away—it says God will wipe them away. This image conveys intimacy and care. Just as a parent gently wipes away a child's tears; our Heavenly Father will personally bring comfort to each of His children. Every sorrow, trauma, loss, and grief will be lovingly erased—not forgotten, but fully healed.

"And there will be no more death." Death—the great enemy that has haunted mankind since the Fall—is finally abolished. In the new creation, death has no power, no presence, and no place. Jesus defeated death at the Cross and in His resurrection, but now we see its total banishment from the new order of things.

"Neither sorrow, nor crying, neither will there be any more pain." The emotional and physical suffering that characterizes our current existence will be limited. "Sorrow" speaks to mental anguish. "Crying" reflects the outcry of the heart in distress. "Pain" includes not just physical pain but the deep ache of loss and brokenness. In New Jerusalem, none of it remains. This is a realm where healing is complete, and joy is full.

"For the former things are passed away." The phrase "former things" includes everything tied to the fallen world: sickness, injustice, heartache, loss, evil, sin, and death. All the burdens of the old creation will be permanently removed. This is not a temporary relief but a total transformation. The order of life as we know it is replaced by a new reality infused with God's holiness, peace, and joy.

Revelation 21:4 is the fulfillment of God's promise to "make all things new" (verse 5). It marks the end of humanity's pain and the beginning of eternal wholeness. This is the eternal comfort of the redeemed—a future where God Himself is our Comforter, where the curse is reversed, and every wound is healed. It's not just paradise regained—it's paradise perfected.

OLD TESTAMENT FORESHADOWS REVELATION:

And the ransomed of the LORD shall return, and come to Zion with songs and everlasting joy upon their heads: they shall obtain joy and gladness, and sorrow and sighing shall flee away. (Isaiah 35:10)

"Sorrow and sighing shall flee away" echoes the promise in Revelation 21:4: "neither sorrow, nor crying, neither shall there be any more pain." The imagery of "everlasting joy" parallels the eternal comfort and restoration promised in the new creation. This is a prophetic vision of God's people living in redeemed joy, free from the former world's suffering.

THE REVELATION OF JESUS CHRIST REVEALS:

[21:5] And He that sat upon the throne said, behold, I make all things new. And He said to me, Write: for these words are true and faithful.

This powerful verse captures the divine voice of God Himself seated on the throne—affirming His authority, His creative power, and the certainty of His promises. This is not just a declaration of future hope—it's a *guarantee* rooted in the character of the One who sits enthroned over all of creation.

"Behold, I make all things new." This phrase is sweeping in scope. Not some things. Not most things. All things. The entire order of reality as we know it—tainted by sin, decay, and death—is being replaced by something radically new. This is not just a restoration of the old, but a complete transformation. Just as God once declared "Let there be light" in Genesis 1, now He proclaims a second Genesis—a new beginning for the heavens, the earth, and redeemed humanity.

This echoes Isaiah 65:17: "For behold, I create new heavens and a new earth; and the former shall not be remembered, nor come into mind." It also parallels 2 Corinthians 5:17 where Paul says that anyone in Christ is "a new creature: old things are passed away; behold, all things are become new."

"And He said to me, Write." God commands John to write this down—intended to be preserved as eternal truth for the Church through the ages. God Himself emphasizes its importance. There is urgency and certainty in this command.

"For these words are true and faithful." This phrase is heaven's signature. These words aren't metaphorical wishes or poetic ideals. They are true—reliable, real—and faithful—trustworthy, guaranteed to come to pass. This is covenant language, echoing how God is often described in the Old Testament: as "Faithful and True" in all His works and promises (Deuteronomy 7:9; Psalm 33:4).

Revelation 21:5 offers assurance. In a world where everything seems broken or uncertain, God promises: "Behold, I make all things new." And He seals that promise with His own authority and character. It's not a maybe. It's a guarantee.

OLD TESTAMENT FORESHADOWS REVELATION:

Behold, I will do a new thing; now it shall spring forth; shall you not know it? I will even make a way in the wilderness, and rivers in the desert. (Isaiah 43:19)

This verse in Isaiah reflects God's promise to bring about radical transformation and restoration. Just as He once delivered Israel from Egypt, He promises a future act of redemption that breaks with past patterns—something new, unexpected, and filled with hope.

THE REVELATION OF JESUS CHRIST REVEALS:

21:6 And He said to me, It is done. I am Alpha and Omega, the Beginning and the End. I will give to him that is athirst of the fountain of the water of life freely.

This verse echoes a divine finality—"It is done"—a phrase that signals the completion of God's redemptive plan. Just as Christ cried, "It is finished" on the Cross (John 19:30) to declare the completion of salvation's purchase, here in Revelation 21:6, God proclaims the consummation of that plan in eternity. The old order has passed away (verse 4), and now a new eternal reality is established where God dwells with man forever.

"I am Alpha and Omega, the Beginning and the End." This powerful declaration frames God's sovereignty over all time and creation. Alpha and Omega are the first and last letters of the Greek alphabet, signifying that God is the origin and the conclusion of all things. He is preexistent before time and the eternal purpose toward which all creation moves. This is the third time in Revelation this title is used (Revelation 1:8, 22:13), underscoring the unchanging, eternal nature of God.

"I will give to him that is athirst of the fountain of the water of life freely." This is a promise of eternal satisfaction, offered to all who recognize their spiritual thirst and turn to God. The "water of life" symbolizes eternal sustenance, joy, and fellowship with God, reminiscent of Jesus' invitation to the Samaritan woman:

Jesus answered and said unto her, If you knew the gift of God, and who it is that says to you, Give Me to drink; you would have asked of Him, and He would have given you living water. (John 4:10)

The phrase "freely" emphasizes grace—this is not something one earns, but a gift offered without price to those who come in faith. It is the ultimate fulfillment of Isaiah 55:1: "Ho, everyone that thirsts, come you to the waters . . . without money and without price."

Revelation 21:6 declares the fulfillment of God's plan, the finality of His dominion, and the invitation to eternal life. It brings together God's power, purpose, and provision, assuring all who thirst spiritually that God is both the source and the satisfaction of that thirst—forever.

OLD TESTAMENT FORESHADOWS REVELATION:

Ho, everyone that thirsts, come you to the waters, and he that has no money; come you, buy, and eat; yea, come, buy wine and milk without money and without price. (Isaiah 55:1)

Both verses speak to spiritual thirst—a deep soul hunger only God can satisfy. The invitation is open and free: Isaiah 55:1 emphasizes "without money and without price," and Revelation 21:6 echoes "I will give . . . freely." Isaiah is prophetic of the Messianic age—an age of renewal, grace, and covenant restoration—fulfilled in Revelation's vision of the new heaven and new earth.

This connection highlights the continuity between the Testaments, showing that God's offer of salvation by grace has always been His plan—freely given to those who thirst for Him.

THE REVELATION OF JESUS CHRIST REVEALS:

21:7 He that overcomes will inherit all things; and I will be his God, and he will be My son.

This verse is the covenantal heartbeat of the entire vision of the new heaven and new earth. It is a divine declaration of victory, inheritance, and intimate relationship—all tied to the identity of the "overcomer."

"He that overcomes will inherit all things." Who is the overcomer? Scripture interprets Scripture. In 1 John 5:4–5, John defines the overcomer clearly:

For whatsoever is born of God overcomes the world: and this is the victory that overcomes the world, even our faith. Who is he that overcomes the world, but he that believes that Jesus is the Son of God? (1 John 5:4–5)

This tells us that faith in Christ—not personal performance—is the foundation of our overcoming. Those who trust in Jesus and remain faithful are seen as conquerors, not victims of this fallen world. What does the overcomer inherit? The verse says, "inherit all things." That's staggering. Not just a portion, not just eternal life, but all things—the fullness of God's promises:

- The new heaven and new earth (verse 1)
- The New Jerusalem (verse 2)
- The presence and fellowship of God (verse 3)
- The end of sorrow, pain, and death (verse 4)
- The water of life, freely given (verse 6)

This is the eternal inheritance promised in Romans 8:17:

And if children, then heirs; heirs of God, and joint-heirs with Christ; if so be that we suffer with Him, that we may be also glorified together. (Romans 8:17)

"And I will be his God, and he will be My son." This echoes ancient covenantal language found in 2 Samuel 7:14; Jeremiah 31:33; and Leviticus 26:12. It is the deepest expression of restoration: to be called God's son or daughter, no longer alienated, no longer lost, but fully brought into divine family and purpose.

Yes—this is the ultimate fresh start. Whatever brokenness, loss, or failure we carry, this is God's promise to rewrite the story for those who remain faithful to Him. This isn't just about surviving the trials of life. It's about conquering through Christ and stepping into eternal sonship.

In Revelation 21:7, we're not just promised a place—we're promised a relationship. The overcomer gets God Himself as their reward.

OLD TESTAMENT FORESHADOWS REVELATION:

I will be his Father, and he shall be My son. If he commits iniquity, I will chasten him with the rod of men, and with the stripes of the children of men. (2 Samuel 7:14)

In Revelation 21:7, God declares that the overcomer will "inherit all things" and enter into the ultimate relationship: "I will be his God, and he will be My son." This is the full realization of what was foreshadowed in God's covenant with David—a promise that pointed not only to Messiah Jesus but ultimately to all who belong to Him. Here, we're tracing a golden thread of sonship, inheritance, and covenant that runs from David's throne all the way to the New Jerusalem. Beautiful theology.

THE REVELATION OF JESUS CHRIST REVEALS:

[21:8] But the fearful, and unbelieving, and the abominable, and murderers, and whoremongers, and sorcerers, and idolaters, and all liars, will have their part in the lake which burns with fire and brimstone: which is the second death.

This verse serves as a sobering contrast to the promise of eternal inheritance just stated in Revelation 21:7. While overcomers are promised a divine inheritance and relationship with God as sons and daughters, verse 8 outlines the fate of those who reject God's truth and righteousness. It is one of the most direct and comprehensive descriptions of those excluded from the New Jerusalem and cast instead into the Lake of Fire, the second death.

- Fearful (cowardly)—Those who abandon faith under pressure—ruled by fear, not faith (Mark 4:40; 2 Timothy 1:7–8).
- Unbelieving—Rejecters of the gospel and salvation through Christ (John 3:18; Hebrews 3:12).
- Abominable—Embrace what God calls detestable (Titus 1:16).

- Murderers—Includes killers and those who harbor hatred (1 John 3:15).
- Whoremongers—Unrepentant in sexual sin (1 Corinthians 6:9–10).
- Sorcerers—Practicing witchcraft, occultism, or drug-induced rebellion.
- Idolaters—Worship anything above God—money, self, power, or idols.
- Liars—Living in deception, rejecting truth. (John 8:44).

"Which is the second death." This list is not exhaustive, but representative. All who reject God's grace, persist in sin, and refuse to repent are said to "have their part in the lake which burns with fire and brimstone"—a description of eternal judgment. This is what Scripture calls the second death: not the cessation of existence, but eternal separation from God in conscious torment (Revelation 20:14–15).

- The Lake of Fire is final—There is no repentance, no reversal, no escape.
- Sin will be totally excluded from the new creation—it has no foothold in the New Jerusalem.
- Faith and obedience are non-negotiable—Fear and unbelief are not innocent. Scripture identifies them here with eternal consequences.

This verse is both a warning and a call to action. It compels us to examine our own hearts and cling to Christ, not only as Savior but as Lord. It calls the Church to boldness in the gospel, because this fate awaits those outside of Christ.

OLD TESTAMENT FORESHADOWS REVELATION:

Upon the wicked He shall rain snares, fire and brimstone, and a horrible tempest: this shall be the portion of their cup. (Psalm 11:6)

"Fire and brimstone" directly mirrors the imagery in Revelation 21:8. The phrase "portion of their cup" suggests a just fate—just like Revelation describes the final portion of the wicked as the Lake of Fire. Psalm 11:6 emphasizes God's judgment on the wicked and the inescapable nature of His wrath.

THE REVELATION OF JESUS CHRIST REVEALS:

21:9 And there came to me one of the seven angels which had the seven vials full of the seven last plagues, and talked with me, saying, Come hither, I will show you the Bride, the Lamb's wife.

This verse marks a significant transition in John's vision. One of the very angels who previously poured out God's wrath in the form of the seven last plagues now takes John aside to reveal something glorious and redemptive: the Bride, the Lamb's wife—a dramatic contrast from judgment to reward.

It is significant that the angel who once displayed divine judgment now reveals divine love and fulfillment. This emphasizes that God's justice and mercy are not in conflict but work together to bring about His eternal purposes. The same hand that poured out wrath is now showing grace.

This angel echoes a scene from Revelation 17:1, where a similar phrase is used to introduce the judgment of Babylon the Great, the harlot. But here, instead of showing John the false bride, he is shown the true Bride—the holy New Jerusalem. This literary contrast highlights the difference between the prostitute and the pure, the corrupt city and the consecrated city, the temporal and the eternal.

The "Bride" is symbolic of the Church, the redeemed people of God, now joined in perfect union with Christ for eternity. This term, "Lamb's wife," emphasizes the sacrificial love of Jesus who died as the Lamb to redeem His Bride. This is the culmination of divine love, a marriage made in heaven— literally.

It also echoes Paul's teaching in Ephesians 5:25–27, where the Church is presented as a bride, spotless and holy, having been sanctified by Christ. The "wife" imagery now shows maturity—the relationship is no longer an engagement (as in the Church Age) but has reached its consummation in eternity.

OLD TESTAMENT FORESHADOWS REVELATION:

For as a young man marries a virgin, so shall your sons marry you; and as the bridegroom rejoices over the bride, so shall your God rejoice over you. (Isaiah 62:5)

This verse beautifully anticipates the imagery in Revelation 21:9, where the angel declares, "Come hither, I will show you the Bride, the Lamb's wife." It connects the covenantal joy of the Old Testament with the final, eternal union between Christ (the Lamb) and His redeemed people (the Bride). The prophetic joy of Isaiah—where God rejoices over His people like a bridegroom over a bride—is fully realized in the New Jerusalem, prepared and presented in glory, forever joined with her Savior.

THE REVELATION OF JESUS CHRIST REVEALS:

21:10 And he carried me away in the spirit to a great and high mountain, and showed me that great city, the holy Jerusalem, descending out of heaven from God.

In this verse, John is "carried away in the spirit"—a phrase that marks a major transition or revelation throughout the Book of Revelation (Revelation 1:10, 4:2, 17:3). Here, it signifies a supernatural experience where God gives John a panoramic, divine view of the New Jerusalem.

The "great and high mountain" recalls the imagery used throughout Scripture to depict places of divine revelation—such as Moses receiving the Law on Mount

Sinai (Exodus 19) or the Transfiguration of Jesus on a high mountain (Matthew 17:1–9). Mountains are often symbolic of closeness to God, elevation in perspective, and clarity in revelation.

The "holy Jerusalem" is described as "great" and "descending out of heaven from God." This reiterates that the New Jerusalem is not manmade, but a divine origin—a city whose architect and builder is God Himself (Hebrews 11:10). It's not humanity ascending to heaven, but heaven coming down to dwell with redeemed humanity. This is the fulfillment of what Jesus promised in John 14:2–3—that He was going to prepare a place for us.

This Holy City is the Bride of Christ, now fully revealed in glory, and it becomes the central focus of the eternal state. The descent of the New Jerusalem shows the merging of heaven and earth—the dwelling place of God with man (verse 3). It represents the complete restoration of what was lost in Eden and the consummation of God's redemptive plan.

This verse sets the stage for the detailed description of the city's splendor and divine architecture in the verses that follow—with its foundations, gates, walls, and overwhelming glory—all designed to reflect the glory of the One who inhabits it.

OLD TESTAMENT FORESHADOWS REVELATION:

In visions of God He took me to the land of Israel and set me on a very high mountain, on which was a structure like a city to the south. (Ezekiel 40:2)

Both John and Ezekiel are carried "in the spirit" to a high mountain. Both are shown a divinely designed city—Ezekiel sees a vision of a restored temple-city (Jerusalem), while John sees the New Jerusalem, the eternal city of God. The visions symbolize God's ultimate dwelling with His people and the culmination of His redemptive plan.

THE REVELATION OF JESUS CHRIST REVEALS:

21:11 Having the glory of God: and her light was like to a stone most precious, even like a jasper stone, clear as crystal.

This verse introduces the radiant splendor of the New Jerusalem, emphasizing that the city itself reflects the glory of God. The Greek word for "glory" (*doxa*) speaks of divine brilliance, majesty, and unapproachable light (1 Timothy 6:16). The light that emanates from the city is not its own—it is the manifestation of God's presence, just as the Shekinah glory once filled the tabernacle (Exodus 40:34) and the temple (1 Kings 8:11).

The jasper stone is likely what we now call a diamond—clear as crystal, symbolizing purity, perfection, and eternal value. The brilliance of the city isn't metaphorical—it has a literal radiance, suggesting its entire structure is permeated with light. This echoes the heavenly radiance of Ezekiel's vision (Ezekiel 1:22) and aligns with Paul's prayer in Ephesians 3:17–19, that believers would be filled with the fullness of God.

This description forms a stark contrast to Mystery Babylon, the false woman (Revelation 17:4–5), whose outward adornment masked inner corruption. Unlike her, the New Jerusalem is pure, transparent, and infused with divine glory. It is what Jerusalem in the Millennium foreshadowed—and Abraham foresaw it by faith (Hebrews 11:10).

Finally, the phrase "her light" also personalizes the city—it is not just architecture, it is a bride, filled with the people of God and the presence of God. This aligns with John 3:29, where the Bride belongs to the Bridegroom.

> He that has the bride is the bridegroom: but the friend of the bridegroom, which stands and hears him, rejoices greatly because of the bridegroom's voice; this my joy therefore is fulfilled. (John 3:29)

OLD TESTAMENT FORESHADOWS REVELATION:

> The sun shall be no more your light by day; neither for brightness shall the moon give light unto you: but the LORD shall be unto you an everlasting light, and your God your glory. (Isaiah 60:19)

This Old Testament prophecy finds its full realization in the New Jerusalem, described in Revelation 21:11. The glory of God replaces all created sources of light—His presence becomes the eternal illumination of the new city. This connection underscores the continuity of Scripture, showing how God's promises in the prophets are fulfilled in Revelation's final vision.

THE REVELATION OF JESUS CHRIST REVEALS:

> [21:12] And had a wall great and high, and had twelve gates, and at the gates twelve angels, and names written thereon, which are the names of the twelve tribes of the children of Israel.

This verse unveils the majesty and order of the New Jerusalem, the eternal city of God. Its architecture is not just breathtaking but deeply symbolic.

"And had a wall great and high." Walls in Scripture symbolize both protection and separation. In the New Jerusalem, this wall isn't to keep danger out—evil has already been judged and removed—but to display the security and perfection of God's eternal dwelling. Its great height (measured in verse 17 as 144 cubits or about 216 feet) emphasizes the city's grandeur and the total safety of those within.

"And had twelve gates." There are twelve gates, three on each side (as seen in verse 13), showing equal access from all directions of the world—a powerful image of the global invitation of salvation. These gates are not just entry points; they represent the inclusivity of God's redemptive plan for all who enter through faith and grace.

"And at the gates twelve angels." Angels are stationed at each gate, signifying divine guardianship and holiness. Their presence reminds us that the city is under God's watchful care, where only the righteous, whose names are in the Lamb's Book of Life, may enter (Revelation 21:27).

"And names written thereon, which are the names of the twelve tribes of the children of Israel." This detail reveals continuity between the Old and New Covenants. The names of the twelve sons of Jacob—flawed yet forgiven men— are eternally honored on these gates. It's a testimony to God's covenant faithfulness, His mercy, and His power to redeem imperfect people. Despite their sins—lies, betrayals, and rebellion—these men represent the foundation of God's earthly people, Israel. Their names being on the gates shows that the history of Israel remains eternally significant in God's plan.

This single verse reminds us that God does not erase history—He redeems it. The New Jerusalem stands as a testimony of God's faithfulness to Israel, His mercy toward the sinner, and His eternal reward for the overcomer.

OLD TESTAMENT FORESHADOWS REVELATION:

And these are the goings out of the city on the north side, four thousand and five hundred measures. And the gates of the city shall be after the names of the tribes of Israel: three gates northward; one gate of **Reuben**, one gate of **Judah**, one gate of **Levi**; on the east side, four thousand five hundred cubits, three gates: one gate for **Joseph**, one gate for **Benjamin**, and one gate for **Dan**; on the south side, measuring four thousand five hundred cubits, three gates: one gate for **Simeon**, one gate for **Issachar**, and one gate for **Zebulun**; on the west side, four thousand five hundred cubits with their three gates: one gate for **Gad**, one gate for **Asher**, and one gate for **Naphtali**. (Ezekiel 48:30–34)

Ezekiel's final vision in chapters 40–48 describes a future, ideal city of God—one with twelve gates, each bearing the name of a tribe of Israel, just as Revelation 21:12 does. The alignment of the gates (north, south, east, and west) and their naming pattern directly echoes what John sees in the New Jerusalem. Ezekiel's vision laid the groundwork that Revelation builds upon and fulfills.

THE REVELATION OF JESUS CHRIST REVEALS:

21:13 On the east three gates; on the north three gates; on the south three gates; and on the west three gates.

This verse describes the layout and accessibility of the New Jerusalem, the eternal city of God. The twelve gates are evenly distributed: three on each side of the perfect cube-shaped city (Revelation 21:16). This is not just architectural symmetry—it's symbolic theology.

Symbolism and meaning:

1. **Total Inclusion—A Welcome From Every Direction**—The four directions (north, south, east, west) represent universality and inclusivity. It mirrors God's open invitation to all nations and peoples—no matter where they're from. This is a picture of God's final and eternal gathering of His people from the four corners of the earth (Matthew 24:31; Isaiah 43:5–6).

2. **Echoes of Israel's Camp Arrangement**—This structure mirrors the camp layout of the twelve tribes around the tabernacle in the wilderness (Numbers 2). Each tribe was placed in a specific direction relative to the tabernacle, pointing to God's order, presence, and dwelling among His people. The New Jerusalem is the ultimate tabernacle (Revelation 21:3), where God dwells forever with His people.

3. **Fulfillment of Ezekiel's Prophecy**—This verse parallels Ezekiel 48:30–34, where the prophet envisioned a future Holy City with twelve gates, each named after the tribes of Israel and arranged exactly in this four-sided pattern. John is not inventing a new city but witnessing the fulfillment of Ezekiel's prophetic vision.

Every believer, no matter where they're from, has a gate into God's eternal city. The even spacing of the gates suggests equal access—no privileged entrance, no hidden doorway. It is the culmination of God's redemptive plan: that all who overcome will inherit the promises (Revelation 21:7), and all nations will walk in the light of the city (Revelation 21:24).

This is the geography of grace, the architecture of eternity, and the layout of love—where no one is forgotten and all are welcome.

OLD TESTAMENT FORESHADOWS REVELATION:

Every man of the children of Israel shall pitch by his own standard, with the ensign of their father's house: far off about the tabernacle of the congregation shall they pitch. (Numbers 2:2)

This layout continues in verses 3–31, detailing how three tribes camped on each cardinal direction surrounding the tabernacle. Just as in Revelation 21:13, the order and symmetry reflect God's design for His people—then in the wilderness, and ultimately in the eternal city. The New Jerusalem honors this tribal arrangement, embedding it into the gates of eternity, and demonstrating how the Old Covenant foundation merges into the New Covenant glory.

THE REVELATION OF JESUS CHRIST REVEALS:

^{21:14} And the wall of the city had twelve foundations, and in them the names of the twelve apostles of the Lamb.

Revelation 21:14 reveals the deep significance of the apostles in God's redemptive plan by inscribing their names on the twelve foundations of the New Jerusalem. This imagery underscores their foundational role in the birth of the Church and the spread of the gospel message. The apostles, as eyewitnesses of Christ's ministry, death, and resurrection, laid the doctrinal and spiritual groundwork upon which the global body of believers is built.

The symbolism echoes Ephesians 2:20, which states that the household of God is "built upon the foundation of the apostles and prophets, Jesus Christ Himself being the chief cornerstone." Just as the Old Testament patriarchs are honored in the twelve gates (verse 12), the New Testament apostles are memorialized in the very structure of the city's walls, representing the full covenantal unity between Israel and the Church in God's eternal plan.

It is noteworthy that the verse refers to the "twelve apostles of the Lamb," a title that emphasizes their relationship with Jesus—not simply as disciples, but as those specially sent (Greek: *apostolos*) by Him. While Judas Iscariot forfeited his role, Matthais was chosen by the early church in Acts 1:26 to restore the twelve.

The twelve apostles of the Lamb:

1. Peter (Simon Peter)
2. James (son of Zebedee)
3. John (brother of James)
4. Andrew (Peter's brother)
5. Philip
6. Bartholomew (also known as Nathanael)
7. Matthew (the tax collector)
8. Thomas (also called Didymus)
9. James (son of Alphaeus)
10. Thaddaeus (also called Judas, son of James, or Lebbaeus)
11. Simon the Zealot
12. Matthias (chosen in Acts 1:26 to replace Judas Iscariot)

Some also suggest that Paul, though not one of the twelve, carried apostolic authority uniquely as the "apostle of the Gentiles" (Romans 11:13), yet Revelation 21:14 focuses on the original circle tied directly to Jesus' earthly ministry.

This passage is not just about architecture—it is a testament to grace. Peter, who denied Jesus three times, will have his name on one of the foundations. The inclusion of flawed, human men in the eternal city's foundation reminds us that

God builds His Kingdom not on perfection but on forgiven and transformed lives. Their legacy becomes a perpetual reminder of the gospel's reach and power.

This verse paints a picture of divine completion: the Old Covenant tribes (verse 12) and the New Covenant apostles (verse 14) together form the permanent spiritual structure of the Holy City, reinforcing that salvation comes from the Jews (John 4:22), and access to the city is through the grace of Jesus Christ. Christ remains the chief cornerstone (1 Peter 2:6), and His apostles—redeemed, restored, and remembered—are the pillars upon which the eternal city stands.

OLD TESTAMENT FORESHADOWS REVELATION:

O you afflicted, tossed with tempest, and not comforted, behold, I will lay your stones with fair colors, and lay your foundations with sapphires. And I will make your windows of agates, and your gates of carbuncles, and all your borders of pleasant stones. (Isaiah 54:11–12)

Isaiah speaks prophetically of a glorious, restored Jerusalem whose foundations are laid with precious stones—sapphires, agate, carbuncles— pointing forward to the radiant, perfected New Jerusalem described in Revelation. Isaiah's vision is one of divine craftsmanship and eternal beauty—a city built by the Lord Himself, which aligns perfectly with the heavenly city John sees descending from God. Isaiah's prophecy foreshadows what Revelation 21 fulfills—the merging of God's covenantal promises with a literal and spiritual reality in the eternal age.

The precious foundations in Isaiah represent God's faithfulness and His covenant love for His people, now fulfilled in Revelation's eternal city where the names of the apostles—those who first declared the gospel—are forever inscribed.

THE REVELATION OF JESUS CHRIST REVEALS:

[21:15] And he that talked with me had a golden reed to measure the city, and the gates thereof, and the wall thereof.

This verse continues the awe-inspiring vision of the New Jerusalem. The angel—one of the seven who had poured out the final plagues—now turns to measure the city with a golden reed, a tool symbolizing both perfection and divine authority.

In Scripture, measuring often symbolizes ownership, intentional design, and divine approval. We see similar moments in: Ezekiel 40–42—where a heavenly messenger measures the Millennial Temple; Zechariah 2:1–2—where Jerusalem is measured in anticipation of restoration; and Revelation 11:1—where John is told to measure the temple of God. Each time, measuring communicates that God is taking possession, and that what is being measured is set apart, holy, and under His sovereignty.

"And he that talked with me had a golden reed." Gold is the metal of royalty and divinity in Scripture. That the reed is gold emphasizes the heavenly and perfect nature of the New Jerusalem. This isn't just any city—it is God's dwelling with His people (Revelation 21:3), and even its measurements reflect His eternal glory.

"To measure the city, and the gates thereof, and the wall thereof."

- The City—Measuring its dimensions shows us that the city is not just symbolic—it has real, measurable structure. This reflects the permanence and stability of God's eternal Kingdom.
- The Gates—With twelve gates named after the tribes of Israel (verse 12), their measurement signifies the universal access through God's covenantal plan.
- The Wall—Its height and thickness point to absolute security—evil is forever shut out (Revelation 21:27). This city needs no defenses, but its walls reflect God's complete protection for His people.

The measuring moment isn't just about dimensions—it's about divine order, eternal security, and the perfection of God's eternal design. The angel with the golden reed is confirming that everything John is witnessing is precise, true, and unshakable—built by God Himself for His Bride.

OLD TESTAMENT FORESHADOWS REVELATION:

I lifted up my eyes again, and looked, and behold a man with a measuring line in his hand. Then said I, Where goes you? And he said unto me, To measure Jerusalem, to see what is the breadth thereof, and what is the length thereof. (Zechariah 2:1–2)

In both Zechariah 2:1–2 and Revelation 21:15, Jerusalem is being measured by divine instruction. This symbolic act shows God's intent to dwell with His people and to establish His presence in a city set apart. In Zechariah, the act looks forward to the earthly restoration of Jerusalem. In Revelation, it points to the eternal fulfillment—the New Jerusalem, God's final and perfect dwelling place with man.

THE REVELATION OF JESUS CHRIST REVEALS:

21:16 And the city lies foursquare, and the length is as large as the breadth: and he measured the city with the reed, twelve thousand furlongs. The length and the breadth and the height of it are equal.

This astonishing verse unveils the literal dimensions of the New Jerusalem—an immense, awe-inspiring city that is not merely symbolic, but precisely measured and geometrically perfect. The "twelve thousand furlongs" equates to roughly 1,500 miles (or 2,414 kilometers) in length, width, and height, forming a massive cube that speaks of divine perfection, symmetry, and completeness.

The cube design is deeply significant. It mirrors the Holy of Holies in Solomon's Temple (1 Kings 6:20), which was also a perfect cube—symbolizing the purest and most concentrated presence of God. In Revelation 21, the Holy of Holies is no longer hidden behind a veil or reserved for a high priest. It has expanded to become an entire city—the permanent dwelling place of God Himself and His covenant people.

This cube structure extends vertically for 1,500 miles, far beyond earth's atmosphere—clearly marking this as a supernatural dwelling, unbound by earthly limitations. This is not simply a majestic city; it is the centerpiece of eternity, the throne city of God and the Lamb.

Scripture points to the inhabitants of this glorious city as being none other than the Wife of God (Israel) and the Bride of Christ (the raptured Church)—two distinct yet covenantal peoples of God, united in the eternal plan of redemption. Revelation 21:9–10 emphasizes that the New Jerusalem is "the Bride, the Lamb's wife," descending in full glory and perfection. This suggests that only those in this covenantal relationship—God's Wife and Jesus' Bride—will reside inside the New Jerusalem.

The redeemed from all nations, including Old Testament saints, Tribulation martyrs, and Millennial believers, while glorified, will likely dwell outside the city, surrounding it on the new earth and within the new heaven. Revelation 21:24 confirms this when it states, 'The nations of those who are saved shall walk in its light.' They do not dwell in the city, but they are welcome to approach and bask in the glory that radiates from it.

This cube city is a tangible fulfillment of John 14:2–3 where Jesus said, 'In My Father's house are many mansions . . . I go to prepare a place for you.' The New Jerusalem is that prepared place—custom-built for the Bride of Christ and the eternal dwelling of God's intimate presence with His covenant people.

This is not metaphor. It is majesty. And it's coming.

OLD TESTAMENT FORESHADOWS REVELATION:

And the oracle in the forepart was twenty cubits in length, and twenty cubits in breadth, and twenty cubits in the height thereof: and he overlaid it with pure gold; and so covered the altar which was of cedar. (1 Kings 6:20)

The "oracle" refers to the Holy of Holies in Solomon's Temple—a perfect cube, just like the New Jerusalem. Both are cubed shaped—The Holy of Holies was 20 x 20 x 20 cubits; the New Jerusalem is 12,000 stadia (furlongs) per side—1,500 miles. Both represent God's dwelling—The Holy of Holies housed the Ark and represented the most concentrated presence of God on earth. The New Jerusalem is God's permanent dwelling among men (Revelation 21:3).

What the Holy of Holies foreshadowed, the New Jerusalem fulfills. God's presence is no longer limited to a temple cube—but now expands to a cosmic, eternal cube for His redeemed people.

THE REVELATION OF JESUS CHRIST REVEALS:

21:17 And he measured the wall thereof, a hundred and forty and four cubits, according to the measure of a man, that is, of the angel.

This verse continues the awe-inspiring description of the New Jerusalem by focusing on the measurement of its wall—given as 144 cubits (approximately 216 feet if we use the standard 18-inch cubit). The text clarifies that this measurement is "according to the measure of man, that is, of the angel," meaning it's a literal measurement that both humans and angels would recognize.

"And he measured the wall thereof." There has been debate over whether the 144 cubits refers to the height of the wall or its thickness. Since the city itself reaches a staggering 1,500 miles high, it's unlikely that 216 feet describes its height in this context. It makes much more sense to interpret this as the thickness of the wall—reinforcing the strength, permanence, and impenetrability of God's eternal city.

Walls in biblical times represented protection, identity, and separation. The wall around the New Jerusalem isn't there to keep out danger—as evil has already been judged and excluded (Revelation 20:11–15, 21:8)—but rather as a symbol of divine security and completeness. This massive, thick wall emphasizes the strength and glory of the city, echoing Psalm 125:2:

As the mountains are round about Jerusalem, so the LORD is round about His people from henceforth even forever. (Psalm 125:2)

"A hundred and forty and four cubits." The number 144 may also carry symbolic significance. It is 12 x 12, mirroring the twelve tribes of Israel and the twelve apostles of the Lamb—both of which are etched into the gates and foundations of the city (Revelation 21:12, 14). This number represents the unity of God's redeemed people—Israel and the Church—brought together in perfect harmony.

"According to the measure of man, that is, of the angel." This curious phrase reveals something fascinating: heaven's dimension are tangible. What the angel measures is meant to be understandable to human perception. Heaven is not some ethereal dream-state—it's a real, physical place prepared for real, resurrected people. Jesus said in John 14:2, "I go to prepare a place for you." This verse affirms that the place is measurable, visible, and solid.

Revelation 21:17 gives us not only a literal measurement but also a deeper spiritual reassurance: God's eternal city is secure, precise, and prepared with divine intentionality. The walls speak of safety, the number 144 of covenant completeness, and the angel's measurement reminds us—we're not dreaming. We're going home.

OLD TESTAMENT FORESHADOWS REVELATION:

And behold a wall on the outside of the house round about, and in the man's hand a measuring reed of six cubits long by the cubit and a hand breadth: so he measured the breadth of the building, one reed; and the height, one reed. (Ezekiel 40:5)

Both passages describe an angelic being measuring a holy structure with a reed. Both use the standard cubit measurement known to man. Both are visions of a future, divine dwelling place—Ezekiel's vision of the Millennial Temple, and John's vision of the eternal New Jerusalem. Both symbolize order, exactness, and divine design—God is a God of measurements, boundaries, and structure, even in eternity. This connection reinforces the idea that what was foreshadowed in Ezekiel's temple vision is fulfilled on an eternal scale in the New Jerusalem—a city perfectly measured, gloriously complete, and designed by the Master Architect Himself.

THE REVELATION OF JESUS CHRIST REVEALS:

[21:18] And the building of the wall of it was of jasper: and the city was pure gold, like to clear glass.

This verse offers a breathtaking glimpse into the materials and majesty of the eternal New Jerusalem—God's divine capital city.

"And the building of the wall of it was of jasper." In Revelation 4:3, jasper is also used to describe the appearance of God Himself—so this radiant stone carries symbolic weight. While earthly jasper is opaque and varied in color, heavenly jasper seems to be translucent, crystal-like, and brilliant—something more akin to diamond in purity and radiance. This wall isn't just for defense, but for beauty and glory, radiating light and reflecting God's majesty. Its presence is not to keep enemies out (since none exist in eternity), but to highlight the preciousness and holiness of what's within.

"And the city was pure gold, like to clear glass." This detail defies earthly physics. Gold, as we know it, is opaque—but the gold of New Jerusalem is transparent, like clear glass. It speaks of a material reality in eternity that surpasses anything known on earth. The city isn't just symbolic; it's made of real, tangible matter—but that matter is transfigured into something holy, luminous, and spiritually perfect.

The transparency emphasizes two things:

1. **Purity**—No flaw, no corruption, no impurity exists in this eternal dwelling.

2. **Revelation**—Nothing is hidden; everything in the city is open and visible, reflecting perfect communion and no separation between God and man.

This verse paints a picture of ultimate holiness and perfection—not just in structure, but in essence. Gold and jasper, the most precious materials to human understanding, are the building blocks of God's eternal city. It speaks volumes about how highly God values His redeemed people and the place where He will dwell with them forever. Just as the tabernacle and temple were made with precise detail and costly materials, the New Jerusalem is constructed with divine splendor, reflecting God's glory, purity, and eternal purpose.

OLD TESTAMENT FORESHADOWS REVELATION:

So Solomon overlaid the house within with pure gold: and he made a partition by the chains of gold before the oracle; and he overlaid it with gold. And the whole house he overlaid with gold, until he had finished all the house: also the whole altar that was by the oracle he overlaid with gold. (1 Kings 6:21–22)

Solomon's Temple within was overlaid entirely in pure gold—symbolizing divine presence and holiness. Similarly, New Jerusalem is described in heavenly architectural terms, not only echoing the temple but surpassing it in glory and eternal permanence. The use of precious materials (gold, jasper) in both passages reflects the sanctity of God's dwelling place, and in Revelation, it shows the ultimate fulfillment of the Old Testament temple types in God's eternal city.

THE REVELATION OF JESUS CHRIST REVEALS:

21:19 And the foundations of the wall of the city were garnished with all manner of precious stones. The first foundation was jasper; the second, sapphire; the third, a chalcedony; the fourth, an emerald.

This verse unveils the breathtaking foundation of the New Jerusalem—not made of concrete or stone, but garnished with twelve radiant, precious stones, each glowing with a purity and brilliance that only heaven could produce.

These aren't randomly chosen gems. The stones listed each have the ability to radiate pure light. That's no small detail. On earth, many gemstones absorb or distort light—but these heavenly stones will perfectly reflect the glory of God shining through the New Jerusalem (Revelation 21:23). The result? A stunning kaleidoscope of divine color. Each hue, perfectly refracted by the pure light of God, becomes a testimony of beauty, redemption, and divine artistry.

This is not just decoration—it's declaration. It tells us something about God:

- He spares nothing when preparing a place for His people.
- He honors His promises—naming foundations after apostles, gates after tribes.
- He creates beauty from brokenness—just as many apostles and patriarchs had troubled pasts.

Let's not miss the emotional power here. Some of the names etched into these eternal structures—Jacob's sons, the apostles—were once liars, doubters, cowards, and traitors. And yet their names endure. Why? Because God isn't looking for perfection—He's looking for those covered by the blood of the Lamb.

So, if you're ever tempted to wonder, "Will I make it?"—just remember: The same grace that got those rascals in (yes, even Peter, the denier . . . even Judah, the betrayer of Joseph) is the same grace that will welcome you. Praise God for the mercy, majesty, and matchless beauty of the coming city!

OLD TESTAMENT FORESHADOWS REVELATION:

O you afflicted, tossed with tempest, and not comforted, behold, I will lay your stones with fair colors, and lay your foundations with sapphires. And I will make your windows of agates, and your gates of carbuncles, and all your borders of pleasant stones. (Isaiah 54:11–12)

Isaiah 54:11–12 prophetically speaks of God's restoration of Zion with precious stones—almost identical to the imagery in Revelation 21:19. This passage is poetic and prophetic, pointing to a future glorified city—which many scholars believe is a foretelling of the New Jerusalem. It includes references to foundations and gates made of gems—exactly what John sees in Revelation. It highlights beauty, stability, and divine craftsmanship, which are central themes in the Revelation vision.

THE REVELATION OF JESUS CHRIST REVEALS:

21:20 The fifth, sardonyx; the sixth, sardius; the seventh, chrysolite; the eighth, beryl; the ninth, a topaz; the tenth, a chrysoprasus; the eleventh, a jacinth; the twelfth, an amethyst.

This verse continues the dazzling description of the twelve foundations of the walls of New Jerusalem, each one adorned with a unique and radiant gemstone. These stones reflect more than mere beauty—they reveal the manifold grace, order, and glory of God.

Peter spoke of the "manifold grace of God" (1 Peter 4:10), and the word "manifold" literally means variegated or many-colored. That is precisely what is being displayed here. Each stone reflects a different hue of God's redemptive plan, and together, they form a visual testament to His covenantal faithfulness.

These gemstones closely resemble those embedded in the breastplate of the high priest (Exodus 28:15–21, 39:10–14), where each stone represented one of the twelve tribes of Israel. In Revelation, those same tribes are honored again— this time not as wanderers in the wilderness, but as part of the eternal foundation of God's Holy City. While the specific identification of these stones across languages and centuries remains debated, the symbolism is unmistakable: God's people are precious, colorful, and eternally remembered.

Some scholars also connected these stones to the Mazzaroth—the ancient Hebrew arrangement of constellations—which many believe tells the story of redemption written in the stars (Job 38:32). John's order here appears reversed from the traditional sequence of the Mazzaroth, possibly symbolizing heaven's inversion of earthly systems or a divine reset of creation's order in eternity.

This gemstone imagery echoes Ezekiel 28:13, which describes Eden, the garden of God, adorned with many of these same stones. The message? What was lost in Eden through sin is now restored in New Jerusalem through grace. We are returning—not just to Eden—but to a better Eden, infused with glory and permanence.

These foundation stones aren't just decoration—they're divine declarations. Each one sings of God's character, His covenant, His creativity, and His care for His people. In the New Jerusalem, beauty is not ornamental—it's theological.

OLD TESTAMENT FORESHADOWS REVELATION:

Now I have prepared with all my might for the house of my God the gold for things to be made of gold, and the silver for things of silver, and the brass for things of brass, the iron for things of iron, and wood for things of wood; onyx stones, and stones to be set, glistering stones, and of diverse colors, and all manner of precious stones, and marble stones in abundance. (1 Chronicles 29:2)

This verse shows King David's preparation for building the temple of God, which include diverse and colorful precious stones—a direct connection to the twelve jeweled foundations of the New Jerusalem in Revelation 21:20. The imagery here reinforces the idea of God's dwelling place being adorned with beauty, glory, and symbolism.

THE REVELATION OF JESUS CHRIST REVEALS:

21:21 And the twelve gates were twelve pearls; every single gate was of one pearl: and the street of the city was pure gold, as it were transparent glass.

This verse paints one of the most iconic and awe-inspiring images of heaven—the pearly gates and the street of gold—but far more than symbolic, it is a revelation of God's beauty, grace, and divine value system.

"And the twelve gates were twelve pearls; every single gate was of one pearl." Each of the twelve gates is made of a single pearl, an astonishing detail that speaks volumes about heaven's glory and suffering's redemptive power.

- A pearl is the only precious gem formed through suffering—a grain of sand irritates an oyster, and over time, it produces something beautiful.
- These massive pearls speak of the sacrifice of Christ and the sufferings of the saints that led to the formation of the Church.
- Walking through each gate is a reminder that access to this eternal city was not without cost—yet the outcome is eternal beauty.

"And the street of the city was pure gold, as it were transparent glass." Interestingly, the text speaks of a singular street—not many streets, but one main street—perhaps symbolizing unity, righteousness, and oneness in Christ.

- The street is made of pure gold, so refined and holy that it appears like transparent glass—a quality unknown to earthly gold.
- This is not the gold of earth—which we treasure here—but a gold that has been made so pure in heaven it is translucent, signifying absolute purity, holiness, and clarity.
- Gold, the most precious of metals to man, is reduced to pavement in God's city. What we esteem most here, God uses as a foundation—showing us that heaven's glory far surpasses earth's treasures.

Everything about the New Jerusalem reflects the character of God—His purity, perfection, glory, and holiness. Even the infrastructure is infused with symbolism: Pearl gates remind us of the suffering that leads to beauty. A golden street points to a sanctified path where nothing impure may walk. Transparent glass reflects light—meaning God's glory will shine throughout the city in unfiltered radiance. This is not just architecture; it's theology in stone and metal. Every step taken on that golden street will be a reminder that we walk in God's finished work, surrounded by glory, welcomed through grace.

OLD TESTAMENT FORESHADOWS REVELATION:

The gold and the crystal cannot equal it: and the exchange of it shall not be for jewels of fine gold. No mention shall be made of coral, or of pearls: for the price of wisdom is above rubies. The topaz of Ethiopia shall not equal it, neither shall it be valued with pure gold. (Job 28:17–19)

Job 28:17–19 poetically compares wisdom to the most precious materials known to man, including gold, pearls, and jewels—the very same elements used to construct the New Jerusalem. While Job emphasizes the incomparable value of divine wisdom, Revelation 21:21 shows us the literal fulfillment of divine wisdom—a city built by God where even the Mainstreet is of gold and gates are giant pearls. The use of such priceless materials as building elements in heaven illustrates the abundance, beauty, and supremacy of God's eternal dwelling—and how heaven's glory surpasses all earthly imagination.

THE REVELATION OF JESUS CHRIST REVEALS:

21:22 And I saw no temple therein: for the LORD God Almighty and the Lamb are the temple of it.

This verse reveals one of the most profound truths about the New Jerusalem: there is no temple in this eternal city. That may come as a surprise to those familiar with biblical history, where the temple was the central meeting place between God and man. But here, in the New Jerusalem, no building is necessary—because God Himself is the temple. His immediate, unfiltered presence permeates every inch of the city.

- In the Old Testament—The tabernacle (Exodus) and later the temple (1 Kings) were essential as places where God's glory dwelled and where sacrifices were made. But even then, access was limited—the high priest alone could enter the Holy of Holies, and only once a year.
- In the New Covenant—Jesus referred to His own body as the true temple (John 2:19–21), showing that the ultimate purpose of the temple was to point to Him. On the Cross, when Jesus died, the veil of the temple was torn (Matthew 27:51), symbolizing direct access to God was now possible through Him.
- In the Eternal State—In the New Jerusalem, we don't go to a temple to meet God—we dwell with Him. The LORD God Almighty (the Father) and the Lamb (Jesus Christ) are the temple. Their presence fills the city, making every place holy ground.

This verse completes a powerful narrative arc:

- In Eden—God walked with man.
- In the tabernacle and temple—He dwelt among them.
- In Christ—He dwelt within human flesh.
- In the Church—He dwells in believers through the Holy Spirit.
- But in the New Jerusalem—God and the Lamb will dwell face-to-face with His people, forever.

There's no longer a need for symbolic spaces of worship—because worship becomes our reality. The presence of God is unmediated, unending, and undeniably central. The Lamb, our Redeemer, and God, our Creator, are now the very structure, sanctuary, and center of our eternal lives.

OLD TESTAMENT FORESHADOWS REVELATION:

It was round about eighteen thousand measures: and the name of the city from that day shall be, The LORD is there. (Ezekiel 48:35)

Ezekiel's vision ends with a future city—not just with a temple but with the declaration that God Himself dwells there. The name "YHWH Shammah" means "The LORD is here," foreshadowing the direct, permanent presence of God with His people, just as Revelation 21:22 describes. The emphasis shifts from a holy building to a holy presence—God is no longer symbolically housed in a temple. He is the temple. This parallels Revelation 21:22 perfectly: in eternity, we won't go to a sacred place to meet God—His presence will be the sacred place.

THE REVELATION OF JESUS CHRIST REVEALS:

$^{21:23}$ And the city had no need of the sun, neither of the moon, to shine in it: for the glory of God did lighten it, and the Lamb is the light thereof.

This stunning verse reveals a profound truth about the New Jerusalem—a city illuminated not by created light but by the uncreated glory of God Himself.

"And the city had no need of the sun, neither of the moon, to shine in it." The verse doesn't say the sun and moon are destroyed—it says the city *has no need* of them. This is key: it highlights the superior radiance of God's presence. The Shekinah glory that once hovered over the Ark of the Covenant now permanently lights the entire city. Just as in the wilderness, God's presence was their guiding light (Exodus 13:21), now He Himself is the eternal light.

"For the glory of God did lighten it, and the Lamb is the light thereof." Jesus, the Lamb, is not only our Savior—He is our everlasting source of light. This is the fulfillment of John 8:12, where Jesus declared, "I am the light of the world." In the New Jerusalem, this isn't metaphorical—it's literal. His light banishes all darkness, physically and spiritually.

In the tabernacle and temple, the menorah represented the light of God's presence. Now, there's no lampstand—Christ Himself is the lamp. This completes the prophetic picture of Isaiah 60:19 (Revelation 21:11).

Because the glory of God is fully present, there is no night in the city (Revelation 21:25). This glory light is not reflected—it is emitted. God's own essence is the light source, and the Lamb—Jesus—shares in that radiance. It also speaks of eternal accessibility: no darkness, no fear, no separation.

The New Jerusalem is not governed by the rhythms of earthly time, nor by the limitations of natural light. It is governed by the presence of God, who will dwell forever with His people in unapproachable yet welcoming light. As Paul wrote in 1 Timothy 6:16, "Who only has immortality, dwelling in the light which no man can approach unto; whom no man has seen, nor can see: to whom be honor and power everlasting. Amen."—and yet, we will see Him face to face.

This verse proclaims the ultimate fulfillment of God's plan: His people, in His city, in His light—forever.

OLD TESTAMENT FORESHADOWS REVELATION:

But it shall be one day which shall be known to the LORD, not day, nor night: but it shall come to pass, that at evening time it shall be light. (Zechariah 14:7)

This prophetic verse from Zechariah speaks of a supernatural light that replaces the normal cycle of day and night—a light that remains even at evening time. It anticipates the divine illumination of the future Kingdom, harmonizing beautifully with the eternal light that fills the New Jerusalem in Revelation 21:23.

———◆◆◆———

"Ann, I've been wondering . . . if the New Jerusalem doesn't need the sun or moon because it's lit by God's glory, then what does the rest of the new earth look like?" Irene asked, curiosity sparking in her voice.

I smiled, delighted by the question. "Ooh, I love that you're thinking about this! Let's unpack it. Revelation 21:23 says the city—the New Jerusalem—'has no need' of the sun or moon, because the glory of God lights it, and the Lamb is its lamp. But catch that phrasing: *no need*. It doesn't say the sun and moon are gone entirely—just that they're unnecessary within the city."

"So they might still exist . . . just not needed inside the city?"

I nodded. "Exactly. Outside the city—on the new earth—there are still nations. Revelation 21:24 says, 'The nations of them which are saved shall walk in the light of it.' That suggests the city's light radiates outward, illuminating the world—but it doesn't say the sun and moon are gone completely. So yes, I think natural rhythms like day and night could still exist out there."

"That makes sense," Irene said thoughtfully. "Especially if people are planting vineyards or harvesting fruit. You'd still need rhythm and order, right?"

I smiled. "Exactly. Revelation 22:2 says the Tree of Life yields fruit every month—that's a clear time marker. Not for pressure or deadlines, but for a steady rhythm of abundance. It's not the end of time itself—just the end of time under the curse."

"So time still exists," Irene said slowly, "but not as something to fear. It's no longer running out—it's something we live within, joyfully?"

I nodded, my expression warm. "Exactly. In the Eternal Age, time isn't erased—it's redeemed. No aging, no decay—just divine rhythm. It's more like *kairos* time—God-ordained moments—rather than *chronos*, the ticking clocks."

"So fascinating," Irene murmured. "And I love how it all circles back to Genesis—like God is restoring everything to what it was meant to be."

I smiled, my voice reverent. "Yes! The Bible opens with 'Let there be light'— before the sun or moon were even created. In Eden, there was both: the sun and the presence of God's light. And it ends with that divine light shining forever. The same Spirit who hovered over the waters in Genesis 1 will dwell with us, face to face, in the New Jerusalem. It's full circle—restored, redeemed, and radiant."

"That's such a powerful picture," Irene said softly. "Not floating souls in the sky, but real people, in real places, doing real things . . . in glory."

I nodded, my eyes shining.

"Amen, sister. We won't be bored—we'll be fulfilled. The Eternal Age isn't the end of the story—it's the beginning of forever."

THE REVELATION OF JESUS CHRIST REVEALS:

21:24 And the nations of them which are saved shall walk in the light of it: and the kings of the earth do bring their glory and honor into it.

This verse offers a breathtaking glimpse into life on the new earth in the eternal age. While the New Jerusalem serves as the central city—radiating the glory of God—it is not the only place where redeemed people will dwell. In fact, "the nations of them which are saved" implies that glorified saints from all ethnicities and cultures will inhabit the new earth, surrounding the New Jerusalem and walking in its divine light.

"And the nations of them which are saved." This phrase highlights the inclusivity and global reach of God's redemptive plan. Salvation will have touched people from every tribe, tongue, and nation (Revelation 5:9). These "nations" are not rebellious political entities, but redeemed communities of glorified believers, now unified in worship and obedience to Christ.

"Shall walk in the light of it." The New Jerusalem, illuminated by the glory of God and the Lamb (Revelation 21:23), becomes the source of spiritual and literal light. These nations shall walk in the uncreated light of God's presence. This echoes Isaiah 60:3: "And the Gentiles shall come to your light, and kings to the brightness of your rising."

"And the kings of the earth do bring their glory and honor into it." This is a picture of honoring God with the fullness of redeemed culture and leadership. These "kings" are likely glorified rulers or representatives from among the saved nations, now submitting all authority and honor to Jesus Christ—who is King of kings, Lord of lords. They bring the best of what they once stewarded on earth, not elevate themselves, but to glorify God in this eternal Kingdom.

Revelation 21:24 reminds us that heaven is not homogenous—it is a Kingdom of diversity, redemption, and light. The nations live in peace, walk in divine light, and willingly offer all their glory to God. This is not just the end of history—it's the beginning of perfect fellowship, not only with God but with one another, in a radiant new creation.

OLD TESTAMENT FORESHADOWS REVELATION:

The kings of Tarshish and of the isles shall bring presents: the kings of Sheba and Seba shall offer gifts. Yea, all kings shall fall down before Him: all nations shall serve Him. (Psalm 72:10–11)

The kings bringing gifts in Psalm 72:10–11 parallels "the kings of the earth do bring their glory and honor into it." "All nations shall serve Him" corresponds to "the nations of them which are saved shall walk in the light of it." This psalm is a Messianic prophecy of Christ's eternal reign, which aligns perfectly with the Revelation 21:24 scene of the glorified nations in the new earth under Christ's light and lordship.

THE REVELATION OF JESUS CHRIST REVEALS:

21:25 And the gates of it shall not be shut at all by day: for there shall be no night there.

This verse presents a powerful symbol of eternal security, peace, and divine presence in the New Jerusalem. In ancient cities, gates were shut at night or during times of threat to protect inhabitants from enemies or danger. Here, however, the gates of the New Jerusalem will never be shut—because there is no more danger, no more threat, no more night.

The phrase "for there shall be no night there" reminds us that the city is perpetually illuminated by the glory of God and the Lamb (Revelation 21:23). There is no darkness—literal or symbolic. Spiritually, night often represents fear, uncertainty, or sin. In the New Jerusalem, none of these exist anymore. God's presence ensures unending light, unending clarity and unending peace.

Because sin has been judged and evil has been eternally banished (Revelation 20:14–15), there is no need for security systems or barriers. The gates remain open, testifying to the absolute safety of all who dwell in God's presence. Every redeemed soul can come and go in perfect freedom.

The gates of the New Jerusalem are not only open—they are inviting. Revelation 21:24 tells us, "the nations of them which are saved shall walk in the light of it," meaning those outside the city will live in the radiance that emanates from it. While the light may not cover the entire new earth, it clearly extends far enough to guide and welcome the redeemed from every nation. These ever-open gates are a powerful symbol: the work of redemption is complete, access to God is unhindered, and His promise stands fulfilled—"They shall be His people, and He shall be their God" (Revelation 21:3).

OLD TESTAMENT FORESHADOWS REVELATION:

Therefore your gates shall be open continually; they shall not be shut day nor night; that men may bring unto you the forces of the Gentiles, and that their kings may be brought. (Isaiah 60:11)

Isaiah 60:11 aligns closely with Revelation 21:25, both in imagery and in theological message. It speaks of eternally open gates, the incoming glory of nations, and uninterrupted divine presence, all of which are fulfilled in the eternal state described in Revelation 21.

THE REVELATION OF JESUS CHRIST REVEALS:

[21:26] And they shall bring the glory and honor of the nations into it.

This verse speaks to the dignified procession of the redeemed nations into the New Jerusalem. After describing the city's eternal openness in verse 25, John emphasizes what will be brought into this glorious city—"the glory and honor of the nations."

"And they shall bring." This is a continuation from Verse 24, where it is said that "the kings of the earth bring their glory and honor into it." It implies movement, reverence, and the voluntary offering of all that is noble, pure, and exalted from the redeemed peoples of the earth to the very presence of God.

"The glory and honor of the nations into it." These words suggest that while cultural distinctions between nations may still exist in the new earth, only the righteous essence of those cultures will be present—free from sin, corruption, or division. Think of it as the best of humanity's creativity, craftsmanship, and worship, all offered to the Lamb is a continual act of tribute. This is not material wealth but rather the spiritual richness and redeemed excellence of the nations—their worship, righteousness, obedience, and praise.

This phrase beautifully expresses the unified diversity of God's Kingdom: one people under Christ, yet still rich with individual and national identities, all sanctified and harmonized for God's glory.

In eternity, there is no nationalism, racism, or cultural superiority—only a redeemed world that reflects the multi-faceted beauty of God through its glorified people. All "glory and honor" will be laid at His feet (Revelation 4:10–11), and the New Jerusalem becomes the eternal sanctuary where the worship of the nations flows freely, perpetually.

OLD TESTAMENT FORESHADOWS REVELATION:

And I will shake all nations, and the desire of all nations shall come: and I will fill this house with glory, says the LORD of hosts. (Haggai 2:7)

Haggai 2:7 is a prophecy about the future glory of God's house—ultimately fulfilled in the New Jerusalem. The phrase "desire of all nations shall come" has been understood by many as both a Messianic reference and a picture of the nations bringing their glory into God's dwelling place. This mirrors Revelation 21:26, where the redeemed nations bring their glory and honor into the eternal city.

THE REVELATION OF JESUS CHRIST REVEALS:

21:27 And there shall in no wise enter into it any thing that defiles, neither whatsoever works abomination, or makes a lie: but they which are written in the Lamb's Book of Life.

This verse is the final safeguard—the divine boundary—around the holiness of the New Jerusalem. It assures us that the eternal city will be utterly undefiled, free forever from sin, corruption, deceit, and moral compromise. It's a declaration of eternal purity and a reaffirmation that God's redemptive plan has fully restored what was lost in Eden.

The phrase "in no wise enter into it" uses the strongest Greek double negative possible, meaning "absolutely never under any circumstances." Nothing impure, no evil deed, no hidden lie, no corrupt soul will ever cross the threshold of that city. This is the absolute fulfillment of holiness, something humanity has longed for but never achieved on its own. This verse shows that all the effects of the Fall—sin, lies, wickedness, abominations—will be permanently excluded from God's eternal dwelling. The separation between light and darkness will be complete and irreversible.

The only ones permitted into the New Jerusalem are those whose names are written in the Lamb's Book of Life. This book, referenced earlier in Revelation (13:8, 20:15), contains the names of those who have placed their trust in the

Lamb—Jesus Christ, the crucified and risen Savior. Their righteousness is not their own, but the righteousness of Christ, imputed to them by faith. It is by grace alone that they have access to this city, not by works, merit, or heritage (Ephesians 2:8–9).

This verse reveals the completion of God's original intention from creation— to dwell with a holy people, free from sin and united with Him forever (Ephesians 2:7; Titus 2:14). What began with the presence of God walking in the garden of Eden is now perfected in the eternal city, where He will dwell with the redeemed for all eternity.

Revelation 21:27 isn't just a look forward—it's a reminder to live with eternity in view. God's holiness is not optional. Those written in the Lamb's Book of Life are not perfect people—but they are redeemed people, made new by grace, and committed to walking in truth. This verse urges each of us to examine our hearts and ensure that our names are written in His book—sealed by faith in Christ.

OLD TESTAMENT FORESHADOWS REVELATION:

So shall you know that I am the LORD your God dwelling in Zion, My holy mountain: then shall Jerusalem be holy, and there shall no strangers pass through her any more. (Joel 3:17)

This verse clearly reflects the same theme found in Revelation 21:27—only those who are holy and belong to God will have access to His dwelling place. No stranger, no defiled or unclean individual, will enter. Joel 3:17 anticipates the exclusive purity and sanctity of the eternal city, foreshadowing the New Jerusalem where only those written in the Lamb's Book of Life may enter.

SUMMARY OF REVELATION 21

Revelation 21 unveils the eternal future for the redeemed—a breathtaking picture of the new heaven, the new earth, and the New Jerusalem. After the final judgment in chapter 20:11–15, John sees a new creation where the old heaven and earth have passed away and there is no more sea (Revelation 21:1), symbolizing the removal of chaos and separation.

Descending from heaven, John sees the Holy City, New Jerusalem, prepared as a bride adorned for her husband (Revelation 21:2). A loud voice proclaims the fulfillment of God's eternal plan: "The tabernacle of God is with men" (Revelation 21:3). God will now dwell with His people forever—wiping away all tears, eradicating death, sorrow, pain, and all former things (Revelation 21:4).

Seated on the throne, God declares, "Behold, I make all things new" and affirms His identity as Alpha and Omega, offering the water of life freely to those who thirst (Revelation 21:5–6). Overcomers will inherit all things and be called sons of God (Revelation 21:7), but the wicked—cowards, unbelievers, liars, and immoral—will face the second death in the Lake of Fire (Revelation 21:8).

One of the seven angels takes John to a high mountain to reveal the New Jerusalem in detail (Revelation 21:9–10). The city is immense—1,500 miles in length, width, and height—forming a perfect cube (Revelation 21:16), mirroring the Holy of Holies in Solomon's Temple (1 Kings 6:20). The city radiates with God's glory, with walls of jasper, gates of pearl, and a Mainstreet of pure, transparent gold (Revelation 21:11–21). The names of the twelve tribes of Israel are on the gates, and the names of the twelve apostles are on the foundations, symbolizing the unity of God's covenant people (Revelation 21:12–14).

There is no temple in the city—because the LORD God Almighty and the Lamb are its temple (Revelation 21:22). There is no sun or moon, for the glory of God lights the city, and the Lamb is its light (Revelation 21:23). The saved nations walk in its light and bring their glory into it (Revelation 21:24), and its gates are never shut, for there is no night there (Revelation 21:25). Only those written in the Lamb's Book of Life may enter; no defilement or evil will be allowed (Revelation 21:27).

KEY TAKEAWAYS

- The new creation—A new heaven and earth replace the former, now cleansed of all sin and sorrow.
- God's dwelling among men—Fulfillment of the eternal plan: God lives with His people forever.
- The New Jerusalem—A perfect, radiant city that functions as the Holy of Holies for the redeemed.
- Unity of God's people—The twelve tribes and twelve apostles signify the union of Israel and the Church.
- No need for sun, moon, or temple—God's presence is the light and the temple in the eternal city.
- Only the redeemed enter—Nothing impure enters; only those written in the Lamb's Book of Life dwell there.

Revelation 21 is the ultimate vision of hope. It declares that all sorrow and death will end, and that God's people will live forever in His presence, in a place of unimaginable beauty and joy. The New Jerusalem is not only a city—it is the final fulfillment of God's promise to dwell with His people, forever.

Chapter 20

Revelation 22: The Eternal Kingdom

THE LAST CHAPTER OF GOD'S LOVE STORY—Revelation 22 opens with a glimpse into the heart of eternity—a world restored, perfected, and radiant with the presence of God. At the center of the New Jerusalem flows the river of the water of life, clear as crystal, issuing from the throne of God and of the Lamb. This river doesn't just quench thirst—it nourishes the soul. It runs through a city where time and decay no longer exist. On either side of this life-giving stream stands the Tree of Life, no longer guarded or forbidden, but freely accessible, bearing twelve kinds of fruit—one for every month—it's leaves bringing healing to the nations. What was lost in Eden has been fully, gloriously restored.

Gone is the curse that once marred creation. In its place stands a city of light and righteousness, where the servants of God dwell in and around it in perfect harmony with their Creator. No more barriers. No more separation. The redeemed will see God's face and bear His name upon their foreheads—a mark not of servitude, but of beloved belonging. There is no night in this eternal city. No need for sun or lamp, because the Lord GOD Himself gives light, and His people will reign with Him forever and ever.

As the vision closes, the angel reminds John that everything he has seen is faithful and true. These are not dreams or distant hopes, but sure promises that will come to pass. Jesus Himself speaks into the final chapter of the Bible with urgency: "Behold, I come quickly." These are words of comfort and also of call—a reminder to stay watchful, faithful, and ready.

In the quiet hush of eternity's threshold, a final invitation is offered: "Let him who is thirsty come." It is the last call of grace in Scripture—a wide-open door for any who long to drink freely from the water of life. There is no entrance fee, no qualification, only desire and faith.

John, overwhelmed by the majesty of what he's witnessed, falls in worship. But the angel directs him to worship God alone. He is told not to seal up the book, for the time is near. Let the holy remain holy, and the wicked remain wicked—because the day of reckoning is coming. To those who overcome, a blessing awaits. But to any who tamper with the words of this prophecy—adding or taking away—there is a dire warning.

And then, in what may be the most tender moment in Scripture, Jesus speaks once more: "Surely I come quickly." And John, speaking not only for himself, but for the entire Bride of Christ, answers with trembling hope, "Even so, come, Lord Jesus." The final words of Revelation—and the Bible—echo a promise and a prayer: Grace to all who love Him. And a longing that has filled the heart of every believer since time began—Come, Lord Jesus.

DO YOU REALLY KNOW HIM?

He is not just the centerpiece of history—He is the Author of it. Jesus is the King of the Jews by heritage, the King of Israel by covenant, and the King of all nations by sovereign right. He is the timeless ruler, the One who reigns above the rise and fall of empires. Heaven calls Him the King of Glory. Earth will bow to Him as King of kings. Hell trembles at the mention of His name—for He is the Lord of lords.

He is the Prophet who surpasses Moses, the Priest whose authority exceeds Melchizedek, and the Warrior Champion whose victory makes Joshua's conquest look like a shadow. He is the sacrificed Son in place of Isaac, the rightful heir from the line of David, and the rejected brother exalted—just like Joseph. But no earthly title captures Him fully.

Creation shouts His glory—the skies preach His fame. He is the One who is, who was, and who is to come. The Beginning and the End. The Alpha and the Omega. The Aleph and the Tav. The A and the Z. He is the radiance of God in flesh, the Lamb who was slain yet lives forevermore. He is the Word, the Light, the Living Bread, and the Door. He is the great "I AM" who spoke from the burning bush. The Captain of heaven's armies. The Holy One who goes before us, behind us, and within us.

He is immeasurably strong, endlessly faithful, unshakably just, and lavishly merciful. In Him dwells the fullness of the Godhead in bodily form. He is the Kinsman Redeemer who stepped into our mess, the Avenger of Blood who rights every wrong, the Refuge for the weary, the Priest who intercedes without end, and the reigning King whose throne is everlasting.

He is the beauty behind every masterpiece, the brilliance behind every truth, and the mystery that confounds every critic. He is the Miracle of every age—the perfection of all that is good. And yet, He is not distant or abstract. He wrote His love letter in crimson ink on the Cross of Calvary, in blood that still speaks.

He crafted the hill He was crucified on. The hands that stretched the heavens were pierced for you. Nails didn't hold Him there—love did. A love that laid down divinity to lift us into glory. A love that chose the Cross so you could be chosen. He became nothing, so you could inherit everything.

He invites the tempted, restores the broken, and revives the weary. He cleanses the unclean, frees the bound, and welcomes the forgotten. He walks with the outcast, defends the defenseless, and raises the dead. He heals, helps, holds, hears. He saves.

His promises never expire. His grace never weakens. His truth never bends. His mercy never ends. His power never falters. His throne never shakes. His love never fails.

No one can define Him. No system can contain Him. No trial can defeat Him. No grave could keep Him. Herod tried. Pilate tried. The Pharisees tried. But He rose—because He is risen. And He's returning.

He will never be replaced, overthrown, or forgotten. His name is above every name. And one day, every knee will bow, every tongue will confess: Jesus Christ is Lord.

He is the glory of heaven, the treasure of earth, and the heartbeat of eternity. The question is—do you know Him?

We sit in a cozy, sun-drenched study filled with worn leather chairs and walls lined with well-loved Bibles, commentaries, and journals. A teacup gently steams on the small table between Irene and I, positioned near a large window that overlooks a blooming park. The atmosphere is hushed, reverent, and intimate—perfect for deep scriptural reflection.

I leaned back in my chair, tracing the edge of my Bible's page as my thoughts swirl. "Irene, do you ever get the sense that the Book of Revelation isn't just about the end of the Bible—but about the whole Bible?"

Irene nods, her fingers wrapped around the warm teacup, eyes catching the golden light streaming through the window. "Yes, Ann. Revelation isn't simply the final chapter—it's the grand unveiling of everything that came before it. It's like a lens that suddenly brings Genesis, the law, the prophets, the gospels, and the church into sharper focus. The story God began in Genesis doesn't just conclude in Revelation—it finds its completion there. Full circle."

"Exactly, Irene. Genesis opens with, 'In the beginning, God created the heavens and the earth.' Revelation closes with a new heaven and a new earth—not just new in time, but new in kind. What was once corrupted is now glorified. Revelation isn't a sequel—it's the fulfillment of the entire divine drama."

Irene nodded thoughtfully. "The symbols we see in Genesis echo through Revelation—but refined by the journey of Scripture. The Tree of Life, lost and guarded by cherubim in Eden, reappears in Revelation—no longer forbidden, but freely accessible to all who overcome. It's like God never let go of Eden. He carried that hope through Abraham, Moses, David, the prophets—and fulfilled it in the Lamb."

I leaned in. "Exactly! And speaking of the Lamb—Genesis gave us the first sacrifice when God clothed Adam and Eve with skins. Exodus gave us the Passover Lamb. Isaiah foretold the Suffering Servant. John the Baptist cried, 'Behold, the Lamb of God.' And Revelation? Revelation crowns Him. 'Worthy is the Lamb who was slain!' The entire Bible leads to that moment."

"Yes! Even Babylon's fall brings it full circle," Irene said, eyes lighting with conviction. "Genesis gave us Nimrod and the Tower of Babel—the arrogance of man trying to build apart from God. Revelation doesn't forget. It reveals Babylon not just as a place, but as a spiritual system—one that's infected humanity for generations. And then it shows us its final collapse. God's justice, fulfilled."

I leaned forward. "And think about this—back in Genesis, God walked with man in the cool of the day. But in Revelation? 'Behold, the tabernacle of God is with men.' Not just a garden—but a city. Not just a passing visit—but a permanent dwelling. That's what the whole Bible has been moving toward: God with us, forever."

"Revelation also unveils the fullness of the covenants," I said, voice low with awe. "Genesis introduced the promise to Abraham—'in your seed all nations will be blessed.' Revelation reveals the Seed: Christ. And those in Him? A vast multitude from every nation, tribe, and tongue. The Bible didn't shift directions—it matured into fulfillment."

Irene nodded thoughtfully. "And the imagery of water—it carries through, Ann. Genesis gave us rivers that nourished Eden. Revelation gives us the river of life, flowing straight from the throne of God. Genesis introduced the sea that separated lands and people. But Revelation? 'There shall be no more sea.' The barrier is gone. Separation erased."

"It even ties back to the serpent," I said, my voice firm. "The enemy who slithered into Genesis is finally thrown into the Lake of Fire in Revelation. His rebellion, his lies—they're judged. Finished. Revelation isn't just prophecy—it's divine closure. The bruised heel becomes the crushed head."

Irene's eyes lit with understanding. "And in that, Ann, it's unmistakable: Revelation isn't the end—it's the unveiling. Not just apocalypse, but *apokalypsis*—the great reveal. The entire Word of God pulls back the curtain. We finally see: the Lamb, the throne, the saints, the city, the glory. What was once whispered in shadow is now declared in light."

Thinking out loud, I murmured, "The New Testament is in the Old Testament concealed; the Old Testament is in the New Testament revealed."

Irene nodded slowly, a thoughtful smile tugging at her lips. "From garden to city. From exile to homecoming. From promise to possession. Revelation isn't just the ending—it's the moment the whole story comes into focus."

"It's like God has been writing one long, beautiful, redemptive story—His love letter to us. And in Revelation . . . He finally places the period. Or maybe the exclamation point."

Irene smiled softly. "Yes, Ann. 'Surely I am coming quickly.' That's not just the ending—it's the invitation. And the whole Bible has been preparing our hearts for it."

Then, I reached forward and turned the page.

"And now," I said softly, "the river begins."

Revelation 22 opens not as a new scene, but as the continuation—the culmination—of all we've seen. The Lamb is on the throne, and from that throne flows the river of life, clear as crystal. A new Eden. A new creation. A new forever. Let's step into the final chapter.

THE REVELATION OF JESUS CHRIST REVEALS:

22:1 And he showed me a pure river of water of life, clear as crystal, proceeding out of the throne of God and of the Lamb.

This opening verse of Revelation 22 is breathtaking in both its imagery and theological depth. After being shown the glory of the New Jerusalem—the Holy City descending from heaven—John's attention is now drawn to a singular feature at the heart of that city: a pure river of the water of life.

This is not a symbolic river, but a literal, eternal river, described as "clear as crystal." Its purity reflects the sinless, undefiled nature of the eternal order. There is no pollution, no death, no decay—only perfect, living water, flowing perpetually from the source of all life: the throne of God and of the Lamb. This union—God the Father and Jesus the Lamb—is central. Their shared throne in the New Jerusalem is the very seat of divine authority, glory, and provision.

The river is not only beautiful, but life-giving. It is called the "water of life" because it flows from the One who is the Life (John 14:6). Just as Jesus once said to the woman at the well in John 4:14, "Whosoever drinks of the water that I shall give him shall never thirst," this eternal river is the fulfillment of that promise. It nourishes, refreshes, and sustains all who dwell in the city—not just physically, but spiritually and eternally.

This river also hearkens back to Eden, where a river flowed out of the Garden and watered it (Genesis 2:10). In a profound way, Revelation 22:1 reveals Eden restored—but on a far grander scale. This river is not hidden behind cherubim and a flaming sword—it is wide open to the redeemed, a gift from God to His people in their eternal home.

The river's origin is key. It proceeds directly from under the throne of God and of the Lamb. This imagery tells us that everything in the eternal order flows from divine authority, divine love, and divine grace. Jesus is both King and Shepherd, and from His rule flows everlasting life to His people.

Therefore, Revelation 22:1 sets the tone for the final chapter of Scripture: the story of paradise restored, where divine intimacy, provision, and peace now flow eternally to those written in the Lamb's Book of Life. This river is not only central to the geography of the city—it's central to the joy of eternity.

OLD TESTAMENT FORESHADOWS REVELATION:

> Afterward he brought me again unto the door of the house; and, behold, waters issued out from under the threshold of the house eastward: for the forefront of the house stood toward the east, and the waters came down from under from the right side of the house, at the south side of the altar. (Ezekiel 47:1)

In Ezekiel 47:1, the prophet sees a vision of a river flowing from the temple in the Millennial Kingdom—a preview of divine restoration and life-giving blessing. In Revelation 22:1, John sees a similar river flowing from the throne of God and the Lamb in the New Jerusalem—a final and eternal fulfillment of that promise. Both passages depict: Water proceeding from God's dwelling place. A source of life and restoration flowing outward. And a vision of healing, purity, and divine presence. It's the movement from the Millennial Temple (Ezekiel) to Eternal Throne (Revelation)—from partial fulfillment to ultimate glory.

THE REVELATION OF JESUS CHRIST REVEALS:

22:2 In the midst of the street of it, and on either side of the river, was there the Tree of Life, which bare twelve manner of fruits, and yielded her fruit every month: and the leaves of the tree were for the healing of the nations.

This verse is both a fulfillment and a restoration. What began in Genesis now comes full circle in Revelation. The Tree of Life, first introduced in the garden of Eden (Genesis 2:9), vanished from Scripture after the fall of Adam and Eve. Its reappearance in the New Jerusalem signals not only the end of the curse but the beginning of eternal healing and wholeness for redeemed humanity.

In Eden, Adam and Eve were banished from the Tree of Life to prevent eternal life in a fallen, sinful state (Genesis 3:22–24). God placed cherubim with flaming swords to guard the tree—a divine act of mercy. If man had eaten from it after sinning, he would have lived eternally separated from God in a state of damnation.

Now, in Revelation 22, the Tree of Life is back—not in a garden, but in the eternal city of God. It lines both sides of the river that flows from the throne of God and the Lamb. This tree is no longer guarded; it is freely accessible to the redeemed. What was once forbidden is now a gift, because Christ has removed the curse and made all things new (Revelation 21:5).

It bears twelve kinds of fruit, each in its season—symbolizing divine variety, abundance, and continual nourishment. Every month brings a fresh supply, indicating that in eternity, time may still unfold in some rhythm or cycle, but without decay or lack.

"The leaves of the tree are for the healing of the nations"—a poetic and powerful declaration. There will be no sickness, no sorrow, no division among peoples. This healing refers not to curing diseases, but to perpetual peace, wholeness, and unity—*shalom* in its truest form. The nations, once divided at Babel, once at war through history, are now united in worship and fellowship under the Lamb.

This verse is rich in restoration theology. It speaks to God's faithfulness to complete what He began—from Eden to eternity, from exile to access, from curse to communion. The Tree of Life is more than a symbol; it is the evidence that paradise lost has become paradise regained—not just for individuals, but for all redeemed creation.

OLD TESTAMENT FORESHADOWS REVELATION:

And by the river upon the bank thereof, on this side and on that side, shall grow all kinds of trees for food, whose leaf shall not fade, neither shall the fruit thereof fail: it shall bring forth new fruit according to his months, because their waters they issued out of the sanctuary: and the fruit thereof shall be for food, and the leaf thereof for medicine. (Ezekiel 47:12)

This prophetic passage, Ezekiel 47:12, beautifully foreshadows the Tree of Life described in Revelation 22:2—bearing fruit each month and producing leaves for healing. It confirms the theme of divine restoration, provision, and healing for the nations in the eternal Kingdom of God.

THE REVELATION OF JESUS CHRIST REVEALS:

22:3 And there will be no more curse: but the throne of God and of the Lamb will be in it; and His servants will serve Him.

This verse delivers one of the most profound and hopeful declarations in all of Scripture: the curse is gone—forever. This is a direct reversal of Genesis 3, where sin entered the world, the ground was cursed, toil began, pain was introduced, and death followed. Revelation 22:3 announces the full and final redemption of creation. The curse of sin, which has haunted humanity since Eden, is not just lifted—it is eradicated in the presence of God.

The throne of God and of the Lamb being present in the New Jerusalem signifies unified, eternal governance and intimacy. No longer will God's presence be hidden behind veils or accessed only through priests or intermediaries. His throne is right in the middle of the city, and His servants shall serve Him—a reminder that heaven will not be idle, but filled with meaningful, joyful worship and purpose.

The phrase "His servants shall serve Him" reflects restored relationship and redeemed labor. The word "serve" here (Greek: *latreuo*) implies both worship and priestly service. In eternity, God's people will experience the fullness of what they were always created for: to dwell in His presence and serve with delight.

Theologically, this verse suggests the reversal of entropy: the laws of decay and death—what we know scientifically as the second law of thermodynamics—no longer apply. Nothing will break down. Nothing will decay. Everything remains in perfect harmony, including time, space, purpose, and joy. God's glory will infuse every aspect of existence, and all of creation will thrive under His eternal reign.

OLD TESTAMENT FORESHADOWS REVELATION:

And men shall dwell in it, and there shall be no more utter destruction; but Jerusalem shall be safely inhabited. (Zechariah 14:11)

This prophetic verse points forward to a restored, curse-free Jerusalem—echoing the vision John receives of the New Jerusalem, where the curse is lifted, and God Himself dwells with His people.

THE REVELATION OF JESUS CHRIST REVEALS:

22:4 And they will see His face; and His name will be on their foreheads.

This verse is one of the most awe-inspiring promises in all of Scripture—it speaks of direct, unfiltered access to the very face of God. Throughout the Bible, to see God's face was a terrifying and unreachable hope. In Exodus 33:20, God told Moses, "You cannot see my face: for there shall no man see Me, and live." And yet here, in the New Jerusalem, the redeemed will not only live—but thrive— in the full, unveiled presence of God.

To "see His face" signifies intimacy, acceptance, and eternal fellowship. It is the ultimate restoration of what was lost in Eden. Adam and Eve once walked with God, but sin brought separation. Now, through Christ, that separation is completely erased. Seeing His face represents perfect communion, endless joy, and total transformation.

The second part—"His name will be on their foreheads"—speaks of ownership, identity, and consecration. In contrast to the mark of the beast on the foreheads of the wicked (Revelation 13:16–17), God's people are sealed with His name, publicly declaring their loyalty and belonging to the Lamb. This name is not merely written externally—it reflects an inner reality: we belong to Him, and He belongs to us. This is the fulfillment of every longing of the heart—and the destiny of every true believer.

OLD TESTAMENT FORESHADOWS REVELATION:

The LORD bless you, and keep you: The LORD make His face shine upon you, and be gracious unto you: The LORD lift up His countenance upon you, and give you peace. And they shall put my name upon the children of Israel; and I will bless them. (Numbers 6:24–27)

This priestly blessing, given by God through Moses to Aaron, reflects the deep longing of Israel to be in God's favor—to see His face, experience His grace, and live in His peace. In the Old Testament, the idea of God's face shining upon someone symbolized divine favor, closeness, and blessing, even though direct sight of God was not possible due to sin. Revelation 22:4 fulfills this ancient desire—what was once a hope spoken over Israel becomes an eternal reality for the redeemed. No longer mediated by priests or concealed by veils, the face of God is now beheld without fear, and His name marks us forever as His own.

THE REVELATION OF JESUS CHRIST REVEALS:

22:5 And there will be no night there; and they need no candle, neither light of the sun; for the Lord GOD gives them light: and they shall reign forever and ever.

This verse captures the eternal radiance and unbroken fellowship of the redeemed with God in the New Jerusalem. The absence of night is not just a physical reality—it symbolizes the removal of all spiritual darkness, fear, danger, and separation. In the eternal state, there will never again be a moment without the presence and glory of God.

There is no need for candlelight or sunlight, because God Himself is the light—both literally and spiritually. This divine illumination reflects perfect clarity, understanding, peace, and joy. It is the fulfillment of what Jesus declared in John 8:12: "I am the light of the world: he that follows Me shall not walk in darkness, but shall have the light of life."

The final phrase, "they shall reign forever and ever," speaks of the eternal destiny and authority of the redeemed. We are not merely passive citizens of heaven—we are co-heirs with Christ, entrusted with eternal stewardship and reigning with Him in a kingdom that will never end (2 Timothy 2:12; Revelation 5:10). This reign is one of perfect righteousness, joy, and purpose—free from corruption, sin, or decay.

This verse brings Revelation to its grand crescendo: an everlasting light, an eternal reign, and a redeemed people forever in the presence of their King.

OLD TESTAMENT FORESHADOWS REVELATION:

The sun shall be no more your light by day; neither for brightness shall the moon give light unto you: but the LORD shall be unto you an everlasting light, and your God your glory. Your sun shall no more go down; neither shall your moon withdraw itself: for the LORD shall be your everlasting light, and the days of your mourning shall be ended. (Isaiah 60:19–20)

This prophetic passage from Isaiah perfectly mirrors the imagery in Revelation 22:5. Both affirm that God Himself becomes the light of His people—removing the need for created sources of illumination—and both promise eternal joy, peace, and the end of sorrow. It's a beautiful demonstration of how the Bible, from beginning to end, tells one unified story of redemption and restoration.

THE REVELATION OF JESUS CHRIST REVEALS:

[22:6] And he said to me: These sayings are faithful and true: and the Lord GOD of the holy prophets sent His angel to show to His servants the things which must shortly be done.

Revelation 22:6 serves as a divine seal of authenticity for everything revealed throughout the book. The angel declares, "These sayings are faithful and true"—echoing earlier affirmations in Revelation 21:5, reinforcing the trustworthiness of the prophetic vision. This isn't mythology or metaphor; it's reality. It's God's solemn assurance that everything John has seen will come to pass.

The verse also highlights that "the Lord GOD of the holy prophets"—the same God who spoke through Isaiah, Jeremiah, Daniel, and the rest—"sent His angel to show to His servants the things which must shortly be done." This statement bridges the Old and New Testaments, uniting the prophetic voices of Scripture under one divine Author. Just as God revealed future events to the prophets of old, He now reveals the final unfolding of His redemptive plan to John.

The phrase "must shortly be done" underscores the imminence and urgency of these events. Though centuries have passed since John penned these words, they remain relevant because God's timeline is not our own (2 Peter 3:8). The point is not to mark our calendars but to ready our hearts. Heaven is not just our future destination—it is our present motivation.

This verse re-centers our faith in the certainty of Christ's return and the fulfillment of every promise. It reminds us that this isn't just about prophecy—it's about a Person, Immanuel, "God with us," whose presence will be fully realized in the eternal dwelling place of God and His people. Revelation 22:6 invites the believer to live with expectation, urgency, and hope, knowing that He who promised is faithful and true.

OLD TESTAMENT FORESHADOWS REVELATION:

God is not a man, that He should lie; neither the son of man, that He should repent: has He said, and shall He not do it? Or has He spoken, and shall He not make it good? (Numbers 23:19)

Revelation 22:6 emphasizes that "these sayings are faithful and true," and Numbers 23:19 reinforces the trustworthiness and unchanging nature of God's Word. Both verses confirm that what God declares, He will certainly fulfill. The idea of divine integrity and the certainty of prophetic fulfillment is central to both texts. This connection underlines that the visions given to John in Revelation are not symbolic fantasies, but faithful, true declarations from the God who never lies.

THE REVELATION OF JESUS CHRIST REVEALS:

$^{22.7}$ Behold, I come quickly: blessed is he that keeps the sayings of the prophecy of this book.

This verse is the first of three times in Revelation 22 where Jesus Himself declares, "Behold, I come quickly" (verses 12 and 20). The urgency in His words is not necessarily a reference to immediate chronological time, but rather to the suddenness and certainty of His coming when it occurs. The Greek word for "quickly" (*tachu*) conveys swiftness and immediacy—He will return suddenly, like lightning flashing across the sky (Luke 17:24).

The beatitude—"blessed is he that keeps the sayings of the prophecy of this book"—reminds us that Revelation is not merely a book to be studied, debated, or admired, but a call to obedience and faithfulness. This echoes the blessing found at the very beginning of the book in Revelation 1:3, linking the start and end of the prophecy with the same exhortation: read it, hear it, and keep it.

To "keep" the saying means to treasure, guard, and live by them. It is an invitation not to sensationalism or idle curiosity, but to holy living in light of Christ's return. Jesus is not giving a vague suggestion—He is issuing a divine warning, filled with hope and urgency. The return of Christ is both imminent and incentivizing—every believer is called to stay awake, remain faithful, and walk in obedience until He comes.

This verse re-centers the reader on the ultimate message of Revelation: Jesus is coming soon, and it is the wise, faithful servant who will be found ready.

OLD TESTAMENT FORESHADOWS REVELATION:

Thus says the LORD, Keep your judgment, and do justice: for My salvation is near to come, and My righteousness to be revealed. (Isaiah 56:1)

This verse shares key themes with Revelation 22:7. "My salvation is near to come" aligns with "Behold, I come quickly." Isaiah exhorts people to keep judgment and do justice, just as Revelation blesses those who keep the sayings of the prophecy. Both verses encourage living righteously in view of what is soon to be revealed. Isaiah 56:1 highlights the urgency and the blessing associated with faithful obedience just before the manifestation of God's final salvation—making it a rich prophetic companion to Revelation's closing call.

THE REVELATION OF JESUS CHRIST REVEALS:

22:8 And I John saw these things, and heard them. And when I had heard and seen, I fell down to worship before the feet of the angel which showed me these things.

This verse captures the awe and overwhelming reverence that the apostle John experienced as he received the final visions of God's redemptive plan. It emphasizes the vivid reality of what John saw and heard. These were not merely symbolic dreams or abstract ideas—they were actual revelations from the Lord, communicated through an angelic messenger. John's response—falling down to worship—reveals the emotional and spiritual weight of the encounter.

However, this act also points to a recurring human weakness: the temptation to misdirect worship. Despite his deep spiritual maturity, John again finds himself falling at the feet of an angel (as he did in Revelation 19:10). The power and glory surrounding the angel were so intense that even John mistook the messenger for the One deserving worship. This reminds us that even the most faithful believers can be overwhelmed in the presence of the divine and must be constantly reoriented to give God alone the glory.

Theologically, this verse is a powerful warning: no matter how noble or radiant the messenger, worship belongs to God alone. The role of angels—even when delivering monumental truths—is to point us upward, not to become the focus of our devotion.

John's transparency in sharing this moment reveals his humility and underscores a profound truth: even those closest to God need reminders to keep their worship rightly directed.

OLD TESTAMENT FORESHADOWS REVELATION:

And it came to pass, when the flame went up toward heaven from off the altar, that the Angel of the Lord ascended in the flame of the altar. And Manoah and his wife looked on it, and fell on their faces to the ground. (Judges 13:20)

In Revelation 22:8, John is overwhelmed by the glory of what he has seen and heard, and instinctively falls to worship the angel delivering the message. Similarly, in Judges 13, Manoah and his wife witness the Angel of the Lord ascending in the flame and instinctively fall to the ground in awe and fear. In both cases, there is a misdirected act of reverence—not necessarily out of idolatry, but from an overwhelming sense of divine presence. The angel in Revelation immediately corrects John (verse 9), just as the angelic encounter in Judges leads Manoah to realize the seriousness of divine manifestations. This connection underscores a recurring biblical truth: human awe in the presence of the supernatural must be rightly aligned—to worship God alone.

THE REVELATION OF JESUS CHRIST REVEALS:

22:9 Then says he to me, See you do it not: for I am your fellow-servant, and of your brethren the prophets, and of them which keep the sayings of this book: worship God.

This verse serves as a powerful reminder of the exclusive worship due to God alone. Again, John, overwhelmed by the majesty and gravity of what he has seen and heard, falls at the feet of the angel to worship. But the angel stops him immediately with a correction that echoes both humility and theological clarity. "See you do it not."

The angel identifies himself not as an object of veneration, but as a fellow-servant, one among the prophets and those who obey the words of Revelation. In this rebuke, we hear a clear declaration: no matter how glorious or supernatural the messenger may appear, worship belongs only to God.

The instruction to "worship God" is not a suggestion—it's a command, anchoring the final chapters of Revelation in the central theme of true worship.

Throughout the book, we've seen a war between true and false worship: the Lamb versus the Antichrist, heavenly songs versus demonic deception. This verse crystallizes the conclusion: only God is worthy.

Interestingly, this is not the first time John attempted to worship an angel (Revelation 9:10), and again, he is corrected. The repetition may show how easily—even for the most faithful—we can be caught up in the glory of divine encounters, but still miss the target of our adoration.

From a broader perspective, this moment also reaffirms the continuity of God's servants across the ages: angels, prophets, and saints are all on the same mission—pointing creation to the Creator. As we close in on the final moments of Revelation, we're reminded that at the heart of prophecy, of history, and of eternity is this single command: Worship God.

OLD TESTAMENT FORESHADOWS REVELATION:

You shalt have no other gods before Me. You shalt not make unto you any graven image, or any likeness of any thing that is in heaven above, or that is in the earth beneath, or that is in the water under the earth. You shalt not bow down yourself to them, nor serve them: for I the LORD your God am a jealous God, visiting the iniquity of the fathers upon the children unto the third and fourth generation of them that hate Me. (Exodus 20:3–5)

The Old Testament passage lays the foundation for exclusive worship of God, and Revelation 22:9 reaffirms this principle in the New Testament's final chapter. The angel, though glorious, refuses worship—just as God commanded that worship be reserved for Him alone.

THE REVELATION OF JESUS CHRIST REVEALS:

22:10 And he says to me, Seal not the sayings of the prophecy of this book: for the time is at hand.

This verse stands in bold contrast to Daniel 12:4 and 12:9, where the prophet is commanded to "seal up the book until the time of the end." In Daniel's day, much of the prophetic vision was for a distant future. But in Revelation 22:10, the command is reversed—John is told not to seal the book, because "the time is at hand." The implication is profound: the final phase of God's redemptive plan has already been set in motion.

The phrase "the time is at hand" translates from the Greek word *kairos*, which refers to an opportune, appointed time—a decisive moment—not merely chronological time (*chronos*). This is not suggesting that the events must unfold immediately in our human perception, but rather that everything needed for their fulfillment is already in place. The stage is set. The actors are in position. Nothing more needs to be added to God's prophetic clock before these things unfold.

Additionally, the command to "seal not" emphasizes urgency and accessibility. The message of Revelation is not to be hidden or reserved for an elite few. It is meant to be read, studied, and proclaimed by believers everywhere. The blessing of Revelation 1:3—"Blessed is he that reads, and they that hear the words of this prophecy"—is directly tied to this openness. God wants His people to be aware, alert, and ready.

This verse reminds us that prophecy is not merely for fascination, but for preparation. The events described in Revelation are not idle predictions—they are unfolding realities. The call is for urgency in faith, clarity in truth, and boldness in testimony. The time to awaken is now.

OLD TESTAMENT FORESHADOWS REVELATION:

Now go, write it before them in a table, and note it in a book, that it may be for the time to come forever and ever. (Isaiah 30:8)

In Isaiah 30:8, God tells the prophet to write the message in a book for future generations—to make it accessible, not hidden or sealed. It reflects God's desire for His Word to be preserved, declared, and available for all time, especially as His judgment and mercy unfold. Similarly, Revelation 22:10 affirms that the time has arrived, and God's message is not to be sealed anymore, but openly declared. This demonstrates a prophetic continuity: what was once written for the future (Isaiah) is now revealed and ready (Revelation).

THE REVELATION OF JESUS CHRIST REVEALS:

[22:11] He that is unjust, let him be unjust still: and he which is filthy, let him be filthy still: and he that is righteous, let him be righteous still: and he that is holy, let him be holy still.

This sobering verse reveals a powerful truth about finality. As the end of the age draws near, the message becomes clear: there is a point when the condition of every soul will be fixed for eternity. Those who have chosen rebellion, wickedness, or moral defilement will remain in that state. Likewise, those who have chosen Christ, righteousness, and holiness will be eternally sealed in their redeemed state.

This echoes the principle seen throughout Scripture: a day is coming when the time to repent will end. The door of grace, open for so long, will finally shut. Just as in the days of Noah, when the ark was sealed and no one else could enter (Genesis 7:16), so too will the opportunity for salvation come to a close.

God is not unjust—He has given every opportunity. But in the end, our eternal destinies are locked by the choices we made in this life.

This verse also serves as a warning to the complacent. It's not a call to fatalism, but a last call to urgency. Just before Christ's return, there will be no time left for soul-searching or delayed repentance. As 2 Peter 3:3–4 notes, scoffers will say "all things continue as they were," but the sudden arrival of judgment will prove them wrong.

> Knowing this first, that there shall come in the last days scoffers, walking after their own lusts, and saying, Where is the promise of His coming? For since the fathers fell asleep, all things continue as they were from the beginning of the creation. (2 Peter 3:3–4)

Those who are unjust and filthy have refused God's grace, and so their condition becomes irreversible. On the other hand, the righteous and holy are not made so by their works, but by the redemptive blood of the Lamb. Their state, too, becomes eternally fixed—not as a burden, but as a blessed inheritance.

Therefore, Revelation 22:11 is not just a statement of fact—it's a prophetic line drawn in the sand. When Christ comes, how He finds you is how you will remain forever. This is the ultimate dividing line of eternity. Let it stir us to walk in holiness and to share the gospel while the time of grace remains open.

OLD TESTAMENT FORESHADOWS REVELATION:

> But when I speak with you, I will open your mouth, and you shalt say unto them, Thus says the Lord GOD; He that hears, let him hear; and he that forbears, let him forbear: for they are a rebellious house. (Ezekiel 3:27)

This echoes the same principle of personal accountability and final response to divine revelation. Just as John is told in Revelation 22:11 that the unjust will remain unjust and the righteous will remain righteous, Ezekiel 3:27 is told that some will hear and respond, while others will ignore and remain rebellious. The message has been proclaimed—now comes the moment of personal choice and eternal consequence.

THE REVELATION OF JESUS CHRIST REVEALS:

> [22:12] And, behold, I come quickly; and My reward is with Me, to give every man according as his work shall be.

This verse powerfully reaffirms one of the central themes of the Book of Revelation: Jesus is coming—suddenly, certainly, and personally. Again, the word "quickly" (Greek: *tachy*) doesn't necessarily imply "soon" in terms of human chronology, but rather speaks of suddenness and swiftness—when He comes, it will be without delay or warning.

Christ is not coming empty-handed. He says, "My reward is with Me," which reflects not only His awareness of every believer's labor and faithfulness but also

His role as Judge and King. This statement echoes Isaiah 40:10, "His reward is with Him, and His work before Him," drawing upon prophetic imagery to emphasize that He brings both justice and blessing.

"To give every man according as his work shall be" makes clear that personal responsibility and faithfulness matter. Though salvation is by grace through faith (Ephesians 2:8–9), our works will be judged for reward (2 Corinthians 5:10). This judgment is not about condemnation for the believer but evaluation for reward, based on obedience, sacrifice, and spiritual fruit.

> For by grace are you saved through faith; and that not of yourselves: it is the gift of God: Not of works, lest any man should boast. For we are His workmanship, created in Christ Jesus unto good works, which God has before ordained that we should walk in them. (Ephesians 2:8–9)

> For we must all appear before the Judgment Seat of Christ; that every one may receive the things done in his body, according to that he has done, whether it be good or bad. (2 Corinthians 5:10)

This verse also serves as a wake-up call to avoid complacency. The promise of Jesus' return should never lead to passivity or procrastination. Instead, it should fuel holiness, urgency, and dedication, reminding us that we are stewards of time, talents, and truth.

Ultimately, Revelation 22:12 is a call to live intentionally and watchfully, with the assurance that Christ sees all, remembers all, and will reward justly when He appears.

OLD TESTAMENT FORESHADOWS REVELATION:

> Behold, the Lord GOD will come with a strong hand, and His arm shall rule for Him: behold, His reward is with Him, and His work before Him. (Isaiah 40:10)

This verse is remarkably similar in both language and meaning. Isaiah 40:10 prophesies the coming of the Lord with power and justice, bringing His reward and executing His righteous purposes. It highlights the Lord's sovereignty, the certainty of His coming, and His intention to reward or judge according to each person's deeds—the same themes that are echoed in Revelation 22:12.

This connection bridges the prophetic anticipation in the Old Testament with its fulfillment in the New Testament, showing the consistency of God's justice and His plan from beginning to end.

THE REVELATION OF JESUS CHRIST REVEALS:

[22:13] I am Alpha and Omega, the Beginning and the End, the First and the Last.

This majestic declaration—repeated for the fourth time in Revelation (Revelation 1:8, 1:11, 21:6)—reaffirms Christ's absolute divinity, sovereignty, and eternal nature. It is one of the most powerful "I AM" statements in Scripture, encompassing all dimensions of time, space, and authority. By calling Himself:

- Alpha and Omega—the first and last letters of the Greek alphabet—Jesus is saying, "I am the Author and the Conclusion of everything."
- The Beginning and the End—He is the origin of all creation and the goal toward which all history moves.
- The First and the Last—echoing Isaiah 44:6, a clear affirmation of His oneness with Yahweh (God the Father).

In this climactic moment of Revelation, Jesus is not merely presenting Himself as Savior, but also as Judge and Ruler over all creation. This is the final affirmation of His unchanging, eternal identity—that He is the same yesterday, today, and forever (Hebrews 13:8). All power, all history, all prophecy, and all destinies culminate in Him.

Jesus Christ the same yesterday, and today, and forever. (Hebrews 13:8)

Revelation 22:13 also continues the tone of urgency and finality begun in verse 12—"Behold, I come quickly." The Judge is not distant. His return is imminent. And when He comes, His judgment will be righteous, His rewards just, and His rule eternal.

Ultimately, Revelation 22:13 is both a warning and a comfort: a warning to the unrepentant that Christ's authority is final, and a comfort to the faithful that the One who is coming is the eternal King who holds everything together, from Alpha to Omega.

OLD TESTAMENT FORESHADOWS REVELATION:

Thus says the LORD the King of Israel, and His Redeemer the LORD of hosts;
I am the First, and I am the Last; and beside Me there is no God. (Isaiah 44:6)

This link strongly reinforces the divine identity of Jesus Christ. In Revelation 22:13, Jesus uses titles that were once reserved for Yahweh (God the Father) alone, affirming His eternal nature, deity, and role as supreme judge of all creation. It brings full circle the message of Scripture—from the prophetic declaration in Isaiah 44:6 to the final revelation in John's vision.

THE REVELATION OF JESUS CHRIST REVEALS:

22:14 Blessed are they that do His commandments, that they may have right to the Tree of Life, and may enter in through the gates into the city.

This verse brings the grand conclusion of Scripture into sharp focus—blessing is promised not merely to those who believe, but to those whose belief compels them to obey. The word "blessed" here speaks of a deep, enduring happiness—a state of divine approval and favor. It echoes the beatitudes of Jesus, where inner joy is promised to the faithful in spirit and conduct (Matthew 5).

The phrase "they that do His commandments" ties the entire biblical narrative together. From Eden to Sinai, from the prophets to the teachings of Jesus, obedience has always been a marker of covenant faithfulness. It is not legalism—it is the evidence of love. As Jesus said in John 14:15, "If you love Me, keep My commandments."

The reward for this covenant obedience is twofold:

1. **Access to the Tree of Life**—The very tree Adam and Eve were barred from in Genesis 3:22–24 now becomes the reward of the righteous. It signifies eternal life, not just in duration but in quality—full, flourishing, uninterrupted communion with God.

2. **Entrance through the Gates into the City**—This speaks of full citizenship in the New Jerusalem. Not as visitors, but as rightful heirs. The gates, named after the twelve tribes of Israel (Revelation 21:12), are always open for those who belong to the Lamb.

This verse, then, stands as a powerful reminder that salvation is not simply about escape from judgment, but about restoration to paradise, access to divine life, and belonging to the everlasting city of God. The commandments are not burdens—they are the road markers guiding us to our eternal home.

OLD TESTAMENT FORESHADOWS REVELATION:

Blessed are the undefiled in the way, who walk in the law of the LORD. Blessed are they that keep His testimonies, and that seek Him with the whole heart. (Psalm 119:1–2)

Both passages emphasize blessing upon those who obey God's commandments. In Psalm 119:1–2, the focus is on those who walk in God's law—highlighting covenant faithfulness and wholehearted devotion. In Revelation 22:14, the blessing is expanded into eternity: obedience leads to access to the Tree of Life and entrance into the eternal city.

THE REVELATION OF JESUS CHRIST REVEALS:

[22:15] For without are dogs, and sorcerers, and whoremongers, and murderers, and idolaters, and whosoever loves and makes a lie.

This verse delivers a stark contrast to the blessings described just one verse earlier. While verse 14 celebrates the blessed—those who do His commandments and gain access to the Tree of Life and the gates of the Holy City—verse 15 identifies those excluded from that eternal glory.

The word "without" doesn't merely mean outside the walls of the city. It represents being cut off—eternally excluded from the presence of God, and cast into the Lake of Fire (Revelation 20:15, 21:8). These are not merely people who sinned, but those who persisted in sin, unrepentant and unchanged:

- Dogs—In ancient times, dogs were not cute pets—they were considered unclean scavengers. The term "dog" became a spiritual insult for those morally depraved (Isaiah 56:10–11; Deuteronomy 23:18; Philippians 3:2). It also became a Jewish euphemism for Gentiles (Matthew 15:26) and false teachers. In this context, it refers to people characterized by spiritual impurity and moral filth.

- Sorcerers—From the Greek *pharmakoi*, referring to users of drugs and magic arts. In biblical terms, this represents those who engage in occult practices—invoking demonic power in opposition to God.

- Whoremongers—Those who engage in sexual immorality (Greek: *pornos*)—including fornication, adultery, cohabitation outside of marriage, pornography, and other acts that violate God's design for sexuality. This term also encompasses unrepentant lifestyles that persist in rejecting biblical boundaries, including identities or behaviors that fall under LGBTQIA+ when they are in contradiction to God's intended order for male and female, marriage, and purity (1 Corinthians 6:9–10; Hebrews 13:4).

- Murderers—This includes not only those who commit physical acts of killing, but also those who harbor hatred in their hearts (1 John 3:15, as Jesus equated unjust anger with murder (Matthew 5:21–22). It also extends to those who take innocent life—including unborn life. The Bible consistently upholds the value of human life from the womb (Psalm 139:13–16; Jeremiah 1:5), and unrepentant participation in or promotion of abortion falls under this sobering category.

- Idolaters—Those who elevate anything or anyone above God in their hearts and lives. This includes not only the worship of physical idols or statues, but also the modern-day idols of money, fame, power, relationships, entertainment, career success, self-image, and even religion when it replaces true devotion to Christ. An idol is anything that captures our allegiance, affections, or trust more than God Himself (Exodus 20:3–5; Colossians 3:5; 1 John 5:21).

- Liars—Not just those who tell lies, but those who love and make them—delighting in falsehood, deceit, and distortion of truth. This is a deeply moral indictment against habitual dishonesty and deception (Revelation 21:8).

This verse mirrors the final separation found in Jesus' own teaching—the sheep from the goats, the wheat from the tares. It reinforces that salvation is not merely a matter of profession, but one of transformation. True faith results in obedience. Those who enter the city are those who have been washed by the blood of the Lamb and walk in righteousness—not perfection, but pursuit of holiness through Christ.

This verse should be read as both a warning and a call to repentance. It underscores the importance of living a life aligned with God's Word and turning away from willful rebellion. And it reminds us that access to the city is not automatic—it's a result of being written in the Lamb's Book of Life (Revelation 21:27).

OLD TESTAMENT FORESHADOWS REVELATION:

They that sanctify themselves, and purify themselves in the gardens behind one tree in the midst, eating swine's flesh, and the abomination, and the mouse, shall be consumed together, says the LORD. (Isaiah 66:17)

This verse, like Revelation 22:15, addresses those who persist in abominable practices—people who outwardly appear religious but are inwardly corrupt. Isaiah 66:17 is condemning false worship, ritual impurity, and rebellion— categories that match the exclusion list in Revelation: idolaters, sorcerers, and those who love lies.

THE REVELATION OF JESUS CHRIST REVEALS:

22:16 I Jesus have sent My angel to testify to you these things in the churches. I AM the Root and the Offspring of David, and the Bright and Morning Star.

This verse stands as one of the most personal and direct affirmations in all of Scripture—spoken by Jesus Himself. After all the angelic proclamations and apocalyptic visions of the Book of Revelation, here Jesus breaks through with unmistakable clarity, saying, "I, Jesus . . ." No titles, no symbolism—just the unmistakable name that changed history. It is His personal stamp of authorship and authority on everything revealed in this book.

Jesus describes Himself with two profound titles that reflect both His divine eternity and His human lineage. This is more than poetic language—it's theological gold. Jesus is declaring that He is both before David and after David. He is David's Source ("Root") and David's Son ("Offspring").

1. **I AM the Root**—As the Root, Christ pre-existed David. He is eternal, uncreated, and the One from whom David himself drew life and purpose. Isaiah 11:1 and 11:10 speak of the Messiah as the "Root of Jesse," affirming this truth.

2. **And the Offspring of David**—As the Offspring, Christ came through David's earthly lineage—fulfilling the Messianic promise that the Savior would descend from David's house (2 Samuel 7:12–16; Luke 1:32–33).

Only Jesus could be both Creator and Descendant, both Ancient of Days and Son of Man. As He said in John 8:58, "Before Abraham was, I AM."

"And the Bright and Morning Star." This title speaks of hope, promise, and new beginnings. The "morning star" appears just before dawn—it's the signal that night is over and the day is about to begin. Christ is that light that pierces the darkest night of human history, promising that the eternal day is coming. This echoes the prophecy in Numbers 24:17, ". . . there shall come a Star out of Jacob . . ." and affirms that Jesus is the radiant fulfillment of all prophetic hope.

In calling Himself the Morning Star, Jesus also reminds us that His return is imminent. Just as the morning star rises suddenly and brilliantly, so too will Christ return to establish His eternal Kingdom. This metaphor is full of encouragement for the Church—it tells us that no matter how dark the world becomes, the light of Jesus will soon rise in glory.

What makes this verse all the more beautiful is that Jesus specifically says He sent His angel to testify these things "to the churches." Revelation is not meant to be a confusing riddle or merely a timeline of doom—it is a message of hope, victory, and warning for the body of Christ. Jesus wants His Bride to be awake, prepared, and filled with longing for His appearing.

In Revelation 22:16, we encounter the Jesus of eternity, the Jesus of history, and the Jesus of personal redemption—all in one sentence.

- He is the Root—our divine origin.
- He is the Offspring—our human Redeemer.
- He is the Morning Star—our eternal hope.

This verse reminds us that everything in Scripture—from Genesis to Revelation—centers on Christ. He is the Alpha and the Omega. The One who laid the foundation of the earth is also the One who will reign in the New Jerusalem.

Let every heart be stirred by His voice, and every eye look for His return. The One who came once as the Lamb is coming again as the King—and His light will never be dimmed.

OLD TESTAMENT FORESHADOWS REVELATION:

And in that day there shall be a Root of Jesse (David's father), who shall stand as a banner to the people; to it shall the Gentiles seek: and His resting place shall be glorious. (Isaiah 11:10)

"Root of Jesse" in Isaiah 11:10 is the same as "Root of David" in Revelation 22:16—both refer to Jesus as the preexistent source of David's line. The offspring of David shows His earthly descent through the Davidic covenant. Isaiah's mention of the Gentiles seeking Him is fulfilled in the New Testament age, and culminates in Revelation's final vision of the eternal Kingdom, where both Jew and Gentile dwell in the light of the Lamb. And the Bright and Morning Star? It's a messianic image that heralds the dawn of a new day—eternal life, peace, and the fulfillment of every promise God has made.

THE REVELATION OF JESUS CHRIST REVEALS:

[22:17] And the Spirit and the Bride say, Come. And let him that hears say, Come. And let him that is athirst come. And whosoever will, let him take the water of life freely.

This verse is one of the most tender and powerful invitations in all of Scripture—a final divine call echoing from the heart of God to the soul of mankind. It is the last invitation in the Bible, and it reflects both the urgency and the mercy of the gospel.

"And the Spirit and the Bride say, Come." The Holy Spirit—the divine agent of conviction and comfort—and the Bride of Christ (the Church) both issue a united plea for the return of Jesus and also extend the call to the lost to come to Him. It's a shared yearning: for Christ's return, and for the salvation of those still outside the gates. The Church, empowered by the Holy Spirit, does not remain silent in the last hour. She invites.

"And let him that hears say, Come." This is a call to every individual who has received the Word—to join in the invitation. Anyone who hears the message is now commissioned to become a messenger. Evangelism is never passive. If you've heard the gospel; you're now invited to echo the call: Come to Christ.

"And let him that is athirst come." This speaks directly to the heart of those who are spiritually dry, empty, and longing. Are you thirsty? Come. Jesus offers the water of life, clear as crystal, flowing from the throne of God (Revelation 22:1). This is not a forced religion, but a free and refreshing relationship.

"And whosoever will, let him take the water of life freely." Here is the global call—the open gate. No pedigree, no price tag, no prerequisites. Just willingness. The word "freely" hammers home the grace of God. The gospel is not earned. It's not for sale. It's a gift. Anyone, anywhere, who wills to come—may.

This verse isn't just an invitation—it's the gospel in one line. From Genesis to Revelation, God calls us back to Himself. And in this last chapter of the Bible, that call is still open. No matter where you are or what you've done, the door is still open, and the Holy Spirit and the Bride are still saying: Come.

OLD TESTAMENT FORESHADOWS REVELATION:

And it shall come to pass, that whosoever shall call on the name of the LORD shall be delivered: for in Mount Zion and in Jerusalem shall be deliverance, as the LORD has said, and in the remnant whom the LORD shall call. (Joel 2:32)

This verse aligns beautifully with Revelation 22:17, echoing the heart of God's invitation across both Testaments. Joel 2:32 uses the word "whosoever," just as Revelation does, offering a universal call that extends grace to all, regardless of past or background. In Joel, the appeal is to "call on the name of the LORD," while Revelation urges all to "come" and "take the water of life freely"—both emphasizing salvation as a gift of mercy, not merit.

Joel's context centers on the Day of the Lord, highlighting the urgency of responding before judgment comes. Likewise, Revelation issues one final, open invitation before eternity is sealed. Together, they form a seamless thread from Old to New: God always provides a way—and always invites.

THE REVELATION OF JESUS CHRIST REVEALS:

22:18 For I testify to every man that hears the words of the prophecy of this book, If any man shall add to these things, God will add to him the plagues that are written in this book.

This verse stands as one of the most solemn and sobering warnings in all of Scripture. Here, the glorified Christ—through the apostle John—issues a final and unambiguous command: do not tamper with the prophecy of this book.

This is not merely a cautionary footnote—it is a heavenly declaration of the sanctity and finality of the Book of Revelation. God is asserting His authority as the ultimate Author, placing divine boundaries around His Word. Just as the Law had warnings (Deuteronomy 4:2 and 12:32), Revelation closes the canon with a similar and stronger tone. Adding to God's Word is not innovation—it is spiritual trespass.

To "add" to this prophecy could involve:

- Inserting false teachings or extra-biblical revelations.
- Distorting the meaning through personal agenda or manipulation.
- Altering prophecy to fit political, cultural, or theological trends.

The result? The offender will receive the very plagues described throughout the book—plagues meant for unrepentant sinners and followers of the beast. This is no small matter; God links the eternal destiny of a person to how they handle His prophetic Word.

Although this verse directly refers to the Book of Revelation, many theologians believe it carries implications for the entirety of Scripture, as

Revelation is the final book of the Bible, serving as the prophetic and theological conclusion of God's revealed Word. It is the last seal of the canon of divine truth.

In an age of spiritual relativism, where truth is often customized or watered down, this verse reminds us that God's Word is not a draft—it's final, holy, and eternal. We are stewards of it, not editors.

This verse is not about instilling fear but ensuring reverence. It reminds believers, teachers, and readers of every generation that God guards His Word fiercely—not to exclude people, but to preserve the truth that sets them free.

OLD TESTAMENT FORESHADOWS REVELATION:

You shall not add unto the word which I command you, neither shall you diminish ought from it, that you may keep the commandments of the LORD your God which I command you. (Deuteronomy 4:2)

This verse lays the foundational principle that God's Word is complete authoritative, and inviolable. Just as Moses warned Israel not to add or subtract from God's commandments, John echoes the same in the final chapter of Revelation, applying it directly to the prophecy of this book.

THE REVELATION OF JESUS CHRIST REVEALS:

22:19 And if any man will take away from the words of the book of this prophecy, God will take away his part out of the Book of Life, and out of the Holy City, and from the things which are written in this book.

This verse contains one of the most solemn and sobering warning in all of Scripture. It is the second half of a divine safeguard (along with verse 18), reinforcing the sacredness, authority, and finality of God's revealed Word—especially the prophecy contained in the Book of Revelation. To alter it is to tamper with the very will and Word of the Almighty.

Much like the warning in Deuteronomy 4:2, where God forbade Israel from adding to or taking away from His commandments, John records Jesus' final warning to the Church: do not subtract a single word from this prophecy. To do so is to tamper with the very fabric of eternal truth, and the consequences are just as eternal.

The punishment described here is profound: the one who removes from this prophecy will have his part taken away from the Book of Life, from the Holy City, and from the things written in this book. This isn't merely symbolic loss—it is eternal exclusion. The implication is that those who deliberately distort, deny, or diminish the Word of God reveal their true nature as unbelievers or false teachers, never truly born again, and will therefore face separation from all of God's promises.

The reference to the Book of Life underscores the seriousness. Throughout Scripture, the Book of Life represents the names of the redeemed—those who will enter heaven and dwell in the New Jerusalem (Revelation 3:5, 20:15, 21:27). To have one's portion removed from it is to be denied entry into eternal life.

This passage echoes Psalm 138:2, where it is said that God has "magnified His Word above all His name," emphasizing the preeminence and inviolability of His revelation.

> I will worship toward Your holy temple, and praise Your name for Your loving-kindness and for Your truth: for You have magnified Your word above all Your name. (Psalm 138:2)

It also connects with 2 Peter 3:16, where Peter warns of unstable men who twist Scripture "to their own destruction." Those who distort God's message for personal gain, power, or doctrinal error do so at the cost of their own souls.

> As also in all his (Paul) epistles, speaking in them of these thing; in which are some things hard to be understood, which they that are unlearned and unstable twist, as they do also the other Scriptures, unto their own destruction. (2 Peter 3:16)

God's Word is not a draft in progress—it is a sealed and complete testimony. This verse reminds us to approach Scripture with reverence, to proclaim it faithfully, and to resist every temptation to soften, alter, or omit what is difficult or unpopular. To guard the Word is to guard the truth—and ultimately, our own inheritance in the Holy City.

OLD TESTAMENT FORESHADOWS REVELATION:

> What thing soever I command, you, observe to do it: you shalt not add thereto, nor diminish from it. (Deuteronomy 12:32)

These Old Testament commands set the foundation for Revelation's final warning: God's Word is not open to revision. From Moses to John, the canon of Scripture has always been under God's sovereign protection. Revelation 22:19 is the final bookend to a theme that spans the entire Bible—God's Word is sacred, sealed, and settled forever.

THE REVELATION OF JESUS CHRIST REVEALS:

> 22:20 He which testify these things says, Surely I come quickly. Amen. Even so, come, Lord Jesus.

This verse stands as one of the most powerful and emotionally charged declarations in all of Scripture. Here, Jesus Himself speaks—the faithful witness, the Alpha and Omega, the Lamb upon the throne—affirming His promise for the final time: "Surely I come quickly." The repetition of this declaration (also in verses 7 and 12 of this same chapter) emphasizes its certainty, urgency, and imminence. Though the world may grow skeptical, Christ's words are trustworthy. His return is not in doubt—it is guaranteed.

"Amen. Even so, come, Lord Jesus," echoes the longing of every faithful heart across time. The word "Amen" signifies agreement—"Yes, Lord, so be it." It is not passive, but expectant. And "Even so, come" is a cry of yearning and submission, the soul's call for the King to return and make all things new.

From Genesis to Revelation, Scripture has always pointed toward the culmination of God's redemptive plan: the return of the Messiah and the restoration of all creation. This final promise from Jesus is not just the end of a vision—it is the anchor of Christian hope. It assures believers that justice will reign, evil will be judged, and God's Kingdom will fully manifest.

This final "come" is layered in beauty. It mirrors the invitation of verse 17, where the Spirit and the Bride say, "Come." Heaven calls us, and now the saints call back to heaven. There is a divine conversation in the closing moments of Revelation—an echo between the throne of God and the heart of the believer.

In a world longing for peace, justice, and healing, this verse reminds us that the ultimate answer is not found in human systems or efforts but in the return of Jesus Christ. The prayer of Revelation is the prayer of the church through the ages: "Even so, come, Lord Jesus."

OLD TESTAMENT FORESHADOWS REVELATION:

Behold, the LORD has proclaimed to the end of the world, Say to the daughter of Zion, Behold, your salvation comes; behold, His reward is with Him, and His work before Him. (Isaiah 62:11)

Both verses speak of the coming of the Lord with reward in hand, directly connecting the Old Testament hope with the New Testament fulfillment. Isaiah's prophecy anticipates a Messianic arrival—a declaration of imminent salvation. This anticipatory tone mirrors Jesus' final words in Revelation, "Surely I come quickly." The phrase "His reward is with Him" is also echoed in Revelation 22:12, tying the promise of return and reward into a consistent biblical thread.

This connection beautifully demonstrates how the hope of the Messiah's coming was deeply embedded in the prophetic writings and fully affirmed in the final pages of Revelation.

THE REVELATION OF JESUS CHRIST REVEALS:

22:21 The grace of our Lord Jesus Christ be with you all. Amen.

This final verse of Revelation—and of the entire Bible—closes the Scriptures with one of the most powerful and comforting declarations in all of God's Word:

grace. After the majesty of New Jerusalem, the judgment of the wicked, the reward of the righteous, the invitation to come, and the promise of Jesus' imminent return, what is the last word to mankind? Grace.

1. **Grace as the Final Word**—The Bible opens with God's creative power, and it closes with His redemptive favor. From Genesis to Revelation, the unfolding story of humanity is not merely about failure and judgment, but about a grace that triumphs—a divine, unearned favor that calls the sinner, sanctifies the saint, and sustains the soul.

   By ending with grace, we are reminded that the entire journey—from Eden's fall to the New Jerusalem's glory—has always been rooted in God's mercy toward His creation.

2. **The Grace of Jesus—Not Just God in General**—John specifies: "The grace of our Lord Jesus Christ." This grace is not an abstract concept; it's found in the person of Jesus—His death, His resurrection, and His promise to return. This grace is both the means of our salvation and the strength of our perseverance.

   For by grace are you saved through faith; and that not of yourselves: it is the gift of God. (Ephesians 2:8)

   And He said unto me, 'My grace is sufficient for you: for My strength is made perfect in weakness.' Most gladly therefore will I rather glory in my infirmities, that the power of Christ may rest upon me. (2 Corinthians 12:9)

3. **Universal Benediction**—The phrase "be with you all" is inclusive and compassionate. It reflects the heart of God that none should perish, but that all should come to repentance. Even at the end, the invitation remains wide open to the whole world.

   For God so loved the world that He gave His only begotten Son, that whoever believes in Him should not perish but have everlasting life. (John 3:16)

   John, having witnessed the end of time, the judgment of the wicked, the victory of Christ, and the eternal glory of the saints, signs off with a pastoral blessing for every reader: May grace be with you. No matter your past. No matter where you are. Let grace find you.

4. **Amen—Let it be so, Lord**—The word *Amen* seals the canon of Scripture with certainty, affirmation, and faith. It echoes the heart-cry of the Church—"Let it be so, Lord." It's not just a conclusion; it's a declaration of trust in everything God has revealed.

The final word of the Bible is not judgment. It's not fear. It's grace. God's last word to a broken world is an invitation to life, joy, and eternal fellowship through Jesus Christ. It is a fitting end to the greatest love story ever told.

OLD TESTAMENT FORESHADOWS REVELATION:

For the Lord GOD is a sun and shield: the LORD will give grace and glory: no good thing will He withhold from them that walk uprightly. (Psalm 84:11)

This verse directly mentions grace, just as Revelation 22:21 does. It shows that grace is not a New Testament concept alone, but deeply rooted in the nature of God even in the Old Covenant. Psalm 84:11 speaks of God's presence, protection, and generosity, all of which are consummated in the eternal fellowship described in Revelation 22. The combination of grace and glory in this verse mirrors the final blessings of Revelation—where glory has come, and grace remains. This Old Testament verse connects beautifully with the closing benediction of the Bible, reminding us that God's grace has always been His gift to the faithful—from Eden to eternity.

SUMMARY OF REVELATION 22

Revelation 22 is the triumphant finale of the Bible, unveiling the eternal state of God's redeemed creation. The chapter opens with a vision of a pure river of the water of life, clear as crystal, flowing from the throne of God and of the Lamb. This life-giving stream represents the continuous, unending refreshment that comes from God's presence (Revelation 22:1). On both sides of the river stands the Tree of Life—once barred from mankind after the Fall, now restored. It bears twelve kinds of fruit, each in season, and its leaves are for the healing of the nations, symbolizing total restoration and wholeness (Revelation 22:2).

The curse that began in Eden is finally and forever lifted. The throne of God and the Lamb now dwells with humanity in the New Jerusalem, and His servants serve Him in perfect joy and purpose. They will see His face—a privilege no one could experience in the Old Covenant—and His name will be written on their foreheads, signifying identity, belongings, and ownership. There will be no night, no sun, and no candle—because God Himself is the light, and His people will reign with Him forever and ever (Revelation 22:3–5).

John is told not to seal the words of the prophecy, for the time is at hand. The invitation remains open, and the call to readiness is urgent (Revelation 22:6–10). Jesus speaks: "Behold, I come quickly." A blessing is promised to those who keep the words of this prophecy (Revelation 22:7, 12–14). The chapter ends with one final, open invitation to all: "The Holy Spirit and the Bride say, Come . . .

whosoever will, let him take the water of life freely." Christ identifies Himself as the Root and Offspring of David, and the Bright and Morning Star—highlighting both His divine preexistence and His rightful kingship (Revelation 22:16–17).

As the final words are spoken, the reader is reminded that Jesus is coming soon. And the response of the faithful echoes throughout the ages: "Even so, come, Lord Jesus." The last word of the Bible is not judgment, but grace: "The grace of our Lord Jesus Christ be with you all. Amen" (Revelation 22:20–21).

KEY TAKEAWAYS

- The river of life—Flowing from God's throne, it represents eternal refreshment and unbroken fellowship with God.
- The Tree of Life restored—A symbol of healing, abundance, and eternal life, now freely accessible to the redeemed.
- No more curse—Sin, death, and decay are forever eradicated; the eternal state is one of purity and joy.
- Face-to-face fellowship—Believers will behold God's face and bear His name, signifying intimacy and belonging.
- Eternal light and reign—God Himself is the light, and His people will reign with Him forever.
- Final invitation—The gospel call remains open to all who thirst, urging every heart to come and receive the water of life.
- The promise of Christ's return—Jesus declares three times in this chapter that He is coming quickly—prompting readiness and hope.
- A closing blessing—The Bible ends with grace, inviting all to receive and rest in the finished work of Christ.

Revelation 22 is a divine crescendo that ties together every promise, every prophecy, and every purpose of God throughout Scripture. It assures believers that paradise lost is paradise regained—and infinitely more. It is both a final warning and a glorious invitation to dwell with God forever. The King is coming, and His Kingdom will have no end.

Epilogue
The Mystery Revealed

WHAT WAS HIDDEN NOW SEEN—*The Trumpet I: The Ancient Prophecy That Reveals America's Final Hour* closed with an Afterword—an invitation to choose. *The Trumpet II: The Prophecy Continues—America's Final Hour Unveiled* concludes not with a farewell, but with fulfillment. This Epilogue offers a glimpse beyond the choice: the mystery uncovered, the King unveiled, and eternity made visible.

The sun hung low in the sky, casting a warm, golden glow across the quiet hillside where Irene and I sat on a weathered stone bench beneath a blooming cherry tree. In the distance, the silhouette of a city shimmered—perhaps only a city of this world, or maybe a symbolic glimmer of what is to come. The air was still, stirred only by the gentle rustle of leaves and the occasional birdsong. Between us, a well-worn Bible rested open, its pages lifting slightly in the breeze, as if even the Word itself were alive with anticipation.

This overlook had become sacred to us—a place where Scripture and life had braided together over countless cups of tea and pages of prophecy. But today felt different. Today marked the end of a long and sacred journey.

The conversation began not with urgency, but with quiet reverence. Irene gazed at the sky, speaking softly—more to the wind than to me—as the golden light deepened into a hue like flame, as though heaven itself leaned closer to listen.

"Ann, can you believe it? We started this journey trying to find America in prophecy . . . but what we really discovered was a King who reigns over every nation—and a forever home in a city not built by human hands."

I smiled, my heart full. "I couldn't have said it better myself, Irene. At first, we were chasing headlines and timelines, piecing together history in hopes of finding clarity. And we did. But what we uncovered along the way was so much more than geopolitical insight. We found a revelation of Jesus in all His glory. From Genesis to Revelation, every page whispers His name."

Irene smirked, her eyes distant with memory. "I still remember how overwhelmed I felt the first time I read Revelation 17 and 18. The weight of what Mystery Babylon represents—the parallels to America, the sins that rise like smoke to heaven—it was sobering. And yet, even then, God never left us in the dark. Even in judgment, there's always mercy. Even in waring, there's always an invitation."

I nodded, my voice low with conviction. "That's exactly why Revelation is so often misunderstood. People see the beasts and the bowls of wrath and think it's a horror story. But it's not. It's a hope story. It's about the Lamb who triumphs. The Bride who prepares herself. And Jesus Christ the King of kings and Lord of lords who keeps His promises—and comes back for His own."

I leaned forward, voice low with awe. "I keep thinking about the contrast. Babylon falls—but the New Jerusalem descends. One city is consumed by judgment, the other shines with the glory of God. One is filled with abominations, the other with righteousness. It's like God is crying out: 'You have a choice. Come out of her, My people!'"

Irene nodded solemnly. "That's exactly what He's saying. And not just to the world—but to the Church. Come out of compromise. Come out of mixture. Come out of comfort. God isn't only preparing a place for us—He's preparing us for that place."

I exhaled slowly, wonder softening my voice. "You know what amazes me the most? That cube-shaped city—the New Jerusalem. It's not just symbolic. It has dimensions. Foundations. Gates. Mainstreet. It's real. Tangible. Holy. And somehow . . . it's our forever home."

Irene smiled, eyes reflecting the awe we both felt. "The measurements boggle the mind—1,500 miles long, wide, and high. It stretches beyond earth's atmosphere, into the heavens. And each gate bears the name of a tribe of Israel. Every foundation stone carries the name of an apostle. That tells you everything—this city is built for both God's covenant people and the Church. His Wife and His Son's Bride. Together. One redeemed family."

I leaned forward, eyes bright. "I love that. For all our differences, we'll be united in Him—Jew and Gentile. No denominations. No borders. Just redeemed souls, washed in the blood, dwelling in light."

Irene nodded, her voice soft with awe. "And think about this: the nations walk by the city's light. That tells us the New Jerusalem may not be the only dwelling place in eternity. The new earth is alive—populated. Nations are there. Redeemed kings bring their glory into the city. God didn't just save people—He's redeeming creation itself."

Irene tilted her head, curiosity dancing in her eyes. "Ann, do you think we'll still explore? Build? Create? Or will it all just be endless praise in the throne room?"

I smiled. "Why not both? We were made in God's image—and that doesn't stop in eternity. We're eternal image-bearers: creators, thinkers, stewards. The new earth will be Eden restored, but glorified. With perfect minds and glorified bodies, we'll live curse-free, fully alive. Worship won't be limited to song—it will be expressed in everything we do. Every act—whether crafting, discovering, or adventuring—will glorify the Lamb."

Irene sighed, her voice soft. "And no more tears . . . no death, no sorrow, no pain. That's the part that gets me. All the losses, all the trauma, all the brokenness we've carried through life—it will be wiped away forever."

I smiled gently. "I used to think that verse meant we'd forget everything. But now I wonder—what if it means He redeems everything? That every scar becomes a story of grace. Every tear, a testimony. That we'll remember not to mourn, but to magnify His mercy—for what He brought us through."

Irene nodded, eyes glistening. "That makes me want to fall on my knees in worship. We were so focused on America's place in prophecy—but now I see, it was always about Jesus' place in us."

I leaned in. "And that's the mystery revealed. Yes, America matters. She's in the story. But she's not the point—she's just one piece of a far greater puzzle. The real story is about a throne, a Lamb, and a wedding that's been unfolding since Eden."

"It all comes full circle, doesn't it, Ann? From the Tree of Life lost in Genesis—to the Tree of Life restored in Revelation. From the first Adam who fell . . . to the last Adam who conquered. From a garden we were exiled from . . . to a city we're invited into."

I nodded, voice low with awe. "And it's all grace. Not because we earned it—but because He finished it. 'It is done,' He said. The Alpha and the Omega has written the final word. And now, the Holy Spirit and the Bride say, *Come.*"

"Ann, I began this journey to decode prophecy . . . but I'm ending it with a deeper love for the Author behind it all."

I smiled. "That's the beauty of Revelation. It doesn't just reveal events—it reveals Jesus. And once you see Him as He truly is—faithful, victorious, radiant with glory—you're never the same. You're forever changed."

Irene sighed. "So . . . what do we do now?"

I smiled. "We keep watching. We stay sober. We stay rooted in the Word. We sound the alarm when it's needed—and we extend the invitation always. But most of all, we stay in love with Jesus."

"Amen, Ann," she whispered. "This world is not our home. But that city . . . that radiant cube gleaming with glory . . . that's where we're going."

"And until then," I said softly, "we walk in the light. We live like citizens of heaven. Because soon—very soon—we'll see the face of the One we've longed for."

Irene's eyes glistened. "Yes . . . the King of kings is coming."

And as the last light slipped below the horizon, I understood: the story wasn't ending—it was only just beginning. The veil had lifted. The mystery unveiled. The King of kings, revealed.

That America is not the focus—Jesus is.

That Revelation is not fear—it's fulfillment.

That we are not left guessing—but invited in.

So as the final page turns, the Bride lifts her eyes—not with dread, but with devotion. Her lamp is full. Her heart is ready. Her spirit cries out with longing.

And the Holy Spirit and the Bride say, "Come."

He which testifies these things says, Surely I come quickly. Amen. Even so, come, Lord Jesus! (Revelation 22:20)

THE END

Acknowledgments

THANK YOU GOD, OUR CREATOR—for the greatest book in the world—the Holy Bible—written to unfold the wisdom of Yor ways, to illuminate the path of truth, and to draw every seeking heart closer to You. Writing this book was a sacred undertaking that could not have been accomplished alone; it was shaped by the blending of Your inspired Word and the thoughts, ideas, experiences, and lives—past and present—of those who have touched my heart deeply.

I must first express my deepest appreciation to my husband, Eric. I am forever grateful to God that I get to be your wife. "Thank you" seems far too small. I would be absolutely nowhere without you. Your faith, love, encouragement, and unwavering support have been my anchor. You are my best friend, my true companion, and the one who continually motivates me to teach the truth. I am blessed beyond measure to walk this life by your side. You are easy to love—and you have my whole heart forever. I love you!

I would also like to acknowledge my three sons: Matthew, John, and Jared. When death knocked at my door in 2007, you three were the reason for my desperate prayer and promise to God: "Let me live to finish raising my boys, and I will do anything You ask." It took years of growing and surrendering, but nine years later, I finally understood: God had been preparing me all along to fulfill that vow.

The past is finished. The future rests in God's hands. The time is now. *The Trumpet I: The Ancient Prophecy That Reveals America's Final Hour* and *The*

Trumpet II: The Prophecy Continues—America's Final Hour Unveiled, which began as a seed of obedience, is beyond anything I could have imagined when this journey first began. Matthew, John, and Jared—you are the precious treasures of my life. Thank you for the honor of being your mother. I love you more deeply than words could ever express.

I also want to thank Pastors John and Brenda Kilpatrick and Church of His Presence. Your sermons, your worship, and your steadfast leadership have fueled my spirit. You are my family, and I love each and every one of you.

To the many who have poured into my life across the globe with love, encouragement, and truth: Thank you to the faithful translators who labored to bring the Holy Scriptures from Hebrew, Greek, and Aramaic into English. Thank you to Pastor Steve Cioccolanti (Discover Ministries), Reverend Rick Joyner (MorningStar Ministries), the late J. Barton Payne (Covenant Theological Seminary), and Evangelist Tiff Shuttlesworth (Lost Lamb Association). Your teachings, writings, and ministries have helped shape and sharpen my understanding of biblical prophecy.

To all my family, friends, and teachers throughout this life: I live in gratitude for you. The time we have shared has enriched my soul and taught me lessons in grace, resilience, and the fullness of love. Every encounter, every challenge, every joy has helped forge the journey that led me here.

Most importantly, I give thanks to my Lord and Savior, Jesus Christ, whose unfailing faithfulness carries me through every challenge.

And to You, Everlasting Almighty God—thank You for awakening me to my purpose and calling. Thank You for inspiring, sustaining, and completing this work. *The Trumpet I: The Ancient Prophecy That Reveals America's Final Hour* and *The Trumpet II: The Prophecy Continues—America's Final Hour Unveiled* are Yours, unfolding Your masterpiece, the Book of Revelation, in new and refreshing ways. May this book bring forth the progressive revelation of Your great love and truth to every heart You are calling.

To the dear reader:

May this work not only inform you but ignite you.

May it lead you to your own purpose and calling in this critical hour.

May it draw you ever closer to the One who wrote your name before the foundations of the world.

All glory to God.

Author Photo © 2023 Edwin Wolfe

ABOUT THE AUTHOR—Lori Ann Moeszinger, affectionately known as "L," is the founder and creative force behind The Ridge Publishing Group and its family of imprints. A prolific American author, blogger, and publisher, Lori brings a passion for clarity, truth, and inspiration to everything she writes. Nestled in the lakeside beauty of Coeur d'Alene, Idaho, she draws daily inspiration from God's creation, her husbands' unwavering support, and the quiet companionship of their two beloved dogs.

Holding a Juris Doctorate in Law, along with an Associate's degree in Paralegal Studies, and a Bachelor's degree in Business Administration, Lori transitioned from a legal career to full-time authorship and publishing, embracing the freedom to pursue her calling. Since 2016, she has devoted her life to the study of biblical prophecy and Scripture, bringing both depth and urgency to her writing.

Under the byline L. A. Moeszinger, she writes extensively on business, law, and the publishing industry, helping authors bring their dreams to life. Under her full name, Lori Ann Moeszinger, she explores biblical truths, prophetic insights, and personal reflections rooted in faith. Her New Youniversity Chronicles and The Manhattan Diaries series showcase her versatile storytelling gifts across multiple genres and voices.

At the heart of all she writes is a deep conviction: that faith is the foundation for life, that blessings are to be shared, and that diligence is a divine calling. Her books are more than words—they are invitations to prepare, to believe, and to live with eternal purpose.

LATEST RELEASES

For More Information . . .

If you would like to explore more of what you've read in *The Vanishing*—or dive deeper into related teachings, prophetic studies, biblical insights, and the call to prepare for Christ's return—or if you're seeking salvation, discipleship, or a deeper understanding of God's end-time purposes, you are warmly invited to connect further. Write to:

The Ridge Publishing Group
P.O. Box 549
Coeur d'Alene, Idaho 83816

You can also discover the multifaceted worlds Lori Ann Moeszinger has woven through her books, blogs, and ministries. Each platform is designed to equip, inspire, and walk alongside you in your journey of faith, purpose, and readiness.

Parent Platforms:

RidgePublishingGroup.com—Home base for all Lori's imprints, books, publishing updates, and new releases.

PublisherAndHerWorld.com—Blog site offering publishing insights, author tools, and faith-based reflections for Christian writers.

Ministry Platforms:

GuardiansofBiblicalTruth.com—Focused on Bible teaching, prophecy, and end-time preparation.

Jesus-Says.com—Home of *Coffee with God*, featuring daily inspiration, personal testimonies, and Scripture-rooted teachings.

Author Platforms:

LAMoeszinger.com—Lori's personal author site with theological writings, spiritual reflections, and upcoming projects.

NewYouniversityChronicles.com—A movement for faith-driven personal growth through the *New Youniversity Chronicles* and *The Manhattan Diaries* book series.

ManhattanChronicles.com—Where urban life, cultural reflection, and spiritual depth meet.

Publishing and Writer Support Platforms:

AuthorsDoor.com—Tools, training, and encouragement for indie authors.

AuthorsRedDoor.com—A blog site for writers pursuing excellence in publishing, marketing and writing—offering wisdom, strategies, and encouragement.

Children, Young Adult, and Family Adventures:

EthanFoxBooks.com—Enter the world of Ethan Fox, where wonder meets character-building adventure.

KidsStagram.com—Creative content and blog posts for young readers and families.

STAY CONNECTED

We invite you to join our online communities and become part of a growing network of watchmen, believers, writers, seekers, and young adventurers preparing for what lies ahead. Explore, engage, and grow deeper through our private Facebook groups and social spaces:

- Ethan Fox KidsStagram Fan Zone—A creative and inspiring space for young readers, families, and fans of Ethan Fox's adventures.
- Publisher and Her World Forum—A supportive community for writers and publishing entrepreneurs seeking guidance, encouragement, and industry insights.

- Guardians of Biblical Truth Forum—A gathering place for believers to study Scripture, explore prophecy, share testimonies, and strengthen their walk with Christ.
- AuthorsDoor Strategy Forum—A mastermind group for authors and independent publishers dedicated to writing, marketing, and publishing strategies that make an impact.

You can find links to these private groups, as well as *free* newsletter subscriptions, resources, and more across our websites.

EXPLORE OUR YOUTUBE CHANNELS

Discover a rich library of content across nine unique YouTube channels under The Ridge Publishing Group umbrella. From biblical teaching and prophetic insight to author features and publishing resources, our channels include:

- Publisher Website
  - o Publisher and Her World at Ridge Publishing Group
- Author Website
  - o Live with LAM #Shorts
- Guardians of Biblical Truth
  - o Guardians of Biblical Truths
  - o Coffee with God! Jesus-Says #Shorts
- AuthorsDoor Group
  - o AuthorsDoor Group
  - o Authors Red Door #Shorts
- Ethan Fox Books
  - o Ethan Fox Live
  - o Ethan Fox KidsStagram Book Club Circle
  - o KidsStagram Ethan Fox Books #Shorts

Each channel offers curated videos designed to inform, encourage, and equip viewers for deeper spiritual understanding and creative inspiration. Subscribe and journey with us through truth, storytelling, and timeless wisdom.

Stay watchful. Stay ready. Stay connected.